DISCOVERING MEANINGS IN ELEMENTARY SCHOOL MATHEMATICS

DISCOVERING MEANINGS IN ELEMENTARY SCHOOL MATHEMATICS

EIGHTH EDITION

FOSTER E. GROSSNICKLE
Professor Emeritus, Jersey City State College

LELAND M. PERRY
Professor of Teacher Education
California State University, Long Beach

JOHN RECKZEH
Professor Emeritus, Jersey City State College

Holt, Rinehart and Winston, Inc.
Fort Worth   Chicago   San Francisco
Philadelphia   Montreal   Toronto   London   Sydney   Tokyo

Publisher: Ted Buchholz
Acquisitions Editor: Jo-Anne Weaver
Project Editor: Michael D. Hinshaw
Production Manager: Kenneth A. Dunaway
Art & Design Supervisor: John Ritland
Cover Designer: Pat Sloan

Cover photographs: Upper left and lower right by Leland Perry; all other cover photographs are HRW photos by Richard Haynes. The photograph on page v courtesy of John Reckzeh. The photograph on page x by AP/Wide World photos. All other photographs by Leland Perry, except where noted by Billie Perry.

GW-BASIC® is a registered trademark of Microsoft Corporation. Apple is a registered trademark of Apple Computers, Inc.

Library of Congress Cataloging-in-Publication Data

Grossnickle, Foster E. (Foster Earl), 1896–
    Discovering meanings in elementary school mathematics.

    Rev. ed. of: Discovering meanings in elementary school mathematics / Foster E. Grossnickle . . . [et al.]. 7th ed. c1983.
    Includes bibliographical references.
    1. Mathematics—Study and teaching (Elementary) I. Perry, Leland M.   II. Reckzeh, John. III. Discovering meanings in elementary school mathematics.   IV. Title.
    QA135.5.G7   1990   372.7   89-24731

ISBN 0-03-030987-5

Address for editorial correspondence: Holt, Rinehart and Winston, Inc., 301 Commerce Street, Suite 3700, Fort Worth, TX 76102

Address for orders: Holt, Rinehart and Winston, Inc., 6277 Sea Harbor Drive, Orlando, Florida 32887. 1-800-782-4479, or
1-800-433-0001 (in Florida)

PRINTED IN THE UNITED STATES OF AMERICA

0 1 2 3   039   9 8 7 6 5 4 3 2

Holt, Rinehart and Winston, Inc.
The Dryden Press
Saunders College Publishing

This eighth edition is dedicated to Foster E. Grossnickle. He served many years as a professor of mathematics and chairman of the mathematics department at Jersey City State College. He was co-author of the Winston Arithmetic Series, which was later published by Holt, Rinehart and Winston. He co-authored all eight editions of *Discovering Meanings in Elementary School Mathematics*. He has published many articles in more than a dozen national education journals and in yearbooks of the National Society for the Study of Education and the National Council of Teachers of Mathematics. He has contributed a substantial amount of money to scholarships throughout his career.

Preface

The first edition of this text came off the press in 1947. In the more than forty years since that time there have been four major movements in the teaching and learning of arithmetic and mathematics at the elementary school level:

1. Meaningful Approach, mid-1930s to 1960

2. New Math, 1960 to early 1970s

3. Back to Basics, early 1970s to 1980

4. Problem solving, 1980 to present

Before the mid-1930s the major approach to teaching arithmetic was based on the stimulus-response theory, which led to *telling* and *drilling* approaches. Little emphasis was given to understanding.

The *meaningful approach*, which continues to remain valid in a modern mathematics program, was based on the belief that pupils should *understand* what they learn and should be able to *use numbers* in problem situations having social significance. The meaningful approach emphasized using manipulative aids and visual materials to develop understanding of concepts and language before symbolic representation. Reinforcement (drill and practice) became a part of the learning process. The meaning theory emphasized that computational skills be taught in such a way that children learn to compute intelligently—that is, they know and understand why things work as they do and are able to reconstruct forgotten processes and facts.

In the early 1960s *new mathematics* was introduced into the elementary curriculum. In 1957 the Soviet Union had put Sputnik I into orbit. This achievement demonstrated that Russia was ahead of the United States in space technology, the basis of which is a knowledge of mathematics and science. Consequently, great pressures were brought on the schools to improve their mathematics and science programs. The mathematics program developed and implemented in elementary schools was popularly known as the New Math and emphasized mathematical structure, set terminology, set symbolism, set operations, study of bases other than ten, and topics from algebra, geometry, and statistics. Two major changes were made that proved to be effective. First, curriculum was changed from arithmetic to mathematics and thus included a study of arithmetic, geometry, algebra, and other topics. Second, the mathematical concept of meaning was expanded to include *structure* (positing that a limited number of properties control basic operations). These two additions to the program are vital today in the teaching of mathematics in the elementary school. Some of the topics of New Math proved too difficult and too abstract for many pupils, however, and these topics were dropped from the elementary mathematics curriculum. The Back-to-Basics movement was not effective and was replaced by *problem solving* as a major emphasis since 1980.

The seven different editions of *Discovering Meanings in Elementary School Mathematics* have been tailored to meet prevailing theories of learning mathematics. This eighth edition is structured to prepare teachers to teach mathematics in the elementary schools during the 1990s. Any effective program for the 1990s must prepare the teacher to meet the changes resulting from the use of calculators and computers in our modern society.

Features of the Eighth Edition

This new edition perpetuates the tried-and-tested procedures that characterized previous editions and has several new features as well.

Use of Learning Principles

The writers identify six basic principles of teaching and learning in the first chapter. These principles are used as the basis for lesson planning and in introducing major topics throughout the text.

Three New Chapters

Chapters 5, 17, and 18 are new to this edition. Chapter 5 deals with mathematics for preschool and kindergarten children. The program in many schools for dealing with four- and five-year-old children from homes in which both parents are working is fragmentary. The program in Chapter 5 gives patterns and procedures for dealing with these groups, and makes recommendations that are based upon tested procedures in the classroom.

Chapter 17 treats statistics and probability. Both topics are found in current mathematics textbooks for pupils in the upper grades of the elementary school. The simplicity of the treatment of probability in this text should enable the teacher to present this topic very effectively to a class.

Chapter 18 discusses the perplexing problem of helping minorities and limited-English-proficient pupils learn mathematics.

Calculator and Computer Activities

The wide use of calculators and computers has changed the curriculum in elementary school mathematics. Calculator sections are given at the end of most chapters. The work dealing with the calculator emphasizes the ability of this instrument to reduce computational time, therefore giving the pupil more time to devote to problem analysis. Computer activities also appear at the end of most chapters. Appendix B contains an introduction to programming in LOGO, a computer language very useful in studying geometry. A computer disk that contains more than 80 BASIC programs accompanies the Instructor's Manual, with permission to copy for the use of interested students.

Estimation

Educators have long advocated teaching estimation of the answer to a given example or problem, but this has been done sparingly and ineffectively. Estimation is important to help pupils determine if an answer to a problem or example is sensible and will often detect errors in entry into calculators and computers. The exercises at the end of most chapters offer opportunities to practice estimation. Methods of estimation are discussed in Chapters 8 and 10.

Unification of Common Fractions, Decimals, and Percents

The final new feature of this edition is the unification of teaching common fractions, decimals, and percents. Traditionally, these topics were taught in sequence. With the increased use of the metric system and work with decimals instead of common fractions in computers and calculators, the curriculum must be changed to meet this situation. Pupils learn that these notations may be used as different ways for expressing the same number. To emphasize this idea, these different topics are included in the same chapters.

Increased Emphasis on Problem Solving

This edition gives major emphasis to problem solving—the heart of the mathematics program. Chapter 6 deals with problem solving and this topic is a central consideration in most of the chapters of the book.

Acknowledgments

The writers wish to acknowledge their indebtedness to a number of people who read the copy and offered valuable suggestions for improving it, including:

Ernest Duncan, Rutgers University; Mary Jo Lass, California State University—Long Beach; Billie Rae Perry, Iva Meairs Elementary; Patricia Doerr, Louisiana State University; Robert Joyner, East Carolina University; Heather Carter, University of Texas—Austin; Martha Drobnak, Grove City College; Durward Richardson, East Texas State University; Kathleen J. Nickerson, University of Rhode Island.

We especially express our indebtedness to the late Leo J. Brueckner, who co-wrote the first five editions of this text. His insight into how children learn mathematics and how to implement that vision laid the foundation for the entire series.

The writers are grateful to the professionals of Holt, Rinehart and Winston for their contributions to making this eighth edition a reality. Special recognition is due Ted Buchholz, Publisher and Editor-in-Chief; Jo-Anne Weaver, Education Acquisitions Editor; and Michael D. Hinshaw, Project Editor.

The writers, of course, assume full responsibility for the content of this text.

Foster E. Grossnickle
Leland M. Perry
John Reckzeh

Contents

■ *CHAPTER 5*

TEACHING MATHEMATICS TO PRESCHOOL AND KINDERGARTEN CHILDREN 72

■ *CHAPTER 6*

PROBLEM SOLVING 94

■ *CHAPTER 7*

DISCOVERING MEANINGS FOR BASIC ADDITION AND SUBTRACTION FACTS 116

■ *CHAPTER 11*

FRACTIONS, DECIMALS, AND PERCENTS   216

■ *CHAPTER 12*

ADDITION AND SUBTRACTION OF FRACTIONS AND DECIMALS   242

■ *CHAPTER 13*

MULTIPLICATION AND DIVISION OF FRACTIONS AND DECIMALS: PERCENTS   265

■ *CHAPTER 17*

STATISTICS AND PROBABILITY   364

■ *CHAPTER 18*

TEACHING MINORITIES AND LIMITED-ENGLISH-PROFICIENT PUPILS   382

Florence Griffith Joyner seems to be running on air as she nears the finish line in the 200-meter dash of the 1988 Olympic Games in Seoul, Korea. This was her second record-setting gold medal performance of the week. She thrilled audiences around the world while winning one silver and three gold medals.

The great progress achieved in technology and science in recent years has affected our daily lives. A good example is the field of communications: any significant event can now be seen throughout the world, either as it occurs or within minutes of its occurrence. For instance, a worldwide audience was able to watch the 1988 Olympic Games from opening to closing ceremonies, as clearly as if the viewers were in the stadium. Early in the century, viewers would have had to rely on photographs published many days—or even weeks—later. As remote as the connection may sometimes seem between world events and the elementary school classroom, it is mathematics that has provided the basis for the technology that so shapes our world and our cultures.

Foundations for a Modern Program in Elementary School Mathematics

ACHIEVEMENT GOALS

After studying this chapter, you should be able to:

1. Describe the four basic features of the meaningful approach to mathematics.

2. Identify what was new about New Math.

3. List four of the goals in elementary school mathematics for the 1990s.

4. Suggest ways to promote readiness and motivation for learning mathematics in the elementary school.

5. Illustrate four levels of growth in learning mathematics in the elementary school.

6. Suggest the types of reinforcement necessary for mastering the objectives of the mathematics program.

VOCABULARY

These terms are defined or illustrated in the Glossary.

Algorithm
Back to Basics
Cognitive
Diagnosis
Expanded notation
Expository method
of teaching
Guided discovery
Manipulative
materials

Mastery level
Mathematical
structure
Number pattern
Quantitative
thinking
Symbolic level

In recent years numerous national reports have been published expressing concerns about our educational system, often including recommendations for educational reforms. Several of these reports have addressed needed changes in the teaching and learning of mathematics, including *Everybody Counts* (published in 1989 by the National Research Council), and *Curriculum and Evaluation Standards for School Mathematics* (published in 1989 by the National Council of Teachers of Mathematics). During the decade of the 1990s, concerted efforts will be made to implement these reforms.

Mathematics is the foundation for the technology that is rapidly changing our culture. A modern program for the teaching of mathematics in the elementary school must provide the optimum conditions for pupils to understand concepts and develop skills essential for continued study in this field. Such a program prepares learners not only to deal effectively with current quantitative problems but also to look to the future, thus preparing our youth to cope with situations presently unforeseen.

From Past to Present

A program for the 1990s is the outgrowth of programs and theories of learning that have been tried in years past. These have in turn served as the basis for the development of newer, better programs.

If we examine major movements in the teaching of arithmetic and elementary school mathematics since the early 1940s, we can identify some procedures that have met the test of time and should be continued as essential parts of a modern elementary mathematics program. We must avoid repeating the mistakes of the past and learn to take advantage of the features that produced effective learning.

The Meaningful Approach

In 1935 William A. Brownell published an article advocating that the learner should understand what is learned and apply it to socially significant situations.[1] This widely accepted plan of learning is known as the meaning theory of learning and was dominant in our schools from the early 1940s through the early 1960s. Brownell's research led him to advocate these four features of a modern program in arithmetic:

1. Work with manipulatives and pictures before dealing with abstract symbols.

2. Understand our base-ten number system and such terms as *place value, number properties,* and *relationships of the four operations.*

3. Apply the learning in solving problems in social situations familiar to the learner.

4. Have pupils learn by discovery rather than by teacher telling. Discovery learning involves activities that enable a pupil to learn without being told. The teacher's role changes from telling and showing to one of using leading questions to direct the learners to discover the answer.

The meaningful approach was a sound and workable program for teaching *arithmetic* to children. However, in the view of leading mathematics educators, the program was too limited. Children needed an early start with such other topics in mathematics as algebra and geometry .

The New Math Approach

In 1957 the Soviet Union launched Sputnik I, the first manmade satellite to orbit the

---

1. W. A. Brownell, "Psychological Considerations in the Learning and Teaching of Arithmetic," *The Teaching of Arithmetic,* tenth yearbook (Reston, VA: National Council of Teachers of Mathematics, 1935), pp. 1–31.

earth. This achievement demonstrated that the USSR was ahead of the United States in space technology which is based on a knowledge of mathematics and science. This event challenged America's ability to excel in space exploration, which is dependent upon technicians who are well-grounded in mathematics and science. As a result, major coordinated efforts were made to improve the curricula of mathematics and science in grades 1 through 12.

A major influence on the development of New Mathematics programs was the School Mathematics Study Group (SMSG) founded in 1958 at Yale University and directed by Dr. Edward G. Begle.[2] The materials published by SMSG stressed mathematical structure, a set of principles and properties that provides a basis for the logical study of mathematics as a system. Before 1960, many of the structural concepts and much of the vocabulary introduced by SMSG were not encountered in the curriculum until late high school.

OPPOSITION TO THE NEW MATH

When major changes are made in any kind of social program, opposition is inevitable. The New Math program was not fully successful for several reasons:

1. Teachers were not adequately prepared to understand and teach the New Math curriculum.

2. Parents did not understand the subject matter and criticized the schools for teaching mathematics that neither they nor their children could understand.

3. Set terminology and symbolism were alien to parents, pupils, and most teachers, so

discontent was expressed both vocally and in the media.

4. Achievement in mathematics, according to national surveys, showed a decline soon after the introduction of the New Math program. This was especially true for the Scholastic Aptitude Test (SAT). The SAT scores are used for determining admission to many colleges and universities throughout this country.

5. Social applications of number in familiar situations and problems were omitted or limited in the New Math program. Motivation for learning mathematics ebbed as a result.

6. There was a rising tide among parents and in the media for a return to the "basics."

The New Math program ran into difficulty in the schools because it involved too much *new* mathematics, introduced too fast, with too little emphasis on social usefulness. The revolt against New Math led to the Back-to-Basics movement.

CONTRIBUTIONS OF NEW MATH

Although the New Math had defects, it made significant contributions to the mathematics program in the elementary school, of which two were: (1) The curriculum was broadened to include beginnings of both algebra and geometry as well as arithmetic. (2) New Math broadened the concept of mathematical meanings. According to the meaning theory of learning, the chief element was an understanding of our number system. New Math introduced some laws or number properties that control the four basic operations on numbers. These properties, which constitute structure, are discussed in Chapter 14. These two contributions of New Math are now recognized in modern curricula and in elementary school mathematics textbooks.

2. For a historical account of the group's workings see William Wooton, *SMSG: The Making of a Curriculum* (New Haven: Yale University Press, 1965).

Back to Basics

The Back-to-Basics movement during the early 1970s involved a return to a program that stressed learning to compute with speed and accuracy. Many of the topics introduced during the New Math days were dropped. The emphasis on the structural aspects of mathematics gave way to memorized rules and procedures, learned through drill and practice.

The Back-to-Basics movement, with its emphasis on rote learning, did not enhance the *understanding* of elementary mathematics. Concerted efforts to prepare children for tests in basic skills were often at the expense of experiences in the learning cycle, such as working with concrete materials and applying knowledge to real-life problem situations.[3]

Future Programs

Each of the movements discussed in this chapter was a valid attempt to improve the teaching and learning of elementary mathematics. Each emphasized certain objectives and approaches. However, because of the dynamic nature and the diversity of American public education, these principles were neither fully accepted nor implemented by many teachers. Future elementary school mathematics programs will have to meet the challenges of the changing times.

Effective teachers of elementary school mathematics are competent, well-informed, skillful, caring individuals. Beyond that, effective teachers must demonstrate three important competencies:

1. Teachers must have a good background in mathematics, understand how children learn, and be skillful in dealing with them in the teaching-learning process.

3. Fred M. Hechinger, "The Back-to-Basics Impact," *Today's Education,* 67 (February/March 1978):32.

2. Teachers must understand the psychology of the teaching-learning process.

3. Teachers must strive continually to keep informed of new and improved approaches.

Principles of Teaching and Learning Mathematics

An effective program of elementary mathematics is made up of units and lessons. These are planned, implemented, and evaluated in accordance with selected psychological principles of teaching and learning mathematics. These principles have evolved over the years—beginning with the research and writings of pioneers such as Piaget, Brownell, Bruner, and Gagné—and have been validated by the practical experiences of outstanding teachers. These psychological principles of teaching and learning are used throughout this text:

1. Establish goals and objectives.

2. Determine readiness and make provisions to develop it.

3. Provide motivation.

4. Provide growth through guided discovery and directed teaching from concrete to abstract.

5. Provide reinforcement.

6. Diagnose and evaluate.

Establishing Goals and Objectives

PRINCIPLE **1.** BOTH TEACHER AND PUPILS SHOULD CLEARLY UNDERSTAND WHAT IS TO BE LEARNED AND HOW TO GO ABOUT THE LEARNING PROCESS.

Effective learning must be based upon carefully selected and clearly stated program goals and learning objectives. Program goals serve to guide the development and evaluation of the mathematics curriculum and teaching methods. Learning objectives are an outgrowth of program goals and serve to guide the planning, teaching, and evaluating units of study and lessons.

In 1989, the National Council of Teachers of Mathematics published *Curriculum and Evaluation Standards for School Mathematics*. In that document five general goals that should be addressed in the mathematics curriculum were identified:

1. Learning to value mathematics.

2. Becoming confident in one's own ability.

3. Becoming a mathematical problem solver.

4. Learning to communicate mathematically.

5. Learning to reason mathematically[4].

LEARNING OBJECTIVES

Pupils in the elementary school are expected to progress toward the achievement of program goals through a series of well-planned lessons. Each lesson or series of lessons within a unit of study must include clearly identified learning objectives in four categories: cognitive, skillful, social, and attitudinal.

Cognitive Objectives The central objective of any lesson or series of lessons must be *to develop an intelligent system of mathematical thinking in problem situations*.

To think mathematically in problem situations, pupils must develop *cognitive objectives* such as the following:

1. To understand, recall, and use the language of mathematics.

2. To be able to reason logically.

3. To demonstrate the ability to solve problems by making drawings, writing equations, guessing, and testing.

4. To become proficient in estimation in order to determine the reasonableness of answers.

5. To draw conclusions and make judgment based on mathematical thinking.[5]

Skillful Objectives A modern mathematics program includes a wide variety of skills children need to acquire, such as:

1. To be able to perform the four fundamental operations with understanding using different algorithms.

2. To perform mental computation and estimation.

3. To use a calculator to reduce computation time.

4. To read graphs and tables and to be able to record data graphically.

Social Objectives The mathematics pupils learn should be applied to socially significant situations in the children's everyday lives. Social objectives help pupils see how mathematics is used in their lives and in the lives of members of our society. Social applications include telling time, managing money, making change, understanding interest, computing sales tax, understanding the measurement concept, and being able to make measurements (see Chapter 15).

Attitudinal Objectives An attitudinal objective involves the pupil's attitude toward learning mathematics. Pupils who develop a favorable attitude for mathematics are interested in learning more about it, rate it as one of their favorite subjects. They realize that the subject has value and importance in society.

4. National Council of Teachers of Mathematics, *Curriculum and Evaluation Standards for School Mathematics* (Reston, VA: NCTM, March 1989), pp. 5–6.

5. See Benjamin S. Bloom (ed.), *Taxonomy of Educational Objectives: The Classification of Educational Goals, Handbook I: Cognitive Domain* (New York: David McKay, 1965).

Determining and Developing Readiness

PRINCIPLE 2. READINESS IS THE KIND OF PU-PIL BACKGROUND THAT WILL ENABLE THEM TO SUCCEED IN LEARNING A NEW TOPIC.

The teacher must first determine the state of readiness of each child for learning activities and then implement different approaches to develop readiness for those who have deficiencies.

Three important considerations relate to the concept of readiness: (1) prerequisite skills, (2) levels of abstractness, and (3) psychological factors.

PREREQUISITE SKILLS

Consideration should be given to each pupil's mastery of prerequisite skills. Many topics in mathematics proceed sequentially, from simple concepts and skills to more complex ones, an aspect of the mathematics continuum arranged into "levels of difficulty." Pupils who have not adequately mastered certain prerequisites to a new topic may have problems learning the more difficult topic. For example, pupils who have not mastered dividing by a one-place divisor will not succeed when asked to divide by a two-place divisor.

Since success on a particular skill in mathematics is largely dependent upon mastery of prerequisite skills, a task analysis for each major sequential topic in mathematics should be completed and children assessed for mastery of prerequisite skills. For pupils found deficient, provisions need to be made through review and remediation to develop required background while at the same time giving them an opportunity to continue to progress through the core curriculum.

LEVELS OF ABSTRACTNESS

Levels of abstractness progress from exploration and discovery with the use of con-crete objects through pictures to symbols. A pupil may be considered ready for a new topic in mathematics if he or she has, among other things, attained a level of abstract thinking high enough to profit from instruction on the new topic. Although the development of beginning concepts and skills should start at the concrete level, a pupil who is still counting objects to determine the sum $9 + 6 = \boxed{}$ is not ready to solve addition examples of the type $27 + 28 = \boxed{}$.

PSYCHOLOGICAL FACTORS

Psychological factors such as self-confidence and attitude toward learning mathematics comprise a third consideration of readiness. For pupils to obtain greatest benefits from learning activities, they should pay attention, actively participate, respond and communicate, enjoy, and value mathematics.

To implement the principle of readiness the teacher needs to take two actions for each class member: (1) Determine the degree of readiness in terms of the mathematics continuum, levels of abstractness, and psychological considerations; (2) plan to develop readiness for pupils who are deficient. Obviously, provisions must be made for individual differences (see Chapter 4).

Providing Motivation

PRINCIPLE 3. LEARNING IS MOST ECONOMI-CAL WHEN HIGHLY MOTIVATED BY ADVANTA-GEOUS PSYCHOLOGICAL AND SOCIAL CONDI-TIONS.

A motivated child is one who is stimulated willingly to participate actively in learning activities. Motivation may come from many sources, but psychologists generally classify them into the two categories of *external* and *intrinsic*. External factors are the result of rewards such as praise by teacher or parent, bonus points, time off for good behavior, and stars on a chart. Intrinsic factors are inner feelings that create a drive to learn more about a given topic or subject. Although a teacher may need to use external motivation to get children started learning, intrinsic motivation is the more effective of the two.

Behavior is complex and caused by many factors, so no one factor can explain the diversity of behavior that even one person displays. Most teachers know that there are certain things that motivate learning and others that cause pupils to lose interest in learning. Research and practice have shown that the following techniques increase motivation:

1. Relate learning to its usefulness. Discuss with the class the many uses of mathematics in their lives and in the community.

2. Make clear to the pupils what is to be learned and explain why and how to go about it.

3. Provide appropriate readiness and background experiences.

4. Use a wide variety of learning materials. Pupils need to progress through the levels of abstraction, beginning with manipulatives and ending with symbols.

5. Make sure each child experiences a degree of success. Nothing succeeds like success. Failure kills motivation.

6. Make learning enjoyable and interesting. Children enjoy working together on group activities and games.

7. Vary the teaching–learning methods. Some lessons need to be guided discovery with manipulatives, drawings, and symbols. Other lessons should be teacher-directed with active participation by the pupils.

8. Keep pupils informed of where they stand in terms of achievement of learning objectives and what needs to be done for future successes.

Providing Growth Through Guided Discovery

PRINCIPLE 4. LEARNING IS A GROWTH PROCESS FACILITATED BY GUIDED DISCOVERY AND DIRECTED TEACHING THROUGH FOUR STAGES: MANIPULATIVE, VISUAL, SYMBOLIC, AND MASTERY.

Three facts are central to the acquisition of mathematical concepts and skills. First, much of mathematics is sequential. Second, learning is a growth process. Third, a pupil understands concepts better and retains them longer if given an opportunity to discover them.

LEVELS OF ABSTRACTNESS

To foster the acquisition of mathematical concepts and skills, one must recognize that there are levels of cognitive development.

Bruner formulated three levels of learning:

1. *Manipulative.* At the first level, the child manipulates objects or things.

2. *Pictures.* At the second level, the child deals with pictures or images of objects but does not manipulate the objects.

3. *Symbols.* At the third level, the child deals with symbols or numerals and no longer deals with tangible or concrete objects.[6]

Throughout this text we stress four levels of learning:

1. *Manipulative level.* At this level the child manipulates objects and works with various manipulative materials such as blocks, abacuses, fraction kits, measuring devices, and the like. During this level, the child starts to develop a vocabulary of mathematical terms and processes. Atten-

6. Jerome S. Burner, Rose R. Oliver, and Patricia M. Greenfield, *Studies in Cognitive Growth* (New York: Wiley, 1966), p. 12.

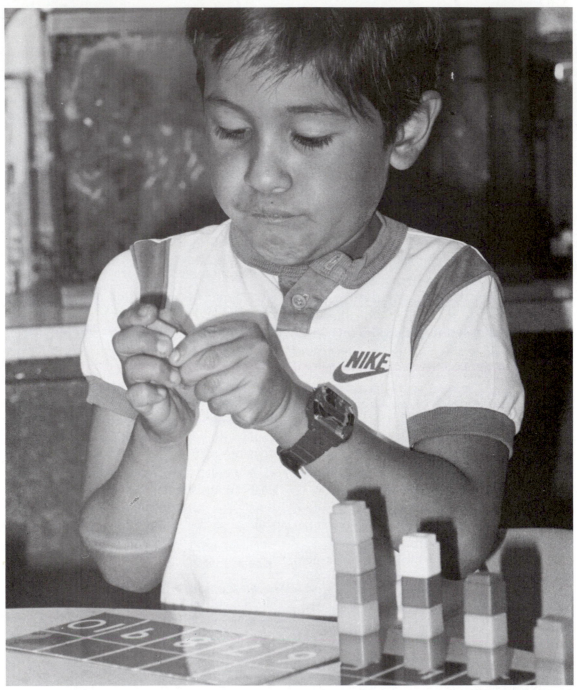

A pupil makes some number discoveries with Unifix cubes.

tion to problem solving and guided discovery is central to any learning situation where manipulatives are to be used.

2. *Visual level.* At this level the child creates drawings of mathematical concepts and learns from pictures of mathematical situations. Translating a mathematical situation represented with manipulatives to a drawing is an important step in learning as a bridge between the concrete and abstract notations. Also at the visual level are materials such as films, filmstrips, videotapes, and computer simulations. All modern mathematics textbooks for children include a wide variety of pictures.

3. *Symbolic level.* At this level the pupil records the situations represented by objects, drawings, and pictures with symbols, signs, and other kinds of notations. This level starts with "expanded notation" and concludes with the standard way to write numerals and algorithms. For example, a pupil may represent 15 as one bundle of ten sticks and five single sticks at the concrete level. At the picture level the child may draw a picture of the objects; at the expanded notation level the child records 1 ten 5 ones = 15.

4. *Mastery level.* At this level the student has satisfactorily achieved the learning objectives for a particular topic. (*Evaluation* is the process of determining the extent to which pupils have mastered learning objectives; see Chapter 3.)

GUIDED DISCOVERY

Guided discovery means that the teacher directs the class through a sequence of activities and provides questions and appropriate discussions until the desired answer or concept is found. The activities may involve manipulatives, visuals, or symbolic materials. As Paul Cobb points out, *constructivism* views teachers and pupils as "active meaning-makers who continually give contextually based meanings to each others' words and actions as they interact."[7]

For some children, however, independent self-discovery is not easy and teachers, pressed for time, sometimes resort to "telling approaches," which are the least effective during early stages of learning.

During a discovery learning experience, children should be given opportunities to explore and create new ideas, patterns, and processes. Teachers can use the following techniques:

1. Use instructional materials in a way that encourages pupils to think for themselves at various levels of abstractness.

2. Give encouragement and suggestions. No child can be expected to discover independently all the essential meanings in mathematics.

3. Provide guidance when necessary. The skillful teacher will create several different situations involving the new topic. Some children may need to use manipulative materials, while others will profit from pictures and drawings, self-made or otherwise.

4. After pupils have been given ample opportunity to explore and discover, they should be engaged in a discussion of what they have done and what they have discovered. Pupils need to talk and have discussions in order to learn effectively.

Teachers must plan experiences carefully so that one experience leads logically to the next, and each is guided so that desirable learning results. In a good textbook series, the important mathematical topics are arranged according to levels of difficulty. But no textbook can possibly provide the variety of experiences needed by children working at different levels of abstraction. The teacher can help by asking the right questions, provoking new lines of thought, giv-

7. Paul Cobb, "The Tension Between Theories of Learning and Instruction in Mathematics," *Educational Psychologist.* Special issue: "Learning Mathematics from Instruction," *23* (Spring 1988): 88.

ing praise when deserved, and giving encouragement when needed. The teacher can provide hints or clues when a child is discouraged and progress is temporarily blocked.

After pupils have been given an opportunity to discover basic concepts with the teacher's guidance, the pupils then must have the opportunity to discuss basic concepts. Then the teacher guides the class to understand the *structural* aspects of mathematics—patterns, relationships, principles, and properties that characterize a mathematical system (see Chapter 14).

DIRECTED TEACHING

After initial discovery experiences with appropriate instructional materials, the teacher should provide opportunities for pupils to fully understand the major concepts and language of the new topic. At this stage of the lesson development the teacher may need to use a type of directed instruction. Directed instruction, expository teaching, or teaching by telling has long been used for instruction in mathematics. The approach is based upon the *transmission view* of teaching, which Cobb describes as one that emphasizes the teacher's words and actions as if "they carry meanings in and of themselves that are waiting to be apprehended by students, or they can serve to draw students' attention to mathematical structures in the environment. These structures might, for example, be embodied in manipulative materials, pictures, diagrams, or problem statements."[8]

Children cannot develop a full understanding of mathematics without special help from the teacher. Instruction must include guided discovery during initial phases of concept development, followed by directed teaching during the latter phases of concept development as needed.

8. Cobb, p. 88.

Any major educational movement has been misinterpreted by some teachers, and *discovery* is no exception. It is completely unrealistic to think that all the pupils in a class will discover the desired concept when given a set of manipulatives without any guidance. Careful supervision and guidance will lead some members of the class to the desired discovery, but the teacher must make every effort to see that all pupils finally understand the desired concept. Recognition of this necessity leads to *guided discovery* rather than discovery. Current terminology often uses the term *directed teaching* to refer to the place in the lesson where the teacher takes charge and makes the final summary with the help of the members of the class.

Providing Reinforcement

PRINCIPLE 5. REINFORCEMENT THROUGH PRACTICE AND APPLICATIONS IS ESSENTIAL FOR MASTERY.

Fixation of concepts and skills is essential for mastery-level achievement. Reinforcement is delivered through practice activities and by the child's participating in a variety of applications in measurement and problem-solving situations.

TYPES OF PRACTICE

There are two different kinds of practice: varied purposeful practice and repetitive practice, also called drill. Varied purposeful practice is designed to increase mathematical understanding and to move the learner toward more mature, economical abstract thinking at the symbolic level of learning. Repetitive drill is necessary to fix a desired skill and to increase the proficiency of using the skills taught.

Both types of practice must involve thinking, and both are necessary in a modern program. Each type of practice needs to be given with a specific objective in mind. Special attention must be paid to the time and the amount of practice needed by each learner.

The use of calculators and computer programs offers the opportunity to provide both types of practice discussed above. Subsequent chapters include illustrations of practice activities that have been found useful in helping pupils master concepts and skills in mathematics.

Diagnosing and Evaluating

PRINCIPLE 6. EVALUATION IS NECESSARY TO DETERMINE THE EXTENT TO WHICH PUPILS HAVE ACHIEVED STATED GOALS AND OBJECTIVES.

During the teaching–learning process the teacher is continually evaluating and diagnosing pupils' learning. Evaluation is the process of periodically assessing the extent to which each pupil has progressed toward achieving learning objectives. Diagnosis is the process of identifying the reasons children may be having difficulty in achieving that objective. Remediation is the process of treating deficiencies in learning mathematics. Evaluation and diagnosis are discussed in detail in Chapter 3 and are treated in subsequent chapters.

Principles Applied to a Sample Lesson

The following paragraphs describe a third-grade lesson in addition of two two-digit numbers with *regrouping*. The teaching–learning approaches that were used exemplify the principles of learning that we identified.

Illustrative Lesson

A problem arose in connection with a shopping experience when a third-grade class had to find the answer to the addition example $37 + 15 = \square$. The class had not yet learned the *regrouping* step that was involved. The teacher first stated the problem as follows:

"If you went to the store and bought two items, a tablet for 37 cents and a pencil for 15 cents, how much did both items cost?" The teacher then wrote the example in vertical form on the chalkboard to focus the attention of the class to the new step.

$$\begin{array}{r} 37 \\ + 15 \\ \hline \end{array}$$

The teacher asked the children to think of a way to find the answer using what they already knew about number.

One boy suggested that we take 37 pennies and 15 pennies and count them to find the total, but this would take too long. Another child suggested that a shorter way would be to use dimes and pennies. Several pupils suggested that *base-ten blocks* could be used to solve the problem. Each pupil had a kit of base-ten blocks. The teacher asked each child to represent 37 in terms of 3 tens and 7 ones (3 longs and 7 cubes), and 15 as 1 ten and 5 ones (1 long and 5 cubes). The children had no difficulty in representing these two numbers with the base-ten blocks.

The teacher then directed the pupils to *join* the objects used to represent the two numbers and find out how many tens and how many ones there would be. The pupils concluded that the answer was 4 longs and 12 cubes (4 tens and 12 ones). The pupils were then asked if the answer 4 tens 12 ones helped them to find the total cost of the two articles. One pupil suggested that the 12 ones could be changed to 1 ten 2 ones. The teacher asked the other pupils to perform the *regrouping* with their materials so that the result was a sum of 5 tens 2 ones, or 52.

The teacher now felt that the class was ready to learn the new step for regrouping

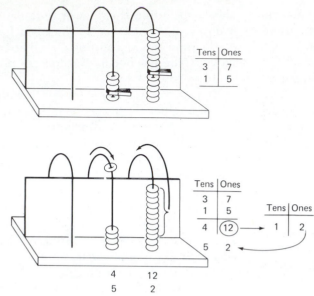

Represent 3 tens 7 ones
and 1 ten 5 ones
on the abacus.

Join beads at the tens-
place and at the ones-
place = 4 tens 12 ones.

The ones place is now
overloaded, so regrouping
will be necessary.

Regroup the 12 ones to
1 ten 2 ones by removing
ten beads from the
ones place in exchange
for one bead at the
tens place.

Answer: 5 tens 2 ones = 52.

Figure 1.1
Use of the abacus in showing regrouping in addition

in addition. To make sure that the new step was understood, the teacher had a pupil use an 18-bead abacus to demonstrate the procedure, as shown in Figure 1.1.

First, the pupil showed 15 on the abacus by moving one bead to the tens-rod and by moving 5 beads to the ones-rod. Then he showed 37 by moving 3 beads to the tens place and 7 beads to the ones place. The two sets of beads were separated by clothespins. Next, he joined the ones-place beads and the tens-place beads by removing the clothespin; the result was 4 beads in the tens place and 12 beads in the ones place. Because there were "too many ones" (the ones place was *overloaded*), he then regrouped the 12 ones by exchanging 10 beads in the ones place for 1 bead in the tens place. This exchange left only 2 beads in the ones place, while 5 beads occupied the tens place.

One girl volunteered to write out her

steps on the chalkboard and give a reason for each step:

A. Add the ones and the tens:

3 tens	7 ones
1 ten	5 ones
4 tens	12 ones

B. Rename 12 ones to 1 ten 2 ones.

C. So our answer is 5 tens 2 ones.

Principles of Learning Implicit in the Lesson

In the following sections, we analyze the principles of learning that underlie the procedures used in the preceding lesson.

1. *Learning experiences should be purposeful and realistic.* The need to learn the new step in addition arose in a realistic problem situation. The teacher believed that

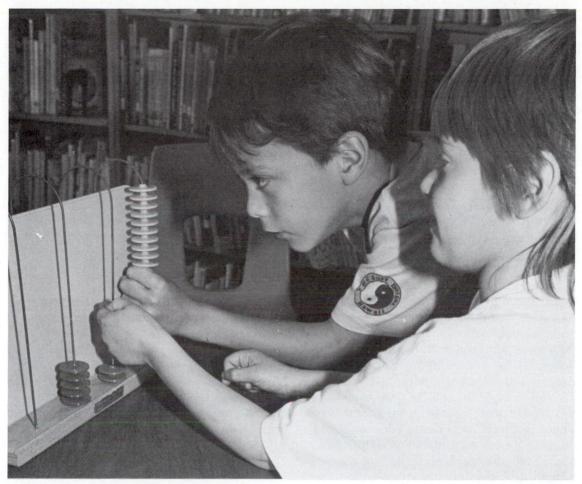

Pupils explore regrouping with an abacus.

(Photo by Leland Perry)

learning is most effective when its basis is problem solving. The purpose for the lesson was to solve a problem that required a new step in addition—that is, regrouping when the sum of the one-place numbers is ten or more.

2. *Readiness is essential for learning.* Before this lesson, the pupils already had considerable experience with basic addition situations and had used a variety of instructional materials. Each pupil was ready for the types of experiences involved in this lesson.

3. *Learning requires a high level of motivation.* In this lesson, motivation resulted from the need to solve a real-life problem and the opportunity for each pupil to participate actively in learning activities. The teacher did not do all the telling; children were asked to share their thoughts with the class.

Next, the teacher had the children read the presentation in their textbook, which used a similar example. The class explained each step in the presentation.

Now the teacher was ready to discuss

how to handle the ones when the sum is 10 or more, as illustrated in (a) and (b).

(a)   37   (b)   37   (c)   37
    + 15   + 15   + 15
    ⎯⎯⎯   ⎯⎯⎯   ⎯⎯⎯
     ⑫   52   52

(with a "1" written above the tens column in (b), connected by an arrow from the circled 12 in (a))

The class told why the 1 ten from the sum in (a) is written above the 3 tens in (b).

The class used the pattern in (b) to add in further examples. The pupils use the pattern in (c) after they are able to think the 1 ten without writing it in the tens place. When students reach this stage, they are approaching the mastery level of learning.

4. *Learning is a growth process facilitated through guided discovery and directed teaching during four stages: concrete, visual, symbolic, and mastery.*

Discovery played an important role in the lesson. Using symbolic notations and a variety of activities with manipulative materials, the teacher led the children to discover the answer to the problem in several ways. These methods were meaningful to the children and easy to understand. The teacher made sure that each child had an opportunity to discover the steps that were necessary to understand the written record. The regrouping step was demonstrated on an abacus and with written notations. The pupils' discoveries with manipulative materials enabled them to follow the teacher's demonstration so that later they will be able to understand regrouping in addition.

The emphasis in this lesson was on regrouping in addition. The number patterns used were related to the structural properties of place value and regrouping. The technique of writing 37 as 3 tens and 7 ones was used to help children understand the meaning of place value. When 12 ones was regrouped, the structural property of naming a number in different *equal* forms was emphasized. That is, the fact that 12 ones is

regrouped as 1 ten 2 ones was an important insight in mathematics.

The pupils used manipulative materials to find solutions to the problem. The pupil explained the different steps in a solution, thereby demonstrating that they understood the work and would be able to interpret the printed page. Then the teacher had the class read the presentation of the same problem in the textbook. The initial presentation of a basic operation is never complete until the pupil is able to read and interpret the textbook presentation.

5. *Reinforcement through practice and application is essential for mastery.* In this lesson the teacher did not assign practice exercises to "fix" the steps being learned until the children understood them. The assigned practice followed naturally from the class discussion. The children were encouraged to use a variety of approaches to find solutions to the examples assigned. Drill was not appropriate at this stage of learning.

6. *Evaluate and diagnose.* As the lesson progressed the teacher evaluated and diagnosed the learning of each pupil through careful observations. (See Chapter 3.)

Summary

The current technological revolution makes it imperative that the study of elementary mathematics develop understanding of concepts and applications as a preparation for a rapidly changing social and economic society.

Between 1940 and 1980 three movements changed mathematics programs in the elementary schools. Each movement had a major theme, and each had deficiencies. Elements of each approach still appeal to some elementary school teachers, so one can find evidence of each movement in some classrooms.

In the early 1940s the meaningful approach was introduced into the schools. This approach emphasized working with manipulatives, understanding our number system, applying learning to social situations, and having pupils discover meanings in elementary arithmetic. Unfortunately, this approach emphasized only arithmetic, and children needed an early start with topics from geometry and algebra.

New Math, introduced in the early 1960s, brought major changes in the content of mathematics in the elementary school, emphasizing structure and including new topics in mathematics. New Math made two significant contributions to elementary school mathematics. First, it broadened the curriculum and changed a program solely devoted to arithmetic to a program of mathematics. Second, it broadened the concept of meaning to include structure. A few aspects of the New Math program proved to be of questionable value, but the beneficial results were superior to a limited number of deficiencies.

The Back-to-Basics movement prompted a re-examination of the mathematics curriculum in order to determine the most essential content to be taught in the elementary schools. It resulted in several changes in elementary textbooks that in turn produced changes in what was taught to pupils. Many New Math topics were either reduced or dropped from the curriculum, and more pages of the textbook were devoted to drill exercises. In response to Back-to-Basics, many leading mathematics educators feared a return to overemphasis on learning computational skills through rote drill.

Elementary school mathematics programs of the 1990s need to be implemented by teachers who understand mathematics, who know how children learn and develop, who understand the teaching–learning process, and who strive to keep informed of new and improved approaches.

Modern elementary school mathematics programs should be guided by the following six essential principles of teaching and learning mathematics:

1. Both teacher and pupils should understand clearly what is to be learned and how to go about the learning process.

2. Readiness is the kind of background that will enable a pupil to succeed in learning a new topic.

3. Learning is most economical when it is highly motivated by advantageous psychological and social conditions.

4. Learning is a growth process that is facilitated through guided discovery and directed teaching during four stages: concrete, visual, symbolic, and mastery.

5. Reinforcement through practice and applications is essential for mastery.

6. Evaluation is necessary to determine the extent to which pupils have achieved the stated goals and objectives.

Teachers should make every effort to implement the principles of teaching and learning discussed in this chapter and elaborated in later chapters. Traditional rote methods that stress repetitive drill as the basis of learning should be discarded in favor of approaches that emphasize the discovery of meanings in elementary school mathematics. These approaches are the keys to the successful teaching and learning of elementary mathematics. The teacher plays an important role in a program of this kind.

Exercises

1. In what ways did New Math differ fom the meaningful approach?
2. What improvements in the elementary school mathematics program could result from new technology?

3. Examine and criticize the objectives listed in the teacher's edition of a recently published textbook on elementary mathematics for a particular grade level.

4. You are working with a group of sixth graders who are not interested in learning mathematics. What are some techniques you could use to motivate these students?

5. What are the differences between the discovery approach to teaching and learning elementary school mathematics and the transmission view of teaching?

6. What are some objections to having pupils learn mathematics through rote drill without understanding mathematical meanings?

7. What is the specific meaning of evaluation, diagnosis, and remediation?

Outline for Lesson Planning

I. *IDENTIFICATION DATA:*
Topic, grade, name, date, etc.

II. *OBJECTIVES:*
Write objectives in terms of what the pupils are expected to learn: concepts, language, skills, procedures, properties, patterns, problem-solving strategies, etc.

III. *TASK ANALYSIS:*
Analyze the lesson topic in terms of what prerequisites are needed for success and what aspects of the topic will be taught later.

IV. *MATERIALS NEEDED:*
List the manipulatives, visuals, and other materials that will be needed during the lesson development.

V. *ANTICIPATORY SET:*
Indicate ways to get the lesson started, such as review, warmups, mental math, sharing, questioning, story problems, etc.

VI. *THE TEACHING/LEARNING SEQUENCE:*
Outline the sequence to be followed in the development of the lesson with an emphasis on guided discovery and sharing of thinking by pupils.

VII. *LESSON CLOSURE:*
State how the lesson will be concluded: summarize, review, generalize, reinforce, test, enrich, etc. Here is the place in the lesson to give an assignment for group and independent work.

VIII. *EVALUATION:*
Indicate ways assessment of pupils' learning will be accomplished in terms of the stated objectives.

IX. *NEEDED MODIFICATIONS FOR INDIVIDUAL PUPILS:*
After the lesson make notes of special needs of individuals who need remediation, reteaching, and/or enrichment.

Selected Readings

The Agenda in Action, 1983 Yearbook. Reston, VA: The National Council of Teachers of Mathematics, 1983.

Copeland, Richard W. *How Children Learn Mathematics. Fourth Education.* New York: Macmillan, 1984. Chapters 1 and 2.

Cruikshank, Douglas E., and Linda Jensen Sheffield. *Teaching Mathematics to Elementary School Children.* Columbus, OH: Merrill, 1988. Chapter 1.

Everybody Counts, A Report to the Nation on the Future of Mathematics Education by the National Research Council. Washington, D.C.: National Academy Press, 1989.

Kennedy, Leonard M., and Steve Tipps. *Guiding Children's Learning of Mathematics, 5th ed.* Belmont, CA: Wadsworth, 1988. Chapters 1 and 2.

Marks, John L., et al. *Teaching Elementary Scool for Understanding.* New York: McGraw-Hill, 1985, Chapters 1 and 2.

Piaget, Jean, *The Child's Concept of Number.* New York: Norton, 1965.

Post, Thomas R., *Teaching Mathematics in Grades K–8.* Boston: Allyn & Bacon, 1988. Chapter 1.

Reys, Robert E., et al. *Helping Children Learn Mathematics*, 2nd ed. Englewood Cliffs, NJ: Prentice-Hall, 1989, Chapter 1.

Trafton, Paul R. (ed.). *New Directions for Elementary School Mathematics*, The 1989 NCTM Yearbook Reston, VA: National Council of Teachers of Mathematics, 1989. Chapter 1.

See also issues of *The Arithmetic Teacher* and the *Journal for Research in Mathematics Education.*

The Classroom as a Learning Laboratory

ACHIEVEMENT GOALS

After studying this chapter, you should be able to:

1. Explain how working with manipulatives leads pupils to the symbolic stage of learning.

2. Identify what is needed to implement the laboratory approach.

3. Outline three guidelines for the proper use of manipulatives.

4. Identify different kinds of learning centers and tell what is needed for proper operation.

5. Describe the proper way to use the textbook in an elementary program.

6. Outline the major advantages and disadvantages of calculator use.

7. Identify the role of computers in the elementary school.

VOCABULARY

These terms are defined or illustrated in the Glossary.

Associate picture
Calculator logic
Computer memory
Computer program
Expressive
   vocabulary

Functional picture
Hardware
Interpretative
   vocabulary
Learning
   laboratory
Scope and
   sequence
Software

To learn mathematics with understanding, pupils must be actively involved in *doing* mathematics. The classroom must therefore be a *learning laboratory* where children are given a wide variety of activities. These activities include working with manipulatives, viewing visuals, participating in guided discovery and class discussions, solving problems, and studying the textbook. Such activities often lead to exploring and working with mathematics in other subject areas, in the home, and in the community. The teacher orchestrates the activities in ways that encourage individual pupil initiative.

Value of the Laboratory Approach

Extensive research has verified the value of the laboratory approach in learning elementary school mathematics. In this approach a class uses concrete objects and manipulatives to begin the study of a mathematical concept. Working with manipulatives helps pupils visualize mathematical concepts. Discussing and interpreting these concepts, with the teacher's guidance, provides the basis for a transition to the visual level of learning and then to the symbolic stage. Pupils reach the mastery level of learning after they have had appropriate reinforcement experiences with writing, studying the textbook, and solving problems.

As pupils move to higher grade levels, learning experiences tend to be more symbolic and verbal. Guided discovery is a major activity in learning mathematics that requires questions, answers, and discussion directed by the teacher. Reading the textbook and solving problems are essential activities at the symbolic level. The teacher must always be alert for opportunities to use manipulatives and visuals at any grade level. Fractions, percents, geometry, and statistics all should be introduced with manipulative and visual aids.

Learning Mathematics Is Enhanced by Language Experiences

Working in groups in laboratory activities encourages pupils to *talk* about mathematics. As pupils work with materials and equipment they should be encouraged to "think out loud." They should listen to others describe a mathematics concept or procedure, answer questions, pose questions, and tell about experiences. Critical thinking is stimulated by verbal exchanges about mathematics.

As pupils of different ability levels and interests work together on various activities and projects in the laboratory setting, each child may learn something different that can be shared with others. Sharing often helps pupils gain insights into the topic being studied.

Implementing the Laboratory Approach

Flexible Organization Plan

Working in groups should not be limited to the traditional three groups. The basis for deciding how many groups to form and which pupils to be assigned to each group depends upon the type of activity and materials involved as well as class composition. Flexibility in physical arrangements is often essential for maximum learning.

Working with manipulatives can be provided during whole-class activities through teacher-directed lessons, but appropriate materials must be used and pupils must be actively involved in guided discovery. Usually it is advisable to provide experiences with manipulatives in a small-group setting. When possible, pupils needing similar remediation should be in the same group. Pupils in another small group may be rapid learners investigating an advanced topic in mathematics. Some other pupils may be in cooperative learning groups of four or five children from different achievement levels working toward the same objective.

Manipulative Materials

Manipulative materials are objects that pupils can feel, touch, handle, and move. The objects can be blocks, or other kinds of objects and devices such as base-ten blocks, abacuses, fraction parts, and the like. At the concrete level, pupils deal with manipulatives as they discover solutions to problems.

Research Findings

The work of many researchers, including Piaget and Bruner, supports the view that the first stage of the learning cycle should be at the concrete level. Since 1960, more than a hundred research studies have reported on the positive effects of various manipulative materials on pupils learning elementary mathematical concepts and skills. These studies were made in programs that emphasized discovery as the result of pupil exploration with appropriate instructional aids.

Parham performed a meta-analysis of 64 studies and compared the use and nonuse of manipulative materials on student achievement.[1] The analysis showed that elementary school pupils using manipulatives scored on achievement tests at approximately the 85th percentile, while the nonusers scored at about the 50th percentile. The conclusion was that manipulative materials do have a positive effect on student achievement in mathematics.

A great majority of research studies shows that the use of manipulatives to introduce new topics in elementary school mathematics is highly desirable. The vital problem

pertains to the selection and proper use of *appropriate* manipulatives.

Selection of Manipulatives

Hundreds of types of manipulatives are on the market for pupils to use as they learn elementary mathematics. The choice of materials is critical. Each type of manipulative should be selected with these criteria in mind:

1. *The aid should represent the concept involved and be useful in developing appropriate mathematical language.* The teacher can use a balance to illustrate the idea of "equal" in a number sentence.

2. *The aid should be available to the pupils to use during the discovery experience.* Sometimes a teacher uses a demonstration aid to show pupils an idea. To gain full benefit from the manipulative, many children need hands-on experience. Demonstration models are useful, especially when they provide for pupil participation.

3. *The aid should provide an easy transition to a drawing or picture of the idea that leads to more abstract notations.* For example, base-ten blocks are easy to draw to represent the base-ten concept, which in turn is easy to represent with symbolic notations. An abacus used to demonstrate the idea of place value is easy to represent with a picture, then with symbols. Manipulatives have not served their purpose until they are no longer needed.

4. *Manipulative aids should be attractive, durable, multipurpose if possible, and of interest to pupils.* Commercially distributed manipulatives typically meet these criteria, but they are sometimes very expensive. Nevertheless, many times the purchase of manipulatives can be a school project, and several teachers can share them at different times of the year, reducing the cost per pupil. In many instances, manipulatives can

---

1. Jaynie Loftin Parham, "A Meta-Analysis of the Use of Manipulative Materials and Student Achievement in Elementary School Mathematics." *Dissertation Abstracts International*, Vol. 44, July 1983, p. 96A.

(Photo by Leland Perry)

Pupils use the balance to better understand the concept, "equal".

be homemade by teachers, parents, or pupils. Homemade manipulatives may be as good as or better than commercial aids, particularly if the pupils help in their constructions.

5. *Manipulative aids need to be easy to store.* The storage of manipulatives could be made a school project and the materials could be stored in a mathematics laboratory, the library, or in some other storage area. No one classroom is supposed to be equipped with all the materials suggested in this book. It is the teacher's responsibility to select a few of the suggested materials that

best meet the needs of the children. Two manipulatives used effectively are better than a dozen hidden in a closet.

Examples of Recommended Manipulatives

The following section presents a brief description of a few manipulatives available for a modern program from which a teacher can select those most appropriate for the topics taught at a particular grade level. Throughout most of the following chapters of this book examples will be provided of many other manipulatives.

- **Objects for counting.** Any discrete thing can be counted, such as real objects, blocks, and people.
- **Ten-ten bead frame.** A ten-ten bead frame is a good manipulative to help pupils see the "tenness" of our number system. It can also be used to help children count by 2s, 5s, and by 10s (see Chapter 5).
- **The hundred board.** From counting objects comes the formation of number concepts—how many, which one, before, between, and after. One of the best aids for teaching these is the hundred board (see Chapter 5).
- **Unifix Cubes.** Unifix cubes constitute a durable, colorful, and flexible manipulative aid. They are made out of plastic, come in ten colors, and interlock.
- **Cuisenaire Rods.** Cuisenaire rods are useful in showing patterns, in ordering in size from shortest to longest, and in studying number operations. The Cuisenaire rods start with a centimeter cube that is colored white. All the other rods are in different colors and differ in length by one centimeter.

A pupil uses both the length of a rod and its color to help identify the number represented.

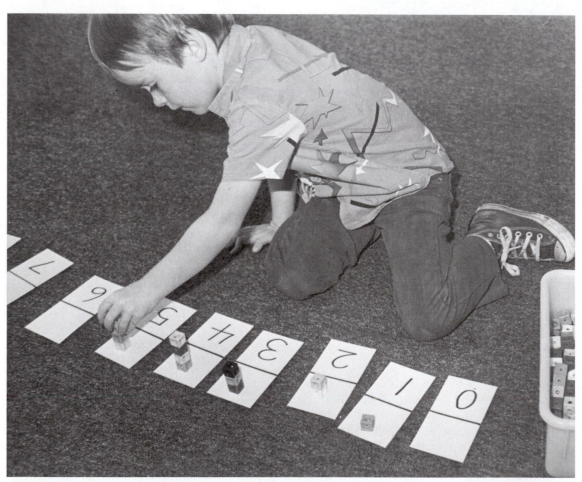

A pupil associates blocks with the correct numerals.

(Photo by Leland Perry)

(Photo by Leland Perry)

Pupils puzzle out sequencing and ordering with Cuisenaire rods.

- **Attribute Blocks.** Attribute blocks are valuable for building patterns, sorting, ordering and classifying. Unifix cubes, Cuisenaire rods, and geometric solids with holes through their center are also helpful for these purposes.

Attribute blocks are made up of the following pieces:

1. Five shapes—square, circle, rectangle, triangle, and hexagon.

2. For each shape there are two sizes—large and small.

3. For each shape and each size there are three colors—red, blue, yellow.

4. For each shape and each size and each color there are two thicknesses—thick and thin.

(How many pieces in a set?)

BASE-TEN CONCEPTS

Our system of number has a base of ten. This means when we have ten ones we may regroup them into one set of ten, and when we have ten tens we may regroup these into one set of one hundred.

Three types of materials are essential for developing the concept and language associated with base ten:

1. Sticks or straws and rubber bands for grouping by tens.

2. Base-ten blocks. The most durable base-ten blocks are made from hardwood and scored to indicate the number of ones in each piece. The design on the ones shown in the Figure 2.1 is metric, in which the smallest unit is a cubic centimeter. This type of aid may also be used for metric projects.

3. Money—pennies, dimes, and dollars.

BASE TEN BLOCKS

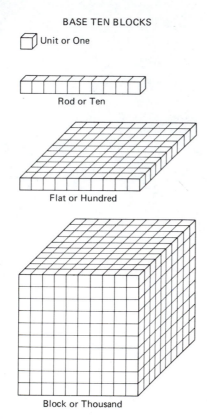

Unit or One

Rod or Ten

Flat or Hundred

Block or Thousand

Figure 2.1
Base-ten blocks

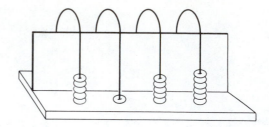

Figure 2.2
A modern computing abacus

mend is a modern "computing abacus"; its major value is to demonstrate the idea of *place value* and the idea of regrouping in addition and subtraction. Figure 2.2 shows a modern computing abacus constructed with bent metal rods with eighteen wooden beads on each rod. (See Chapter 1 for a sample lesson using this type of abacus.)

Aids for basic number facts and number operations appear in Chapters 7 and 9.

Aids for fractional numbers are shown in Chapters 11 and 12.

Aids for geometry are shown in Chapter 16.

Aids for measurement are shown in Chapter 15.

Many times a single manipulative may be used for a variety of different topics in mathematics. Table 2.1 shows several manipulatives with their multiple uses.

Proper Use of Manipulatives

The proper use of manipulatives involves the following three procedures:

1. Use manipulatives with all pupils during the exploratory level of learning to assist pupils to discover patterns, relationships, and number concepts. The major purpose of using manipulatives is to help each pupil bridge the gap from the concrete level of learning to more abstract representations.

PLACE-VALUE CONCEPTS

Place value is a very special concept in our system of notation. It means that the *position* of a digit in a numeral determines its value. The Hindu priests who invented the place-value idea we use today in our system of notation used a counting board. A model of this type of abacus is easily made out of cardboard, and many objects could be used as the counters. The type of abacus we recom-

Table 2.1 Manipulative Use Chart

Manipulative	Numeration								Geometry and Measurement								
	Counting	Discrimination	Sorting and ordering	Pattern relations	Place value	Addition/Subtraction	Multiplication/Division	Fractions	Decimals	Boundaries and regions	Geometric relationships	Symmetry	Linear	Volume	Weight	Graphing	Money
Abacus	X				X												
Attribute blocks	X	X	X	X		X				X	X	X					
Base-ten blocks	X	X	X			X	X	X	X				X	X	X		
Geoboards		X		X				X		X	X	X	X				
Pattern blocks	X	X	X	X		X	X	X		X	X	X				X	X
Unifix cubes	X	X	X	X	X	X	X	X					X	X		X	
Pocket place value chart					X	X	X		X								

2. Use different types of organizational plans. Some activities with manipulatives can be done with the whole class; others are best accomplished in small groups. Learning centers may be set up within the classroom where pupils can be scheduled to perform assigned tasks. If possible, a school mathematics laboratory could be established where pupils have the opportunity to study under the direction of a specialist. The laboratory may also be a school-level computer laboratory where instruction and direction is provided by a specialist in mathematics and computers.

3. Give pupils problems to solve with their manipulatives. Give them time to work out solutions. Have them work in pairs or in teams, and encourage them to discuss various ways to approach the solution to the problem. During the time pupils share dis-

coveries they gain important insights into mathematics.

Multimedia Materials

Visual materials include pictures, diagrams, charts, films, filmstrips, and books. The mathematics textbook generally includes many pictures, diagrams, and charts for pupils to examine and discuss. Audio materials include tapes for listening centers. Audiovisual materials include motion-picture films, filmstrips with audiotapes, and videotapes.

Many school districts have available a multimedia center which has on file filmstrips, motion pictures, and videotapes for teachers to check out and use. Multimedia materials are useful when they provide experiences otherwise unavailable such as weighing objects on the moon. These materials offer unique opportunities to motivate children and to enrich their learning of mathematics.

Learning Centers

A desirable part of the laboratory approach is the establishment of one or more learning centers within the classroom or in a special room set up for that purpose. A learning center is a place that is equipped with special materials where pupils can go individually or in small groups to participate in special learning activities. Several types of learning centers are a measurement center, a practice center with drill and practice kits, a listening center with audiotapes and earphones, and a visual center with sound filmstrips or loops.

Designing a Learning Center

These steps should be taken in designing a learning center:

1. Determine the purpose of the center. Learning centers may serve one or more purposes. They may provide enrichment, reinforcement, opportunities for discovery, applications, and problem-solving activities.

2. Carefully select the materials to be in the center. The materials need to be available to each pupil for individual work.

3. Plan activities to fit the maturity level of the pupils.

4. Provide written instructions for the use of the center in language that is understood by the pupils.

5. Provide assistance by a parent volunteer, an aide, or a cross-age tutor as available.

6. Establish standards of behavior such as rules for movement and for talking. Make

clear what the pupils are to do when finished.

7. Develop some kind of recordkeeping system so pupils can be held accountable for learning accomplished.

8. Have follow-up discussions of how things went in the center and how the center can be improved.

The Mathematics Textbook

All publishers of modern textbooks for elementary school mathematics provide a variety of materials in addition to the pupils' textbooks. One of the most beneficial publications is the Teacher's Edition for each grade level. This book should be required reading for each teacher. A Teacher's Edition typically includes the following features:

- Suggestions for yearly and unit planning.
- Scope and sequence chart showing the grade placement of topics as well as the sequence of teaching for each topic.
- Suggested lesson plans for each unit and each lesson including objectives, prelesson activities, suggested manipulatives, lesson development, follow-up activities, enrichments, games, etc.
- Diagnostic tests, unit tests, and end-of-year tests.
- Practice exercises.
- Suggestions for calculator and computer activities.

In addition to the Teacher's Edition, many textbook publishers have developed kits of manipulative materials, workbooks to go along with the textbook, supplementary problem-solving pamphlets, audiovisual tapes for various topics in mathematics, and computer disks.

The pupil's textbook is typically very attractive with many colored pictures, developmental activities, word problems, and practice examples. It is unfortunate that many pupils are unable to read and understand the contents of their mathematics textbook. The following list of suggestions will help pupils reach that goal.

Building the Mathematics Vocabulary

Every pupil has two vocabularies: the expressive and the interpretative. The *expressive vocabulary* is the one used in speaking and writing; the *interpretative vocabulary* relates to listening and reading. Often a teacher will talk and hope that the children are listening. To promote effective learning, teachers should listen and have the pupils talk.

Any mathematics textbook contains some words that are unfamiliar to many children. The teacher should read each new word in a lesson and then write it on the chalkboard. The children should also read the word and say in their own words what the word means. A dictionary should be consulted if none of the children can define a term adequately. Some textbooks list the terms introduced in a chapter and indicate the page on which each term is presented. These lists are valuable aids for reviewing the vocabulary in that chapter. Each chapter in this text has a list of terms that may be unfamiliar to readers. These terms are explained in the Glossary to help readers understand the subject under discussion.

Reading and Understanding Number Symbols

To read mathematics, one must learn certain words and symbols unique to the subject. Some symbols have more than one meaning; for example, the period (.) can represent a decimal point, as in 2.5, or a sign of multiplication, as in 2·5. Some pupils find the symbolism of mathematics an obstacle to reading the textbook. Consider the symbolism involved in designating the basic operation of multiplication.

$$3 \times 4 \qquad \begin{array}{r} 4 \\ \times\ 3 \\ \hline \end{array} \qquad 3{\cdot}4 \qquad 3(4) \qquad (3)(4)$$

The pupil must be able to interpret each of these designations. These and similar symbols raise the reading level of a mathematics textbook.

The list given here is the symbolic representation for multiplication. Have the class give the verbal representation. Some of the phrases or statements would be: "multiply," "find the product," "three times four," "three fours," "perform multiplication," "write the number sentence," and so on.

Improving Reading in Problem Solving

To solve verbal problems the first thing pupils must do is to read the problem carefully and identify the problem question. (How to solve verbal problems is covered in Chapter 6.) Pupils who have difficulty in reading verbal problems need special assistance in this type of reading. The teacher should have a pupil who articulates well read a problem aloud. Each pupil should identify the problem question and then solve the problem. Further help may be needed at this point.

Using Pictures

All elementary school mathematics textbooks contain pictures that should be used as reading exercises. Nearly all these pictures can be classified as either associative or functional. An *associate picture* shows a scene connected with an activity or event, such as children at play on an outing. A *functional picture* contains data that are essential to the solution of the problem on that page or that enrich the meaning of a concept.

Have the class explain or describe a picture. When pupils tell what they see in the picture or how they interpret it, they exercise their expressive vocabularies. Have pupils make up one or more problems about a picture so as to exercise their interpretative vocabularies. The teacher can direct the activity by having the class make up a problem dealing with a particular operation, such as subtraction.

The text may have quantitative tables, such as height and weight charts. Teachers should make certain that students learn how to read and interpret the data in tabular form.

Conventional Reading versus Mathematical Reading

Reading a mathematics text is not like reading conventional material, in which a thread of continuity holds the interest of the reader, who seeks recreation or information. Most readers are curious to know the outcome of a story or news item or wish to add to their knowledge of the subject at hand. In contrast, most of the reading in elementary mathematics textbooks contains verbal problems, where there is no thread of continuity. In most cases pupils do not know what the outcome of the problem will be. The reader's chief source of interest in reading mathematics textbooks is the desire to excel and to get the correct answer. Often, readers require much extra time for reading a mathematics text so as to take in all the details, to read equations in two directions, to glance at tables or charts, and to translate symbols into words.

The adage that every teacher should be a teacher of English, both oral (spoken) and silent (reading), is very true for elementary mathematics. The teacher not only must give professional instruction in mathematics but also must be skillful in giving instruction in reading and interpreting the textbook.

Calculators

In the early 1970s hand-held calculators were expensive, and few elementary pupils could afford one. Pupils often were not allowed to bring them into the classroom.

Current research indicates that calculators are an effective learning tool, but, as with other educational materials, if misused they can be a liability instead of an asset. Ray Hembree reports that although research has given a green light to the use of calculators, fewer than 20 percent of elementary teachers employ calculators during instruction.[2]

Concerns About Calculator Use

Many teachers are reluctant to use calculators extensively in the elementary school mathematics program because of a variety of concerns, each of which can be avoided with proper instruction.[3]

PUPILS MAY NOT MASTER PENCIL-AND-PAPER COMPUTATION

Teachers are concerned that pupils who are permitted to use calculators will not develop an adequate mastery of computational skills needed to pass competency tests required for school graduation and for admission to college programs. This fear is well founded if calculators rather than manipulative and visual materials are used during initial phases of instruction on basic concepts and procedures. It is now generally agreed that the use of calculators does not eliminate the need for pupils to acquire basic computational skills. Hembree and Donald Dessart found, however, that a use of calculators can *improve* the average student's basic skills with pencil and paper,

2. Ray Hembree, "Research Gives Calculators a Green Light," *Arithmetic Teacher*, 33 (September 1986): 18–22.

3. See Thomas Dick, "The Continuing Calculator Controversy," *Arithmetic Teacher* 35 (April 1988): 37–41.

both in basic operations and problem solving.[4]

PUPILS MAY NOT LEARN TO THINK

There are two advantages to the use of calculators in problem solving. First, using calculators greatly reduces computational time and thus allows more time for problem analysis. The vital thinking involved in solving a verbal problem consists in the selection of the operation or operations rather than performing the computation. Second, more realistic problems can be solved when a calculator is available. Most textbook problems are designed so that the computation is easy and the answer is usually a whole number. In real life, problems rarely satisfy these conditions.

CALCULATORS MAY NOT WORK PROPERLY

Calculators can malfunction and batteries do run down. A simple test to determine whether the calculator is performing properly is to key in the following *in the order given*: 12 + 34 − 5.6 × 7.8 ÷ 90. If the answer is 3.501333. . ., the calculator is working properly. The example uses all ten digits in order (except zero is used last), and all four operations. The example and answer can be written on a tape and attached to the calculator for easy reference. Various calculators have different operating systems. Some will give the indicated answer when numbers and operations are pressed in the sequence indicated above. Pressing *equal* after each operation will give the desired results on most calculators. Experiment. If your calculator does not give the above answer, make a note of your answer. One way to solve this problem is to have the same type of calculator available for pupils to use during classroom work.

Even when calculators are working properly, pupils may not get the correct answer because they press incorrect keys and fail to press correct ones hard enough.

CALCULATORS MAY NOT HELP PUPILS DEAL WITH FRACTIONS

Most calculators available for classroom use are not efficient for computing with common fractions, although some newer, more expensive calculators do perform operations on common fractions. Calculators do not compute the remainder directly in long division. The calculator will give the quotient 6.75 for the division 162/24. This apparent disadvantage can be turned into an opportunity to reinforce the relation between the divisor and remainder. Multiplying 24 by .75 will indicate the remainder of 18.

Research Findings on the Use of Calculators

When pupils grow to adulthood they will use calculators in a variety of ways; it is the school's responsibility to teach them to use calculators properly. The use of a calculator will not keep pupils from learning to compute and will contribute to improvements in problem solving. The Fourth Assessment of Educational Progress in Mathematics found that when some pupils were allowed to use calculators on certain problem-solving items, the pupils who used calculators scored from 10 to 40 percent higher on problems involving whole numbers and decimals than the pupils who did not use calculators.[5] And David Williams concluded from his research that the only true obstacle to the use of calculators in an elementary school math-

4. Ray Hembree and Donald J. Dessart, "Effects of Hand-Held Calculators in Precollege Mathematics Education: A Meta-Analysis," *Journal for Research in Mathematics Education 17* (March 1986): 83–89.

5. Vicky L. Kouba, et.al., "Results of the Fourth NAEP Assessment of Mathematics: Number, Operations, and Word Problems," *Arithmetic Teacher, 35* (April 1988): 14–19.

ematics program is the negative attitudes of teachers and parents.[6]

Advantages of Using the Calculator

A calculator that is available to every pupil has the following advantages:

1. It is portable. It can be available when and where computation is necessary.

2. It is inexpensive. A six-function calculator may be purchased for five dollars or less.

3. A traditional paper-and-pencil solution may require 90 percent of the solution time on computation and 10 percent of the time on problem analysis. Calculator use may reverse this situation. In this sense, calculator usage tends to enhance thinking rather than diminish it.

4. Pupil reluctance to do the computation required to check problem solutions may be reduced when a calculator is available.

5. Calculators reduce the drudgery of computation and allow the use of numbers that represent real-life situations.

Using the Calculator for Estimation

The calculator is a valuable tool for learning to estimate if the following steps are taken when a computation is to be made:

1. Estimate the answer for the computation.

2. Perform the computation on the calculator.

3. Determine the error in the estimate.

4. Compare the error with the correct answer. If the pupil has the background in percent, estimate the percent of error. Otherwise, determine whether the error is more or less than one tenth of the correct answer. An estimate with an error of 10 percent or

less is usually considered acceptable. It will verify the position of the decimal point.

Learning to estimate without a calculator or computer is difficult because it is usually necessary to perform the computation to determine the error in the estimate.

Computers in the Elementary School

The small desk computer, not much larger than an office typewriter, is now more than ten years old. First known as the microcomputer, it is now called a personal computer, often abbreviated PC. We use the word *computer* to mean a micro or personal computer. More than 95 percent of schools have one or more computers, and their impact on education is steadily increasing.

The Computer Laboratory

It is not yet economically practical for each pupil to have a computer. Many schools have a separate computer lab that often contains one computer per pupil for a class assigned to this lab. Groups of two or three pupils at each computer may have advantages in some situations.

A pair of pupils can type information efficiently if one reads and checks screen entries as the other types. The pair should alternate between reading and typing for maximum benefit.

A full-time teacher knowledgeable about computers is essential to supervise and direct activities for maximum use of these expensive machines. Ideally, the lab should be available to pupils after school and on weekends. At a minimum, pupils should have at least one hour of instruction per week. Time for remedial work, tutorials, and enrichment should also be available.

The National Academy of Sciences has urged that all K–12 students be given access

---

6. David E. Williams, "A Calculator-Integrated Curriculum: The Time is Now," *Arithmetic Teacher, 34* (February 1987): 8–9.

to calculators and computers in mathematics classes. The use of technology can enhance each student's "math power"—the ability to reason and to apply principles of mathematics. Robert Rothman predicts that by the year 2000 all students will have hand-held calculators and will be using computers in school.[7]

Research Findings

James Kulick and colleagues reviewed 28 research studies on computer-assisted instruction and concluded that it had positive effects on the achievement of children. The computer users scored higher in achievement than the traditional groups.[8]

Patricia Wilson reviewed the research on microcomputer use in the elementary school and arrived at these conclusions:

Young children can program in BASIC and LOGO.

Open-ended software and programming can help students develop problem-solving abilities.

Mathematics instruction supplemented by drill and practice programs may improve mathematical skills.

Students using microcomputers have positive attitudes toward mathematics.

Children work together effectively on mathematics tasks.

Students work on computer activities longer than other activities and talk more about these tasks.

Using the microcomputer to teach mathematics is enhanced by teacher direction.[9]

7. Robert Rothman, "Computers, Calculators in Math Urged," *Education Week*, April 20, 1988, p. 9.

8. James A. Kulick, Chen-Lin C. Kulik, and Robert L. Bangert-Drowns, "Effectiveness of Computer-Based Education in Elementary Schools," *Computers in Human Behavior*, 1 (September 1985): 59–74.

9. Patricia Wilson and Glenda Lappan, "Microcomputer Use in the Elementary School," *Arithmetic Teacher*, 35 (December 1987): 33–34.

Educational Uses of a Computer

The computer can perform many tasks in a school. Some of these are:

1. Furnishes tutorial and remedial work. A tutorial program for a third-grade pupil may be a remedial or reinforcement program for a fourth- or fifth-grade pupil.

2. Provides practice in mental arithmetic and estimation. The computer can provide this practice more efficiently than any other medium.

3. Engages pupils in problem solving. The computer opens an entirely new level of problem-solving opportunities for pupils at the elementary school level (see Chapter 6).

4. Makes simulation possible. The computer can make available many aspects of real-life situations (see Chapter 17 for probability simulations).

Vocabulary

Computer use has generated a technical vocabulary containing many words and acronyms, such as *hardware*, *software*, *DOS*, *RAM*, and *ROM*. Pupils should not be required to define or describe these words. It is more effective to have pupils learn these terms as they use the computer. Requiring pupils to define or describe too many technical words can adversely affect their attitude toward computers.

Teachers should use the vocabulary so that the pupils become familiar with it as they use the computer. The computer manual must be available, and pupils should be encouraged to read it. A copy of the essential features and vocabulary for the computer may be placed on the classroom bulletin board. Common computer words that pupils encounter are included in the glossary of this text.

Hardware and Software

Hardware refers to the computer and the physical objects connected to it, such as a disk drive or a printer. *Software* refers to any program that tells the computer to perform a specified task. Software is usually stored on disk but must be transferred to computer memory in order to tell the computer what to do. Without software, a computer is practically useless to anyone but a skilled programmer. A computer should never be purchased until one is certain that software is available at an affordable price to make the computer perform the desired tasks.

Choosing Software

If a computer is to be used efficiently, the cost of software will eventually exceed the cost of the computer. This hard fact requires careful examination of software before it is purchased.

The Educational Management ERIC Clearinghouse, located in Portland, Oregon, evaluates educational software. References can be found in the *Resources in Education Index* under "Computer Software Reviews."

Do not invest a substantial sum in software without having exhausted every means of obtaining information about it. If at all possible, observe the software in action at another school or obtain it on a trial basis so that it can be returned if it does not prove satisfactory. If neither of these options is possible, buy a single package and let an experienced teacher use it in the classroom to see if it performs as expected.

This text will not recommend specific items of software. An item that works well in one school may be unsatisfactory in another. A specific item may be the best at the time of this writing but may be out of date in a year or so. In addition to educational software that is used for teaching, remedia-

tion or enrichment, every school should have a word processor, a spreadsheet, a data base, a paint program, and a graph program in its software library. Without these it is not possible for the computer to be used to its full capacity.

1. A word processor enables a teacher to make and store a record for each pupil as well as to make tests, instruction sheets, memos, and a variety of other communications. It is a major tool for any writing task, mathematical or otherwise. It is probably the most used item of software over the entire computer-use spectrum.

2. A spreadsheet will keep track of grades and averages and perform a wide range of calculations quickly. It is then possible to examine a problem for a given set of data, change one or more entries, and almost immediately compare the results. This capability provides an efficient procedure for finding the best solution for many problems. The spreadsheet was a major factor in persuading industry to use the personal computer.

3. A data base, also widely used in industry, allows storing information, such as pupil records, that can be accessed very quickly for reference or updating. Data bases are more specialized than the word processor and have features that make them more efficient, but they are also more restrictive in the way that they will accept data.

4. Practically every computer available in the schools has at least one combination program that includes a word processor, a data base, and a spreadsheet. This combination program enables the teacher to do all of the tasks described previously in addition to allowing efficient transfer of data from one program to another. A separate word processor, spreadsheet, or data base may be more powerful than its counterpart in the combination program. These combination programs are probably used by more teachers than any others.

5. A paint program enables a teacher or pupil to draw geometric figures, freehand drawings, simple graphs, and a wide range of graphics. Many drawings and diagrams that will supplement or replace some manipulative material can be constructed. LOGO is an essential tool for interactive geometry that enables pupils to tell the computer what to do and obtain immediate output. A paint program can produce complex pictures quickly that would be a major programming task with LOGO or BASIC. Paint programs make it possible to write tests with geometric figures interwoven with text. Tutorials and remedial work can also be constructed efficiently. A paint program is an absolute necessity for mathematics and has many applications in other areas.

6. A graph program is also essential. It will draw bar graphs, circle graphs, and line graphs from data entered into the computer and make data that pupils have collected come alive. The data should be discussed and a freehand graph drawn before the computer graph is constructed. Graphs can be printed and copies placed on the bulletin board.

While the best advice on choosing software is to see it in use before buying, there are some useful criteria to apply when considering a test purchase:

1. How long does the software take from the time the disk is entered to the time that it is ready for pupil use? Some software can use up an appreciable part of a period loading and getting ready for use.

2. Is the sound an effective part of the learning process? Can it be turned off or adjusted? Sound can be a distraction in a crowded learning laboratory.

3. Is each disk limited to use on a single computer or is it legal to use on any computer? Many software disks are licensed to a single machine and cannot legally be transferred to others.

4. If the disk is limited, can an arrangement be made with the software company that will allow it to be used on any computer and to make legal copies?

5. Is the disk copy-protected? A copy-protected disk often causes complications when transferred to a hard disk. It is important to make legal copies of any disk for safekeeping so that use of the program is not disrupted when one disk fails. Many manufacturers provide a back-up disk when their program is copy-protected. Such a copy must be kept in a safe place.

Remember, however, that copyrighted software cannot be copied legally. It is criminal to do so and can lead to severe legal penalties.

Software Sources

Here is a partial list of companies that specialize in educational software.

Davidson and Associates
3135 Kashima Street
Torrence, CA 90505

Milliken Publishing Company
1100 Research Blvd.
St. Louis, MO 63132-0579

Minnesota Educational Computing Consortium (MECC)
3490 Lexington Avenue No.
St. Paul, MN 55126

This company was formed to produce educational software and has been in existence for more than ten years. A major source of educational software at reasonable prices, it has a large variety of math programs. It has special arrangements with schools for mass use and is considered by many as offering some of the most economical software available.

Scott Resources
PO Box 2121B
Fort Collins, CO 80522

Spinnaker
One Cambridge Road
Cambridge, MA 02139

Sunburst Communications
39 Washington Avenue
Pleasantville, NY 10570-2898

Send for catalog. This company has a wide variety of programs in problem solving as well as other aspects of mathematics for most brands of computers.

Practically every major publishing company, including Holt, Rinehart and Winston, has a line of software that may be related to its textbook publications.

Periodicals

At least one magazine is published for each computer found in substantial number in the schools. The school library should subscribe to one or more such magazines for each different type of computer in the school. These magazines have articles about many phases of the computer and often evaluate available software. A section that contains answers to questions from readers may solve problems encountered in your school.

There are also computer magazines that discuss computers in general and have separate sections for each of the more popular computers. These magazines are helpful in obtaining a more balanced view of what is happening in the world of computers.

For Apple II Computers

A+ and **Incider**
Nibble

For Apple Macintosh

MacUser
MacWorld

IBM and Compatible Computers

PC Magazine
PC World

For all computers

Computer Shopper
Compute

The Arithmetic Teacher

The Arithmetic Teacher, published by the National Council of Teachers of Mathematics, is dedicated to the teaching of mathematics in the elementary school. Each issue usually has one or two articles on the use of the computer and about a half-dozen software programs are evaluated. Computer programs in both BASIC and LOGO are often included, with recommendations for classroom use. The magazine also carries many advertisements for current educational materials, software, and books.

Arithmetic Teacher
1906 Association Drive
Reston, VA 22091

User Groups

A user group is a collection of individuals interested in computers who meet regularly to exchange information. Some are concerned only with a specific computer; others are concerned with computers in general.

Computer Shopper has a list of about ten pages of user groups in each state with the address and phone number of the secretary. The listing indicates which computer the group is interested in or that it is concerned with all computers.

If a user group interested in the computer(s) in your school exists in your area, a teacher should join. Information may be available from this source that cannot be obtained easily in any other way.

Telecommunications

Some states have central data bases specifically designed to supply information to schools whose computers have modems. (A modem is a device that translates a computer signal to a form that can be transmitted over phone lines.) The school transmits a question to the central data base and the central unit can send back an answer immediately if it is available.

Commercial data bases charge for membership and for time spent on the computer to find and transmit an answer. The phone call may be free or not, often depending on whether the call is local or long distance.

The options of each local situation in terms of cost and availability of the type of information available are worth examining.

The best-known commercial data bases are Delphi, Genie, and The Source. They carry news, sports, travel information, and educational programs and have ways for groups with a common interest to communicate with each other.

Summary

A mathematics classroom designed to function as a laboratory must have several types of materials: manipulatives, audiovisual materials, mathematics textbooks, calculators, and computers.

A child's first exposure to abstract mathematics should be through discovery experiences with concrete materials. Manipulatives must be carefully selected and properly used. Their main purpose is to help each child move with understanding to the picture and symbolic levels of learning. Research has verified the value of using manipulatives in mathematics.

Learning centers are a desirable part of the laboratory approach.

The mathematics textbook is an integral part of a modern program. Pupils must be given instruction in mathematical reading so that they can interpret the word problems given and understand the basic topics provided at the picture and symbolic levels.

Pupils should be allowed to use handheld calculators during selected problem-solving activities. The use of computers should be an essential part of the laboratory approach to teaching and learning mathematics.

Exercises

1. Visit a school supply store and make a list of manipulatives for teaching mathematics that are in stock.

2. Select a manipulative and evaluate it in terms of the following criteria:
   a. Does the aid represent a major mathematical concept?
   b. Is the aid attractive, durable, multipurpose?
   c. Can the aid be homemade?
   d. Is the manipulative designed for individual pupil use? For teacher demonstration?
   e. Will the aid help the pupil move to higher levels of thinking?

3. Examine the Teacher's Edition of a major series of mathematics in the elementary school texts. Outline the various manipulatives recommended for specific topics.

4. Design a learning center. Name the type of center and state its purpose. Describe the materials and pupil activities. Explain how pupils' work is to be evaluated.

5. Discuss the pros and cons of using calculators: (a) in grades K–2; (b) in grades 3–4; (c) in grades 4–5.

6. Visit a computer laboratory in an elementary school. Describe the plan for implementing the effective use of computers for K–6 pupils for learning elementary mathematics.

Selected Readings

Berger, Emil J. (ed.). *Instructional Aids in Mathematics,* 34th Yearbook. Reston, VA: National Council of Teachers of Mathematics, 1973.

Bitter, Gary G., and Ruth A. Camuse. *Using a Microcomputer in the Classroom,* 2nd ed. Englewood Cliffs, NJ: Prentice-Hall, 1988.

Bitter, Gary G., and Jerald L. Mikesell. *Activities Handbook for Teaching with the Hand-Held Calculator.* Boston: Allyn & Bacon, 1980.

Cathcart, George W. (ed.). *The Mathematics Laboratory: Readings from* The Arithmetic Teacher. Reston, VA: National Council of Teachers of Mathematics, 1977.

Hansen, Viggo P., and Marilyn J. Zweng (eds.). *Computers in Mathematics Education,* 1984 Yearbook. Reston, VA: National Council of Teachers of Mathematics, 1984.

Higgins, John L., and Larry A. Sacks. *Mathematics Laboratories: 150 Activities and Games for Elementary Schools.* Columbus, OH: ERIC/SMEAC, Ohio State University, December 1974.

Krause, Marina C. *Multicultural Mathematics Materials.* Reston, VA: National Council of Teachers of Mathematics, 1983.

Martinez, Michael E., and Nancy A. Mead. *Computer Competence: The First National Assessment.* Princeton, NJ: Educational Testing Service, April 1988.

Post, Thomas R. "The Role of Manipulative Materials in the Learning of Mathematical Concepts" in *Selected Issues in Mathematics Education,* edited by Mary Montgomery Lindquist. Berkeley, CA: McCutchan Publishing Corporation, 1980. Pp. 109–131.

Reys, Robert E., and Thomas R. Post. *The Mathematics Laboratory: Theory to Practice.* Boston: Prindle, Weber & Schmidt, 1973.

Smith, Seaton E., Jr., and Carl A. Backman. *Games and Puzzles for Elementary and Middle School Mathematics: Readings from* The Arithmetic Teacher. Reston, VA: National Council of Teachers of Mathematics, 1975.

Vochko, Lee E. *Manipulative Activities and Games in the Mathematics Classroom.* Washington, D.C.: National Education Association, 1979.

See also issues of *The Arithmetic Teacher* and the *Journal for Research in Mathematics Education.*

Evaluation and Diagnosis

ACHIEVEMENT GOALS

After studying this chapter, you should be able to:

1. Identify the functions of evaluation in elementary mathematics.

2. List the essential steps in the evaluation process.

3. Discuss the role of educational goals and objectives in evaluation.

4. Enumerate various techniques for assessing mathematical achievement.

5. Outline the advantages and disadvantages of objective tests.

6. Summarize the most important characteristics of standardized norm-referenced and criterion-referenced tests.

7. Prepare different types of objective test items for measuring selected objectives in elementary school mathematics.

8. Describe the elements and techniques of effective diagnosis in mathematics.

9. Name ways to interpret and utilize the results of appraisals.

10. Identify ways to evaluate (a) the curriculum, (b) methods of teaching, and (c) instructional materials.

VOCABULARY

These terms are defined or illustrated in the Glossary.

Assessment
Continuum
Criterion-
  referenced test
Diagnosis
Formative
  evaluation

Norm-referenced
  test
Reliability
Standardized tests
Summative
  evaluation
Validity

Evaluation is the process of measuring and judging the extent to which an individual or program has attained identified goals and objectives. Diagnosis is the process of determining where and why deficiencies occur. Remediation is the treatment of these deficiencies.

Evaluation is an integral part of the teaching–learning process. For pupils who have not satisfactorily attained the stated objectives, diagnosis is necessary. To succeed in mathematics pupils must be given special instruction. Emphasis needs to be placed on concepts they fail to understand and skills in which they are deficient.

Evaluation also applies to the process of assessing the extent to which a program is meeting stated goals and objectives. When groups of pupils are not achieving a satisfactory level in mathematics, diagnosis is needed to identify weaknesses in the program design and implementation. Once the causes of deficiencies have been identified, remedial measures can then be taken (see Chapter 4).

Functions of Evaluation

Two types of evaluation processes are commonly used in elementary school mathematics programs.[1] These are *summative* and *formative* evaluation. *Summative* evaluation is used by teachers to measure the achievement of different groups or classes, and by administrators to compare the achievement of different groups or classes. Many schools use standardized tests for this type of evaluation. Well-constructed standardized achievement tests provide valuable information as to where each pupil stands in comparison with other children of about the same age and grade. These tests

1. Benjamin S. Bloom et al., *Handbook on Formative and Summative Evaluation of Student Learning* (New York: McGraw-Hill, 1971).

can also be used to measure a pupil's growth over a given period of time and offer valuable insights into the child's level of achievement.

Formative evaluation measures the extent to which children have mastered specific learning tasks. This type of evaluation provides feedback to both the teacher and the pupil, enabling each to make the necessary adjustments for continued progress. This process identifies specific areas in which mastery is lacking so that the teacher can arrange to provide needed additional instruction.

One way to determine how well a student is learning the subject is by giving frequent short tests or quizzes, not designed for purposes of assigning grades. The results of a well-constructed test for a cluster of mathematical concepts and/or skills provide valuable information about each child's specific strengths and weaknesses.

The Evaluation Process

There are four essential steps in the evaluation process:

1. Formulating the educational goals and objectives.

2. Selecting and constructing measuring instruments.

3. Securing a record of achievement.

4. Interpreting assessment results.

Formulating the Educational Goals and Objectives

The first essential step of any instructional program is to define and clarify the program's goals and objectives. Likewise, the first essential step of any evaluation program is to identify the goals and objectives toward which the children have been working. In Chapter 1 we list the major goals and objectives for teaching elementary school mathematics.

Broad objectives help to lend general direction to a program. Evaluation of a program's effectiveness for groups of children can be done in terms of these general objectives. More specific objectives are necessary for lesson planning and for appraising progress on a particular concept, skill, or application in elementary mathematics.

The effectiveness of the evaluation depends largely on how closely the objectives measured match the accepted objectives. When objectives to be evaluated are stated too narrowly, a teacher may direct class activities to specific test items. There is evidence that the Back-to-Basics movement encouraged teachers to stress computation at the expense of the concepts involved and problem-solving abilities.

One major objective of elementary school mathematics is to enable students to apply the tools of mathematics to solve problems both in the classroom and in everyday life. Outcomes are most effective when they form the background for quantitative thinking. To deal effectively with number in quantitative problem situations, many specific objectives must be attained. Learning to compute with reasonable speed and accuracy is certainly essential in problem solving. A child may demonstrate mastery of computational skills and yet be unable to solve problems successfully.

The Many Types of Objectives

Objectives can take various forms. They can emphasize *final* outcomes or concentrate on the process of learning. They can be stated in *broad* terms or state very specific *narrow* tasks to be performed.

Objectives of daily lessons need to deal with specific outcomes. For example, one of the major objectives of a mathematics program is understanding the number system.

This understanding implies that the learner can demonstrate:

1. The meaning of base ten.

2. Place value of a digit to the left or right of the ones place.

3. What happens to the total value of a digit when it is moved a certain number of places to the left or right in a numeral.

Another major objective in elementary school mathematics is for children to understand the meanings involved in computational algorithms. To analyze this objective, a task analysis is needed to determine the types of skills and understandings that are required for any particular algorithm. For example, the child's understanding of multiplication facts can be analyzed and delineated to include the following specific tasks:

1. Using objects to model basic multiplication facts.

2. Modeling basic facts on a number line.

3. Using arrays as a model.

4. Show that multiplication can be used to find the sum of a number of equal addends.

5. Recognizing the sign × and the words *factor* and *product*.

6. Writing multiples of a given one-digit number.

7. Understanding the commutative property of multiplication.

8. Generalizing facts with a factor of zero or one.

9. Using multiplication in solving one-step problems.

All Objectives Need to Be Appraised

Evaluations of mathematics achievement should include an assessment of all of the program's goals and objectives, including knowledge, skills, problem solving, problem-solving processes, and student attitudes toward mathematics. Hoepfner et al. have listed four major *categories* of goals for elementary school mathematics for the purpose of evaluating standardized tests of mathematics content.[2]

I. Understanding mathematical concepts
    a. Knowledge of numbers
    b. Knowledge of numeral systems and number properties
    c. Knowledge basic to algebra
II. Performing arithmetic operations
    a. Whole-number computation
    b. Computation with fractions
    c. Decimal and percentage computation
III. Applying and valuing mathematics
    a. Solution of word problems
    b. Personal use and appreciation of mathematics
IV. Geometry and measurement skills
    a. Knowledge of geometric figures and relations
    b. Measurement knowledge and skills
    c. Use of tables, graphs, and statistical concepts

In this chapter, we place major emphasis on evaluating and diagnosing children's achievement within a classroom situation at a particular grade level. The following is a list of some sources of objectives that the classroom teacher should have available.

Goals and Objectives of the National Assessment of Educational Progress, Educational Testing Service, Rosedale Road, Princeton, NJ 08541-0001.

Goals and objectives at the state level, in terms of curriculum frameworks in mathematics and statements of various commissions. Information about state-level goals and objectives is given in

state Department of Education publications, found in most district administrative offices.

District-level statement of goals and objectives for mathematics. Every district should have a document that lists the goals and objectives in mathematics, usually at each grade level and in terms of priorities.

Grade-level objectives for a particular school. Each school faculty should have an agreed-upon list of major goals and objectives in mathematics at each grade level in the school.

Selecting and Constructing Measurement Instruments

After goals and objectives have been determined, the second step in evaluation is to select and construct measurement instruments.

Methods of Evaluation

Just as there are many different objectives in elementary school mathematics, there are many different techniques for assessing outcomes of learning. The most valuable methods are:

I. Standardized, norm-referenced tests
    1. Survey achievement tests
        (a) Group tests
        (b) Individualized tests
    2. Mathematics achievement tests
        (a) Readiness
        (b) Diagnostic
        (c) Survey
II. Criterion-referenced tests
    1. Standardized
    2. Nonstandardized
III. Tests within an instructional program
    1. Textbook tests

2. Ralph Hoepfner et al., *CSE Elementary School Test Evaluations* (Los Angeles: Center for the Study of Evaluation, 1976).

(a) Readiness, pretests
(b) Placement tests
(c) End-of-unit tests
2. Teacher-made tests

IV. Teacher assessments of how children learn
1. Observations of daily work
2. Clinical interviews with the pupils
3. Demonstrations by the learners
4. Analysis of daily written work
5. Approaches to problem-situation activities

V. Affective assessments
1. Interest inventories
2. Rating scales and questionnaires
3. Behavior checklists and sociometric procedures

All of the above types of evaluation are needed to assist the teacher in drawing conclusions about pupils' educational needs, their progress toward achieving objectives, and improvements needed in the instructional program.[3]

Although test scores are useful in evaluating achievement in mathematics, there are goals that are not adequately measured by conventional tests. For example, the thinking involved in problem solving cannot be evaluated by test scores alone. For the most part, the thinking approaches in problem solving are assessed by the classroom teacher by observing how children solve problems, through clinical interviews, and by examining a child's written record of problem-solving activities.

Values of Objective Tests

A teacher's major task is to facilitate learning by each child. Objective tests verify and document that specific knowledge has

3. *Curriculum and Evaluation Standards for School Mathematics* (Reston, VA: National Council of Teachers of Mathematics, March 1989), p. 193.

been acquired and that certain learning objectives have been achieved.

An *objective test* is systematically constructed, administered, and scored such that the judgment of the scorer does not affect the results. Objective tests help to focus attention on selected important learning outcomes and provide a written record of the performance of each pupil. When pupils expect to be tested, their motivation to learn tends to increase. Although it is difficult to construct meaningful objective test questions, objective tests are relatively easy to administer and to score. An analysis of the results of a test should become a written record of a child's degree of mastery of certain objectives.

As they progress through school, pupils take many different objective tests for a variety of purposes. They need to develop a "test wiseness" in order to score well on objective tests. The tests that are included in the instructional program should provide valuable experiences for learning how to take a test. This experience in turn should help reduce test anxiety, which afflicts many students.

Shortcomings of Objective Tests

Objective tests have many shortcomings. They are sometimes used only to measure memorized responses. Memorization is the lowest level of cognitive functioning. Tests can also fail to indicate a full understanding of mathematical concepts. When a test score represents the number of correct answers, there is no attention given to the thought process that went into finding the answers.

Values of Teacher Assessments

One of the most important methods of evaluating learning in elementary school mathematics occurs as part of the ongoing activity of the class. The teacher who is a good observer, a perceptive listener, and an insightful interviewer will know a great deal about how and what the children are learning.

Selection of Norm-Referenced Standardized Tests

Many excellent standardized tests in elementary school mathematics are available for survey purposes. Table 3.1 lists some of the most widely used tests in the United States. Although they are very much alike in outward appearance and content, the tests differ widely in their emphasis on different objectives and on content.

Characteristics of Norm-Referenced Standardized Tests

A norm-referenced standardized test is primarily concerned with cognitive tasks that can be measured objectively with pencil and paper. Achievement is defined in terms of the number of correct items, translated for comparison purposes into various tables called *norm tables*. The items on a norm-referenced test are selected and arranged systematically in order to rank the pupils from high to low scores. The procedures for administering and scoring the test are uniform.

VALIDITY

A test is *valid* if it measures accurately what it is designed to measure. There are several methods for determining the validity of the results. One approach is if the results of a test closely match the objectives of the program, then the results of the test should be considered a valid indication of each pupil's achievement.

RELIABILITY

A test is *reliable* if it measures accurately and consistently. In other words, the children get approximately the same scores if

Table 3.1 Norm-Referenced Standardized Tests

California Achievement Test, Grades K–12.

Comprehensive Test of Basic Skills, Form U, Grades K–12. CTB/McGraw-Hill, Del Monte Research Park, Monterey, CA 93904.

Comprehensive Assessment Program, Grades K–12. A basic skills test for each grade level that includes mathematics. The tests are both norm-referenced and criterion-referenced. Available from American Testronics, P.O. Box 2270, Iowa City, IA 52244.

Iowa Test of Basic Skills, Grades 3–9, multilevel battery. Houghton Mifflin, Test Department, Box 1970, Iowa City, IA 52240.

Key Math Diagnostic Arithmetic Test, revised. Individualized in test book, continuous by strands.

Peabody Individual Achievement Test. Individualized in test book, math section continuous K–12. American Guidance Service, Publisher's Building, Circle Pines, MN 55014.

Sequential Test of Education Progress, III. Grades 4–12. Addison-Wesley Testing Service, 2725 Sand Hill Road, Menlo Park, CA 94025.

SRA Achievement Series, Grades K–12. Science Research Associates, 155 North Wacker Drive, Chicago, IL 60606.

Metropolitan Achievement Test, Grades K–12.

Stanford Achievement Test, Grades 2–9.

Stanford Diagnostic Mathematics Test, Grades 2–12. Psychological Corporation, 757 Third Avenue, New York, NY 10017.

measured again. For example, a watch is a reliable timepiece if it measures 60 minutes per hour. It is a valid measure if it gives the correct time. A watch set to give the correct time in the Eastern time zone will not give a valid time in another zone. A test can be reliable and not valid, but a valid test must be reliable.

A test is only a sample of a pupil's knowledge of a subject. The true measure would be derived from an unlimited sampling of a subject. Since tests of unlimited sampling are impossible, limited sampling is used. The test scores are corrected for error of measurement. Statistical procedures beyond the scope of this text are used to correct such errors.

EASE OF ADMINISTERING AND SCORING

The test should have clear directions for administering and scoring. This is the case for most tests, which are constructed for machine scoring by a computer. The computer will do a complete detailed analysis of the test results for each pupil.

NORMS

To establish norms for a given test, standardized tests are given to a large sample of pupils of the same chronological age or grade level. A norm can be expressed in different ways: as a mean, median, grade equivalent, or percentile rank.

The *mean* is another name for the arithmetic average. The sum of the raw scores on a test divided by the number of scores is the mean.

(Photo by Billie Perry)

Teacher and pupil work through the Key Math Diagnostic Arithmetic Test to diagnose learning difficulties.

The *median* is the middle number, or the mean of two middle numbers, of a set of numbers arranged in order of size.

The *grade equivalent* is the most frequently used statistic derived from a norm-referenced test. For children who score within the "average range," the grade-equivalent derived score is fairly accurate and useful in determining the general performance expected for each pupil in the typical mathematics program. Grade equivalents that are one year or more above or below grade level are subject to misinterpretation.

A grade-equivalent score on a standardized test should not be used as an indicator of mastery of the subject matter at a particular grade level. For example, if a second-grade pupil scores at the 4.0 grade level in mathematics, this does not mean that this learner has mastered average fourth-grade work. The pupil has scored well above average second-graders in mathematics, but if he or she were given a test designed for fourth-graders, it is very unlikely that the score would equal a 4.0 grade equivalent. Consequently, grade equivalents are not appropriate for placing children in the grade levels that match their scores. Many other factors must be considered before a child is placed in a grade level with children a year or more older or younger.[4]

Another frequently used score derived from a standardized test is *percentile rank*. Again, percentile is a statistical, relatively simple concept. The raw scores of a particular group of children who take the same test at the same time under similar conditions can be arranged from highest to lowest and percentile ranks calculated. By percentile rank, we mean that for a particular score the percentile equivalent represents the percent of children who took the test that scored at or below that point. Percentiles range from 1 to 99. A rank at the 50th percentile means that 50 percent of the children scored at or below the score associated with this ranking. A raw score of 62 may assign a pupil to the 50th percentile. There may be 15 pupils who have the same score.[5]

Nonstandardized Objective Tests

Nonstandardized objective tests are used by teachers and school administrators for a variety of purposes. They can be used for both summative and formative evaluation. In summative evaluation, pupils' scores are ranked from highest to lowest, and various statistics are used to describe the relative position of a child in terms of the mean, median, standard deviation, and so on. Summative evaluation provides information about the top, middle, and lowest students at a particular grade level. Standardized tests are more reliable and valid for this purpose than other kinds of nonstandardized assessments.

If a nonstandardized objective test is used for formative evaluation, the results should indicate what children have learned in each unit of the instructional program. The results of a nonstandardized objective test should indicate the extent to which each pupil has mastered the specific learning objectives.

The most frequently used type of teacher-made test in mathematics is one in which pupils are given a series of examples to work, problems to solve, and/or exercises to complete. Pupils are asked to show their work and circle their answers. The teacher not only counts the correct answers, but also tries to determine why the pupils obtained incorrect answers. Tests of this type

4. See the *Test Coordinator's Handbook, Forms C and D, California Achievement Tests* (Monterey, CA: CTB/ McGraw-Hill, 1978), p. 53.

5. Chris Pipho, "The Uses of Test Scores," *Phi Delta Kappan, 70* (December 1988): 278–279.

are valuable as daily, weekly, and/or monthly quizzes. They are closely related to the instructional program and provide both the pupil and the teacher with evidence of the pupil's achievement on topics currently being studied.

In addition to the types of exercises we have mentioned, the most widely used types of items for nonstandardized objective tests are: (a) simple recall, (b) multiple-choice, (c) alternate response, and (d) matching. In the next sections, we present a sample of each type of test, with directions for the pupil. For summative evaluation of these items, the number of correct answers would be needed. For formative evaluation, an item-by-item analysis of rights and wrongs for each pupil would be needed.

SIMPLE RECALL OR COMPLETION ITEMS

To complete simple recall items, the pupil is instructed to write the correct answer in the blank. The pupil's score is the number of correct answers. Here are some simple recall items on the topic of place value.

1. The total value of the 2 in 325 is _____.

2. The cardinal value of the 4 in 347 is _____.

3. The digit that names the number of greatest total value in the numeral 149 is _____.

4. The value of the place two places to the left of the ones place is _____.

The answers to the above items are 20, 4, 1, and 100, respectively.

MULTIPLE-CHOICE ITEMS

Multiple-choice items are used most often on standardized tests. Although these questions are difficult to write, they are relatively easy to score. The pupils should be instructed to write on the blank the letter of the answer that makes the statement true.

The score for each pupil is the number of correct answers. Here are some multiple-choice items on the topic of fractions.

_____ **1.** The fraction $\frac{2}{3}$ can be renamed:

(a) $\frac{4}{9}$ (b) $\frac{3}{2}$ (c) $\frac{9}{12}$ (d) $\frac{12}{18}$

_____ **2.** The fraction $\frac{3}{4}$ can be renamed:

(a) $\frac{3+1}{4+1}$ (b) $\frac{3-1}{4-1}$

(c) $\frac{3 \times 2}{4 \times 2}$ (d) $\frac{3 \times 3}{4 \times 4}$

_____ **3.** The sum of $\frac{1}{2} + \frac{1}{3}$ is:

(a) $\frac{5}{6}$ (b) $\frac{1}{5}$ (c) $\frac{2}{5}$ (d) $\frac{1}{6}$

_____ **4.** To divide a fraction by 2:
(a) divide the denominator by 2.
(b) divide both the numerator and denominator by 2.
(c) multiply the denominator by 2.
(d) multiply either the numerator or the denominator by 2.

The answers to the above items are d, c, a, c, respectively.

TRUE OR FALSE ITEMS

To answer true or false items, the pupil must mark a statement as true (+) or false (0) or answer a question yes or no. Here are some true or false items on the topic of basic operations.

_____ **1.** Addition and subtraction are opposite operations.

_____ **2.** Multiplication will "undo" addition.

_____ **3.** The commutative property holds for both addition and subtraction.

_____ **4.** The sum of zero and a number is that number.

The answers to the above items are +, 0, 0, +.

Because there is a 50 percent chance that

a pupil will answer a true or false item correctly, we recommend a correction for guessing. For quick hand scoring of a true/false test, circle each wrong answer and mark each omission with a dash. Do not mark the correct answers. A pupil's score is the total number of items *attempted*, minus twice the number of items missed. To find the number of items attempted, subtract the number of omissions from the total number of questions on the test. A pupil's score *(S)* equals the total number attempted *(T)* minus twice the number of wrong items (2W): $S = T - 2W$.

MATCHING TESTS

A matching test consists of a list of five to ten statements in a left-hand column and a corresponding list of possible answers in a right-hand column. Usually, the right-hand column contains one or two more items than the left-hand column. The pupil is instructed to fill in the blank with the letter from column II that matches the statement (or question) in column I. The score is the number of correct matchings. Here is a sample matching test on the topic of number properties.

I

_____ **1.** Associative property

_____ **2.** Commutative property

_____ **3.** Distributive property

_____ **4.** Identity element for addition

_____ **5.** Identity element for multiplication

II

(a) $2 \times 3 = 3 \times 2$

(b) $2(3 + 4) = (2 \times 3) \times (2 \times 4)$

(c) $(3 + 2) + 4 = 3 + (2 + 4)$

(d) one

(e) $3 \times (2 + 4) = (3 \times 2) + 4$

(f) zero

(g) $2(\ell + w) = (2 \times \ell) + (2 \times w)$

The answers to the above matching test are as follows: c, a, g, f, and d, respectively.

Sources of Test Items

There are several sources of test items in mathematics. In addition to items contained in standardized and criterion-referenced tests, almost every textbook series in elementary mathematics now includes several different kinds of test items. Table 3.2 presents a list of selected criterion-referenced tests, with the publisher from whom they can be obtained.

Table 3.2 Criterion-Referenced Tests

Criterion-Referenced Mathematics Objectives and Item Bank.
The item bank contains 100 objectives with 5 to 8 multiple-choice items each for grades 1 through 8. Objectives deal with such topics as numeration, whole number operations, decimals, fractions, integers, geometry, graphs and charts, problem solving. Available from Institute for Educational Research, 793 N. Main Street, Glen Ellyn, IL 60137.

Diagnostic Mathematics Inventory.
Seven levels, grades 1.5–7.5 with 37–179 multiple-choice items per level and 5–10 items per objective. CTB/McGraw Hill, 2500 Garden Road, Monterey, CA 93940.

Tests of Achievement in Basic Skills.
Seven levels, survey tests, K–12, with one item per objective grouped in clusters. Educational Industrial Testing Service, P.O. Box 7234, San Diego, CA 92107.

Sequential Assessment of Mathematics Inventories (SAMI) Standardized Inventory.
K–grade 8. Provides a comprehensive profile of a pupil's overall standing in mathematics. The Psychological Corporation, San Antonio, TX 78283-3854.

Assessing Attitudes Toward Mathematics

A favorable attitude toward aspects of mathematics cannot be measured directly, but can be inferred from a variety of observational techniques, which show that the pupil:

1. Willingly participates in learning activities.

2. Enjoys working with mathematics.

3. Is interested in learning.

4. Appreciates the value of mathematics for future study and for activities outside of school.

The most common way of measuring attitudes toward mathematics has been to use some type of questionnaire. The attitudes of pupils in the primary grades can be mea-sured best by observational techniques and personal interviews. If a written response from each child is needed, the teacher can read the questions to the pupils and have them mark, on the form with "faces," the face that best describes their answers. Pupils in the upper grades can use a checklist such as that shown in Table 3.3. Attitude scales are relatively easy to create and administer, but are difficult to interpret.

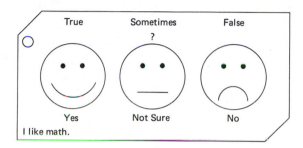

Table 3.3 Inventory of Attitudes Toward Mathematics

Directions: Put a checkmark in the column that best describes your answer for each statement below.

Attitude	Always	Sometimes	Never
I like mathematics.			
I enjoy working problems and puzzles in mathematics.			
I think mathematics is useful.			
I make good grades in mathematics.			
I want to continue my study in mathematics.			
I complete mathematics assignments on time.			
I use mathematics outside of school.			
I work hard in mathematics.			
I find mathematics easy.			
I do well on tests on mathematics.			

Note: Score "Always" 3 points, "Sometimes" 2 points, and "Never" 1 point. Maximum score is 30, minimum score is 10.

Two major difficulties of using a test to measure attitudes are the reliability and validity of the instrument. It is difficult to judge the extent to which a score on an attitude scale is a true picture of a pupil's attitude toward mathematics.

Diagnosis Using a Continuum

There are four phases to diagnosis:

1. Determining what children are expected to understand, be able to do, and how they feel about mathematics.

2. Collecting data about the child's attitudes and interests, and the extent to which the pupil performs identified tasks, and demonstrates understanding.

3. Analyzing the data to determine specific weaknesses and the probable causes of deficiencies.

4. Setting in motion appropriate prescriptions for improved learning.

One way to carry out diagnosis is to use a *mathematics continuum* for each level of instruction. The mathematics continuum should be created at the local school by teachers at each grade level following these steps:

1. Record all the achievements expected in terms of behavioral objectives.
   a. Identify items that should have been mastered.
   b. Determine what knowledge is essential to the instructional program.
   c. Specify objectives that will provide readiness experiences for the next level of instruction.
2. Group objectives into categories such as
   a. Concepts (understanding desired).
   b. Operations (skills developed).
   c. Measurement/applications/problem solving.
3. Prepare a record sheet listing objectives in the left-hand column and leaving space for recording observations on the right.
4. For each child, use information from a variety of sources to code performances in terms of level of achievement.
   a. Performs at the readiness stage. (R)
   b. In the development level, ready for directed instruction. (D)
   c. Has mastered the objective and needs reinforcement and enrichment. (M)
5. Analyze data for all students and set up the instructional program to meet the needs of the children.

Diagnostic Techniques

The techniques one should use to diagnose difficulties in learning elementary school mathematics depend on the kind of diagnosis to be made. There are three levels of diagnosis: general diagnosis, analytical diagnosis, and case study procedures.

General Diagnosis

General diagnosis implies the use of systematic and comprehensive tests and other types of evaluation procedures. The results of standardized tests are the most efficient means of measuring pupils' general level of achievement. To be of maximum value, the tests should be administered early in the school year.

When standardized achievement tests are not available, informal inventory tests of the work done in previous grades should be administered early in the year. These tests are available in most mathematics textbooks, or can be prepared by individual teachers. The inventory test can be constructed so that a quick analysis of total scores and those for each section of the test will not only give a fairly satisfactory measure of the individual pupil's general level of ability but will also indicate to both teacher and pupil the areas in which the pupil is strong and those in which carefully planned review, even re-teaching, may be necessary.

Analytical Diagnosis

Analytical diagnosis is designed to identify a pupil's specific weakness in mathematics achievement. The results of a survey test will show how a pupil's achievement compares with the norm for his or her age group. A low score on a survey test does not indicate the specific phase or cause of the low achievement. Analytical diagnostic tests are used for this purpose.

A survey test covers a wide range of subject matter in a given area, such as multiplication of whole numbers or fractional numbers. There is only a limited sampling of specific types of examples. On the other hand, a diagnostic test deals with a small segment of subject matter with intensive sampling of a given topic. This feature of the test enables one to reliably diagnose the point at which the pupil has difficulty with a topic.

Sampling of a Diagnostic Test

A diagnostic test in addition of fractions should contain subunits, such as a unit dealing with fractions expressed with like denominators, with unlike denominators when one is a common denominator, and with unlike denominators when a common denominator is not given.

The subunit of a diagnostic test, at right, in addition of fractions covers unlike but related denominators. The three examples in each set contain the same difficulty. In order to make a reliable diagnosis one would need at least three samples of the same difficulty so as to distinguish between a *chance* error and a *constant* error. A chance error occurs at random and is not repeated in a similar number situation. A con-stant, or systematic, error recurs in similar number situations because the pupil has faulty or limited knowledge of the number involved. If only one of the responses to the three similar examples is incorrect, the error is due to chance. If at least two of the three responses are incorrect, the error is systematic.

The test can be expanded to include examples involving mixed fractions, in order to sample all the types of examples involving adding fractions with unlike but related denominators. If a pupil gets at least two examples incorrect within a set, the new step in the solution is the source of the difficulty. The teacher is now able to apply the correct remedial measures, which enable the pupil to deal with that particular type of fraction example.

Diagnostic Test in Addition of Fractions
(Denominators are unlike but related)

I.	$\dfrac{1}{2}$	$\dfrac{1}{4}$	$\dfrac{2}{5}$	The sum is in the simplest form.
	$\dfrac{1}{4}$	$\dfrac{3}{8}$	$\dfrac{3}{10}$	
II.	$\dfrac{7}{8}$	$\dfrac{5}{6}$	$\dfrac{3}{4}$	Same as Set I except the sum is greater than 1.
	$\dfrac{1}{2}$	$\dfrac{1}{3}$	$\dfrac{1}{2}$	
III.	$\dfrac{1}{3}$	$\dfrac{1}{2}$	$\dfrac{1}{5}$	The sum must be renamed to be in the simplest form.
	$\dfrac{1}{6}$	$\dfrac{1}{6}$	$\dfrac{3}{10}$	
IV.	$\dfrac{1}{2}$	$\dfrac{7}{10}$	$\dfrac{5}{6}$	Same as Set III except the sum is greater than 1.
	$\dfrac{5}{6}$	$\dfrac{1}{2}$	$\dfrac{2}{3}$	

Effective diagnosis requires assessments of various subskills within a particular operation. For example, to determine the extent to which children have mastered division by one-place divisors, one would need a test consisting of several examples of this type. If a student solved most of the examples correctly with reasonable speed, it may be assumed that the pupil can also deal effectively with all the subskills involved. On the other hand, if a student misses several examples, then one would need to administer a diagnostic test made up of the subskills of division by a one-place divisor.

So many skills are involved in division by a one-place divisor that it is difficult to find a reliable diagnostic test to point out the source of most errors in the operation. The errors made with a one-place divisor stem from a deficiency in one or more of the following abilities:

1. Identification of the number of places in the quotient

2. Knowledge of division facts

3. Knowledge of multiplication facts

4. Renaming in subtraction

5. Repeating the operation (bringing down the next dividend digit)

A pupil should be able to estimate that the quotient of $3\overline{)452}$ will be a three-place number. Then that pupil should have no difficulty in dealing with the zero in the quotient. The most frequent incorrect answer to the example is 15 r 2.

The teacher should give an example with a divisor ranging from 6 to 9 to sample a pupil's ability to deal with other knowledge needed for division by a one-place divisor. Consider the example $8\overline{)543}$. The solution involves renaming in subtraction, a difficult fact in both division and multiplication, and a repetition of the procedure after bringing down the digit in the ones place in the dividend.

A diagnostic test must have in-depth sampling of a given skill. For division by a one-place divisor, such a test should include a good sampling of both division and multiplication facts, as well as a sampling of renaming in subtraction with a final remainder, and several examples. An analysis of the child's work, along with an interview, should effectively locate various difficulties that need to be remediated. Success in dividing by one-place divisors depends largely on proficiency in the required subskills. If a child is not proficient in working examples of this type, that learner cannot be expected to solve problems that involve division.

Case Study Procedures

Case study procedures apply diagnostic techniques that enable the teacher to analyze in detail the performance or achievement of a pupil having learning difficulties. These procedures are clinical, and are best adapted to the study of the work of individual pupils or groups of pupils. Case study diagnosis of learning difficulties in elementary school mathematics includes the following procedures:

1. Analysis of written work to discover faulty responses, such as:
   a. Numerals written incorrectly, such as reversal in the primary grades.
   b. Types of examples worked incorrectly.
   c. Nature of computational errors made in tests and in regular daily written work.
2. Analysis of oral statements:
   a. Faulty thought processes are revealed by having each pupil "say aloud" the steps in working difficult examples or problems.

b. Reading difficulties are revealed by having each pupil read the problem aloud.

c. Faulty thinking is revealed by having each pupil tell how to solve a given problem.

3. Personal interview to secure information by asking the pupils:
   a. About their thought processes in working an example.
   b. To test their understanding of a number operation.
   c. About methods of solving a problem.
   d. About interests, attitudes, and methods of work.

4. Questionnaires and inquiry blanks:
   a. Securing interest ratings of topics in mathematics.
   b. Reports from classmates, parents, and teachers.
   c. Study habits and methods of work.

5. Observation in the course of daily work provides evidence of:
   a. The use of counting and other inefficient methods.
   b. Rate of work.
   c. Study habits; use of reference books.
   d. Factors affecting performance, such as health and vision.
   e. Methods of using a measuring device.

6. Analysis of available records:
   a. Anecdotal records.
   b. School cumulative records.

7. Administration of diagnostic tests given in textbooks or workbooks or prepared by the teacher.

Summary

The major purpose of evaluation and diagnosis is to improve instruction. Evaluation can be summative or formative. Summative evaluation describes a pupil's overall performance, such as with a grade on a unit of work or in a course. Formative evaluation indicates the extent to which each pupil has achieved specific learning objectives.

The stages in the evaluation process include: (1) establishing goals and objectives, (2) selecting and/or constructing assessment instruments, (3) securing a record of achievement, and (4) interpreting assessment results.

Standardized tests can be norm-referenced or criterion-referenced. Norm-referenced tests are designed to rank-order pupils' achievement. Criterion-referenced tests determine the pupils' mastery of various learning objectives.

Tests used to measure achievement must be valid, or represent accurately the pupils' true performance. Tests also must be reliable, meaning that they need to measure concepts and skills consistently.

The test that is the most useful and frequently used in elementary mathematics is that which is an integral part of the day-to-day instructional program. Teacher-made tests provide valuable information on how well each pupil is learning mathematics. They also provide diagnostic data that can assist the teacher in planning for proper remediation as well as appropriate enrichment.

Diagnosis involves four components: (a) setting individual learning objectives, (b) assessing the child's status in terms of the objectives, (c) analyzing the child's strengths and weaknesses, and (d) providing appropriate remediation and/or enrichment. An effective teacher diagnoses pupil progress daily and suggests to each child, in individual conferences, ways to improve performance.

Exercises

1. What are several purposes for evaluating mathematics achievement in the elementary school?

2. Explain the difference between summative and formative evaluation. Under what conditions should each be used?

3. Why is it necessary to establish a set of accepted objectives in mathematics as a first step in evaluation?

4. What are the values and limitations of norm-referenced standardized tests? of criterion-referenced tests?

5. Examine the types of tests that are included in a mathematics textbook. Evaluate the tests.

6. Identify several ways a teacher can assess a pupil's ability to solve word problems in mathematics.

7. Why may the results of a standardized test for a given school be considerably above or below the norm published by the testing company?

8. How could the fact that a pupil operates at the exploratory level affect his or her score on a standardized test?

9. Explain the difference between evaluation and testing. What is the teacher's role in each?

10. Explain the difference between testing and diagnosing. What is the teacher's role in each?

11. Give an illustration of general diagnosis, analytical diagnosis, and case study procedures.

12. Obtain the results of a mathematics test for some class. Analyze the errors and indicate the type of remedial measures you would apply.

Selected Readings

Anderson, Lorin W. *Assessing Affective Characteristics in the Schools*. Needham Heights, MA: Allyn & Bacon, 1981.

Beyond Standardized Testing. Reston, VA: National Association of Secondary Principals, 1988.

Braswell, James S., and Alicia A. Dodd. *Mathematics Tests*. Reston, VA: National Council of Teachers of Mathematics, 1988.

Fennell, Francis M. *Elementary Mathematics Diagnosis and Correction Kit*. West Nyack, NY: Center for Applied Research in Education, 1981.

Freeman, Howard E., et. al. *A Closer Look at Standardized Tests*, Research Series No. 53. East Lansing: Michigan State University, 1979.

Gronlund, Norman E. *Measurement and Evaluation in Teaching*, 4th ed. New York: Macmillan, 1981.

Hopkins, Charles D., and Richard L. Antes. *Classroom Testing—Construction*. Itasca, IL: F. E. Peacock, 1979.

Hopkins, Kenneth, D., and Julian C. Stanley. *Educational and Psychological Measurement and Evaluation*. Englewood Cliffs, NJ: Prentice-Hall, 1981.

How to Evaluate Your Mathematics Program. Reston, VA: National Council of Teachers of Mathematics, 1981.

Mehrens, William A., and Irvin J. Lehmann. *Standardized Tests in Education*, 4th ed. New York: Holt, Rinehart and Winston, 1984.

Reisman, Fredricka K. *Diagnostic Teaching of Elementary School Mathematics*. Chicago: Rand McNally, 1977.

Suydam, Marilyn N. *Evaluation in the Mathematics Classroom*. Columbus, OH: ERIC Science, Mathematics and Environmental Education Clearinghouse, January 1974.

Trafton, Paul R., and Albert P. Shulte. *New Directions for Elementary School Mathematics*, 1989 Yearbook, Reston, VA: National Council of Teachers of Mathematics, 1989. Chap. 5.

Tyler, Ralph W., and Richard M. Wolf (Eds). *Crucial Issues in Testing*. 1973 Yearbook of the National Society for the Study of Education. Berkeley, CA: McCutchan, 1973.

Underhill, Bob, Ed Uprichard, and Jim Heddens. *Diagnosing Mathematical Difficulties*. Columbus, OH: Charles E. Merrill, 1980.

Accommodating Individual Differences

ACHIEVEMENT GOALS

After studying this chapter, you should be able to:

1. Summarize the many ways that pupils at the same grade level differ from one another.

2. Discuss organizational approaches that have been used over the years to accommodate individual differences.

3. Enumerate several techniques to deal with individual differences within the self-contained classroom.

4. Describe individualized approaches for dealing with individual differences.

5. Identify the characteristics of slow learners and rapid learners.

6. Suggest ways to provide appropriate instruction for both slow and rapid learners.

7. Explain the differences between horizontal and vertical enrichment and how each can be used effectively to adjust for individual differences in mathematics.

VOCABULARY

These terms are defined or illustrated in the Glossary.

Academic
acceleration
Heterogeneous
class
Homogeneous
class

Horizontal
enrichment
Vertical
enrichment

"One of the thorniest issues facing educators is how to organizationally deal with students who exhibit differential talents, abilities, achievements, and interests in the study of mathematics."[1]

A variety of factors influences the way pupils learn mathematics. They vary in intelligence, in academic achievement, in family environment, in cultural and ethnic backgrounds, in emotional and social maturity, in language fluency, in motivation, and in physical appearance.

One of the greatest challenges a teacher faces is to accommodate differences among pupils in a classroom. Great effort should be made to adjust the instructional program to provide for these differences and to encourage all pupils to achieve according to their potentials.

How Children Differ

Children differ from one another in many ways. Some of these differences fall within the normal range, and so no special adjustments in the instructional program are needed. On the other hand, other differences are so pronounced that provisions must be made in order for optimum learning to take place.

According to recent estimates, at least 20 percent of the pupils in a typical classroom deviate so much from the norm that drastic measures must be taken to create successful educational experiences and appropriate personal-social development.

Intellectual Differences

Children differ in levels of intellectual functioning. The intellectual capacity of children has traditionally been measured

using an IQ (Intelligence Quotient) test. The IQ of a 5-year-old child who has a mental age of 6, as measured by the test, would be $(6 \div 5) \times 100 = 120$, or stated in general terms, 100 times the quotient of mental age divided by the chronological age. According to the Wechsler Intelligence Scales for children, approximately 16 percent of elementary school children have IQs of 115 or higher and are classified as rapid learners. Less than 3 percent have IQs of 130 or more and are classified as gifted. Approximately 16 percent have IQs of 85 or less and are classified as slow learners.

The validity of the IQ test is the subject of continuing intense debate, and some critics claim that the test discriminates against children from lower socioeconomic backgrounds. At best, the test measures only one dimension of a child's ability.

Achievement Differences

One obvious way to see how children differ is to examine the results of a standardized achievement test in mathematics.

In one self-contained fifth-grade class, there may be children who score all the way from the second-grade level to the seventh-grade level. The achievement level is a function of the pupil's rate of learning. Pupils in the top quarter of the norm group are among the rapid learners in mathematics, whereas the pupils who score in the lowest quarter are among the slow learners. The middle 50 percent are relatively homogeneous in their abilities to achieve in mathematics. The pupils in a class who have about the same IQ are considered to be homogeneous for that trait. If IQ is not considered a factor in selecting a class, then the pupils are considered to be heterogeneous for that trait.

Different Family Environments

Children come from very different home environments. Children from affluent

1. *Curriculum and Evaluation Standards for School Mathematics*, Working Draft (Reston, VA: National Council of Teachers of Mathematics, October 1987), p. 16.

This group of fifth-graders shows the physical differences that may exist within a single class.

(Photo by Leland Perry)

homes who have well-educated parents usually come to school with a rich background of experiences and tend to be average or rapid learners. In contrast, children of parents who are economically poor and uneducated often tend to be slow learners.

The home also influences the child's attitudes toward mathematics. Research has shown a positive correlation between the child's attitude toward mathematics and the parents' attitude toward this subject. Sharon Wilhelm and Douglas Brooks found that mothers have considerable influence on their daughters' anxiety about mathematics, and fathers influence their sons' attitudes. The mother influences both the son's and daughter's self-concept.[2]

2. Sharon Wilhelm and Douglas M. Brooks, "The Relationship between Pupil Attitudes toward Mathematics and Parental Attitudes toward Mathematics," *Educational Research Quarterly*, Summer 1980, 5:14–15.

Cultural and Ethnic Backgrounds

Children also differ in their cultural and ethnic backgrounds. Motivation to learn varies from culture to culture, as do children's interests and the value placed on educational achievement.

Educational Factors

Educational factors influence levels of academic achievement. Children who have progressed through an effective, meaningful, sequential mathematics program such as that advocated here, tend to be average and rapid learners. Pupils who have experienced a minimum, drill-type program limited to learning computational techniques and memorizing basic facts usually have difficulty at the upper levels of elementary mathematics.

Organizational Approaches to Accommodating Individual Differences

There is a growing concern in American education with regard to social promotion policies. By social promotions, we mean the practice of making sure that pupils are kept with their own age group as they progress through a typical elementary school program. There have been several plans to break this tradition such as ability grouping, nonpromotion practices, and departmentalized teaching.

Ability grouping puts all the slow learners together, and the result tends to be that they are unable to break out of the "low track." Nonpromotion forces the child to repeat a grade, usually with no different results than occurred initially. Departmentalized teaching is not widely practiced at the elementary school level because this approach works no better than learning in the self-contained classroom.

Tracking by Ability

Most of the elementary schools of the United States are organized by age groups into graded self-contained classrooms. However, some schools attempt to narrow the range of achievement in elementary school mathematics by assigning pupils to homogeneous classes on the basis of ability or achievement. This practice has not produced desired results. After reviewing relevant research literature, Robert Slavin concluded that assigning pupils to a self-contained classroom according to ability or general achievement did not lead to improved achievement.[3] In addition, it was found that pupils were isolated into classes that stereotyped children. Pupils in the low class were given fewer opportunities to learn. Further, the low classes frequently were made up of minority and limited-English-speaking pupils.[4]

Departmental Plan

Some schools have pupils spend most of the schoolday in the self-contained classroom with their peers but regroup the children by achievement level for about an hour at the same time each day for instruction in mathematics. This plan places together pupils who have similar achievement levels, thus allowing teachers to vary their pace and level of instruction to respond to pupils' needs.[5]

According to Slavin, research is unclear on the effectiveness of this plan in terms of achievement in mathematics, although there

3. Slavin, Robert E., *Ability Grouping and Student Achievement in the Elementary Schools: A Best-Evidence Synthesis* (Baltimore: Johns Hopkins, June 1986), p. 74.

4. Jeannie Oakes, "Tracking: Can Schools Take a Different Route?," *NEA Today,* 6 (January 1988): 41–47.

5. Laurie Maxwell, *Making the Most of Ability Grouping—Research in Brief* (Washington, D.C.: Office of Educational Research and Improvement, November 1986).

is some evidence that such a plan can be instructionally effective.[6]

To accommodate individual differences within the self-contained classroom, the teacher should develop and use whatever approaches seem to work for different children. By and large, teaching exceptional children merely requires applying good teaching practices.

1. Establish learning objectives and adjust to meet individual needs.

2. Be flexible and provide a variety of learning activities with a variety of materials.

3. Accept and respect each child. Give praise and encouragement.

4. Foster independence and self-discipline.

5. Be positive about mathematics; make learning fun and exciting.

Dealing with Individual Differences Within the Self-Contained Classroom

There are a variety of ways to adjust for individual differences within a typical self-contained classroom in elementary school mathematics. Two easily administered approaches are varying the difficulty of the subject matter, and varying the level of maturity of operation.

Pupils of average ability will be able to complete the adopted textbook. Slow learners cannot be expected to master all the topics treated in a regular program, whereas fast learners need in-depth enrichment of the subject matter in areas such as problem solving.

One of the most effective ways to adjust for individual differences in a heterogeneous class is to vary the amount of time pupils operate at different levels of maturity. The slow learners operate at the exploratory level with concrete materials, while

6. Slavin, *Ability Grouping*, p. 74.

the fast learners operate at the mastery level. Most of the pupils participate in appropriate learning experiences at the symbolic level.

There are two advantages to having students operate at different levels of maturity. First, the program is relatively easy to administer. All the pupils start each unit of the mathematics program together, as a group. Introductory exploratory experiences are provided to all children. The teacher divides the class into subgroups, based on the particular needs of each child. The groupings are kept flexible so if a pupil in the exploratory group working with concrete materials moves to the stage of working with numerals and symbols, that child then joins the subgroup that operates at the symbolic level. In the same way, a pupil can advance or fall back to the next higher or lower subgroup.

The second advantage of having pupils operate at different levels of maturity is its effectiveness within the framework of class organization. The conventional curriculum is geared to the pupil of average ability. Most mathematics textbooks include a series of ten or more units or chapters to be completed in blocks of two or three weeks each during the school year. The time is constant for each unit, and the variables are the subject matter and the degree of mastery. Average pupils devote some time to exploratory activities. Laboratory materials are useful for all children, but some pupils need to spend more time with them than others. All children at the symbolic level need some systematic instruction by the teacher.

The most able pupils need fewer exploratory experiences. They can easily grasp structural aspects of various topics at the symbolic level.

The slow learners spend much of their time in each unit at the concrete level. They are able to progress to the simple aspects of the symbolic level during the time spent on each unit. These children generally need reinforcement and practice with additional learning experiences beyond those covered in the normal class period.

Children learning mathematics will have different needs at different times. Teachers should consider making the following adjustments for individuals and for groups.

1. *Vary the time.* Some pupils may need extra time to complete the following activities:
   a. Work with laboratory materials.
   b. Practice on basic facts and computational exercises.
   c. A learning-center task.
   d. Work on a measurement project.
   e. A problem-solving assignment.

2. *Vary the space.* Not every pupil can learn mathematics successfully out of a book and by just watching the teacher show and tell. Special spaces need to be created for small-group work, areas such as practice centers, laboratory stations, demonstration materials, and listening posts. In addition, many schools provide a learning laboratory outside the classroom so that exceptional children who have special needs receive special assistance.

3. *Vary the people.* Learning is fostered by having different individuals present and working with the material. As well, it is impossible for the teacher to be with the children constantly while they are studying mathematics. There are many ways to arrange having other people be of assistance to children as they learn mathematics.
   a. Work in small study groups, not homogeneously arranged. Rapid learners can serve as leaders.
   b. Work in small study groups, arranged homogeneously. Children tend to learn from one another as they discuss their work.
   c. Use older pupils to assist younger pupils who need extra help (cross-age tutors).
   d. Instructional aides help to direct pupils and meet their special needs.
   e. Parents can assist as volunteers in the classroom and as tutors at home.

4. *Vary the curriculum.* Some topics can be presented to the whole class. Other special topics can be selected by individual students. Some aspects of the mathematics curriculum should be adjusted to the individual interests of each pupil.

5. *Vary the instructional materials.* Instructional materials should be varied and adjusted to individual needs. Special learning centers, practice materials, calculators and computers, and multiple textbooks can be varied as is appropriate to the students' individual needs.

6. *Vary the methods of teaching.* Vary the teaching approaches by providing some balance among the following techniques.
   a. Self-discovery, guided discovery, and teacher presentations.
   b. Self-paced, individualized work, small group discussions, and whole-class, teacher-directed demonstrations.
   c. Teacher-controlled developmental activities, independent assigned seatwork.

Mastery Learning—A Group-Based Approach

Group-paced mastery learning, pioneered by Benjamin Bloom,[7] may be seen as one form of flexible within-class ability groupings in that students are assigned after each lesson to a heterogeneous team of three to five pupils to complete assigned tasks. The traditional assumption has been that in order to adjust adequately for individual differences in learning mathematics, teachers must group children into three ability

7. Benjamin B. Bloom, *Human Characteristics and School Learning* (New York: McGraw-Hill, 1976).

groups for instruction. Research has not supported this contention. As Callahan and Glennon report, "simply narrowing the ability range does not necessarily result in better adjustment of method or content and does not necessarily result in increased achievement."[8]

The mastery-learning approach has been proposed as a way to give all students an opportunity to achieve at a higher level of mastery. It is an effective way to organize instruction not only to reach students who lack basic mathematical skills, but also to promote rapid learners to go beyond the minimum requirements.

The premise of mastery learning is that a student can master a subject if he or she spends enough time in learning it. The time that each pupil needs is determined by three factors: (1) the pupil's aptitude, (2) the quality of instruction, and (3) the capacity of the student to understand.[9] With the mastery-learning approach, virtually all pupils can learn well and master most of what they are taught. Instruction is organized according to the following sequence.

1. Specific learning objectives that all students are expected to master are established.

2. A comprehensive unit test is prepared.

3. After an initial period of instruction with the whole class, taking perhaps 50 to 75 percent of the total time allotted for completion of the unit, a unit test is given to all pupils. The results will show how each pupil has progressed toward mastery of the objectives.

8. Leroy G. Callahan and Vincent J. Glennon, *Elementary School Mathematics—A Guide to Current Research* (Washington, D.C.: Association for Supervision and Curriculum Development, 1975), pp. 94–95.

9. Judith Harle Hector, "Organizing for Mastery Learning: A Group-based Approach." In *Organizing for Mathematics Instruction*, 1977 Yearbook (Reston, VA: National Council of Teachers of Mathematics, 1977), Chapter 8, pp. 131–145.

4. Then a set of alternative approaches is developed, to reteach the items on the test missed by each pupil. These approaches may include one or more of the following situations:

 a. Small-group study sessions, with or without a leader.
 b. Individual tutoring by peers, by cross-age tutors, by an instructional aide, or by a rapid learner in the class.
 c. Learning centers including laboratory materials, audiovisual tapes, filmstrips, and the like.
 d. Alternative learning aids including different text materials, workbooks, and various practice materials.
 e. Computers and minicalculators with directed instruction and individualized approaches.

Pupils who have mastered all of the learning objectives of the unit are given opportunities to serve as tutors of slower students and are given the option of working on a variety of enrichment activities. (The topic of teaching the rapid learner is discussed in a later section of this chapter.)

5. A specific length of time is set aside for alternative approaches; and all students are expected to complete their assignment, even if out-of-class time is necessary.

6. At the end of the unit, a final test is administered and graded. It is likely that at least 80 percent of the pupils will have mastered the objectives of the unit. With mastery, the pupils will have developed a complete understanding of a concept or operation and be able to use it out of habit. Occasional chance errors will occur, however.

Cooperative Learning Groups

Cooperative learning uses *heterogeneous* groups of from three to five members who work together to achieve the learning objectives of the assignment. Cooperative learning is only one kind of approach used by the teacher to enhance learning. Before cooperative learning groups begin to work, the teacher must make clear the learning objectives to be accomplished and ways the members of the group can work together. The teacher must also establish an incentive structure to assure that each learner is motivated to participate. Pupils need to be given the opportunity to communicate and interact in an integrated structure with no one individual dominating the activities.[10]

Research shows that cooperative goal structures lead to more effective problem solving than competitive groups. Each pupil in a cooperative learning group achieves as much or more as a part of the group than if that child studied alone. Cooperative learning increases social interactions, brings about positive attitudes toward school, and results in fewer discipline problems than individualistic approaches.

Individualized, Self-paced Learning

Individualized, self-paced learning is essential to any good instructional program. Some authorities advocate the exclusive use of this approach in teaching and learning elementary school mathematics. Individualized, self-paced instruction includes the following basic components:

1. *Learning objectives.* Objectives to be achieved by each pupil are identified and written in a hierarchy from simple to complex, with a summary achievement profile sheet for each learner.

2. *Tests.* A variety of tests is used. Placement tests are used to determine readiness for each block of instruction so that each pupil can be placed at the proper level on the continuum. Progress tests are administered individually, as the child progresses through the learning materials. Mastery tests are used to determine required levels of achievement.

3. *Learning prescriptions.* Based on diagnostic data, each child is given appropriate learning materials, usually a programmed workbook. Pupils are expected to try to progress through the materials on their own, asking for help only when necessary. The rate of learning is set by the pupil.

4. *Record-keeping system.* Progress records are kept for each pupil. A system of recording the objectives that have been mastered is maintained.

To make individualized instruction more personal, the teacher should confer with each pupil about personal objectives, with regard to both content and time. Encourage the pupils to use different kinds of learning materials as they proceed through the content.

Individualized learning has been used successfully by many teachers to adapt instruction to the very slow and the very rapid learners. However, it has doubtful value as an approach for all the students in a class.

Combining student teams with individualized instruction in mathematics produces significant gains in grades 3 and 5, according to Slavin and others.[11]

Characteristics of Slow Learners

Children become slow learners of elementary mathematics for many different reasons. To treat the causes of slow learning adequately, you need to understand the characteristics of each slow learner. Slow

10. Robert Slavin, *Cooperative Learning in Student Teams: What Research Says to the Teacher,* rev. ed. (Washington, D.C.: National Education Association, 1986).

11. Robert E. Slavin, et. al., "Combining Student Teams and Individualized Instruction in Mathematics: An Extended Evaluation," *Resources in Education,* May 1983. ED2316519.

learners are most often found to possess the following characteristics.

1. *Below average in intelligence.* Slow learners are usually low in intellectual functioning, although this is not always true. Some low achievers have normal intelligence, but are slow for other reasons.

   Children of very low intelligence generally have limited vocabularies, use faulty grammar, and have low functional reading skills. They usually have difficulty in drawing conclusions, in making generalizations, and in seeing relationships. They have trouble remembering things, and find it difficult to solve word problems.

2. *Poor adjustment to school.* Slow learners typically do not like school very much. They have a short attention span, and are distracted easily. Most slow learners are poor test takers, and are low achievers in several subjects. Many times they cause discipline problems in the classroom and in the school.

3. *Physical deficiencies.* Slow learners are sometimes not as well developed physically as normal learners. Some have poor diets. They are ill a lot, and miss more school than the average pupil. Many slow learners have problems with their eyes and ears.

4. *Psychological and emotional problems.* Slow learners generally lack interest in learning-related tasks. They have a low level of motivation to learn.

5. *Poverty-level homes.* It is estimated that at least 20 percent of the families in the United States live at the poverty level. In some urban areas, this figure can exceed 50 percent.

   Poverty often produces low educational achievement. Many children at the poverty level are disadvantaged by:
   a. Limited language development.
   b. Lack of balanced meals; generally poor nutrition.
   c. Inadequate medical care.
   d. Less family stability; many broken homes.
   e. Negative attitudes toward school.
   f. Lack of parental encouragement to try in school or to help at home. (See Chapter 18.)

6. *Handicaps.* Slow learners sometimes have serious physical and/or intellectual handicaps. In the past, these pupils were assigned to special education classes. But, since the passage of Public Law 94–142 in 1975, many handicapped children are being "mainstreamed" into the normal self-contained classroom. Often the handicapped child needs to make some type of adjustment to the instructional program in order to learn successfully. Generally, the teacher deals individually with the slow learners in this group of children, and includes them in other aspects of the instructional program as it becomes appropriate.

Providing Appropriate Instruction for Slow Learners

A great many children are unsuccessful in achieving adequate levels of performance in elementary mathematics. A child's lack of success can be the result of a variety of causes. To improve a child's learning of mathematics, the teacher must be able to diagnose each child's deficiencies and identify the specific reasons for the lack of appropriate achievement. Effective instruction for the slow learner requires two major efforts:

1. Treatment needs to be directed toward the causes for poor achievement.

2. Instruction should concentrate on specific diagnosed difficulties in mathematics.

The methods by which slow learners master the concepts and skills of mathematics are not unique or very different from those used by children of greater ability. A large number of slow learners function successfully within the typical self-contained classroom by applying the approaches discussed in the section "Dealing with Individual Differences Within the Self-contained Classroom."

There are, however, a few slow learners who are so retarded that special adjustments in the instructional approaches are needed for them to make any kind of progress in mathematics.

Recommended Adjustments for the Slow Learner

Here are some of the most useful ways to adjust instruction for slow learners:

1. Select content that involves personal survival skills, such as work with money, time, and measurement. Avoid limiting the curriculum to computation. Content of mathematics for the slow learner should be the kind that pupils will want and be able to learn naturally.

2. Present material at a level and pace that will ensure success. Begin at a point slightly below the child's deficiency. Do not repeat a procedure that has already resulted in failure. Pupils should never participate in learning situations in which they face repeated failure. Teach for success and proceed slowly.

3. Provide extensive opportunities for the pupil to work with laboratory materials at the exploratory level. Have pupils use concrete objects as they solve practical problems. Much of the current effort to accommodate slow learners has centered on the laboratory approach. (See Chapter 2.)

Use a wide variety of visual aids—such as pictures and diagrams—so that the learner can visualize the situation involved and grasp the meaning of steps to be taken in the new operation. Supplemental readers, pictures, and illustrations of mathematics in daily life are all valuable ways to visualize learning experiences.

4. Give diagnostic tests systematically to locate weak areas at the early stages of learning. Reteach in a simpler way, if this is necessary. Link skills to concepts, for understanding is important to slow learners. Keep each child informed of his or her progress, and provide immediate positive reinforcement.

5. Insist on an understanding and mastery of each step before presenting new work to avoid the practicing of errors and faulty procedures.

6. Spread the presentation of a new process or topic over a longer period of time than average learners would require.

7. Allow slow learners more time and variety to practice exercises than are required by average learners to develop skills. To avoid monotony, vary the exercises by using games in social situations.

8. Give frequent, short practice exercises, rather than a few long ones, to allow for the short attention span of slow learners.

9. During the introduction of a new topic, provide the pupil with the basic skills and concepts needed for success in the new work.

10. If possible, assign to slow learners only those textbook activities and problems that are not likely to create frustration. Most publishers of elementary textbooks provide suggestions about materials that can be used in a laboratory setting for slow learners.

11. Conduct frequent observational checks of children's work habits. Use individual interviews to uncover evidences of difficulty, faulty methods, and lack of comprehension.

12. Have pupils tell their thought pattern as they solve a problem or perform a computation. This is one of the best ways to diagnose a pupil's difficulty in mathematics.

13. Give considerable guidance to reading activities so that children develop reading skills connected with the use of the textbook and supplementary materials.

14. Work to change the attitudes of slow learners toward school and mathematics. Since most slow learners are not highly motivated toward school work, a reward system helps to stress the value of learning.

15. Involve the parents in the plan to improve learning. When parents are willing to cooperate and limit the time the child spends watching television and require that assigned homework be completed, progress is almost always improved.

16. Avoid isolating slow learners from other children. They need to learn not only from pupils who serve as good models but also from those who serve as individual tutors.

Characteristics of Rapid Learners

In a typical self-contained classroom of heterogeneous pupils, there should be approximately as many rapid learners as slow learners. As we stated earlier, the average class will consist of approximately 16 percent slow learners and 16 percent rapid learners. The middle two-thirds of the group are classified as average learners. Among the group of about one-sixth rapid learners, perhaps 2 or 3 percent may be among the academically gifted of the total population. Thus, in any one classroom, there usually will be rapid learners of mathematics and even one or more gifted pupils.[12]

Rapid learners have some of the same characteristics as gifted pupils, but not in the same intensity. Most rapid learners are found to possess the following characteristics.

1. *Above average in intelligence.* Rapid learners are usually above average in general intelligence. Most have well-developed language patterns, which tend to help them score higher than average on IQ tests that place an emphasis on verbal ability.

Rapid learners:
a. Are alert, curious, and observant.
b. Have good memories and reason well.
c. Enjoy asking and answering questions.
d. Are good problem solvers.
e. Discover patterns and relationships among numbers.

2. *High achievement in mathematical reasoning.* Ability in mathematics does not necessarily go hand in hand with measured intelligence, although there is a high positive correlation between the two. An effective and simple way to identify fast learners of mathematics is to select those pupils who achieve one or more grade levels above average in mathematics. High achievers in mathematics are the rapid learners.

3. *Well adjusted to school.* Fast learners are well adjusted and self-sufficient. They have wide interests and enjoy mathematics activities, especially games and applications.

4. *High socioeconomic status.* Pupils who are fast learners often come from home environments that enjoy a relatively high socioeconomic status.

5. *Task commitment.* Fast learners are often very task oriented. They approach problems and learning in mathematics with considerable zeal and determination.[13]

12. Foster E. Grossnickle and Leland M. Perry, "Dealing with the Gifted in Elementary School Mathematics," *Focus on Learning Problems in Mathematics* (Framingham, MA: Center for Teaching/Learning Mathematics, Summer Edition, 1984), pp. 65–80.

13. H. Laurence Ridge and Joseph S. Renzulli, "Teaching Mathematics to the Talented and Gifted." In *The Mathematical Education of Exceptional Children and Youth* (Reston, VA: National Council of Teachers of Mathematics, 1981), pp. 200–201.

6. *Creativity.* Often, fast learners are also highly creative. Rapid learners are usually versatile and flexible in their thinking. They are willing to take chances, or run the risk of being wrong. They seem to have an intuition about how ideas fit into the right order and structure in problem-solving activities. They show confidence and are inventive in their approaches to problem-solving and mathematics situations.[14]

7. *Social adjustment.* Rapid learners are typically well accepted socially. They are usually competitive and forceful in their behavior. They exhibit a great deal of independence in their work in mathematics, and work well both in group and individualized situations.[15]

Providing Appropriate Instruction for Rapid Learners

A great many children in the self-contained classrooms of American schools are not being challenged sufficiently in elementary school mathematics. In the typical learning environment, a child who is a rapid learner in mathematics often completes only the standard program provided in the adopted textbook.

A well-planned program for pupils of average ability is inadequate for the fast learner because fast learners can:

1. Achieve at a more rapid rate than the average pupil.

2. Achieve at a higher level of content than the average learner.

3. Generalize and discover different solutions to problems that pupils of average ability are unable to solve.

Organizational Patterns for Rapid Learners

Many rapid learners perform up to their potential within the organizational patterns discussed in the section "Dealing with Individual Differences Within the Self-contained Classroom." All these plans involve some type of grouping, which is necessary for effective mathematics programs at all levels. After he examined the research evidence on grouping, E. G. Begle concluded: "The evidence is quite clear that most able students should be grouped together, separate from the rest of the student population."[16]

This is not to imply that rapid learners should be isolated and segregated from other pupils at all times as they learn mathematics. Often the teacher will want to group students in ways other than by level of achievement. Nevertheless, there must be some basis for the groups, which also must be kept flexible. Sometimes, the teacher will want to instruct the class as a group, as when a new topic or game is presented or a measurement activity is demonstrated. At other times, subgroups may be formed for special purposes, such as: (1) laboratory activities, (2) practice on skills, (3) learning-center tasks, and (4) problem-solving activities. At times, the teacher may guide a small-group discussion of a mathematics topic, or work with an individual pupil who needs help.

In addition to the organizational plans we have discussed, there are two other basic plans for the self-contained classroom: (1) use of specialist teachers, and (2) creation of special classes.[17]

14. Ibid., pp. 208–209.

15. James J. Gallagher, "Mathematics for the Gifted." In *Teaching the Gifted Child*, 2nd ed. (Boston: Allyn & Bacon, 1975), pp. 95–118.

16. E. G. Begle, *Critical Variables in Mathematics Education* (Washington, DC: Mathematics Association of America and the National Council of Teachers of Mathematics 1979), p. 106.

17. James Hersberger and Grayson Wheatley, "A Proposed Model for a Gifted Elementary School Mathematics Program," *Gifted Child Quarterly*, Winter 1980, 24:37–40.

Use of Specialist Teachers

Many educators believe that there is a need for teachers who are specialists in mathematics to strengthen the program for mathematically talented children.

In some schools, mathematically talented pupils are sent to special mathematics rooms where they work for periods of time with a teacher who has a rich mathematical background in a variety of very challenging topics.

Some states provide funding so that schools may establish programs taught by teachers trained to deal with gifted and talented children.

Creation of Special Classes

Some communities provide special classes for talented and gifted children. These pupils work with a special teacher—sometimes full time, sometimes part time. Sometimes classes are recruited from several schools, and in some areas classes contain children of several age levels for economic reasons. There also is grouping in extracurricular activities, such as math clubs.

Adjusting the Curriculum for Fast Learners

Acceleration and *enrichment* are two widely used means of adjusting the curriculum for the rapid learners in mathematics. Acceleration enables the talented pupil to progress through the mathematics program at a faster than normal rate. Enrichment provides the talented child with an opportunity to participate in the basic mathematics program, plus extension activities in both the breadth and depth of mathematics.

ACCELERATION

Acceleration can be achieved by means of: (1) academic acceleration, (2) the un-

graded classroom, and (3) skipping a grade.

1. *Academic acceleration.* Academic acceleration permits a talented child to progress through the graded textbooks in mathematics at a pace faster than normal. Thus, when a fast learner in grade 3 finishes the mathematics textbook for that grade, this pupil is given a mathematics textbook for grade 4. Similarly, the pattern is repeated for the mathematics textbook for grade 5. Hence, a pupil may be a member of the third grade but yet have completed the work in mathematics as given in textbooks for grades 4 and 5.

2. *The ungraded classroom.* The organizational approach of the ungraded classroom provides for acceleration by two different procedures. First, it permits a talented child to enter kindergarten or grade 1 at an earlier age than the standard age. Second, the child is permitted to complete three grades of work in two years, by progressing according to his or her ability to achieve. The major difference between the ungraded plan and academic acceleration is the instructional approaches that are used. In the ungraded classroom, the child has opportunities to work with other pupils in a variety of activities, but this is not so in an academic acceleration program.

3. *Skipping a grade.* Skipping a grade is based on two assumptions that often prove false:

a. A talented learner is talented in all subject areas.

b. A talented learner can acquire the skills and concepts achieved in the grade skipped at the next grade level.

Children often have a given talent or aptitude and are not equally talented in all subject areas. It is possible that a specific skill or concept necessary for progress in a sequential subject, such as mathematics, may not be acquired when a grade is skipped. For this reason we do not recommend skipping a grade unless there is no other way to provide enrichment.

ENRICHMENT

Enrichment is a widely accepted means of providing appropriate learning experiences for children who are talented in elementary school mathematics. Enrichment for the rapid learner implies that the material covered will be broader and deeper than that which is normally included in the basic mathematics program, but will be related to and grow out of this standard program. There are two kinds of enrichment: horizontal enrichment, and vertical enrichment.

1. *Horizontal enrichment*. Horizontal enrichment includes *more* learning experiences on the level of the pupil's present achievement status. With horizontal enrichment, the content being studied is broader in scope than that which occurs in textbooks at that grade level. Often this type of enrichment is interpreted to mean "more of the same." That is, when a fast learner completes the assigned textbook work, the teacher merely assigns the same type of exercises from another book or hands out a ditto to work on the same material. Talented learners are not challenged by this sort of busy work. Most elementary school mathematics textbooks suggest horizontal enrichment activities of the following types:
   a. Performing a laboratory activity and keeping a record of steps.
   b. Picking a topic for further study, such as a study of ways that primitive cultures used number, measured, or used money.
   c. Creating a bulletin board display about the topic under study.
   d. Playing games.
   e. Working with the minicalculator.
   f. Completing a puzzle or other type of recreational activity.
   g. Writing word problems.
   h. Completing problems a second time with a minicalculator.
   i. Viewing a film or filmstrip on the topic being studied.

2. *Vertical enrichment*. Vertical enrichment provides advanced work or further specialization in the same area of learning. This type of enrichment increases the quality of the work being offered so as to widen and deepen understanding in a given area. Vertical enrichment leads to *power* in mathematics. Among the experiences that can be used to develop mathematical power are:
   a. Discovering varied methods of solving examples that involve number operations.
   b. Discovering varied methods of solving verbal problems.
   c. Identifying mathematical properties applied in operations.
   d. Developing an understanding of how the basic properties of mathematics are applied in shortcut procedures.
   e. Independent study of the operational procedures in available reference materials.
   f. Independent study of topics related to the applications of mathematics.
   g. Studying topics without class instruction. The leader confers with the teacher for guidance in the assignment.
   h. Independent study of subject matter through the use of adequate programmed materials and other textbooks.
   i. Studying the newer kinds of computational devices and machines.
   j. Verbalizing generalizations, rules, and conclusions in concise language.
   k. Solving and making puzzles requiring the application of basic mathematical properties.

Mathematics textbooks suggest a wide variety of activities that enrich the learning of mathematics for the more able children in grades 1 through 6. Some of the more widely used methods are:

a. Exploration of the uses of mathematics in all curriculum areas, especially science, health, music, and social studies.
b. Starred problems within instructional units that require independent research, reading, and logical inquiry.
c. List of topics and problems for special investigation and report.
d. Challenges for the more capable learners.
e. Solving equations and formulas.
f. Mathematical puzzles and recreations.
g. Geometrical constructions and proofs.
h. Activities leading to the discovery of principles, generalizations, and relationships.
i. Field work requiring the application of mathematical procedures, especially geometry.
j. Mathematics scrapbooks—individual or class.
k. "Brain twisters."
l. The preparation of exhibits, displays, and collections.
m. Excursions and field trips.
n. Mathematics clubs.
o. Sections of the textbook labeled "Challenges" or "Extensions," in which the material is keyed to the main body of the text. Extensions are designed to create power in dealing with number.
p. Supplementary books dealing with programming and electronic computers. If the school has a microcomputer, students should learn how to operate it.

THE SCHOOL LIBRARY

Library resources should be used continually to enrich the work in mathematics. The library is the heart of an enrichment program for superior learners with special interest in mathematics. These students are likely to browse widely among all kinds of available printed materials, seeking information on matters of interest. Independent reading and study are a high-level type of learning that the teacher should encourage and facilitate by having available a well-selected variety of printed materials, including general books, reference books, magazines, bulletins, schedules, and the like.

Motivating Superior Learners

How can the teacher help pupils to set goals that will challenge them? What can be done to motivate them? To what extent should external inducements and artificial stimuli—such as grades, examinations, rewards, and punishments—be used to stimulate them to greater efforts?

Ideally, motivation should help pupils to develop purposes, interests, and expectations that will direct their efforts and activities toward the fulfillment of long-range ambitions and goals. Some children reveal at an early age a marked aptitude in mathematics that should be guided and developed by the school. The experiences of young children in the home and elsewhere may have stimulated them to explore a variety of everyday uses of mathematics. This impetus should be expanded and encouraged by the whole staff of the school. It is unfortunate that lack of motivation accounts for the failure of a large number of talented youths to complete mathematics courses within their secondary education or continue the study of mathematics at the college level.

Some of the motivational techniques used by schools are:

1. Honor rolls.
2. Invitations to membership in mathematics clubs.
3. Student interviews with counselors and teachers.

4. Letters to parents praising unusual achievements.

5. Scholarship luncheons and banquets.

6. Mathematics contests.

7. The availability of a wide variety of books and mathematical devices and instruments. Some elementary schools have set up mathematics workrooms in which children can work when they wish. (For mathematics laboratories, see Chapter 2.)

8. Centers of interest in classrooms.

Summary

Children are alike as well as different in many ways. For the teacher, the challenge is to know when children should learn mathematics as a group, all performing similar activities, and when to differentiate the curriculum and methods of teaching.

Each individual child has strengths and weaknesses. To accommodate individual differences, the teacher should adjust the program so that each child lives up to his or her potential. Adjustments can be made in content difficulty, in levels of maturity, in time, in space, in materials used, and in teaching approaches.

The mastery-learning approach is a whole-class approach that provides small-group and individualized instruction. The ungraded approach helps ensure continuous growth for all pupils. There should be some type of grouping according to achievement in mathematics and the needs of the pupils.

There are many reasons why pupils become low achievers. The teacher should treat the causes, if possible. Use diagnostic techniques and remediate weaknesses. Slow learners need more time at the exploratory level with laboratory activities than average pupils. Time is an important factor in achievement for slow learners.

The pupil who is talented at mathematics needs to be challenged with the structural aspects of mathematics. Emphasize patterns, relationships, properties, and alternative algorithms. Fast learners need to study advanced topics in mathematics not normally found in a typical program. They need a variety of problem-solving experiences that involve estimating, alternative solutions, and more abstract thinking at the symbolic level. They need extensive applications of mathematics. Limited acceleration is desirable for the gifted child who is outstanding in most aspects of the curriculum.

Both slow and fast learners need various forms of enrichment. We recommend horizontal enrichment for slow learners, while the fast learner needs activities that will lead to the development of power in mathematics.

A teacher needs to maintain an attitude of experimentation—a willingness to be flexible and adaptable—trying different approaches with different groupings of children, and systematically studying results.

There is no one best approach to accommodate individual differences. Both the teacher and the pupils need to create approaches to learning that will produce optimum growth in mathematics for each child.

Exercises

1. How does grouping a class according to levels of maturity adjust for differences in ability in elementary school mathematics?

2. A year-long course of study is planned for a given grade. Is subject matter or time a variable or a constant? Or are both time and subject matter constants? If time is a constant and subject matter is a variable, how will that affect the course of study?

3. List at least five characteristics of slow learners; of fast learners.

4. Evaluate this statement: Slow learners and fast learners should be taught in segregated groups.

5. What is meant by the ungraded elementary school? Tell why you do or do not approve of it.

6. What is the difference between a slow learner and a slow achiever?

7. If homogeneous groups are formed, enumerate at least three factors that should be considered in the formation of the groups.

8. Under what conditions would you approve of acceleration as an acceptable means of adjusting the program for fast learners in mathematics?

9. Give five different solutions for finding the product of 15 and 45. Do not include the standard algorithm for multiplication of two two-digit numbers.

Selected Readings

Bartkovich, Kevin G., and William C. George, *Teaching the Gifted and Talented in the Mathematics Classroom.* Washington, D.C.: National Education Association, 1980.

Bloom, Benjamin S. *All Our Children Learning.* New York: McGraw-Hill, 1980.

Callahan, Leroy G., and Vincent J. Glennon. *Elementary School Mathematics— A Guide to Current Research.* Washington, D.C.: Association for Supervision and Curriculum Development, 1975.

Fox, Lynn. *Programs for the Gifted and Talented.* Part I, 78th Yearbook of the National Society for the Study of Education. Chicago: University of Chicago Press, 1979.

Gallagher, James J. "Mathematics for the Gifted." In *Teaching the Gifted Child,* 2nd ed. Needham Heights, MA: Allyn & Bacon, 1975, Pp. 95–118.

Glennon, Vincent J. (ed.). *The Mathematical Education of Exceptional Children and Youth—An Interdisciplinary Approach.* Reston, VA: National Council of Teachers of Mathematics, 1981.

Hector, Judith Harle. "Organizing for Mastery Learning: A Grouped-based Approach." In *Organizing for Mathematics Instruction,* 1977 Yearbook. Reston, VA: National Council of Teachers of Mathematics, 1977. Pp. 131–145.

Howell, Daisy, et al. *Activities for Teaching Mathematics to Low Achievers.* Jackson: University of Mississippi Press, 1974.

Hurwitz, Abraham B., et al. *Number Games to Improve Your Child's Arithmetic.* New York: Funk & Wagnalls, 1975.

Hurwitz, Abraham B., et al. *More Number Games—Mathematics Made Easy through Play.* New York: Funk & Wagnalls, 1976.

Kennedy, Leonard M., and Ruth L. Michon. *Games for Individualizing Mathematics Learning.* Columbus, OH: Charles E. Merrill, 1973.

Lamon, William E. (ed.). *Focus on Learning Problems in Mathematics.* Framingham, MA: Center for Teaching/Learning Mathematics, 1984.

Smith, Seaton E., Jr., and Carl A. Beckman (eds). *Games and Puzzles for Elementary and Middle School Mathematics.* Reston, VA: National Council of Teachers of Mathematics, 1975.

Sobel, Max A., and Evan M. Maletsky. *Teaching Mathematics: A Sourcebook of Aids, Activities, and Strategies,* 2nd ed. Englewood Cliffs, NJ: Prentice-Hall, 1988.

Trafton, Paul R., and Albert P. Shulte. *New Directions for Elementary School Mathematics,* 1989 Yearbook. Reston, VA: National Council of Teachers of Mathematics, 1989. Chapter 21.

Teaching Mathematics to Preschool and Kindergarten Children

ACHIEVEMENT GOALS

After studying this chapter, you should be able to:

1. Enumerate the advantages of preschool and kindergarten programs.

2. Outline the distinguishing features of a mathematics program for young children.

3. Discuss the role of the teacher in establishing an appropriate learning environment, in using the textbook, and in working with children and with parents.

4. List the strands of the preschool and kindergarten program and suggest two or more activities for each.

5. Justify the use of computers for young children and suggest some guides for their use.

VOCABULARY

These terms are defined or illustrated in the Glossary.

Attribute blocks
Cognitive
Continuum
Preoperational
  period

Sequence
Seriation
Strand

Educators and psychologists have documented the importance of guiding the intellectual, emotional, and social development of young children. Children learn very rapidly during the early years and need to be encouraged to think about the experiences they have and be guided in their learning.

Many parents and teachers have taken seriously the conclusion reached by Benjamin Bloom that "if a child does not develop appropriate learning during the first few years of life, then he or she is likely to face the likelihood of failure throughout school."[1]

Increased Interest in Schooling for Young Children

During the past decade there has been a renewed interest in the education of very young children. Kindergarten programs are universally provided throughout the United States, and preschool programs are growing rapidly. The percent of 3- and 4-year-olds enrolled in preschool programs rose dramatically over a 25-year period from about 10 percent in the mid-1960s to over 40 percent in the late 1980s. Preschool enrollments are expected to continue to increase because of the following factors: (1) increased number of children, (2) increased participation of women in the workforce, (3) the public's enthusiasm for early childhood programs, and (4) the growing availability of nursery school programs.[2]

Kinds of Programs for Young Children

Along with the increase in enrollments in programs for 3-, 4-, and 5-year-olds there

has also developed a wide range of opinions about the most appropriate kinds of program for these young children. Some professionals and parents believe that there should be an increased emphasis on early introduction of academic skills with textbooks, seatwork, formal directed instruction, and drill. Others are convinced that these young children need experiences that will help them live as young children with richness and vigor; experiences that will give them outlets for their energy, imagination, curiosity, sociability, and creativity.[3]

The first four years of the life of a child are critical. Physically, the child learns to control body parts, learns to sit, to walk, and to manipulate objects. Socially, the young child becomes aware of others, is interested in peers, and begins to develop working-together skills. Intellectually, the child learns to use language, to draw, to recognize symbols, to communicate, and develops thinking skills. Young children need to be nurtured and guided by caring adults during this crucial period of development in order to have the best chance of success later in school.

Most authorities in preschool education believe that programs for very young children should include mainly child-centered activities. In a child-centered program the children are *active learners* who learn most effectively from experiences that they help plan and carry out themselves. In terms of mathematics, preschool children tend to base their judgments about number and amount on the appearance of concrete objects.[4]

1. Benjamin S. Bloom, *Stability and Change in Human Characteristics* (New York: Wiley, 1964), p. 88.

2. Audrey Pendleton, "Preschool Enrollments: Trends and Implications," *The Condition of Education*, 1986 edition (Washington, D.C.: United States Department of Education, 1986), pp. 124–133.

3. James L. Hymes, Jr. "Public School for Four-Year-Olds," *Young Children*, 42 (January 1987): 51–52.

4. David P. Weihart, "Basics for Preschoolers: The High/Scope Approach," in *A Better Start: New Choices for Early Learning*, edited by Fred M. Hechinger (New York: Walker, 1986).

Research Confirms Values of Preschool Education

Longitudinal studies of children enrolled in preschool programs, especially Head Start programs for disadvantaged pupils, have demonstrated the advantages of early learning. One recent 14-year study of preschoolers was conducted by the Frank Porter Graham Child Development Center at the University of North Carolina. Dr. Craig Ramey, the physician who directed the research, concluded that by the time the children had completed second grade their IQ had increased an average of ten points, and they experienced only about one-half as many school failures as pupils without preschool experiences. In addition, pupils in the program demonstrated improved language skills and improved their achievement-test scores from below the 25th percentile to near the national average.[5]

Programs for Young Children

Programs for very young children should not focus on formal academic training in subjects such as reading, writing, and mathematics. Rather, programs should provide opportunities for children to actively engage in interesting play activities with selected materials. They should interact with their peers, with older children, and with adults.[6]

Lawrence Schweinhart conducted a comprehensive study of three types of preschool programs:

1. *Programmed-learning.* In this type of program, the teacher initiated the learning activities and the pupils responded. Objectives were clearly defined and tasks were clearly prescribed. The emphasis was placed on preacademic learning.

2. *Open-framework.* In this model, the teacher and the pupils worked together in planning and implementing key learning activities designed to develop intellectual and social skills.

3. *Child-centered.* In the child-centered approach, the child initiated the learning and the teacher responded to the child's needs and interest. The teacher's role was to encourage active free play on the part of the child.

Schweinhart and his associates found that preschool experiences in any one of the three models improved children's intellectual performance. The open-framework model was the most effective in terms of developing social behavior. It was concluded that although preschool programs could be based upon any one of the above approaches, formal academic programs represented by teacher-directed learning models should be avoided.[7]

The Kindergarten Curriculum

The kindergarten curriculum is more structured and has more of an academic orientation than preschool programs. Yet the kindergarten program needs to be more flexible and activity-oriented than the rest of the school program. Today's kindergarten should stress socialization and overall development of children with a majority of time spent on play activities, games, work

5. Craig T. Ramey and Dale C. Farran, "Intervening with High-Risk Families via Infant Daycare," *Resources in Education*, April 1983, ED-230289.

6. Lilian G. Katz, "Early Education: What Should Young Children Be Doing?" Chapter 9 in *Early Schooling, The National Debate,* edited by Sharon L Kagan and Edward F. Zigler (New Haven, CT: Yale University Press, 1987), p. 161.

7. Lawrence J. Schweinhart et al., "Three Preschool Curriculum Models: How Children Are Affected," in *A Better Start: New Choices for Early Learning,* edited by Fred M. Hechinger (New York: Walker, 1986), pp. 41–55.

in learning centers, art and music, and in oral language development.[8]

Research has shown that kindergarten programs that stress working with manipulatives, playing games, doing puzzles, and taking field trips are superior to extensive work in the textbook, completing worksheets, doing seatwork drill, participating in choral responses, and filling out ditto sheets.[9]

Oral language development is central to learning beginning concepts of mathematics. The use of talk during mathematics activities provides content and structure to thinking.

Learning Mathematics

In terms of learning mathematics, the National Association for the Education of Young Children recommends that young children learn through exploration and discovery activities using manipulative materials and by solving meaningful problems. Mathematics activities should be integrated with other areas such as science and social studies. Children should be provided with many opportunities for spontaneous play through projects and through many situations of daily living. The Association believes that children need playful interactions with objects and people in order to develop physically, socially, and intellectually. The curriculum should take into account different rates of growth of young children. All aspects of child development should be considered—namely, physical, social, emotional, and cognitive. The integrated curriculum with active learning activities using manipulative materials in small cooperative learning groups provides the most effective approach for young children to learn and grow.

The preschool program should involve play activities with many manipulatives, should have storytime, cooking, dramatic play, music, nature walks, and the like. During the preschool years children should (1) increase their attention span and learn to stick to a task until completed, (2) develop a positive attitude toward school, and (3) acquire a pleasing, healthy personality.[10]

The Teacher's Role

Establish the Learning Environment

The teacher of young children should establish a rich learning environment by providing the materials, utilizing the space, and coordinating the individuals who will make possible physical, social, emotional, and intellectual stimulation needed for optimum development. Teachers should not "lecture" pupils but should provide opportunities for meaningful experiences and for the exchange of ideas. The teacher's role should be to comfort the children, set limits, provide for crisis intervention, deal with emotions, help pupils share, and guide them toward the development of self-control.[11]

Use the Textbook as a Guide

The typical Teacher's Edition of a modern textbook series in elementary school mathematics has many excellent suggestions for planning and implementing effective pro-

8. Joanne R. Nurss and Walter L. Hodges, "Early Childhood Education," *Encyclopedia of Educational Research* (New York: Free Press, 1982), pp. 489–507.

9. Ruth K. Rowl and Francis S. O'Tuel, "Mathematics Achievement in Young Children Is Increased with a Cognitively Oriented Curriculum," *Resources in Education*, March 1988, pp. 1–10. ERIC ED 227-933.

10. "NAEYC Position Statement on Developmentally Appropriate Practice in the Primary Grades, Serving 5-Through 8-Year-Olds," *Young Children*, 43 (January 1988): 64–84.

11. David Elkind, "Educating the Very Young: A Call for Clear Thinking," *NEA Today*, 6 (January 1988): 22–27.

grams. The idea-packed Teacher's Edition usually provides suggestions for yearly planning, has an overview for each unit with pretests for pupils, and provides a sample lesson plan with objectives, teaching suggestions, follow-up activities, and end-of-unit tests. In most textbooks there are colorful pictures and pencil-and-paper exercises. Unfortunately, many teachers fail to provide the necessary laboratory activities for pupils to use to explore and discover concepts and create appropriate language *prior* to using the textbook lessons. Textbook activities are at the visual and symbolic level and should be used *after* experiences with laboratory materials.

Work with Parents

The teacher also has an important responsibility to work with parents of young children so appropriate learning experiences can be provided in the home and community that will support and reinforce school activities. At frequent intervals the teacher should talk with parents about specific topics that will help the children learn mathematics. Also, the teacher should send home a "progress report" on selected objectives on the mathematics continuum (discussed later), for which the child needs additional reinforcement. In addition, written suggestions such as the following may be sent home:

- Encourage your child to talk about different sizes, shapes, and colors of familiar objects.
- Provide many different counting activities. Have your child count small collections of objects.
- Keep a height and weight record. Make a graph.
- Have a clock for your child to watch. Talk about when different things happen such as time to get up, go to school,

eat lunch, watch a favorite TV program.
- Let your child help you cook—measure ingredients, keep track of cooking time, and so on.
- Encourage your child to read and talk about different numerals and discuss what they mean.
- Give your child a small allowance in various coins. Talk about the names of coins and their values. Practice making change.
- Take your child shopping with you. Practice reading the prices of items. Talk about items that cost more or less than others.
- While riding in the car, talk about road signs, distances, speed limits, and mileages. Count different things.
- Play lots of games with your child—jacks, dominoes, board games, and puzzles.
- Do mental math with games such as "I'm thinking of a number; it's larger than 3 but smaller than ten. You have three guesses, and each time I'll tell you 'more' or 'less.' "

Principles of Teaching and Learning Applied to Young Children

The principles of teaching and learning presented in Chapter 1 should serve as a basis for planning and implementing programs for preschool and kindergarten children. Units of study and daily lesson plans should include the following categories.

I. Goals and Objectives

The major goals in mathematics for primary children are to:

1. Give experiences in problem solving.
2. Help children acquire beginning con-

cepts of number and geometry along with appropriate language development.

3. Provide reasoning activities.

4. Learn to value and enjoy activities involving mathematics.

Objectives should be listed on a continuum. The continuum serves two purposes. It helps in planning activities for learning and it serves as a record of progress for each child.

II. Readiness

Young children come to school with a wide range of background experiences with different aspects of mathematics. They are not passive recipients of knowledge; rather, they are actively and continuously acquiring mathematical concepts and language for themselves through interaction with the environment. In this sense, preschool and kindergarten children spend their time in building readiness for subsequent learning experiences. Everything a pupil learns becomes a readiness for the next stage of development. Readiness is ever-present in every phase of learning mathematics. It is something that is *developed,* not something that just happens. In planning learning activities, the teacher needs to assess the extent of readiness of each child for new learning and then take this information into consideration during learning experiences.

III. Motivation

Young children have natural interest in number and shapes. They tend to be highly self-motivated and are inquiring, active learners. Youngsters gain enjoyment, satisfaction, and intellectual stimulation from interesting play activities. They like stories and pictures and want to actively explore, share and talk. The teacher needs to plan ways to keep children actively engaged in meaningful, interesting, and successful learning experiences.

IV. Growth Through Guided Discovery

Learning is a growth process that is facilitated through discovery during four stages: *manipulative, visual, symbolic,* and *mastery.* The emphasis for young children must be placed on manipulative and visual experiences. According to Piaget, between the ages of 2 and 7 the child is in the *preoperational period* of development. This means that learning takes place mainly as the result of the child's interactions with objects and people. Children can, however, learn to recognize symbols, use language, and make drawings, but they learn best as the result of discovery experiences with concrete objects. Children need to be guided in their intellectual development and in their language development. In planning learning activities, the teacher of young children needs to provide many experiences at the concrete level of learning.

V. Reinforcement

The kinds of reinforcement young children need should be provided through varied purposeful practice in meaningful activities with interesting materials. Many experiences with manipulatives should be provided. Games should be used daily. Paper-and-pencil activities may be used only as a follow-up from experiences with concrete materials. Cooperative learning activities are recommended for reinforcement experiences. Isolated drill is not recommended.

VI. Evaluation of Learning

Young children will learn mathematics at different rates, and these rates will vary for each child at different times of the year.

Thus evaluation should be carried out by keeping a record of each child's performance and how the learner is progressing in meeting objectives. This record should be kept on a continuum that can be developed from materials provided in most Teacher's Manuals. Assessment of progress should be done through observing each pupil's work and through oral questioning. Standardized tests are not recommended for preschool and kindergarten children.

The Strands of the Preschool and Kindergarten Curriculum

Classifying

Very young children interact with the things in their environment in a variety of ways. Most children enjoy sorting things according to some characteristic or attribute. Preschool children need to start sorting by one attribute only. Kindergarten children should begin classifying according to two characteristics.

Give a small group of pupils a box of objects of various-colored geometric shapes (circle, square, rectangle, triangle), sizes (large, medium, small), and ask them to perform the following tasks:

- Sort the objects into two groups. Talk about what plan was followed. Was the classification by color, by shape, or by size?
- Have the children find things that are alike in some way. Talk about the choices and why they are alike.
- Provide an empty box. Tell the pupils to put all the objects with a specific characteristic in the box. Choices are (1) all the same color, (2) all the same shape, or (3) all the same size.
- Classify the objects according to two characteristics. Place in the box the objects that meet such conditions as (1) all large shapes that are red, (2) all purple

triangles, (3) all small square regions.
- Challenge the children to classify by more than one attribute. Talk about their results.

Ordering in a Sequence

Ordering in a sequence is not difficult for young children. To create an orderly sequence the child must be able to identify the attribute being ordered and then arrange the objects from one aspect of the characteristic to the other. For example, pupils may be asked to order the Cuisenaire rods from the shortest to the longest. Pictures of people could be ordered from tallest to shortest. Pictures of animals could be ordered from smallest to largest. For preschool children start with only two or three things to order. Kindergarten children can learn to order five or more things.

Completing Patterns

Among the ways young children learn about patterns with geometric shapes are by copying a pattern picture with objects on a rod, or creating patterns with blocks.

Counting

One of the first things a small child is asked to do by an adult is to count some objects. Research has shown that although counting seems to be a simple procedure, it is a very complex process for the young child to learn and may take up to three years to master.[12]

The procedure involved in counting a set of objects include the following subskills:

1. *Rote counting.* Rote counting is the ability to recite the number names in sequence. Children learn to rote-count early in life as the result of memorization. Most pupils can count to more than ten when

12. Pearla Nesher, "Learning Mathematics—A Cognitive Perpsective," *American Psychologist*, 41 (October 1986): 1114–1122.

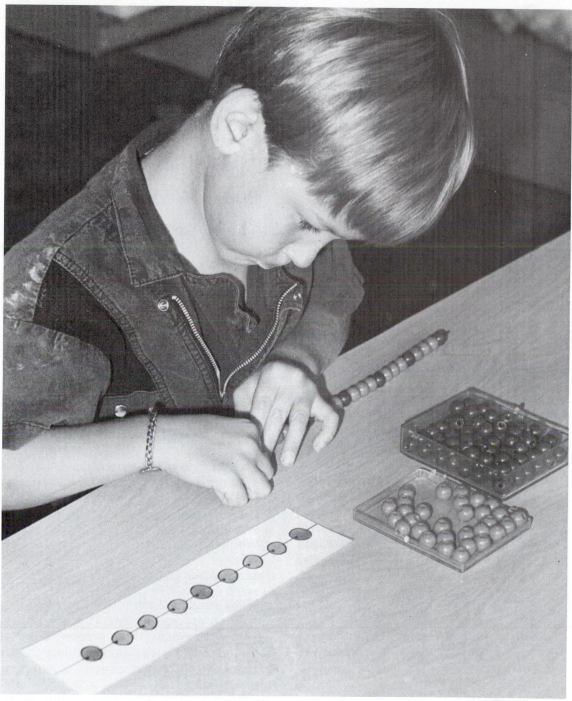

A pupil copies a pattern with beads on a rod.

(Photo by Leland Perry)

they enter kindergarten. Pupils should be provided with many opportunities to practice saying the number names in sequence. Number games, rhymes, and songs provide enjoyable reinforcement. Children may sing "One little, two little, three little Indians" and "One, two, buckle my shoe." Have the pupils count while others are swinging. Have them count the number of children in a small group. Count the number of times you clap your hands. The purpose of these activities is to help pupils remember the number names.

2. *Matching number names to objects.* This activity involves the ability to start with an object and say the number "one" and then point to the next object in a collection and say the next counting number until all objects have been counted. Pupils should be provided with many opportunities to perform a one-to-one matching between objects and number names.

3. *Rational counting.* Rational counting is the process of assigning a cardinal number to a collection to answer the question "How many?" When a child assigns a counting-number name to the last object in a collection, the learner must realize that this becomes the cardinal number of the set. Counting to find how many involves knowing the number names in sequence, matching the names in a one-to-one correspondence with the objects being counted, and then concluding by assigning the last name assigned to the last object as the number of things in the collection.

DEVELOPING NUMBER SENSE

Rational counting provides opportunities for pupils to develop number sense or the cardinal meaning of number. Many counting activities should be provided for young children. At first concentrate on collections of less than ten. Show some objects and have the pupils count to find how many. Make sure each child follows the correct

procedure and understands that the last number matched with the last object is the number name of the collection. Next, put in front of a class a collection of more than ten and ask a child to pick out a specified number of objects less than ten. This is a more difficult task for most children than merely counting a set number of objects.

THE ASSOCIATION OF NUMBER AND NUMERAL

Many children entering kindergarten can recognize the numerals from 1 to 10. Some pupils have difficulty with 6 and 9. However, most beginning kindergarten pupils have trouble associating numerals with different collections of things larger than three. There are many activities that can be provided for young children to learn to associate numerals (digits) with the number of objects in a set.

DOT PATTERNS FOR NUMBERS FROM ONE TO TEN

Young children can usually recognize the number of things in a set of objects or in a picture without counting if a pattern is shown. In fact, it is recommended that pupils be challenged to recognize at a glance the number in a set up to five and the dot patterns to ten. Common dot patterns are shown on dominoes and dice from one to six (see page 81).

DON'T OVEREMPHASIZE COUNTING BY ONES

Often pupils get the idea that to find the number of things in any collection they must count by ones. Overteaching counting strategies may distract from rational thinking. Robert Wirtz recommends that pupils use a 10-frame formed by a 2 by 5 grid drawn on a piece of cardboard. By placing objects on the grid, pupils can see the relationship of the number of objects to five and to ten. This assists them in determining the

Pupils match numerals with dot patterns on an electric board.

(Photo by Leland Perry)

number of objects without counting by ones.[13]

13. Robert Wirtz, *New Beginnings* (Monterey, CA: Curriculum Development Associates, 1980).

"Take a peek" is a good game for youngsters to play for recognition of numbers of five or less. Have the children close their eyes. Place a set number of lima beans under a paper cup. Then have the children open their eyes and raise the cup for about two seconds and cover the beans again. Ask "How many?" Have each pupil try to name the number for "scattered" objects and for objects that have been placed in a set pattern. For numbers from five to ten, place the lima beans in a set pattern, cover with a paper plate, and play the "take a peek" game.

MATCHING AND COMPARING TWO SETS

One-to-one matching of the objects in two collections helps pupils develop the ideas of more than, less than, and equal in number. Preschool children should match sets with five or fewer objects. Kindergarten pupils should begin matching activities with collections of up to ten objects. Many different types of materials may be used for matching—blocks, pictures, and other things. After comparing two unequally numbered sets, the pupils should discuss the idea of which set has more and which has less.

There are many situations in which pupils can match one-to-one: cartons to straws, boxes or crayons to pupils, and pupils to chairs. After performing the matching, pupils should be encouraged to discuss the ideas of more than, less than, and equal.

UNDERSTANDING NUMBERS MORE THAN TEN

Counting numbers from 10 to 15 are usually difficult for children to remember. The number names can be made more meaningful if the collection of 10 to 20 objects is regrouped into a set of ten and some more. Eleven and twelve are the only two number names that do not follow the pattern of "one ten plus some more." For example, "thirteen" can be related to "one-ten-three." A manipulative aid helpful in establishing this pattern of thinking is the ten-ten counting frame (see page 83).

The next step in helping children learn to count to 100 is to have them count by tens. The number names should be related to the "tenness" of our number system: one-ten (ten), two-tens (twenty), three-tens (thirty), etc. Again, the ten-ten counting frame is a useful aid in helping children learn to count to 100 by tens.

NUMBER SEQUENCE AND ORDER

Although children can count by rote as a result of memorization, they may not understand the *order* of the numbers. Understanding the order of numbers involves being able to perform the following tasks:

- Given two consecutive counting numbers, either orally or on a number strip, tell or write what number comes after and comes before. Most children have difficulty in identifying what number comes *before* a given number.
- Given any two consecutive even or odd numbers either orally or on a number strip, tell or write what number comes in between.

One of the best aids for helping children learn about number sequences and order of numbers is the hundred board (see page 84).

Other aids include the number line, and cards individually numbered to be arranged in sequence.

NUMERALS ON CLOCKS AND CALENDARS

Numerals are associated with telling time and on the calendar. Numerals are also on measuring instruments. Young children need to read and understand various uses of numerals and realize that digits are used for purposes other than to name the number of objects in a set. A Judy clock and a calendar should be available in the classroom for children to use. Kindergarten children should learn to tell time on the hour. They should also learn the names of the months of the year and the days of the week.

(Photo by Leland Perry)

These pupils are learning to count by tens on a ten-ten frame.

The hundred board has many uses. Here a pupil counts by twos.

(Photo by Leland Perry)

NUMBER WORDS

Number words are harder to learn than digits—the word *three* is more difficult for the pupil to recognize than the numeral 3. The types of activities provided for children to learn to associate the number of objects in a set are also appropriate for learning to associate number with numeral with the number word. Display cards that show the number word, the dot pattern, and the digit can be made or purchased to use for practice or for bulletin-board displays. A typical set is shown in Figure 5.1.

LEARNING TO WRITE NUMERALS

Once a child can assign a correct number to collections from 1 to 10, it is time to learn to write numerals. Most textbooks provide practice in writing numerals, but prior to practice the child must be carefully guided as to where to start, how to proceed, and where to stop. The following steps are recommended.

Make each numeral with a marking pen on a 5-by-8-inch card. Figure 5.2 shows a widely accepted way to form the numerals. Pupils can use a finger to trace each numeral or can use the numeral as a guide to make the digits.

Many children have difficulty learning to write certain digits. Some of the most common mistakes include:

1. Making the digit backwards (3, 5, and 7 are commonly reversed).

2. Writing a digit from the bottom toward the top (7, 1, and 9 are examples).

3. The numeral 8 is sometimes made incorrectly with two unconnected circles.

4. The numeral 9 is made incorrectly with a circle and a vertical line.

5. The zero is made incorrectly by starting at the bottom and progressing counterclockwise.

Mistakes in making the digits can easily be corrected with careful guidance. The use of an overhead projector permits the teacher to show pupils how to form each numeral. For pupils who display persistent errors in making one or more digits, special techniques may be needed based on a kinesthetic approach. Following a pattern made out of sandpaper may be helpful. Making each digit with a paintbrush or with a wet finger may be helpful. Careful supervision of pupils in small groups as they write the digits is necessary. Sometimes children who have been writing the digits correctly will

Figure 5.1
Cards showing number word, the dot pattern, and the digit

This pupil is matching numerals with words.

(Photo by Leland Perry)

Figure 5.2
Guide for writing numerals

start making reversals and write them in the wrong direction.

ORDINAL NUMBERS

An ordinal number is one that answers the question "Which one?" It is usually learned in the context of a series of things that are placed in line in order and named with the words "first, second, third, fourth," and so forth. Preschool children may learn the ordinal *first*, but should not be expected to understand more than that. Sometimes the word *last* is assigned to the final thing in a series, which is confusing because it may be the third one in a series of three things or the fifth one in a series of five. Kindergarten children find ordinal number very difficult to learn. Two skills must be established for pupils to understand ordinals. First, pupils must learn the ordinal names *in order*. Second, left-to-right progression must be established.

FRACTIONS

Children encounter parts of wholes in everyday activities. Frequently use the expression "Give me half of your . . ." The concept of "a part of a whole" is easily developed under these conditions. First, the parts must be congruent (equal in size and shape). Second, the number of congruent parts must be determined (this becomes the denominator). Third, the number of parts under consideration must be identified (this becomes the numerator of the fraction).

In developing initial fraction concepts, the teacher may take an orange, a paper plate, or a piece of cardboard and cut it into two (or more) congruent parts. Have the pupils discuss the size of the parts and the number of parts. Then take one part and ask "What part of the whole is this one piece?" The pupils should be led to use the language "It is one part out of two." Then relate this idea to the numeral word *one-half* and the numeral ½. Other objects can be used to cut into parts from two to four. The pupils should see the relationship between the total number of parts, the parts being considered, the word, and the numeral used to express each fraction.

One of the best manipulative aids to use in developing concepts of fractions is the circular fraction kit.

GRAPHING

Making a graph uses classification skills. Pupils can participate in graphing activities by using various attributes—colors, favorite foods, kinds of pets, and months of birthdays. First, it is necessary to decide what information is to be collected, for example favorite pets. Second, the teacher needs to construct the basic format for the graph on the chalkboard, bulletin board, or flannelboard. Along the bottom of the graph, write the names of pets on the base and numbers along the left side. Now ask the children to raise their hands for each pet on the graph. For each pet, record a rectangle for each pupil who selects that pet.

MEASUREMENT

Young children should have beginning experiences with measuring height, length, weight, and capacity. When given two

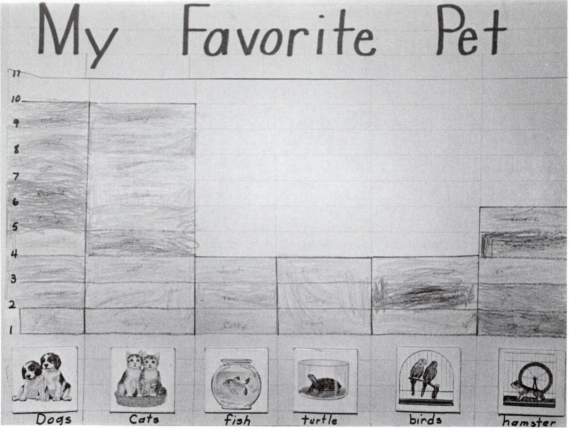

Graph shows pupils' favorite pets.

(Photo by Leland Perry)

heights they should compare to find which is taller or shorter. When given two lengths they should be able to tell which is longer or shorter. When given two amounts of substance in a container they should tell which one has more and which has less. Measurement is discussed in detail in Chapter 15.

MONEY

Children should be given activities involving the recognition of pennies, nickels, dimes, quarters, and dollar bills. A half-dollar should not be used because it is so rarely seen.

During initial activities use real money. Put 10 pennies, 2 nickels, 1 dime, and 1 quarter in a zip-lock bag for each pupil in a small group. Have the pupils identify each side of a coin by name. Discuss how many pennies it takes to make a nickel, how many nickels it takes to make a dime, and so on. Have available several small items (such as a pencil, tablet, eraser, and the like) with price tags on them. Have the pupils show with the coins how much each will cost. Talk about which items cost more than others. Games such as money bingo are fun to play.

GEOMETRY

Preschool and kindergarten classrooms should be stocked with a variety of geome-

Pupils enjoy a game of color-shape bingo.   *(Photo by Leland Perry)*

try models of all sizes and shapes. There should be regions of various colors that are circular, square, triangular, and rectangular. There should be spheres, cones, cylinders, and prisms. These materials should first be used as manipulatives. As they are used they should be named by the teacher, and children should be encouraged to discuss the ways the geoshapes are alike and how they differ. The children should learn the names of and be able to identify and draw squares, triangles, and rectangles. (A comprehensive discussion of geometry is provided in Chapter 16.)

PROBLEM SOLVING

All of the above activities involve different types of problems to be solved. For example, if a pupil has a set of colored cubes, several questions could be asked that would involve solving a problem. "How many cubes are there?" "Show me five red cubes." "If the first four cubes of a pattern are a red cube, a yellow cube, a green cube, and a red cube, what would be the next one?"

Young children are capable of solving a wide variety of problems. They enjoy story problems and are usually successful in solving them when provided with appropriate manipulative materials. Cheryl Ibarra and Mauritz Lindvall found that kindergarten pupils who were given story problems with objects and action performed better than pupils without objects and in "static" situations.[14] (A comprehensive discussion of problem solving appears in Chapter 6.)

14. Cheryl Gibbons Ibarra and Mauritz C. Lindvall, "Factors Associated with the Ability of Kindergarten Children to Solve Simple Arithmetic Story Problems," *Journal of Educational Research*, 75 (January/February 1982): 149–155.

A group of pupils solves a story problem.

(Photo by Leland Perry)

Addition Problems

Story problems involving joining objects in two sets help pupils solve addition problems. For example, the teacher tells the pupils: "Once upon a time there were four little piggies who lived in a circular house. Now show these piggies with your lima beans. There was one little piggie who lived in a square pen. Show this piggie with a lima bean or some kind of marker. Now if all the piggies decided to go to market together, how many would make the trip? How many is four plus one?"

Next the pupils are asked to record the solution of the story problem with a number fact on their chalkboards. Other stories may be used for other number facts. Children find these activities very enjoyable and relatively easy.

Subtraction Problems

Young children find addition problems easier than subtraction problems. Thus, subtraction situations should be used with children after they have a clear understanding of addition facts to sums of six. Subtraction story problems should involve a "take-away" situation, such as "If you had five pennies and lost two of them, how many would you have left?" Pupils should use objects to represent the pennies. They should put out five, take away two of them, and then determine how many are left. The number fact would then be recorded as 5 − 3 = 2.

(A complete discussion of helping pupils understand basic addition and subtraction facts is provided in Chapter 7.)

Using Computers with Preschool and Kindergarten Pupils

Computers have been used with preschool and kindergarten pupils with some success. Ruth Nieboer completed a study with preschool children. A computer activity center was placed in an established preschool environment. The pupils were given the opportunity to select the computer learning center as one of their activities. It was found that pupils improved their fine motor development by working with the keyboard, they improved in their ability to take turns, and they demonstrated problem-solving behavior.[15]

Tonni McCollister and others studied the effects of computer-assisted instruction compared with teacher-directed instruction on arithmetic scores of kindergarten pupils. The children who used the computer treatment performed better on a post-test than pupils who worked with the teacher.[16]

A third study, by Sonja Grover, involved kindergarten pupils working with software designed around cognitive-development principles in comparison with pupils working with other kinds of software. Those working with the cognitive-developmental software scored higher than the other children.[17]

If computers are used in the preschool and kindergarten classroom or in a central computer laboratory, the teacher must be sure the computer programs are well designed. They must fit into the curriculum. The programs should be colorful, in large format, move at an appropriate pace, and give immediate feedback to responses. Avoid programs that are too easy or too difficult.

Schedule pupils to work at the computer in groups of two or three. This encourages discussion as well as taking turns and increases interest.

Computers must not be used as a substitute for exploration and discovery with concrete objects. They cannot replace the teacher's guidance and systematic development of concepts and skills in mathematics.

Summary

Research has confirmed the values of preschool and kindergarten education. Interest in providing appropriate schooling for 3-, 4-, and 5-year-olds has grown rapidly in the last decade. During the 1980s an increased emphasis was placed upon learning academic skills in the preschool and kindergarten programs. The National Association for the Education of Young Children does not endorse this trend. They believe that young children need playful interactions with objects and people. Their major concern is with the overall development of each child—physically, emotionally, socially, and intellectually.

15. Ruth N. Nieboer, "A Study of the Effect of Computers on Preschool Environment," *Resources in Education*, July 1983, ED−234−898.

16. Tonni S. McCollister, et. al., "Effects of Computer Assisted Instruction and Teacher Assisted Instruction on Arithmetic Task Achievement Scores of Kindergarten Children," *Journal of Educational Research* 80 (Nov/Dec 1986): 121–125.

17. Sonja Grover, "A Field Study of the Use of Cognitive-Developmental Principles in Microcomputer Design for Young Children," *Journal of Educational Research*, 79 (July/August 1986): 325–332.

Kindergarten children come to school ready to begin to learn mathematical concepts and skills. The teacher's role is critical in providing a rich learning environment, including well-selected and properly used manipulatives, pictures, and symbolic materials. Young children can profit from work with the computer. Working with parents is of vital importance. The kindergarten curriculum should include a systematic study of various topics in mathematics outlined in this chapter.

The key to successful learning at the preschool and kindergarten levels is to be sure the pupils participate in activities that include both manipulatives and intellectual responses. Children should verbalize what they do when they manipulate objects and what the result is. Learning situations are optimum when the child physically moves objects, then becomes able to discover a pattern or procedure and then verbalize the activity.

Exercises

1. Make a list of the manipulative materials that should be available for (a) preschool children, and (b) kindergarten pupils.

2. Compare the topics presented in this chapter with the contents of at least two contemporary kindergarten textbooks.

3. Prepare a checklist of mathematics concepts and skills that kindergarten pupils should be expected to learn. Have a kindergarten teacher critique your work. Then interview a 5-year-old child to see if he or she can do the things you have listed.

4. Prepare one of the instructional aids suggested in this chapter and use it with one or more pupils.

5. Make a board game to use in a kindergarten classroom. Give the rules for playing and the necessary game pieces; name the specific skill or skills the game reinforces.

6. Make a hundred board as shown on page 84 and try the following activities with two or three young children.
   a. *Naming number patterns.* Use the tags with the blank side showing. Display a set of tags less than five in a pattern. Have the pupil name the number in the set without counting. Then count to verify. Set up sets of tags in pattern to ten. Have the pupil guess and then verify.
   b. *Recognizing numerals.* With the numerals showing, have the child name any numeral. (Later the pupil should learn that a numeral such as 23 can also be named as 2 tens, 3 ones.)
   c. *Counting forward.* Have the child count by ones, pointing to the numerals. Later have pupils count by 5s, 10s, 2s, and so on by pointing to the numerals. Turn the tags over with blank side showing and have the pupil count by 1s, 5s, 10s, 2s as he or she turns the tags over. Then turn over any tag and have the child count by tens from there.

d. *Counting backward.* Have the child count backward by ones pointing to the numerals on the hundred board.

e. *Finding more than, less than.* Have the child tell what number is one more than a given number on the hundred board. Later, have that pupil tell two more, then three more. Have the child tell what number is one less than a given number; two less; three less. Then turn all the tags over with the blank sides showing; turn over one numeral and have the pupil tell the number that is 10 more, 20 more, and so on. Later, ask the child to tell 5 more, 8 more, etc.

f. Finding missing numbers. Turn all the numerals over with blank side out. Then pick any two disks, turn them over, and have the pupil supply the missing numbers in between, just before, and just after the given numbers.

g. *Discovering patterns.* With all numerals showing, have the pupil look for different patterns on the hundred board. Pick a number at the top and read down. What is the relationship? What about the relationship of all the columns?

Selected Readings

Baratta-Lorton, Mary. *Mathematics Their Way.* Menlo Park, CA: Addison-Wesley, 1976.

Baratta-Lorton, Mary. *Workjobs II: Number Activities for Early Childhood.* Menlo Park, CA: Addison-Wesley, 1979.

Croft, Doreen J., and Robert D. Hess. *An Activities Handbook for Teachers of Young Children,* 2nd ed. Boston: Houghton Mifflin, 1975.

Cruikshank, Douglas E., David L. Fitzgerald, and Linda R. Jensen. *Young Children Learning Mathematics.* Needham Heights, MA: Allyn & Bacon, 1980. Pp. 36–40, 342.

Greenes, Carole. *The Mathworks: Handbook of Activities for Helping Students Learn Mathematics.* Palo Alto, CA: Creative Publications, 1978.

Hechinger, Fred M. (ed.). *A Better Start: New Choices for Early Learning.* New York: Walker, 1986.

Here They Come Ready or Not! A Report of the School Readiness Task Force. Sacramento: California State Department of Education, 1988.

Kagan, Sharon, and Edward F. Zigler (eds.). *Early Schooling: The National Debate.* New Haven, CT: Yale University Press, 1987.

Piaget, Jean. *The Child's Conception of Number.* New York: Norton, 1965.

Piaget, Jean, et al. *The Child's Conception of Geometry.* New York: Norton, 1981.

Pitcher, Evelyn Goodenough, et al. *Helping Young Children Learn,* 3rd ed. Columbus, OH: Charles E. Merrill, 1979.

Spodek, Bernard. *Teaching in the Early Years,* 3rd ed. Englewood Cliffs, NJ: Prentice-Hall, 1985.

Steffe, Leslie P. (ed.). *Research on Mathematical Thinking of Young Children.* Reston, VA: National Council of Teachers of Mathematics, 1975.

6

Problem Solving

ACHIEVEMENT GOALS

After studying this chapter, you should be able to:

1. Discuss the role of the calculator and computer in the problem-solving process.

2. Describe the nature of a mathematical problem.

3. List and illustrate a usable set of steps for problem solving.

4. Practice estimation in problem solving and describe its importance.

5. State various types of problems that are suitable for elementary-age pupils and describe how the computer and calculator affect each set.

VOCABULARY

These terms are defined or illustrated in the Glossary.

Deductive
  reasoning
Guess and test
Heuristic
Inductive
  reasoning
Key-word
  approach

Mathematical
  problem
Rate
Strategy
Variable

Problem solving as discussed in this chapter refers to the types of problems typically found in elementary school textbooks, those provided by teachers, and those the computer now makes available to elementary-age pupils. Learning to solve problems requires experience and persistence. Pupils need to develop a sound understanding of the situations that can be described by addition, subtraction, multiplication, and division. There is no standard algorithm for problem solving; pupils have to develop flexible thinking skills in order to approach various problem situations.

In 1980, the National Council of Teachers of Mathematics published *An Agenda for Action*, which designated *problem solving* as the theme for the 1980s. It recommended that problem solving become the central focus of mathematics programs of the future.[1] Again in 1989, the same council reaffirmed its commitment to problem solving by listing it as one of five major goals of mathematics instruction and stated that "the development of each student's ability to solve problems is essential if he or she is to be a productive citizen."[2]

The Nature of Problems and Problem Solving

Polya, the master problem solver and teacher of problem solving, defines problem solving as: "finding an unknown means to a distinctly conceived end. . . . To find a way when no way is known offhand, to find a way out of a difficulty, to find a way around an obstacle. . . . There is no problem unless the individual has the desire to find a solution."[3] In other words, a mathematical problem, whether elementary or advanced, always involves finding an answer to a question that cannot be obtained by a habitual response. This definition of problem solving implies that what is a problem to one person (or at one grade level) will not be perceived as a problem by another.

For example, sixth-graders should be able to give the sum of 6 + 7 with a habitual response. However, this sum cannot be given as a habitual response by pupils who know only addition facts to the sum of 10. There are several ways in which pupils at this stage might solve such a problem:

1. Count a set of 6 objects and a set of 7 objects. Combine them and determine that there are 13 objects.

2. Note that 3 of the objects from the first group can be combined with 7 objects in the second group to make a group of 10 objects; obtaining a group of 10 objects and a group of 3 objects gives a set of 13 objects.

3. Write 6 + 7 as (6 + 4) + 3, which is 10 + 3, or 13. The first two of these solutions are at the concrete level. The third solution is at the symbolic level.

Computation and Mathematics

Many people erroneously equate computation with mathematics. Computation is definitely a part of mathematics, but a full grasp of mathematics requires understanding—computation can be learned by rote with little understanding. The main thrust of a meaningful program in mathematics is to enable pupils to understand the work. This aim is not outmoded even in an age of calculators and computers. The main reason for teaching computation is to help pupils

1. *An Agenda for Action: Recommendations for School Mathematics for the 1980s* (Reston, VA: National Council of Teachers of Mathematics, 1980), p. 29.

2. *Curriculum and Evaluation Standards for School Mathematics* (Reston, VA: National Council of Teachers of Mathematics, March 1989), p. 6.

3. G. Polya, "On Solving Mathematical Problems in High School." In *Problem Solving in School Mathematics* (Reston, VA: National Council of Teachers of Mathematics, 1980), pp. 1–2.

learn the ideas and concepts associated with the basic operations.

Problem Solving Is a Process

Problem solving is a process by which the choice of an appropriate strategy enables a pupil to proceed from what is given in a problem to its solution. Often, the answer is the least important part of the problem-solving process; few of the answers children obtain in school mathematics will have much value in their lives. The ideas used in the process are much more valuable than the answer. Thus, it is important for teachers to determine whether an incorrect answer is due to an error in process or in computation. Do not, however, infer from this discussion that errors in computation are acceptable; rather, keep in mind that overemphasis on answers may impede the pupil's understanding of the process. A pupil with poor computational ability who understands the process can use a calculator to get the answer. A pupil who can compute rapidly and accurately but does not understand the process is lost.

In the field of banking, a computational error that results in an imbalance of a single penny in an account may require as much time to correct as a computational error involving thousands of dollars.

National Assessment

The National Assessment of Educational Progress was established in 1969 by the United States government to assess progress of students in several different subject areas, including mathematics. The assessments measure achievement of 9-, 13-, and 17-year-olds. There have been four national assessments of educational progress in mathematics, conducted in 1973, 1978, 1982, and 1986. In all four national assessments, students were found to be deficient in prob-

lem-solving skills. The results of the 1986 assessment were published in 1988 by the Educational Testing Service.[4]

Vicky Kouba and others, in their analysis of the performance on word problems and problem solving of students on the fourth NAEP of mathematics, concluded that "problem solving continues to be an area of central concern."[5]

Kouba and colleagues found that about 90 percent of the third-grade pupils could solve simple one-step addition problems with whole numbers and 70 percent could solve simple subtraction problems. But only about 21 percent of the 9-year-old pupils tested had mastered basic mathematical operations and beginning problem-solving skills. Only about 30 percent of those pupils tested could solve a simple two-step problem such as "Jane buys a tablet for 49 cents and a pencil for 25 cents. How much change should she get back from $1.00?"

At the age of 13, only 16 percent of the students tested had mastered moderately complex mathematical procedures and reasoning. About 37 percent could solve problems involving simple interest. Only 5 percent solved a problem like this one: "The sale price of a radio after it had been discounted 60% was $136. What was the regular price?"

Ways to Improve Problem Solving

There is no easy way to teach or learn problem solving. It is a "learn-by-doing" activity. A list of strategies may be useful as a

4. *The Mathematics Report Card: Are We Measuring Up? Trends and Achievement Based on the 1986 National Assessment* (Princeton, NJ: Educational Testing Service, June 1988).

5. Vicky L. Kouba, et.al., "Results of the Fourth NAEP Assessment of Mathematics: Number, Operations, and Word Problems," *Arithmetic Teacher*, 8 (April 1988): 19.

guide, but such a list must be altered by individuals on the basis of their experience. Research indicates that skills improve when pupils are given a variety of problems to solve.

Textbook problems cover a broad range of social situations as well as provide experiences in problem solving. These problems provide some of the background needed to become a useful member of our society. A valid criticism of mathematical textbooks of the past is that the range of problems for the elementary school was too limited. The scope of problems has been expanded in recently published textbooks.

Success generates confidence and produces a positive attitude toward problem solving. Every effort should be made to provide problems for pupils that match their ability, but a wider range of problems must be provided for the more able pupils. Children must learn to walk before they can run. An elementary-age pupil should achieve competence in the solution of standard textbook problems before encountering problems with an expanded range and difficulty.

William Nibbelink and others examined problem-solving exercises included in textbooks over the past 30 years and found that problem-solving ability improved under the following conditions:

1. When textbooks included more problem solving exercises.

2. As the pupil's language fluency improved.

3. With improved understanding of mathematical concepts and of the fundamental operations.

4. When teachers provided guidance in the use of problem-solving strategies.[6]

Randall Charles and Frank Lester implemented a systematic approach to problem solving for fifth- and seventh-grade pupils. The investigators emphasized solving a variety of problems with a guided choice of strategies. This approach resulted in uniform benefits when compared to the traditional approach.[7]

A Guide for Problem Solving

The following five steps form a guide for elementary pupils in the solution of typical textbook problems:

1. Read the problem carefully.

2. Identify the problem question and the numbers given and how they are related.

3. Identify the operation or operations—write an equation.

4. Perform the operation or operations—solve the equation.

5. Interpret the answer and check the problem solution.

Read Carefully

It should be obvious that it is necessary to read carefully and understand a problem fully, but the obvious is sometimes overlooked. Almost every problem solver has obtained the wrong answer to a problem that would normally cause little difficulty by failing to note a discrepancy in units or by misreading some aspect of the problem. In the past, careful reading has usually been taken for granted. Recent discussions on problem solving have recognized that reading ability cannot be taken for granted. Reading carefully is now often listed as the first prerequisite for successful problem

6. William H. Nibbelink, et al., "Problem Solving in the Elementary Grades: Textbook Practices and Achievement Trends Over the Past Thirty Years," *Arithmetic Teacher*, 35 (September 1987): 34–37.

7. Randall I. Charles and Frank K. Lester, Jr., "An Evaluation of a Process-Oriented Instructional Program in Mathematical Problem Solving in Grades 5 and 7," *Journal for Research in Mathematics Education*, 15 (January 1984): 15–34.

solving. Careless reading is a major cause of incorrect solutions.

Identify the Problem Question and Numbers Given

Read the problem carefully to identify the problem question, the numbers given, and how they are related.

Reword the problem. It often helps, mentally or on paper, to use the form: Wanted: Given:

Reread the problem to be sure that all the information given has been included as well as some not given but that should be known, such as the number of inches in a foot.

Identify units. Determine if the problem involves money, measurements, percent, or abstract numbers. It is a common error to fail to note that the answer calls for dollars, but the numbers are given in cents. Similarly, an area may be required in square feet, but the dimensions are given in inches. Failure to note such differences will lead to an incorrect answer even though the basic procedures are understood and the computation is correct.

Too much or too little? Determine whether the problem has too much information or not enough. Recent textbooks include problems with too much or too little information. This practice approximates reality. Real-life problems do not always have just the right amount of information.

Identify the Operation

Most textbook problems can be solved with one or two computations. However, a few, such as logic problems, do not require computation.

What is important is to visualize the things represented by the numbers in the problem and what must be done to these quantities to obtain the solution. For example, if a problem asks for the total number of apples in two separate groups, the operation is addition because the apples associated with the given numbers must be combined into a single group. Early work with manipulatives should lead to recognition of how combining, separating, and comparing sets of things can be described by the basic operations.

The pupils should look for rates and learn when they indicate multiplication or division.

Writing an appropriate equation indicates that the pupil has identified the operation correctly. Note that only rarely will one equation be correct: if $N + 3 = 5$ is correct, then $N = 5 - 3$ is also correct.

Performing the Computation

A helpful practice is to have the pupil estimate the answer before performing the computation. Having demonstrated reasonable competence in computation, a pupil should be encouraged to use a calculator or computer so that more time can be spent on problem analysis than on computation. Use of the calculator or computer should encourage estimation due to the opportunities these devices offer for immediately checking the accuracy of the estimate. A major difference between the computation and the estimation indicates that one of the two is in error. Estimation can help: verify the position of the decimal point; detect a malfunction of a computer or calculator; or detect the pressing of a wrong key.

Record and Interpret the Solution

There is no one correct way to record the solution of a problem and interpret the computation. The teacher must make clear to the pupil what is acceptable and what is not. Neatness and well-organized written solutions should be encouraged, but requiring a rigid format may stifle creativity. The minimum information in a written solution should be the nature of the computation and an interpretation of the result of the computation. If computation is done with paper and pencil, it is desirable that the work be shown so that errors can be identified.

The minimum acceptable written numerical answer should include a label. A complete sentence is usually preferable.

Most rate problems can be recorded efficiently as follows:

A.   1 gallon $\longrightarrow$ \$0.93
    10 gallons $\longrightarrow$ 10 × 0.93 $\longrightarrow$ \$9.30

B.   7 gallons $\longrightarrow$ 147 miles
    1 gallon $\longrightarrow$ 147/7 $\longrightarrow$ 21 miles

In problem A, the rate is given. In problem B, the rate is to be found.

If an answer is incorrect, it is important for the pupil to know whether the error is in the computation or in problem analysis or both. In the real world, an error in computation is as bad as an error in problem analysis. In a learning situation, problem analysis is more important, but pupils must not be allowed to develop careless computational habits. If a bridge falls, it is little comfort to an engineer to know that the analysis was correct but the decimal point was in the wrong place. Writing an equation often makes it easy to record the solution. Consider the problem: "How many books can be bought for \$60 if the cost of each book is \$10?"

Solution: Let N = the number of books.
        N × 10 = 60
        Thus, N $\longrightarrow$ 6 books

A problem check should determine if the solution satisfies the problem question. Checking computation is a part of the check but does not check the problem solution. If the wrong operation has been used, the computation may check, but the solution will be incorrect, except in the most unusual circumstances. For example, a pupil who adds 2 + 2 instead of multiplying 2 × 2 will get the correct number for an answer.

Consider the problem: "What number added to 231 is equal to 470?" If the pupil chooses addition as the operation and adds 231 to 470 to get a sum of 701, the addition is correct but the answer is wrong. The problem question requires that the 701, obtained as the answer, must give a sum of 470 when added to 231. Therefore the problem condition is not met and the problem does not check.

Additional Strategies

Books have been written on the nature of problem solving, including the discussion of many strategies. Introducing too many strategies too soon may be more confusing than helpful. The number of strategies an elementary pupil can assimilate is limited but should increase with experience. Start with a few and introduce a new one when an appropriate situation arises. A strategy one pupil finds useful may seem useless to another.

The following additional strategies may be introduced to the class or to individual pupils at appropriate times to broaden the concept of problem solving.

USE SIMPLER NUMBERS

When numbers in a problem seem difficult because of fractions, decimals, or large numbers, rewrite the problem using small whole numbers. For example, it will confuse many pupils when asked to find the cost per pound when a modern scale indicates that 0.79 pounds cost \$2.73. The problem will be more sensible and has the same structure as that of finding the cost of one pound if 5 pounds cost \$10.00. To find the answer in the simple problem, divide the cost by the number of pounds. So the solution to the more complicated problem is to divide 2.73 by 0.79.

LOOK FOR A RATE

A rate compares unlike units by division. Typical quotients are labeled as miles per gallon, feet per minute, or dollars per hour. One-step problems (requiring a single computation) in which a rate is given or wanted can usually be solved by multiplication or division. However, there are exceptions. For example, if one car is traveling 40 mph and another 50 mph, how much faster is the second car going? Two rates are given but must be compared by subtraction to solve the problem.

LOOK FOR A FAMILIAR PATTERN

Determine if the problem is similar to one that has already been solved. With *careless reading*, problems may appear to be similar when they are quite different. Both of the following questions contain the same words, but the transposition of *apples* and *dozen* completely changes the problem.

How many dozen are in 36 apples?
How many apples in 36 dozen?

The importance of careful reading cannot be overemphasized.

GUESS AND TEST

The guess and test method has been recommended as a problem-solving strategy for many years, but it is often impractical for a problem with numbers that require substantial time for computation. The computer has now changed that. The ability to repeat a given set of computations rapidly and accurately enables the computer to solve a great variety of problems by its version of the guess and test strategy. Most of the sample problems, solved by the computer at the end of this chapter, use a FOR-NEXT loop to list a range of possible solutions. The correct answer can then be found by inspection. Guess and test may be reasonable for problems with small numbers without a cal-

culator or computer. For example, a pupil seeking to find the length of time it will take to travel 1000 kilometers at a speed of 75 kilometers per hour may first guess 10 hours, which will give a distance of 750 kilometers. The pupil can learn two things from making this guess. First, the correct answer is more than 10 hours; second, the product of the missing number and 75 must equal 1000, leading to the equation $75n = 1000$. By guessing and testing, the pupil discerns that the answer is sensible and arrives at the correct operation.

KEY WORDS

Key words can be valuable, but they must be used with caution. For example, the word *sum* does not always indicate that addition must be used to solve a problem. To solve the problem question "What number, when added to 18, gives a sum of 31?" the student obtains 13, the answer, by subtraction. The word *sum* suggests that 18 is to be added to an unknown addend. When the sum and one addend are known, the missing addend is determined by subtraction. Here, the problem question would be translated directly as the equation $18 + n = 31$.

If pupils are unclear about the limits of key-word use, meaningful learning may be inhibited. As the previous example illustrates, no word always indicates that one specific operation is required to solve a problem. However, if the word *sum* occurs in a one-step problem, addition or subtraction is required. The problem is then reduced to discovering whether all the addends are known and the sum is to be determined, or whether the sum and all addends but one are known. This discussion applies to words such as difference, product, and quotient.

The word *of* sometimes, but not always, indicates multiplication, as in "Find three-fourths of 40." But the question "Three-fourths of what number is 10?" is solved by division rather than multiplication. When a situation suggests multiplication with a question containing *of*, and the product and one factor are known, division is required for the solution.

An activity that helps strengthen the pupil's vocabulary of words associated with the four operations involves asking for oral or written answers to questions such as the following:

(1) What is the sum of 3 and 5?

(2) The product of what number and 8 is 40?

(3) Eight is 3 less than what number?

(4) Seventeen is how much more than 13?

(5) What is the difference between 9 and 4?

(6) What number is 3 less than 8?

(7) The difference of 8 and what number is 3?

(8) What number is the quotient of 10 divided by 2?

(9) The quotient of what number divided by 2 is 8?

Brief oral exercises performed frequently are more effective than a single extended session. Encourage pupils to write number sentences (equations) for questions of this type. If key words are to be of any value, it is essential that their limitations be understood.

Multistep Problems

Early concrete and symbolic work involves only single-step problems. Only one computation is required to solve single-step problems, which are sometimes called "choose-the-operation" problems. A problem is usually considered to be multistep if its solution requires at least two computations. For example, two computations are required to solve the equation $2n + 13 = 35$, and so a problem that requires this

equation can be considered a two-step problem. There is no easy way to determine whether a problem involves one step or more than one step. The length of the problem and the numbers given or implied will give some indication. It is a good clue when a number usually given in a one-step problem is missing. For example, a problem may ask for the cost of ten books without giving the cost of one book. If the problem is to be solved, enough information must be given so that the cost of one book can be found either directly or indirectly. A proportion could be used to solve this problem without directly determining the cost of one book. Consider the following problem: If 7 books cost \$21, what would be the cost of 10 books priced at the same rate?

Solution: Solve both of the following one-step problems:

Step 1: 7 books $\longrightarrow$ \$21

1 book $\longrightarrow$ $21 \div 7 = 3$

The cost of one book is \$3.

Step 2: 1 book $\longrightarrow$ \$3

10 books $\longrightarrow$ $10 \times 3 = 30$

The cost of 10 books is \$30.

By finding the cost of one book, one solves a problem within a problem, and then is led to the solution of the original problem. The original problem can be solved with a proportion, without specifically finding the cost of one book:

$$\frac{n}{21} = \frac{10}{7}$$

If $n \div 21 = \frac{10}{7}$, then, by the relationship between multiplication and division:

$$n = 21 \times \frac{10}{7} = 30$$

The cost of 10 books is \$30.

By writing an equation, one can avoid breaking a problem into two one-step problems. For example, if Judy buys a head of lettuce for 89 cents and 3 cans of tomatoes at 30 cents per can, what is the total cost? This problem can be solved with two one-step problems. First, find the cost of 3 cans, by multiplying 3 × 30, or 90 cents. Second, add 90 to 89 to get 179, for a total cost of 179 cents, or $1.79. Or the solution can be obtained with a single equation, as shown:

$$n = 3 \times 30 + 89$$
$$n = 179$$

Total cost is 179 cents, or $1.79.

Most problems at the elementary school level can be solved easily and accurately once the correct operation(s) have been chosen. The equation indicates which operation(s) have been chosen.

Additional Types of Problems

The key in solving one-step problems is choosing the correct operation. Often this step is easy for textbook problems, as it is common practice for all the problems in a section to require the same operation that was discussed on previous pages. Although this situation is fine when pupils are first exposed to new operations, it is important, as pupils progress, for them to encounter problems that require a variety of operations. If the text does not include a mixture of problems, the teacher must provide the variety.

If problem solving is truly to be the major emphasis of the 1990s, then pupils must be exposed to a wider variety of problems than are found in traditional elementary programs. A wide variety of problems are suggested in the 1980 yearbook of the National Council, which is devoted to problem solving. Chapters 9, 10, and 11 deal specifically with the elementary program, with addi-

tional material of interest to elementary teachers included in other chapters.[8]

Most of the additional problems that are recommended are less structured than typical textbook problems, suggesting real-life problem situations that often have extraneous or insufficient information. Formulating the problem is often a major step in solving problems of this type. In the next sections, we present some problems similar to those recommended for the elementary program.

Data Organization

If Anne has 3 pennies, 2 nickels, 4 dimes, and 3 quarters, how many different amounts can be formed by choosing one or more of these coins?

It is clear that the smallest amount is 1 cent and the largest is 128 cents. One approach to solving this problem is to make a table such as the following:

Total	Cents	Nickels	Dimes	Quarters
1	1	0	0	0
2	2	0	0	0
3	3	0	0	0
4	cannot be done			
5	0	1	0	0
6	1	1	0	0

This table, which includes a total of 128 lines, is not the most efficient way to solve the problem. A more concise solution would demonstrate that combinations of every number from 1 to 128, except 4, 9, 14, and so on, can be formed. Either approach

8. *Problem Solving in School Mathematics* (Reston, VA: National Council of Teachers of Mathematics, 1980).

will lead to the answer that there are 103 different amounts possible.

Another problem might ask for all the ways that a football team can score 20 points. The most likely method is to score 3 touchdowns and 2 points after 1 touchdown. The least likely way is to score 10 safeties of 2 points each.

Pupils may be asked to gather information about different aspects of their school or community. Pupils can gain practice in measurement and experience in organizing data by recording the heights or weights of pupils in one or more classes. This experience in organizing and interpreting data can be valuable to them in the future, both in and out of school.

Logic Problems

The ability to draw logical conclusions is one of the most basic mathematical skills. On the elementary level, logic should be informal. It can involve *inductive* or *deductive* reasoning.

Inductive conclusions are based on experience. For example, a person watching the traffic on a freeway might conclude that all cars have 4 wheels, which is a false conclusion. Some cars have 3 wheels. An alert pupil might conclude that all numbers ending in 0 or 5 are divisible by 5, which is a correct conclusion.

A deductive conclusion follows an "if then" pattern. In other words, if something is true, then a certain fact must follow. Deductive reasoning is the basis of mathematical proof. In the appropriate mathematical setting, deductive reasoning can prove that every number ending in 0 or 5 is divisible by 5. Although there is little occasion to cover mathematical proof in the first six grades, and few educators recommend it, there is opportunity for informal deductive reasoning that provides readiness for proof.

Many problems contain no numbers but require logic for their solution. One such problem states that Joe will be sent to bed without supper or be spanked, depending on whether he makes a true or false statement. If the statement is true, he will be spanked; if it is false, he will be sent to bed without supper. The problem question is: What statement can Joe make to escape punishment? The answer is: "I will be sent to bed without supper." If he is sent to bed, his statement is true, and so he should be spanked. If he is spanked, his statement becomes false and he should be sent to bed. Thus, no punishment is possible under the stated conditions. Although this problem bears little relation to reality, it does provide an opportunity to demonstrate that if one thing is true, then another must follow.

The logic of this problem is simple without being trivial. Such problems would appeal to fast learners and are meant for enrichment.

Problems Without Numbers

To solve problems without numbers, pupils must think more about the process than about the numbers. Here are some examples:

1. How can one find the cost of one pen by knowing the cost of many pens? Rephrasing the problem as a "many-to-one" or as a "given many, find one" situation can help the pupil identify it as a division problem.

2. How can one find the cost of many books if the cost of one is known? Rephrasing this problem as a "one-to-many" or as a "given one, find many" situation can help the pupil to recognize it as a multiplication problem.

3. How many neckties can be purchased for n dollars?

4. Sam went to the store with some money and bought several pounds of apples at a given price per pound. How much did he have left after the purchase? One way to solve the problem is to multiply the number of pounds times the price per pound and subtract this product from the original amount of money. Pupils can then be asked to substitute their own numbers and solve the problem.

A different type of problem that can be stated without numbers is one that uses *variables* (letters) for numbers. Here are some examples:

1. Find the cost of one book if the cost of *m* books is *n* dollars.

2. Find the cost of *n* blouses if the cost of one blouse is *m* dollars.

3. Sam went to the store with *n* dollars and bought *m* pounds of apples at *t* dollars per pound. How much money did he have after the purchase?

Problems with variables are difficult for most pupils but are excellent enrichment material. If used judiciously, they can reinforce the pupil's understanding of letters in formulas and provide readiness for algebra.

Mental Arithmetic

Problem solving involves high-level mental activity, but the term *mental arithmetic* usually refers specifically to solving problems "in one's head" without using paper and pencil, except to record the answer. Computation in mental arithmetic should be so easy for elementary pupils that it can be done without recording the numbers. Mental arithmetic, popular in the early half of the century, was deemphasized in the days of New Math.

The emphasis in mental arithmetic should be on recognizing procedure and the relationships between numbers. If these problems are adapted to a given grade level, most pupils should be able to find the answer without using paper and pencil. The

following examples are appropriate for grades 5 and 6:

1. How far will a car travel in 15 minutes if it travels 8 kilometers in 5 minutes?

2. The cost of 3 oranges is 40 cents. What is the cost of 6 oranges?

3. What is the total value of the numeral 5 in 3580?

4. What is the quotient of a nonzero number divided by itself?

5. How many centimeters are there in 2 meters?

6. What is the product of $8 \times 7 \times 0$?

7. With the numbers 4, 6, and 10, write a true number sentence using subtraction.

8. The product of two factors is 1. If one factor is 4, what is the other?

9. Thanksgiving day is the fourth Thursday in November. What is the earliest date for Thanksgiving? The latest date?

10. Give two ways a football team can score 16 points without scoring a safety or a 2-point after-touchdown conversion.

There are several types of problems in this sample set, including choice of operation, metrics, place value, number sentences, properties of 1 and 0, the calendar, and problems with multiple answers. Other types can also be included.

Applications

The National Council has published a useful book that stresses the value of applications to the student learning mathematics.[9]

Well-chosen applications will make mathematics more interesting to many pupils and help them to recognize it as a useful subject

9. *A Sourcebook of Applications in School Mathematics* (Reston, VA: National Council of Teachers of Mathematics, 1980).

worth the effort required to learn it. It is unlikely, however, that any one application will interest every student in a class. A sports application, such as batting average, will interest many, while an automobile application may also interest several students, but not necessarily the same group. In order to interest most of the pupils in a class, a variety of applications must be available. The best guide for choosing applications for a given class and grade level is the teacher's experience. The teacher should be alert for new applications and continue to use those that have been successful in the past.

Textbooks contain many applications, but due to space limitations there is not the variety to interest the widest range of pupils. Many suggestions for the elementary level can also be found in the sourcebook of the National Council.

Below are two different types of problems that may interest a substantial number of pupils.

1. Car A travels 25 miles per gallon of gasoline. Car B travels 20 miles per gallon. If the cost of gasoline is $1.00 per gallon, what is the difference in the cost of gasoline for driving each car 10,000 miles?

This is an excellent example of a multistep problem which can be solved by a sequence of one-step problems. Direct pupils as follows: Find the cost per mile for car A and for Car B. Find the difference in cost for one mile and then find the difference in cost for 10,000 miles.

Car A 25 miles $\longrightarrow$ $1.00
        1 mile $\longrightarrow$ 1.00/25 = 0.04
        Cost per mile: $0.04 or 4 cents.
Car B 20 miles $\longrightarrow$ $1.00
        1 mile $\longrightarrow$ 1.00/20 = 0.05
        Cost per mile: $0.05 or 5 cents.
Difference for 1 mile: $\longrightarrow$ $0.01
Difference for 10,000 miles $\longrightarrow$
        10,000 × 0.01 $\longrightarrow$ $100

The following formula illustrates the value of being able to think with variables:

D is the difference in cost for d miles.

m_1 is cost per gallon for car A.

m_2 is cost per gallon for car B.

g is the cost of gasoline per gallon.

d is the number of miles.

$$D = \frac{(m_1 - m_2) \times g \times d}{m_1 \times m_2}$$

For our problem, $m_1 = 25$, $m_2 = 20$, $g = \$1.00$, and $d = 10,000$. The problem is to find D.

$$D = \frac{(25 - 20) \times 1 \times 10,000}{25 \times 20} = \frac{50,000}{500}$$

The difference in cost is $100.

This distance formula not only can be used to solve the above problem but will solve any problem in which all but one of the variables are known.

2. The cost of electricity is now a much bigger factor in the household budget than ever before. Problems involving the cost of specific items, such as television sets, stereos, and toasters may interest a substantial number of pupils. By law, almost every electric appliance must carry a statement of its power consumption. This information is given in watts or amperes (usually abbreviated as *amps*). The power in watts *(w)* is the product of the electromotive force in volts *(e)* and the current in amps *(a)*, or $w = ae$. If the current is 8 amperes and the electromotive force is 120 volts, then the power is 8 × 120, or 960 watts.

The quantity of electricity is measured in kilowatt-hours. A kilowatt, as the standard metric prefix indicates, is equal to 1000 watts. A kilowatt-hour is the quantity of electricity used by an appliance, rated at one kilowatt of power, in one hour. The formula for the cost of electricity is $C = ktc$ where:

C is the cost for t hours of use

k is the power rating in kilowatts

t is the number of hours in use

c is the cost per kilowatt-hour

Since most home devices list power in watts rather than kilowatts, the formula is usually more useful in the following form:

$$C = \frac{wtc}{1000}, \text{ where } w = \text{power in watts}$$

For example, a 100-watt bulb burned for 24 hours at 10 cents per kilowatt-hour will cost:

$$C = \frac{100 \times 24 \times 10}{1000} = 24$$

The cost for 24 hours of use is 24 cents, or $.24.

The problem would probably interest more pupils if a television set or stereo were involved. Most television sets use about 100 watts of power.

Providing for Individual Differences

Every mathematics teacher faces the problem of how to provide for individual differences in learning, but the problem is especially acute in teaching problem solving. One plan that is often used is to have the slow learners solve a few problems, the average pupils a few more, and the fast learners still more. But unless the problems are carefully graded in difficulty, this plan will not effectively accommodate individual differences in problem solving.

Another effective plan that is easy to implement is to have pupils of varying ability give more than one solution for a problem. Have slow learners give one solution and the faster learners two or more solutions to a given problem. The following problem is an illustration of the plan.

Jim buys 3 cans of corn for $2.00. At this rate, what is the cost of 12 cans? Ask the class for an answer. One approach may be to think that 12 cans should cost 4 times as much as 3 cans, so the answer is $4 \times \$2.00 = \$8.00$.

A second solution might be to solve the problem by proportion:

$$\frac{\$2.00}{3 \text{ cans}} = \frac{?}{12 \text{ cans}}$$

A third solution might be that the cost of 1 can is 1/3 the cost of 3 cans, or 2/3 of a dollar. Therefore, 12 cans will cost $12 \times 2/3 = \$8.00$. A pupil may ask why $12 \times .66$ gives an answer of $7.92 instead of $8.00. Class discussion should lead to the use of the calculator to show that 2 divided by 3 $= 0.6666666 \ldots$ Thus, $12 \times .6666$ equals 7.9992, which rounds off to $8.00.

Ask the class which solution is most likely to be used by business. Point out that calculators, cash registers, and computers use decimals almost exclusively. The example should help pupils understand why most financial transactions are carried out with four or more decimal places. One cannot use decimals effectively without understand the rounding process.

The above problem offers a wide range of opportunities for discussion and solution, with each pupil having the opportunity to contribute on the basis of ability and understanding.

Great effort should be made to prevent the slower learner from feeling inept so that it is useless to make any effort. The majority of problems should be on a level that almost the entire class can solve, with all pupils encouraged to find two or more solutions. Build a class attitude that leads to class discussion. When possible, use guided discovery to lead the class to a solution that has not been proposed.

Activities to Strengthen Problem Solving

1. Whenever possible, have pupils reword textbook problems by using the form:
Given:
Wanted:

2. Write the numbers for each problem in a set of textbook problems on the chalkboard. Have pupils identify things associated with each number and show how numbers are related.

3. Ask pupils to make up their own problems for a specific operation.

4. Write an equation on the chalkboard. Ask pupils to write a problem for which the equation will lead to a solution.

5. Conduct frequent brief oral exercises to strengthen pupils' mathematical vocabulary.

6. Conduct frequent, brief oral exercises with one-step problems that can be solved mentally.

7. Encourage pupils to give a variety of solutions to a problem.

Functions

The function concept is one of the most basic ideas in mathematics. Although advanced work with functions is usually delayed until secondary school and college, it is important that elementary pupils work with the function concept in its simple forms.

A formal definition of a function says that it is a set of *ordered pairs* where each first element has a unique second element. The inch-foot relation is a function. One foot corresponds to 12 inches, generating the *ordered pair* (1,12). Although we sometimes refer to the square root function, technically it is a relation because the square root of 4 is not unique. In the set of integers, the square root of 4 is both $^+2$ and $^-2$. No em-

phasis should be placed on this distinction at the elementary school level.

Functions can be represented with tables, graphs, and formulas. All three of these representations should be used throughout the elementary program. The computer can deal effectively with all three of these representations. A computer can readily create a table from the fact that the number of inches is 12 times the number of feet. Other examples occur throughout this text.

Problem Solving with the Calculator

Chapter 2 discusses uses and limitations of the calculator in the classroom. This sequence illustrates what may be one of the most useful applications of the calculator to problem solving.

Problem 1. The cost of oil is $20 a barrel. What is the cost of 5 barrels?

Problem 2. The cost of oil is $18.73 a barrel. What is the cost of 750 barrels?

Problem 3. The cost of oil is D dollars per barrel. What is the cost of N barrels?

The sequence above is a specific example of a process that will use the calculator to help the pupil understand that the computation required for the solution of a problem is not dependent on the complexity of the numbers.

It is desirable that the first problem in the sequence can be solved mentally. If an individual requires paper and pencil, there should be no objection to its use. This problem should be simple enough so that a calculator should not be used except as a check for the mental arithmetic.

The second problem should use numbers that occur in real-life situations (but cannot easily be solved mentally) and can be

A student solves a problem with a calculator.

(Photo by Leland Perry)

solved efficiently by using the calculator. The pupils should recognize that the two problems are identical except for the complexity of the computation.

By repeating this sequence in a wide variety of problem situations, the pupil should more readily recognize the distinction between analyzing the problem and performing the computation.

Note that a rate is given in all three problems as dollars per barrel and that the problem is to find the cost of more than one barrel. This situation is sometimes described as going from one to many, a description that may be useful if not overemphasized. Trying to learn problem solving by memorizing types of problems may succeed for a limited number of types, but pupils often have difficulty with mathematics by trying to perform by memory rather than by thinking. A good memory is an asset in learning almost any discipline, but it is no substitute for thinking. Overemphasis on memory may inhibit thinking.

Problem Solving with a Computer

This introduction to problem solving on the computer emphasizes interaction between the pupil and the computer. The pupil types information into the keyboard and the computer responds by displaying output for the pupil to interpret. This is an ideal way for pupils to learn how to use a computer.

It is desirable that every pupil be given the opportunity to work with a computer and have some exposure to at least one of the programming languages. It is not educationally sound to insist that every pupil learn to program on an advanced level. It is as important to give talented and motivated pupils the opportunity to work with a computer as it is to provide gifted athletes the opportunity to develop their skills.

Three Major Features of the Computer

The computer has three capabilities that have made it an essential part of our lives. It can:

1. Store large quantities of information of all types and retrieve any item efficiently.
2. Repeat instructions quickly and accurately.
3. Make decisions.

ABILITY TO STORE AND RETRIEVE
INFORMATION EFFICIENTLY

The majority of adults in this country are listed on several computers, including those of government, banks, credit card companies, and stores. The Internal Revenue Service has every taxpayer's name and tax record stored on a computer file that can be retrieved quickly.

ABILITY TO REPEAT INSTRUCTIONS RAPIDLY
AND ACCURATELY

A LOOP is a technical name for the procedure in which a computer performs an instruction or a set of instructions repeatedly. We will say that a loop has two or more cycles. The computer performs a given set of instructions in each cycle.

A FOR-NEXT loop is one of the most common routines that tells a computer to repeat instructions. It starts with an instruction of the type FOR J = A TO B and ends with the instruction NEXT J.

The set to be repeated must be listed between the FOR instruction and the NEXT instruction. Most early FOR-NEXT loops start with an instruction similar to: FOR J = 1 TO 10 or FOR N = 1 to 30. The NEXT instruction acts as a counter and tells the computer to exit the loop after it completes the last cycle.

Program P6.1, a three-line program listed on the next page, contains a loop of 20 cycles. The comma in line 20 tells the computer to display the output of each cycle in two columns.

Enter program P6.1 into computer memory by typing each of the three lines exactly as listed below. Press RETURN after entering each line.

The RUN instruction tells the computer to execute the program that is in its memory.

The output for P6.1 displays the value of J from 1 to 20 in the left hand column. The right hand column displays the value of 40/J. When 40/J is a whole number, J and 40/J

Pupils solve problems on a computer.

(Photo by Leland Perry)

form a pair of divisors or factors with a product of 40. We tell the computer to test from 1 to 20 rather than from 1 to 40 because no whole number, other than itself, can have a divisor greater than one-half of that number. Therefore, the number 40 can have no divisors greater than 20, except 40, and the divisors for 40 are listed in the first line of output.

```
PROGRAM P6.1
  10 FOR J = 1 TO 20
  20 PRINT J, 40/J
  30 NEXT J
```

```
RUN
1          40
2          20
3          13.333333
4          10
5          8
--------------------------
8          5
9          4.4444444
10         4
--------------------------
20         2
```

Inspection of the two-column output tells us that 1 and 40, 2 and 20, 4 and 10, and 5 and 8 are pairs of divisors of 40. Each pair has a product of 40. Each pair of divisors occurs twice, except (1,40), with the order of the factors reversed.

This program illustrates the power of the guess and test method when used with the ability of the computer to repeat efficiently and accurately. The computer divides 40 by each number from 1 to 20 and prints the number in the left column and the quotient in the right column, illustrating that factors occur in pairs. If 8 is a factor of 40, then 40 ÷ 8 must also be a factor of 40. Inspection allows us to identify immediately the pairs of factors of 40.

ABILITY TO MAKE DECISIONS

The IF-THEN instruction allows the computer to make decisions.

Obtain Program P6.2 by retyping line 20 in Program P6.1 as follows:

```
20 IF INT(40/J) = 40/J THEN
PRINT J,40/J
```

Retyping a line with a given line number replaces that line with the line that has just been typed.

Run the program to discover that the display now includes only pairs of divisors and duplicates but displays no pairs of non-divisors.

The INTEGER function (INT) eliminates the decimal portion of any numeral. $INT(3.7) = INT(3.1) = 3$. $INT(40/3) = 13$. $INT(40/4) = 10$.

$INT(N)$ displays the largest whole number in N.

Therefore, 40 is divisible by J if and only if $INT(40/J) = 40/J$.

The IF-THEN instruction requires that the computer can recognize whether a statement is true or false.

$INT(40/3) = 40/3$ is false because $INT(40/3) = 13$ and $40/3 = 13.333333$

$INT(40/4) = 40/4$ is true because both expressions are equal to 10.

When the IF statement in an IF-THEN instruction is true, the computer executes the THEN instruction.

In the first cycle of the loop in program P6.2, the computer encounters the IF statement: IF $INT(40/1) = 40/1$.

Because this statement is true, the computer executes the THEN instruction and prints the pair 1 and 40.

In the second cycle, because $INT(40/2) = 40/2$ is a true statement, the computer prints the pair 2 and 20.

However, in the third cycle, the statement $INT(40/3) = 40/3$ is false so the computer ignores the THEN instruction and proceeds to the fourth cycle of the loop and so on.

Program P6.2 lists pairs of divisors, with some duplicates, for the number 40. To find factors for another divisor we must retype lines 10 and 20. The INPUT instruction allows entry from the keyboard after the program is run. Inserting the INPUT instruction allows us to choose a number for the computer to find divisors after the program is run.

The INPUT instruction stops the program and displays an INPUT PROMT, often a question mark, to indicate that the computer is waiting for information from the keyboard.

Because the pairs of factors repeat in opposite order after the square root of the number N, we eliminate repetition by testing from 1 to the square root of N, as indicated in line 20.

```
PROGRAM P6.3
10 INPUT "ENTER NUMBER TO
FACTOR" ;N
20 FOR J = 1 to SQR(N)
30 IF INT(N/J) = N/J THEN
PRINT J,N/J
40 NEXT J
```

The INPUT instruction in line 10 will display an instruction between quotes and display a blinking cursor to indicate that the computer is waiting for information from the keyboard.

RUN tells the computer to execute the program in its memory. A program remains in memory until one types NEW or turns off the computer.

When you type 40 into the keyboard and press return, the first line of the display, ENTER NUMBER TO FACTOR 40, is followed by the 4 pairs of divisors of 40. Each time RUN is entered, with the program in memory, the computer will ask for a number to factor.

The following examples illustrate the display of Program P6.3 when it is run 3 times with successive inputs of 40, 1001, and 101.

```
RUN
ENTER NUMBER TO FACTOR: 40
1              40
2              20
4              10
5              8
RUN
ENTER   NUMBER   TO   FACTOR:
1001
1              1001
7              143
11             91
13             77
RUN
ENTER   NUMBER   TO   FACTOR:
101
1              101
```

You may be startled when you enter 111111 to factor in Program P6.3.

Computer Solutions

Educators have complained for many years about the narrow range of textbook problems. Most of these problems provide useful social information as well as practice in problem analysis and computation. However, for the most part, the analysis usually requires the identification of one or two operations. The answers are almost always whole numbers so that pupils do not get bogged down in computation and lose sight of the problem.

The computer now makes it possible to present problems with a much wider range of activities. The problems in this section and in the problem-solving sections that follow illustrate how the computer can provide solutions that would be completely beyond the scope of elementary pupils without it. The number of problems in this text is restricted because of space and programming limitations. Commercial programs are limited only by the internal memory of the computer and the imagination of the programmer. A wide variety of problem-solving software is available commercially; it is essential to keep abreast of program availability. Some major sources are listed in the introduction to computers in Chapter 2.

This text will emphasize the use of the FOR-NEXT loop with the guess and test procedure. It usually requires a three- or four-line program that can be entered in the computer in little more than a minute. It has an amazing variety of applications and is truly interactive.

Guess and Test

1. Tillie's age is 3 more than twice her brother's age and the sum of their ages is 60. What is her age?

If her brother's age is N, give two expressions for Tillie's age.

Answer: $2 * N + 3$ and $60 - N$

What must we do to find a solution?

Answer: Find a value of N that will make the two expressions for Tillie's age equal. This is an easy algebra activity at the proper level, but not for most elementary pupils. Use the following FOR-NEXT loop.

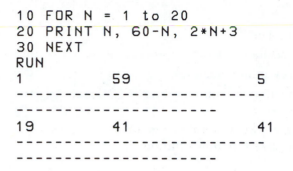

```
10 FOR N = 1 to 20
20 PRINT N, 60-N, 2*N+3
30 NEXT
RUN
1            59              5
------------------------------
--------------------------
19           41             41
------------------------------
--------------------------
```

The brother's age is 19 and Tillie's age is 41. Sum = 60, 2 × 19 + 3 = 41

To make the computer use its decision-making power to display the answer, replace line 20 with the following:

```
IF 60-N = 2*N+3 THEN PRINT
"BOY'S AGE:"; N;" TILLIE'S
AGE:";60-N
```

2. 5 times a number is the product of 6 and 3 less than the number. Use the following FOR-NEXT loop to find the number:

```
10 FOR N = 1 TO 20
20 PRINT N, 5*N, 6*(N - 3)
30 NEXT
```

Inspection of the output will show that when N = 18, 5 × N and 6x(N − 3) are both equal to 90.

3. Replace line 20 so that the computer will display the answer.

```
IF 5*N = 6*(N-3)
THEN PRINT
"NUMBER = ";N
```

Summary

There is no algorithm for problem solving. Problem solving requires careful reading, critical thinking, and persistence.

A mathematical problem is one that cannot be answered by a habitual response.

Thus a basic fact may be a problem to an early elementary pupil but should be a habitual response later on.

Recent elementary mathematics textbooks have expanded the range of problems to include problems with too much and too little information, problems without words, logic problems, probability problems and more.

The following guide is similar to those found in a variety of texts dealing with mathematics:

1. Read the problem carefully.

2. Identify the problem question, the numbers given, and how they are related.

3. Identify the operation or operations (write an equation).

4. Perform the operation or operations (solve the equation).

5. Interpret the answer and check.

This guide is just that and requires repeated application to become a useful tool. It will become more meaningful if constantly referred to at appropriate times in class discussions and in individual conferences when discussing problem solutions.

Checking the computation is essential but it does not check the problem. Always estimate the answer before performing the computation, whether it is on paper or pencil, calculator or computer.

There are many strategies for problem solving and the computer has added more. Use judgment on when and how many strategies to introduce to pupils. Too many may be worse than too few. Introduce a new strategy with the introduction of an appropriate problem whose solution will be facilitated by it. Recognize that there are individual differences in use of strategies. Do not force them on unwilling pupils. Encourage multiple solutions of problems to challenge more able pupils.

Encourage use of the calculator, with proper guidance, and the computer. Attempt to make computers available for those with motivation and ability.

Exercises

1. Define a mathematical problem.

2. Illustrate a disadvantage of the key-word approach.

3. Discuss the role of memory in mathematics.

4. What was the conclusion drawn from the fourth National Assessment in mathematics?

5. Find the cost of 7 items if the cost of 3 items is $21.
   (a) What is probably the easiest mental solution?
   (b) Solve by proportion.
   (c) Solve by first finding the cost of 1 item.
   (d) Solve by guess and test.

6. How much change will Al get from a $20.00 bill if he buys 3 pairs of socks for $5.00 and a shirt for $11.50?
   (a) Solve with two one-step problems.
   (b) Solve with an equation. What are the steps to solve this problem on a calculator?

7. Give an example of a sequence of three problems that will enable the calculator to help one obtain a better understanding of the relation between problem analysis and computation.

8. Write a program that will solve the equation $11*N^2 + 3 = 399$.

9. Write a program that will find the smallest number divisible by 24 and 27.

10. Describe the output of the following program:

```
10 FOR J = 1 TO 10
20 PRINT 11*J + 7
30 NEXT
```

11. A blacksmith shoes a horse, a job that requires 24 nails. He charges 1 cent for the first nail, 2 cents for the second nail, 4 cents for the third nail and so on. What was the charge for shoeing the horse? Solve this problem with a calculator. Then write a computer program that will solve it.

Selected Readings

An Agenda for Action: Recommendations for School Mathematics in the 1980s. Reston, VA: National Council of Teachers of Mathematics, 1980.

James W. Heddens and William R. Speer. *Today's Mathematics*, 6th ed. Chicago: Science Research Associates, 1988. Unit 4, pp. 82–110.

Leonard M. Kennedy and Steve Tipps. *Guiding Children's Learning of Mathematics*, 5th ed. Belmont, CA: Wadsworth, 1988. Chapter 5, pp. 113–160.

Steven Krulik and Jesse A. Rudnick. *Problem Solving: A Handbook for Teachers.* Needham Heights, MA: Allyn & Bacon, 1980.

John L. Marks, et. al. *Teaching Elementary School Mathematics for Understanding*, 5th ed. New York: McGraw-Hill, 1985. Chapter 11, pp. 313–342.

Mathematics in Early Childhood, 37th Yearbook. Reston, VA: National Council of Teachers of Mathematics, 1975.

James L. Overholt, et al. *Math Problem Solving for Grades 4 Through 8*. Needham Heights, MA: Allyn & Bacon, 1984.

Thomas R. Post. *Teaching Mathematics in Grades K–8*. Needham Heights, MA: Allyn & Bacon, Inc., 1988. Chapter 3, pp. 40–75.

Problem Solving in School Mathematics, 1980 Yearbook. Reston, VA: National Council of Teachers of Mathematics, 1980.

Robert E. Reys, et al. *Helping Children Learn Mathematics*, 2nd ed. Englewood Cliffs, NJ: Prentice-Hall, 1989. Chapter 3, pp. 26–41.

Trafton, Paul R., and Albert P. Shulte. *New Directions for Elementary School Mathematics*, 1989 Yearbook. Reston, Va: National Council of Teachers of Mathematics, 1989. Chapter 3.

Discovering Meanings for Basic Addition and Subtraction Facts

ACHIEVEMENT GOALS

After studying this chapter, you should be able to:

1. Define a basic fact.

2. Designate the grade placement for teaching the basic facts in addition and subtraction.

3. Outline the order in which basic addition and subtraction facts should be presented to pupils.

4. Plan, write, and implement lesson plans showing the teaching-learning sequence needed to develop a mastery of basic facts in addition and subtraction based on the principles discussed in Chapter 1.

5. Explain ways of teaching verbal problems involving the basic facts.

6. Discuss the role of drill and practice as a part of a modern program of mathematics in the elementary school.

7. Write and use computer programs designed to help children understand and become skillful in dealing with basic facts in addition and subtraction.

8. Suggest ways addition and subtraction may be applied to solving problems of time, money, and measurement situations.

9. List the things each pupil should be able to do to demonstrate a mastery of basic facts in addition and subtraction.

VOCABULARY

These terms are defined or illustrated in the Glossary.

Addend
*Associative property for addition
*Base
Basic fact
*Commutative property for addition
Difference

Equation
Expanded notation
*Identity element
*Minuend
Number family
Open sentence
Place value
*Subtrahend

*Do not use terms marked with an asterisk with kindergarten and first-grade pupils.

Our modern society uses calculators and computers almost exclusively to perform complicated calculations rapidly and accurately. Therefore it should not be necessary for pupils in the elementary school to spend a large amount of time learning to perform difficult pencil-and-paper computations. Rather, children's learning should be directed toward discovering and developing an understanding of number and basic concepts of number operations, their patterns, relationships, and properties. They should learn thinking strategies. Special emphasis must be placed upon how number operations are used in problem-solving situations. Children should master computation with basic facts, simple multidigit numbers, estimation, and mental math. Calculators, computers, and games should be used by pupils to extend and reinforce their learning.

Pupils should learn to enjoy working with numbers and number operations in problem-solving situations. They should actively participate in various learning experiences, value mathematics as an important subject for study, and develop confidence in their ability to understand and do mathematics.

Meaning of a Basic Fact

Mathematically, a basic addition fact is an equation that consists of any pair of one-digit numbers (addends) such as (3, 5) and their sum. If the two numbers are unequal, there are two addition facts. For example, the number pair (3, 5) can be used to form two addition facts: $5 + 3 = 8$ and $3 + 5 = 8$. The order of two addends can be changed without changing the sum (commutative property for addition). If the numbers are equal, the addition fact is called a *double*. There are 100 basic addition facts.

For each addition fact with two unequal numbers there are two subtraction facts. For the addition facts, $2 + 3 = 5$ and $3 + 2 = 5$, the two corresponding subtraction facts are $5 - 2 = 3$ and $5 - 3 = 2$. For the operation of addition we start with a pair of numbers (addends) and are asked to find the sum. Mathematically, subtraction is the *inverse* of addition. For subtraction we start with a number corresponding to a sum (minuend) and a second number corresponding to a known addend (subtrahend), and are asked to find the missing addend (difference). Mathematically, subtraction "undoes" addition. Thus, there are 100 basic subtraction facts.

The mathematical definitions and vocabulary of addition and subtraction are not taught to pupils in the early stages of learning. Addition is taught initially as starting with two sets of objects, showing the action of putting them together, and then determining how many are in the combined set. For subtraction, pupils initially learn to start with one set, show the action of removing a number of objects from that set, and then determine how many are left. This is the "take-away" interpretation of subtraction. A second "action" situation for subtraction is to start with two sets and compare them to find their difference. This is the "comparison" interpretation of subtraction. The "missing addend" interpretation of subtraction (called the additive concept), should not be presented to pupils until after they understand the "take-away" and "comparison" interpretations of subtraction discussed later in this chapter.

Recommended Grade Placement

Many elementary school mathematics textbooks used during the 1980s presented all 100 addition and 100 subtraction facts at the first-grade level. The National Council of Teachers of Mathematics recommended in 1987 that the easy addition facts and the corresponding subtraction facts be mastered by first-grade pupils. The easy facts have sums of 10 or less. It was further recommended that the development of the addition facts having sums from 11 to 18, and the corresponding subtraction facts, be presented at the second-grade level. In this way children are given more time for the development of concepts and skills at the exploratory level using concrete objects. Also, more time can be spent on problem-solving activities, logical thinking with drawings and patterns, and on other topics in mathematics such as measurement, geometry, and graphing.[1]

Order for Teaching the "Easy" Basic Addition and Subtraction Facts

The sequence for teaching the basic addition and subtraction facts with sums and minuends of 10 or less is many times determined by the mathematics textbook used in the elementary classroom. In a few textbooks the addition and subtraction facts are taught simultaneously. However, in most recently published textbooks, addition facts having sums of 10 or less are presented first and then the corresponding subtraction facts are presented. We recommend that the addition and subtraction facts be presented separately during the initial instruction. The concepts and notations are new. To present both operations at the same time may result in a learning difficulty. Therefore we recommend that addition facts having sums of 10 or less be introduced separately from the corresponding facts in subtraction.

1. *Curriculum and Evaluation Standards for School Mathematics*, Working Draft (Reston, VA: National Council of Teachers of Mathematics, 1987), p. 38.

Sequence for Presenting the Addition Facts with Sums of 10 or Less

The addition facts with sums of 10 or less may be taught in the following sequence:

(1) Teach ten addition facts for numbers 2 through 6 with sums not more than 10, which include the following:
  (a) Four doubles: $2 + 2 = 4$
  $$3 + 3 = 6$$
  $$4 + 4 = 8$$
  $$5 + 5 = 10$$
  (b) Six facts with sums 8 or less that start with a larger number:
  $3 + 2 = 5 \qquad 4 + 2 = 6$
  $5 + 2 = 7 \qquad 6 + 2 = 8$
  $4 + 3 = 7 \qquad 5 + 3 = 8$
  Both the horizontal (shown above) and the vertical forms of each fact should be presented to pupils.

(2) Teach the facts which are "derived" by changing the order of the addends in 1(b). A pupil who knows these facts should be able to figure out the "commuted" facts easily.

(3) Teach basic facts in which 1 or 0 is one of the numbers to be added as generalizations: If *one* is to be added to a number, then the sum is one more than that number, and if zero is to be added to a number, the sum is that number. Of the 100 basic addition facts, 36 have an addend of 0 or 1.

(4) Teach the six facts with sums of 9 or 10 starting with a larger number:
  $5 + 4 = 9 \qquad 6 + 3 = 9$
  $7 + 2 = 9 \qquad 8 + 2 = 10$
  $6 + 4 = 10 \qquad 7 + 3 = 10$

(5) Teach the six "commuted" facts for sums of 9 or 10.

As pupils develop a good understanding of addition involving the beginning facts, give special emphasis to the "nine-" and "ten-facts." The "ten-facts" are very special in elementary mathematics because our number base is ten. The "nine" facts are usually easy for pupils to remember if they realize that any addition fact (not involving zero) that starts with 9 can be renamed ten and one less than the second number. Thus, $9 + 6 = 10 + 5$, or 15.

As the facts that have sums of 9 or more are explored, pupils should be encouraged to use the thinking strategies discussed on page 121. However, instant recall of easy facts is very desirable prior to studying number pairs that have sums more than 10.

In summary, of the 64 addition facts with sums 10 or less, there are 16 that must receive special emphasis, usually in the first grade. These are: 4 doubles, 6 facts that sum 8 or less, and 6 facts that sum 8 or 9. The other 48 basic addition facts are easily remembered by pupils because of the following generalizations:

1. If you change the order of the addends, the sum will remain the same.

2. When one is an addend, the sum is one more than the other addend.

3. When zero is one of the addends, the sum is the other addend.

After pupils understand the addition facts to sums of 10, they are ready to learn the corresponding subtraction facts, discussed later in this chapter.

Teaching Facts with Sums of 10 or Less

In planning and teaching basic facts in addition, the principles discussed in Chapter 1 should be followed in developing a series of lessons.

I. Objectives

The following objectives should be considered for inclusion in each lesson plan. Each pupil should be able to:

1. Relate addition to the process of "putting together" two sets.

2. Name each of the two collections and their sum with number words and write their numerals.

3. Follow an addition story and create the solution with manipulatives.

4. Show an addition fact with a drawing.

5. Write an addition fact in both horizontal and vertical forms, then read them.

6. Verify the correctness of a fact by relating it to other known facts.

7. Tell an addition story given an addition fact.

8. Given any two one-digit numbers, respond quickly and accurately with the correct sum.

II. Readiness

Readiness activities, similar to those described in Chapter 5, provide the background for learning the basic facts in addition and subtraction. These include classifying, ordering in a sequence, completing patterns, counting, number sense, matching and comparing two sets, number sequence and order, and reading and writing numerals. Children who have never had these experiences should be given this background as they participate in meaningful activities designed to explore addition and subtraction situations.

III. Motivation

Young children are usually highly motivated to learn mathematics, especially in programs that utilize manipulative materials and learning-center activities. The teacher should give positive reinforcement and praise for each child's efforts. Make sure that each child succeeds. Learning activities need to be interesting and enjoyable.

IV. Growth Through Guided Discovery

Learning basic addition facts involves a growth process that is facilitated through guided discovery and directed teaching. Pupils should start at a low level of abstraction and progress through higher levels in pursuit of mastery. These levels are:

1. BEGIN WITH A PROBLEM THAT IS VITAL TO THE CLASS

Word problems should evolve from actual, everyday occurrences and should be personalized by using the names of children in the class. Problems should involve things, people, money, time, and other measurement units.

2. USE MANIPULATIVES

Manipulative materials are essential for pupils to use for exploring basic number operations. Manipulating concrete objects helps children realize that addition is related to joining sets. Using manipulatives helps pupils find the correct answer, develop appropriate language, and explore thinking strategies. Objects may be placed in a circular or rectangular region when dealing with sets of small numbers.

To help pupils "sense" the number of objects in each set without having to count by ones, the things can be arranged in a standard dot pattern or placed on a drawing of a "ten-ten frame," shown in Figure 7.1.[2]

2. See Charles S. Thompson and John Van de Walle, "The Power of 10," *Arithmetic Teacher, 32* (November 1984): 6–11.

Pupils write an addition fact for a problem.

(Photo by Leland Perry)

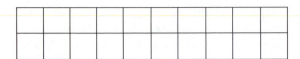

Figure 7.1
A "ten-ten" frame

The aid can be drawn on a piece of cardboard, and objects, markers, cubes, or disks can be used as manipulatives. For a problem such as "There are three birds sitting on a fence and two more join them. How many birds are there now?" Have each child put three objects in the upper row and two in the lower row. Then have them move the two in the lower row to the upper row for a sum of 5. To help children visualize and recognize a number without counting, each of four five-block sections should be made a different color.

3. DRAW AND VIEW PICTURES

As children solve word problems with manipulatives, they should be guided in making some kind of drawing that represents the beginning numbers, the action of "putting together," and the resultant sum. Use the addition problem "Billie has 4 pennies. Her mother gave her 2 more. How many pennies does she now have?"

Most mathematics textbooks for the primary grades give pictures showing problem situations. Figure 7.2 shows the solution to the preceding problem.

4. WRITE NUMBER EQUATIONS

Pupils must learn to write a number sequence, or equation, using basic facts. As a part of the teaching–learning sequence, pupils should be led to tell the number story with words and write the number fact with signs and symbols. Pupils enjoy making up their own word problems. Ask children to make up an addition problem with one-digit numbers for their classmates to solve. Another helpful exercise is for the teacher to write an addition fact on the chalkboard and have each child think of and share a problem for that example.

5. GUIDE PUPILS TO DEVELOP THINKING STRATEGIES

As children work with the easy addition facts, they should be led to examine the following *thinking strategies* and explore some generalizations.

(a) The order of a pair of addends may be changed without changing the sum (The Commutative Property), that is:
$4 + 2 = 6; 2 + 4 = 6$

(b) If one is added to a number, the sum is the next counting number, that is:
$5 + 1 = 6; 8 + 1 = 9; 7 + 1 = 8$

(c) If zero is added to a number, the sum is that number, (The Identity Property for Addition) that is:
$7 + 0 = 7; 4 + 0 = 4$

(d) An addition example may have more than two addends, in which case the

Start with 4.

Four and mother's 2 joined.

Now have 6.

Figure 7.2
Joining 4 and 2

way the numbers are grouped will not affect the sum. For example, the numbers 3 and 5 may be represented with objects in different groupings:

(1) Start with: ### #####
    3 + 5 =

(2) Rearrange as: ### ### ##
    3 + 3 + 2 = 6 + 2

(3) Rearrange as: #### ####
    4 + 4, two 4's!

(4) Rearrange as: ## ## ## ##
    four 2's!

Pupils find that if an addition fact can be renamed so one pair is a double, the sum is easy to find.

(e) At the symbolic level, if a certain number is added to one addend and the same number is subtracted from another addend, the sum does not change.

This idea works well when the two numbers differ by 2. The example 3 + 5 = ? could be renamed to 4 + 4 by adding 1 to the 3 and subtracting 1 from the 5. This is an application of the associative property:

$$3 + (1 + 4) = (3 + 1) + 4; 4 + 4 = 8.$$

It is also an application of the property of compensation.

V. Reinforcement

Young children who are actively involved in activities suggested above usually learn the beginning addition facts with little need for repetitive drill. In fact, the best way to provide reinforcement for the basic facts is to provide opportunities for children to use the facts they are learning in meaningful applications of time, money, and measurements.

VI. Evaluate Learning

Evaluation takes place continuously as pupils are learning the basic facts. The teacher should observe children as they are working and provide for extra assistance and guidance as needed. Some teachers find it helpful to prepare for each child a list of objectives to be accomplished. Then, during learning activities, each objective is checked off and dated when the child has achieved it.

Teaching Subtraction Facts

The teacher should follow the same pattern for introducing the subtraction facts that was used for introducing the addition facts. In both situations, the basic principles in Chapter 1 are applied. The following discussion applies to planning a series of subtraction lessons over a period of time.

I. Objectives

Consider the following objectives for inclusion in lesson plans designed to develop an understanding of the easy subtraction facts.

1. Relate subtraction to one of three situations: (a) take away, (b) comparison, (c) additive.

2. Follow a subtraction story and create the solution with manipulatives.

3. Show a subtraction fact with an appropriate drawing.

4. Write a subtraction fact in both horizontal and vertical forms, then read them.

5. Tell a subtraction story for a given subtraction fact.

6. Given any addition fact with unequal addends, write 2 subtraction facts.

7. Respond quickly and accurately with the difference between a minuend and a subtrahend of a basic fact.

II. Readiness

After pupils have a good understanding of basic addition facts to sums of 10 or less, they should be ready to learn the corresponding subtraction facts.

III. Motivation

The teacher should continue to emphasize story problems, working with manipulatives, and positive reinforcement. Pupils need to understand what they are learning and should enjoy a high degree of success.

IV. Growth Through Guided Discovery

1. BEGIN WITH A PROBLEM SITUATION

There are three different types of problem settings for subtraction. Each subtraction concept should be introduced with a different kind of problem.

(a) *Take-away.* John had 8 salted nuts. He ate 5. How many were left?

(b) *Comparison.* Lola had 6 dolls. Letha had 4 dolls. How many more dolls did Lola have than Letha?

(c) *Additive.* Rita needed 8 stamps to fill a page in her stamp book. She had only 6. How many more stamps did she need to fill the page?

The sequence of lessons should start with the "take-away" concept. After pupils have a good understanding of this concept, explore the "comparison" concept. Last, present the "additive" concept. Presenting more than one concept in any one introductory lesson may confuse pupils. Presenting a more difficult concept before the pupils are ready may also lead to confusion.

2. USE MANIPULATIVES

(a) Take-Away Problems During initial instruction, the take-away interpretation of subtraction for minuends of 10 or less may be explored in problem settings with the use of objects. For young children, taking away zero objects from a collection is not a real situation, but taking away all of the objects resulting with zero remaining is real to them. The solution of a take-away problem involves three steps: (1) Represent how many to start with. (2) Remove a specified number. (3) Determine how many are left. For subtraction facts of 10 or less, these steps are very simple for most children to perform.

(b) Comparison Problems For a comparison situation, two sets of objects are "compared" to find the difference. Given the problem "John has 6 pennies and Maria has 4 . . . ," three questions can be asked.

(1) How many more pennies does John have than Maria?" (What is the difference between 6 and 4?)

(2) How many pennies does Maria need to have the same number as John?" (What can be added to 4 to sum 6?)

(3) How many pennies could John spend and still have as many as Maria?" (What can be subtracted from 6 to result in 4?)

The problem in comparison subtraction is to determine the number difference between two sets. This is more difficult for most pupils than the take-away problem. Once the pupil learns to arrange the objects in each set for easy one-for-one matching, the solution to the question "How many more in one set than the other?" is relatively easy.

(c) Additive Problems The additive-type problem should be presented last because it is the most difficult for pupils to solve. For example, "Josie's daddy promised to give her $5.00 for her birthday. He gave her only $3.00. How much did he owe her?"

The thinking involved in the solution of the above problem is: What do I add to 3 to have a sum of 5 or, $3 + \boxed{} = 5$ or $\boxed{} + 3 = 5$. This is the "missing addend" interpretation of subtraction.

The "additive" situation may be illustrated by having the pupil represent with objects the number promised or needed. Then the pupil could cover with a hand or a piece of paper the number already received. The number of objects showing is the "number owed" or the "number needed."

3. WORK WITH PICTURES

Drawing a picture of a take-away subtraction problem requires three actions:

(a) Represent with a drawing the number that you start with.

(b) Repeat this picture and show that a number is *removed*. This is the number to be subtracted.

(c) Indicate the number left.

The drawings in Figure 7.3 show the solution to the problem "Jose has 4 rabbits. One rabbit ran away. How many rabbits did Jose have left?"

For a comparison problem, the solution can be obtained from one drawing. For example, "Angela has 6 dolls and Jessica has 4 dolls. How many more dolls does Angela have than Jessica?"

Represent Angela's dolls: # # # # # #
Represent Jessica's dolls: # # # #
Match one-for-one, and the difference is 2. Angela has two more dolls than Jessica. Also, we can see from the drawing that Angela could give two dolls away and have the same number as Jessica. Jessica would need two more dolls to have the same number as Angela.

Most elementary school mathematics textbooks have pictures of subtraction situations for pupils to use in telling and writing subtraction stories.

4. TRANSLATE SUBTRACTION STORIES TO NUMBER FACTS

Subtraction stories may be *take-away*, *comparison*, or *additive*. This can be illustrated with the subtraction fact $5 - 2 = 3$, read "five minus two equals three." The story problem for a take-away situation is described as "Five take away two leaves three." For a comparison situation, the story is "If we compare five and two, the difference will be three." The language for an additive situation is "What number should be added to two to make five?"

The additive concept is similar to the comparison concept; both may use the term *more*, which suggests addition. Because of the similarity to the additive concept, pupils must be instructed not to rely on a "key word," but to understand the meaning of the problem presented. Although the verbal cue is different in each problem, the solution involves subtraction.

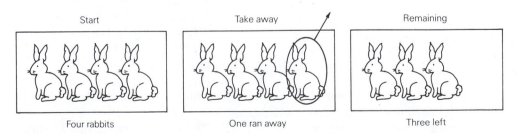

Figure 7.3
Picture story demonstrating "four take away one leaves three."

5. CREATE SUBTRACTION STORIES

Children should be asked to make up their own subtraction stories. For each story, ask if it is a take-away subtraction, a comparison situation, or an additive problem. Have the pupils solve each other's story problems. Then write a basic subtraction example on the chalkboard, such as 8 − 2 = ? or 2 + ? = 8, and ask each pupil to make up either a take-away, a comparison example, or an additive problem.

V. Reinforcement

DISCOVER NUMBER PATTERNS

Patterns play an important role in everyday life and are a large part of the way the world is organized and understood. As pupils study operations on whole numbers, fractions, and decimals, they should be encouraged to look for patterns.

The following is an example of a simple pattern formed from a series of addition facts. Each fact uses the number 2 as the first addend, with each subsequent addend increased by one. The rule is: Each sum will also be increased by one.

2 + 2 = 4	2 + 5 = 7
2 + 3 = 5	2 + 6 = 8
2 + 4 = 6	2 + 7 = 9

With this information, the answer to 2 + 7 has to be 9.

When pupils discover that they can derive a new fact from a series of known facts arranged in an orderly series, they no longer need to manipulate objects to find answers. This gives them a powerful thinking strategy to use to discover unknown facts and to assist them in remembering facts that they have previously studied but may have forgotten.

EXAMINE THE NUMBER FAMILY RELATIONSHIP

A number family is the set of facts in addition that has the same sum and the corresponding subtraction facts. For example, the set of addition and subtraction facts in the family of *five* is:

0 + 5 = 5	5 − 0 = 5
1 + 4 = 5	5 − 1 = 4
2 + 3 = 5	5 − 2 = 3
3 + 2 = 5	5 − 3 = 2
4 + 1 = 5	5 − 4 = 1
5 + 0 = 5	5 − 5 = 0

The above series of addition and subtraction facts represents an organized pattern. By examining the pattern the child should be able to discover some generalizations about the relationship between addition and subtraction. Have pupils see if they can write all the addition and subtraction facts for other families up to a sum of ten. Make sure they record the facts in an orderly pattern. See if they can discover the "rule" to predict how many facts there should be for a given sum and minuend in both operations.

Teaching Addition and Subtraction Facts with Sums Greater Than 10

I. Objectives

The learning objectives for basic addition and subtraction facts having sums greater than 10 are generally the same as for the facts having sums of 10 or less. For facts having sums greater than 10, more emphasis is given to thinking strategies while the work with manipulatives is lessened, but more structured.

II. Determining and Developing Readiness

Prior to presenting addition facts that include sums more than 10 and the related subtraction facts, the teacher should diagnose each pupil's readiness for learning this topic. For pupils who are still mastering the facts with sums less than 10, additional reinforcement should be provided as lessons on sums more than 10 progress. Activities similar to those described earlier in this chapter provide the background for learning the harder basic facts in addition and subtraction.

III. Providing Motivation

The teacher should continue to give positive reinforcement for each child's efforts. Make sure that each child succeeds, and provide learning activities that are interesting and enjoyable.

IV. Growth Through Guided Discovery

Lessons designed to develop meanings of the addition facts with sums more than 10 and the corresponding subtraction facts should continue to emphasize guided discovery. This means that each lesson should start with a problem to solve. The pupils should be encouraged to use manipulatives, drawings, and thinking strategies to arrive at solutions.

1. PROBLEM SOLVING

When addition and subtraction facts involving sums greater than 10 are introduced, pupils should have had many experiences in dealing with problem situations with sums of 10 or less and the corresponding subtraction examples. The class should be able to understand problems, determine the operation needed for a solution, and perform the operation at the symbolic level with a reasonable degree of speed and accuracy. Children who are lagging require additional practice and reinforcement, which is suggested later in this chapter.

2. USE MANIPULATIVE MATERIALS

When addition and subtraction facts with sums more than 10 are introduced, pupils should not have to use manipulatives as much as they did during earlier work with these operations. However, because the sum is more than 10, the use of manipulatives on a "ten-ten" frame either made out of egg cartons or drawn on a piece of cardboard, may be of value to most children during initial discovery experiences.

(a) *State a problem.* "There are 7 boys in the class that plan to join the Cub Scouts and 5 girls who plan to join the Brownie Scouts. How many pupils plan to join the Scouts?"

(b) *Discover solution with manipulatives.* Have pupils represent the two addends with objects on their "ten-ten" frame as follows:

#	#	#	#	#	#	#			
#	#	#	#	#					

Have several pupils describe how they arrived at an answer. Some possible approaches might be:

(1) Counting by ones.

(2) Starting with 7 and counting 5 more. Pupils who use counting strategies to solve addition problems need to review some of the thinking strategies discussed earlier in this chapter so they will have no need to count by ones to find sums.

(3) Recognizing that on the "ten-ten" frame there is a double 5, then two more.

(4) Taking an object from the top row and putting it in the bottom row to make the number pair 6 + 6.

(5) Making a ten.

When a sum is more than 10, in our system of number we rename it as tens and ones. So $7 + 5 = 10 + 2$ or 12. With the aid of the "ten-ten" frame, pupils can be guided to discover that they can take enough from the bottom row to make a ten in the top row. Visually it is easy to see that three is needed to make a ten, which leaves two in the bottom row. The answer now is easy to see, 1 ten 2 ones or twelve.

The easiest set of facts to use in demonstrating this procedure involves 9 as an addend. For example, when one number is 9 and the other addend is 2 or more, the property of compensation may be applied. The sum of the number pair (9, 4) may be found by adding 1 to 9 and subtracting 1 from 4. Then the example becomes $10 + 3 = 13$. A pupil may use manipulatives to discover the pattern. The thought pattern requires more mental operations than when a direct procedure is used. The direct thought pattern is "9 + 4 is 13." The greater the number of mental operations involved, the greater the possibility for error. With teacher guidance, pupils should decide whether to make the three mental responses "$9 + 1 = 10, 4 - 1 = 3, 10 + 3 = 13$" or give one mental response, "$9 + 4 = 13$."

For each pair of unequal numbers with a sum of 11 through 18, there are two addition facts and two subtraction facts. For each of the two subtraction facts there are three types of problem setting: take-away, comparison, and additive. When a problem involving addition is solved, the teacher should ask the pupils to create subtraction problems using the sum as the minuend and one of the addends as the subtrahend.

V. Reinforcement

EXAMINE ALTERNATIVE WAYS TO APPROACH SUBTRACTION FACTS

Mastering the addition facts seems to be easier for pupils than mastering the subtraction facts. At this stage some pupils have a tendency to count backward. In order to help children *avoid* solving subtraction problems by counting backward, the following thinking strategies may be explored.

RELATE TO AN ADDITION FACT

If the subtraction fact is $15 - 7$, encourage the pupil to think of this as "What do I add to 7 to have a sum of 15?" Knowledge of the addition facts should be very helpful in arriving at answers to subtraction facts. Examples written in vertical form make it easier to "see" this "missing addend" approach.

$$
\begin{array}{cccc}
14 \quad \overset{14^{*}}{\underline{}} & 17 & 12 & 15 \\
\underline{-\ 7} \quad \overset{7}{\underset{+}{}} & \underline{-\ 9} & \underline{-\ 6} & \underline{-\ 8} \\
\uparrow \quad ? & & &
\end{array}
$$

$* \ ? + 7 = 14$

In each example, start at the bottom of the example, where the answer will be recorded, and move upward. The thinking involved to solve the first example is "What added to 7 equals 14?"

USE A THINKING STRATEGY

Thinking strategies are helpful for pupils who otherwise have difficulty in remembering answers to basic facts and for those who enjoy exploring alternative algorithms. A thinking strategy should not involve counting by ones.

Some pupils find it helpful to break the minuend into a ten and ones, then subtract the known addend from the ten and add that difference to the ones part of the renamed addend. In the subtraction example $15 - 7 = ?$, rename the 15 as $10 + 5$. Then subtract the 7 from $10 = 3$ and add that to $5 = 8$.

Another thinking strategy involves adding the same number to both the minuend and subtrahend. According to the property of compensation, doing this will not change the difference. But to simplify thought, add a number to the subtrahend that will make it 10. In order not to change the difference, add this same number to the minuend. The record of work follows:

$$
\begin{array}{ccc}
17 & (17 + 2) = & 19 \\
- \ 8 & -(\ 8 + 2) = & - \ 10 \\
\end{array}
$$

The difference is 9

USE TEXTBOOK DEVELOPMENT

Most commercially prepared textbooks in mathematics for the elementary school have developmental lessons on the topics discussed in this chapter. The problem is, the textbook is written at the visual level, with pictures and symbolic notations. Many times suggestions are made in the Teacher's Edition for prelesson activities and ways to start lessons. But if the teacher does not provide the suggested experiences with manipulatives and does not follow through with the "getting started" ideas, then the full value of the developmental lesson may be lost.

PROVIDE DRILL ACTIVITIES

Through drill activities children can learn to respond to mathematical situations spontaneously and with assurance. The teacher should look carefully to see that pupils understand what they are doing or else they will practice incorrect procedures. By itself, extra drill cannot cure *error patterns*. It is the teacher's role to discover why pupils make errors, teach them to avoid mistakes, and, finally, provide suitable drill when apparent that each child understands (1) what to do, (2) why it is done, and (3) how to proceed. Under these conditions, drill will help children memorize the basic facts.

Interesting drill activities can be provided by using flash cards, games, calculators, *tachistoscopic* devices (electronic and self-powered), computers, and by other means. An example of a self-powered tachistoscope is shown in Figure 7.4. This tachistoscope is easily constructed. Using any type of stiff

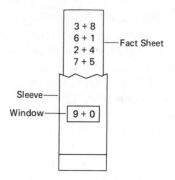

Figure 7.4

paper, make a sleeve, with a "window" cut into it, that fits snugly over an appropriate list of basic pairs. The child simply pulls the list through the sleeve and gives the answer to each pair as it appears in the window. Answers to the pairs can be written on the back of the list. A window can also be cut into the back of the sleeve to reveal the answers and make quick checking possible.

Electronic tachistoscopic devices that are programmed to display difficult or easy facts are also available. Many of these devices give immediate feedback, telling a child if a correct or incorrect answer has been given by flashing a smile or frown. Some devices tell the number of answers that are correct. Electronic devices have been shown to be strong motivators for some children.

The teacher should try to provide practice activities that use a fact in several settings. Progress records should be kept. When the objective is to help the children learn to memorize, drill sessions should be short.

The *addition crows* shown in Figure 7.5 assist pupils in adding 8 to other one-digit numbers. The crows are made of sturdy cardboard and are small enough to be held in a child's hand comfortably. The small circle (on the front, A) is cut to form an aperture through which numerals on a wheel, fastened to the back of the crow, will appear

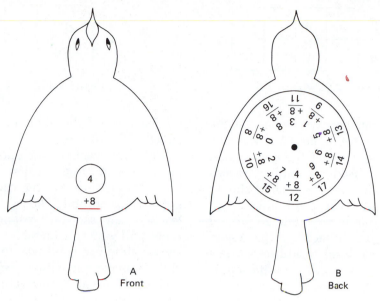

Figure 7.5

as the wheel is turned. The pupil adds to the number 8 the numeral that appears and then rotates the wheel until the next numeral appears. Write the answers on the back of the wheel (see B) for self-checking. Many variations of this design are possible.

Pupils solve *cross-number puzzles* (Figure 7.6) by writing in the missing numerals. This type of puzzle can be used after teaching a given number pair, such as (2, 3), shown in puzzles a, b, and c. Pupils will not be able to fill in the squares in the sum until they have learned the sum of all number pairs given.

Cover-up is the name of a game in which each child has 13 markers and a copy of the activity sheet (see Figure 7.7). Two dice, or cubes with the numerals 1 through 6 on each cube, are needed for each group of children playing. The players take turns tossing the cubes and "cover up" on the activity sheet either the sum or the difference of the two numbers rolled in the toss. The other players should check the arithmetic. If there is no play (because the sum or differ-

ence is already covered), the cubes are passed to the next player. The first player to cover his or her activity sheet is the winner.

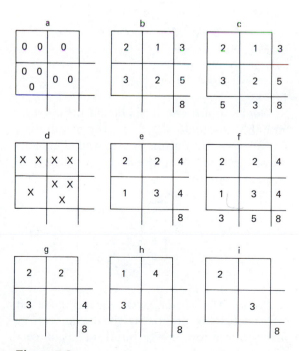

Figure 7.6

0	1	2	3	4	5	6
	7	8	9	10	11	12

Figure 7.7

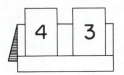

Figure 7.8

This activity can be extended to let the children record all the possible ways to make each number using the two cubes. Charts could be used for pupils' record sheets. When completed, each chart should list all the ways to make each number.

A *number fact circle* has numerals around the outside and one numeral in the center. This device can be used to add or subtract the numbers on the outside of the circle with number on the inside of the circle. If a record of the answers is necessary, the child can write the fact and the answer on a sheet of paper.

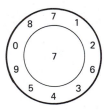

Magic squares will challenge pupils who are able to create a 3 × 3 array of numbers in which all columns, rows, and diagonals have the same sum. Below is an example of a magic square.

8	1	6
3	5	7
4	9	2

"Show Me" cards, as shown in Figure 7.8, are useful for practicing the basic facts in each operation. Each pupil needs a card

holder, a set of the digits 0 through 9, and an extra 1 card.

When the teacher calls out a fact, the pupil selects the digit card(s) that illustrates the answer, inserts the card(s) into the holder pocket, and holds it up so that the teacher can see the response. Response times will vary considerably. In drill, the response time is a good way to see whether a child is answering without counting. "Show Me" cards are also very valuable for place-value activities.

Many teachers make *tape recordings* of the facts. The pupils use headsets to listen to the tape and write sums or differences as the tape is played. The teacher may include the answers at the end of the tape for self-checking. Commercially produced tapes are also available, and several textbook publishers offer tapes compatible with their series. Let children make their own tapes and compete to find the answer.

Some drill activities can be effective learning-center situations. Each activity should be viewed as an "idea starter"—that is, teachers need to expand these ideas and prepare additional, and similar, activities. For example, give each pupil several objects. Have the pupils make a set of 6 objects and a set of 7 objects, representing the addends as 6 + 7 = □. Next bring the objects together and place on a ten-ten frame to show how many there are in both sets. The teacher should ask "How many all together?" The desired answer is 13. Children need to figure out the number of tens they have and then the number of ones before being able to give the answer 13. In this case, let the child verbalize the number of tens and ones before expecting the desired answer. Work many examples before going on to more difficult problems.

FIND MISSING PARTS OF BASIC FACTS

Practice sheets with addition and subtraction facts given with any one of the three numbers missing is very challenging to pupils and helps the teacher discover if a pupil understands the relationship between addition and subtraction. The following are a few examples that could be included on such a practice sheet.

$$9 + \boxed{} = 11 \qquad 6 + 8 = \boxed{}$$
$$\boxed{} - 4 = 9 \qquad 14 - \boxed{} = 8$$
$$\boxed{} + 6 = 10 \qquad 15 - 9 = \boxed{}$$

Column Addition

Column addition involves examples with three or more addends. In a problem setting, there are more than two numbers to be added. When adding a column of three one-place numbers, add the first pair, then add that sum to the third addend. One difficulty most pupils have in carrying out this procedure is remembering the first sum, which is an "unseen" numeral. A second difficulty occurs when the first pair results in a two-digit sum. For primary-grade children who are still striving to master basic addition facts, the second difficulty can be avoided. Select the first two addends of a three-addend column that have a sum less than 10. The first difficulty, that of an unseen numeral, can be solved by having the child record the first subsum either in the column or off to the side (see Chapter 8).

VI. Evaluating Learning

All of the learning experiences and activities suggested in this chapter are designed to assist pupils to reach the *mastery level* of learning. In order for a pupil to be evaluated as having mastered the basic addition and subtraction facts, he or she must be able to perform the following tasks:

1. Demonstrate the solution to a problem involving a basic addition or subtraction fact with manipulatives.

2. Show the solution to a problem with a drawing.

3. Write the fact in both vertical and horizontal forms, then read them.

4. Verify the answer to the fact from other known facts by showing a pattern and by applying a thinking strategy.

5. From a verbal problem be able to tell a number story and write a correct number equation.

6. Give two addition and two subtraction facts for any pair of unequal single-digit numbers.

7. For any sum, write all the members of that family as addition and subtraction facts.

8. Identify addends and sum in an equation.

9. Given any addition or subtraction fact with one number missing, name the missing number.

10. Give the answer to the basic addition and subtraction facts with assurance and without hesitation.

11. Given any basic addition or subtraction fact, construct a verbal problem and show its solution.

Problem Solving

With only the basic facts available problem solving is necessarily limited, but important basic concepts can and should be introduced. Once the facts are established, it is essential to place more emphasis on the transition to symbolic notation and begin to emphasize place value concept.

1. Arrange the following to represent a two-digit number and write the numeral:

xxxxxxxxxxxx

    Answer: x̲x̲x̲x̲x̲x̲x̲x̲x̲x̲ xx =
    one ten + two = 10 + 2 = 12

Because few pupils can tell the difference between a group of 9, 10, or 11 at a glance, it is useful to underline groups of 10. It may also be useful to write 6 as x̲x̲x̲x̲x̲ x, 7 as x̲x̲x̲x̲x̲ xx, 8 as x̲x̲x̲x̲x̲ xxx, and 9 as x̲x̲x̲x̲x̲ xxxx. Pupils should discover early that x̲x̲x̲x̲x̲ + x̲x̲x̲x̲x̲ = x̲x̲x̲x̲x̲x̲x̲x̲x̲x̲.

2. June has this many pennies: x̲x̲x̲x̲x̲ xxx
  . . .is given this many: x̲x̲x̲x̲x̲ xxxx
   How many does she now have?

x̲x̲x̲x̲x̲ xxx + x̲x̲x̲x̲x̲ xxxx →

x̲x̲x̲x̲x̲x̲x̲x̲x̲x̲ x̲x̲x̲x̲x̲ xx
       8 + 9 = 10 + 7 = 17

3. Joe has this many cookies:
    x̲x̲x̲x̲x̲x̲x̲x̲x̲x̲ xxxx
  He eats this many: x̲x̲x̲x̲x̲ xxx
  How many are left?
  x̲x̲x̲x̲x̲ x̲x̲x̲x̲x̲ xxxx take away x̲x̲x̲x̲x̲ xxx
  Answer: x̲x̲x̲x̲x̲ x
  Symbolic: 14 − 8 = 6

The work can be done first with concrete materials before moving to pictures and symbolic representation. When a pupil encounters these situations for the first time, the response is not habitual and is a problem that requires a solution.

Even and Odd

Patterns are vital in many problem-solving situations.

Write the following and ask the pupils to assign numerals to each set and extend the pattern:

xx   xx xx   xx xx xx   xx xx xx xx

The pupil should be able to write the numerals 2, 4, 6, and 8 and then be able to extend the pattern to 10 and 12 and beyond.

Now introduce the following pattern and ask for a similar extension:

x   xx x   xx xx x   xx xx xx x

The pupil should be able to write 1, 3, 5, 7 and extend the pattern to 9, 11, and beyond.

These activities are done with only the basic facts and counting available.

Now name the first set as even numbers and the second set as odd numbers. Ask the class to describe the difference.

The following questions should lead to interesting guided discoveries:

How can we describe even numbers? One possible answer: An even number can be represented by pairs of x's.

How can we describe odd numbers? Possible answer: When we attempt to represent an odd number in pairs of x's, there is always a single x left over.

How can we get from one even number to the next? from one odd number to the next?

How can we change an even number into an odd number? an odd number into an even number?

What kind of number is:

1. The sum of two even numbers?

2. The sum of two odd numbers?

3. The sum of an even and an odd number?

Nonroutine Problems and Patterns

Always be on the alert for problems that do not fit into the standard mode found in textbooks that will reinforce the skills being learned at a given time. Learning facts, algorithms, and concepts should involve problem solving. To obtain a complete solution, the following requires not only the basic facts but also an organized plan.

1. Find the smallest number that is the sum of three distinct non-zero digits. The sum of the numbers must be written in sequence. $3 + 4$ is in sequence but $4 + 3$ is not. Answer: $6 = 1 + 2 + 3$.

2. How many different answers are possible if the sequence requirement is removed? A plan is necessary here if the answer is to be found efficiently without omitting any possibilities.

$1 + 2 + 3 = 6$	$2 + 3 + 1 = 6$
$3 + 1 + 2 = 6$	$1 + 3 + 2 = 6$
$2 + 1 + 3 = 6$	$3 + 2 + 1 = 6$

The plan is simple but not obvious to pupils at this level: Examine all possibilities beginning with 1, with 2 and with 3.

3. What is the answer to problem 1 if the digit zero is allowed?

Answer: $0 + 1 + 2 = 3$

4. Write all possible answers if the sequence requirement is removed.

5. Find all possible combinations of three distinct digits in sequence that have a sum of 9. Plan: start with 1 and examine all possibilities. Then start with 2, and so on. The word distinct means that no two digits in the sum can be alike. $1 + 4 + 4$ is not an acceptable solution.

Answer: $1 + 2 + 6 = 9$ $1 + 3 + 5 = 9$
$2 + 3 + 4 = 9$

The sequence requirement eliminates all answers beginning with 3, 4, 5, and so on.

6. Use the property of compensation to convert the first solution into the second. Answer: $1 + (2+1) + (6-1) = 1 + 3 + 5$. Compensation is the process of adding a number to one addend and then subtracting the same number from another addend so that the sum is unchanged. This process is the equivalent of adding zero.

Enrichment

A pupil's first introduction to variables should be with the variable in the form of a frame. Answers should be inserted in the frame.

$\square = 3 + 7$	$3 + 7 = \square$
$4 + \square = 9$	$\square + \triangle = 6$
$N = 3 + 7$	$3 + 7 = N$
$4 + N = 9$	$A + B = 6$

The transition from frames to letter variables, as illustrated above, is essential for entering instructions into the computer. When letter variables have been introduced, try the following:

What is the value of $N + N$ when $N = 1$, 2, 3 . . .?

Guide the class to recognize that $N + N$ will always be an even number for all replacements of N by a whole number.

Repeat the same procedure for $N + N + 1$ to help the class discover that this expression will always give an odd number. An alert pupil may notice that $N + N + 1$ must be odd because adding 1 to an even number gives an odd number.

The following two FOR-NEXT programs will display 10 even numbers and 10 odd numbers respectively and verify the previous conclusions about the result of substituting whole numbers for $N + N$ and $N + N + 1$.

```
10 FOR N = 0 TO 10
20 PRINT N,N + N
30 NEXT
```

```
10 FOR N = 0 TO 10
20 PRINT N,N + N + 1
30 NEXT
```

Encourage pupils to try other sets of numbers in line 10 other than 0 and 10.

Have pupils write any digit and add 3, then add 7, subtract 4, and then subtract the original number to get a sum of 6. Now have the pupil write a different digit and repeat the process to again get the answer 6. Ask why.

Answer: The result must be $3 + 7 - 4 = 6$ because the original pupil entry is added and subtracted, the equivalent of adding 0.

If a computer is available, enter the following program and run it to demonstrate that the answer for both expressions is the same for N equals 1 to 20 for a convincing demonstration.

```
10 FOR N = 1 TO 20
20 PRINT 3 + 7 - 4, N + 3
+ 7 - 4 - N
30 NEXT
```

The comma between the two expressions tells the computer to display the output for the two expressions in two columns. The second column is the same as the first for reasons already stated. Adding and subtracting N is the equivalent of adding 0.

Computer Activities

If more information is wanted about entering programs into the computer, refer to the computer section in the Appendix and review the work with FOR-NEXT loops in the problem-solving section of Chapter 6.

Initial work with facts in the symbolic form should be in the vertical mode, but the horizontal mode has been neglected far too often in the past. Enter lines 10–60 and then lines 90 and 100. This program will ask for the completion of a basic fact and provide the correct answer for immediate verification for a pupil entry. If lines 70, 80 and 110 are inserted, the program will indicate whether a response is right or wrong and will display the number of correct and incorrect answers after 5 questions.

The program is written in Basic. Refer to the Appendix for changes required for IBM computers and compatibles.

The REM in lines 25, 65 and 125 stands for remark and provides information to help understand the program. These REMS have no effect on the running of the program and are only seen when program is listed.

DO NOT ENTER REMs

```
Program P7.1
 10  HOME: VTAB 9
 20  IF C + W > 4 THEN 110
 25  REM  CHANGING 4 IN LINE
20 WILL CHANGE THE NUMBER OF
QUESTIONS REQUIRED BEFORE
CORRECT AND INCORRECT RE-
SPONSES ARE DISPLAYED.
THIS LINE SHOULD BE ENTERED
WITH THE ORIGINAL SET BUT
WILL NOT BE USED UNTIL LINES
70, 80 AND 110 ARE ENTERED.
 30   A = 1 + INT(9*RND(1))
 40   B = 1 + INT(9*RND(1))
 50   PRINT A ; "+"; B ;
"=";
 60   INPUT " "; N
 65   REM FOR MENTAL ARITH-
METIC, REPLACE N BY N$ SO
THE COMPUTER WILL CONTINUE
WITHOUT A KEYBOARD ENTRY
 70  IF N = A + B THEN PRINT
     "GOOD WORK!": INPUT Z$
     : C = C+1:GOTO 10
 80  PRINT "WRONG ANSWER": W
     = W + 1
 90  PRINT A; "+" ; B ; "="
     ; A + B
100  INPUT Z$ : GOTO 10
105 REM THE COLON IN LINES
80 AND 100 ALLOWS US TO
PLACE TWO INSTRUCTIONS ON A
LINE. COLONS IN LINE 70 AL-
LOW 4 INSTRUCTIONS WITH ONE
LINE NUMBER BUT THEY ARE NOT
USED WHEN IF STATEMENT IS
FALSE.
 110 PRINT "NUMBER RIGHT";
C ; "   NUMBER WRONG";W
```

Program P7.2 reinforces the relation between addition and subtraction.

```
PROGRAM P7.2
  10   HOME: VTAB 9
  20   A = 1 + INT(9*RND(1))
  30   B = 1 + INT(9*RND(1))
  40   PRINT "IF "; A ; "+"
       ; B ; " = "; A + B;
       "THEN:"
  50   PRINT
  60   PRINT A + B ; " - " ;
       A ; "= "
  70   INPUT " ";Z$
  80   PRINT
  90   PRINT A + B; " - "; A
       ; " = "; B
 100   PRINT A + B; " - "; B
       ; " = "; A
```

Summary

Use of calculators and computers has reduced the number of pencil-and-paper calculations adults perform. Today's school children should learn to use these instruments on a regular basis. However, in order to use the calculator and computer successfully and to compute with pencil and paper, it is necessary for pupils to master the basic facts. Children need to develop thinking strategies to apply to problem situations. Manipulative materials are vital in giving pupils an opportunity to build concrete models of problem situations and to help them develop thinking strategies. Work with manipulatives should lead children to the visual and symbolic levels of thinking. Exploring patterns and working with number properties help pupils understand and remember basic facts.

Reinforcement activities should be used after children have been introduced to the facts in problem situations that are solved with manipulatives, drawings, and symbolic notations. After it is clear that pupils understand the concepts of addition and subtraction, drill and practice activities are appropriate. Activities with calculators and computers should be provided. All reinforcement activities should be chosen with the intent of helping pupils gain a deeper understanding of the operations and to help them memorize the basic facts.

Exercises

1. Prepare a lesson plan designed to introduce pupils to the easy addition facts.

2. Prepare and teach a lesson to a small group of pupils that stresses thinking strategies for number pairs that have sums more than ten.

3. Manipulatives should be used to help children find correct answers, to develop appropriate language, and to develop thinking strategies. Make and use a manipulative to demonstrate these three functions.

4. Explain how a teacher should determine whether a pupil is ready for drill activities on the basic facts.

5. Agree or disagree with each statement below and give one or more reasons for your position.
   (a) Calculators should be used in the first grade to introduce basic addition facts.

(b) Activities such as sorting, matching, and classifying provide readiness for learning the basic facts.

(c) The facts involving one and zero should be taught first.

(d) Pupils should be permitted to count on their fingers to find sums more than 10.

(e) It is more important for a pupil to develop a positive attitude toward mathematics than to become a successful problem solver.

6. Design and teach a lesson on the relationship between addition and subtraction.

7. Write several "real-life" problems for first- and second-graders that can be solved with the aid of manipulatives.

8. A pupil knows the basic addition facts but cannot add a column of three or more numbers. What remedial measures should be taken?

9. A teacher remarked, "I teach all the addition facts and then all the subtraction facts." Evaluate this procedure.

10. Discuss the role of the computer in teaching basic addition and subtraction facts to first- and second-graders.

References

Copeland, Richard W. *How Children Learn Mathematics: Teaching Implications of Piaget's Research*, 4th ed. New York: Macmillan, 1984. Chapter 7.

Cruikshank, Douglas E., and Linda Jensen Sheffield. *Teaching Mathematics to Elementary School Children: A Foundation for the Future.* Columbus, OH: Merrill, 1988. Chapter 4.

Engelhardt, Jon M., Robert B. Ashlock, and James H. Wiebe. *Helping Children Understand and Use Numerals.* Needham Heights, MA: Allyn & Bacon, 1984.

Heddens, James W., and William R. Speer. *Today's Mathematics*, 6th ed. Chicago: Science Research Associates, 1988. Unit 6.

Kennedy, Leonard M., and Steve Tipps. *Guiding Children's Learning of Mathematics*, 5th ed. Belmont, CA: Wadsworth, 1988. Chapter 9.

Marks, John L., Arthur A. Hiatt, and Evelyn M. Neufeld. *Teaching Elementary School Mathematics for Understanding.* New York: McGraw-Hill, 1985. Chapter 4.

Suydam, Marilyn N., and Robert E. Reys (eds.). *Developing Computational Skills*, 1978 Yearbook. Reston, VA: National Council of Teachers of Mathematics, 1978. Chapter 2.

Post, Thomas R. (ed.). *Teaching Mathematics in Grades K–8: Research-Based Methods.* Needham Heights, MA: Allyn & Bacon, 1988. Chapter 5.

CHAPTER

8

Addition and Subtraction of Multidigit Numbers

ACHIEVEMENT GOALS

After studying this chapter, you should be able to:

1. Enumerate several new approaches for teaching addition and subtraction of multi-digit numbers.

2. Identify the sequence of examples for addition and subtraction of multidigit numbers with and without regrouping.[1]

3. Outline the sequence for guiding pupil discovery of the meanings, language, and procedures involved in adding and subtracting multidigit numbers, with and without regrouping.

4. State addition and subtraction word problems that are useful in introducing and reinforcing these operations.

5. Discuss the proper use of base-ten materials and place-value devices in teaching addition and subtraction of multidigit numbers.

6. Show the transition from manipulatives to visuals, to expanded notation and to the standard forms of notation.

7. Explain the thinking involved in performing higher-decade addition, without and with bridging.

8. Prepare and implement activities to develop pupils' understanding and skills by using calculators and computer programs.

VOCABULARY

These terms are defined or illustrated in the Glossary.

Addend
Adding by endings
Algorithm
Bridging the
  decade
Column impasse
Comparison
  subtraction
Decomposition
  method
Difference

Equal additions
  method
Expanded notation
Higher-decade
  addition
Minuend
Multiples
Regrouping
Renaming
Subtrahend

1. The term *regrouping* is used when working with manipulatives in a situation where a place is "over-loaded" with more than nine objects. Pupils learn to "regroup" ten things into one set of ten. The term *re-name* is used in symbolic notations. In this book we use the two terms interchangeably.

Approaches to teaching addition and subtraction with multidigit numbers need to be based upon the principles of teaching and learning discussed in Chapter 1.

Goals and objectives for teaching addition and subtraction of multidigit numbers must emphasize the importance of having the pupils *understand* the mathematics to be learned. Pupils need to be skillful in *doing* mathematics, *know* what they are doing, and be able to *explain* the procedures involved. In order for a class to be skillful with multidigit numbers in addition and subtraction, each pupil must know the basic facts, understand the algorithm, and apply this knowledge for solving problems.

New Approaches to Teaching Operations on Multidigit Numbers

During the past decade there have been several proposals to change the teaching and learning of mathematics in the elementary school. These include problem solving, grade placement, place value, manipulatives, calculator use, estimation, and computers.

Problem Solving

One significant proposal has been to give more emphasis to problem solving than in the past quarter-century. According to the data collected from four National Assessments of Educational Progress in Mathematics many pupils have difficulty when solving problems beyond the routine, one-step variety.[2] It is therefore recommended that problem solving receive more emphasis in programs of the 1990s. Word problems need to be used in introducing a new operation, in developing the meanings and skills involved, in providing reinforcement, and in studying various applications of mathematics.

Grade Placement

In the past, pupils have studied all the basic addition and subtraction facts in first grade and have been introduced to addition and subtraction of multidigit numbers with and without regrouping in the second grade. We believe that regrouping should be delayed until the third grade. The National Council of Teachers of Mathematics has recommended that most work with multidigit addition and subtraction be explored and developed during the third grade.[3]

Base, Place Value, and Regrouping

Many pupils do not fully understand the concepts and language associated with our base-ten system, place-value notations, and the regrouping process. The fourth National Assessment of Mathematics found that place-value questions involving tens were answered correctly by only about two-thirds of the third-grade pupils tested. In dealing with place-value notations beyond tens, fewer than 50 percent of the pupils were successful. For addition, 84 percent of the third-grade pupils tested could add two two-digit numbers with regrouping, but only 48 percent could add four two-digit numbers. For subtraction, 70 percent could subtract a two-digit number from a two-digit number with regrouping, but only 50 percent could subtract a three-digit number from a three-digit number with regrouping.

Kouba and others concluded that part of the difficulty pupils have in dealing with multidigit numbers is their lack of under-

2. Vicky L. Kouba, et. al., "Results of the Fourth NAEP Assessment of Mathematics: Number, Operations, and Word Problems," *Arithmetic Teacher*, 35 (April 1988): 17–19.

3. *Curriculum and Evaluation Standards for School Mathematics*, Working Draft (Reston, VA: National Council of Teachers of Mathematics, 1987), p. 38.

standing of place value and its relationship to the regrouping process.[4] More attention must be given to developing an understanding of the concepts and procedures involved in dealing with multidigit numbers.

Manipulatives

For forty years much research has been reported to support the advantages of using manipulatives in the early stages to help pupils discover meanings, as discussed in Chapter 2. But the instructional materials used for helping children understand base-ten and place-value concepts have often been poorly selected and improperly used. We strongly recommend that base-ten materials and place-value devices be properly used if children are to develop a clear understanding of these important concepts.

Calculator Use

The National Council of Teachers of Mathematics has recommended that pupils use calculators when working with numbers of three digits or more. We endorse this recommendation.

Estimation

With the introduction of the calculator, an *estimate* of a reasonable answer to a word problem should be made prior to calculation. Estimation will need to receive more emphasis in programs of the 1990s, especially when operations involve multidigit numbers.

Computers

Another major innovation in the teaching and learning of elementary school mathematics is the proper use of computers.

At a meeting of the National Education Association in Washington, DC on July 5,

1989, a report was accepted by the Association that a computer should be on the desk of every elementary teacher by 1991 so that the teacher could save paper work and time by recording grades, preparing tests, writing letters to parents and the like.

The report also recommended additional computer training for teachers to be certain that they can take advantage of the computers when available.

Although the report stressed record keeping and elimination of paper work, a computer in the classroom has considerable educational potential, particularly in mathematics.

A wide variety of software programs is now available for use in exploring and practicing many different aspects of elementary mathematics. Many of these programs may be more useful for reinforcement than for introducing concepts.

Addition and Subtraction of Multidigit Numbers Without Regrouping

When pupils have learned the addition and subtraction facts to sums of 9, they can use these facts in examples involving numbers of two or more digits where regrouping is not encountered. This knowledge is based on the concept of place value. Within a place-value number system, it is possible to add or subtract the numbers named in like places in the numerals.

The teacher can use the following sequence of activities to introduce addition and subtraction of two-place numbers without regrouping. In general, examples should be presented to pupils in the following order:

(a) Addition of a one-place number to a two-place number (see higher-decade addition):

---

4. Kouba, et al., pp. 14–19.

$$
\begin{array}{r} 15 \\ +\ 2 \\ \hline \end{array}
\qquad
\begin{array}{r} 21 \\ +\ 3 \\ \hline \end{array}
\qquad
\begin{array}{r} 42 \\ +\ 4 \\ \hline \end{array}
$$

(b) Addition of two two-digit numbers that are multiples of ten:

$$
\begin{array}{r} 30 \\ +20 \\ \hline \end{array}
\qquad
\begin{array}{r} 40 \\ +30 \\ \hline \end{array}
\qquad
\begin{array}{r} 50 \\ +10 \\ \hline \end{array}
$$

(c) Addition of two two-digit numbers without renaming:

$$
\begin{array}{r} 31 \\ +24 \\ \hline \end{array}
\qquad
\begin{array}{r} 14 \\ +82 \\ \hline \end{array}
\qquad
\begin{array}{r} 40 \\ +53 \\ \hline \end{array}
$$

(d) Subtraction of a one-digit number from a two-digit number:

$$
\begin{array}{r} 26 \\ -\ 5 \\ \hline \end{array}
\qquad
\begin{array}{r} 35 \\ -\ 2 \\ \hline \end{array}
\qquad
\begin{array}{r} 44 \\ -\ 1 \\ \hline \end{array}
$$

(e) Subtraction of two two-digit numbers that are multiples of ten:

$$
\begin{array}{r} 50 \\ -20 \\ \hline \end{array}
\qquad
\begin{array}{r} 40 \\ -10 \\ \hline \end{array}
\qquad
\begin{array}{r} 60 \\ -30 \\ \hline \end{array}
$$

(f) Subtraction of two two-digit numbers without renaming:

$$
\begin{array}{r} 35 \\ -14 \\ \hline \end{array}
\qquad
\begin{array}{r} 73 \\ -32 \\ \hline \end{array}
\qquad
\begin{array}{r} 65 \\ -13 \\ \hline \end{array}
$$

In some elementary mathematics programs, addition and subtraction algorithms are presented more or less simultaneously for each level of difficulty. In this plan, the addition and subtraction examples in groups (a) and (d) would be presented simultaneously. Groups (b) and (e) would be taught together, as would (c) and (f). Some programs use the *sequential* approach of (a) through (f), as discussed briefly in the subsequent examples.

Lesson Planning for an Addition Lesson

The following is a description of a lesson designed to teach pupils the topic of adding two two-place numbers without regrouping, using base-ten materials.

I. Objectives

During and at the end of this lesson (or series of lessons) each pupil will:

1. Demonstrate the solution to word problems:
   (a) By using base-ten blocks
   (b) By showing a visual picture of base-ten drawings
   (c) By using base-ten expanded notation
   (d) By recording the numerals in standard form.

2. Name the ones place, the tens place, and the sum of each example.

3. Tell that adding numbers at the tens place involves the same basic facts as those in the ones place.

4. Show that changing the order of two numbers added does not change the sum.

II. Readiness

This lesson could be presented to first- or second-grade pupils. Because there is no regrouping involved, the facts used should be very familiar to each pupil. Pupils should have had experience working with base-ten materials and should be able to rename a two-place number such as 32 as 3 tens 2 ones and demonstrate with manipulatives. Pupils who are still learning their basic facts can also participate in this lesson, but they will use manipulatives to solve the problems given. Pupils who have a mastery of the basic facts can move quickly from manipulatives to the visual and symbolic levels of notation.

III. Motivation

A base-ten manipulative will be used for this lesson for motivation and to help pupils understand the nature of *base ten* in our system of numeration. That is, when children use sticks for counting, and they have counted ten sticks (ten ones), they should be guided to discover that these ten ones can be bundled into one set of ten and named "one ten." Likewise, when pupils collect ten bundles of ten, these can be regrouped into one set of one hundred. The understanding of these ideas is essential when pupils encounter the need for regrouping in addition and subtraction of multidigit numbers.

Perhaps the most durable type of the base-ten materials is the set of base-ten blocks made from hardwood or plastic. The "ones-block" is a centimeter cube; the "tens-block" is ten centimeter long, scored to indicate the number of units; the "hundreds-block" is made from ten "ten-blocks" made into a ten- by- ten-centimeter square. The "thousand-block" is a cube that is ten by ten by ten centimeters.

IV. Guided Discovery

START WITH A WORD PROBLEM

The addition lesson should be introduced with the need to find the answer to an addition example such as 32 + 25 = ☐ resulting from some type of social experience. For example, if Billie has 32 trading cards

A group can work with base-ten blocks.

(Photo by Leland Perry)

and John has 25, how many do they have all together (what is the sum)? Each child should have access to a set of base-ten materials, but it is not necessary for each child to have a set. When discovery experiences such as these require materials, small groups of pupils in which two to four pupils share a set of blocks can be established. After the problem is stated the teacher asks the pupils to use the base-ten materials to explore ways of finding the answer.

EXPLORE WITH BASE-TEN MATERIALS

Most pupils will easily associate 32 with 3 tens and 2 ones. With base-ten blocks, this can be represented with 3 longs (3 one-ten blocks) and 2 ones (small cubes), and 25 can be represented with 2 longs and 5 ones. Then the pupils are directed to join the two sets and are asked: "There are how many ones, and how many tens?"

PICTORIAL AND SYMBOLIC NOTATIONS

The sequence of recording what just happened is essential for enriched understanding. Most textbooks used by pupils show pictures of base-ten blocks and then the numeral in standard form. But these pictures are drawn by artists and are usually shown in color. They are nice to look at, but there is a doubt as to whether or not pictures drawn by somebody else are as valuable as pictures drawn by pupils. First, children should decide what simple picture can be drawn to represent ones and tens. For the purpose of this discussion, suppose the pupils use a dot for a one and a circle for a ten. (Later, a square can be used for a hundred.) These are simple drawings to make and they do relate to geometry. Now the pupils are asked to represent the solution to 32 + 25 = ☐ with drawings, with expanded notation, and with standard notations. A typical response is shown in Figure 8.1.

Drawings

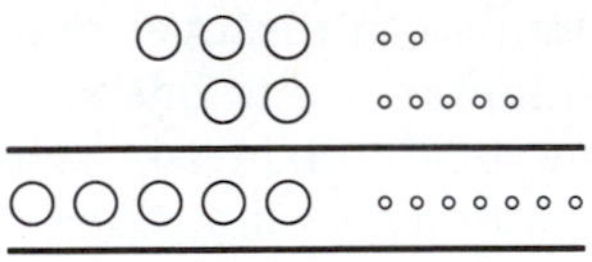

Expanded Notation

3 tens	2 ones	30 + 2
2 tens	5 ones	20 + 5
5 tens	7 ones	50 + 7
		57

Standard Form

$$
\begin{array}{r}
32 \\
+\,25 \\
\hline
57
\end{array}
$$

Figure 8.1
Various ways to find the sum of 32 + 25

CLASS DISCUSSION

The next step in the lesson should be for the teacher to lead a discussion of the major ideas involved when adding two multidigit numbers and the sum of the numbers in any place does not exceed nine.

V. Reinforcement

The children's mathematics textbook provides valuable exercises that can be used as follow-up to this lesson. Follow-up activities should also include more problems in which pupils will be asked to estimate their answer prior to calculation. Pupils should use a calculator to solve word problems involving larger numbers. Computer programs that involve adding multidigit numbers may be used for additional reinforcement and practice.

VI. Evaluation

During the lesson and at the conclusion the teacher should determine the extent to which each pupil can perform the objectives stated. This can be done through observation, by giving a pencil-and-paper quiz, or by having the pupils complete exercises in the textbook.

A Subtraction Lesson

A subtraction lesson should follow the same sequence as the addition lesson presented above. In the following description of a lesson involving subtracting a two-place number from a two-place number without regrouping, a place-value device will be used rather than base-ten materials.

I. Objectives

At the completion of this lesson (or series of lessons), each pupil should be able to:

1. Demonstrate the solution to word problems by:
  (a) Using a place-value device
  (b) Showing a visual picture with a place-value drawing
  (c) Using place-value in expanded notation
  (d) Recording the numerals in standard form.

2. Name the ones place and the tens place, the number we start with and the number to be subtracted.

3. Explain that subtracting numbers at the tens place involves the same basic facts as those in the ones place.

II. Readiness

Pupils should be ready for this lesson after they have succeeded on the addition lesson. The subtraction facts used are all "easy" subtraction facts. The new procedure involved in this lesson is working with a place-value device and with place-value drawings.

III. Guided Discovery

WORD PROBLEM

Begin with a problem that involves a "take-away" process, whereby ones are taken from ones and tens are taken from tens without regrouping. A typical problem could be: "Mary has 35 cents. She spent 14 cents at the store. How much does she have left?"

USE A PLACE-VALUE DEVICE

The pupils can solve this problem with some kind of place-value device, of which the three most useful are: (a) a counting-board abacus, (b) an 18-bead computing abacus, and (c) a place-value pocket chart. (In this lesson we will use a place-value pocket chart as shown in Figure 8.2.)

First, have the pupils represent the 35 cents on the place-value chart by placing 3 tickets in the tens place and 5 tickets in the ones place. Next, have them take away 4 ones and 1 ten. Then have them determine how many are left. This sequence is shown in Figure 8.2.

The transition from visualizing numbers with base-ten materials to their representations on a place-value device is an important step in concept learning. Representing a number on a place-value device is a more

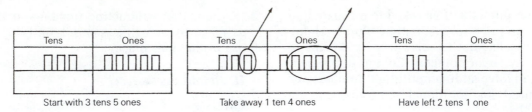

Start with 3 tens 5 ones   Take away 1 ten 4 ones   Have left 2 tens 1 one

Figure 8.2
Showing 35 − 14 on a Place-Value Chart

abstract representation of a two-place number than with base-ten materials. Three tens represented by three bundles of ten sticks each, for example, are shown on a place-value chart as three single sticks in the tens place. The position to the left of the ones place on the device gives each stick the value of one ten.

Addition of Two Two-Digit Numbers with Regrouping

One of the greatest difficulties pupils have in adding multidigit numbers is with regrouping, which is necessary when the numbers at any place in the sum *overload* that place. In the example 38 + 16 the sum in the ones place is 14 ones, as shown below in base-ten long form and in place-value form:

		Tens	Ones
3 tens	8 ones	3	8
+1 ten	6 ones	+1	6
4 tens	14 ones	4	14

To be in "standard form," the final answer to an addition example must have digits of 9 or less at each place. Consequently, the 14 ones must be renamed 1 ten 4 ones, resulting in a sum of 5 tens 4 ones, or 54.

Readiness for renaming involves:

1. A mastery of the addition facts to sums of 18.

2. Ability to regroup many single objects

into bundles of tens and ones and to regroup with other types of base-ten materials.

3. Ability to regroup on a place-value device—that is, the ability to exchange ten in the ones place for one in the tens place.

4. A well-developed understanding of and proficiency in working with two two-digit numbers without regrouping.

Review of Demonstration Lesson

A demonstration lesson illustrating the principles of teaching and learning mathematics was included at the end of Chapter 1. Since it centered on the teaching and learning of addition of multidigit numbers with regrouping, we suggest that readers review that lesson, presented on pages 11–12, before continuing with this chapter.

Summary of the Steps for Regrouping

We can summarize the steps used to develop the addition algorithm for multidigit numbers with regrouping as follows:

1. Start with a problem setting. The problem must involve numbers that, when added, will "overload" the ones place. The following is a good example: Dick delivers 25 papers on Saturday and 48 papers on Sunday. How many papers does he deliver? The pupils should be able to write one of the following addition examples for this problem:

(a) $25 + 48 = \square$ (c) $\begin{array}{r} 25 \\ +48 \\ \hline \end{array}$

(b) $48 + 25 = \square$ (d) $\begin{array}{r} 48 \\ +25 \\ \hline \end{array}$

These notations are at the most advanced symbolic level. A less abstract base-ten notation for (a) would be:

$$\begin{array}{r} 2 \text{ tens } 5 \text{ ones} \\ + \ 4 \text{ tens } 8 \text{ ones} \\ \hline \end{array}$$

The following is another way to record example (c) with a place-value grid:

Tens	Ones
2	5
+4	8

This type of notation can be developed by working with a place-value device.

2. Have pupils solve the problem at the concrete level by using base-ten materials. The desired result of this activity is for the pupils to discover the need to regroup the 13 ones as 1 ten 3 ones. From their experience with base-ten materials pupils can generalize that "ten ones can be regrouped into one ten." This concept can be shown by exchanging ten pennies for one dime, ten cubes for one long, or ten single sticks for one bundle of ten. Although various types of materials can be used, only one type should be used in each presentation.

3. Have the pupils write in long form the numerals for the addition example illustrated by the base-ten materials.

4. Discuss with the pupils the standard algorithm for writing the problem in (b). Ask them to use the standard form to solve the problem. If necessary, refer again to base-ten materials to clarify the operation.

(a) $\begin{array}{r} \overset{1}{2}5 \\ +48 \\ \hline 73 \end{array}$ (b) $\begin{array}{r} 25 \\ +48 \\ \hline 73 \end{array}$

Three-Place Addends

When teaching addition involving renaming, deal first with two-place addends, then with three-place addends in which an overloaded place occurs: (a) in the ones place only, (b) in the tens place only, (c) in both the ones place and the tens place, (d) in the hundreds place only, (e) in two or more places, and (f) in each place given.

(a) $\begin{array}{r} 248 \\ +327 \\ \hline \end{array}$ (b) $\begin{array}{r} 482 \\ +256 \\ \hline \end{array}$ (c) $\begin{array}{r} 567 \\ +384 \\ \hline \end{array}$

(d) $\begin{array}{r} 824 \\ +632 \\ \hline \end{array}$ (e) $\begin{array}{r} 869 \\ +356 \\ \hline \end{array}$ (f) $\begin{array}{r} 487 \\ +635 \\ \hline \end{array}$

By the time pupils are ready to work three-place addends with renaming in one or more places, they should be able to operate entirely at the symbolic level.

The major value of working with three-place addends with and without regrouping is to discover how to deal with an overloaded place in a sum regardless of the number of digits in the addends.

Use a calculator for adding larger numbers.

Higher-Decade Addition

Higher-decade addition involves finding the sum of a one-place number and a two-place number in one mental process. This kind of adding may not involve bridging the decades, as in $15 + 3$—or it may bridge the decade, as in $15 + 7$. We shall first discuss the nonbridging type.

Without Bridging the Decade

The most logical and easiest procedure to follow when the sum is in the same decade as the two-digit number is to "think forward" and find the sum in one mental response. A pupil performs higher-decade addition without bridging the decade if the thought pattern is "15 + 3 = 18." If the ones-place number has a sum less than 10, the answer can be found by proceeding forward from the tens place to the ones place. Here are some examples of higher-decade addition without bridging:

(a) 13   (b) 21   (c) 34   (d) 53   (e) 65
　　+ 4　　　+ 8　　　+ 3　　　+ 5　　　+ 2

Bridging the Decade

In some higher-decade addition examples the sum of the pair of ones-place numbers is ten or more. The first step in higher-decade addition is to determine if the sum of the numbers in the ones place is less than 10 or 10 or more. If the sum is less than 10, the sum does not bridge the decade. On the other hand, if one determines at a glance that the sum of the ones-place numbers is 10 or more, rename the tens-place number to the next decade and think the "ending" of the sum of the ones-place digits. This is the reason this technique is sometimes called adding by endings. The following are examples of higher-decade addition where bridging the decade occurs:

(a) 26   (b) 35   (c) 48   (d) 59   (e) 67
　　+ 6　　　+ 8　　　+ 7　　　+ 5　　　+ 4

Higher-Decade in Column Addition

Higher-decade addition can occur at any point in a column of digits where a subsum is a two-digit number, as in this example:

4
8
7
9

The thinking involved in adding this column is:

1. The first pair of numbers is a basic fact: 4 + 8 = 12

2. The 12 can be recorded in the column below the 8.

3. The next step is to add 12 + 7, higher decade, without bridging,

4. The 19 can be recorded in the column below the 7.

5. In an instant one thinks that the sum of the ones-place numbers is ten or more, so bridge the decade to 20 and then think 8, the "ending" of the basic fact 9 + 9.

In the column below, the subsums are verbalized in sequence downward as: "Twelve, seventeen, twenty-four, thirty-two."

3
9
5
7
8

Higher-Decade Addition in Multiplication

Higher-decade addition is encountered in multiplication in examples such as:

64
× 8

After multiplying 8 × 4, the 2 is recorded in the ones place and the 3 tens above the 6 tens. The next multiplication is 8 × 6 tens = 48 tens plus 3 tens. This involves higher-decade addition with bridging.

Higher-decade addition is a less important topic today than it was before the use of calculators became widespread. Although mental addition of long columns of numbers is rare these days, this skill will assist children in learning multiplication and division.

Examples (f) through (h) show that a two-digit number ending in 6, when added to 5, always ends in 1, but in the next higher decade. Children should practice this form of addition on examples in which the sum is less than 50:

(f)   16   (g)   26   (h)   36
    + 5   + 5   + 5

1. Have pupils give the sums when the examples are written:

(a) In sequence in vertical form:

12   22   32
+3   +3   +3

The number pair 2 + 3 is the key fact in each example in the set.

(b) In sequence in equation form:

$12 + 3 = \square$ $22 + 3 = \square$
$32 + 3 = \square$ $42 + 3 = \square$

(c) Out of sequence, using the same key facts:

$12 + 3 = \square$ $32 + 3 = \square$
$22 + 3 = \square$ $42 + 3 = \square$

(d) Out of sequence, using different key facts:

$11 + 4 = \square$ $13 + 5 = \square$
$25 + 2 = \square$ $33 + 3 = \square$

(e) On a number line and bridging the decade, as shown in Figure 8.3:

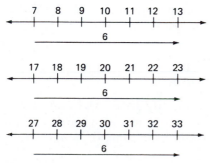

Figure 8.3

2. The following type of exercise helps pupils learn to bridge the decade:

$8 + 4 = 10 + \square$ $6 + 7 = \square + 3$
$18 + 4 = 20 + \square$ $16 + 7 = \square + 3$
$28 + 4 = 30 + \square$ $26 + 7 = \square + 3$

3. Creating tables is an effective way to practice adding by endings. For example, the sum in Table (a) does not bridge the decade but it does in Table (b):

(a)

+	12	22	32
3			
7			
4			

(b)

+	17	27	37
4			
5			
7			

4. A short oral exercise in which the class deals with dictated numbers is recommended. The teacher writes a numeral, such as 4, on the chalkboard and dictates numbers, such as 12, 28, or 35. The two-place numeral is unseen; hence the pupil must think this number and add it to the visible number 4. The exercise can be varied so that all numerals are unseen. The pupil is directed to add a ones-place number, such as 6, to each number dictated.

Practicing Higher-Decade Addition in Column Addition

When children first begin to use higher-decade addition in columns, the exercises should be limited to three addends with the sum of the first two ranging from 10 to 18. Write exercises in the fashion shown here and leave a space between the second and third addends (downward) for pupils to write the two-digit subsum of the first two addends, if needed. In the following sequence it is recommended that the pupil enter partial sums in the parentheses.

1. No bridging:

8	7	5	9
9	8	6	5
(17)	( )	( )	( )
2	3	4	5
19			

2. Bridging in each example:

7	8	7	5
8	9	6	9
(15)	( )	( )	( )
6	5	8	9
21			

3. Mixed examples, with some bridging and some not bridging.

7	8	9	8	8
6	8	6	3	5
(13)	( )	( )	( )	( )
3	7	6	3	8
16				

The first example in each group above can be solved with the suggested notations. Pupils should practice working other similar examples.

After pupils become proficient in adding a column of three addends with and without bridging and understand the process, they can practice with four addends. Let the children write the subsums until they are no longer needed.

Mastery Level of Higher-Decade Addition

At the mastery level, pupils are able to add a column downward by *thinking* each subsum (forward) and without writing the subsums. Mastery is shown in the solution of the following example:

6	The pupil should think the follow-
8	ing subsums: "Fourteen, twenty-
7	one, twenty-five, thirty-four."
4	
9	
34	

This approach is called the "direct method" of adding a column. The sum can be checked by adding the column upward and thinking: "Thirteen, twenty, twenty-eight, thirty-four."

We recommend that column addition be taught first with the direct method. Later, you can use a search-for pattern as an alternative approach. Alternative approaches are presented at the end of this chapter.

Multidigit Subtraction with Regrouping

Young children have long had difficulty in subtracting multidigit numbers when regrouping is required. The fourth National Assessment of Educational Progress in Mathematics found only 70 percent could subtract a two-digit number from a two-digit number with renaming required in the ones-place, such as:

$$\begin{array}{r} 6\,4 \\ -3\,7 \\ \hline \end{array}$$

When renaming was required at both the ones-place and the tens-place in multidigit numbers, only 50 percent of the third-grade pupils tested answered correctly.[5]

The Difficulty

The difficulty arises when the minuend in the subtraction fact at a particular place is less than the subtrahend, as in the following example:

5. Kouba et. al., p. 15.

```
  862
- 328
```

In the ones place there is a *column impasse*, because 2 − 8 has *no answer* in the set of whole numbers. When subtracting multidigit numbers, pupils must be able to recognize a column impasse, or else they will arrive at incorrect answers.

Manipulatives Needed

The sequence for teaching subtraction of two two-digit numbers that require regrouping is similar to the sequence for subtracting multidigit numbers without regrouping, except the new difficulty is there are not enough ones in the ones place of the minuend. The process is to regroup the minuend by changing a ten into ten ones.

Textbook writers generally show pictures of base-ten materials much more frequently than they recommend and show place-value devices. Place-value devices represent a more abstract representation of number and the regrouping process than base-ten materials do, but for full understanding of addition and subtraction of multidigit numbers with and without regrouping, place-value devices are strongly recommended.

Proper use of the place-value chart demands that one stick in the tens place represents 1 ten. To show regrouping, the teacher should take one stick from the tens place and put 10 sticks in the ones place, saying that one stick in the tens place represents 10 sticks in the ones place.

Two Approaches

How do pupils deal with a column impasse? When pupils cannot solve a problem, such as 2 − 8, they must ask themselves, "What can be done to make subtraction at the ones place possible?"

There are two basic approaches to over-come a column impasse in multidigit subtraction. These are (1) the *decomposition method* and (2) the *equal-addition approach*.

In the past, research has generally favored the decomposition method, which is easily understood.

The Decomposition Method

In the decomposition method, the minuend is renamed so that there is a basic subtraction fact at each place in the example.

1. Begin with a "take-away" problem having a column impasse in the ones place.

> Matthew has 3 dimes and 2 pennies. He goes to the store to buy a new metric ruler. The price of the ruler is 16¢. The sign on the cash register says MUST USE EXACT CHANGE. Matthew needs 1 dime and 6 pennies. What will Matthew have to do before he can buy the ruler?

Pupils might suggest the simple solution that Matthew *change* one of his dimes into 10 pennies. This solution gets at the heart of regrouping in subtraction, which is if more ones are needed, the logical solution would be to regroup one of the tens in the tens place as 10 ones. Pupils have little trouble seeing that 1 dime = 10 pennies and that 1 ten = 10 ones.

2. Have pupils explore regrouping 1 ten to 10 ones with dimes and pennies (real or models). See Figure 8.4, page 150.

(a) Start with 3 dimes 2 pennies.

(b) Change 1 dime to 10 pennies.

(c) Now name the coins as 2 dimes 12 pennies.

3. Using the long form of base-ten notation, provide practice exercises that involve renaming (that is, rename 1 ten to 10 ones). Ask pupils to show their work.

(a) 3 tens   4 ones =   2 tens   ___ ones

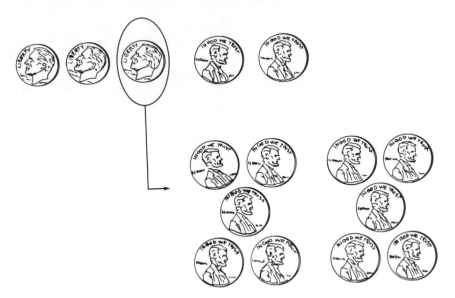

Figure 8.4

(b) 4 tens   2 ones = ___ tens   12 ones

(c) 5 tens   5 ones =   4 ___   ___ ones

4. Give pupils a practice sheet with several subtraction examples involving two two-digit numbers. Have some of the examples require no regrouping and some examples require regrouping as a first step in the solution. Ask the pupils to mark the examples in which the minuend must be regrouped before subtracting. Ask the pupils to give their reasons for marking the examples they thought would need to be regrouped.

5. Give pupils several word problems to solve by using base-ten materials. Have them draw pictures of their solutions. Make a record of the solution with expanded notation. For example, give them the following problem:

> A second-grade class grew 74 carrots in their garden. They pulled 26 carrots for a school party. How many carrots were left in the garden? Have the children use base-ten or place-value materials to solve the problem; then draw the picture and record the notations.

6. Have the pupils study the presentation of this topic in their textbooks. Recent textbooks use a variety of pictures and notations to illustrate the process of regrouping and subtracting.

7. Give pupils practice exercises at the symbolic level, requiring both expanded notation and standard algorithm form.

After pupils understand how to regroup 1 ten to 10 ones with manipulative materials and can use this procedure to solve multi-digit subtraction with and without regrouping, they can be expected to work at the symbolic level without using manipulative materials. Table 8.1 illustrates the symbolic level of subtraction with regrouping.

Multiple Regrouping in Subtraction

After the pupils understand how to rename 1 ten to 10 ones and have had symbolic-level practice in regrouping for more ones, give them problems that require regrouping at the tens place, as in the examples:

$$\begin{array}{r} 825 \\ -362 \end{array} \qquad \begin{array}{r} 528 \\ -365 \end{array} \qquad \begin{array}{r} 614 \\ -261 \end{array}$$

Table 8.1 Subtraction with Regrouping at Symbolic Level

Example	Expanded Form Tens Ones	Tens Ones	Developmental Algorithm	Standard Algorithm
			6 (14)	
74 = 7 4	=	6 14	7 4	74
−26 = −2 6	=	−2 6	−2 6	−26
		4 8	4 8	48

Special attention needs to be paid to examples involving zero in the tens place in the minuend, as in the example:

302
−186

Tens	Ones
⌐29	12⌐
⌊30	2⌋
−18	6

More ones are needed at the ones place, but there are zero tens. What can be done? The 3 hundreds can be viewed as 30 tens; after one of the 30 tens is changed to 10 ones, 29 tens are left in the minuend. Now we can subtract.

The thought pattern to subtract in the above example by the decomposition method is "6 from 12 = 6; 8 from 9 = 1; 1 from 2 = 1."

Checks for Addition and Subtraction

Children should be taught effective ways to check addition:

1. Find the sum by adding in the opposite direction.

2. If there are more than five or six addends, form two examples and find the sum of each. Then add the two sums.

3. Use a calculator.

Effective checks for subtraction are:

4. Add the difference and the subtrahend.

This sum must equal the minuend. If $a - b = c$, then $a = b + c$.

5. Subtract the difference from the minuend to find the subtrahend, such that $a - c = b$.

6. Use a calculator.

Alternative Approaches to Addition

Fast learners often discover other ways to perform the basic operations. This practice should be encouraged. In this section we give examples showing alternative approaches that can be used for enrichment.

After pupils have mastered addition of two two-place numbers with and without regrouping the sum, alternative approaches to addition can be introduced.

238
+ 95
200
120
+ 13
333

This algorithm is designed to strengthen the understanding of place value and build a readiness for a better understanding of the renaming step in the standard algorithm.

The sum of two addends is found by writing 200; adding 30 and 90; adding 8 and 5.

Another alternative approach to adding two or more numbers is to rename the addends so as not to change the sum. This can be done by the property of *compensation for addition*: when a number is added to or subtracted from one of the addends, the sum will not change as long as the opposite operation is performed on a second addend, as illustrated in the following example:

$$
\begin{array}{rl}
36 & +4 = \\
+44 & -4 = \\
\hline
\end{array}
\qquad
\begin{array}{r}
40 \\
40 \\
\hline
80
\end{array}
$$

$$
\begin{array}{rl}
82 & -2 = \\
+96 & +2 = \\
\hline
\end{array}
\qquad
\begin{array}{r}
80 \\
98 \\
\hline
178
\end{array}
$$

Alternative Approaches to Subtraction with Regrouping

After pupils have developed a meaningful understanding of the *decomposition method* of adjusting a column impasse, the teacher can introduce other alternative techniques. One of the alternatives, described here, is based on the mathematical property of *compensation for subtraction*—that is, the same number can be added to both the minuend and the subtrahend without changing the difference. This technique is commonly referred to as the *equal additions* or the *equal addends* approach. The meaning of this method is best demonstrated with a comparison-type subtraction problem, in which two numbers or measures are compared to determine the difference. The idea is that if both lengths are increased by the same measure, the difference would remain the same.

```
 8 cm ┐            18 cm ┐
-5 cm ┘           -15 cm ┘

 3 cm              3 cm
```

If we started with a problem requiring regrouping, would adding 10 to both the minuend and subtrahend take care of the column impasse? In the following example there is still a column impasse, even after adding 10 to both numbers. How does the property of compensation help?

$$
\begin{array}{rl}
62 & = 60 + 2 \\
-46 & = 40 + 6
\end{array}
\;\rightarrow\;
\begin{array}{r}
60 + 12 \\
50 + 6 \\
\hline
10 + 6 = 16
\end{array}
$$

In the example above, 10 is added to the minuend in the form of *10 ones* and to the subtrahend in the form of *1 ten!* When this technique is applied to the example, the minuend and subtrahend both increase in value by 10. However, the minuend becomes 6 tens 12 ones, and the subtrahend becomes 5 tens 6 ones, a shift that eliminates the column impasse without changing the difference. The thought pattern to subtract in the example below by the equal additions method is "7 from 13 = 6; 4 from 10 = 6; 5 from 8 = 3."

$$
\begin{array}{r}
803 \\
-437 \\
\end{array}
\qquad
\begin{array}{r}
8\overset{10}{0}\overset{13}{3} \\
-4\,37 \\
\hline
5\,4
\end{array}
$$

Calculator Activities

The calculator is of limited use for a pupil in the early stage of learning the addition algorithm. A young pupil may make as many errors by pressing incorrect keys on a calculator as in using the standard algorithm for addition using paper and pencil. A good guide after the basic facts are learned is, using mental arithmetic when possible, estimate, compute, use the calculator to check.

A useful game for two pupils with one calculator proceeds as follows:

1. The first player enters a number from 1 through 5 and hands the calculator to the second player.

2. The second player adds a number from 1 through 5 and hands the calculator back to the first player.

3. The first player adds a number from 1 through 5 and hands the calculator to the second player.

This continues until a player reaches the goal of 31 to win the game. The game offers an excellent opportunity to analyze the process for a winning strategy. A starting point is to recognize that a pupil who obtains a sum of 25 can win. The next step is to discover that a pupil who obtains a sum of 19 can get to 25 and so on. This leads to a winning strategy of starting with 1 and successively reaching sums of 7, 13, 19, 25, and 31.

The game can be altered by choosing any goal, such as 100, and using any range, such as 1–10. Each new game requires a new analysis and a different strategy. It is possible to choose a goal and range so that the second player can find a strategy that will always win. However, the 31 game is ideal for a beginning and many pupils will play the game without the calculator, providing useful mental activity.

An interesting class activity can be for the teacher to play the class and write the totals on the chalkboard. The teacher should avoid the numbers in the winning sequence in early stages and challenge the class to find the winning strategy.

The following illustrates a fundamental multiplication–division relation and an interesting number property. Ask the pupils to:

1. Enter any three-digit number in the calculator, multiply by 1000, and add the original number to that product;

2. Divide this sum by 91;

3. Divide the number in the calculator by 11 to get the original number.

If an entire class participates, it is impressive for the teacher to take a calculator from several pupils after step 2 and obtain the original number in each case by dividing by 11. Pupils should be challenged to discover how this is done. Multiplying a number by 1000 and adding the number is equivalent

to multiplying the original number by 1001. Dividing by 91 and then by 11 is equivalent to the single division by 91×11, or 1001. Therefore the procedure multiplies the number by 1001 and then, in an indirect way, divides it by 1001. Vary the procedure: Have the pupil divide by 77 in place of 91 and then divide by 13 or divide by 143 and then divide by 7.

A little-known variation on an old trick is to have pupils enter their favorite nonzero digit on the calculator and multiply it by 333667. Use the calculator and multiply by 333. If the pupil has entered 7, the calculator will now display 777777777, and so on. The original trick asks the pupil to multiply by 9×12345679 to get the nine-digit display of the favorite digit. The variation suggested here relies on the fact that $12345679 = 37 \times 333667$ and that $9 \times 37 = 333$.

One pair of factors for 11111111 is 10001*1111 and 1111 factors into 11×101. Ask pupils to enter any number and multiply by 11111111 and divide this entry successively by 10001 and 11. Use the calculator and divide by 101 to obtain the original number.

Mental Arithmetic and Estimation

Estimation and mental arithmetic are now recognized as essential skills in this age of calculators and computers. Estimation is most useful when it is done mentally but can be of value when done with paper and pencil.

Estimation is useful because it can.:

1. Verify the position of the decimal point and detect other large errors when computing with decimals.

2. Detect malfunctions in calculators and computers as well as errors of entry due to accidentally pressing an incorrect key.

3. Encourage the development of number sense and mental arithmetic.

4. Allow one to make purchasing and other decisions without pencil and paper or computing equipment.

5. Increase the speed of computation. A mental operation is many times as fast as one done with paper and pencil. Paper-and-pencil estimation can be faster than the corresponding standard algorithm.

The computer has no peer in providing activities that will help an individual acquire skill in mental arithmetic and estimation.

The computer can provide random numbers in a program and provide an unlimited number of exercises on any given level. Textbooks have an obvious limit for the number of exercises they can provide for any topic.

A motivated pupil can get more useful practice in several minutes using a computer than can be obtained in much more time with the use of printed material. A few minutes a day can develop a substantial increase in efficiency.

The ability to master basic facts in the four operations has always been a major educational goal. One cannot compute efficiently without reasonable mastery of the basic facts.

Estimation for Addition

Estimation is usually performed with numbers rounded to one significant digit. Thus, 12343 rounds to 10000 and 486 rounds to 500. It may sometimes be useful to round to two significant digits so that 12343 rounds to 12000 and 486 rounds to 490.

Rounding to a single nonzero digit usually provides reasonable accuracy for most estimation in addition and subtraction. For ease of execution and speed, it is probably best to round up and down alternately with-

out following the traditional rounding pattern. No one method of estimation is always the most accurate.

Program PE8.1 asks for a choice of the number of addends. When the choice is made, the computer displays a column of four-digit numbers with the number of addends requested. A carriage return without a keyboard entry allows for the check of a mental estimate on some computers.

The advantage of typing the estimate is that the computer will display the error and percent error in addition to the correct answer.

```
PE8.1
  10 HOME : VTAB 4
  20 INPUT "ENTER NUMBER OF
     ADDENDS ";N1
  30 FOR J = 1 TO N1
  40 N = 1000 + INT(9000 *
     RND(1))
  50 PRINT TAB(17) N
  60 S = S + N
  70 NEXT J
  80 PRINT
  90 INPUT "ENTER ESTIMATE";
     E
 100 PRINT "CORRECT AN-
     SWER  "; S
 110 ER = ABS(E - S)
 120 PRINT
 130 PRINT "ERROR = ";ER
 140 PRINT
 150 PRINT "%ERROR = ";
     INT(1000 * ER/S +
     .5)/10;"%"
```

Example A represents an initial output for Program PE8.1.

```
                         9123
                         5474
Example A                1997
                         1321
                         7810
                      +  4848
                        ─────
                        30573
```

Estimating with traditional rounding gives :
$9 + 5 + 2 + 1 + 8 + 5 = 30$, leading to
an estimate of 30000, with an error less than
2 percent.

Alternate rounding can be done efficiently by adding the first digits of each of
the addends with no rounding and then
adding one-half the number of addends to
the total of the first digits. This procedure is
equivalent to rounding up for every other
addend. For Example A, this method of alternate rounding leads to $9 + 5 + 1 + 1 + 7 + 4 + \underline{3} = 30$, giving an estimate of
30000.

The two methods often give slightly different results, but both usually give acceptable estimates.

Estimation for Subtraction

Program PE8.2 provides displays of four-digit subtraction examples for estimation or
practice with subtraction. The computer
displays the correct answer, the error and
percent error. When a carriage return is
pressed without a keyboard entry, the answer will be displayed but, as with PE8.1,
without a keyboard entry, evaluation of the
estimate is not possible. Rounding to two
digits usually gives a very good estimate for
subtraction.

```
PROGRAM PE8.2
  10 HOME : VTAB 8
  20 PRINT "ESTIMATE THE
     FOLLOWING SUBTRACTION: "
  30 PRINT: PRINT
  40 A = 1000 + INT(9000 *
     RND(1))
  50 B = 1000 + INT(9000 *
     RND(1))
  60 IF A - B < 1000 THEN 40
  70 PRINT TAB(16)A
  80 PRINT TAB(16)B
  90 INPUT " ENTER ESTIMATE
     "; E
 100 PRINT " CORRECT ANSWER";
     A - B
```

```
 110 ER = ABS(E - (A- B))
 120 PRINT
 130 PRINT "ERROR = "; ER
 140 S = A - B
 150 PRINT "%ERROR = ";
     INT(1000 * ER/S + .5)/
     10;"%"
```

Problem Solving

Traditional textbook problems almost always have just the right amount of information necessary for a solution. Real-life
problems may have too much or not
enough. Educators have recommended that
pupils encounter problems with too much
or not enough information.

The following includes problems with too
much, not enough, or just the right amount
of information. Label each one T, N, or R for
too much, not enough, and just right, respectively. If there is too much information,
tell what can be omitted. If there is not
enough information, tell what is needed.

1. Jose bought two pairs of socks. What is
the total cost?

2. Sue bought a blouse, a pair of jeans,
and a comb. If the cost of the blouse is $8
and the jeans cost $20, how much more did
the blouse cost than the comb?

3. Carmella worked 3 hours, 4 hours, and
5 hours on successive days in the first week
and 4 hours on each of 5 days in the second
week. If she earns $5 an hour, on which day
in the second week did she earn the most?

4. Sue has 5 fewer records than Kim.
How many records does Kim have?

5. Georgia has $3 less than Karen. How
much does Georgia have if Karen has $20?

6. Tom is 3 inches taller than Gina. How
much shorter is Gina than Tom?

Answers: 1. N, cost per pair of socks; 2.
N, cost of comb; 3. T, First-week informa-

tion, Jan earned the same amount each day.
4. N, number of Sue's records. 5; R, George
has $17; 6. R, Gina is 3 inches shorter than
Tom.

Write an equation for each of the following. Let N represent the number that is
wanted.

7. Zula's book cost $5 more than June's
book. June's book cost $7. What is the cost
of Zula's book?

8. Sam's book cost $5 more than Ella's
book. Sam's book cost $7. What is the cost
of Ella's book?

9. Dom buys a book for $4, a pen for $1,
and a notebook for $2. How much did he
have left if he started with $10?

Answers: 7. $N = 5 + 7$; 8. $N + 5 = 7$; 9.
$N = 10 - 4 - 1 - 2 = 3$.

The following procedure allows practice
in addition and estimation of addition without a computer. There are two patterns to
discover.

10. Discover how each number is determined after the initial pair is chosen.

11. Discover a short cut for finding the
sum.

1	3	2	5
2	5	1	3
3	8	3	8
5	13	4	11
8	21	7	19
13	34	11	30
Sum: 32	84	28	76

Answers—10: Each number after the first
arbitrary pair is the sum of the previous two
numbers in the column. 11. The sum is always four times the fifth number in the column.

A pupil can start with any two small
numbers, equal or unequal, and write four
additional addends by following the pattern. An estimate can then be checked by
multiplying the fifth addend by 4. The size
of the addends is controlled by the size of
the first two digits.

12. What is the smallest sum possible with
this procedure allowing the use of zero? not
allowing the use of zero?

Answer: $0 + 1 + 1 + 2 + 3 + 5 = 12$.
$1 + 1 + 2 + 3 + 5 + 8 = 20$

13. Construct an example with this pattern that uses only even numbers.

Answer: $0 + 2 + 2 + 4 + 6 + 10 = 24$

14. Is it possible to construct an example
with this pattern that uses only odd numbers?

Answer: No, because the sum of two odd
numbers is even, so it would be impossible
to have six consecutive odd numbers with
this pattern.

Enrichment

Write and solve the equation for the following problem.

15. Gene had a goal of G dollars for three
days' work cutting grass. The first day he
earned $3 more than his goal, the second
day $5 less than his goal, and on the third
day he earned $8 less than his goal. The total earning for the three days was $20 more
than his goal. What was the number of dollars for his goal?

Plan: Write the equation in words:
Goal plus 3 plus Goal minus 5 plus Goal
minus 8 equals Goal plus 20.

$G + 20 = G + 3 + G - 5 + G - 8$

This is an easy equation to solve for a pupil at a higher grade level but cannot be
done by most pupils in the middle grades.
It is accessible with a guess-and-test approach and a calculator. The computation is
not difficult without a calculator, but a calculator minimizes the drudgery for most pupils.

What is the smallest possible goal that
makes sense?

Answer: $9. The problem implies that
Gene earned something every day. A goal of
less than $9 would imply no earning or a
loss for that day.

Make a table as follows and start with a guess of $10:

GOAL   TOTAL(GOAL + 20)
  10   30
  20   40
TOTAL(G + 3 + G − 5 + G − 8)
   10 + 3 + 10 − 5 + 10 − 8 = 20
   20 + 3 + 20 − 5 + 20 − 8 = 50

Answer by guess and test: The guess of 10 and of 20 indicate that the goal is between the two. Common sense would dictate starting in the middle. A guess of 15 gives the same value for G + 20 and G + 3 + G − 5 + G − 8, indicating that the goal for three days was $15 and the total amount earned was $35.

Now enter the following in a computer and observe the simplicity of the guess-and-test solution with a FOR-NEXT loop:

```
10 FOR G = 10 TO 20
20 PRINT G, G+20,
   G+3 + G-5 + G - 8
30 NEXT G
RUN
10          30          20
11          31          23
12          32          26
. . . . . . . . . . . . . . . . . . . . . .
15          35          35
. . . . . . . . . . . . . . . . . . . . . .
20          40          50
```

The three columns are identical with the paper-and-pencil guess-and-test solutions, but the answer is obtained almost immediately when the program is run. The numbers in this example were carefully chosen for illustrative purposes. The solution for complex algebraic expressions would make guess and test impractical without the computer. Guess and test is a powerful tool for problem solving with the computer.

16. Find the number such that if 91 is added to it, the sum is 8 times the original number.

Use the computer to guess and test:

```
10 FOR N = 1 TO 20
20 PRINT N, N + 91, 8*N
30 NEXT N
RUN
1              92              8
. . . . . . . . . . . . . . . . . . . . . .
13            104            104
. . . . . . . . . . . . . . . . . . . . . .
20            111            160
```
The number is 13: 13 + 91 = 8 * 13 = 104

Summary

Developmental algorithms often are written differently from the standard algorithm because their purpose is different. Developmental algorithms are used to build a child's understanding of the operation, whereas the standard form is gradually taught after such an understanding has been developed.

Aids such as base-ten materials and place-value charts are valuable in demonstrating to children the operations of addition and subtraction. Place-value materials are usually introduced after base-ten materials, because they represent a number more abstractly.

Addition and subtraction without regrouping should be taught before addition and subtraction with regrouping. Texts differ on the specific sequence for each and also as to whether addition and subtraction algorithms should be presented simultaneously. A good technique is to introduce the algorithm with a story as the problem situation. Have the children use concrete materials to demonstrate how they would go about solving the problem in the story and have them write the corresponding algorithms as they work.

Teachers must keep in mind that before children can be expected to operate on numbers at a symbolic level they will need much practice with concrete materials and developmental algorithms. Some children will learn faster than others. Teachers will need to adjust their techniques to meet the needs of each child.

Children should be taught to add downward in column addition and to check their work by adding in the opposite direction. They should be taught to check subtraction by adding the difference to the subtrahend, so that the sum equals the minuend. Students should learn to use a calculator to check both addition and subtraction. Computer programs provide excellent activities for practice, estimation, and enrichment.

Exercise 8.1

1. Discuss the concept of place value as it relates to teaching addition and subtraction algorithms.

2. Design a sequence of activities for developing the algorithm for the addition of multidigit numbers without regrouping.

3. Design a sequence of activities for developing the algorithm for the subtraction of multidigit numbers without regrouping.

4. Complete a sequence of activities, for both addition and subtraction, in which regrouping is necessary.

5. Prepare a talk on the readiness activities for addition and subtraction. Indicate the nature of readiness and how it is achieved.

6. Distinguish between checking an answer for accuracy and checking for reasonableness.

7. Give the relevant thought pattern for, discuss, and solve each of the following problems.
   a. Sandra gave the clerk $1.00 for a glass of orange juice and received 55¢ in change. What did the orange juice cost?
   b. Each weekend Jane delivers 25 papers on Saturday and 42 papers on Sunday. How many papers does she deliver each weekend?
   c. The larger of two numbers is 54, and their difference is 15. What is the smaller number?
   d. The sum of the measure of three sides of a triangle is 56 centimeters. The length of one side is 21 cm and the length of another side is 18 cm. What is the length of the third side?

8. Give the thought pattern to subtract in the example below by the decomposition method; by the equal additions method.

$$\begin{array}{r} 5002 \\ -1309 \\ \hline \end{array}$$

Selected Readings

Cruikshank, Douglas E., and Linda Jensen Sheffield. *Teaching Mathematics to Elementary School Children: A Foundation for the Future.* Columbus, OH: Merrill, 1988. Chapter 4.

Heddens, James W., and William R. Speer. *Today's Mathematics*, 6th ed. Chicago; Science Research Associates, 1988. Unit 6.

Kennedy, Leonard M., and Steve Tipps. *Guiding Children's Learning of Mathematics*, 5th ed. Belmont, CA: Wadsworth, 1988. Chapter 9.

Marks, John L., Arthur A. Hiatt, and Evelyn M. Neufeld. *Teaching Elementary School Mathematics for Understanding*. New York: McGraw-Hill, 1985. Chapter 4.

Reys, Robert E., Marilyn N. Suydam, and Mary M. Lindquist. *Helping Children Learn Mathematics*, 2nd ed. Englewood Cliffs, NJ: Prentice-Hall, 1989. Chapter 9.

Suydam, Marilyn N., and Robert E. Reys (eds.). *Developing Computational Skills*, 1978 Yearbook. Reston, VA: National Council of Teachers of Mathematics, 1978. Chapter 5.

Post, Thomas R. (ed.). *Teaching Mathematics in Grades K–8: Research-Based Methods*. Needham Heights, MA: Allyn & Bacon, 1988. Chapter 5.

Discovering Meanings For Multiplication and Division Facts

ACHIEVEMENT GOALS

After studying this chapter, you should be able to:

1. Identify the sequence in which basic multiplication and division facts are learned.

2. Describe different kinds of multiplication situations.

3. Illustrate the differences between measurement and partitive division situations.

4. Show children how to use manipulatives to solve multiplication and division problems.

5. Use drawings to demonstrate solutions to multiplication and division problems.

6. Discuss ways to bridge the gap from using objects to notation.

7. Illustrate the commutative, distributive, and associative properties for multiplication.

8. Summarize ways to help pupils master basic multiplication and division facts.

9. Explain how to make division with remainders meaningful to pupils.

10. Write different kinds of verbal problems involving multiplication and division situations and show how each could be solved (a) with objects, (b) with drawings, and (c) with numbers.

11. Demonstrate the use of calculators and computer programs in helping children master multiplication and division facts.

VOCABULARY

These terms are defined or illustrated in the Glossary.

Array
Associative
  property
Commutative
  property
Distributive
  property
Factor
Identity

Inverse operation
Measurement
  division
Partition division
Quotient
Rational numbers
Remainder
Sequence

Learning to perform the operations of multiplication and division is an important goal of mathematics in the elementary school. Mastery of these operations, however, must be viewed as more than instant recall of basic facts and memorized algorithms. Mastery must include an understanding of these operations, how they are related to other operations, and patterns and properties. Classroom instruction must focus on problem-solving and reasoning skills. More attention must be given to discovering mathematical concepts and in using multiplication and division in practical applications than in many conventional programs in the past. Time spent on drill and practice activities should follow guided discovery and should continue until the pupil can give a habitual response to any given fact.

Relationships Among the Fundamental Operations

The four fundamental operations are related to one another. Addition describes the process of joining two or more collections. When two or more groups are equal in number, the joining process can also be described by multiplication. For example, the addition fact $6 + 6 = 12$ can be renamed as the multiplication fact $2 \times 6 = 12$. Subtraction describes the process of separating a collection into two parts. The process of separating a group of things into two or more smaller groups equal in number can also be described by division. Division can be performed by successive subtraction. The example $18 \div 6$ can be solved by subtracting 6 from 18 three times.

Grade Placement

The grade placement and sequence for teaching the basic facts in multiplication and division that follows is recommended by the National Council of Teachers of Mathematics.[1]

Easy Facts

Grades K – 1: Provide experiences with objects in problem situations.

Grade 2: Develop an understanding of the operations and ways to answer fact problems.

Grade 3: Practice the facts for recall within three seconds.

Hard Facts

Grade 2: Explore by using objects in problem situations.

Grade 3: Develop an understanding of the operations and strategies for finding answers to problems.

Grade 4: Practice the facts for recall of each within three seconds.

The National Council recommends a time limit of three seconds for a pupil to give the answer to a number pair in multiplication for grades 3 and 4. It is difficult to give a specific time limit for a number pair, but the smaller the time interval the more effective the learning.

Sequence for Teaching Multiplication and Division Facts

We recommend the following sequence for teaching multiplication and division facts:

(1) Present factors 2 through 5 with products to 25. This includes:

[1]*Curriculum and Evaluation Standards for School Mathematics*, Working Draft (Reston, VA: National Council of Teachers of Mathematics, 1987), p. 38.

(a) Four doubles: 2×2, 3×3,
4×4, 5×5
(b) Six easy facts: 2×3, 2×4, 2×5
3×4, 3×5, 4×5
(c) The facts in (b) "commuted"

(2) The zero and one multiplication facts taught in problem settings, generalized as follows:
(a) When zero is a factor, the product is zero.
(b) When one is a factor, the product is the other factor.

(3) Present the division facts that correspond to the multiplication facts in (1) above in a problem context:
(a) Start with a measurement-type problem (discussed later).
(b) Show the relationship between division and multiplication. For example:

$3 \times 4 = 12$ $4 \times 3 = 12$
$12 \div 4 = 3$ $12 \div 3 = 4$

(4) Demonstrate that the answer of any number divided by 1 is that number.

(5) During the third grade present the remaining multiplication and division facts derived from the following:
(a) Four doubles: 6×6, 7×7, 8×8, 9×9
(b) 22 facts, these "commuted" and the corresponding division facts:

2×6, 3×6, 4×6, 5×6
2×7, 3×7, 4×7, 5×7, 6×7
2×8, 3×8, 4×8, 5×8, 6×8, 7×8
2×9, 3×9, 4×9, 5×9, 6×9, 7×9, 8×9

The difficulty of the facts given has not been verified by research but represents our best judgment. The teacher may not agree with the inclusion of some of the facts in the list. The 2s and the 5s in multiplication usually are considered easy for the pupil to learn. The facts having products greater than 25 for the 6s, 7s, 8s, and 9s are the difficult facts in multiplication.

Teaching Basic Multiplication Facts

In planning and teaching basic facts in multiplication and division, the principles discussed in Chapter 1 should be followed in developing a series of lessons.

I. Objectives

The following objectives for the multiplication facts should be considered for inclusion in a series of lessons:

1. Relate multiplication to "putting together sets equal in number."

2. Rename a multiplication fact with addends.

3. Follow a multiplication story problem and create the solution with (a) manipulatives, (b) visuals, and (c) symbolic notations.

4. Write a multiplication fact in both horizontal and vertical forms.

5. Given a word problem involving multiplication, name the factors and the product.

6. Verify the correctness of a fact by relating it to other known facts, by showing a pattern, or by applying a property.

7. Given a multiplication fact, make a problem to fit.

8. Given any pair of basic factors, respond quickly and accurately with the correct product.

II. Readiness

Children's first experiences with multiplication facts are with everyday situations in which they put together things that are equal in number. When pupils learn the "doubles" in addition, they should relate this to multiplying by two. For example, 3 + 3 = 6 can be related to the multiplication fact 2 × 3 = 6. Long before children can understand multiplication they can solve real-life problems involving groups that are equal in number by manipulating objects and by drawing and examining pictures.

Children are ready for a study of the easy multiplication facts after they have a good understanding of the basic addition and subtraction facts.

III. Motivation

Young children are usually not as highly motivated to learn multiplication facts as they are to learn addition and subtraction facts. Multiplication facts are more difficult to represent with manipulatives and are harder to remember. Thus, special approaches must be used to help children want to master multiplication. These include: (a) relating multiplication to real-life problems, (b) using manipulatives to show patterns, (c) drawing and discussing arrays, and (d) examining the commutative, associative, and distributive properties. Activities that tend to enhance motivation are reinforcement with interesting games, using calculators, and having children work with computer programs.

IV. Guided Discovery

The teaching–learning sequence for the multiplication facts is as follows:

1. Start with a simple verbal problem involving a basic fact in multiplication.

2. Give children manipulatives to use and discuss in solving the problem.

3. Guide each child in using and discussing drawings to represent the problem-solving process.

4. Emphasize how manipulatives and drawings are useful for showing the symbolic notation for a multiplication fact.

5. Examine the commutative, associative, and distributive properties as appropriate.

1. MULTIPLICATION PROBLEMS

There is basically one type of problem that can be solved by multiplication: given one, find many. This is often introduced as combining two or more sets equal in number.

(a) If one toy costs $2.00, how much will three of them cost?

$$\$ \quad \$$$
$$\$ \quad \$$$
$$\$ \quad \$$$

(b) There are 5 sticks of gum in each package. If John buys 3 packages, how many sticks of gum would he get?
5 + 5 + 5 = ? or 3 × 5 = ?

2. USING MANIPULATIVES

The following discussion illustrates how problems can be solved at the exploratory level of learning by using manipulative materials.

Problem 1: You receive an allowance of $3.00 per week. How much will you receive in four weeks?

Young children should be encouraged to solve this problem by using an appropriate substitute for dollar bills, as follows:

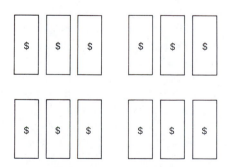

Once the materials are arranged to match the problem situation, the answer can be found by counting by 3s.

Pupils create an array with blocks.

(Photo by Leland Perry)

Problem 2: We are going to plant some pansies in a box. We have 4 rows and plant 3 pansies in each row. How many pansies will we need?

Because it is not convenient to have the children use real pansies to solve this problem, you should supply objects or drawings to serve as substitutes in the configuration below:

The physical or visual model then represents 4 threes, or 3 + 3 + 3 + 3, which equals 12.

3. SHOWING MULTIPLICATION WITH
DRAWINGS

The children can be taught to make marks on paper to represent real objects in a problem situation and in its solution.

Problem: How many eyes do five children have?

The problem situation and its solution are shown with drawings below:

Problem: You have 5 flowers in each of 2 vases. How many flowers are there in all?

An *array* is a type of drawing that is one of the best ways for children to gain an understanding of multiplication and division.

1. Represent 5 flowers with five dots.

2. Draw two sets of 5 dots for 2 vases.

3. The array is a 2 by 5 figure, containing 10 dots in all. So there will be 10 flowers.

4. FROM OBJECTS TO THE SYMBOLIC LEVEL

These activities are recommended to help children understand the patterns for learning the multiplication facts with factors of 2 through 5.

1. *From counters to multiplication and division facts.* Use counters to show any multiplication example.
    (a) For factors 2 and 3 show two arrangements with counters:

$$\begin{matrix} & & \circ & \circ \\ \circ & \circ & \circ & \quad \circ & \circ \\ \circ & \circ & \circ & \quad \circ & \circ \end{matrix}$$

    (b) Write as equal addends:
        $3 + 3 = 6$ $2 + 2 + 2 = 6$
    (c) Relate to multiplication facts:

"Two 3s equal 6." $2 \times 3 = 6$
"Three 2s equal 6." $3 \times 2 = 6$
    (d) Relate to division facts:
        "6 broken into 2 equal parts is 3 in each part," or "How many 2s are there in 6?" $6 \div 2 = 3$
        "6 broken into 3 equal parts is 2 in each part," or "How many 3s are there in 6?" $6 \div 3 = 2$

In situations like (a) above, each child should be able to *represent with objects, draw an array, show on a number line,* and *write appropriate number sentences.*

2. *From arrays to multiplication facts.* Draw two arrays, such as:

    (a) Interpret the array with addends:
        $4 + 4 + 4 = 12$
        $3 + 3 + 3 + 3 = 12$
    (b) Interpret the array as a multiplication fact:
        $3 \times 4 = 12$ $4 \times 3 = 12$
    (c) Therefore: $3 \times 4 = 4 \times 3$ (Illustrates the commutative property for multiplication.)

Symbolic Level   At the symbolic level pupils solve verbal problems by following a sequential pattern. The steps are:

(a) State the number story

(b) Write an equation

(c) Solve the equation and check the computation

(d) Interpret the answer

Problem: A page of Nell's stamp album contains 4 rows of 5 stamps each. There are how many stamps on the page?

1. *State* the number story: Four rows of 5 stamps equal how many stamps?

2. *Write* an equation:
$$4 \times 5 = \square.$$
3. *Solve* and *check*: $4 \times 5 = 20$; $5 + 5 + 5 + 5 = 20$; $5 \times 4 = 20$; $5 (2 + 2) = 10 + 10 = 20$.

4. *Interpret*: The page contains 20 stamps.

Teaching Basic Division Facts

For any pair of unequal one-digit numbers (not 0) there are two multiplication facts and two division facts. Thus, for the factors (3,5) there are the following four basic facts:

$3 \times 5 = 15$, $5 \times 3 = 15$,
$15 \div 5 = 3$, $15 \div 3 = 5$

Terminology

The terms *factor* and *product* are relatively easy for pupils to learn and use. However, the terms for division are more difficult. In the following example:

$$\begin{array}{r} 5 \\ 3\overline{)15} \end{array}$$

The 3 is called the *divisor*, the 15 is the *dividend*, and the 5 is the *quotient*. Most elementary textbooks do not use the division terminology in the early stages of learning. Some authors relate division to multiplication by referring to the dividend as the "known product" and the divisor as the "known factor." This terminology is often confusing to pupils, especially in problem settings. Pupils wonder why they start with a product and a known factor. We recommend that the numbers in division be named according to their meaning in a problem situation. In the problem: "Enzo has $15 and wants to buy some $3 gifts. How many can she buy?" The $15 is the amount of money Enzo starts with and $3 is the value of each gift. The problem is to find how many times $3 can be subtracted from $15.

The exact division terms should be delayed until the pupils have had consider-able experience with division and need to know the terminology to record the parts of a division algorithm.

I. Objectives

The following objectives for teaching the division facts should be considered for inclusion in a series of lessons.

1. Relate division to a "taking apart by equals" process.

2. Solve measurement-type problems with (a) manipulatives, (b) visuals, and (c) successive subtractions, and (d) symbolic notations.

3. Solve a partitive-type problem with (a) manipulatives, (b) visuals, and (c) symbolic notations.

4. Write a division fact in two different ways:
(a) $3\overline{)15}$ and $15 \div 3 = ?$

5. Verify the correctness of a division fact by relating it to a corresponding multiplication fact or by examining a pattern of division facts.

6. Given any basic division fact, write a measurement or partitive problem to fit the fact.

7. Respond within three seconds with the correct quotient to any basic division fact.

II. Readiness

Division facts are the most difficult for pupils to master. Consequently children need to have had experience with multiplication facts and subtraction prior to a study of division.

III. Motivation

Pupils may be motivated to learn division facts with the following activities: (a) use real-life problems, (b) provide manipulatives, (c) encourage visuals, and (d) relate division to multiplication and to subtracting equals.

IV. Guided Discovery

The teaching–learning sequence for division follows the same sequence as previously discussed for multiplication.

TWO DIVISION PROBLEM SITUATIONS

Division undoes multiplication in the form of N × A = P where N is the number of equal groups and A is the number of items in each group and P is the product or total number of items in N groups.

Measurement division answers the question: How many groups, equal in number, are contained in a given group?

Partition division answers the question: How many items are in each of N groups equal in number?   It cannot be determined whether the division required to solve 12 ÷ 3 = ? is measurement or partition until it is known whether the 3 represents the number of equal groups (partition) or the number in each of the equal groups (measurement).

Here are some examples of measurement division problems:

1. At 3¢ each, how many candies could you buy for 15¢?

2. There are 15 children to play a game with 3 children on each team. How many teams of 3 will there be?

3. You have a candy bar 15 cm long and want to cut it in pieces 3 cm long. How many pieces will there be?

4. There are 15 roses in a bunch. It takes 3 roses to make a bouquet. How many bouquets can be made?

The solutions to these problems require a *measuring* process, in which one would ask "How many *a's* are there in *b?*"

1. Three cents measures 15¢ five times.

2. If we separated 15 children into groups of 3 children, we would have 5 groups.

3. Three cm measures 15 cm five times.

4. Fifteen roses can be separated into 5 bouquets of 3 roses each.

Here are some examples of partitive division problems:

1. Tom paid 20¢ for 4 candies. How much did each cost?

2. There are 2 cars and 8 children. The same number of children ride in each car. How many will ride in each car?

3. You have 8 cookies to share equally with a friend. How many will each of you get?

4. You have 8 big blocks the same size to build 2 towers the same height. How many blocks will you use for each tower?

The teacher should not overemphasize the distinction in spite of the difference between partitive and measurement division. Once a pupil has found an equation to solve the problem the computation is the same, whether the problem is a partitive or a measurement situation. Whether a problem is a partitive or measurement situation is relevant when it is time to interpret the quotient.

Showing Division with Drawings

Problem: How many pieces of candy at 3¢ each can you buy for 12¢?

1. Draw 12 pennies.

ООООООООООО

2. Mark off (measure) by 3s.

ООО ООО ООО ООО

3. Because each set of 3¢ equals one piece of candy, the number of candies is the number of sets of 3s, which is 4.

Problem: You pay 5¢ for one pencil. How many can you buy for 15¢?

Solution: Draw an array with dots as follows:

1. Represent 5¢ • • • • •   1 pencil
with five dots.

2. You have 10¢   2 pencils,
left. Draw another • • • • •   for 10¢
set of five dots.

3. You have 5¢   3 pencils,
left. Draw another • • • • •   for 15¢
five dots.

When complete, the 3 by 5 array contains
5 dots 3 times. It contains 15 dots, showing
that 3 × 5 = 15 and 15 ÷ 5 = 3. Thus 5¢
measures 15¢ three times.

The Number Line

Many elementary mathematics textbooks use the *number line* to illustrate the
meanings of multiplication and division.

Problem: A rubber ball costs $3. How
many can you buy for $15?

Solution with a number line:

1. Draw a number line of 15 spaces to
represent $15.

2. Starting at 15, mark off line segments
by moving to the left 3 units at a time, with
each move representing $3.

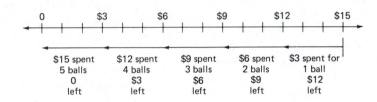

Exercise 9.1

1. Given a collection of objects represented by an array such as this:

○ ○ ○ ○ ○

○ ○ ○ ○ ○

○ ○ ○ ○ ○

   (a) Write two addition facts with *unequal* addends.
   (b) Write two addition examples with *equal* addends.
   (c) Write two multiplication facts.
   (d) Write two division facts.
   (e) For each division fact:
      (1) Write a word problem illustrating a partitive division situa-
          tion.
      (2) Write a word problem illustrating a measurement division sit-
          uation.

2. In solving each of the following word problems, first identify the kind
   of problem situation (multiplication, partitive division, measurement
   division), then represent the solution with drawings, and, third, write
   an equation.
   (a) Jay bought 4 pencils at 8¢ each. How much did he spend on pen-
       cils?

(b) Scott has 35¢ to spend on graph paper. Each sheet costs 5¢ How many sheets can he buy?

(c) It takes Mary 8 minutes to walk to school one way. How long does it take her to walk to and from school each day?

(d) Steve walks at the rate of 4 miles per hour. How long does it take him to walk 12 miles?

(e) Lucy has $10 to spend on her five-day vacation. On the average, how much can she spend each day?

(f) Mark has saved $25 for airplane models, and he wants to buy 5 models. On the average, how much can he spend on each one?

Properties for Multiplication and Division of Whole Numbers

In this chapter we are concerned only with one-place whole numbers and their products. In teaching multiplication and division to beginning children, one should not stress mathematical properties. Rather, the emphasis should be on the exploratory-level solution with real objects and drawings.

The activities at the symbolic level enable the pupil to discover *patterns* and *relationships* among the multiplication and division facts. These discoveries should minimize the need for exploratory materials, and enrich the pupils' understanding of the facts so that they can easily be recalled in doing later work.

The Commutative Property

The commutative property for multiplication means that the order of two factors does not affect the product. In symbolic-level activities, have the pupils rename a number pair to discover that the order of the factors does not affect the product:

$2 \times 3 = 3 \times 2$
$2 \times 4 = \square \times 2$
$2 \times 5 = 5 \times \square$

Relationship between Equal Addends and Multiplication

Equal addends can be related to multiplication; for example, $3 + 3$ can be renamed

as 2×3, and conversely, 3×4 can be renamed with addends as $4 + 4 + 4$. At the symbolic level, pupils can be expected to write a number sentence using both equal addends and factors:

$2 \times 3 = 3 + \square$
$2 \times 5 = \square + \square$
$4 \times 2 = 2 + \square + \square + \square$
$4 + 4 = 2 \times \square$
$3 + 3 + 3 = \square \times \square$
$5 + 5 + 5 + 5 = \square \times 5$

Relationship between Subtraction and Division

At the symbolic level, pupils should be able to discover for themselves the relationship between subtraction and division. Give them examples in which equal numbers are subtracted from a given number and ask them to rename them into division examples:

$6 - 3 = 3; 3 - 3 = 0;$
How many 3s in 6, or $6 \div 3 = 2$
$8 - 4 = 4; 4 - 4 = 0;$
How many 4s in 8, or $8 \div 4 = 2$
$10 - 5 = 5; 5 - 5 = 0;$
How many 5s in 10, or $10 \div 5 = 2$

Relationship between Multiplication and Division

Each multiplication fact involving two different nonzero factors can be renamed as two division facts; for example, $4 \times 5 = 20$ can be renamed as $20 \div 4 = 5$ and $20 \div 5 = 4$.

The pupils should be able to complete these number sentences by writing the correct answers in the frames:

$$2 \times 3 = \square \qquad \square \div 3 = 2$$
$$2 \times \square = 8 \qquad 8 \div \square = 2$$
$$\square \times 5 = 10 \qquad 10 \div \square = 5$$

SPECIAL PROPERTY OF ONE AS A FACTOR OR DIVISOR

Multiplying by one illustrates the *identity property for multiplication* because the product of any factor and one equals the given factor $n \times 1 = n$. The earliest that the teacher should introduce *one* as the identity element for multiplication is probably after the children have completely understood and mastered the multiplication facts for factors of 2 through 5.

SPECIAL PROPERTY OF ZERO AS A FACTOR OR DIVISOR

When zero is one of two factors, the product is always zero. Illustrate this concept by using zero as addends, then relating it to multiplication:

$$0 + 0 + 0 = 0 \qquad 0 + 0 + 0 + 0 = 0$$
$$3 \times 0 = 0 \qquad 4 \times 0 = 0$$

Applying the commutative property, if $3 \times 0 = 0$, then $0 \times 3 = 0$. *When 0 is a factor, the product is 0. When 0 is a divisor, division is impossible.*

PRODUCTS OF FACTORS 2 THROUGH 9

Pupils should be encouraged to use exploratory materials in multiplying number pairs with products of 25 or less. But for number pairs having products greater than 25, manipulative materials should be used sparingly. Arrays can be helpful with these facts, especially in helping children to understand the distributive property of multiplication over addition.

The Distributive Property

Once pupils have mastered the multiplication facts to products of up to 25, they should learn the facts with products to 81 at the symbolic level by means of patterns and properties, rather than manipulative materials. A good visual approach to learn products greater than 25 is the *array*. For a problem with one factor greater than 5, students should be asked to rename that factor as the sum of two addends as follows:

Problem: Find the product of 5×8 by using the distributive property of multiplication over addition.

Solution with an array: Draw an array such that 8 is renamed as two different addends: $7 + 1$, $6 + 2$, $5 + 3$, $4 + 4$. Because the purpose of this activity is to find the product by using two known multiplication facts, the addends of 6 and 7 should not be used. Rename the 8 in the factors 5×8 as $(5 + 3)$ and write the number sentence $5 \times (5 + 3) = \square$. The array for this number sentence is:

```
x  x  x  x  x   O  O  O
x  x  x  x  x   O  O  O
x  x  x  x  x   O  O  O
x  x  x  x  x   O  O  O
x  x  x  x  x   O  O  O
```

Pupils should now be able to see two multiplication facts in the array: the x-array forms a 5 by 5 array for $5 \times 5 = 25$, and the o-array forms a 5 by 3 array for $5 \times 3 = 15$. The product is then the sum of the numbers in the two arrays, or $25 + 15 = 40$. So $5 \times (5 + 3) = (5 \times 5) + (5 \times 3) = 25 + 15 = 40$. Applying the commutative property, when we know that $5 \times 8 = 40$, we also know that $8 \times 5 = 40$.

In the same way, pupils can find the product of any pair of one-digit factors by renaming one factor and then applying the distributive property. The *double array* serves as a visual aid to demonstrate how the distributive property works.

The Associative Property of Multiplication

The *associative property of multiplication* is stated in symbolic form as $a \times (b \times c) = (a \times b) \times c$. In other words, in an example with three factors, the number b can be associated first with *either c or a* without changing the product. Sometimes this property is described as regrouping three factors without changing the order. With numbers, the associative property works as follows:

$$3 \times (2 \times 4) = (3 \times 2) \times 4$$

$$3 \times 8 \quad = \quad 6 \times 4$$

$$24 \quad = \quad 24$$

A useful application of the associative property of multiplication is to make new facts from old ones in the following manner:

1. Start with a two-factor example.
$4 \times 6 = \square$

2. Rename the factor 6 as 2×3.
$4 \times (2 \times 3) = \square$

3. Associate the 2 with the 4.
$(4 \times 2) \times 3 = \square$

4. Multiply $(4 \times 2) = 8$ and substitute.
$8 \times 3 = \square$

5. Therefore $4 \times 6 = 8 \times 3 = 24$.

Mastering the Facts in Multiplication and Division

After pupils understand the facts in multiplication and division, in problem settings and with patterns, take different approaches to help them achieve mastery of these facts.

One aspect of mastery is instant recall of number facts. The following activities at the symbolic and mastery levels should strengthen the learner's grasp of the facts and help fixate the learning of them so that pupils attain the mastery level.

1. Construct tables from which a product or factor is missing, and ask the pupil to write the missing numeral. Tables (a), (b), and (c) are short but can be expanded to include all the facts for a given factor, such as 2 in table (a).

(a)

×	2	3	4
2	4	?	?

(b)

×	3	7	8
2	?	?	?

(c)

	3	4	?	7	?
2	2 × 3	?	12	?	18

A vertical table, as shown in (d), illustrates the commutative property of multiplication:

(d)

×	2
3	3 × 2
?	8
5	?
6	?
?	18

2. Have pupils complete open sentences to discover the relationships between addition and multiplication and between multiplication and division:

$$3 + 3 = \square \qquad 3 \times 4 = \square$$
$$2 \times 3 = \square \qquad 4 + 4 + \triangle = \square$$
$$15 \div 3 = \square \qquad 21 \div 3 = \square$$
$$3 \times \square = 15 \qquad \square \times 3 = 21$$

Just as the squares and triangles in number sentences hold a place for a numeral, a circle is frequently used to hold a place for a sign of operation, such as $+$, $\times$, $-$, or $\div$.

To complete each of the following number sentences, pupils must replace the circle with the sign of operation that will make the sentence true:

$$2 \bigcirc 4 = 8 \qquad 8 \bigcirc 2 = 16$$
$$12 \bigcirc 4 = 3 \qquad 8 \bigcirc 4 = 2$$

3. Have pupils fill in the missing data in each category at the bottom of this page. Follow the pattern established in the first row.

4. Write the products or quotients of the number pairs below:

5	6	3	9
$\times 3$	$\times 4$	$\times 7$	$\times 5$

$4\overline{)20}$	$3\overline{)24}$	$9\overline{)0}$	$6\overline{)30}$

5. Write the other number sentences when one of the related facts is given, as in the following examples:

$$3 \times 7 = 21 \qquad 7 \times 3 = 21$$
$$21 \div 7 = 3 \qquad 21 \div 3 = 7$$

6. Give a product and have the class write all the basic multiplication facts that have that product. In initial work of this type, the teacher should write equations using a given product, such as 12:

(a) $\triangle + \square = 12$ $\qquad$ (b) $\triangle \times \square = 12$
$\square + \triangle = 12$ $\qquad\qquad$ $\square \times \triangle = 12$

The equations in (a) and (b) illustrate the commutative property. Tell the class that different pairs of numbers are used in (a) and (b), and have the class write the corresponding equations in division.

Pupils should learn to distinguish between the equations $\square \times \square = 16$ and $\triangle \times \square = 16$. When both frames are squares, the same number is represented twice; when a square and a triangle are used, the numbers can be the same or different. The equation $4 \times 4 = 16$ can be correct for both $\square \times \square = 16$ and $\triangle \times \square = 16$, but only the equation $2 \times 8 = 16$ is correct for the latter.

7. Give a set of whole numbers, such as 3, 4, 12, and have the class write the four basic facts that use these numbers.

The set may include a variable, such as [3, n, 15]. The equations formed from these numbers are $3 \times n = 15$, $n \times 3 = 15$, $15 \div n = 3$, and $15 \div 3 = n$.

8. Have pupils write in sequence the nu-

Array	Set Sentence	Abbreviated Set Sentence	Addition Equation	Multiplication Equation	Number Line
• • • • • •	Two sets of 3 books is a set of $\square$ books	Two 3s are n	$3 + 3 = \square$	$2 \times 3 = \square$	0 3 6
?	?	Two 5s are n	?	?	?
?	?	?	?	$2 \times 6 = \square$	?

merals for the numbers from 3 to 30 for the 3s, from 4 to 40 for the 4s, and so on. Then cross off each third numeral for the 3s and every fourth numeral for the 4s. As they cross off each numeral, the pupils write the number pair for that product. If they cross off 21, the number pair is 3 and 7. They would then write the following four facts derived from this number pair: $3 \times 7 = 21$, $7 \times 3 = 21$, $21 \div 3 = 7$, and $21 \div 7 = 3$.

9. Draw more complex tables than those in item 1, which should be used after a few facts have been introduced. Create and use tables of this type after many facts have been introduced.

Tables (c) and (d) show how many pupils can develop number sentences from given data. Table (e) can be used effectively to show the inverse relationship between multiplication and division.

(c)

×	2	4
3	□	△
5	t	n

$3 \times 2 = □$ $3 \times 4 = △$
$5 \times 2 = t$ $5 \times 4 = n$

(d)

×	2	n	△
3	t	12	15
□	10	20	25

$3 \times 2 = t$ $□ \times 2 = 10$
$3 \times n = 12$ $□ \times n = 20$
$3 \times △ = 15$ $□ \times △ = 25$

(e)

×	?	?	?
3	6	12	15
5	10	?	?

10. Have pupils discover patterns by filling in the blanks with the numbers that belong in a series of this type:

(a) 1, 2, 3, 4, _____, _____, _____.
(b) 2, 4, 6, 8 _____, _____, _____.
(c) 3, 6, 9, 12, _____, _____, _____.
(d) 6, 12, 18, 24, _____, _____, _____.

Pupils do two things with the table. First, they write the three numerals that name the numbers for the blanks. Second, they rename each of the numbers in the series by writing a number pair whose product is equal to the given number. Renaming the numbers in series (a) involves the identity element. The first and fourth numbers in each series can be renamed as follows:

(a) $1 \times 1 = 1$ $4 \times 1 = 4$
(b) $1 \times 2 = 2$ $4 \times 2 = 8$
(c) $1 \times 3 = 3$ $4 \times 3 = 12$
(d) $1 \times 6 = 6$ $4 \times 6 = 24$

Formation of Tables

Table for the Facts in Multiplication and Division

When the teacher introduces a set of facts, have pupils construct a table that includes these facts, for example, the set of facts for the 2s, 3s, and 4s. After all the facts in multiplication have been introduced, each pupil should make a composite table of these facts. Some of these tables can be displayed on the classroom bulletin board. A composite shows the orderly arrangement of a set of factors and products.

Table 9.1 is a composite table for all the facts in multiplication and division. The pupil must understand that division by 0 is not permissible. The numerals at the beginning of each row and at the top of each column name the factors of the product, which appears in both a column and a row.

Table 9.1 Composite Table of Multiplication and Division Facts

X	0	1	2	3	4	5	6	7	8	9
0	0	0	0	0	0	0	0	0	0	0
1	0	1	2	3	4	5	6	7	8	9
2	0	2	4	6	8	10	12	14	16	18
3	0	3	6	**9**	12	15	18	21	24	27
4	0	4	8	12	**16**	20	24	28	32	36
5	0	5	10	15	20	**25**	30	35	40	45
6	0	6	12	18	24	30	**36**	42	48	54
7	0	7	14	21	28	35	42	**49**	56	63
8	0	8	16	24	32	40	48	56	**64**	72
9	0	9	18	27	36	45	54	63	72	**81**

There are two unequal factors for each product, except the products named along the diagonal that runs from the upper left-hand corner of the table to the lower right-hand corner. These products are the squares of the numbers from 0 through 9. The square of a number is the product of that number and itself. Each pair of unequal nonzero factors forms a set of four related facts, two in multiplication and two in division.

Interpreting a Composite Table

Each pupil's composite table of multiplication facts should be done on cross-ruled paper so that the products will be in rows and columns. Give the class some time to make discoveries about the table. Have pupils tell about or identify their discoveries. Write a table of the facts on the chalkboard, and have the class answer the following questions:

1. Each succeeding number in a row increases by what amount?

2. Each succeeding number in a column increases by what amount?

3. Any number in a row or column can be found by adding what number to the preceding number?

4. If a number in a row is divided by the factor (not 0) at the beginning of the row, what number will be the quotient?

5. Reverse the procedure in item 4.

6. When one factor is 0, what is the product?

7. When one factor is 1, what is the product?

8. What property does item 7 represent?

9. Use the table to show the commutative property of multiplication.

10. Use the table to show the distributive property in the equation $3 \times 7 = \square$ by renaming 7 as $(2 + 5)$.

11. The numbers along the diagonal that runs from the upper left to lower right are the squares of the numbers from 0 to 9 inclusive. Are the factors of each product equal or unequal?

12. Are the squares even or odd?

13. In which rows or columns are all the products even numbers? Is the number at the head of each of these rows or columns odd or even?

14. In which row or column does an odd product follow an even product? Is the number at the head of each of these rows or columns odd or even?

15. From problems 13 and 14, complete the following:

(a) The product of two even numbers is _____.

(b) The product of two odd numbers is _____.

(c) The product of an even and an odd number is _____.

16. Write the squares given along the diagonal. Find the difference between consecutive (next in order) squares. What name is given to the set of numbers of the differences? (The first 9 odd numbers.)

17. What is the sum of the first 3 odd numbers in problem 16? The first 5 odd numbers? The first 8 odd numbers? The first n odd numbers?

18. What is the sum of the numbers in the column headed by 1? by 2? by 3?

19. Write the sum of the numbers in the remaining columns in problem 18 without adding the numbers.

The list of questions about the table can be expanded to include the differences between consecutive products along imaginary lines drawn parallel to the diagonals.

The teacher need not have the class answer all the questions listed. It is important, however, for the pupils to make a table and discuss some of its characteristics. Use the principle of guided discovery to have the class explore the table.

Making a Table from Known Facts

All students in a class should make a table, such as the table of 4s. Certain facts involving the 4s are given. New facts are derived from the known facts. The teacher challenges each pupil to discover as many ways as possible to find a new fact. As each new fact or element in a table is verified, this fact can be used to discover other facts in a table. For example, to make a table of the 4s from known facts, assume that the following facts are known:

$1 \times 4 = 4$
$2 \times 4 = 8$
.
.
.
$10 \times 4 = 40$

The next step is to derive the fact 3×4

$= 12$. The class suggests all the possible ways to find the fact by using only the facts assumed to be known and also basic knowledge of multiplication. The class should be able to verify that $3 \times 4 = 12$ with the following discoveries:

> "Since 1 four is 4 and 2 fours are 8, add 4 and 8 to find 3 fours." This method applies the distributive property.
> "Add 3 fours."
> "Add 4 threes."

The next step is to find the fact $4 \times 4 = 16$. The thought pattern may be as follows:

> "Add 1 four to the product of 3 fours."
> "Add 4 fours."
> "Since 2 fours are 8, 4 fours will be twice as much, or 16."
> "Since 10 fours are 40, 5 fours will be half as much, or 20. The 4 fours will be 1 less four, or $20 - 4 = 16$."

These answers are typical of those that pupils will give to express the relationships among multiplication facts in a table. The teacher should provide pupils with the opportunities to discover some of these relationships.

Applying the Distributive Property

Tables involving the 2s, 5s, and 10s are the easiest to learn. If pupils know these facts, they can find the facts in other tables by applying the distributive property.

Multiplication facts involving the 3s can be derived from a knowledge of the 2s by renaming 3 as (2 + 1) and applying the distributive property:

$2 \times (2 + 1) = 4 + 2 = 6$
$3 \times (2 + 1) = 6 + 3 = 9$

The facts involving the 4s can be derived by two procedures. The first is by doubling each fact in the table of the 2s. Thus, $2 \times 2 = 4$; hence 2×4 will be $2 \times (2 + 2)$, or 8. The second way is to rename 4 as (5 − 1) and apply the distributive property.

The facts involving the 6s can be determined from a knowledge of the 5s. First rename 6 as (5 + 1) and then apply the distributive property. Similarly, the facts involving the 7s can be found by renaming 7 as (5 + 2), and then proceeding as described.

The facts involving the 8s can be found by two procedures, as we did for the 4s. First double each fact in the table of the 4s. Second, rename 8 as (10 − 2) and apply the distributive property. Finally, the facts involving the 9s can be derived from the 10s by renaming 9 as (10 − 1), and proceeding as described.

The aim of these activities for deriving facts by new procedures is to supplement and deepen pupils' insight into number relationships among the multiplication facts.

Number Patterns

The 9s form some very interesting patterns in multiplication. Encourage the class to discover some of the patterns. Extending the table or the few facts given should enable the pupils to make the following two discoveries about the products:

$$9 \times 1 = 9$$
$$9 \times 2 = 18$$
$$9 \times 3 = 27$$

1. The sum of the numbers named by the digits in each product is 9.

2. The ones digit in each succeeding product decreases by 1 and the tens digit increases by 1.

Students can discover the truth of the second statement by renaming 9 as (10 − 1) and applying the distributive property.

Since 9 is one less than the decimal base of our number system, and 11 is one more than the base, these facts can be used to form a pattern for the tables of the 9s and 11s.

$$1 \times 9 = 10 - 1 \qquad 1 \times 11 = 10 + 1$$

$$2 \times 9 = 20 - 2 \qquad 2 \times 11 = 20 + 2$$
$$3 \times 9 = 30 - 3 \qquad 3 \times 11 = 30 + 3$$

An intriguing application of the 9s in multiplication enables us to find the difference between a two-place number and the number with the digits reversed:

$$\begin{array}{r} 21 \\ -12 \\ \hline 9 \end{array} \qquad\qquad \begin{array}{r} 31 \\ -13 \\ \hline 18 \end{array}$$

$$2 - 1 = \triangle \qquad 3 - 1 = \triangle$$
$$\triangle \times 9 = \square \qquad \triangle \times 9 = \square$$

After a few illustrations, the pupils should discover the pattern for finding the difference between any two-place number and the number with the digits reversed. Fast learners should be able to arrive at the generalization. Generalizing with regard to a pattern is much more difficult than discovering the pattern.

Changing Sequence of Factors

In a table of the multiplication facts, such as the 6s, one factor is 6 and the other factor consists of the 10 digits in order. An interesting pattern is formed by changing the sequence of the factors as shown in (a) and (b):

(a)
$$6 \times 6 = 36$$
$$7 \times 5 = 35$$
$$8 \times 4 = 32$$
$$\cdot$$
$$\cdot$$
$$\cdot$$
$$11 \times 1 = 11$$

(b)
$$6 \times 5 = 30$$
$$7 \times 4 = 28$$
$$8 \times 3 = 24$$
$$\cdot$$
$$\cdot$$
$$\cdot$$
$$11 \times 0 = 0$$

Supply the class with a few facts for a table, and ask the pupils to discover the pattern and supply the missing numerals. In the examples given, the pupils should be able to discover the pattern for writing missing numerals for the sequence of either the factors or the products. In (a) the difference of the products is the series of odd numbers; in (b) the difference is the series of even numbers.

Division with Remainders

Unfortunately, not all numbers of things can be regrouped into parts of equal number. For example, 16 cannot be distributed into groups of 5 without having one left over. After having a great deal of experience with no remainders, children at the exploratory level should be given some problem situations that have remainders. The following problems and solutions illustrate the ways to help children understand division with remainders.

Problem: How many teams of 5 girls each can be formed from 12 girls?

1. Use girls—have 12 girls line up, and have the girls get into groups of 5. Clearly, there are 2 groups. (2 girls are left unassigned).

2. Make a drawing to show the formation of teams:

3. Write a number sentence:
   $12 \div 5 = 2 \text{ r } 2$.

4. State the solution, "From 12 girls, there can be 2 teams of 5 girls, with 2 girls remaining."

Problem: John's father wants to give each of his three children an equal weekly allowance, If he has 16 one-dollar bills, how much will each child get?

1. Lay out the 16 one-dollar bills, paper money, or markers.

2. Go through a "sharing process" and distribute the dollar bills to the three children. Remove $3 and give $1 to each child. Repeat this five times. (See illustration below.)

3. Show that after the sharing process, each child will have 5 one-dollar bills, with one bill left over.

4. Use the drawing in step 2 to write the number sentence
   $16 \div 3 = 5$, remainder 1. (5 r 1)

Practicing Division with Remainders Greater than Zero

There is no whole number that will make the equations $3 \times \square = 7$ or $7 \div 3 = \square$ true. Although 7 is not a multiple of 3, with rational numbers, division can be used to find the number that will make the sentence $7 \div 3 = \square$ true. When 7 is divided by 3, there is a remainder greater than zero.

At the symbolic level, there are three different procedures for finding a one-place quotient of a nonmultiple of a one-place divisor:

1. Number sequences
2. Open sentences
3. The division algorithm

1. Pupils write the numbers in sequence up to 10 times the divisor, circling the multiples of the divisor 3 as shown:

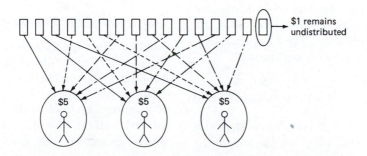

$1 remains undistributed

0 1 2 ③ 4 5 ⑥ 7 8 ⑨
10 11 ⑫ 13 14 ⑮ 16 17 ⑱ 19
20 ㉑ 22 23 ㉔ 25 26 ㉗ 28 29

Then use both multiplication and division to express the nonmultiples of three in a number sequence. For example, the different ways to write the number pair 13 ÷ 3 are:

$$13 = (3 \times 4) + 1 \qquad 13 \div 3 = 4 \text{ r } 1$$

The two number sentences show the relationship between multiplication and division. The r in 4 r 1 stands for "remainder." An effective teaching technique is to have each pupil write a few number sentences that have been derived from sequences on a number line.

2. Have the class solve open sentences of the following type:

$16 = 3 \times \square + 1 \qquad \square \div 6 = 3 \text{ r } 4$
$21 \div 4 = \square \text{ r } 1 \qquad 14 = \square \times 5 + 4$
$\square \div 3 = 4 \text{ r } 2 \qquad 23 \div 3 = \square \text{ r } 2$
$27 = 4 \times 6 + \square \qquad \square \div 5 = 2 \text{ r } 4$
$15 \div 6 = 2 \text{ r } \square \qquad 20 = 3 \times \square + 2$

3. Have the class use the division algorithm as shown in example (a).

(a) $\quad \dfrac{5 \text{ r } 2}{3\overline{)17}}$
$\quad \underline{15}$
$\quad\ \ 2$

Have pupils who are unable to give the quotient and the remainder in the manner illustrated express the dividend as the sum of two addends and then apply the distributive property of division. For example, a pupil who does not know the largest multiple of 6 in 52 may rename 52 as 36 + 16 or 30 + 22. One of the addends should be a multiple of 6. The example can now be written as:

$$52 \div 6 = (36 + 16) \div 6$$
$$= (36 \div 6) + (16 \div 6)$$

The quotient of 36 ÷ 6 is 6. Since 16 is not a multiple of 6, and 12 is the largest multi-

ple of 6 that is less than 16, 16 ÷ 6 = (12 ÷ 6), with a remainder of 4. Therefore, 52 ÷ 6 = (48 + 4) ÷ 6. The quotient is 8, with a remainder of 4. The same answer can be found by using division, as shown in example (b). The pupil did not recall the largest multiple of 6 that is less than 52, but did know that 6 × 6 = 36.

(b) $6\overline{)52}$
$\quad \underline{36} \quad$ 6 (6 divides 36, 6 times)
$\quad 16$
$\quad \underline{12} \quad$ 2 (6 divides 12, 2 times)
$\quad\ \ 4 \quad$ 8 (6 divides 48, 8 times with a remainder of 4)

$$52 = 6 \times 8 + 4$$

The pupil indicated that 6 × 6 = 36 in the first step. After the subtraction, there is a remainder of 16 and 12 which is divided as shown in the second step. The final quotient is 6 + 2, or 8, with a remainder of 4. The same answer can be found by repeated subtraction of 6 from 52. The short forms in (c) and (d) for (17, 3), q = 5 and r = 2, so that:

(c) $17 = 5 \times 3 + 2$, or $\quad\dfrac{5 \text{ r } 2}{3\overline{)17}}$

For (3, 17), q = 0 and r = 3, so that:

(d) $3 = 0 \times 17 + 3$, or $\quad\dfrac{0 \text{ r } 3}{17\overline{)3}}$

If the remainder is greater than the divisor, the division is not complete. It is true that 17 = 4 × 3 + 5, but 4 is not considered to be the quotient, since 5 is not less than the divisor 3.

Expressing the Remainder in Division

When division is performed on a number that is not a multiple of the divisor, the remainder will be greater than 0. The way to express that remainder depends on the kind of numbers on which the operation is performed and on the division situation. For whole numbers, the quotient can be expressed only as a whole number with a remainder. For rational numbers, the quotient can be expressed in fractional form, as shown here for 8 ÷ 3:

$$\frac{8}{3} = \frac{6 + 2}{3} = \frac{6}{3} + \frac{2}{3} = 2 + \frac{2}{3}, \text{ or } 2\frac{2}{3}.$$

The Remainder in Problem Situations

In division there are two situations that require different representations of the remainder. In one the remainder is expressed as part of the quotient, with the quotient expressed as a fractional number. An illustration of this situation is the following problem.

A piece of wire 9 feet long is cut into 4 pieces of equal length. What is the length of each piece?

The length of each piece is 2¼ feet. It makes no sense to give this answer as 2 with remainder 1. With fractional numbers, it is possible to divide 9 by 4 and express the quotient as 2¼; with whole numbers this problem cannot be solved. The need to solve problems of this kind prompted the expansion of the number system to include fractional numbers.

The other division situation requires that the remainder be expressed as a remainder and not as part of the quotient. This condition prevails in the set of whole numbers. An illustration of this situation is the following problem.

How many groups of 4 children can be formed from 9 children?

The answer is 2 with a remainder of 1. A quotient of 2¼ is meaningless in this situation.

The way to express quotients in division situations involving nonmultiples of the divisor depends on the situation. The pupils must be able to interpret the answer. The structure of the number system is such that the division process can be applied to any two whole numbers (divisor not 0). The

quotient of $a \div b$ is q, with a remainder $r(r < b)$. If a is a multiple of b, r is 0.

Mathematical Answers Not Always Applicable

Interpreting a remainder in division relies on social usage and the good judgment of the teacher. This is shown by the following two problems:

1. A grocer sells 3 oranges for 50¢. Find the cost of 1 orange.

2. If 91 pupils are to be transported and a bus will hold only 45 pupils, how many buses will be needed?

The mathematical answer to problem 1 is 16⅔¢. Since fractional parts of a cent do not exist, the cost of one orange is 17¢.

The conventional answer to problem 2 is 2 buses and 1 child remaining. In a real situation one child would not be left out of the group, because some arrangement would be made to get 46 pupils on one of the buses.

Calculator Activities

Calculator use is limited when dealing with single-digit multiplication. It can be more useful in early work with division facts. However, the calculator becomes an essential tool when the pupil encounters problems in multiplication and division with numbers from everyday situations, business, and industry.

Most current inexpensive calculators have a repeat capability. For these calculators, early work with multiplication facts can be reinforced as follows.

Place 3 in the calculator and add 3. On most calculators this is done by pressing "+" and then pressing the equal key. If the calculator has a repeat, pressing the equal sign repeatedly will add 3 as many times as is desired. This activity can be useful in demonstrating that multiplication of whole numbers can be performed by repeated addition.

After a total of 6 addends gives a sum of 18, use the calculator to multiply 6×3 to see that the results of the two procedures are the same. This activity produces the multiplication table for the 3s and can be used to reinforce the basic facts for 3. By starting with 5 and adding 5 and repeating, practice can be had for the table of 5s and so on.

In a similar manner, the pupil can subtract 4 successively from 24 and count to see that there are six 4s in 24. This should be checked by using the calculator to see that $24 / 4 = 6$. It is also instructive to use the same procedure to see that $24 / 6 = 4$, an important structural relation in division. Finally use the repeated subtraction procedure to show that there are four 7s in 30 with a remainder of 2.

The calculator is useful to help pupils understand the following:

1. $\dfrac{30}{7} = 4\dfrac{2}{7}$

2. $\dfrac{30}{7} = 4r2$

3. $\dfrac{30}{7} = 4.285714$

4. $R = 30 - 7 \times 4 = 2$

5. $R = \dfrac{2}{7} \times 7 = 2$

6. $R = .285714 \times 7 = 2$, approximately.

Step 1 illustrates a common form for the quotient of $\frac{30}{7}$.

Step 2 illustrates a form of the quotient often used in the division algorithm. It is useless if the divisor is not known.

Step 3 illustrates the answer obtained with a calculator. The number of decimal places will vary with the calculator.

Step 4 shows that the remainder is the difference between the dividend and the highest multiple of the divisor contained in the dividend.

Step 5 shows the divisor times the fractional part of the quotient, $\frac{2}{7} \times 7 = 2$, is the remainder.

Step 6 uses the decimal equivalent of $\frac{2}{7}$ multiplied by 7 to get the remainder. If enough decimal places are used, the product will be the integer 2 but $.28 \times 7 = 1.96$. Because the remainder must be an integer, 1.96 rounds to the correct answer 2. This is an excellent opportunity to multiply 7 by $\frac{2}{7}$ expressed as a decimal to 2, 3 or 4 or more places. Ability to round intelligently is essential for efficient use of decimals.

Computers and calculators do not accept commas for numbers in computation. Ask each pupil in a class to enter a favorite digit; multiply by 239, then by 4649. It may be more effective for the teacher to perform the second multiplication on several calculators. Each calculator will display a numeral with 7 digits, all of which are the favorite digit entered by the pupil.

Ask a pupil to enter any number and multiply by 1111111, divide by 4649 and then divide by 239 to display the original number. In an alternate approach, the teacher performs the second division by 4649 and hands the calculator back to the pupil with the original number on display. Use a computer to show that $1111111 = 239 \times 4649$ and remind the pupils that dividing by 4649 and then by 239 is the same as dividing by 1111111.

Problem Solving

When introduced at an appropriate stage in the learning cycle, the activities in FIG. 9.1 all require responses that are not habitual. Each activity will reinforce the learning of basic facts as well as other multiplication and division concepts. They also will reduce some of the boredom resulting from the repetition of facts that is often necessary

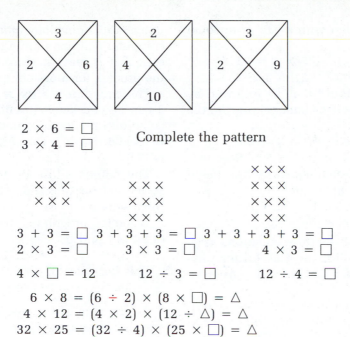

FIG. 9.1

to enable a pupil to perform algorithms with reasonable efficiency.

Latter activities use the property of compensation for multiplication. It requires that if one factor in a product is divided by a number N, another factor in the same product must be multiplied by N if the product is to remain unchanged. This property can be used to obtain one fact from another:

1. Why does the property of compensation work?

Answer: Multiplying a factor by 2 multiplies the product by 2. Dividing a factor by 2 divides the product by 2. Multiplication by 2 is undone with division by 2 because of the inverse relation between multiplication and division.

$$4 \times 6 = (4 \times 2) \times (6 \div 2) =$$
$$8 \times 3 = 24$$
$$9 \times 4 = (9 \div 3) \times (4 \times 3) =$$
$$3 \times 12 = 36$$

The procedure should be extended beyond basic facts. It is particularly useful in obtaining factors of 10, 100 or 1000.

$$48 \times 5 = (48 \div 2) \times (5 \times 2)$$
$$= 24 \times 10 = 240$$
$$84 \times 25 = (84 \div 4) \times (25 \times 4)$$
$$= 21 \times 100 = 2100$$
$$108 \times 50 = (108 \div 2) \times (50 \times 2)$$
$$= 54 \times 100 = 5400$$
$$96 \times 125 = (96 \div 8) \times (125 \times 8)$$
$$= 12 \times 1000 = 12000$$

For enrichment, extend this concept:
$$18 \times 15 = (18 \times 3) \times 5 =$$
$$9 \times 3 \times 10 = 270$$
$$24 \times 75 = (24 \times 3) \times 25 =$$
$$6 \times 3 \times 100 = 1800$$

These and similar examples provide excellent practice in mental arithmetic. The ideal procedure is to estimate the answer first before performing the computation. However, most pupils should record beginning work with pencil and paper and gradually proceed to mental arithmetic.

Early work with facts should be reinforced by asking pupils to write the four equations associated with a pair of unequal digits, as (3, 7):

$$3 \times 7 = 21 \qquad 7 \times 3 = 21$$
$$21 \div 7 = 3 \qquad 21 \div 3 = 7$$

This activity should then be followed by giving a complete fact, and asking for the other three facts:

$$9 \times 7 = 63 \rightarrow 7 \times 9 = 63,$$
$$63 \div 9 = 7 \text{ and } 63 \div 7 = 9.$$

The three additional equations associated with $4 \times N = 36$ are:

$$N \times 4 = 36, 4 = 36 \div N,$$
$$\text{and } N = 36 \div 4.$$

1. Ask which of the three equations associated $5 \times N = 35$ is most useful for solving the equation: $5 \times N = 35$. Answer: $N = 35 \div 5$.

The natural consequence for these activities is to write equations for problems, one of the basic strategies for problem solving.

Use an equation to solve the following problems. If there is too much or not enough information, indicate the omission or the surplus:

2. What is the cost of 7 items if the cost of one item is 12 cents?

Solution: $N = 7 \times 12 = 84$. The cost of 7 items is 84 cents.

Check to see if the answer is sensible: It must be between 5×12 and 10×12 or between 60 and 120 and closer to 60. The answer is sensible.

3. If the cost of 8 pounds of seed is $56, what is the cost of one pound?

Solution: $8 \times N = 56 \rightarrow N = 56 \div 8 \rightarrow N = 7$. The cost of one pound is $7. The answer is sensible because 7 is between $56 \div 10$ and $56 \div 5$.

4. Aretha has $24 that she wants to divide equally among her 3 sisters. How much will each sister get?

Solution: $N = 24 \div 3 \rightarrow N = 8$. Each sister will get $8. The answer is sensible because 8 is between $24 \div 2$ and $24 \div 4$ or between 6 and 12.

Each of the above solutions can be checked by a calculator or with the computer in its immediate mode. A check in the computer's programming mode is trivial except that it may increase understanding of the process for more complex situations.

The equation $8 \times N = 56$ from problem 3 can be checked without transforming the equation into an equivalent form:

10 FOR N = 1 TO 10: PRINT N, 8 * N: NEXT

The colons allow us to place three instructions on the same line instead of on three separate lines.

When the program is run, the seventh line of output will be:

$$7 \qquad 56$$

This indicates that when $N = 7$ then $8 \times N = 56$, the required solution.

5. The sum of the ages of a grandmother and her grandson is 60. In 20 years, the grandmother will be three times as old as the grandson is at that time. How old is each now?

Plan: If the grandson's age is now A, what is the expression for the grandmother's age? Answer: $60 - A$

Write expressions for the boy's and grandmother's age in 20 years.

Answer: $A + 20, 60 - A + 20$

Use the output of the following FOR-NEXT LOOP to solve the problem:

10 for A = 1 to 10
20 PRINT A, A + 20, 60 − A + 20
30 NEXT A

The output for the 5th line is:

$$5 \qquad 25 \qquad 75$$

This output tells us that the boy is now 5 years old and the grandmother is $60 - 5$ or 55 years old. In 20 years, the boy will be 25 and the grandmother will be 75, three times as old.

6. The sum of two numbers is 100 and one number is three times the other. Find the numbers. The solution just obtained for problem 5, 75 and 25, meets the conditions for this problem. At a glance, the problems seem different. However, when 20 is added to both the boy's and grandmother's age, the

problems become identical. Check the output of the FOR-NEXT loop and see that the sum of the two numbers in each line of output is 100. The ability to apply the solution of one problem to that of another is a basic strategy in mathematics.

Find the Pattern

7. The following three sequences have the same pattern. Each sequence starts with a two-digit number and terminates with a fourth one-digit number if the pattern is followed.

```
88  64  24  8
79  63  18  8
98  72  14  4
```

Answer: Each number, after the first, in all three sequences is the product of the two digits in the preceding number.

8. Write a fourth sequence using this pattern.

Answer: The first three numbers must be two-digit and the fourth one-digit. The sequence 34 12 2 is incorrect. Try 66.

Read Carefully:

9. A man shops at 5 stores and spends all but $5 dollars. He made no expenditure at any other store. How much did he have left?

10. Find the product of all ten digits mentally.

11. A pupil incorrectly divides by 7 instead of multiplying by 7 to get an answer of 5. What is the correct answer?

Answers: 9. $5   10. Zero   11. 245

Enrichment

12. Jackie cashes a check and, by error, is given cents for dollars and dollars for cents. The original check has twice as many cents as dollars. If she received 594 cents more than the amount of the correct check, what was the amount of the original check?

Write an expression for the correct check: 100 * N + 2 * N

Write an expression for the incorrect check: 100 * 2 * N + N

Interpret the output of the following FOR-NEXT loop to get the answer:

```
10 FOR N = 1 TO 10
20 PRINT N, 100 * N + 2 *
N + 594, 100 * 2 * N + N
30 NEXT N
RUN
1          696          201
2          798          402
3          900          603
4          1002         804
5          1104         1005
6          1206         1206
```

The center column displays the value of the original check plus 594 cents for each value of N. The right-hand column displays the value of the incorrect check. The output shows that the two are equal when N = 6.

This problem can be done with paper and pencil if, after computing values for N = 1 and N = 2, it is recognized that the middle column increases by 102 and the right-hand column increases by 201. A calculator can lead to a solution rather quickly, using its repeat mode.

If the following lines are inserted, the computer will recognize the answer and print: N = 6   Original check: $6.12

```
20 IF 100 * N + 2 * N + 594
= 100 * 2 * N + N THEN 100
100 PRINT
110 PRINT "N = ";N;"
ORIGINAL CHECK = $"; N + 2 *
N/100
```

13. Find two numbers with a sum of 60 so that one is three times the other.

Use guess and test with a FOR-NEXT loop.

```
10 FOR N = 1 TO 20
20 PRINT N, 60 - N, (60 - N)/N
30 PRINT
40 NEXT N
```

```
RUN
1                59         59
2                58         29
- - - - - - - - - -
10               50          5
- - - - - - - - - -
15               45          3
```

Answer: The numbers are 45 and 15. Sum = 60 and $45 \div 15 = 3$.

The computer will use its decision-making ability to eliminate the need for inspection and print the answer if line 20 is retyped with:

```
20 IF (60 - N) / N = 3 THEN
PRINT "THE NUMBERS ARE ";60
- N; " AND ";N
```

Computer Activities

Program P9.1 provides practice in simplifying products by applying the law of compensation to obtain factors of 10 or 100.

```
PROGRAM P9.1
  10 HOME : VTAB 9
  20 A = 4 + INT(12 * RND(1))
  30 PRINT 2 * A;" X 5 = "; A;
     " X ";
  40 INPUT "";Z$
  50 PRINT 2 * A;" X 5 = "; A;
     " X 10 = ";10 * A
  60 PRINT
  70 PRINT 8 * A;" X 25 = "
     ; 2*A; " X ";
  80 INPUT "";Z$
  90 PRINT 8 * A;" X 25 = "
     2*A; " X 100 = ";
     2*A*100
 100 INPUT ""; Z$: GOTO 10
 110 REM LINE 100 TELLS THE
COMPUTER TO REPEAT WHEN RE-
TURN IS PRESSED BUT IT MAKES
THE PROGRAM AN INFINITE LOOP
SO THAT YOU MUST HOLD DOWN
THE CONTROL KEY AND PRESS C
TO EXIT THE PROGRAM.
```

Program P9.2 provides practice in using the distributive property to obtain new facts from old.

```
PROGRAM P9.2
  10 HOME : VTAB 9
  20 A = 2 + INT(4 * RND(1))
  30 B = 6 + INT(4 * RND(1))
  40 PRINT A;" X ";B; " = "
     ;A; " X 5 + "; A;
     " X ";
  50 INPUT "";Z$
  60 PRINT A;" X ";B; " = "
     ;A; " X 5 + "; A; " X ";
     B - 5; " = ";A*5
```

Summary

Once pupils clearly understand the operations of addition and subtraction of whole numbers, the study of multiplication and division facts follows naturally. Pupils who understand addition as the operation that describes the combining of two groups of objects are ready to explore the process of combining two or more parts equal in number. This process can be described as either addition, as in $7 + 7 = 14$, or multiplication, $2 \times 7 = 14$. Likewise, pupils who are proficient at separating a collection into two parts and can describe this process as subtraction are ready to separate a group of objects into two or more parts equal in number and describe this process with division.

Pupils should be introduced to multiplication and division facts in problem situations. Experiences with manipulative materials serve to help pupils understand the meaning of these operations. Pupils should then learn to show multiplication and division facts with drawings and later with symbolic notations. The use of notations should flow from exploratory experiences with objects and drawings. Careful attention must be paid to bridging the gap from working with objects to solving problems at the symbolic level of thinking.

Pupils at the symbolic level are ready to study the properties of multiplication and division. The teacher must strive to help pupils discover the meanings of each property in terms of patterns and relationships. The relationship between multiplication and division can be stressed at the symbolic level of learning.

Mastery of the facts in multiplication and division requires (a) an ability to respond to each fact quickly and accurately, without using supplementary aids, (b) an understanding of the meaning of each operation and ability to show facts with drawings and with objects, and (c) an ability to solve word problems and verify the correctness of the solutions.

Calculators and computer programs offer a multitude of ways of providing reinforcement and enrichment to multiplication and division problems.

Exercise 9.2

The first six problems in this exercise use the facts in multiplication or division. Give the thought pattern you would use in teaching these problems to a class at the third-grade level:

1. If each team contains 5 players, how many players would there be on 4 teams?

2. There are 3 feet in a yard. What is the length in feet of a string 8 yards long?

3. One day, Jim rode his bicycle 18 km. He rode at an average rate of 6 km per hour. How many hours did he ride that day?

4. How many packages of 5 cookies each can be made with 35 cookies?

5. There are 8 trees in a row. How many trees are there in 5 rows?

6. How many 25¢ stamps can you buy with $4.00?

7. What properties of multiplication are common to addition?

8. Show how finding this product illustrates the distributive property:

   32
   × 3

9. Show why it is impossible to divide by 0.

10. Give four ways a pupil can discover the product of 3 × 8, or verify the product if he or she knows the 3s through the 5s.

11. Identify each of the following problems as either a *partitive* or a *measurement* situation:
    (a) How many yards are there in 15 feet?
    (b) How many quarts are there in 6 pints?
    (c) At 25 miles per gallon, how many gallons of gasoline are needed to travel 100 miles?
    (d) A car used 3 gallons of gasoline on a 60-mile trip. What was the average mileage per gallon?
    (e) There are 40 tulip bulbs in 5 rows of equal length. How many bulbs are there in a row?

12. Some pupils use the algorithm shown in (a) to find the quotient of the example 53 ÷ 8. Other pupils use the one shown in (b). Evaluate these procedures:

(a) 53 ÷ 8 = 6 r 5

(b)
```
8)53
  40 | 5
  13
   8 | 1
   5 | 6    Thus 53 ÷ 8 = 6 r 5
```

13. A teacher writes the following number sentences on the chalkboard and asks the class to fill in the table. One pupil asks why the numbers behave as they do. Give a satisfactory answer to this question.

$1 \times 9 + 1 = 10$

$2 \times 9 + 2 = 20$

$10 \times 9 + \triangle = \square$

14. Write the set of tables for the 2s, 4s, and 8s. Identify at least three distinguishing features of the products or of the sequence of the digits in the products.

15. List the ways to show that multiplication and division are opposites.

16. State two word problems that fit each of the following:

(a) $n \div 4 = 5$ (b) $n \times 6 = 30$ (c) $\dfrac{16}{n} = 3 \text{ r } 1$

Selected Readings

Ashlock, Robert B., et. al. *Guiding Each Child's Learning of Mathematics.* Columbus, OH: Charles E. Merrill Publishing Company, 1983. Chapter 9.

Heddens, James W., and William R. Speer. *Today's Mathematics,* 6th ed. Chicago: Science Research Associates, 1988. Unit 7.

Kennedy, Leonard M., and Steve Tipps. *Guiding Children's Learning of Mathematics,* 5th ed. Belmont, CA: Wadsworth, 1988. Chapter 10.

Marks, John L., et. al. *Teaching Elementary School Mathematics for Understanding,* 5th ed. New York: McGraw-Hill, 1985. Chapter 5.

Post, Thomas R. *Teaching Mathematics in Grades K–8.* Needham Heights, MA: Allyn & Bacon, 1988. Chapter 6.

Reys, Robert E., et. al. *Helping Children Learn Mathematics,* 2nd ed. Englewood Cliffs, NJ: Prentice-Hall, 1989. Chapter 9.

Riedesel, C. Alan. *Teaching Elementary School Mathematics,* 4th ed. Englewood Cliffs, NJ: Prentice-Hall, 1985. Chapters 8 and 9.

Suydam, Marilyn N., and Robert E. Reys (eds.). *Developing Computational Skills,* 1978 Yearbook. Reston, VA: National Council of Teachers of Mathematics, 1978. Chapter 7.

Trafton, Paul R., and Albert P. Shulte. *New Directions for Elementary School Mathematics,* 1989 Yearbook. Reston, VA: National Council of Teachers of Mathematics, Chapter 10.

Algorithms for Multiplication and Division of Multidigit Numbers

ACHIEVEMENT GOALS

After studying this chapter, you should be able to:

1. Identify the grade placement and sequence for teaching multiplication and division of multidigit whole numbers.

2. List the objectives for teaching multiplication and division of multidigit numbers.

3. Enumerate what pupils should understand and be able to do as readiness for studying multiplication and division.

4. Describe the teaching–learning sequence for multiplication and division that involves:

    (a) Stating appropriate problems to solve
    (b) Using well-selected manipulatives
    (c) Creating visual models of the multiplication and division operations
    (d) Translating multiplication and division into symbolic notations

5. Explain various ways to reinforce learning by using practice activities, calculators, and computer programs.

VOCABULARY

These terms are defined or illustrated in the Glossary.

Adding by endings	Higher-decade
Algorithm	multiplication
Bridging a decade	Multiple
Dividend	Multiplicand
Divisible	Multiplier
Divisor	Product
Expanded notation	Quotient
Factor	Regrouping
Higher-decade	Remainder
addition	

Multiplication and division of multidigit whole numbers can be performed in a variety of ways. Meaningful learning requires that pupils grow in their understanding of these operations. They do this by having opportunities for discovering solutions to problems by using base and place-value devices, by drawing visual representations, and by translating these approaches into symbolic notations. One standard algorithm performed by following a series of memorized steps and rules is no longer acceptable. Pupils should construct their own meanings by thinking and reasoning as they explore a variety of approaches to multiplication and division problems. For complete understanding, pupils need to learn techniques of estimating products and quotients and explore how these operations are used in measurement, geometry, statistics, and probability.

Finally, today's pupils should be taught to perform multiplication and division of multidigit numbers with the aid of calculators and computers. Critics of using these modern machines assert that "things won't be the same as they were when one struggled with pencil and paper arithmetic . . . [but] they are wrong in thinking that pencil and paper arithmetic is ideal, and that what replaces it is not viable."[1]

The impact of the use of calculators and computers requires a re-examination of what pupils need to learn about multiplication and division of multidigit whole numbers. Renewed emphasis should be placed on understanding how and why procedures work and how these operations are used in problem-solving situations.

Grade Placement and Sequence

In the 1980s, multiplication and division of multidigit numbers was typically presented and developed at the third-grade level. The following sequence and grade placement for multiplication and division of multidigit numbers is based on the recommendation of the National Council of Teachers of Mathematics.[2]

(1) Multiplication of a two- or three-digit number by a one-digit number:
   Third grade— Explore in problem situations with manipulatives and visuals (no regrouping).
   Fourth grade—develop meaningful connections between manipulations of physical objects and symbolic procedures, without and with regrouping.

(2) Multiplication of two-digit numbers by two-digit numbers:
   Fourth grade—explore in problem situations with manipulatives and visuals without and with regrouping. Develop meaningful symbolic notations and procedures.

(3) Division involving one-digit quotients, one-digit divisors, without and with remainders:
   Third grade— explore in problem situations with manipulatives and visuals.
   Fourth grade—develop meaningful connections between manipulatives and symbolic procedures.

(4) Division involving two- or three-digit numbers by one-digit numbers:
   Fourth grade—explore in problem settings with manipulatives and visuals. Develop

1. Philip J. Davis and Reuben Hersh, *The Mathematical Experience* (Boston: Houghton Mifflin, 1981), p. 33.

2. *Curriculum and Evaluation Standards for School Mathematics*, Working Draft (Reston, VA: National Council of Teachers of Mathematics, 1987), p. 39.

meaningful algorithms. Fifth grade— reteach and reinforce.

(5) Division involving more than two-digit divisors should be solved by using a calculator.

We recommend that pupils be taught to deal with multiplicands (the number multiplied) of up to three digits, but the multiplier should have no more than two digits. However, three-place numbers ending in zero are acceptable. In division, we recommend that pupils be taught to deal with dividends (the number divided) containing four or less digits, and with divisors of up to 100. More important than the number of digits to be used, however, is that the pupils learn and understand the algorithms so that they can be applied in problem-solving situations. It is of little value to learn these procedures without understanding them.

Results of the Fourth National Assessment

The Fourth National Assessment of Educational Progress in Mathematics included a limited number of multiplication and division items. Vicky Kouba and others[3] interpreted the data as follows:

Percent Correct by Grade

Type of Example	Third	Seventh
43 × 2	56	94
413 × 3	7	77
42 ÷ 3	20	—

3. Vicky L. Kouba, et. al., "Results of the Fourth NAEP Assessment of Mathematics: Number, Operations, and Word Problems," *Arithmetic Teacher,* 35 (April 1988): 15–16.

These data show that third-grade pupils have an inadequate understanding of multidigit multiplication and division, although these topics have traditionally been taught at the third-grade level. This fact supports our recommendation to delay the development of these tasks until the fourth grade.

Teaching Multiplication of a Two-Digit Number by a One-Digit Number

In planning and teaching multiplication with multidigit whole numbers, the principles discussed in Chapter 1 should be followed in developing a series of lessons. Graph paper is a good teaching aid to help pupils write the digits in the correct places when dealing with multidigit numbers. The squares on the paper must be large enough for a pupil to write digits in them.

I. Objectives

The following objectives should be achieved by pupils during a series of lessons on multiplication of multidigit numbers:

1. Given a word problem of combining sets equal in number, recognize that multiplication can be used for arriving at the answer.

2. Solve in a variety of ways examples of a two-digit number multiplied by a one-digit number, without regrouping and then with regrouping.

3. Demonstrate the commutative, associative, and distributive properties of multiplication.

4. Name the factors and the product.

5. Solve word problems involving multidigit multiplication.

6. Estimate reasonable answers and verify.

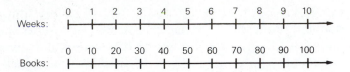

II. Readiness

Pupils are ready for a study of multidigit multiplication when they:

- Have developed a reasonable degree of understanding of and proficiency in working with the basic multiplication facts
- Can represent base-ten concepts with manipulatives and with visuals
- Can represent place-value concepts with manipulatives and with visuals, understand and perform regrouping in addition and subtraction, round numbers
- Can make reasonable estimates of sums and differences

If pupils are deficient in one or more of these prerequisites, special provisions need to be made for reteaching and reinforcement activities as they are being introduced to multidigit multiplication.

As a readiness for multiplication of multidigit numbers without and with regrouping, the pupils should solve word problems that involve multiplying a multiple of ten by a one-digit number, such as "Each month Francisco reads 10 books. How many does he read in four months?"

1. Show solution with base-ten manipulatives:

2. Count by tens: ten, twenty, thirty, forty.

3. Use a double number line as shown above.

4. Make a multiples table:

$$1 \times 10 = 10$$
$$2 \times 10 = 20$$
$$3 \times 10 = 30$$
$$4 \times 10 = \boxed{}$$

The same kinds of activities should be provided for multiplication problems with a multiplicand that is a multiple of 100 by a one-digit multiplier.

BUILDING AND STUDYING MULTIPLES TABLES

Another readiness activity for multidigit multiplication and division is learning how to build, study, and use multiples tables. The table on page 191 is for the multiples of 8:

Discuss with pupils the relationships shown in the table:

1. What is the difference between any two consecutive multiples?

2. What are two division facts that can be stated for each multiple? For example, the two division facts that can be stated for the multiple 56 are: 56 divided by 8 = 7 and 56 divided by 7 = 8. Another language pattern for division is: 8 divides 56 seven times, and 7 divides 56 eight times.

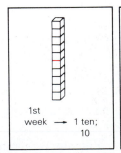

1st week → 1 ten; 10

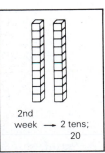

2nd week → 2 tens; 20

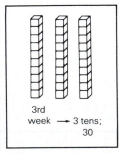

3rd week → 3 tens; 30

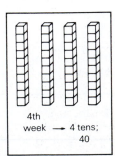

4th week → 4 tens; 40

GUIDE No.	Multiples of 8:	Meanings/Procedures	
1 →	8	$1 \times 8 = 8; 8 \div 8 = 1$	
2 →	16	$2 \times 8 = 16; 16 \div 8 = 2$; double 1st multiple	
3 →	24	$3 \times 8 = 24$; Add the 1st and 2nd multiples →	$8 + 16 = 24$
4 →	32	$4 \times 8 = 32$; Double the 2nd multiple →	$2 \times 16 = 32$
5 →	40	$5 \times 8 = 40$; Add the 2nd and 3rd multiple →	$16 + 24 = 40$
6 →	48	$6 \times 8 = 48$; Double the 3rd multiple →	$2 \times 24 = 48$
7 →	56	$7 \times 8 = 56$; Add the 3rd and 4th multiple →	$24 + 32 = 56$
8 →	64	$8 \times 8 = 64$; Double the 4th multiple →	$2 \times 32 = 64$
9 →	72	$9 \times 8 = 72$; Add the 4th and 5th multiples →	$32 + 40 = 72$

3. Discuss changing the table to show multiples for 80 and for 800. How do the products change?

4. Using the techniques shown above, create a multiples table for a two-digit number such as 15.

III. Motivation

Most pupils who have been successful in dealing with the readiness concepts and skills enumerated probably will continue to be motivated to study multidigit multiplication. The pupils who are having difficulty in mastering multiplication facts will need special activities to heighten their interest for this more advanced work. All pupils will be more strongly motivated toward a study of this topic by using these techniques:

- Show usefulness in problem-solving settings.
- Give opportunities to use base-ten and place-value manipulatives during introductory lessons.
- Have pupils learn to draw pictures.
- Use expanded notation.

- Discuss the meanings of the various procedures.
- Use calculators, games, and computer programs for reinforcement.

IV. Guided Discovery

WITHOUT REGROUPING

Multiplying a two-digit number by a one-digit number without regrouping requires pupils to understand that each digit in each place of the multiplicand must be multiplied by the multiplier. Introduce multiplication of a multidigit number by a one-place number, no regrouping, with a problem of the following type: A box will hold 12 cookies. How many cookies will 3 boxes hold?

(a) Use base-ten blocks or a place-value chart or an abacus to show $12 + 12 + 12$ and then show with drawings (see page 192):

(b) Demonstrate with expanded and standard notations:

```
1 ten  2 ones      10 + 2       12        12
×       3        ×      3      × 3       × 3
─────────────    ──────────    ────      ────
3 tens 6 ones      30 + 6        6         36
     36              36         30
                                ────
                                 36
```

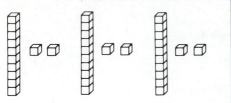

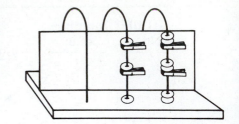

Tens	Ones
⊓	⊓⊓
⊓	⊓⊓
⊓	⊓⊓

WITH REGROUPING

One of the major difficulties pupils encounter when multiplying multidigit numbers is when a place is overloaded with a two-place number. The process of renaming and recording numerals is sometimes taught as a memorized rule of "carrying" with little understanding. Pupils should experience the following steps:

1. Start with a word problem that involves renaming in the ones place. For example, "Nancy has a stamp collection book that holds 16 stamps on each page. How many stamps will 3 pages hold?"

2. Have the pupils solve this problem with base-ten materials such as base-ten blocks or with a place-value chart. Pupils should discover that when 3 sets of 16 are shown with manipulatives, there will be a total of 3 tens and 18 ones. The 18 ones should then be regrouped as 1 ten 8 ones and added to the 3 tens. The result is 4 tens 8 ones, or 48 for the product.

3. Use expanded notation and the standard notation:

(a)	(b)	(c)	(d)	(e)
1 ten 6 ones	10 + 6	16	$\overset{1}{1}6$	16
× 3	× 3	× 3	× 3	× 3
3 tens 18 ones	30 + 18	18	48	48
		30		
		48		

The next step involves "renaming and recording." After the product of 3 × 6 is found to be 18 in (c), the 18 is then renamed as 1 ten 8 ones. The 1 *recorded* above the 1

ten in the multiplicand is added to the product of 3 × 1 found in (d). This is often referred to as "carrying," when in fact it is a technique of *recording* the digit in the tens place so it can be added to the product of the second multiplication. In the final step, pupils should be encouraged to find the product without recording the regrouped 10 as in (e).

4. Check using addition.

V. Reinforcement

After pupils understand the process of renaming in multiplication when the ones place is overloaded (with a number more than 9), additional practice should be given at the symbolic level. Manipulatives and drawings should not be needed by most pupils. Further, not all examples need to be introduced with word problems. Pupils should be encouraged to use various ways to multiply a two-digit number by a one-digit number.

APPLY PROPERTIES OF MULTIPLICATION

For a complete understanding of the operation of multiplication, pupils should be given the opportunity to explore the ways the properties of multiplication can be applied to give alternate ways of solving and checking examples.

Relate to Equal Addends. A multiplication example can be related to repeated addition. The example 4 × 25 can be renamed 25 + 25 + 25 + 25 = 100

The Associative Property. For 3 × 18, the associative property can be used to change the example as follows:

1. Rename 18 as 2 × 9: $3 \times (2 \times 9)$

2. Associate the 2 with the 3: $(3 \times 2) \times 9$

3. The new example becomes: $6 \times 9 = 54$

For 6 × 15, the example can be changed as follows:

1. Rename the 6 as 3 × 2: $(3 \times 2) \times 15$

2. Associate the 2 with the 15 : $3 \times (2 \times 15)$

3. The new example becomes: $3 \times 30 = 90$

The factors of a multiplication example may be rearranged into any order without changing the product. This is a consequence of the commutative and associative properties of multiplication. For the example 6 × 15, both factors may be renamed as factors and then rearranged into any order.

1. Rename 6 as (3 × 2) and 15 as (3 × 5) : $3 \times 2 \times 3 \times 5$

2. Rearrange the factors as $(2 \times 5) \times (3 \times 3)$

3. Rename and find the product: $10 \times 9 = 90$

Even before multiplication by a two-digit number is introduced pupils can apply the associate property to solve 25 × 84 as follows:

1. Rename 84 as 4 × 21: $25 \times (4 \times 21)$

2. Associate 4 with 25: $(25 \times 4) \times 21$

3. Rename and write the product: $100 \times 21 = 2100$

The Distributive Property. For 3 × 24, the distributive property can be used to change the example as follows:

1. Rename 24 as (20 + 4): $3 \times (20 + 4)$

2. Distribute the 3 "over the addends": $(3 \times 20) + (3 \times 4)$

3. Rename each addend and write the sum: $60 + 12 = 72$

A factor may also be distributed "over subtraction" as follows:

1. For 25 × 9, rename 9 as 10 − 1: $25 \times (10 - 1)$

2. Apply the distributive property: $(25 \times 10) - (25 \times 1)$

3. Rename and subtract: $250 - 25 = 225$.

Adding by Endings in Multiplication

Higher-decade addition is the process of adding a two-place number and a one-place number in one mental response. This process is also called "adding by endings." Adding by endings occurs in multiplication as shown in the following example:

Step 1: Multiply 6 × 8 = 48

$$\begin{array}{r} 38 \\ \times 6 \\ \hline 48 = 40 + 8 \end{array}$$

Step 2: Rename 48 as 4 tens 8 ones

Step 3: Record the 8 ones in the product, and the 4 above the tens place digit in multiplicand

$$\begin{array}{r} 4 \\ 38 \\ \times 6 \\ \hline 8 \end{array}$$

Step 4: Multiply 6 × 3 (tens) = 18, then add the 4 (tens) = 18 + 4 = 22 (tens)

$$\begin{array}{r} 4 \\ 38 \\ \times\ \ 6 \\ \hline 228 \end{array}$$

Several different procedures can be followed to practice adding by endings as it occurs in multiplication. First, pupils should review adding by endings in column addition. They should be lead to see that in some examples "bridging the decade" occurs, while in some other examples the sum stays in the same decade. To highlight these two situations, two practice sheets could be used.

(1) A sheet of addition and multiplication examples where the sum will be in the same decade as the two-digit number:

A. 15   24   32   64   81   56
    + 2   + 3   + 5   + 4   + 7   + 2

Each of the higher-decade addition examples in A would occur in B. In the first example in B, $3 \times 5 + 2$ is the first example in A.

B. 57   68   47   85   98   83
    × 3   × 4   × 8   × 8   × 9   × 7

(2) A sheet of addition and multiplication examples where the sum is one decade more than the two-digit number (bridging occurs):

A. 48   54   45   64   27   28
    + 4   + 7   + 8   + 7   + 5   + 6

Each of the higher-decade addition examples in A would occur in B.

B. 65   68   59   89   36   49
    × 8   × 9   × 9   × 8   × 9   × 7

Multiplying a Two-Digit Number by a Two-Digit Number

Once pupils have a good understanding of multiplying by a one-digit number they are ready to multiply by a two-digit number. The new difficulty is learning how to multiply by a number in the tens place. Word problems should be used to introduce this topic. Manipulatives should not be used. Almost all of the work should be done at the symbolic level.

Using Multiples of Ten as Factors

The first type of examples should involve one factor that is a multiple of ten.

(1) Start with a word problem: Gloria's father earns $30 an hour. How much will he earn in 2 hours?

(2) Discuss strategies for solving the problem:
   (a) Use 30 as an addend 2 times.
   (b) Multiply 2×30
   (c) Rename 2×30 as $2 \times (3 \times 10)$
       $= (2 \times 3) \times 10 = 6 \times 10$

(3) Generalize that multiplying 2×30 is just like multiplying 2×3 tens to give 6 tens. The word *tens* can be changed to a numeral by annexing 0 to the right of 6 to make the product 60.

(4) Reinforce with additional problems/examples such as:

   10   20   30   40   50
   × 2   × 3   × 4   × 5   × 6

$2 \times 10 = 2 \times 1 \text{ ten } = 2 \text{ tens } = 20$
$3 \times 20 = 3 \times 2 \text{ tens } = 6 \text{ tens } = \underline{\ \ }$
$4 \times 30 = 4 \times \underline{\ \ } \text{ tens } = \underline{\ \ } \text{ tens } = \underline{\ \ }$
$5 \times 40 = \underline{\ \ } \times 4 \text{ tens } = \underline{\ \ } \text{ tens } = \underline{\ \ }$
$6 \times 50 = \underline{\ \ } \times \underline{\ \ } \text{ tens } = \underline{\ \ } \text{ tens } = \underline{\ \ }$

The second kind of problem should include both factors that are multiples of ten.

(1) If Ralph's father earns $20 per hour, how much would he make in 40 hours?

(2) Discuss strategies:
   (a) Write as an equation: $40 \times 20 = ?$
   (b) Rename 40 as (4×10) and 20 as (2×10)
   (c) Rearrange the factors: $(4 \times 2) \times (10 \times 10) = 8 \times 100$

(3) Generalize: $20 \times 10 = 200$
       $20 \times 20 = 400$
       $20 \times 30 = 600$
       $20 \times 40 = \underline{\ \ \ \ }$

When we multiply 2 tens times 4 tens we get 8 *hundreds*. Multiplying 20×40 is the same as multiplying 8×100.

(4) Provide additional problems/examples:

   20   30   40   20   50   10
   ×40   ×20   ×20   ×30   ×10   ×80

The third kind of problem has two two-digit numbers, but only the multiplier is a multiple of ten.

(1) Charles rides his bike 43 miles a week. How far will he ride in 20 weeks?

(2) Discuss strategies:
(a) Write the equation: $20 \times 43 = ?$
(b) Use the associative property:
$(2 \times 10) \times 43$
$2 \times (10 \times 43)$
$2 \times 430 = 860$
(d) Use the distributive property:
$20 \times (40 + 3)$
$(20 \times 40) + (20 \times 3)$
$800 + 60 = 860$

(3) Generalize:
Multiplying 20×43 is just like multiplying 2×43 except that the 6 has to be written in the tens place instead of the ones place.

$$\begin{array}{r} 43 \\ \times\ 20 \\ \hline 860 \end{array}$$

(4) Reinforcement: Provide additional problems/examples of this type.

Neither Factor a Multiple of Ten

When pupils encounter multiplication examples in which neither factor is a multiple of ten they perform a multiplication for each digit in the multiplier times each digit in the multiplicand. For the example 23×32, four multiplications are actually performed, as the result of the distributive property of multiplication over addition: $(20 + 3) \times (30 + 2)$ is renamed as:

$(20 \times 30) + (20 \times 2) + (3 \times 30) + (3 \times 2)$

In actual practice, the multiplication is performed in reverse order in the following vertical form:

$$\begin{array}{r} 32 \\ \times\ 23 \\ \hline 6\ (3 \times 2) \\ 90\ (3 \times 30) \\ 40\ (20 \times 2) \\ 600\ (20 \times 30) \\ \hline \end{array}$$

The four partial products are shortened to two for the standard algorithm as follows:

$$\begin{array}{r} 32 \\ \times\ 23 \\ \hline 96\ (3 \times 32) \\ 640\ (20 \times 32) \\ \hline 736 \end{array}$$

Alternative Approaches for Enrichment

Many pupils enjoy learning historical approaches to computation. There are two interesting procedures for multiplication of multidigit numbers. One is the *duplation* method and the other is the *Russian Peasant* approach.

Duplation Multiplication

Duplation, as the name implies, is a technique of finding products by doubling numbers. For the example 23×42, the following table is formed. On the left-hand side, start with 1 and double each step until there are enough numbers to find a sum of 23. These are actually the products of powers of two starting with 2^0, which equals 1. Two squared equals 4, two to the third power equals 8, and so forth. In the right-hand column, start with 42 and double it each step. Then find the numbers in the left-hand column that sum 23 and add the corresponding numbers in the right-hand column for the product.

1	42	(1×42)
2	84	(2×42)
4	168	(4×42)
8	336	(8×42)
16	672	(16×42)

$16 + 4 + 2 + 1 = 23$, so $672 + 168 + 84 + 42 = 966$, the product of 23×42.

This method allows pupils to find products by doubling and adding. It is excellent practice and a very interesting approach for most pupils.

Russian Peasant Multiplication

Russian Peasant multiplication is also a very interesting approach to multidigit multiplication. It uses a two-column approach and for the same example yields the same numbers. However, the rules are different than in duplation.

For the example 23 × 42, start two columns with the two numbers, 23 on the left and 42 on the right. For each step on the left-hand column record one-half the previous number, dropping the fractional part of the quotient. For each corresponding step on the right-hand column double each subsequent number. Continue until the quotient in the left-hand column is 1. Examine the numbers in the left-hand column and circle each *ODD* number. The product is the sum of each of the corresponding numbers in the right-hand column, including the original number if it is opposite an odd number.

23	42	(1 × 42)
11	84	(2 × 42)
5	168	(4 × 42)
2	336	(8 × 42)
1	672	(16 × 42)

The numbers 1, 5, 11, and 23 are odd. So the sum of 672 + 168 + 84 + 42 = 966, the product of 23 × 42. Note that this methods picks the same powers of 2 as in the duplication method: (1 × 42) + (2 × 42) + (4 × 42) + (16 × 42) = (1 + 2 + 4 + 16) × 42 = 23 × 42 = 966.

Teaching Multidigit Division

I. Objectives

The following objectives should be achieved by pupils during a series of lessons on division of multidigit numbers:

1. Given a word problem that can be solved by subtracting equal numbers, recognize that division can be used for arriving at the answer.

2. Solve examples of a two- or three-digit number divided by a one-digit number, without and with regrouping and represent with:
   (a) Base-ten and place-value materials
   (b) Drawings including a special array
   (c) Expanded notation
   (d) Long and standard algorithms

3. Demonstrate the renaming of the dividend so that each subtraction is a multiple of the divisor.

4. Name the dividend, the divisor, and the quotient.

5. Show that multiplication and division are inverse operations in that division can be checked by multiplying.

6. Solve word problems involving multidigit division by using pencil-and-paper techniques, calculators, and computer programs.

II. Readiness

As a readiness for division of multidigit numbers without and with regrouping the dividend, pupils should demonstrate a near mastery of the following:

- The basic multiplication and division facts
- Base-ten concepts, place-value concepts, and renaming numbers
- The relationship between multiplication and division:

$6 \times 8 = 48; 48 \div 6 = 8$
$8 \times 6 = 48; 48 \div 8 = 6$
$6)\overline{48}$ 6 divides 48 eight times because 6 × 8 = 48

- The multiples concept: pupils can write a multiples table for one-digit and two-digit numbers
- Measurement- and partitive-type word problems involving basic division facts, solving them with manipulatives, with drawings, and with symbolic notations.

III. Motivation

Division is the most difficult of the whole-number operations taught in the elementary school. Pupils consequently are usually less motivated to work with this operation than with the other three. Several techniques are useful in increasing pupils' motivation toward learning division:

- Use division problems that occur in the pupils' lives.
- Start with problems without remainders that are easily related to the basic multiplication and division facts.
- Use manipulatives only for demonstration purposes. When emphasis is placed on using objects to solve multidigit division problems, many complications arise.
- Use simple drawings to illustrate the steps in solving a division example.
- Emphasize alternative approaches to solving division problems at the symbolic level.
- Help pupils learn how to arrive at an estimate of the quotient.
- Make frequent use of the calculator.
- Use computer programs that emphasize the meaning of the division operation

The best way to motivate learning is to make sure each pupil understands and succeeds.

Teaching Division by a One-Digit Divisor

Division by a one-digit divisor may follow the procedure and language of measurement division or of partitive division. In measurement division, the problem is to find the number of times the divisor can be subtracted from the dividend. When the divisor is a one-digit number and the dividend is a multidigit number, working with manipulatives and drawings is very cumbersome. For the measurement problem: There are 68

people driving to work in cars. In each car there are 2 persons. How many cars are there? To solve this problem with manipulatives, pupils would have to lay out 68 objects, then separate them into sets of two. This would not only take a considerable amount of time but it will not illustrate the advantage of using place-value concepts in division. We therefore recommend that partition division problems be used to develop the ideas and procedures for dividing by a one-digit divisor.

(1) Start with a word problem: Elizabeth has $68 to give equally to her two children for Christmas. How much will each get?

(2) Solve with manipulatives. Use play money, lay out 6 ten-dollar bills and 8 one-dollar bills. Then divide the 6 ten-dollar bills into two equal parts and do the same with the 8 one-dollar bills. Determine that each child will get 3 ten-dollar bills and 4 one-dollar bills, or $34 each.

(3) Use base-ten drawings as shown on page 198.

(4) Translate into expanded and standard notations:

$$\begin{array}{c} 3 \text{ tens } 4 \text{ ones} \\ 2\overline{)6 \text{ tens } 8 \text{ ones}} \end{array} \qquad \begin{array}{c} 30 + 4 \\ 2\overline{)60 + 8} \end{array}$$

$$2\overline{)68} = \frac{60 + 8}{2} = \frac{60}{2} + \frac{8}{2} = 30 + 4 = 34$$

This problem shows the procedure for dividing by a one-digit divisor when regrouping is not involved. Each addend in the dividend represents a number divisible by the divisor. Problems of this type are infrequent in everyday affairs.

Division Involving Renaming the Dividend

(1) Start with a word problem: A class of 72 pupils is to be separated into three groups equal in number. How many pupils will be in each group?

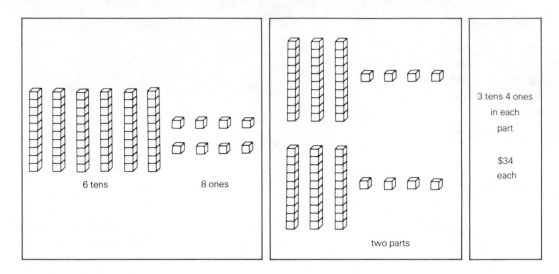

6 tens   8 ones

two parts

3 tens 4 ones in each part

$34 each

(2) Explore the solution with manipulatives. Use base-ten blocks. Lay out 7 tens and 2 ones. Ask the pupils to separate the 7 tens into 3 parts. They discover that 6 tens can be placed into 3 parts, but one ten remains undivided. Discuss what to do with the one ten. Pupils will suggest to regroup the one ten into ten ones. Then 12 ones can be separated into 3 parts, with 4 ones in each group. Children conclude that when 72 is separated into 3 equal numbered parts, there are 24 in each group.

(3) Translate into expanded and standard notations: Rename 72 as 70 + 2. Since 70 is not a multiple of 3, it should be renamed as 60 + 12.

$$\frac{72}{3} = \frac{60}{3} + \frac{12}{3} = 20 + 4 = 24$$

(4) Provide other problems/examples that require renaming the dividend as addends that are multiples of the divisor for pupils to solve.

The Subtractive Method

The solution to measurement-type division problems can be shown by successive subtraction. For the problem, "Peter has 72 cents. He wants to buy candies priced at 3 cents each. How many can he buy?" It is too tedious and time-consuming to use successive subtraction of 3s to solve this problem. However, it is practical and useful to successively subtract *multiples* of 3 as shown below:

```
3)72
  30      10 (×3)
  42
  30      10 (×3)
  12
  12       4 (×3)
        24 sets of 3s.
```

We see in the first step there are 10 threes, in the second step there are 10 threes, and in the last step there are 4 threes. So there are 24 threes in 72.

In using the subtractive method, sometimes called the *Greenwood* method, the idea is to search for the largest multiple of the divisor at each step. In the preceding example, the largest multiple is 60 (20 × 3). Also, rather than recording the partial quotients along the right side, they may be recorded above the dividend to indicate place value. This is sometimes called the *pyramid* method of recording partial quotients.

The successive subtraction method can be

used to solve the following problem: "There are 96 children to be transported on a field trip in vans. If each van holds 8 children, how many will be needed?

```
8)96
   80      10 (8 vans will take 80 children)
   16
   16      2 (2 vans will take 16 children)
```

A total of 12 vans are needed.

The pyramid method is similar to the subtractive method but has a specific requirement for placing partial quotients to emphasize place value. The example on the right illustrates the pyramid method using the same example previously used to demonstrate the subtractive method. All partial quotients and the final quotient are placed above the dividend with digits in the appropriate column to indicate place value.

```
        24
         4
        10
        10
 3)72
        30    10 × 3
        42
        30    10 × 3
        12
        12     4 × 3
         0
```

Division with a Remainder

Unfortunately, the dividend is not always a multiple of the divisor. When this is true, there will be a "remainder." For example, there will be a remainder in this problem: "Charles has $142 to spend on transportation. A bus pass costs $8 a week. How many weeks can he ride the bus?

(1) 1 week → $8

(2) 10 weeks→ $80

(3) After 10 weeks he has $62 left to spend: 142 − 80 = 62.

(4) 7 weeks → $56

Therefore he can ride 17 weeks and have $6 remaining unspent. To check the example, 17 × $8 = $136; $136 + $6 = $142.

In some division problems it is necessary to rename the remainder as a fraction to become a part of the quotient. For example, the problem "Charles wants to save $50 out of his earnings over a 4-week period for Christmas presents. How much will he have to save each week?" The quotient 12 with a remainder of 2 does not give the solution to the problem. The remainder 2 divided by 4 gives ½, so Charles will have to save $12.50 each week.

Determining Number of Digits in the Quotient

An important step in a division example is to determine the number of digits in the quotient. For the example $7)\overline{1547}$, 7 × 10 = 70, 7 × 100 = 700, 7 × 1000 = 7000, so the quotient is more than 100 and less than 1000, or a three-digit number.

One of the distinguishing features of division is the place in the dividend to start the algorithm. In addition, subtraction, and multiplication we begin the algorithm with the ones place and proceed toward the left. In division, the procedure is in the opposite order. To divide 64 by 2, a child divides 6 tens by 2 and 4 ones by 2. In the multiplication algorithm, we multiply the ones and then the tens. The teacher should guide pupils to make this discovery by asking questions about the starting place for each operation.

Research has shown that the best readiness for division with a multidigit quotient is the ability to divide by a one-digit divisor, as in $3)\overline{72}$. If the pupils *understand* the sequence of steps in solving this example, they should have little difficulty in learning the sequence for $21\overline{)672}$.

Estimation of the Quotient

When pupils are introduced to the standard algorithm for division by a two-place divisor they need to know how to estimate the quotient.

There are many ways to estimate the quotient, but two most used are known as the *one-rule* or the *two-rule* procedure. According to the one-rule plan, the divisor is rounded down. For example, the divisors in the 20s, such as 21 to 29, are rounded to 20. In the two-rule plan the traditional procedure for rounding a two-place number is followed. For example, divisors 21 − 24 are rounded to 20 and the divisors 25 − 29 are rounded to 30. The question arises as to which method is superior. Limited research on the question indicates that there is no significant difference between the two.

When the one-rule plan is used, the estimated quotient will either be the true quotient or too large. If it is too large, the estimated quotient must be reduced by one until the true quotient is found. Excluding divisors in the teens, the estimated quotient may be 3 more than the true quotient, as in $29\overline{)180}$. If the one-rule method is used, 29 is rounded to 20 and the estimated quotient is 9. If the two-rule method is used, 29 is rounded to 30 and the true quotient of 6 is obtained.

The two-rule method will give the true quotient more often than the one rule method. In either method, the pupil should multiply the trial quotient by the true divisor to determine if the estimated quotient is too large or too small and make corrections accordingly.

Checking Division

When the dividend is a multiple of the divisor, division can be checked by multi-plying the quotient by the divisor. If the product is the dividend, then the example is correct. When there is a remainder, the same procedure is used with the additional step of adding the remainder to the product of the quotient and the divisor.

Dividing by a Two-Digit Divisor

Divisors That Are Multiples of Ten

Division by a two-place divisor should be introduced with a divisor that is a multiple of 10. For example, "Tickets are arranged in bundles of 20. How many bundles can be formed with 480 tickets?"

First, guide the pupils to estimate the number of digits in the quotient by thinking $20 \times 10 = 200$, $20 \times 100 = 2000$, so the quotient is more than 10 and less than 100, or a two-place number.

```
(1)  20)480                           (2)      4
         400     (20 × 20)                    20
          80                           20)480
          80     ( 4 × 20)                   400
          24                                  80
                                              80
(3)       24
     20)480
          40
          80
          80
```

The pupils think in (3) the number of 20s in 48 tens is the same as the number of 2s in 4. Write 2 in the tens place. Use a similar pattern for the next quotient figure.

Divisors Not Multiples of Ten

After the class can divide by divisors that are multiples of 10, the next step involves dividing by a divisor that is not a multiple of 10. Consider this problem: "A high school senior class of 432 students plans a trip by bus to Washington, D.C. If each bus holds 54 students, how many buses are needed?"

(1) Determine the number of digits in the quotient—10 × 54 is greater than 432 → One-digit quotient

$$54\overline{)432}$$
$$\underline{432}$$
$$8$$

(2) Multiply 5 × 54 = 270. The quotient is more than 5.

(3) Round 54 to 50 and estimate the number of 50s in 432, which is 8.

(4) Write 8 in the ones place in the quotient and multiply as shown. *Eight buses are needed.*

After pupils know how to divide an example when the estimated quotient is the true quotient, they are ready to solve an example in which the estimated quotient is not the true quotient.

Consider the problem: "There are 156 first-grade pupils to be assigned to classrooms. If there are 26 in each room, how many classrooms will there be?" (How many 26s in 156?)

(1) Determine the number of digits in the quotient. If the quotient is 10 or more, there will need to be 260 pupils or more. Since there are only 156, the quotient is a one-place number.

$$26\overline{)156}$$
$$\underline{156}$$
$$6$$

(2) Multiply 5 × 26 = 130. The quotient is more than 5.

(3) There may be as many 26s in 156 as there are 20s in 156 or 2s in 15, which is 7. Multiply 7 × 26 = 182. Since 182 is greater than 156, reduce the estimated quotient to 6. In step 2 we found 5 × 26 = 130 and in step 3 we found that 7 × 26 = 182. Therefore an estimate of 6 is sensible. Multiply 6 × 26 = 156, so the correct quotient is 6. *Six classrooms are needed.*

The Quotient is a Two-Place Number

After a class knows how to divide when the quotient is a one-place number, it is easy to solve an example when the quotient is a two-place number.

Problem: "An average of 64 orange trees can be planted on an acre. How many acres are needed to plant 1024 trees?"

(1) Determine the number of digits in the quotient: 100 × 64 = 6400 which is greater than 1024 so the quotient will be a two-digit number.

$$64\overline{)1024}$$
$$\underline{640}$$
$$384$$
$$\underline{384}$$
$$16$$

(2) Estimate the number of 60s in 102 tens to be 1 ten.

(3) Multiply and subtract as shown.

(4) Estimate the number of 60s in 384 ones as the number of 6s in 38 which is 6.

(5) Multiply 6 × 64 = 384. *It will take 16 acres.*

(6) Check by multiplying 16 × 64 = 1024.

The Multiples Approach

Slow learners and pupils who have difficulty with the standard algorithm may find the multiple approach a helpful intermediate form that eliminates most of the difficulty in determining quotient figures.

Problem: "Leonard wants to buy a video camera that costs $1176.00. If he can save $42 per week, how many weeks will it take him to save the $1176?"

First prepare a multiples table for 42 (see page 191):

```
 1 —  42
 2 —  84
 3 — 126
 4 — 168
 5 — 210
 6 — 252
 7 — 294
 8 — 336
 9 — 378
10 — 420
```

When the multiples table is completed, proceed as follows:

(1) To find how many 42s are in 117, note

that 117 is between $2 \times 42 = 84$ and $3 \times 42 = 126$. The answer is 2 tens or 20. Place 2 in the tens place of the quotient and 84 below 117 tens in the dividend.

$$
\begin{array}{r}
2 \\
42\overline{)1176} \\
84 \\
\hline
336
\end{array}
$$

(2) Subtract $117 - 84 = 33$ in the tens place and bring down the 6 in the ones place to get 336 ones.

(3) Return to the multiples table to find that $8 \times 42 = 336$. Place the 8 in the quotient and 336 under 336.

$$
\begin{array}{r}
28 \\
42\overline{)1176} \\
84 \\
\hline
336 \\
336 \\
\hline
\end{array}
$$

The Standard Algorithm

Pupils should be able to use the standard algorithm routinely to solve division problems with one- or two-digit divisors. The steps for solving $42\overline{)1172}$ are as follows:

(1) Determine the number of quotient digits: $10 \times 42 = 420$; $100 \times 42 = 4200$; So the quotient has 2 digits.

$$
\begin{array}{r}
28 \\
42\overline{)1176} \\
840 \\
\hline
336 \\
336 \\
\hline
\end{array}
$$

(2) Estimate that there are approximately three sets of 42 tens in 117 tens, about the same as the number of 4s in 12.

(3) Multiply $3 \times 42 = 126$ to test the estimated quotient of 3 and find that it is too large.

(4) Revise the estimated quotient to obtain the true quotient of 2, and multiply and subtract as shown.

(5) Think that 42 is contained in 332 about the same number of times that 4 is contained in 32, which is 8.

(6) Test: $8 \times 42 = 336$.

(7) Check: $28 \times 42 = 1176$.

Work with the standard algorithm should emphasize:

(1) The determination of the number of digits in the quotient.

(2) Obtaining the estimated quotient and correcting it, if necessary, to find the true quotient with its place value.

(3) Understanding the steps in the standard algorithm.

Understanding is more important than computation within a specified time limit. Once this understanding is achieved, the pupil should use the calculator for most divisors with two or more digits.

The use of the calculator should enable the pupil to encounter more real-life problems than found in traditional textbook situations. The latter usually use divisions in which the dividend is a multiple of the divisor.

Calculator Activities

The calculator should be used to encourage mental arithmetic and to extend problems with simple numbers to similar problems with everyday numbers. The following sequence of pairs of problems illustrates one approach.

Ask the class for a mental response for how many items at $2 each can be purchased for $10. Now have pupils use the calculator to determine how many computers at $678 can be purchased for $12,500. Remind the class not to enter commas for numbers used for computation on the calculator. The sequence is: $12500 \div 678 = 18.436578$. Thus, 18 computers can be purchased.

Ask the class how many $3 items can be purchased for $20. A mental response should be 6 with $2 left over. The mental computation for the remainder should be to subtract 3 × 6 from 20. The remainder can be found with the calculator as follows:

(1) 20 ÷ 3 = 6.6666666 (on some calculators the quotient will appear as 6.6666667)

(2) Subtract 6 from 6.6666666 to obtain the decimal part of the quotient → 0.6666666

(3) Multiply this difference by 3 (the divisor) to get 1.999999, which is then rounded to 2. (On calculators that show the quotient 6.6666667, when 6 is subtracted and the difference is multiplied by 3, the product will be 2.)

Now ask how many computers at $829 each can be purchased for $20,000. The steps on the calculator are: Enter 20000, press the division key, enter 829, press equal. The answer is 24.125452. The solution to the problem is 24 computers at $829 each can be purchased for a little less than $20,000. There are two ways to find how much money is left over (the remainder).

(1) 24 × 829 = 19896. This gives the cost of 24 computers at $829 each.

(2) 20000 − 19896 = 104. The amount left unspent is $104.

The second method is performed with a series of steps on the calculator: Enter 20000, press the divide sign, enter 829, press the equal sign, and 24.125452 shows on the display. Now press the minus sign, enter 24, and obtain 0.125452 (the decimal part of the quotient) appears on the display. Next multiply that by 829 (the divisor) and 103.9997 will appear on the display on most calculators. This number should be rounded to show a remainder of $104. (More expensive scientific calculators will show: 20000 ÷ 829 = 24.125452; 24.125452 − 24 × 829 = 104.)

Depending on the ability of the class, it may be an excellent readiness activity for algebra to ask how many items at A dollars each can be purchased for B dollars. This leads to the formula N = B/A, where N is the number of items that can be purchased. This approach can be a useful extension of the work with formulas for area as well as the percent and probability formulas.

Estimating Multiplication of Two-Digit Numbers

Most pupils will attain skill in estimation by using a computer that provides random examples with immediate evaluations for estimates. Program PE10.1 on page 207 provides random pairs of two-digit numbers and asks for an estimate. When the estimate is entered on the keyboard, the computer displays the correct answer, the error and the percent error. With this constant evaluation, one can obtain meaningful practice for improving performance.

An estimate with an error of 5 percent or less is often as useful as the exact answer. Estimates with errors of more than 10 percent are less useful but will usually verify the position of the decimal point and often detect large errors.

Even if pupils have not had formal work with percent, using this program will provide readiness. The key idea is that an error of 15 for a correct answer of 100 is a 15 percent error while an error of 15 for a correct answer of 1000 is a 1.5 percent error. The listing of error and percent error for estimates will help pupils recognize the difference between absolute error (precision) and relative or percent error (accuracy).

Good estimates must be based on sound mathematics. We present three methods that produce acceptable estimates. Our discussion is limited to estimation for the product of a pair of two-digit numbers because products of larger numbers can be estimated by rounding to two significant digits. One can estimate 23458 × 3424 by estimating 23 × 34 and annexing five zeros.

In the initial learning stage, pupils should record each step with paper and pencil for the estimation method under discussion. As experience is gained, more able pupils will automatically proceed to mental computation because it is much quicker. The procedure will be better understood and remembered if it has been recorded during the learning process.

Method 1

This method consists of using traditional rounding (round up for a ones digit of 5 or more) for each number to a single significant digit and then multiplying as shown in the middle column in the table below.

These illustrations indicate the simplicity and wide range of accuracy, or lack of it, obtained with Method 1. The only knowledge required is ability to round traditionally, mastery of basic facts, and ability to annex the correct number of zeros. Number sense can improve some estimates. For example, 25 × 25 should be estimated as 20 × 30 instead of 30 × 30 because rounding both numbers up obviously creates a large error. Likewise 95 × 95 should be rounded to 90 × 100.

Method 2

Method 2 requires rounding both factors down to obtain a lower bound, rounding both factors up to obtain an upper bound, and then interpolating.

Apply Method 2 to estimate 23 × 34 as follows:

(1) Round down to 20 × 30 to obtain a *lower bound* of 600.

(2) Round up to 30 × 40 to obtain an *upper bound* of 1200.

(3) This step, optional but desirable, averages the upper and lower bounds to obtain 900 for the midpoint of the interval between the bounds.

(4) Interpolate to choose an estimate that is a multiple of 100.
For 23 × 34, the estimate must lie between 600 and 900. Use the midpoint to obtain an estimate of 700 or 800.

Method 2 involves rounding up *and* down to find upper and lower bounds followed by interpolation, with or without the midpoint.

The middle column in the table on page 205 shows how to record this method:

Method 2 is more complex than Method 1. It is not easy to evaluate for accuracy because it depends on the ability to interpolate mentally. Method 2, with experience,

Factors	Product	Estimate	Error	% Error
23 × 34	782	20 × 30 or 600	182	23%
23 × 48	1104	20 × 50 or 1000	104	9%
32 × 57	1824	30 × 60 or 1800	24	1%
41 × 26	1066	40 × 30 or 1200	134	13%
25 × 25	625	30 × 30 or 900	275	44%
95 × 95	9025	100 × 100 or 10,000	975	11%

Factors	Product	Estimate	Error	% Error
23 × 34	782	600—900—1200→ 800	18	2%
23 × 48	1104	800—1150—1500→ 1150	46	4%
32 × 57	1824	1500—1950—2400→ 1950	126	7%
41 × 26	1066	800—1150—1500→ 1000	134	13%
25 × 25	625	400—650—900→ 650	25	4%
95 × 95	9025	8100—9050—10000→ 9050	25	.3%

can usually provide more accurate results than Method 1. Placing the estimate between the largest and smallest possible values is very desirable for any estimate. Computer Program PE10.1 on page 207 provides efficient practice in estimation and interpolation.

Method 3

The following shows how to use the distributive property to find the product of a pair of two-digit numbers, the major structural idea behind the multiplication algorithm.

Example A
$$
\begin{aligned}
23 \times 34 &= (20 + 3) \times (30 + 4) \\
&= [(20 + 3) \times 30] + \\
&\quad [(20 + 3) \times 4] \\
&= [(30 \times 20) + (30 \times 3)] \\
&\quad + [(4 \times 20) + (4 \times 3)] \\
&= 600 + 90 + 80 + 12 \\
&= 782
\end{aligned}
$$

Example B shows an intermediate form of the standard multiplication algorithm. Multiplying is performed from left to right rather than from right to left, as in the standard algorithm. Note that the partial products in example B are identical with those in example A. Example B has been taught in some countries for the reasons shown here. Use of first three partial products and

rounding, as illustrated in example C, produces a good estimate.

Example B

$$
\begin{array}{r}
34 \\
\times\ 23 \\
\hline
\end{array}
$$

20 × 30 →	600
20 × 4 →	80
3 × 30 →	90
3 × 4 →	12
	782

Example C

$$
\begin{array}{r}
34 \\
\times\ 23 \\
\hline
\end{array}
$$

20 × 30 →	600
20 × 4 rounded →	100
3 × 30 rounded →	100
Estimate →	800

Method 3 uses an abbreviated form, shown in example C. Finding the estimate for 23 × 34 is performed as follows:

(1) Use the first partial product in example C as the initial estimate, 20 × 30 = 600. It is the product of the total value of the two tens digits, the same as the first step in Method 2. When both ones digits are less than 5, this product is identical with the estimate obtained with Method 1.

(2) Find the second and third partial products from example C by multiplying each ones digit times the tens digit of the other

Factors	Product	Estimate	Error	% Error
23 × 48	1104	800 + 100 + 200 = 1100	4	.4%
32 × 57	1824	1500 + 100 + 200 = 1800	24	1%
41 × 26	1066	800 + 0 + 200 = 1000	66	6%
25 × 25	625	400 + 100 + 100 = 600	25	4%
95 × 95	9025	8100 + 500 + 500 = 9100	75	1%

numeral and round to nearest hundred: $3 \times 30 = 90$ and $4 \times 20 = 80$. Round as illustrated in example C to obtain an estimate of $600 + 100 + 100 = 800$. % error = 2.3%

(3) Optional for experts: Method 3 estimates usually have an error less than 5 percent, except in the teens and twenties. Choosing not to round can produce more accurate estimates in some situations, particularly in the teens. Not rounding in step 2 and adding is one step short of the algorithm shown in example B. The product of the ones digits is dropped for the estimate. Ignoring the ones digits can produce substantial error.

The corrections in step 2 must always be added because the initial estimate is too small. The suggested rounding allows the estimate to be obtained by adding three multiples of 100.

The above table illustrates the estimates for Method 3, using the same numbers as those for Methods 1 and 2. The pupil should record the three addends vertically. The tabular display shown here in the middle column is horizontal to conserve space.

Summary for Estimation of Two-Digit Numbers

Estimation involves making controlled errors so that the estimate, with practice, can be made mentally. It is also desirable in that the paper-and-pencil record can be written more efficiently than the standard algorithm.

All pupils should start estimation of multiplication with Method 1, which emphasizes basic rounding of the product of two single-digit multiples of 10. Using Program PE10.1 (on page 207) to provide practice will alert the pupils that the error level of this program is often larger than desirable.

There is no one way to obtain estimates. Different approaches can produce similar results. A combined use of Methods 1 and 3 provides one of the more efficient procedures for obtaining estimates for the product of a pair of two-digit numbers that is usually less than 5 percent and rarely much more.

Use Method 1 if one factor rounds up and the other rounds down when both numbers are in the 40s and above.

Example (a) shows a product within the acceptable range and example (b) shows one outside the suggested range.

(a) $41 \times 96 \rightarrow 40 \times 100 = 4000$
   error: 64   1.6%
(b) $24 \times 95 \rightarrow 20 \times 100 = 2000$
   error: 304   13.2%

When the product is out of this range, use Method 2 or 3; the latter usually provides more accurate estimates. Experience can lead to a wide variety of refinements, too numerous to list.

Compensating for the error caused by rounding is one of the most fundamental ways of improving estimates. For example, in the estimate for 26 × 91, rounding 26 to 30 produces an error of 4 × 91 or about 360 while rounding 91 to 90 produces an error in the opposite direction of 26. Using this information to reduce the estimate by 300 will make the error less than 2 percent. This type of number sense can be applied to most methods of estimation to produce more accurate results.

The situation determines the acceptable error in estimation. However, for most purposes, any estimate less than 10 percent is useful and an error less than 5 percent can often be used in place of the exact answer.

```
PE10.1
  10 HOME: VTAB 10
  20 A = 21 + INT(60*RND(1))
  30 B = 21 + INT(70*RND(1))
  40 PRINT "ESTIMATE ";A;" X
     ";B;" = ";
  50 INPUT "";N
  60 PRINT "ANSWER    ";A;" X
     ";B; ";A*B
  70 PRINT
  80 E = ABS(N - A*B)
  90 PRINT "ERROR = "; E
  100 PRINT "%ERROR =
      ";INT(1000*E/(A*B) +
      .5)/10;"%"
```

Program PE10.2 allows PUPIL TO ENTER any number in place of random computer selection. To obtain program PE10.2 from PE10.1, replace line 20 with `20 INPUT " "; A` and line 30 with `30 INPUT " ";B`

Estimating Division

The first step in estimating division is to determine the number of digits in the quotients, as for the division algorithm. The following is an abbreviation of the method described on pages 199–200 for using the division algorithm to divide by a two-digit

number. Remember that annexing n zeros to a whole number multiplies that number by 10^n. For example, $2300 = 23 \times 10^2$ and $230000 = 23 \times 10^4$.

Step 1. Annex the smallest number of zeros to the divisor that makes it larger than the dividend.

Step 2. The number of quotient digits is equal to the number of zeros required in step 1.

For 12534/34, 3 zeros must be annexed to make the divisor 34 larger than the dividend 12534. This means that $3400 < 12534 < 34000$ so that the quotient is between 100 and 1000 and must contain 3 digits.

For 74239/53, 4 zeros must be annexed to 53 to make it larger than 74239. Therefore, $53000 < 74239 < 530000$ so that the quotient must be between 1000 and 10000 and contains 4 digits.

Estimating division involves 3 steps:

(1) Determine the number of quotient digits.

(2) Round the dividend to two significant digits and the divisor to one and divide.

(3) Interpret the quotient from step 2 in terms of the number of quotient digits from step 1 to obtain the estimate.

The following illustrates these steps for 1235/28:

(1) The number of quotient digits is two because annexing two zeros to 28 makes it larger than 1235. Therefore, $280 < 1235 < 2800$, and the quotient is between 10 and 100 so there are two quotient digits.

(2) Round 1235 to 12 and 28 to 3 and divide: $12/3 = 4$

(3) The first estimate is 40 because we know the quotient has two digits. This estimate can be refined by noting that because we rounded up, our trial divisor is too large, and the estimated quotient of 40 is too small. Any estimate between 40 and 45 is

reasonable. The correct answer, to the nearest whole number, is 44.

It may be helpful to write a sequence of dashes indicating the number of quotient digits before making final estimate.

Three dashes, ___ ___ ___, indicate 3 quotient digits.

The following suggests a written record for estimating division:

4567/23 2300 < 4567 < 23000
1. 3 quotient digits
2. 46 / 2 → 23   Too large
3. Estimate: <u>200</u>   1% error

9302/34 3400 < 9302 < 34000.
1. 3 quotient digits
2. 93/3 = 31   Too large
3. Estimate: <u>290</u>   6% error

Program 10.3 provides practice for estimating division in the same way that PE10.1 provides practice for multiplication. This program will provide an activity that will, with continued practice, improve estimation.

```
PROGRAM PE10.3
  10 HOME: VTAB 10
  20 A = 21 + INT(10000 *
     RND(1))
  30 B = 21 + INT(30 *
     RND(1))
  40 PRINT "ESTIMATE TO
     NEAREST WHOLE NUMBER:"
  50 PRINT : PRINT
  60 PRINT A ;" / "; B;
     " = ";
  70 INPUT ""; N
  80 PRINT A; " / "; B;
     " = "; INT (A / B + .5)
  90 PRINT
 100 E = ABS(N - INT(A / B
     + .5))
 110 PRINT
     "ERROR = ";E
 120 PRINT " %ERROR =
     ";INT(1000*E/(A/B)
     + .5)/ 10;"%"
```

Program PE10.4 is to PE10.3 as PE10.2 is to PE10.1 because it enables the reader to enter the dividend and divisor rather than accept the random choice of the computer in PE10.3. To get program PE10.4, place PE10.3 in memory and retype lines 20 and 30 as follows:

```
20 INPUT "ENTER DIVIDEND
   "; A
30 INPUT "ENTER DIVISOR
   "; B
```

Successful estimation for division is closely tied to the standard algorithm. Determining the number of quotient digits is the same. Interpreting the quotient of the rounded dividend and divisor may vary.

Calculator Activities

The calculator can be used to check the accuracy of an estimation. Use the following problems to practice estimation. After making an estimate, use a calculator to check your work. Do as much of the computation mentally as you can. Use paper and pencil if necessary but round to get approximate results. With practice, the paper and pencil work should be less demanding than traditional computation.

(1) A business man has $35000 to spend on machinery. If the cost of each machine is $5700, how many of these items can he buy?

(2) A farmer has 723 acres and obtains an average of 213 bushels of corn per acre. How many bushels of corn does the farmer grow?

(3) A retail store grosses $7400 per week. What is the gross income of that store for a year?

(4) The quantity of water passing a given point on a river is 37500 cu. ft. per hour. How many cu. ft. of water pass by this point in a day? in a year?

(5) A ship crosses a 158-mile body of water in 24 hours. What is its average rate of speed in miles per hour?

(6) A car travels a distance of 16 miles in 23 minutes. What is its average speed in miles per hour? In km per hour?

(7) A can containing 9 ounces of a vegetable costs $1 dollar. What is the approximate cost in cents per pound?

(8) A case holds 48 bars of soap. A truck can carry 210 cases of soap. If each bar of soap costs 60 cents, What is the value, in dollars, of a truck load of soap carrying its maximum?

Answers are given as indicated operations so that you must use a calculator or computer to check your estimate.
(1) 35000/5700; (2) 723 × 213; (3) 7400 × 52; (4) 37500 × 24; part 2; 37500 × 24 × 365; (5) 158/24; (6) 16/23 × 60; part 2; 16 × 23 × 60 × 1.6; (7) (100/9) × 16; (8) (48 × 210 × 60)/100.

If a computer is available, it may be instructive to check your work with programs PE10.2 and PE10.4

Ask pupils to enter the following three subtractions in their calculators: 321 − 123, 654 − 456, and 987 − 789 to find that the answer for all three subtractions is 198. Ask why. Guide the class to discover that 321 − 123 = (3 × 100 + 2 × 10 + 1) − (1 × 100 + 2 × 10 + 3) = 2 × 100 + 1 − 3 = 198. Help them to recognize that 654 − 456 also leads to (2 × 100) + 0 + (1 − 3), as does 987 − 789, because the difference between the first and third digits is the same and the middle digits are equal with a difference of zero.

Now subtract 741 − 147; 852 − 258; and 963 − 369 to get identical answers of 594. Again ask why. It should be easier to lead the class to see that all three subtractions reduce to 6 × 100 + 2 − 8 = 594.

Now ask for another pair of numbers that will give similar results. The number of

such pairs is infinite. The previous two sets of three subtractions are easy to enter because the digits are in a single row or column for each entry. Use 621 − 126 and 954 − 459 as an example of two subtractions with the same value in which the digits are not in the same row or column.

Challenge the class to find pairs of subtractions with four-digit numbers with equal differences. One of the easiest is:

9632 − 2369 = 8521 − 1258 = 7263.

With about eight or ten of these examples on the chalkboard, ask if there is a common pattern for all the differences. Tell the class to find the sum of the digits in each difference and ask the question again.

What do all the sums of the digits have in common?

Ask for completion of the following pattern with each difference:

198 → 1 + 9 + 8 = 18 → 1 + 8 → 9,
495 → 18 → 9, 7253 → 18 → 9.

Enter any number in the calculator and subtract another number with the same digits in a different order.

654321 − 154362 = 499959 sum of digits → 45 → 9
654321 − 452316 = 202005 sum of digits → 9

Statement A: the sum of the digits is a multiple of 9 for any difference between a number and another with the same digits arranged in a different order.

Examine the following pattern:

456 = 4 × 100 + 5 × 10 + 6 = 4 × (99 + 1) + 5 × (9 + 1) + 6
= (4 × 99 + 5 × 9) + (4 + 5 + 6)

Repeat this pattern to lead to the discovery that any number can be expressed as a multiple of 9 plus the sum of the digits. The distributive property then demands that: If the sum of the digits is divisible by 9, the number is divisible by 9. This statement and statement A lead to the following conclusion:

The difference of any pair of numbers having the same digits in a different order is divisible by 9.

This last fact has been used by accountants for many years. If they expect a certain answer and get a different one, the first step is to subtract the two answers and add the digits of this difference to see if the number is divisible by 9. If the difference is divisible by 9, the most probable cause of error is an incorrect entry involving the interchange of two of the digits, a common error by people who must enter many numbers into a ledger, calculator, or computer.

The same principle led to the following number trick. Ask a friend to enter any five-digit number into the calculator. Now ask that a rearrangement of the digits be subtracted, smaller from larger. Now ask for the sum of all of the digits except one, with the condition that zero cannot be omitted. Find the difference between this sum and the next largest multiple of 9 to find the deleted digit. If zero is deleted, one cannot tell whether zero or 9 was omitted. Example: $95423 - 45932 = 49491$. If 4 is omitted, the sum is 23 and $27 - 23$ is 4. The sum without 9 is 18, a multiple of 9, indicating that 9 has been omitted, assuming that zero was not removed.

Casting Out Nines

The previous activities lead to a rationalization of the casting-out-nines procedure:

$$
\begin{array}{llll}
(1) & 232 \;-\; & 7 & \\
& \times\, 24 \;-\; & \times\, 6 & \\
\cline{1-2}
& 928 & 42 \;-\; 6 & \\
& 464 & & \\
\cline{1-2}
& 5568 \;-\; & 24 \;-\; 6 &
\end{array}
\qquad
\begin{array}{llll}
(2) & 123 \;-\; & 6 & \\
& \times\, 101 \;-\; & \times\, 2 & \\
\cline{1-2}
& 123 & 12 \;-\; 3 & \\
& 123 & & \\
\cline{1-2}
& 1353 \;-\; & 12 \;-\; 3 &
\end{array}
$$

Examples (1) and (2) show a standard notation for checking multiplication by casting out nines. The **7** on the right in example A is called the excess of nines because it is the remainder obtained when 232 is divided by nine. Have the class verify this by dividing mentally or using the calculator to get $232/9 = 25.777$ and multiply $.777 \times 9$ to get 6.993, which rounds to 7.

The check depends on the fact that the product of the excesses of 9 must equal the excess of the product. Unfortunately, a check by casting out nines should never be introduced without making pupils aware that the example may check but still be incorrect. This is illustrated in example (2). Any example will check by casting out nines if the error is a multiple of 9. The correct answer in example (2) is 12423. The difference between the correct answer and the incorrect one, $12423 - 1353 = 11070$, is a multiple of 9. The error in example (2) is a place-value error caused by ignoring the zero in the factor 101. Example (2) is an excellent example of the value of estimation. Estimate 101×123. Any answer slightly more than 12300 is acceptable, demonstrating that the answer 1353 is not sensible.

Checking by casting out nines is not reliable unless combined with sound estimation.

Exercise 10.1
Solve the following eight problems. If there is too much or too little information, list the surplus or deficient information. Answers are in Appendix D.
1. A company buys 3500 tons of steel for $245,000. The company sells the steel at twice the price it paid for it. How much will it charge a customer for 750 tons of steel? (a) Find cost per ton to the company.

(b) the selling price per ton. (c) Find the company's charge for 750 tons.

2. A car travels 118 miles in 3 hours. If gas costs $1 per gallon, how much will it cost to drive 500 miles? Write a proportion that will solve this problem.

3. If a car uses 13 gallons of fuel for 285 miles, how many gallons will it use, at this rate, for 950 miles? Write a proportion that will solve the problem.

4. A fence is to be 33 meters in length with a post every 3 meters. How many posts are needed?

5. How long will it take a clock to strike 12 if it strikes once a second?

6. A car travels M miles in T minutes. At this rate, how many miles will the car travel in 1 minute?

    Gauss, a famous mathematician, is said to have mentally calculated the sum of the whole numbers from 1 to 100 when he was about 5 years old. Take some time to think about it. Can you discover a pattern that will make it easier to calculate?

7. Estimate the sum of numbers from 1 to 100.

8. Give sum of the first and last, of the second and next-to-last of the sum: $1 + 2 + 3 + \ldots + 98 + 99 + 100$.

    (a) Calculate the sum.

    Use the short cut to find the following sums:

    (b) $1 + 2 + 3 + \cdots + 20 = \underline{\hspace{1cm}} \times 21 = \square$

    (c) $2 + 3 + 4 + \cdots + 30 = \underline{\hspace{1cm}} \times \underline{\hspace{1cm}} = \square$

    (d) $10 + 11 + 12 + 13 + 14 + 15 = \underline{\hspace{1cm}} \times \underline{\hspace{1cm}} = \square$

Use the Computer

The computer can be used to solve problem 8 very efficiently:

```
10 T = 0
20 FOR N = 1 TO 100
30 T = T + N
40 NEXT
50 PRINT T
```

The program consists of a loop of 100 cycles in which N has the values 1, 2, 3 . . . . 100. In each cycle the computer adds the value of N to T so that T has the values 1, 1 + 2, 3 + 4, and so on. Therefore each cycle contains the sum of the whole numbers up to that point and finally displays the

sum of the first hundred whole numbers to be 5050.

The program can be made more flexible by inserting the following:

```
5 INPUT "ENTER NUMBER OF
   TERMS "; N1
20 FOR N = 1 TO N1
```

The program now gives a choice for the number of terms to be added, starting with 1.

How can you use the program just completed to find the sum from 9 to 16? Answer: Find sum from 1 to 16 and subtract the sum, using the program, from 1 to 9.

The sum of two numbers is 30 and the product is 209. Find the answer by examining the output of the following FOR-NEXT loop:

```
10 FOR J = 1 TO 30
20 PRINT J, J * (30 - J)
30 NEXT
RUN
```
. . . .
```
10                     200
11                     209
```
. . . .

The numbers are 11 and 19. Sum = 30
Product = 209
Insert lines 20 and 100 to tell the computer to display the answer.

```
20 IF J * (30 - J) = 209
   THEN 100
100 PRINT "THE NUMBERS ARE
    ";J;" AND ";30 - J
```

The following single line also will work:

```
20 IF J*(30 - J)=209 THEN
   PRINT " THE NUMBERS ARE
   ";J; " AND " ; 30 - J:N
```

Estimate

Estimate 24 × 61 by Method 1 and 3:
Method 1: 20 × 60 = 1200. This is an error of 18 percent. This is suitable for checking the position of the decimal point. Method 3: 1200 + 200 + 0 = 1400. This is an error of about 4 percent.

Estimate 237 × 6114 Hint: Multiply 200 × 6000 = 1,200,000 to establish the position of the decimal point (number of digits).

Read Carefully

(1) Two coins have a value of 55 cents and one is not a nickle. Identify the coins.
Answer: One is not a nickle and one is.

(2) Doreen says she has the same number of brothers as sisters. What will her brother say about his sisters? He can say "I have two more sisters than I have brothers."
Answer: Test with a family of two boys and three girls. Each girl can say "I have the same number of brothers as sisters" but each boy can say "I have two more sisters than brothers."

Patterns

(1) Complete the following pattern. :

(a) 1 3 5 7 ____ ____
Complete (b), using sums from (a):
(b) 4 9 16 ____ ____
Use (b) to complete (c)
(c) 2 × 2, 3 × 3, 4 × ____, 5 × ____
Answer for (b): 1 + 3 = 4, 4 + 5 = 9,
and so on.
Answer for (c): 4 × 4, 5 × 5
Follow instructions for previous pattern:
(d) 2 4 6 8 ____ ____
(e) 6 12 20 ____ ____ ____
(f) 2 × 3; 3 × 4, 4 × 5, 5 × ____,
    6 × ____
   Answer for (e): 2 + 4 = 6, 6 + 6 =
   12, 8 + 12 = 20, 30, 42
   Answer for (f): 6 = 2 × 3, 12 = 3
   × 4, 20 = 4 × 5, 5 × 6, 6 × 7

(g) 8 × 9 = ____   7 × 10 = ____
    6 × 11 = ____
Complete the next 3 numbers without multiplying ____ ____ ____
Answer: 72, 70, 60, 52, 42

Subtract successive terms and write sequence: ____ ____ ____ ____ ____
Answer: 2, 4, 6, 8 . . . .

(2) Follow instructions for previous pattern:
8 × 8 = ____ 7 × 9 = ____ 6 × 10 = ____   ____   ____   ____
Complete the last 3 numbers in sequence without multiplying. *Answer: 64 63 60 55 48 39*

Subtract successive terms and write sequence ____ ____ ____ ____ ____
Answer: 1 3 5 7 9

(3) Fill in the blanks on the right to obtain a square with the same sum in each row and each column and each diagonal are the same. What is the sum? Answer: 15

	1	
3	5	7
4		2

(4) The missing numbers in the squares on the right are on the two diagonals. They can be filled in the following manner. Place 16 in the upper left-hand corner and count along the first row. Do not enter numbers in positions already occupied, but when you get to the empty place at the end of the row place the number of your count, 13, in the empty place. Now move to the beginning of the next row and continue to count with 12 but do not enter it because the place is occupied. Place 11 in the empty space and continue in this manner, ending with 1 in the lower right-hand spot. Examine the completed square. What is the sum of all rows, columns, and diagonals? Answer: 34

	2	3	
5			8
9			12
	14	15	

	2		13
5	11	10	8
9		6	12
	14	15	1

Fill in the blanks in the above to complete the magic square so that all rows, columns, and diagonals have the same sum. If both of the previous 4 × 4 squares are completed correctly, they will be identical.

Find at least 6 different sets of 4 numbers from the preceding square with a sum of 34 with numbers not in the same row or column. For example: 16 + 4 + 1 + 13 = 34. Many answers are possible.

(5) Explain how to get the following square from that in Problem (3) and why the sum for each row, column, and diagonal is 9 more than the sum in the original square.

11	4	9
6	8	10
7	12	5

Answer: Each item in the latter square is 3 more than before, so the sum of any row—column or diagonal—is 3 + 3 + 3, or 9 more than before.

Summary

Multiplication and division of multidigit numbers will increasingly be performed with the aid of calculators and computers in everyday life. Pupils should learn to use these machines. However, pupils will still need to study the operations of multiplication and division for an understanding of how they are performed and the algorithms involved. Multiplication and division should be tied closely to problem situations. The teaching–learning sequence should start with a word problem. The pupils should use manipulatives and visuals in beginning discovery experiences as they study the thinking approaches for the solution to simple problems. Gradually pupils should move away from manipulatives toward representing their thinking at the symbolic level. Pupils should not use manipulatives to solve problems involving two-digit multipliers and two-digit divisors.

Learning to estimate products and quotients is an important learning objective. In some instances a good estimate of an answer may be sufficient for making a decision. At other times the exact answer is required. If a calculator is used for computation, estimation is essential to assure accuracy. In division, both estimation of the number of digits in the quotient and estimating the trial quotient require careful teaching.

Computer programs can be used effectively to develop concepts and skills of multiplication and division. They can also provide vital drill and practice.

Exercise 10.2

Give the thought pattern you would use to introduce problems 1 through 6 to a class in grades 4, 5, or 6. Discuss the remaining problems.

1. A diagram has 15 rows of 24 stars each. How many stars does the diagram contain?

2. A car averages 26 miles per gallon of fuel. At that rate, how many gallons of fuel would be needed for a trip of 910 miles?

3. Kathy bought a 5-pound roast at a shopping center for $1.98 a pound. She gave the cashier $20. How much change did she get?

4. The average temperature one day was the average of the highest and lowest temperatures on that day. The highest temperature was 69° and the lowest 43°. What was the average temperature that day?

5. A spool contained 36 yards of ribbon. After 15 yards were used, how many pieces 3 yards in length could be cut from the remaining ribbon?

6. When 10 is added to the product of two factors, the sum is 190. One of the factors is 12. What is the other factor?

7. Write 34 as 30 + 4 and 57 as 50 + 7 and multiply, using the distributive property.

8. Use upper and lower limits to estimate the product of 36 × 53.

9. Evaluate the multiple method of division.

10. Some teachers do not present methods for estimating quotients. Pupils multiply the divisor by the digits, beginning with 1. Evaluate this plan.

11. Refer to sets (a) and (b), and give all the examples that use the members of each set. (a) 12, 15, 180 (b) 912, 16, 57

12. Enumerate some of the procedures a teacher might use to help a slow learner succeed at division with a two-place divisor, as well as ways to challenge the quick learners.

13. Find the products in A and B. Write the generalization that applies to any set of products when one factor is constant.

A:	36	36	36	36
	×4	×9	×15	×20
B:	12	14	23	45
	×5	×5	×5	×5

14. Examine examples A and B, and find the quotients. Write the generalization pertaining to the quotient in A and in B.

A: 3)60   4)60   12)60   20)60

B: 15)30   15)75   15)120   15)450

15. In the example 9 × 48, it is necessary to add 7 to 36 to find the product. Write a two-place number that, when multiplied by a one-

place number, it is necessary to add: (a) 4 to 36 (b) 5 to 32 (c) 7 to 64

16. Reword each of the problems in one of the following ways: Given 1, find 4; Given 1, find 8; Given 4, find 1; Given 8, find 1; How many 4s are there in 32?; How many 8s are there in 32?
    a. The cost of four books is $32. What does one book cost?
    b. How many pounds of meat can be bought for $32 if one pound costs $4?
    c. What is the cost of eight items if one item costs $32?
    d. Find the cost of 4 quarts of liquid if one quart costs $32.
    e. How many books, at $8 each, can be purchased for $32?
    f. What is the cost of one item if eight items cost $32?

Selected Readings

Ashlock, Robert B., et. al. *Guiding Each Child's Learning of Mathematics*. Columbus, OH: Charles E. Merrill, 1983. Chapter 9.

Heddens, James W., and William R. Speer. *Today's Mathematics*, 6th ed. Chicago: Science Research Associates, 1988. Unit 7.

Kennedy, Leonard M., and Steve Tipps. *Guiding Children's Learning of Mathematics*, 5th ed. Belmont, CA: Wadsworth, 1988. Chapter 10.

Marks, John L., et. al. *Teaching Elementary School Mathematics for Understanding*, 5th ed. New York: McGraw-Hill, 1985. Chapter 5.

Post, Thomas R. *Teaching Mathematics in Grades K–8*. Needham Heights, MA: Allyn & Bacon, 1988. Chapter 6.

Reys, Robert E., et. al. *Helping Children Learn Mathematics*, 2nd ed. Englewood Cliffs, NJ: Prentice-Hall, 1989. Chapter 9 .

Riedesel, C. Alan. *Teaching Elementary School Mathematics*, 4th ed. Englewood Cliffs, NJ: Prentice-Hall, 1985. Chapters 8 and 9.

Suydam, Marilyn N., and Robert E. Reys (eds.). *Developing Computational Skills*, 1978 Yearbook. Reston, VA: National Council of Teachers of Mathematics, 1978. Chapter 7.

Fractions, Decimals, and Percents

ACHIEVEMENT GOALS

After studying this chapter, you should be able to:

1. Summarize the historical development of fractions and decimals.

2. Discuss the teaching of fractions in the elementary school.

3. Identify the grade placement and sequence for teaching fractions, decimals and percents.

4. Evaluate the results of the fourth National Assessment of Achievement in Mathematics relating to fractions, decimals, and percents.

5. Explain why it is necessary to introduce decimals early in the elementary curriculum.

6. Write word problems to illustrate basic meanings of fractions, decimals, and percents.

7. Illustrate three different manipulatives for representing fractions.

8. Describe how to make the transition from manipulatives to visuals to the symbolic level and to mastery in teaching all forms of fractions.

9. List ways to introduce common fractions and decimals together.

10. Change from one form to another for fractions, decimals, and percents—using a calculator or a computer when appropriate.

VOCABULARY

The following terms are defined or illustrated in the Glossary.

Congruent
Denominator
Equal fractions
Like fractions
Numerator
Proper fraction

Rational numbers
Region
Renaming fractions
Unit fraction
Unlike fractions

The study of common fractions, decimals, and percents has always been difficult for elementary school children. Traditionally these topics were studied separately, with common fractions taught in the primary grades and decimals and percents delayed until the upper grades. In programs of the future there will be a closer relationship in the teaching of common fractions, decimals, and percents because of the widespread use of calculators, the introduction of metric measures, the increased use of decimals in everyday affairs, and the increased emphasis being placed on understanding the relationships among these numbers.

Historical Perspective

The word *fractions* comes from the Latin word *franger*, "to break." Over the years fractions have been called artificial numbers, vulgar numbers, indicated division, rational numbers, and ratios. Historically, common fractions were first invented to meet a need in measurement when the number of units could not be expressed as a counting number. Ancient cultures not only created subdivision of units, they also invented ways of recording a part of a unit. For example, the Egyptians used unit fractions (numerators of one) to represent parts of units. They used an oval with one of their numerals written underneath to signify a fraction. The Romans divided each of their units into twelfths (which is where the 12-ounce Troy pound originated). The Babylonian astronomers divided a circle into sixty parts. From that we got sixty seconds in a minute and sixty minutes in an hour. Later, the Hindus developed a system in which a whole measuring unit could be divided into any number of congruent parts, and any number of these parts could be considered. If the numeral 3 was written vertically over a 4 this meant that a unit was partitioned into 4 congruent parts and 3 were to be considered. In time the bar was added to indicate that the pair of numbers written vertically signified a fraction. The bar also denoted division. Addition and subtraction of numerators of like fractions came next, followed by multiplication and division of fractions.

Decimals are a relatively recent innovation. The Dutch mathematician Simon Stevin wrote *LaDisme*, the first systematic description of decimals, in the late sixteenth century, but decimals were not in widespread use until about 200 years ago. Even today different countries denote decimals differently. The decimal 3.8 is represented in England as 3'8, and in most of Europe as 3,8 but in the Scandinavian countries as $3,^{8}$.

Percents have been used in business and industry for many years, but are more prevalent today than ever before in everyday conversations to qualify such terms as inflation, prime rate, sales tax, and discount. Our word *percent* comes from the Latin *per centum* ("per hundred"). A 6 percent sales tax means a tax of $6.00 per $100 spent, or at the rate of 6 per 100. A 60 percent chance of rain means that the chances for rain are 60 out of 100, or 6 out of 10, or 3 chances out of 5. Thus 60% = 60/100 = 0.60.

Traditionally, the sequence of topics in the elementary curriculum followed to the historical development of fractions. First teach the idea of a part of a measuring unit. Then present a part of a collection. This was followed by equivalent fractions. Later decimals were introduced, followed by percents. Today, a growing trend is to present decimal concepts earlier and relate them more closely to common fraction ideas.

Grade Placement and Sequence

The National Council of Teachers of Mathematics has recommended that in the primary grades emphasis be placed upon understanding whole numbers, common fractions, and decimals. The Council suggests that physical materials and diagrams be used to develop concepts and language that then will assist pupils to understand the symbolic notations of fractions and decimals. Pupils should explore the relationships between common fractions and decimals with models to understand how these numbers are used in measurement and problem-solving situations. A study of adding and subtracting like fractions and decimals is appropriate for third- and fourth-graders so long as these operations are done with physical models for the purpose of solving real-life problems.

In grades 4 through 6 pupils should continue to study the relationship between common fractions and decimals with the introduction of percents. Students need to understand the four fundamental operations using common fractions and decimals (and percents) and how these are used in problem-solving situations drawn from topics such as measurement, geometry, and statistics.[1]

The authors agree with these recommendations. Some textbook publishers have already started to implement these recommendations—usually starting at the third-grade level, when fractions and decimals are presented in the same chapter. For example, in *Mathematics Unlimited*, published in 1987 by Holt, Rinehart and Winston, for grade 3, Chapter 8 is "Fractions and Decimals."

It is important to introduce decimals early in the curriculum for several reasons:

1. Calculators and computers deal almost entirely with decimals for computations with fractional numbers.

2. Pupils are using calculators and computers more frequently and may see decimal answers on these machines and in stores before they encounter them in class.

3. Decimals are appearing in many places that once used common fractions. The supermarket scale is an excellent example. Many if not most scales for weighing meats are now calibrated in decimals. The weight on a package of meat is now most likely to be listed as a decimal.

4. Metric measures are being used frequently in business and industry. Many highway signs list distances in kilometers as well as miles. Manufacturing companies in the United States have changed to the metric system in order to be able to exchange tools and parts with other countries.

5. It is impractical to express athletic records as fractions. Batting averages, team standings, and other records are always expressed as decimals, usually to the thousandths place.

National Assessment of Educational Progress in Mathematics

The fourth National Assessment of Educational Progress in Mathematics had a limited number of items for third-graders.[2] Only 60 percent of the pupils tested could identify with a common fraction a shaded part of a whole region. Only 50 percent could write "three-fourths" as ¾, and only about 25 percent knew how many fourths make a whole.

Performance of seventh-graders who took the test on fractions, decimals, and percents was very low, probably because of the lack of understanding of the concepts and procedures involved. A summary of the percent correct for selected items follows on page 219.

The topics of fractions, decimals, and percents should be taught with understanding

1. *Curriculum and Evaluation Standards for School Mathematics*, Working Draft (Reston, VA: National Council of Teachers of Mathematics, 1987), pp. 46–47.

[2]Vicky L. Kouba, et. al., "Results of the Fourth NAEP Assessment of Mathematics, Number, Operations, and Word Problems," *The Arithmetic Teacher* 35 (April 1988): 16–17.

Item	Percent Correct
Identify a point on a number line with a common fraction	40
Which is larger, $\frac{3}{5}$ or $\frac{2}{6}$?	67
$7\frac{1}{6} - 3\frac{1}{2}$	32
$4 \times 2\frac{1}{4}$	56
6.002 + .02 + 100.4	59
4.3 − .53	43
7.2 × 2.5	62
Divide .0884 by 3.4.	36
4% of 75	32
30 is what percent of 60?	43
9 is what percent of 225?	20
12 is 15% of what number?	22
Express 0.9 as a percent.	30

through a series of developmental lessons. Lessons should start with a word problem pupils can solve with manipulatives and/or visual representations, then move to appropriate symbolization.

Concepts of Fractions, Decimals, and Percents

Fractions, decimals, and percents are different notations for the same number. Thus, $\frac{1}{2}$, 0.5, and 50% may be used as different names or numerals for the same number.

At the elementary school level the term *fraction* usually implies a *common fraction* in the form of A over B, where A can be any whole number and B can be any nonzero number. It is now common in books and magazines to use a slash notation (A/B), rather than the vertical form with a bar. On the computer, the slash (/) is the standard symbol for division.

Although it is correct to refer to common fractions, decimal fractions, and percents as fractions, we will use *fraction* to designate a common fraction and *decimal* to designate a decimal fraction.

Common Fractions

There are several concepts that may be related to a common fraction. Originally, the term was intended to mean a "part of a measuring unit." This "part of a whole" notion is the first concept introduced to young children. The denominator (D) names the number of congruent parts into which a whole object or drawing has been divided. The numerator (N) indicates the number of parts under consideration. Essentially, the idea is to represent N "out of" D. Several textbook series combine the topic of fractions with geometry and use geometry regions to demonstrate parts of wholes visually. When the topic of measurement with conventional units is presented to pupils, parts of measurement should be discussed and represented with fractions.

A second concept presented in the elementary curriculum is the "part of a set" idea. Typically pupils may be given a small number of objects, such as four, with one object one color (maybe red) and the others some other color, perhaps white. The child is supposed to recognize that "one out of four" is red, so one-fourth of the collection is red. This interpretation of fractions can be used to explore the topic of equal fractions.

A third concept is that of indicated division. The fraction $\frac{3}{4}$ can be read "3 divided by 4." In the problem "Three oranges are to be shared among four children. How much will each receive?" The answer is $\frac{3}{4}$ of an orange. Three divided by four is three-fourths! This interpretation is useful when pupils learn to change a fraction to a decimal by division.

When pupils first learn to divide by a one-digit divisor, in some problem situations there will be a remainder that represents an unrealistic situation. For example, "John's father has $9.00 to divide equally between his two children. How much will each receive?" With a whole-number quotient, the answer is $4.00 with a $1.00 remainder. Realistically, each child should receive $4.50.

A fourth application of a fraction is probability. The concept of probability is related to expressing the chance a certain event will happen out of a certain number of times. If an event can succeed in S ways and fail F ways, the probability of the event succeeding is $S/(S + F)$. Probability is used frequently in statistics (see Chapter 17).

A fifth concept of a fraction is more advanced and different from the above ideas and one that is frequently used in comparing two different measures and in solving proportions. The *rate/ratio* idea is not the same as the "out of" concept. Rather it is an "is to" idea. For example, in a certain class the ratio of boys to girls is 1 to 2. If there are 24 pupils, how many boys are there? The solution is not ½ of 24 or 12. The solution involves thinking that a ratio of 1 boy to 2 girls is 1 boy "out of" 3 students. So ⅓ of 24, or 8, is the number of boys.

A rate indicates the relationship that is expressed with unlike quantities for measures, as miles per hour. Again, this is not an "out of" concept, but rather an "is to" idea. In the problem "Ronald rode his bike 24 miles in 2 hours, how many miles per hour was that?" The problem is solved by thinking: 24 is to 2 as what is to 1? The proportion is $^{24}/_2 = N/1$, or $N = 12$.

From Common Fractions to Decimals

With few exceptions, calculators and computers represent numbers as decimals for calculations. The few calculators that can compute with common fractions are not readily available in the elementary school.

Fractions such as ½, ¼, ⅓, ⅔, ⅙, ⅜, and ¹/₁₂ are frequently encountered in daily situations and are relatively easy to understand. (Fractions with denominators of 2, 3, 4, 5, 8, 10, 12, 16, and 32 constitute well over 95 percent of all the fractions used in business and social living.) Computation with fractions such as ½, ¼, and ⅜ can easily be carried out on a calculator because they can be renamed with a *terminating* decimal. In fact, any fraction with a denominator that is divisible by 2 and/or 5 *only* can be expressed as a terminating decimal; otherwise the decimal is a *nonterminating* decimal. The fraction ⅓ is a nonterminating decimal, 0.3333333..., often written as .3 with a "bar" over the 3 indicating that the 3 repeats infinitely. The fraction ⅐ yields the nonterminating decimal 0.142857142857.... Since the 142857 repeats, a bar can be written over it. The set of digits that repeat in a nonterminating decimal is called the *repetend*. The repetends for ⅑, ¹/₁₁, and ¹/₂₂ are 0.$\overline{1}$, 0.$\overline{09}$, and 0.0$\overline{45}$, respectively.

Rounding and Accuracy

Two basic ideas about computation with approximate numbers are:

1. All measurements are approximate.

2. Any answer resulting from computation with approximate data should be no more accurate than the least accurate number in the computation.

A nonterminating decimal can be treated the same as any other approximate number after it has been rounded. All approximate numbers should be rounded to a number of decimal places that is suitable to the situation in which they are used.

A boy measures the radius of a circle to be 8.7 centimeters. He then uses a calculator to find the circumference by multiplying 2 × 8.7 × 3.14 to get the circumference of 54.636. The circumference is 54.6 centimeters. To use more decimal places gives an answer more accurate than the least accurate measurement, 8.7 cm, in the computation.

Most pupils use the value of **pi** (π) as $3\frac{1}{7}$, 3.14, 3.1416, and 3.14159 without realizing that all are approximations for a nonterminating decimal. For most everyday situations, $3\frac{1}{7}$ or 3.14 is accurate enough. In some very precise applications, the value of **pi** may need to be as many as ten decimal places.

With proper rounding and a calculator, nonterminating decimals are as easy to use as terminating decimals. For everyday situations, pupils must learn to use a calculator or computer to deal with numbers efficiently.

If fractions such as $\frac{1}{3}$, $\frac{1}{6}$, and $\frac{1}{12}$ could be expressed as one or two decimal places, most common fractions would disappear from everyday usage because it is much easier to deal with decimals than with common fractions. However, for a common fraction to be expressed as a decimal it must be possible to rename the denominator as ten or a multiple of ten. Many commonly used measures in everyday life are not subdivided by tens. For example, the clock is subdivided into quarters, halves, sixtieths, twelfths, and twenty-fourths. The calendar has seven days per week and twelve months per year. Most of the time at home when children share fruit, pies, pizzas, and the like the parts are divided into other than ten. Housewives are likely to continue to use recipes that call for $\frac{1}{2}$, $\frac{1}{3}$, $\frac{3}{4}$ of a cup in cooking. Stock market quotations are usually given in the fractional parts of halves, fourths, and eighths. A Troy pound is 12 ounces; gold is measured in Troy ounces. An ounce of gold is heavier than an ounce of lead, which is measured at 16 ounces to the pound. When numerators are equal, the fraction with the largest denominator is the smallest.

Many of the most-used common fractions do not have an exact decimal equivalent, a serious obstacle for removing them from everyday usage. Mathematics programs of the future must therefore continue to teach both common fractions and decimal fractions. The chief benefit of teaching common fractions is their widespread use in everyday activities, while adaptability to computing machines is the chief advantage of decimals.

From Decimals to Percents

The word *percent* indicates "per hundred." It is easy to change from a two-place decimal to a percent or vice versa. For example, .25 = 25% and 25% = 25/100 = .25. The two notations, 25 hundredths and 25 percent, are two ways to represent the same number. For that reason these notations are not to be discovered by the pupils; instead the teacher should show pupils how to write different numerals to name the same number. A class is ready to deal with percent as soon as fractions and decimals are understood to show different notations for the same number.

Percents are used in business, especially in merchandising and banking. It is easier to speak about an interest rate of 6 percent than about 6 hundredths. A business organization may compare the sales or income for a given month with the corresponding month a year earlier. The change in the two amounts may be given in large numbers that are difficult to interpret. When they are expressed as percent, the change is more readily understood. However, percents are usually expressed in decimals for computation. Interest rates, sales taxes, income tax rates, discounts, and profits are all expressed in percent for ease in communication.

Teaching Common Fraction Concepts

Children begin learning about fractions in kindergarten, a learning that continues throughout the elementary school years.

The pattern used for introducing a new topic with whole numbers should be followed for teaching fractions.

I. Objectives

The major outcomes from lessons on the topic of fractions are:

1. To develop an understanding of the concepts and language of:
   (a) Part of a whole
   (b) Part of a measuring unit
   (c) Part of a set
   (d) Indicated division
   (e) Probability
   (f) Ratios/Rates
2. To be able to solve word problems involving the above concepts by using:
   (a) Manipulatives
   (b) Visuals
   (c) Symbol notations
3. To compare two or more fractions to determine which is more than or less than the others.
4. For any given fraction, to write one or more equal fractions.
5. To perform the four fundamental operations with fractions

II. Readiness

Pupils are ready to learn about fractions when they start kindergarten. They first learn the "part of a whole" concept, using unit fractions. After they understand this idea, they are ready to explore a part of a set. Understanding a part of a set then leads to a study of equal fractions. At about the third-grade level pupils should study the relationship between common fractions and decimals. At about the fourth-grade level, pupils should start studying probability, ratios, and percents. Each of these topics serves as a readiness for subsequent topics. In this chapter the emphasis is on developing *concepts* of common fractions and deci-

mals. Subsequent chapters discuss the four fundamental operations and also deal with probability, ratio, and percent.

III. Motivation

As with the study of whole numbers, pupils will be more highly motivated to study the concepts of fractions when they have an opportunity to:

- Explore the many uses of fractions in everyday life
- Use appropriate manipulatives in the beginning phases of learning
- Learn to make drawings of their ideas and explore visuals of fractions
- Understand and succeed in working with fractions
- Solve real-life problems.

IV. Guided Discovery

The first step in guided discovery is to provide pupils with practical problems to solve. Many problems involving time and measurement use fractions. Often textbook series present the part-of-a-whole concept in relation to geometric figures to the exclusion of using fractions in everyday affairs (such as ½ of an orange, ⅓ of a candy bar, a quarter of an hour, and the like).

The second step is to encourage pupils to use appropriate manipulatives to solve problems and for the teacher to demonstrate concepts of fractions with manipulatives and visuals.

MATERIALS FOR TEACHING MEANINGS OF FRACTIONS

Young children need to use manipulative materials and visual aids to solve problems involving fractions. Among the most common and useful items are real objects, drawings, the flannelboard, the pupil fraction kit, the number line, and groups of objects.

The kindergarten child's first contact with

Students can make their own flannelboard cutouts.

(Photo by Leland Perry)

fractions usually comes as a part of a whole object. Typically, the teacher takes an orange and cuts it into two equal-sized parts and discusses the concept of "half an orange" and the fact that "two halves make a whole." Pupils can also use a piece of cardboard, a ribbon, a piece of string, or anything else that can be cut into congruent parts. Do not overlook sets of congruent objects, such as a set of blocks, a set of checkers, or a set of matched books, to illustrate halves, thirds, and the like.

Direct the pupils to name the number of equal-sized parts in the whole thing, the part considered, and the name of the fractional part of the whole.

AN EXAMPLE OF GUIDED DISCOVERY

A teacher-directed activity to help pupils understand the concept of a part of a region may be performed with a piece of paper. Fold a rectangular piece of paper so that overlapping parts are congruent. Hold the folded paper before the class and ask:

(a) How many parts are formed by the fold?

(b) Each region is what part of the whole?

(c) How many halves make a whole?

Now give each pupil a 4-by-6-inch piece of paper and have him or her perform a similar fold. Check to see that the two regions are congruent. Next, fold the demonstration paper at a right angle to the original fold. Have the class count the number of resulting parts. Then have each pupil perform the same activity and answer the same sequence of questions.

Write the numeral to represent one fractional part, such as ¼. Each pupil marks his or her fractional part. Now ask: How many halves are needed to make a whole? How many fourths? How many thirds? The answer to the last question shows whether the pupil can make the correct generalization. The same and similar questions should be repeated at various intervals for these fractions and other familiar fractions, such as eighths and tenths. The pupil who gives a correct answer has learned a major concept pertaining to a fraction.

Next, have pupils draw a rectangle on ruled paper and divide the figure to show halves and fourths.

FLANNELBOARD

The *flannelboard* is a useful aid in early work with fractions. The teacher's kit should include a set of congruent parts of circular and rectangular regions. The cutouts should be made or covered with flannel or some other material with a heavy nap

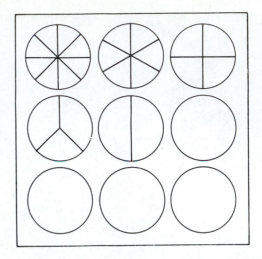

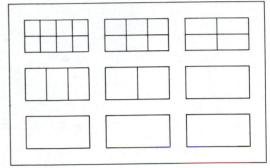

Figure 11.1
Flannelboard cutouts

so that they adhere to the flannelboard. They should be large enough for the parts to be seen easily by the pupils. The use of different colors on either side of a cutout, for example red and green, clarifies a demonstration of fractional numbers on a flannelboard. Figure 11.1 shows some sample flannelboard demonstrations.

PUPIL'S FRACTION KIT

Each pupil should have a *fraction kit* to work with while developing an understanding of the meanings of fractions. Student fraction kits should contain cutouts that are similar to but smaller than the cutouts used for class demonstrations with the flannel-board. The children should store their cut-outs in manila envelopes. As the teacher shows or illustrates various fraction parts with the demonstration kit on the flannel-board the pupils should perform the same activities with their fraction kits.

DRAWINGS

Simple *drawings* on the chalkboard are readily seen by the entire class and can encourage desirable class discussion. Free-hand drawings are usually acceptable, particularly in early work. It avoids the delays that are involved with figures carefully drawn with a ruler or compass. When there is a need for accurate drawings, try to have them placed on the chalkboard before the lesson begins.

Draw a rectangle. Divide it into approximately two congruent parts. Shade one of the parts with diagonal lines. Ask what part of the entire rectangle is shaded. Ask how many parts it takes to make the complete rectangle. Repeat these activities with circles. If freehand circles cannot be drawn with reasonable accuracy, a piece of chalk tied to a string can quickly produce accurate circles. Use squares and any other figures with symmetry that can to be divided into congruent parts.

NUMBER LINES

A *number line* is useful for illustrating the meanings of different fractions as parts of a line-segment unit. A model of a line segment is easy to make both for demonstration purposes and for each pupil. It is versatile because (1) it can be drawn in different unit lengths, (2) it can be partitioned into many congruent parts, and (3) once parts are shown, it is easy to consider one or more parts as a fractional part of the whole unit.

Beginning work with the number line should be on unit segments. Pupils should understand that a segment of any length can represent a unit segment as long as the left endpoint is labeled as 0, and the right endpoint is labeled as 1. The midpoint can then be named as one-half, and each of the two segments can be assigned a length of one-half. To avoid confusion in introductory work, emphasize fractions as the lengths of segments rather than as names for points. When congruent segments are used, compare different parts to illustrate the relationships of greater than, equal to, and less than.

$$0 \quad \frac{1}{4} \quad \frac{2}{4} \quad \frac{3}{4} \quad 1$$
$$\frac{1}{2}$$

ADDITIONAL MODELING OF FRACTIONS

Pupils gain their first insights into fractional numbers by modeling with the various instructional aids discussed before. When a region on the flannelboard is separated into two congruent parts, each is one-half of the original region. Fourths, sixths, and eighths can easily be modeled in this manner.

If a rectangular shape is folded along the line segment connecting the midpoints of opposite sides, the resulting rectangular area is one-half of the original shape. Likewise, if that area is folded again, each part is one-fourth of the original area. Pupils should model such fractions as halves, fourths, and eighths. They can represent these fractions by folding paper, by making drawings, or both.

An effective way to introduce eighths is to have pupils fold rectangular sheets of paper in eighths. The student should discover

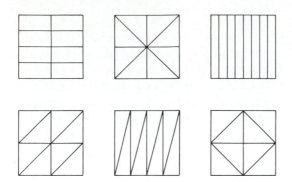

Figure 11.2
Various shapes of eighths of a square

four items in the container, and so on. Similar activities can be used with containers with three, four, and five pockets.

USE OF DRAWINGS

All of the aids we have described can be drawn on paper and discussed. One additional visual model to help understand different fractions is a *fraction strip*, such as:

that an eighth is one-half of a fourth and that a fourth is equal to two eighths. Similarly, they should discover other relationships among halves, fourths, and eighths.

Next have the pupils model eighths by folding a square sheet of paper. Then encourage them to draw line segments in the square region so that eighths are shown. Encourage the class to demonstrate as many ways as possible of representing eighths in a square region. Most of the pupils will discover three of the six ways shown in Figure 11.2.

MODELING PARTS OF A COLLECTION

Fractions can be used to describe parts of a collection. Two or more objects can represent a whole, just as line segments of different lengths can represent one. Thus, one object can be one-third of a collection of three objects, or one-fourth of a collection of four items.

One way to help children understand fractions as representing parts of a collection is to cut up egg cartons with various numbers of pockets in a single row. Put one item in each pocket of a two-pocket container, stating that each item is one-half of the two items in the container. Put two items in each pocket of the same container and note that two items are one-half of the

Different patterns of geometric shapes can be drawn on heavy cardboard, and some can be colored. For each picture, raise the questions:

1. How many are shaded? → 3
2. How many in all? ⟶ 4
3. What part is shaded? ⟶ ¾

PROBLEM-SOLVING ACTIVITIES

Pupils enjoy using their fraction kits to solve oral story problems. Tell them a story about some part of a whole and have them solve the problem with manipulative materials. For example, "Charles bought a pizza that was cut into six pieces. If he ate one piece, what part of the whole pizza was this?"

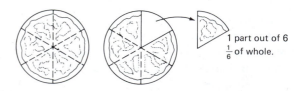

1 part out of 6
$\frac{1}{6}$ of whole.

The pupils will refer to the circular cutout in their fraction kits that is cut into six congruent pieces. Each piece can represent one-sixth of the whole pizza.

Have them use rectangular pieces to solve the following problem: "Jose's garden was divided into three equal-sized plots. If he planted tomatoes in one plot and carrots in another, what part of the garden was planted in tomatoes and carrots?" The solution to this problem involves the addition of the like fractions ⅓ and ⅓ at the exploratory level. Most pupils will readily discover the answer, that 2 plots out of 3 is ⅔ of the whole garden.

To represent a part of a collection is more difficult than finding a part of a whole. Students find solutions by using manipulative materials. For example, "Mike brought five marbles to school. Two were black and three were white. What part of the marbles was black?" The pupils can solve this problem by using a five-pocket egg carton. By distributing one marble in each pocket in the order black, black, white, white, white as shown, pupils can readily find the answer to the problem as they also answer the following questions:

1. How many marbles are black?

2. How many marbles in the collection?

3. So that is, "Two out of _____?"

4. Two out of five is what part?

5. How do we write that as a fraction?

Keep problems simple. Pupils like problems about everyday matters.

Comparing Fractions

In their initial work, pupils should use cutouts to compare fractions and then make a written record of the experience. They should discover, for example, that the denominator 4 in ¾ indicates the number of

equal-sized parts into which the whole is divided, and the numerator 3 indicates how many of these parts are involved. The students should make two basic generalizations:

1. When the denominators are equal, the larger the numerator, the larger the fraction.

2. When the numerators are equal, the larger the denominator, the smaller the fraction.

The *number line* is an excellent way to demonstrate both of these generalizations. Once pupils recognize that the closer the number is to zero, the smaller it is, or that if *A* is to the left of *B*, then *A* is smaller then *B*.

With the cutouts in their fraction kits, pupils can easily demonstrate the fact that a fraction with the largest denominator (assuming the same numerators) represents the smallest fraction.

Similarly, pupils should use their cutouts to compare like fractions (with equal denominators). They should discover that the value of like fractions changes as the numerator changes. If the pupils arrange cutouts in size from smaller to larger, they will obtain a symbolic record of the result such as that shown in (a). Once again, the pupils see that for like fractions, the larger the numerator the larger the fraction.

$$\text{(a)} \quad \frac{1}{8} \quad \frac{2}{8} \quad \frac{3}{8} \quad \frac{4}{8} \quad \frac{5}{8} \quad \frac{6}{8} \quad \frac{7}{8} \quad \frac{8}{8}$$

V. Reinforcement

Reinforcement activities, typically found in modern textbooks, include working with visuals and symbolic notations. Working with calculators and computer programs is helpful for developing a mastery of the concepts of fractions. The amount of practice needed to make learning effective varies with a pupil's ability.

Teaching Decimals

As children are learning about common fractions the teacher should introduce fractions with denominators of 10. Pupils encounter situations in everyday life in which they see numbers written with a decimal point. Writing money values with dollars and cents is frequent.

The sequence for introducing decimals is the same as for fractions.

I. Objectives

In addition to the objectives for common fractions discussed above, the objectives for decimals are:

1. To develop an understanding that fractions and decimals are different names for the same number.

2. To deal with problem situations in which fractions may be converted to decimal fractions and decimal fractions renamed as common fractions.

3. To learn how to write the corresponding numeral when a numeral is given for either a fraction or a decimal.

II. Readiness

Pupils are ready to begin a study of decimals as soon as they have learned the meaning of a fraction and how to deal with it.

III. Motivation

The same techniques listed for fractions are appropriate as motivation to learn decimals.

IV. Guided Discovery

PROBLEM SITUATIONS

Of utmost importance in learning the concepts associated with decimal fractions is looking for and using a variety of problem situations in which decimals are used. Have pupils search in newspapers and magazines for instances of decimals. From these develop problems involving the concepts associated with decimals for the pupils to solve.

MANIPULATIVES, VISUALS, AND SYMBOLIC NOTATIONS

The manipulatives used to develop the concepts associated with common fractions can be helpful in developing the concepts of decimals. The only difference is that the number of parts to be represented by a decimal numeral must be 10 or a multiple of 10.

Metric measuring instruments are excellent manipulatives for introducing decimals. To measure length, use a foot ruler with a strip of tape the length of the ruler on the back. Then graduate the tape into ten congruent parts. Since 12 inches equals about 30.48 centimeters, take a metric ruler and every 3 centimeters mark off the ten parts for tenths of a foot. Then have pupils measure different lengths with the rulers graduated into ten parts and the standard one graduated into twelve parts. Have the class tell which is larger, an inch ($\frac{1}{12}$ of a foot) or $\frac{1}{10}$ of a foot. Give reasons for the answer. Have the pupils measure other objects in the room that measure less than a foot with the foot ruler graduated into ten parts. Have each pupil record measurements as a fraction, then as a decimal.

Another manipulative for introducing decimals is to use fifths as well as halves. Use a set of five black checkers and five red checkers or any similar set of objects. Start with one red and one black checker and hold them so the entire class can see them. Ask how many checkers are in the set. (Two) Ask what part of the set is black. ($\frac{1}{2}$). Now use a set of four checkers, two red and two black. Ask what part of the set is black. ($\frac{1}{2}$) Ask how the answer could be expressed in fourths, because there are four checkers in the set. Guide the pupils to discover that $\frac{1}{2}$ and $\frac{2}{4}$ are equal. The activity can now be extended to a set of three red and three black, up to five red and five black checkers. This activity should lead pupils to understand that ½ = ²⁄₄ = ³⁄₆ = ⁴⁄₈ = ⁵⁄₁₀.

Ask the pupils how many have used decimals on the calculator or computer. Ask them to tell how ⁵⁄₁₀ would look on a calculator. If they do not know, have a pupil use a calculator and perform the steps "5 divided by 10 = ." The answer will be 0.5. Note that 5/10 and 0.5 may look quite different but the pronunciation is identical; each is named "five tenths."

The teacher should then lead the pupils to understand that decimals are a special kind of fraction for two reasons:

(a) Decimals can only have denominators of 10, 100, 1000, and the like.

(b) The denominators are not written but are determined by the number of decimal places.

The decimal 0.5 is a one-place decimal and has a denominator of 10, consisting of the digit 1 followed by a single zero. The decimal 0.23 is a two-place decimal; its denominator consists of the digit 1 followed by two zeros, and so on.

Base-ten materials were used in dealing with whole numbers. These manipulatives are also useful in developing the concept of decimals. Each pupil should have a kit of decimal squares made of cardboard. A large square represents one. Another square can be divided into ten strips, with each strip representing one-tenth. A third square can be divided into 100 small squares, each representing one-hundredth. Figure 11.3 shows how these squares can be used to represent

Figure 11.4

the number 1.35 (1 one, 3 tenths, and 5 hundredths).

Place-value devices should be used to represent ones, tenths, and hundredths. Figure 11.4 shows a place-value chart with 1.35 represented.

A number line can be used to represent the relation between common fractions and decimals. Two are shown in Figure 11.5.

V. Reinforcement

Reinforcement can consist of additional activities with the materials above. If pupils actively participate in a meaningful way they should understand the concepts of fractions and decimals. Practice activities can be provided through the use of textbook, calculator activities, and computer programs.

Meaning of Tenths

It is useful for students at the early symbolic level to practice renaming familiar common fractions in decimal notation. Here are some sample exercises:

a. Complete the following sequence by filling in the blanks with common fractions:

    ¹⁄₁₀, _____, ³⁄₁₀, _____, ⁵⁄₁₀, _____

b. The following sequence names the same numbers as sequence (a). Fill in the blanks with the appropriate decimal numerals.

    .1, _____, .3, _____, .5, _____

c. Use mixed numbers to complete the following sequence:

    2¹⁄₁₀, _____, 2³⁄₁₀, _____, 2⁵⁄₁₀ _____

Figure 11.3

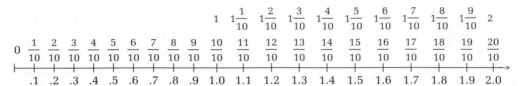

Figure 11.5

d. The following sequence names the same numbers as sequence (c). Fill in the blanks with the appropriate decimal numerals.

2.1, _____, 2.3, _____, 2.5, _____

The activity just described stresses patterns as well as the relationship between common and decimal fractions. The next skill for you to emphasize is renaming decimals as common fractions. Pupils who have difficulty should be given additional exploratory work. Stress two key points in renaming decimals as common fractions:

1. The decimal point identifies the ones place immediately to its left and the tenths place immediately to its right.

2. The unwritten denominator is determined by the number of decimal places (the number of digits to the right of the ones place).

To rename a decimal as a common fraction, it is sufficient to eliminate the decimal point and write the correct denominator. The following illustrates early symbolic work of this nature:

a. $0.3 = \dfrac{3}{\square}$ d. $1.8 = \square\dfrac{\square}{10}$

b. $3.2 = 3\dfrac{2}{\square}$ e. $0.9 = \dfrac{9}{\square}$

c. $.5 = \dfrac{\square}{10}$ f. $1.2 = \dfrac{\boxed{}}{10}$

Meaning of Hundredths

The following activity is suitable for early symbolic learning:

a. The decimal 0.1, or .1, is a one-place decimal because it has one digit to the right of the ones place (immediately to the left of the decimal point), and thus has an unwritten denominator of _____.

b. The decimal 0.14, or .14, is a _____-place decimal because it has _____ digits to the right of the ones place.

c. The decimal .14 has an unwritten denominator of _____.

d. The two-place decimal .03 has an unwritten denominator of _____.

e. The one-place decimal 21.3 has an unwritten denominator of _____.

f. $^{37}/_{100} = $ _____(decimal)

g. The common fraction for .75 is _____.

h. A two-place decimal has an unwritten denominator of _____. Complete the following sequences:

i. .01, .02, _____, .04, _____, _____

j. 1.02, 1.04, _____, 1.08, _____, _____

k. .25, .30, _____, _____, .45, _____

MASTERY LEVEL FOR TENTHS AND HUNDREDTHS

Pupils achieve mastery of tenths and hundredths when they become able to change notations from decimals to common fractions and from common fractions to decimals on a habitual basis.

Identifying the Denominator

Table 11.1 shows how the ones place is used as the reference for separating tens and tenths, hundreds and hundredths, thousands and thousandths. The ones place can be regarded as the center of symmetry, with

Thousands	Hundreds	Tens	Ones	Tenths	Hundredths	Thousandths
10^3	10^2	10^1	10^0	10^{-1}	10^{-2}	10^{-3}
1000	100	10	1	.1	.01	.001
1000	100	10	1	$\frac{1}{10}$	$\frac{1}{100}$	$\frac{1}{1000}$

Table 11.1

the tenths place a reflection of tens, and so on. For example, in the numeral 321.23, the 2 one place to the left of the ones place is in the tens place, while the 2 one place to the right of the ones place is in the tenths place, and so on.

A series of questions such as these can give students the opportunity to discover this symmetry:

1. The 4 in 641.35 is one place to the left of the ones place, and therefore is in the _____ place.

2. The 3 in 642.35 is _____ place to the right of the ones place, and therefore is in the _____ place.

3. The 6 in 641.35 is two places to the left of the ones place, and therefore is in the _____ place.

4. The 5 in 641.35 is _____ place(s) to the _____ of the ones place, and therefore is in the _____ place.

Stress the fact that the decimal point identifies the ones place immediately to its left.

It is sometimes stated incorrectly that a decimal has no denominator. Every decimal has an unwritten denominator that is determined by the number of places to the right of the ones place. By completing a table like the one on page 232, pupils will gain an understanding of the pattern for identifying the denominator.

After examining the completed table, students should be able to conclude: The unwritten denominator of a decimal is 10, 100, 1000, and so on, such that the number of zeros following 1 is equal to the number of decimal places. Recognizing the denominator of a decimal fraction should enable pupils to regroup 21 tenths as 2.1 and 2.1 as 21 tenths.

Teaching Percent

The concept of percent is a natural outgrowth of the concept of decimals to the hundredths place. Pupils should learn that percent is used in a variety of situations—to describe sales tax, interest rates, discounts, and so forth. Later they will learn that we only "talk" about percent; to perform calculations percents usually are converted to common fractions or decimals.

I. Objectives

The objectives for percent are the same as for common fractions and decimals with the addition of:

1. To be able to rename a fraction to a decimal to a percent and vice versa.

2. To be able to use information from a graph to solve problems.

3. To interpret situations found in newspapers and magazines that are expressed in percents.

II. Readiness

As soon as pupils learn how to write the decimal equivalent of a fraction, they have

Decimal	Denominator	Number of decimal places	Number of zeros in denominator
.2	10	1	1
0.3	☐	1	☐
.23	100	2	2
1.4	10	☐	☐
2.34	☐	2	☐
0.35	☐	☐	☐
123.13	☐	☐	☐
.10	☐	☐	☐
1243.8	☐	☐	☐

the background for beginning work for percent.

III. Motivation

The same type of activities used for fractions and decimals are useful in motivating pupils to study percents. Since working with percents is very difficult for elementary-age pupils it is especially important that they have a good understanding of this kind of number and relate it to real-life situations. Frequent use should be made of the calculator during the study of percents. Computer programs are helpful in getting and keeping pupils' interest in the study of percents.

IV. Guided Discovery

PROBLEM SITUATIONS

Have pupils search newspapers and magazines for uses of percents. The class should look for advertisements and sales that use percent. Have pupils talk with their parents on how they use percents in their daily lives. The idea here is to gather information about the uses of percents. Have them tell about the reference to percent that they have heard on television. Later in this chapter and in Chapter 12 we discuss solving problems that involve percents.

MANIPULATIVES

One manipulative for introducing percents is a *hundred board*, shown in Figure 11.6 There is no better instructional aid for presenting percent than this kind of board. The following is a activity on the hundred board designed to develop an understanding of percent.

Fraction: $\dfrac{1}{100}$
Decimal: 0.01
Percent: 1%

Show a hundred board to the class. Have the pupils tell how many disks are in one row; how many rows; how many disks on the board.

The teacher removes one disk from the board and asks the class to describe the disk in terms of the total number of disks. The anticipated answer is "one out of a hundred." Now have the class write that as a fraction (1/100), and then as a decimal (0.01). The teacher then indicates that each number may be described as 1% and read

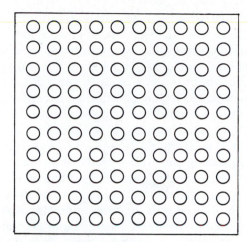

Figure 11.6
A hundred board

"one percent." The teacher leads the pupils to generalize that every number expressed as a percent implies that the percent can be renamed as hundredths and that hundredths can be renamed as percent.

The teacher has the class rename numbers of disks as fractions, decimals, and percents to make sure each pupil understands the relationship that exists among fractions, decimals, and percents. Thus, a row of ten disks on the hundred board can be identified as $\frac{1}{10}$, $\frac{10}{100}$, 0.1, 0.10, and 10%. Similarly, the renaming can be reversed for 50 disks: 50% = $\frac{50}{100}$ = $\frac{5}{10}$ = 0.5 = $\frac{1}{2}$.

V. Reinforcement

RENAMING TO AND FROM PERCENT

1. The key to renaming a percent as a decimal or common fraction or vice versa is recognizing that "percent" and "hundredths" are interchangeable.

   a. 1% = 1 hundredth = .01 = $\frac{1}{100}$

   b. 4% = 4 hundredths = .04 = $\frac{4}{100}$

c. $\dfrac{2}{5} = \dfrac{2}{5} \times 1 = \dfrac{2}{5} \times \dfrac{20}{20} = \dfrac{40}{100}$
   = 40 hundredths = $\square$ %

d. $\dfrac{2}{3} = \dfrac{2}{3} \times \dfrac{33\frac{1}{3}}{33\frac{1}{3}} = \dfrac{66\frac{2}{3}}{100}$

   = 66⅔ hundredths = $\square$ %
   66⅔% is often approximated as 66.7%.

Multiplying by $\dfrac{20}{20}$ or $\dfrac{33\frac{1}{3}}{33\frac{1}{3}}$ illustrates one of the many ways to apply the identity element for multiplication.

2. Complete the following:

   a. $\dfrac{1}{5} \times \dfrac{\square}{20} = \dfrac{\triangle}{100} = \triangle$ hundredths = $\triangle$ %

   b. $.23 = \dfrac{\square}{100} = \square$ hundredths = $\square$ %

   c. $\dfrac{3}{8} = 3 \div 8 = .375 = \dfrac{375}{1000} = \dfrac{37.5}{\square} = \triangle$ %

3. Rename as percents: a. $\frac{1}{10}$ b. $\frac{3}{5}$ c. $\frac{3}{4}$ d. $\frac{1}{3}$

4. Rename as common fractions: a. 7% b. 13% c. 75% d. 10%

5. Rename as decimals: a. 11% b. 10% c. 75% d. 112% e. 3%

Calculator Activities

The calculator is of little value for introductory activities that rely on drawings or manipulation of objects. However, the calculator offers an important opportunity to verify and reinforce basic concepts at the symbolic level.

Earlier introduction of fundamental fraction concepts on the symbolic level is desirable in view of our increased everyday exposure to decimals. The definition of a fraction as the quotient of the numerator and denominator is now much more practical with the calculator available. An excessive amount of paper-and-pencil division is required for effectively verifying that the quotient and part-of-a-whole concept are equivalent.

When the introductory phase for teaching fractions is almost complete, work with manipulatives should have illustrated that $\frac{3}{10}$ = .3, $\frac{1}{2}$ = .5, and similar results. At this point, have pupils use the calculator to confirm these results by dividing each numerator by its denominator.

Allow the pupils to use the calculator to change fractions of their choice to decimals. Some nonterminating decimals will result. This activity offers an excellent opportunity for pupils to discover that when the denominator of a fraction is divisible by any number other than 2 or 5, its equivalent decimal will be nonterminating. Many college graduates have never recognized this fundamental relation between fractions and decimals.

To help pupils discover which decimals are nonterminating, try this procedure: Have the class use calculators to show that $\frac{3}{8}$ = .375. The steps are press 3, press ÷, press 8, press =. Ask what whole numbers divide the denominator. On the chalkboard make a list with two columns, labeled *terminating* and *nonterminating*. When pupils recognize that 2 is the only whole-number divisor, place $\frac{3}{8}$ in the terminating column followed by a 2 in parentheses.

Now use a fraction, such as $\frac{2}{15}$ = .13333..., with a nonterminating decimal equivalent. When the pupils recognize that the only divisors are 3 and 5, place $\frac{2}{15}$ in the column labeled nonterminating with (3,5) in parentheses. Continue this activity. Allow pupils to choose fractions. Supply additional fractions to keep the number of entries in each column about the same. Af-

ter five or six entries in each column, the pattern should begin to emerge. When pupils recognize that fractions with terminating decimal equivalents have a denominator divisible by only 2 or 5 or both, challenge them to see if they can find an exception.

Pupils should use paper-and-pencil division to confirm that $\frac{2}{15}$ produces a nonterminating decimal. Help them recognize that a repeating remainder leads to a nonterminating decimal. This activity offers an excellent opportunity for guided discovery of a property that will increase understanding of the relation between fractions and decimals. Extending the rounding process from whole numbers to decimals may be an appropriate additional activity. It is traditional to round up when the key digit is 5 or more and round down when the key digit is less than 5. The key digit is one place to the right of the rounded place. For example, when rounding to the nearest tenth, the key digit is in the hundredths place.

Use the calculator to convert $\frac{1}{2}$ to 0.5 and $\frac{2}{4}$ to 0.5 to show that $\frac{1}{2}$ and $\frac{2}{4}$ represent the same number. Similar verification may be obtained for each example obtained by manipulatives. Follow this activity by writing a fraction with a single-digit numerator and denominator on the chalkboard. Ask the pupils to rename it. Check each pupil's response with the calculator. Activities of this type should lead to the guided discovery that multiplying numerator and denominator by the same number renames that fraction with an equivalent numeral. The previous generalization is essential for addition and subtraction of fractions in Chapter 12. The calculator is a powerful device for promoting understanding of the relation between common fractions and decimals and should be used frequently to verify computations with common fractions.

Computer activities, discussed at the end of this chapter, can supplement and reinforce the concepts. If calculators are not available, the computer can be used to emulate a calculator.

Another readiness activity is to have pupils find one-half of 10 or one-fourth of 12. Use manipulatives if necessary. Use only examples with small-number, easy answers and nonterminating decimals. When these questions have been answered successfully, ask the pupils how to use a calculator to find these answers. Guide them to remember that ½ and 0.5 are equivalent names for the same number. Ask for a suggestion on how to use a calculator to multiply 10 by ½, leading to the product 0.5 × 10 on the calculator. Follow immediately with the division $10/2$ to introduce the concept that multiplying by ½ and dividing by 2 are equivalent operations, illustrating the principle:

MULTIPLICATION BY A NUMBER CAN BE PERFORMED BY DIVIDING BY ITS RECIPROCAL. DIVISION BY A NUMBER CAN BE PERFORMED BY MULTIPLYING BY ITS RECIPROCAL. (THE RECIPROCAL OF $\frac{4}{1}$ IS $\frac{1}{4}$.)

Use the calculator to show that the pairs ¾ and 8 × .25 both give an answer of 2 while 8 × 4 and $8/.25$ both give an answer of 32. These examples should be recognized as readiness for introduction of the algorithm. The formal vocabulary should be avoided at this point.

Simple verbal problems can be helpful at this time: "Joan has $12.00 and spends one-half of it. How much money is left? If she spends one-fourth of the $12, how much does she spend? Jim has $6 dollars. Joan has twice as much and Sam has one-half as much. How much does Joan have; does Sam have?" These problems should be solved by both multiplication and division. Similar examples, some with decimals, can help pupils recognize that the choice of the operation depends on the situation and not on the numbers.

Problem Solving

Rename as a common fraction, decimal fraction, and percent:
  (a) 3 hundredths   (b) 17 hundredths
  (c) 97 hundredths
Answers: (a) $3/100$, .03, 3% (b) $17/100$, .17, 17% (c) $97/100$, .97, 97%

Rename as common fraction and decimal fraction:
  (a) 3 tenths   (b) 1 tenth
  (c) 9 tenths
Answers: (a) $3/10$, .3 (b) $1/10$, .1 (c) $9/10$, .9

Rename as common fraction and as a decimal:
  (a) 13%   (b) 2%   (c) 113%
Answers: (a) $13/100$, .13   (b) $2/100$, .02 (c) $113/100$, 1.13

Write a proportion for the following. Do not solve.
  (a) The cost of 5 items is 97 cents. Find the cost of 110 items.
  (b) The cost of 1 item is $.03. Find the cost of 75 items.
  (c) The cost of 1 pound is $10 dollars. Find the cost of ½ a pound.
  (d) The cost of 3 pounds is $20 dollars. Find the cost of .75 pounds.
  (e) The cost of 6 grapefruit is $3. Find the cost of 15 grapefruit.
  (f) The cost of 15 tons is $195. Find the cost of ⅗ of a ton.
Answers: (a) $N/97 = 110/5$; (b) $N/.03 = 75/1$; (c) $N/10 = (½)/1$; (d) $N/20 = .75/3$; (e) $N/3 = 15/6$ (f) $N/195 = (⅗)/15$

Use a calculator. Find the repetend for (a) $2/11$ (b) $3/7$ (c) $4/13$.
Answer: (a) $.\overline{18}$ (b) $.\overline{428571}$ (c) $.\overline{307692}$

Many puzzle books use one combination of digits to make another. Three 3s, four 4s, and the like are among the most common. However, the most flexible is the set 1, 2, 3, and 4. The following shows two examples each for the numbers 0, 1, and 2.

For zero: $12 - 4 \times 3$; $3 + 2 - 4 - 1$
For one: $2 + 3 - 1 \times 4$; $2 \times 3 - 4 - 1$
For two: $2 \times 3 - 1 \times 4$, $4 + 2 - 3 - 1$

There are many ways to represent each number from 1 to 12. In an overnight assignment one class found more than thirty ways to represent 11, using square roots, factorials, and decimal notation. Two interesting examples for 11 follow from the fact that 124-3 and $(1 + 4)! + 3 - 2$ are equal to 121 so that the square root of each is 11. Remember $(1 + 4)!$ is 5 factorial or 120. The activity is open-ended and expands when new notations are introduced.

Find at least five different ways of representing 11 with 1,2,3, and 4.

Answer: $42 - 31$, $2 \times 4 + 1 \times 3$, $4 \times 3 + 1 - 2$, $2^3 + 4 - 1$. Other ways are possible.

Find a way of representing 15 with four 4s.

Answer: $4 \times 4 - \dfrac{4}{4}$

Triangular Numbers

The following display shows graphically why the numbers are called triangular. They are referred to frequently as a connection between arithmetic and geometry and provide an excellent exercise in recognizing patterns. As shown below, the first triangular number is 1, the second is 3, and the third is 6. Each new triangular number is formed by annexing a new line of xs to make the next triangle. Each new line added contains 1 more x than the last line that was added.

```
   x          x              x
            x   x          x   x
                         x   x   x

 One(1)    Two(3)       Three(6)
```

Name the fourth, fifth, and sixth triangular numbers.

Answer: 10, 15, 21.

The first triangular number is 1; the second is $1 + 2$. Write the next four triangular numbers in terms of sums of digits added.

Answer: $1 + 2 + 3$, $1 + 2 + 3 + 4$, $1 + 2 + 3 + 4 + 5$

Describe the Nth triangular number in terms of the sum of its addends.

Answer: The Nth triangular number is the sum of the first N-positive integers.

The following program differs from a similar-looking one from the problem-solving section of Chapter 10, page 211.

```
5 INPUT "ENTER THE NUMBER
  OF CYCLES ";N1
10 T = 1
20 FOR N = 1 TO N1
30 T = T * N
40 NEXT
50 PRINT T
```

What does line 30 tell the computer to do on the first cycle of the loop? on the second cycle?

Answer: On the first cycle $N = 1$ and $T = 1$, so the computer stores T*N or 1 in memory with the name of T. On the second cycle, $T = 1$ and $N = 2$, so $T = 1 \times 2$ and the computer stores T in memory with the name of 2. On the next cycle, $T = 2 \times 3$ or 6, and so on.

Run the program with five terms to get a fifth output of 120, the product of $1 \times 2 \times 3 \times 4 \times 5$. This product is called five factorial, written with a 5 followed by an exclamation point: 5!. Factorials occur often in later mathematics and are particularly useful in statistics and probability.

How many zeros are there at the end of the numeral for 4!?

Answer: None. A zero will appear at the end of a factorial each time one of the numbers multiplied contains a factor of 5.

How many zeros for 10 factorial? Answer: Two. The first factor of 5 is in the fifth number, and the second factor of 5 is in the 10th number. Check this by running the program for 10 factors.

How many zeros for 25!? Answer: 6 There is one factor of 5 in 5th, 10th, 15th, and 20th number, and 2 factors of 5 in the 25th number. This cannot be verified on most computers without special programming.

How many ways can one get from town A to town C by way of town B if there are three roads from A to B and two roads from B to C?

Answer: Six ways. Three ways by the first road from A to B and two ways using each road from A to B to make a total of six or 3! ways.

How many different ways are there for three people to watch a ballgame in three adjoining seats?

Answer: Six or 3!. There are three ways to seat the first person, two ways to seat the second, and one way to seat the third. N factorial, N!, represents the number of different arrangements of N things. Each arrangement contains the same items in a different order.

Run the factorial program for N = 15 and get T = 1.30767437E + 12., an abbreviation for $1.29767437 \times 10^{12}$ or approximately 1,307,674,370,000. The answer is approximate because the number is rounded to the nearest 10,000 in the same way that 1234 can be rounded to the nearest 10 as 1230.

Computing with powers of 10 is an essential number skill. Multiplying and dividing by 10, 100, 1000, and the like should be done mentally because it is much faster than any other procedure, including the use of a calculator.

Pupils should use calculators to discover this skill. The calculator can probably teach the process more efficiently than any other method.

The procedure is to challenge the pupil to perform the operations, mentally, if possible, or with a calculator to establish a pattern. The pupils reach the mastery level when the answers are almost instantaneous. Early work should be recorded so the pupils can recognize the pattern more readily. The process should not be learned by rote. It is as legitimate, however, for pupils to reach the mastery level as a result of pattern recognition as it is to recognize that 10 × 21 = 10 × 20 + 10 × 1, which has the effect of moving the 2 and 1 from the tens place to the hundreds place and from the ones place to the tens place respectively—which effectively moves the decimal point one place to the right. For many pupils, work with the calculator will be more convincing. It is disheartening to see college students multiply or divide by 100 using the standard algorithm.

The following is a brief sample of the kinds of computation that should be done almost instantly mentally. In the learning process the pupil should write the entire computation and then check with the calculator.

(a) 234 × 1000 (b) $456/100$ (c) 1.2 × 100
(d) $34/100$ (e) $1/100$ (f) 100   ×   .003
(g) $23.45/1000$ (h) .0001 × 100000 (i) $.01/100$

It is important for calculator and computer users to know how to interpret exponential notation. Change each of the following from exponential notation to standard notation:

(a) 3.45E + 2   (b) 3.45E − 2
(c) 1.2345E + 10 (d) 1.447E − 6
Answers: (a) 345   (b) .0345
(c) 12,345,000,000 (d) .000001447

Change the following to exponential notation:

(a) 123   (b) .123   (c) 1,230,000
(d) .000123
Answers: (a) 1.23E + 2 (b) 1.23E − 1
(c) 1.23E + 6 (d) 1.23E − 4

Estimate

How long will it take to count to 1,000,000 at one count per second?

Answer: $1000000/3600 \rightarrow 100000/400 \rightarrow 1000/4 \rightarrow 250 \rightarrow$ approximately 250 hours. Since we divided by a number that is too small, we can enlarge the estimate. Any number between 260 and 300 is reasonable. The correct answer, rounded, is 278.

With the same rate, how long in years will it take to count to a billion? *Answer:* A billion is 1000 times a million, so multiply an estimate of 278 by 1000, divide by 24 to get days and then by 365 to get years: $278 \times 1000/24/365 \rightarrow 278 \times (1000/365)/24 \rightarrow 278 \times 3/24 \rightarrow 280/8 = 35$ years

There are many ways to do this, but using 280 for 278 and 3 for $1000/35$ followed by using $3/24$ as $1/8$ gives a reasonable answer. The correct answer is 32.

How long will it take to travel a distance equal to the distance to the sun, which is 93,000,000 miles away at a speed of 333,000 miles per hour? *Answer:* $93,000,000/333,000$ can be rewritten as $93 \times 1,000,000/333,000$, or approximately 3×93 or 279 hours. The correct answer rounds to 279 hours. The estimate is almost exact because $1,000,000/333,000 = 3.003$.

Use exponential notation to find how long will it take to fly 93,000,000 miles at the speed of light, 186,000 miles per second.
Answer: $(9.3E + 7/1.86E5 = 9.3/1.86 E2$

Estimate $9.3/1.86$ as $10/2$ to get 5×100 or 500 seconds (8.3 minutes).

The correct answer is 500 seconds. Our estimate is correct because $9.3/1.86$ is equal to 5. These "accidents" of estimation giving a correct answer will not happen often, but good estimation procedures will make it happen occasionally.

Computer Activities

Program P11.1 provides practice in renaming numbers from hundredths to decimals to percent without the visual backup provided by the displays in the previous programs. A typical output, with a time delay between each of the items in the line, is as follows:

`3 HUNDREDTHS = 3/100 = .03 = 3%`

The program is designed for a mental response. The pupil chooses a time delay to provide time for a mental response for items on the line. The total display includes ten such lines. Lines 80, 100, and 120 are called delay loops. They provide the chosen time interval between the display of items on the horizontal line.

Eliminating the semicolon at the end of lines 90, 110, 130, and 150 will provide a vertical rather than a horizontal display. The number 500 in the delay loops may have to be adjusted for some computers.

```
PROGRAM P11.1
 10 HOME : VTAB 5
 20 PRINT "USE FIRST LINE
    OF DISPLAY AS A MODEL.
    MAKE A MENTAL RESPONSE
    FOR EACH ITEM IN THE
    REMAINING LINES."
 30 PRINT
 40 INPUT "ENTER DE-
    LAY(1-10) "; D
 50 PRINT
 60 FOR K = 1 TO 10
 70 A = 2 + INT(25 *
    RND(1))
 80 IF A = 20 THEN A = 9
 90 PRINT A; "HUNDREDTHS = ";
100 FOR J = 1 TO 500 *
    D: NEXT J
110 PRINT A;"/";100;" = ";
120 FOR J = 1 TO 500 * D:
    NEXT J
130 PRINT A / 100;" = ";
140 FOR J = 1 TO D * 500:
    NEXT J
150 PRINT A;"%"
160 PRINT
170 FOR J = 1 TO 500 * D :
    NEXT J
180 NEXT K
```

Program P11.2 provides practice in rounding to the nearest whole number, the nearest tenth, and the nearest hundredth. It also shows the instructions that tell the computer how to round. These instructions will appear in many of the programs that follow. Learning how and when to round is an essential skill for learning to use decimals effectively.

Pupils should have little difficulty in rounding decimals if they have mastered the rounding of whole numbers to tens and hundreds, a skill included in most elementary curricula before the introduction of decimals.

The program also uses adjustable delay loops so that pupils can choose the time delay required for a mental response.

```
PROGRAM P11.2
 10 HOME : VTAB 6
 20 INPUT "ENTER TIME DELAY
    ";D
 30 N = INT(100000 *
    RND(1))/1000
 40 PRINT
 50 PRINT N; " TO THE NEAR-
    EST WHOLE NUMBER: "
 60 PRINT
 70 FOR J = 1 TO D * 500 :
    NEXT J
 80 PRINT "INT(";N;" + .5)
    = ";INT(N + .5)
 90 PRINT:PRINT
100 PRINT N ;" TO THE
    NEAREST 10TH IS: "
110 PRINT
120 FOR J + 1 TO D * 500 :
    NEXT J
130 PRINT "INT(10 * ";N;"+
    .5)/ 10 = "; INT(10
    * N +.5)/10
140 PRINT : PRINT
150 PRINT N; " TO THE
    NEAREST 100TH . = "
160 PRINT
170 FOR J = 1 TO D * 500 :
    NEXT J
180 PRINT INT(100*N +
    .5)/100
```

Summary

In future programs there should be a closer relationship than is traditional in the teaching of the concepts of common fractions and decimals because of the widespread use of calculators and the introduction of metric measures. There should also be increased emphasis on helping pupils understand the meanings associated with fractions and decimals. The fourth National Assessment of Educational Progress in Mathematics found that pupils were generally deficient in understanding of fractions and decimals.

Research and experience have shown that pupils need to explore the solutions of real-life situations involving fractions and decimals with manipulatives, visuals, and symbolic notations. As pupils investigate the concepts associated with fractions, decimals, and percents, they should also learn the mathematical language required to communicate these ideas. Pupils should discover patterns and relationships of these kinds of numbers.

Reinforcement through practice and drill should follow a good understanding of the concepts of fractions, decimals, and percents. Computer programs and calculators should be used extensively for reinforcement.

Exercises 11.1

1. Name three important aids for introducing fractions and decimals.

2. Use a rectangular region to show the following:
   (a) ¾ renamed as 6/8
   (b) 6/10 renamed as ⅗

3. Use a number line to rename the following:
   (a) ⅗ as ⁶⁄₁₀
   (b) ⁶⁄₈ as ¾

4. Express the shaded part of the following figures as a common fraction, decimal, and percent:

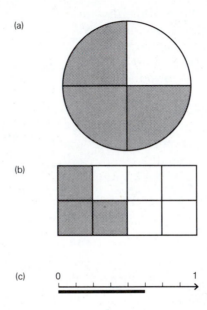

5. Write a proportion to show each of the following rate/ratio relationships:
   (a) Candy sells at 5 pounds for $12. How much will 3 pounds cost?
   (b) The ratio of men to women at a certain university is 5 to 4. If there are 1800 students, how many are men?
   (c) A rocket travels at a rate of 5 miles in 3 seconds. What is the speed in miles per hour?

6. Write a lesson plan to teach common fraction concepts. Include: (a) objectives, (b) readiness, (c) motivation, (d) teaching–learning sequence, (e) evaluation, (f) reinforcement.

7. Examine the Teacher's Edition of an elementary mathematics series. Evaluate the lessons designed to develop concepts of fractions and decimals in terms of the principles developed in this chapter.

Selected Readings

Ashlock, Robert B., et. al. *Guiding Each Child's Learning of Mathematics.* Columbus, OH: Charles E. Merrill, 1983. Chapter 12.

Heddens, James W., and William R. Speer. *Today's Mathematics*, 6th ed. Chicago; Science Research Associates, 1988. Unit 9.

Kennedy, Leonard M., and Steve Tipps. *Guiding Children's Learning of Mathematics*, 5th ed. Belmont, CA: Wadsworth, 1988. Chapters 11 and 12.

Marks, John L., et. al. *Teaching Elementary School Mathematics for Understanding*, 5th ed. New York: McGraw-Hill, 1985. Chapters 8 and 9.

Post, Thomas R. *Teaching Mathematics in Grades K–8*. Needham Heights, MA: Allyn & Bacon, 1988. Chapter 7.

Reys, Robert E., et. al. *Helping Children Learn Mathematics*, 2nd ed. Englewood Cliffs, NJ: Prentice-Hall, 1989. Chapter 11 and 12.

Riedesel, C. Alan. *Teaching Elementary School Mathematics*, 4th ed. Englewood Cliffs, NJ: Prentice-Hall, 1985. Chapters 10 and 11.

Suydam, Marilyn N., and Robert E. Reys (eds.). *Developing Computational Skills*, 1978 Yearbook. Reston., VA: National Council of Teachers of Mathematics, 1978. Chapter 8.

Trafton, Paul R., and Albert P. Shulte, *New Directions for Elementary School Mathematics*, 1989 Yearbook. Reston, VA: National Council of Teachers of Mathematics, 1989. Chapter 13.

See also issues of the *Arithmetic Teacher* and the *Journal for Research in Mathematics Education*.

Addition and Subtraction of Fractions and Decimals

ACHIEVEMENT GOALS

After studying this chapter you should be able to:

1. Express the common properties of, and differences and relationships among common fractions and decimals.

2. State problems where addition and subtraction of fractions and decimals occur.

3. Identify the materials used to teach the meanings of fractions and decimals.

4. Explain how to teach addition and subtraction of fractions and decimals, including (a) stating objectives, (b) assessing readiness, (c) providing appropriate motivation, (d) facilitating growth from the concrete level of learning, through the visual level to the symbol level and finally to mastery.

5. Demonstrate ways an understanding of prime and composite numbers help pupils in finding least common denominators and in reducing fractions to lowest terms.

6. Provide calculator and computer activities for pupils designed to bring about a better understanding of the relationship between fractions and decimals as well as to improve problem-solving skills.

VOCABULARY

These terms are defined or illustrated in the Glossary.

Composite numbers
Equal fractions
Greatest common factor
Improper fraction
Least common denominator

Least common multiple
Like fractions
Lowest terms
Mixed number
Prime number

Addition and subtraction of common fractions were taught prior to working with decimals in earlier mathematics programs in the elementary school. Today there is a growing need that pupils understand the relationships and applications associated with common fractions and decimals. Greater emphasis needs to be given to decimal fractions because of the increased use of calculators to perform computations, the widespread acceptance that will be given metric measure, and the increasing number of computers in elementary schools. Decimal fractions are a natural extension of the whole-number system in terms of base-ten and place value. Pupils who understand these concepts should be able to make the transition to decimal fractions with relative ease. Addition and subtraction of decimals are easily performed by pupils who have mastered these operations on whole numbers.

The study of common fractions, however, will not disappear from the elementary school mathematics curriculum. These numbers will always be a part of the mathematics curriculum. When metric measures become widely used in our society there will be fewer addition and subtraction problems involving the "part of a unit" meaning of common fractions. But the other concepts and uses of common fractions in rate/ratio situations, as indicated division, and as a part of a set, will continue to be important learning objectives.

In future programs, addition and subtraction of fractions and decimals will need to be taught in close association with each other.

Relationships Between Common Fractions and Decimals

Chapter 11 presented concepts of fractions, decimals, and percents. The major differences between common fractions and decimals are:

1. A common fraction may have a denominator of any nonzero number, whereas a decimal has an unwritten denominator that is a power of 10.

2. A common fraction is written with a numerator and a denominator, whereas a decimal fraction is written with a numerator preceded by a decimal point and illustrates an extension of our base-ten and place-value system.

3. Addition and subtraction of common fractions require a common denominator; addition or subtraction of decimals requires the operation on numbers in like places.

4. In some situations it is more appropriate to use the common-fraction form and in other instances it is more appropriate to use the decimal form. The form 25/100 is used in writing a check, but the form $0.25 is used in pricing an item. A discount on an item may be marked as ¼ off or as 25% off. The weatherman could report a 25% chance of rain, and the batting average of a baseball player is reported as .250, meaning an average of one hit in four times at bat.

5. Common fractions and decimals are two different ways of representing rational numbers.

Addition and Subtraction of Like Fractions and Decimals

The most difficult concept for pupils to understand and practice in dealing with fractions is that *fractions as such are not added or subtracted*. Only the *numerators of fractions having equal denominators* are added and subtracted. This concept can best be demonstrated by solving word problems with manipulatives and visual models.

I. Objectives

Upon completion of a series of lessons over a period of time each pupil should achieve the following objectives:

1. Recognize, create, and solve problem situations in which fractions and decimals are to be added or subtracted.

2. Demonstrate the ability to rename fractions to like denominators with understanding.

3. Estimate answers to addition and subtraction problems involving fractions and decimals.

4. Add or subtract fractions and decimals with a reasonable degree of accuracy and speed.

5. Rename fractions to lower or higher terms as appropriate.

II. Readiness

Readiness for addition and subtraction of fractions and decimals involves a good understanding of the "part of a whole" concept of fractions and decimals. Pupils typically study the meanings of fractions during grades K–3. Consequently, almost all pupils should have the necessary background of concepts and skills needed to succeed on this topic. For those who still do not fully understand the "part of a whole" interpretation of a fraction, additional instruction with manipulatives, measuring instruments, and visual models is recommended. Some traditional mathematics programs delayed the teaching of addition and subtraction of fractions until the fourth grade, followed by a study of these operations on decimals. Some of the newer textbook series present addition and subtraction of decimals to tenths and hundredths as early as the third-grade level, prior to introducing addition and subtraction of fractions.

III. Motivation

Teachers should be aware of the need of success so that a pupil develops a favorable attitude for learning mathematics. Pupils in the primary grades are usually more interested in and have a better attitude toward mathematics than pupils in the upper grades. There are several reasons for this situation:

First, primary pupils frequently deal with manipulatives in solving very simple story problems. Manipulatives appropriate for teaching fractions and decimals are not as plentiful nor as easy to use as for teaching operations on whole numbers. These aids are necessary during initial instruction to help bridge the gap to visuals and symbolic notations.

Second, the mathematics taught to primary-age pupils usually emphasizes understanding concepts and procedures in relatively simple language. Often upper-grade pupils are assumed to have had the necessary background for success on more advanced topics in mathematics when in fact they may have not participated in a meaningful program.

Third, problem situations used to illustrate addition and subtraction of fractions and decimals are more complicated than for whole numbers.

IV. Guided Discovery

TEACHING ADDITION AND SUBTRACTION OF DECIMALS

Start With a Word Problem Most primary-age pupils have very little contact with decimal fractions, except perhaps with money notations. But the notation $1.25 is not typically taught as a decimal fraction and read as "one and 25 hundredths of a dollar." Consequently, problems involving money are not the best to use for introducing addition and subtraction of decimals.

Problems involving metric measures are recommended for introducing this topic because they have a base of ten and are studied by most upper-grade pupils. Problems involving one or more units and a tenth of a unit should be used first.

Solve with Manipulatives Pupils first learn about common fractions in kindergarten or in grade 1. When a class first learns to add like fractions, manipulatives are used. After a class can add like fractions, the same procedure with manipulatives is followed for the addition of decimals.

Translate into Symbolic Notation. Because decimal fractions are an extension of the base-ten, place-value whole-number system, pupils should be taught to record addition and subtraction examples in vertical form. Then the operation is performed at each place and an overloaded column or a column impasse is handled with decimals in the same manner as with whole numbers. The only new idea is the name of each decimal place. Pupils should learn that the decimal point is used to identify the ones place.

ADDITION AND SUBTRACTION OF LIKE
FRACTIONS

Start with a Problem Setting Addition of like fractions can be introduced with the following problem:

Joe cut his apple into 4 equal-sized pieces. He gave 1 slice to Raymond and 2 slices to Mary. What part of his apple did he give away?

Solve Problems with Manipulatives Pupils can easily solve the problem above by using an apple, but because it is difficult to cut an apple into equal-sized (congruent) parts, a circular region cut into four congruent pieces is more effective. The pupils should participate in the discussion of each of the following steps:

1. Select a circular region and cut it into four congruent parts. Ask the pupils "How many equal-sized parts are there? What part of the whole is each piece?"

2. Next give a pupil one piece and note that this is one-fourth of the whole. Give another pupil two pieces and ask what part of the whole this is.

3. Next join the one-fourth with the two-fourths and ask the pupils to identify what part of the whole this is. Pupils will easily see that one-fourth + two-fourths equals three-fourths.

Show Solutions with Drawings If cutouts are not available, use a circle on the chalkboard and divide its interior region into fourths by drawing two diameters perpendicular to each other. Now ask a pupil to use chalk and shade in ¼ of the circular region. Another pupil can shade in another ²⁄₄ of the region, and the sentence ¼ + ²⁄₄ = ¾ can be written. The same procedure may be used with rectangular regions. Encourage pupils to use the materials in their fraction kits to solve addition and subtraction problems with fractions.

Record Solutions As pupils use manipulative materials to solve problems involving like fractions, keep appropriate records of the thought process. A record of the solution of the above problem should be recorded (a) in words, (b) with drawings, and (c) in symbolic notation, as follows:

(a) With words:

$$\begin{array}{r} 1 \text{ fourth} \\ +\,2 \text{ fourths} \\ \hline 3 \text{ fourths} \end{array}$$

(b) With drawings:

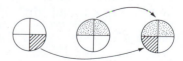

(c) With symbolic notation:

$$\frac{1}{4} + \frac{2}{4} = \frac{3}{4} \text{ or } \begin{array}{r} \frac{1}{4} \\ + \frac{2}{4} \\ \hline \frac{3}{4} \end{array}$$

Problem: David had his pizza cut into 6 equal-sized pieces. If he ate 4 pieces, what part of the pizza would be left?

Pupils can solve this problem by using a circular cutout in their fraction kits cut into six congruent parts.

1. Use the circular region cut into six congruent parts. Ask the pupils, "What is the size of each part?"

2. If David ate four pieces, what part of the pizza was this?

3. How many parts did David start with? Pupils should recognize that there are six parts and the whole region would be six sixths.

4. If David started with six sixths and removed four sixths, how many sixths were left?

Pupils who solve this problem with the use of manipulatives must be guided to operate at a higher level of abstraction. Pupils who feel comfortable in working with manipulatives should record their thinking symbolically.

Problems with Decimals

As pupils are learning to add and subtract fractions they should learn to add and subtract decimals. Consider this problem: Tom lives 0.4 miles from the school he attends. If he rides his bike to and from school, how far does he travel in a round trip?

Fractions

$$\frac{4}{10} + \frac{4}{10} = \frac{8}{10}$$

Decimals

$$\begin{array}{r} 0.4 \\ \underline{0.4} \\ 0.8 \end{array}$$

A round trip is 0.8 miles.

A pupil who can add two like fractions can work intelligently with decimals.

Different Names for the Same Fraction

Pupils must learn that fractions, like whole numbers, can be renamed. For example, 16 can be renamed as 8 + 8, 2 × 8, 10 + 6, etc. $\frac{1}{2}$ can be renamed as $\frac{2}{4}$, $\frac{4}{8}$, $\frac{5}{10}$, 0.5, etc. These fractions are known as *equal* or *equivalent* fractions.

Renaming Fractions to Lower Terms

The sum or difference that results from adding or subtracting fractions may not be expressed in *lowest terms*. A fraction in lowest terms is in *simplified form*, which is usually considered to be in the most acceptable form for a final answer. A fraction is in lowest terms if the numerator and the denominator contain no common factors except 1.

Renaming a fraction means changing the terms of the fraction (numerator and denominator) without changing the value. By working with various instructional materials, young children learn that two-fourths of a circular region can also be named one-half, or that two-fourths make one-half. The fractions $\frac{2}{4}$ and $\frac{1}{2}$ name the same rational number, and so we say that $\frac{2}{4}$ equals $\frac{1}{2}$.

The fractions $\frac{6}{8}$ and $\frac{3}{4}$ name the same number, but $\frac{3}{4}$ is in lowest terms, as the numerator and denominator have no common factors other than one. Traditionally, answers to problems are written in lowest terms. Replacing $\frac{6}{8}$ with $\frac{3}{4}$ is often called "reducing to lowest terms."

Use of Fraction Cutouts

Have the class work with parts of circular regions to rename fractions that are equal. First, have the pupils represent the parts that are needed to make the whole unit. How many halves make one? How many fourths? How many sixths? How many eighths? How many tenths? The pupils will discover that the numerators and denominators for fractions that equal 1 are the same number. That is, $\frac{2}{2}$ = 1; $\frac{3}{3}$ = 1; $\frac{4}{4}$ = 1; $\frac{5}{5}$ = 1, etc.

Next, show the class a flannelboard cutout of *one-half* of a circular region. Pupils should start with the corresponding one-half in their fraction kits and then try to dis-

cover other parts that equal one-half. Pupils will discover that $\frac{4}{8}$ = $\frac{3}{6}$ = $\frac{2}{4}$ = $\frac{1}{2}$ by placing these parts over the one-half region.

Use of A Fraction Chart

Parts of congruent line segments can be used to represent equal fractions. Folding paper is a way to create congruent line segments and discover that several fractions can represent the same length. Have the pupils take an unlined piece of paper and, using a straight edge, draw five horizontal line segments across the page. Note that each line segment represents one unit segment. Have each pupil fold the sheet of paper down the center the long way to create two

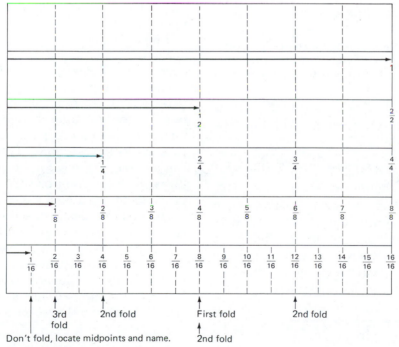

Figure 12.1
A fraction chart

Note: Each horizontal line segment is a number line. Thus, $\frac{1}{8}$ is less than $\frac{2}{8}$, because $\frac{1}{8}$ is to the left of $\frac{2}{8}$ (closer to zero), and $\frac{1}{4}$ is less than $\frac{3}{8}$.

congruent rectangular regions. Now open up the paper and look at the parts of the segments that are formed. Note that the midpoint is named ½, which is the measure of the line segment from the left edge of the paper to the midpoint.

On the second horizontal line segment from the top, draw an arrow just under the segment from the left edge to the midpoint and label the midpoint ½. Continue to fold and label as illustrated in Figure 12.1.

Encourage the pupils to think about what happens to the denominators each time in subsequent line segments. Each time there will be twice as many parts, but each part is one-half the size of the one in the previous line segment, and so the denominators double each time. Each pupil should then make a fraction chart similar to the one shown in Figure 12.1.

Once the pupils have their own fraction chart, they can use it to discover that some line segments can be named with equal fractions. Starting with the bottom line segment, it can be shown that $\frac{4}{16}$ can be named $\frac{2}{8}$ and $\frac{1}{4}$.

Pupils should make additional charts showing ½, ⅕, and ⅒ along with the decimal equivalents.

RENAMING TO LOWEST TERMS AT THE SYMBOLIC LEVEL

The most efficient way of renaming $\frac{8}{12}$ is to use the identity property of 1 for division. Thus any nonzero number divided by one is that number. Also, any nonzero number divided by itself equals one. Thus, at the symbolic level:

$$\frac{8}{12} = \frac{2 \times 4}{3 \times 4} = \frac{2}{3} \longrightarrow \frac{8 \div 4}{12 \div 4} = \frac{2}{3}$$

Once pupils understand the algorithm for multiplication with fractions, the following sequence can be helpful:

$$\frac{8}{12} = \frac{2}{3} \times \frac{4}{4} = \frac{2}{3} \times 1 = \frac{2}{3}$$

However, during the initial instruction on renaming to lowest terms, the correct procedure must be obtained with manipulatives and visuals.

Use these materials to show the following:

$$\frac{1}{2} = \frac{2}{4} \qquad \frac{2}{3} = \frac{4}{6} \qquad \frac{3}{4} = \frac{6}{8}$$

Now use the above equalities and help the pupil discover:

$$\frac{2}{4} = \frac{2 \div 2}{4 \div 2} = \frac{1}{2} \longrightarrow \frac{1}{2} = \frac{1 \times \triangle}{2 \times 2} = \frac{2}{\square}$$

$$\frac{4}{6} = \frac{4 \div \triangle}{6 \div 2} = \frac{\square}{\square} \longrightarrow \frac{2}{3} = \frac{2 \times 2}{3 \times \square} = \frac{\square}{\square}$$

The entire nonverbal sequence is the basis of the traditional verbalization: "Multiplying or dividing both terms (numerator and denominator) of a fraction by the same nonzero number does not change its value (changes the numeral but not the number)."

The difficulty most pupils have when faced with a fraction that is not in lowest terms is to determine the *greatest common factor* (divisor) so that the fraction can be reduced to lowest terms. Three techniques can be used: (1) look for a *common divisor*; (2) write the *factors* of each term; and (3) *prime factor* each term.

The first approach is used by pupils who can immediately recognize a common divisor of the numerator and denominator to be renamed in lowest terms. For example, many pupils can identify 2 as a common factor of the terms 6 and 8 in $\frac{6}{8}$. Then $\frac{6}{8}$ can be reduced to lower terms as follows:

$$\frac{6}{8} = \frac{6 \div 2}{8 \div 2} = \frac{3}{4}$$

Pupils should recognize that if both the numerator and denominator of a fraction are even numbers, then 2 is a common factor (divisor). The difficulty here is that a common divisor may not be the greatest common factor, and so the resulting fraction will not be in *lowest terms*. For example, 2 is a common divisor of 8 and 12 in the fraction $\frac{8}{12}$. The fraction can be reduced to lower terms as follows:

$$\frac{8}{12} = \frac{8 \div 2}{12 \div 2} = \frac{4}{6}$$

Because 2 is not the greatest common factor of 8 and 12, the fraction $\frac{4}{6}$ is not in lowest terms, and so another step is needed. Most pupils recognize that 2 is a common factor of 4 and 6. Thus, each term needs to be divided by two:

$$\frac{4}{6} = \frac{4 \div 2}{6 \div 2} = \frac{2}{3}$$

If a pupil has difficulty identifying the greatest common factor of the terms of a fraction, then we recommend using a more systematic approach.

A second technique for determining the greatest common factor (divisor) of two numbers is the *factor approach*. There are three steps to find the greatest common factor of 8 and 12:

1. Write the factors (divisors) of 8: 1, 2, 4, 8

2. Write the factors (divisors) of 12: 1, 2, 3, 4, 6, 12

3. Examine the factors (divisors) of 8 and 12 and determine the greatest common factors: It is 4.

Since the *greatest common factor* of 8 and 12 is 4, the fraction $\frac{8}{12}$ can be reduced to lowest terms as follows:

$$\frac{8}{12} = \frac{8 \div 4}{12 \div 4} = \frac{2}{3}$$

When the pupil renames a fraction by dividing both terms by the *greatest common factor* (divisor), the resulting equal fraction will be in *lowest terms*.

A third technique for identifying the greatest common factor (divisor) of the terms of a fraction is the *prime factor method*.

$$\frac{8}{12} = \frac{2 \times 2 \times 2}{2 \times 2 \times 3} = \frac{2}{3}$$

Prime and Composite Numbers

The topic of prime and composite numbers was covered in detail in mathematics programs of the past at the elementary school level; more recent programs provide only an introduction to this topic. The chief reason for studying prime numbers at the elementary school level is to assist pupils in reducing fractions to lowest terms and in finding the least common denominator. Because fractions with large denominators are rarely encountered by young pupils, there is little need for a comprehensive treatment of primes and composites.

Every counting number larger than 1 is either a *prime* or *composite number*. A prime number has only one pair of factors—the number itself and 1. Every composite number can be renamed as the product of prime numbers.

Identifying Primes

Elementary-age pupils rarely need to use prime numbers larger than 13 in working with fractions. Prime numbers constitute an interesting mathematical topic that has other applications, such as a study of divisors, multiples, and factors. One of the best methods for identifying the prime numbers beyond 2 and 3 is with a three-column table. First, write the multiples of 6. Then in the left-hand column write numbers that are one less than each multiple. In the right-hand column write numbers that are one more than each multiple. Next, examine the left-hand column. All numbers are prime except 35. Examine the right-hand column. All numbers are prime except 25 and 49.

5	6	7
11	12	13
17	18	19
23	24	(25)
29	30	31
(35)	36	37
41	42	43
47	48	(49)

The table can easily be constructed by pupils. This method also works for numbers larger than 49. Mathematically, every prime number except 2 and 3 can be renamed in the form of $6 \times N$ plus or minus 1. Some composite numbers fit this formula, but any number divided by 6 that has a remainder of 0, 2, 3, or 4 is a composite number.

Prime Factoring

If a number is not prime, it can be renamed as a product of primes. Any number that ends in an even digit, such as 12 or 18, is divisible by 2. If the sum of the digits of any number is divisible by 3, such as 63 or 111, that number is divisible by three. The number 372 is divisible by 2 and by 3, so 372 is divisible by 6. If the sum of the digits of a number is divisible by 9, that number is divisible by 9. A composite number is divisible by 5 if it ends in zero or 5. So 30 and 85 are divisible by 5.

Prime factoring is the technique used to rename a composite number as a product of prime numbers. Two techniques are used to teach pupils to do this: (1) the tree diagram, and (2) successive division by prime factors.

The Tree Diagram

In drawing a tree diagram, as shown in Figure 12.2, start with the original number

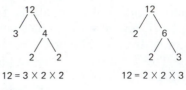

$12 = 3 \times 2 \times 2$ $12 = 2 \times 2 \times 3$

Figure 12.2

and find any two factors. Place each factor at the end of a branch. Whenever a prime number occurs, no further branching takes place. The prime factorization is the product of the primes at the end of each branch. Figure 12.3 illustrates how a tree diagram can be used to find the prime factorization of 84 and 90.

Successive Division by Prime Factors

A more common form of prime factorization follows. For pupils familiar with short division the three divisions on the left can be abbreviated as shown on the right.

$$\frac{42}{2)84} \qquad \frac{21}{2)42} \qquad \frac{7}{3)21} \qquad \begin{array}{r} 2)\overline{84} \\ 2)\overline{42} \\ 3)\overline{21} \\ 7 \end{array}$$

$$84 = 2 \times 2 \times 3 \times 7$$

The original number is divided by the smallest prime number that will divide it. The quotient of this division is then divided by a prime, preferably the smallest such divisor. This procedure is continued until the quotient is a prime. The prime factorization consists of the product of the prime quotient and all the other prime divisors.

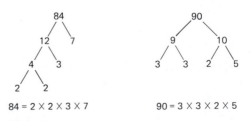

$84 = 2 \times 2 \times 3 \times 7$ $90 = 3 \times 3 \times 2 \times 5$

Figure 12.3

Exercise 12.1

1. By an informal examination, identify the greatest common factor of each of the following pairs of numbers:

   a. 2, 4   c. 10, 15   e. 12, 36

   b. 6, 9   d. 8, 12   f. 6, 21

2. Find the greatest common factor of each of the following pairs of numbers by listing the factors (divisors) of each:

   a. 8, 24   c. 12, 15   e. 12, 20

   b. 9, 12   d. 8, 18   f. 16, 22

3. Find the greatest common factor of each of the following pairs of numbers by the prime factor approach:

   a. 18, 24   c. 24, 36   e. 30, 50

   b. 21, 28   d. 28, 52   f. 35, 42

4. Assume that each pair of numbers in exercises 1 through 3 is a fraction, and rename each to lowest terms.

Finding Prime Factors with a Calculator

The calculator can be useful for finding the prime factors of a number, an often laborious job when done with paper and pencil. To find the prime factors of 504, proceed as follows:

Divide 504 by 2 to get a quotient of 252. Because 252 is even, divide by 2 again to get a quotient of 126. Divide by 2 a third time to get a quotient of 63. Now divide by 3, the next prime number, to get a quotient of 21. Divide by 3 again to get a quotient of 7, terminating the process because 7 is prime. Therefore, $504 = 2 \times 2 \times 2 \times 3 \times 3 \times 7$. Check by multiplying mentally or with the calculator.

The procedure requires knowledge of the sequence of primes: 2, 3, 5, 7, 11, 13, 17, and so on. Start with 2 and divide the number to be factored by 2 until the quotient is no longer even. Continue by dividing by 3 and so on until the final quotient is a prime number.

To prove that 101 is a prime number, it is only necessary to show that 101 is not divisible by 2, 3, 5, and 7, where 7 is the largest prime number less than the square root of 101. If 101 is divisible by 11, the quotient must be less than 11, but it cannot be 8 or 10 because 101 does not have a factor of 2. Also, 101 cannot be divisible by 9 because it does not have a factor of 3. For every factor less than the square root of a number there must be one greater than that square root.

Addition and Subtraction of Unlike Fractions

Mathematically, the statement of how to add and subtract fractions is deceptively simple:

(a) If the fractional numbers are represented by like denominators, use the basic patterns:

$$\frac{a}{c} + \frac{b}{c} = \frac{a + b}{c} \qquad \frac{a}{c} - \frac{b}{c} = \frac{a - b}{c}$$

(b) If the fractions have unlike denominators, rename with like denominators and use the basic pattern shown in (a).

Renaming fractions with unlike denominators to fractions with like denominators often is difficult for elementary school children. Addition or subtraction may involve renaming one or both fractions to higher terms.

Renaming Fractions to Higher Terms

READINESS

As pupils explore renaming fractions to lower terms, they also gain insight into renaming fractions to higher terms. Work with fraction parts, a fraction chart, and the number line should build appropriate readiness for dealing with renaming to higher terms at the symbolic level.

SYMBOLIC LEVEL

At the symbolic level, pupils need a great deal of practice in renaming fractions. The following activities help establish the pattern for renaming:

$$\frac{1}{2} = \frac{1 \times 2}{2 \times 2} = \frac{2}{4} \qquad \frac{1}{2} = \frac{1 \times 3}{2 \times 3} = \frac{3}{6}$$

$$\frac{2}{3} = \frac{2 \times 2}{3 \times 2} = \boxed{} \qquad \frac{2}{3} = \frac{2 \times 3}{3 \times 3} = \boxed{}$$

$$\frac{3}{4} = \frac{3 \times 2}{4 \times 2} = \boxed{} \qquad \frac{3}{4} = \frac{3 \times 3}{4 \times 3} = \boxed{}$$

Pupils can be helped to recognize the pattern in these sentences by means of open sentences like the following:

$$\frac{3}{8} = \frac{3 \times 2}{8 \times \Box} = \frac{6}{\triangle} \qquad \frac{3}{5} = \frac{3 \times 4}{5 \times \triangle} = \frac{12}{\Box}$$

$$\frac{3}{4} = \frac{3 \times \Box}{4 \times 5} = \frac{\triangledown}{20} \qquad \frac{5}{6} = \frac{5 \times \Box}{6 \times \Box} = \frac{10}{12}$$

Note that when a number is assigned to a frame, the same number must be assigned to that frame in a given sentence.

The following patterns can also be used to help pupils rename fractions:

$$\frac{1}{2}, \frac{2}{4}, \frac{3}{6}, \frac{4}{8}, \frac{5}{10}, \cdots$$

$$\frac{2}{3}, \frac{4}{6}, \frac{6}{9}, \frac{8}{12}, \frac{10}{15}, \cdots$$

$$\frac{3}{4}, \frac{6}{8}, \frac{9}{12}, \frac{12}{16}, \frac{15}{20}, \cdots$$

$$\frac{3}{5}, \frac{6}{10}, \frac{9}{15}, \frac{12}{20}, \frac{15}{25}, \cdots$$

The pattern is probably best stated by the open sentence in which the number that can be substituted for the frame is any non-zero number:

$$\frac{3}{5} = \frac{3 \times \Box}{5 \times \Box}$$

This is an application of the identity element for multiplication.

An excellent final exercise would involve the open sentence $\frac{2}{3} = \frac{2 \times \Box}{3 \times \Box}$. Have pupils rewrite it several times, placing a different numeral in the frames:

$$\frac{2}{3} = \frac{2 \times \boxed{3}}{3 \times \boxed{3}} = \frac{6}{9} \qquad \frac{2}{3} = \frac{2 \times \boxed{7}}{3 \times \boxed{7}} = \frac{14}{21}$$

$$\frac{2}{3} = \frac{2 \times \boxed{5}}{3 \times \boxed{5}} = \frac{10}{15} \qquad \frac{2}{3} = \frac{2 \times 10}{3 \times 10} = \frac{20}{30}$$

On the symbolic level, renaming ⅔ as ⁸/₁₂ is performed as follows:

$$\frac{2}{3} = \frac{8}{12} \quad \text{or} \quad \frac{2 \times \boxed{4}}{3 \times \boxed{4}} = \frac{8}{12}$$

The fraction ⅔ can be renamed as ⁸/₁₂ because both the numerator and the denominator are multiplied by the common factor, 4.

RENAMING FOR A SPECIFIC DENOMINATOR

Most renaming to higher terms is done so that addition and subtraction can be performed or so that two fractions can be compared. The thought pattern for finding the unknown number in the given proportion (equation) is as follows:

$$\frac{3}{4} = \frac{\square}{12}$$

(1) $4 \times \triangle = 12$
$\triangle = 12 \div 4$

$$\frac{3 \times \triangle}{4 \times \triangle} = \frac{\square}{12}$$

(2) Now multiply both terms of the fraction ¾ by 3:

$$\frac{3 \times 3}{4 \times 3} = \frac{9}{12}$$

(3) The new numerator = 9, and so

$$\frac{3}{4} = \frac{9}{12}$$

The pupil does not need to repeat the sentences as shown. The three sentences indicate the order in which the frames are to be filled.

Addition and Subtraction of Unlike but Related Fractions

Unlike but related fractions have unlike denominators, but one of the denominators is a common denominator, as in ½ + ⅜. By the time this topic is introduced at the symbolic level, the pupils should have had many experiences in finding equal fractions at the exploratory level. Manipulative and visual materials can be used to verify answers and assist pupils who need more experience at the exploratory level.

Since pupils have already learned that like fractions can be added and subtracted by adding or subtracting the numerators, the new element in adding or subtracting unlike fractions is to find a common denominator and rename each fraction with that denominator.

For unlike but related fractions, one denominator is a multiple of the other. The pupil identifies the larger denominator of

the example, such as 12 in ⅔ + ⁵⁄₁₂, as the common denominator. Then ⅔ can be changed to twelfths by following the pattern shown in the previous section.

Common Denominator Is the Product of the Denominators

Pupils should discover that the product of two denominators is a common denominator but is not always the lowest or least common denominator.

Problem: Nan spent ⅓ of an hour working on her math homework and ¼ of an hour studying her spelling. What part of an hour did it take Nan to do her homework?

Although this problem can be solved at the exploratory level with manipulative materials and visual aids, at this point the pupils should be encouraged to solve the problem at the symbolic level.

1. Can we add ⅓ and ¼ in that form? (No. We need common denominators.)

2. Write some equal fractions for ⅓ and for ¼.

(a) $\dfrac{1}{3} = \dfrac{2}{6} = \dfrac{3}{9} = \dfrac{4}{12} = \dfrac{5}{15} \cdots$

(b) $\dfrac{1}{4} = \dfrac{2}{8} = \dfrac{3}{12} = \dfrac{4}{16} = \dfrac{5}{20} \cdots$

3. Examine the patterns in (a) and (b). Are there any fractions with the same denominators? (Yes, ⁴⁄₁₂ and ³⁄₁₂.)

4. Now we can add the numerators: 4 twelfths + 3 twelfths = 7 twelfths, or ⁷⁄₁₂.

Common Denominator Less Than Product of Denominators

Addition and subtraction of unlike and unrelated fractions involve finding a common denominator that may be less than the product of the denominators. This means that the denominators share a common factor. However, in finding a common denom-inator, pupils should make the following discovery: Look for the larger denominator. If it is not a common denominator, multiply the two denominators. The product will al-ways be a common denominator, but not necessarily the lowest common denomina-tor. One advantage of adding and subtract-ing fractions with lowest common denomi-nators is that the numerators will involve smaller numbers.

We discuss two methods for finding the LCD of two denominators, the multiple method and the prime factor method.

1. To find the LCD with the multiple method, write multiples of each denomina-tor until the two sets have at least one mul-tiple in common. It is desirable in early work to have two or more multiples in com-mon to emphasize that there are many com-mon multiples but only one lowest common multiple. Help pupils discover that the LCD is the lowest common multiple of the two denominators. For ¾ and ⅙ proceed as fol-lows:

Multiples of 4:   4, 8, 12, 16, 20, 24 . . .
Multiples of 6:   6, 12, 18, 24, 36 . . .

Inspection shows that 12 is the LCD but that 24 is also a common denominator.

After pupils understand the process, it is not desirable to list both sets of multiples. The following procedure is more efficient.

Always start with the largest denomina-tor. Write the first multiple of the denomi-nator, and check to see if it is divisible by the other denominators. If not, continue the procedure until the multiple is divisible by all the other denominators.

To find the LCD of 6 and 4, write 6   12.

The LCD is 12 because it is the lowest multiple of 6 divisible by 4.

To find the LCD of 15, 6, and 4, write the multiples of the largest denominator: 15, 30, 45, 60. The LCD is 60 because it is divisible by 15, 6, and 4.

The LCD of 8 and 4 is found on the first trial and indicates that the fractions are un-like but related.

The multiple method can be used effi-ciently to find the LCD when the product of the denominators have no common factor. This situation exists for a limited range of numbers that pupils encounter in the ele-mentary school. This method also promotes mental arithmetic.

2. The prime factor method is included because of its historical importance and for its practical value on the elementary level, especially for large denominators.

Use prime factors to find the LCD of 15, 6, and 4.

We note that to be divisible by 15, the number must have prime factors of 3 and 5. Using an additional factor of 2 will make the number divisible by 6. To make this number divisible by 4, we need to include the prime factor 2 twice. Therefore the LCD $= 2 \times 2 \times 3 \times 5 = 60$.

The LCD of a set of numbers is the prod-uct of all the *different* prime factors con-tained in the set, using each factor the larg-est number of times it occurs in any one number in the set.

The following is an abbreviated form of the prime factor method.

2)15	20	36
2)15	10	18
3)15	5	9
5) 5	5	3
1	1	3

This process of finding the lowest com-mon denominator of 15, 20, and 36 consists of dividing out common prime factors. The prime divisor must divide at least two of the given numbers. If the number does not con-tain the prime divisor, it is brought down intact. The process continues until no two or more numbers (quotients) have a com-mon factor. The lowest common denomina-tor is the product of the divisors and the final quotients, or $2 \times 2 \times 3 \times 5 \times 1 \times 1 \times 3 = 180$.

The existence of calculators and computers reduces the importance of finding the LCD for larger numbers. Fractions with denominators larger than those encountered in the elementary school will usually be changed to decimals.

Exercise 12.2

1. Use the multiple method to find the LCD of the following sets of numbers:

   (a) 12, 30　　(b) 8, 14　　(c) 4, 6, 12

2. Use the prime factor method to find the LCD of the following:

   (a) 10, 12　　(b) 8, 12　　(c) 9, 15

3. Prime factor and then identify which of the following is divisible by 4, by 6, and by *both* 4 and 6:

   (a) 126　(b) 348　(c) 740　(d) 462　(e) 144　(f) 772　(g) 276

4. Identify which of the following is divisible by all three of the numbers 6, 8, and 9:

   (a) 11112　　(b) 1113　　(c) 2808　　(d) 2345　　(e) 40680

5. Identify each of the following as prime or composite: It is not necessary to divide by a prime larger than 13.

   (a) 231　　(b) 137　　(c) 167　　(d) 1001　　(e) 1573

6. Replace n in the following by the smallest digit that will make the number divisible by 9.

   (a) 1n7　　(b) nn6　　(c) 18n　　(d) nnn　　(e) 1n1n　　(f) 100n

Finding LCD With a Calculator

Any calculator with a repeat capability can be helpful in finding the LCD of a set of denominators. For the numbers an elementary pupil will encounter in school or home, the divisions in the following procedures can often be done mentally. Examination of two or three multiples of the largest denominator will often be sufficient. Encourage the pupil to examine the multiples mentally and check the results with the calculator.

To find the LCD of a set of denominators, enter the largest denominator into the calculator and use the repeat function as illustrated in this example:

To find the LCD of 12, 15, and 18, enter 18 into the calculator and press + and then press = repeatedly to find that the multiples of 18 are 36, 54, 72, 90, 108, 126, 144, 162, 180, and so on. It should be clear that 36, 54, 72, 108, 126, and 144 are not divisible by 15 because they do not have a factor of 5. Only numbers that end with a zero or 5 are divisible by 5. The number 90 is not divisible by 12 because it has only one factor of 2. Therefore 180 is the LCD of the set because it is the smallest multiple of 18 divisible by 12 and by 15. If there is any doubt about the division, use the calculator to check. When it is recognized that a multiple in question is not divisible by a number in the set, proceed to the next multiple.

Using prime factors, note that 2 and 3 occur no more than twice in 12, 15, and 18, and 5 occurs no more than once. Therefore the LCD is $2 \times 2 \times 3 \times 3 \times 5 = 180$.

Working with Fractions and Decimals

The major difficulty with changing common fractions to decimals comes when the decimal equivalent is nonterminating. Problems involving common fractions that are renamed as terminating decimals should be used first. If the denominator of a fraction is divisible by only 2, 5, or 10, the decimal equivalent will be terminating.

Jose gained ¾ of a pound in one month. The next month he gained ½ pound. How much did he gain in two months?

Common Fractions

$$\frac{3}{4} = \frac{3}{4}$$
$$+\frac{1}{2} = \frac{2}{4}$$
$$\frac{5}{4} \text{ or } 1\frac{1}{4}$$

Decimal Fractions

$$\begin{array}{r} 0.75 \\ +0.50 \\ \hline 1.25 \end{array}$$

Jose gained 1¼ or 1.25 pounds in two months.

When common fractions are not equivalent to termininating decimals, in most instances the number should be rounded to the nearest hundredths place. Therefore ⅔ should be represented as 0.67 and ⅚ as 0.83.

As soon as pupils learn to find the decimal equivalent of common fractions by division either with pencil and paper or by using a calculator, they no longer have trouble adding and subtracting these numbers.

Adding and Subtracting Fractions with a Calculator

Addition and subtraction of fractions can be checked by conversion to decimals with a calculator. However, this must not be done until the pupils have had sufficient work with the concrete, visual, and symbolic levels to ensure that they understand the process.

To add ½ and ⅓, the following procedure will work on many calculators: Enter 1, press ÷, enter 2, press =. The number 0.5 will appear on the display. Now enter +, enter 1, press ÷, enter 3, press =. The display will show the number 0.8333333, the same answer obtained by taking the sum ⅚ and dividing 5 by 6. If this procedure does not work, convert each fraction to a decimal and then add the two numbers.

If a single-number memory is available, a third procedure is to enter the first fraction as above and store it, enter the second fraction, press +, recall the first fraction from storage and press = to obtain the sum. This procedure can be extended for the addition of as many fractions as desired.

The calculator can be used to demonstrate that 2⁄6 and ⅓ are equivalent by showing that they both have the same nonterminating decimal, 0.333 . . .

One of the difficulties in working with calculators and computers is the fact that they may display rounding errors when working with decimals. For example, an answer that should be 9 may be displayed as 9.000001 or 8.9999999. This situation should not be discussed until pupils encounter it in their computation, when a discussion of rounding becomes natural.

Invent as many sequences of the following type as time allows:

1. Tran worked 2 hours yesterday and 3 hours today. What is the total number of hours she worked both days?

2. Olguin completed ½ of the job yesterday and ¼ of the job today. What is the total fraction of the job completed in both days?

3. Joe completed 0.4 of a job yesterday and 0.2 of the job today. What is the total fraction of the job completed in both days?

The number of variations that can be made to obtain a similar sequence is endless. It is often desirable to start with one of the problems in the pupils' textbook and use it as the basis for completing the sequence.

Addition and Subtraction of Mixed Numbers

Addition and subtraction of mixed numbers should be introduced at the symbolic level because the work involves adding or subtracting whole numbers and then fractions when renaming is not involved.

A mixed number is a rational number greater than one. It is the sum of a counting number and a fraction, such as $1 + \frac{1}{2}$, $2 + \frac{3}{4}$, $5 + \frac{1}{8}$. After pupils understand this form, they can use the short form: $1\frac{1}{2}$, $2\frac{3}{4}$, $5\frac{1}{8}$.

Although pupils may need some work with manipulatives in addition and subtraction with mixed numbers, they should not need as much as with addition and subtraction of fractions less than one. Emphasize how this new work is related to previous work with fractions, whole numbers, and decimals.

Problem: Juan spent 1½ hours working on his math homework and 2¼ hours reading. How much time did he spend altogether on schoolwork?

This problem should be solved by most pupils at the symbolic level with both common fractions and with decimals:

Common Fractions   Decimal Fractions

$$1\frac{1}{2} = 1\frac{2}{4}$$
$$+2\frac{1}{4} = 2\frac{1}{4}$$
$$\overline{3\frac{3}{4}}$$

$$\begin{array}{r} 1.50 \\ +\,2.25 \\ \hline 3.75 \end{array}$$

Juan spent 3¾ hours or 3.75 hours on homework.

Problem: Billie had to ride her bike 3¾ miles to a school picnic. After she had ridden 2¼ miles, how much farther did she have to ride?

Common Fractions   Decimal Fractions

$$3\frac{3}{4}$$
$$-2\frac{1}{4}$$
$$\overline{1\frac{2}{4} \text{ or } 1\frac{1}{2}}$$

$$\begin{array}{r} 3.75 \\ -\,2.25 \\ \hline 1.50 \end{array}$$

Billie has to ride 1½ miles farther, or 1.5 miles more.

Improper Fractions

The sum of ¾ and ⅞ is ¹³⁄₈, which is an *improper fraction.* An improper fraction has a numerator equal to or greater than the denominator. It is traditional in the elementary school program to rename an improper fraction to a mixed number or a whole number, although this is not the accepted procedure in many advanced programs in mathematics. With calculators it is often more efficient to compute with improper fractions than with mixed numbers.

When renaming an improper fraction to a mixed number, the following procedure is recommended:

(a) $\dfrac{5}{4} = \dfrac{4}{4} + \dfrac{1}{4} = 1 + \dfrac{1}{4} = 1\dfrac{1}{4}$

(b) $\dfrac{6}{5} = \dfrac{5}{5} + \dfrac{1}{5} = 1 + \dfrac{1}{5} = 1\dfrac{1}{5}$

(c) $\dfrac{8}{6} = \dfrac{6}{6} + \dfrac{2}{6} = 1 + \dfrac{2}{6} = 1\dfrac{1}{3}$

Subtraction of Mixed Numbers

The teacher should have the class discover the similarity of the procedures in subtracting whole numbers and mixed numbers. In each type renaming of numbers may be necessary. We shall rename a whole number and a mixed number by applying the associative property.

$$43 = 40 + 3$$
$$= (30 + 10) + 3 = 30 + (10 + 3)$$
$$= 30 + 13$$

$$6\frac{1}{3} = 6 + \frac{1}{3} = (5 + 1) + \frac{1}{3}$$

$$= (5 + \frac{3}{3}) + \frac{1}{3} = 5 + (\frac{3}{3} + \frac{1}{3}) = 5\frac{4}{3}$$

Practice exercises in renaming mixed numbers should be given before solving examples involving this operation.

Types of Mixed Numbers in Subtraction

These are four different types of examples in subtraction of mixed numbers. The types and the corresponding types in subtraction of whole numbers are as follows:

(a) $4\frac{1}{3}$ Subtracting a whole number from a mixed number 41
$\underline{-2}$ $\underline{-20}$

(b) $6\frac{3}{4}$ No regrouping needed to subtract 63
$\underline{-2\frac{1}{4}}$ $\underline{-21}$

(c) 4 Interchange of types of numbers in (a) 40
$\underline{-2\frac{1}{3}}$ $\underline{-21}$

(d) $6\frac{1}{3}$ Regrouping needed to subtract 51
$\underline{-2\frac{2}{3}}$ $\underline{-22}$

Most pupils experience little difficulty in subtracting in examples (a) and (b). Many pupils encounter difficulty in solving examples (c) and (d). In (c) a mixed number is to be subtracted from a whole number. In the example $5 - 2\frac{1}{3}$, some pupils obtain the incorrect answer $3\frac{1}{3}$. In this type of example, the whole number must be renamed before the subtraction can be completed, as shown:

$$5 = 4\frac{3}{3}$$
$$\underline{-2\frac{1}{3}} = \underline{-2\frac{1}{3}}$$
$$2\frac{2}{3}$$

Naturally the teacher must have the class learn to rename whole numbers as mixed numbers of the type $5 = 4\frac{3}{3}$.

Subtraction with Regrouping with Mixed Numbers

A positive difference will result only when the number being subtracted from a second number is smaller than the second number. Nevertheless, for mixed numbers, a positive difference can result and yet cause an impasse, if the fractions involved require renaming before the operation can be performed. For example, in $3\frac{1}{4} - 1\frac{3}{4}$ the difference will be positive because $3\frac{1}{4}$ is larger than $1\frac{3}{4}$. However, the fractional part $\frac{3}{4}$ cannot be subtracted from $\frac{1}{4}$ with a positive rational difference. So the $3\frac{1}{4}$ must be renamed for the subtraction of the fractions to be possible:

$$3\frac{1}{4} = 2\frac{5}{4}$$
$$\underline{-1\frac{3}{4}} = \underline{-1\frac{3}{4}}$$
$$\frac{2}{4}$$
$$1\frac{2}{4}$$
$$1\frac{1}{2}$$

1. Cannot subtract $\frac{1}{4} - \frac{3}{4}$ so rename

$$3\frac{1}{4} = 2 + \frac{4}{4} + \frac{1}{4} = 2\frac{5}{4}$$

2. Subtract numerators $5 - 3$ and write over the denominator 4.
3. Subtract $2 - 1$.
4. Rename answer.

RENAME WITH DECIMALS AND SUBTRACT

As pupils work with subtracting mixed numbers these numbers may be renamed as decimals before subtracting. The above example can be solved with decimals as follows:

$$3\frac{1}{4} = \overset{2}{\cancel{3}}.\overset{12}{\cancel{2}}5$$

$$-1\frac{3}{4} = \underline{-1.75}$$

$$1.50$$

Computer Activities

Program P12.1 will display all the prime factors of any number entered at the input prompt, a useful program for finding LCD with prime factors and studying many aspects of number.

```
PROGRAM P12.1
 10 HOME:VTAB 7
 20 PRINT "THE COMPUTER
    WILL DISPLAY THE PRIME
    FACTORS OF THE NUMBER
    THAT YOU ENTER"
 30 PRINT
 40 INPUT "ENTER NUMBER -> ";N
 50 PRINT
 60 PRINT "THE PRIME FAC-
    TORS OF ";N;" ARE:"
 70 PRINT
 80 FOR P = 2 TO N
 90 IF N/P <> INT(N/P) THEN
    130
100 N = N/P
110 PRINT P
120 GOTO 90
130 NEXT P
210 REM P12.1
```

Program P12.2 provides practice in renaming fractions with a new denominator, essential for the addition of fractions.

```
PROGRAM P12.2
 10 HOME:VTAB 8
 20 A = 2 + INT(8 * RND(1))
 30 B = 5 + INT(5 * RND(1))
 40 IF A = > B THEN 20
 50 C = 2 + INT(4* RND(1))
```

```
 60 PRINT "RENAME";A;"/";B;"
    WITH A DENOMINATOR OF ";
    C * B
 70 PRINT
 80 PRINT A;"/";B;" = ";
 90 INPUT "";Z$
100 PRINT
110 PRINT A;"/";B;" = ";A;
    "*";C ;"/";B;"*";C;
    " = ";A * C;"/" ;(B*C)
190 REM P12.2
```

Problem Solving

Pupils can often write equations before they can solve them. The computer can readily solve equations that would be difficult for college math majors. At this time we will restrict ourselves to equations with whole-number solutions. Solve the equation $13*N + 17 = 186$ by examining the output of the following FOR-NEXT loop.

```
10 FOR N = 1 TO 15
20 PRINT N,13* N + 17
30 NEXT
RUN
1         30
--------------------------
10        147
--------------------------
13        186
```

The output demonstrates that $13*N + 17 = 186$ when $N = 13$.

Replacing K with any number in the right-hand column provides an instructor with 15 different equations of the form $13*N + 17 = K$ that have whole-number solutions for N. The variety of equations that can be solved in this manner is almost endless.

A cell is one of the fundamental entities in biology. It reproduces by dividing itself into two cells. If a cell divides into two cells in an hour and each of these cells divides into two cells in the second hour and so on, how long will it take to obtain 1,000,000 cells?

The instruction T = 1 places 1 in memory with the name of T. The instruction T = 2 * T doubles the value of T on each cycle on the loop. The computer enters the cycle with T = 1 and doubles it to 2. The computer enters the second cycle with T = 2 and doubles it to 4 and so on.

```
10 T = 1
20 FOR J = 1 TO 25
30 T = 2*T
40 PRINT J,T
50 NEXT
RUN
1         2
2         4
3         8
4         16
5         32
--------------------------
19        524288
20        1048576
21        2097152
--------------------------
```

The output shows that at the end of 1 hour there are two cells and at the end of 20 hours there will be more than 1,000,000 cells, a startling result for anyone not familiar with exponential growth.

Read Carefully

(a) If a certain cell doubles so that it reaches 1,000,000 cells in 10 hours. When will it reach one-half million?

(b) A train leaves Chicago for New York at 3:27 Central Daylight Time and travels at an average speed of 47.5 miles per hour. Another train leaves New York for Chicago at 5:03 Eastern Standard Time and travels at 44.3 miles per hour. When the two trains meet, which is the farthest from New York? Note the extraneous information.

(c) How much dirt is in a hole 2.7 meters by 12.5 meters by 3.1 meters? (Use your calculator if you need it.)

Answers: (a) 9 Hours

(b) When the trains pass, they are the same distance from New York and the same distance from Chicago.

(c) You don't need it. There is no dirt in the hole.

Magic Squares

Complete the magic square on the right. Find the sum of the middle row. Each row, column, and diagonal must have a sum = 2.4

1.4	☐	1
.4	.8	1.2
☐	1.6	☐

Each of the following squares has the same product. Complete the squares.

A.

4	2	8
☐	4	☐
☐	☐	☐

B.

2	8	32
☐	8	☐
☐	☐	☐

Answer: Square A; 2nd row: 8 4 2, 3rd row, 2,8,4; Product 64
Square B: 2nd row: 128 8 ½, 3rd row: 2 8 32; product 512

Verify that each of the following is a magic square.

1⅓	⅙	¼	1 1/12
5/12	11/12	⅚	⅔
¾	7/12	½	1
⅓	1⅙	1¼	1/12
Sum = 2⅚			

3.2	.4	.6	2.6
1	2.2	2	1.6
1.8	1.4	1.2	2.4
.8	2.8	3	.2
Sum = 6.8			

Be a Math Wizard

The following procedure can be very impressive and make your friends think you are a calculating wizard.

As illustrated on page 261, a friend enters a number and you make your entry.

Your friend enters a second number followed by your entry.

Your friend makes a third entry and you

immediately state the sum of the five numbers. Start with three-digit numbers and expand to four- or five-digit numbers as you gain confidence.

Friend's entry	314
Your entry	685
Friend's entry	831
Your entry	168
Friend's last entry	478
Your instant response	2476

What must be done to the third entry to get an answer immediately?

Test your theory with other examples.

Clue: Add the first two pairs.

The answer will be given later.

Write an Equation

Laura spent the same amount at two different stores and $3 more than that amount at a third store. She had $17 left after these expenditures. If she started with five times the amount spent at the first store, how much was spent at each store?

Fill in the blanks with expressions in N in the following sentence:

She started with A, spent B, spent C, and had E left.

Express A,B,C, and D in terms of N. Hint: Start with B = N.

What is E?

Read the problem again to get a clear picture of the relations between the different amounts.

Answer: $A = 5 \times N, B = N, C = N, D = N + 3, E = 17$.

Rewrite the problem: She started with ____ and spent ____ and ____.

Write the equation.

Answers: She started with $5 \times N$ and spent N and spent N and spent N + 3 and had $17 dollars left.

$5 \times N - N - N - (N + 3) = 17$.

Write a FOR-NEXT loop that will solve this problem.

Guess and test to find an upper and lower

bound. A lower bound is a number that is clearly too small, an upper bound a number that is clearly too large.

$N = 5 \to 25 - 5 - 5 - 8 = 7$. N is too small, a lower bound.

$N = 20 \to 100 - 20 - 20 - 23 = 37$. N is too large, an upper bound.

It is frequently useful to find an upper and lower bound as check for the solution, a guess-and-test procedure. Looking for an upper or lower bound will occasionally lead to a solution, eliminating the need for a computer.

```
10 FOR N= 5 TO 20
15 REM GUESS AND TEST PLACED
   THE ANSWER BETWEEN THESE
   LIMITS
20 PRINT N,5*N-N-N-(N+3)
30 NEXT
RUN
5          7
- - - - - - - - - - - - - - - - - - - - - - - - -

10         17
- - - - - - - - - - - - - - - - - - - - - - - - -
20         37
```

The answer is: N = 10: 5 x 10 - 10 - 10 - (10+3) = 17

An individual with some skill in algebra would replace N + N + (N + 3) with $3 \times N + 3$, usually written as $3N + 3$. Note that the computer requires $3*N+3$ and will not process $3N + 3$ nor $3 \times N + 3$.

The equation would then become: $5 \times N - (3 \times N + 3) = 17$. In line 20 replace $5 * N - N - (N + 3)$ with $5 *N - (3* N + 3)$ and run the program to see that the result is unchanged. Try to simplify the expression further and test your result in line 20.

Solve the following equations using the addition–subtraction relation:

a) $N - 7 = 15 \to N = 15 + 7 = 22$
b) $T + 13 = 20 \to T =$
c) $N - 9 = 3 \to N =$
d) $B + 113 = 115 \to B =$

Solve using the multiplication–division relation:

a) $7 \times R = 84 \rightarrow R = 84 \div 7 = 12$
b) $10 \times A = 47 \rightarrow A =$
c) $6 \times N = 28 \rightarrow N =$
d) $N \div 11 = 5 \rightarrow N =$

To solve $3 \times N + 5 = 23$, we must use both procedures illustrated in the previous two sets.

$3 \times N + 5 = 23 \rightarrow 3 \times N = 23 - 5 = 18$
$3 \times N = 18 \rightarrow N = 18 \div 6 = 3$
Check: $3 \times 6 + 5 = 23$

Solve the following. Be sure to check as just illustrated.

a) $5 \times N - 12 = 28$
b) $8 \times N + 2 = 6$
c) $N/3 + 2 = 7$
d) $3 \times N + \frac{1}{3} = \frac{1}{2}$

Solution for Math Wizard: The two numbers you add must make each pair, your friend's entry and yours, add to 999 or 1000 − 1. This means that 1000 − 1 has been added twice to the third entry of your friend. To add 2000 − 2 to any three-digit number, prefix a 2 and subtract 2 from the ones digit.

$437 + (2000 - 2) = 2435.$

Summary

Future mathematics programs at the elementary school level will require close association between addition and subtraction of fractions and decimals. With the increased use of calculators, computers, and metric measures, more emphasis will be placed on the operations with decimals.

Decimal fractions are an extension of the whole-number system. Fractions that can be renamed as terminating decimals should be used in early addition and subtraction problems. Pupils should be taught to perform addition or subtraction on fractions, then solve the same example with decimals. For fractions renamed as nonterminating decimals, pupils should be taught to round off to the nearest hundredths place before addition or subtraction.

The level of pupil achievement in addition and subtraction of fractions and decimals has been relatively low in the past. The major reason was that basic concepts and procedures of working with these numbers were not taught with adequate meaning and understanding.

Early exploratory activities designed to help pupils discover the meanings and language associated with addition and subtraction of fractions and decimals should involve some work with manipulatives and visuals. However, most of the instruction on this topic should take place at the symbolic level.

Emphasis must be placed on problem solving involving fractions and decimals. As a part of the problem-solving process pupils should learn to estimate an answer prior to performing computation. Extensive use should be made of calculators and computer programs during the study of fractions and decimals.

1. Describe how to solve each of the following problems with common fractions and with decimals: (a) with a manipulative or a visual and (b) with symbolic notations.
   (1) Joe had $10. He spent $2 in one store and $3 in another store. What part of his original amount did he spend?

(2) Olguin had 15 kilometers to walk. He walked 2 kilometers and then rested. He then walked 6 kilometers and rested again. What part of the journey had he finished by the time of the second rest?
(3) Sally estimated that she needed 12 hours to finish sewing her fall outfit. She sewed for 2 hours on Friday night and for another 3 hours on Saturday. What part of her total job did she complete?
(4) Xu-Xu started the day with a quarter in her purse. Her father gave her some money, which she put in her purse without looking. Later she discovered that she had 3 quarters in her purse. How much had her father given her?

2. At the symbolic level, rename $2/3$ and $3/5$ and add:
   (a) with a least common divisor
   (b) with decimals rounded to the hundredths place.
3. Use the prime-factor method to determine the greatest common factor and reduce each of the following fractions to lowest terms:
   (a) $10/24$ (b) $12/30$ (c) $18/40$
4. Rename the following fractions as indicated:
   (a) 5/8 = ____/40 = ____/100 = 0. ____
   (b) 7/12 = ____/60 = ____/100 = 0. ____
   (c) 4/15 = ____/45 = ____/100 = 0. ____
5. Add the following common fractions, then convert each addend to a decimal to the nearest hundredths place and add:
   (a) $3/8 + 2/8 =$ (b) $2/3 + 5/6 =$ (c) $5/6 + 3/8 =$
6. Subtract the following common fractions, then convert each number to a decimal to the nearest hundredths place and subtract:
   (a) $3/4 - 3/8 =$ (b) $5/6 - 2/3 =$ (c) $3\,3/4 - 1\,3/8 =$
7. Find the least common denominator of 12 and 15 by the following methods:
   (a) Listing the multiples of 12 and 15.
   (b) Renaming 12 and 15 with prime factors.
   (c) Dividing out the greatest common prime factors.
8. Use each of the above three methods to find the least common denominator of the following:
   (a) 12 and 18 (b) 20 and 35 (c) 10, 15, and 18

Selected Readings

Ashlock, Robert B., et. al. *Guiding Each Child's Learning of Mathematics*. Columbus, OH: Charles E. Merrill, 1983. Chapter 14.

Heddens, James W., and William R. Speer. *Today's Mathematics*, 6th ed. Chicago: Science Research Associates, 1988. Units 10 and 11.

Kennedy, Leonard M., and Steve Tipps. *Guiding Children's Learning of Mathematics*, 5th ed. Belmont, CA: Wadsworth, 1988. Chapters 11 and 12.

Marks, John L., et. al. *Teaching Elementary School Mathematics for Understanding*, 5th ed. New York: McGraw-Hill, 1985. Chapters 8 and 9.

Post, Thomas R. *Teaching Mathematics in Grades K–8*. Needham Heights, MA: Allyn & Bacon, 1988. Chapter 7.

Reys, Robert E., et. al. *Helping Children Learn Mathematics*, 2nd ed. Englewood Cliffs, NJ: Prentice-Hall, 1989. Chapter 11.

Riedesel, C. Alan. *Teaching Elementary School Mathematics*, 4th ed. Englewood Cliffs, NJ: Prentice-Hall, 1985. Chapters 10 and 11.

Suydam, Marilyn N., and Robert E. Reys (eds.). *Developing Computational Skills*, 1978 Yearbook. Reston, VA: National Council of Teachers of Mathematics, 1978. Chapter 8.

Multiplication and Division of Fractions and Decimals: Percents

ACHIEVEMENT GOALS

After studying this chapter, you should be able to:

1. State word problems involving multiplication and division of fractions, decimals, and percents.

2. Explain how to teach multiplication and division of fractions and decimals, including: (a) stating objectives, (b) assessing readiness, (c) providing appropriate motivation, (d) facilitating growth from the concrete level of learning through the visual level to the symbolic level and finally to mastery.

3. Design a teaching strategy for making percents meaningful to pupils.

4. Provide calculator and computer activities for pupils designed to bring about a better understanding of multiplication and division of fractions, decimals, and percents.

VOCABULARY

These terms are defined or illustrated in the Glossary.

Base (percent)
Complex fractions
Improper fraction
Mixed number
Multiplicative
  identity

Multiplicative
  inverse
Percentage
Rate (percent)
Reciprocal
Unit fraction

Pupils at the elementary school level have always had difficulty with multiplication and division of fractions and decimals. In the Fourth National Assessment of Educational Progress in Mathematics,[1] many of the seventh-grade students who were tested could not work simple multiplication and division examples involving fractions, decimals, and percents as shown by the following:

Example	Correct
(a) 7.2×2.5	62%
(b) $8.4 \div .02$	46%
(c) 4 % of 75	32%
(d) 9 is what percent of 225?	20%

The major reason for the lack of success in dealing with operations on fractions and decimals is the pupils' overall lack of understanding of the underlying concepts of these numbers. Kouba states that "many students appear to be learning mathematical skills at a rote manipulation level without understanding the concepts related to the computation."[2] Special efforts must be made to teach these topics meaningfully.

Multiplication and Division of Fractions and Decimals

I. *Objectives*

Upon completion of a series of lessons over a period of time each pupil should achieve the following objectives:

1. Recognize, create, and solve problem situations in which fractions and decimals are to be multiplied or divided.

2. Use appropriate manipulative, visual, and symbolic approaches in solving problems involving fractions and decimals.

3. Demonstrate the ability to estimate reasonable results when given problems involving multiplication and division of fractions and decimals.

4. Multiply and divide fractions and decimals with a reasonable degree of accuracy and speed.

5. Rename fractions to decimals and decimals to fractions and perform multiplication and division with both forms and compare the results.

II. *Readiness*

Readiness for multiplication and division of fractions and decimals requires a good understanding of the concepts underlying these numbers. Pupils need to have mastered the basic multiplication and division facts with whole numbers in order to succeed with multiplication and division of fractions and decimals. (Percents are not usually multiplied or divided.)

III. *Motivation*

Pupils generally find it difficult to solve problems involving multiplication and division of fractions and decimals. For improved motivation, the concepts and procedures involved in mathematics should be developed with simple problems that are easily understood by pupils. It is often helpful for pupils to replace the fractions by whole numbers in order to obtain a better understanding of the procedures involved for solving a problem. More difficult problems can be solved with the aid of a calculator and computer.

1. Kouba, Vicky L, et. al., "Results of the Fourth NAEP Assessment of Mathematics: Number, Operations, and Word Problems," *Arithmetic Teacher, 35* (April 1988): 16–17.

2. Ibid P. 19.

IV. *Guided Discovery*

MULTIPLICATION OF FRACTIONS

Three kinds of examples are used to introduce pupils to multiplication of fractions:

1. a whole number times a fraction, $3 \times \frac{1}{2}$;

2. a fraction times a whole number, $\frac{3}{4} \times 4$;

3. a fraction times a fraction, $\frac{2}{3} \times \frac{4}{5}$.

These examples seem easy enough to be solved "by the rule"—find the product of the numerators and write it over the product of the denominators. But learning by the rule has not worked in the past. First, these examples need to be stated in a problem setting. Second, the reason for the rule needs to be understood by solving word problems with manipulatives and visuals. Then pupils are ready for the symbolic notations and the "rules."

A WHOLE NUMBER TIMES A FRACTION

(a) *Word Problem* Word problems for a whole number times a fraction can be related to equal additions.

- Tuan picks 3 bags of grapes. If each bag weighs ½ pound, what is the total weight of 3 bags?
- Maria works ½ hour on each of her homework assignments. If she has three assignments, how long will it take her?

(b) *Solve with Manipulatives or Visuals* Pupils can solve each problem by using half-circles on the flannelboard, where each half-circle represents half a pound of grapes or ½ hour, as shown in Figure 13.1.

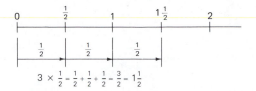

$$3 \times \frac{1}{2} = \frac{1}{2} + \frac{1}{2} + \frac{1}{2} = 1\frac{1}{2}$$

Figure 13.1

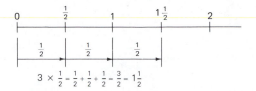

$$3 \times \frac{1}{2} = \frac{1}{2} + \frac{1}{2} + \frac{1}{2} = \frac{3}{2} = 1\frac{1}{2}$$

Figure 13.2

A good visual model is the number line. Each of the problems can be solved on a number line, as shown in Figure 13.2.

(c) *Solve at the Symbolic Level* In both problems $3 \times \frac{1}{2}$ can be renamed as $\frac{1}{2} + \frac{1}{2} + \frac{1}{2} = 1 + \frac{1}{2} = 1\frac{1}{2}$. Three times ½ equals 3 halves, or 1½. The following additional examples illustrate this approach:

$$3 \times \frac{1}{4} = \frac{1}{4} + \frac{1}{4} + \frac{1}{4} = \frac{\square}{4}$$

$$5 \times \frac{1}{2} = \frac{1}{2} + \frac{1}{2} + \frac{1}{2} + \frac{1}{2} + \frac{1}{2} = \frac{5}{\square} = \triangle$$

$$4 \times \frac{1}{3} = \frac{1}{3} + \square + \square + \square = \frac{4}{3} = \triangle$$

FRACTION TIMES A WHOLE NUMBER

The second kind of example should be a fraction times a whole number.

(a) *Word Problems* For the example ½ × 3, the following word problems could be stated:

- A ribbon is 3 feet long. What is the length of one-half of this ribbon?
- Zula has 3 hours to do her two homework assignments. If she wants to spend ½ of her time on each assignment, how many hours will she spend on each?

(b) *Solve with Manipulatives or Visuals* A unit fraction times a whole number such as ½ × 3 involves partitive division. One-half of three means 3 ÷ 2. A number line or a rectangular region can be used to solve this problem, as shown in Figure 13.3.

(c) *Solve at the Symbolic Level* The examples ½ × 3 and 3 × ½ have the same

$$\frac{1}{2} \times 3 = 1\frac{1}{2}$$

Figure 13.3

answer because of the commutative property. The following expansions illustrate this approach:

$$\frac{2}{3} \times 3 = 3 \times \frac{2}{3} = \frac{2}{3} + \Box + \Box = \frac{6}{3} = \Box$$

$$3 \times \frac{3}{4} = \frac{3}{4} + \frac{3}{4} + \frac{3}{4} = \frac{\Box}{4} = \Box$$

$$\frac{3}{4} = \Box \times \frac{1}{4}$$

$$5 \times \frac{3}{4} = 5 \times (3 \times \frac{1}{4}) = \Box$$

MULTIPLICATION OF TWO FRACTIONS

(a) *Word Problems* The third kind of example involves multiplying a fraction by a fraction. For the example ⅔ × ⅘, the following word problems could be stated:

- Mr. Yota owned a lot that was ⅘ of an acre in size. He used ⅔ of the lot for a garden. The garden measured what part of an acre?
- Jason was supposed to run a race that was ⅘ of a mile long. Unfortunately, he finished only ⅔ of that distance. What part of a mile did he run?

(b) *Solve with Visuals* The first problem can be solved by showing ⅘ of an acre with a drawing of a rectangle ABCD divided into five congruent parts, as shown in Figure 13.4. Shade four of the parts to show ⅘ of an acre. The rectangle AFJD represents ⅘ of an acre.

Next, divide the rectangle ABCD horizontally into three congruent parts. Cross-hatch the squares in rectangle AFGH, which represents ⅔ of ⅘ of an acre.

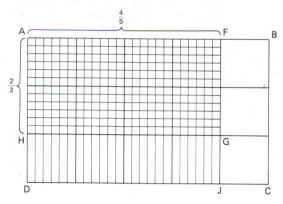

Figure 13.4

Examine Figure 13.4 and answer the following questions:

1. How many squares represent an acre? (15)

2. How many squares represent ⅘ of an acre? (12)

3. How many squares represent ⅔ of ⅘ of an acre? (8) The product of ⅔ × ⅘ = $\frac{\Box}{15}$.

The garden is $\frac{\Box}{15}$ of an acre. Is it more or less than ½ of an acre?

The second problem can be solved on a number line, as shown in Figure 13.5. Draw a unit number line. Divide it into fifths, then into thirds. Next, find ⅔ of ⅘ of the segment.

(c) SYMBOLIC LEVEL

Activities such as those we have described should enable pupils to operate at the symbolic level and understand the work. Pupils at the symbolic level should be taught to find the product of ⅔ and ¾ by proceeding as follows:

$$\frac{2}{3} \times \frac{3}{4} = \frac{2 \times 3}{3 \times 4} = \frac{6}{12} = \frac{1}{2}$$

The algorithm for multiplication of two fractional numbers is the following:

Figure 13.5

$$\frac{a}{b} \times \frac{c}{d} = \frac{a \times c}{b \times d}$$

This algorithm should also be stated verbally as: The *product of two fractions is the product of the numerators divided by the product of the denominators.*

The four examples below are appropriate for students beginning work at the symbolic level:

1. $\dfrac{3}{5} \times \dfrac{4}{7} = \dfrac{\square \times 4}{5 \times 7} = \dfrac{\triangle}{35}$

2. $3 \times \dfrac{4}{5} = \dfrac{3 \times \square}{5} = \dfrac{\triangle}{5}$

3. $\dfrac{2}{3} \times \dfrac{5}{9} = \dfrac{10}{\square}$

4. $\dfrac{2}{7} \times \dfrac{4}{5} = \square$

MASTERY LEVEL

Teachers sometimes assume that pupils have achieved mastery of problems such as ⅔ × ⅘ when they can give the answer ⁸⁄₁₅ as a habitual response. However, additional knowledge is required to achieve mastery of problems like ⅔ × ¾, which are usually performed as follows:

$$\overset{1}{\underset{1}{\frac{\cancel{2}}{\cancel{3}}}} \times \overset{1}{\underset{2}{\frac{\cancel{3}}{\cancel{4}}}} = \frac{1}{2}$$

The pupil must understand that dividing the numerator of the first fraction by 2 and the denominator of the second fraction by 2 divides both the numerator and denominator of the product by 2. Likewise, dividing

the denominator of the first fraction by 3 and the numerator of the second fraction by 3 divides the numerator and the denominator of the product by 3.

In the case of ⅔ × ¾, each numerator is a factor of the numerator of the product by the multiplication algorithm. Similarly, the denominators are factors of the denominator of the product. Therefore, dividing one numerator by 2 divides the numerator of the product by 2. Dividing one denominator by 2 divides the denominator of the product by 2.

Many pupils will find the product as follows:

$$\frac{2}{3} \times \frac{3}{4} = \frac{2 \times 3}{3 \times 4} = \frac{6}{12} = \frac{1}{2}$$

This procedure is correct and acceptable, but is not a mastery-level solution because it is very time-consuming with large numbers. For example:

$$\overset{2}{\underset{9}{\frac{\cancel{26}}{\cancel{27}}}} \times \overset{5}{\underset{7}{\frac{\cancel{15}}{\cancel{91}}}} = \frac{2 \times 5}{9 \times 7} = \frac{10}{63}$$

Multiplying 26 × 15 and 27 × 91 and dividing out a common factor of 39 would be a much more time-consuming process. (This computation is more efficient with decimals on a calculator.)

Multiplication of Decimals

Multiplying a Whole Number and a Decimal

If the distance to Mary's school is 0.3 miles, how far is a round trip?

CONCRETE AND VISUAL LEVELS

The product of 2 and .3 may be found on the concrete and visual levels as follows:

1. Use 2 sets of 3 strips (from student kits) to obtain a set of 6 strips and show that $2 \times .3 = .6$.

2. Use the number line as illustrated:

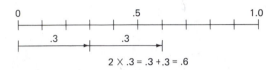

$$2 \times .3 = .3 + .3 = .6$$

SYMBOLIC LEVEL

After the students have done sufficient work with visual materials they can be taught to find products such as $2 \times .3$ in the following ways:

1. Renaming common fractions, such as $2 \times \frac{3}{10} = \frac{6}{10} = 0.6$

2. Using repeated addition, such that $2 \times 0.3 = 0.3 + 0.3 = 0.6$

3. Help pupils recognize that both 2×3 and 2×0.3 give a product with the single numeral 6 but that the position of the decimal point differs in each. Note that 0.3 is between 0 and 1 so that the product 2×0.3 must be between 0×2 and 1×2 or between 0 and 2. Since 0.6 is between 0 and 2, the answer is sensible.

Products Involving Renaming

The methods outlined above also apply to products involving renaming, such as 2×1.6.

1. $2 \times 1.6 = 1.6 + 1.6 = 3.2$

2. $2 \times 1.6 = 2 \times \frac{16}{10} = \frac{32}{10} = 3.2$

3. Apply the distributive property:
$2 \times 1.6 = 2 \times (1 + .6) = 2 + 1.2 = 3.2$

Note that 1.6 is between 1 and 2, so 2×1.6 is between 2×1 and 2×2, or between 2 and 4. The answer 2.8 is sensible because it is between 2 and 4.

The following equations (open sentences) contain a whole-number factor and a one-place decimal factor:

$2 \times 0.3 = \square$
$\square \times 0.4 = 0.8$
$0.3 + 0.3 = 2 \times \square$
$0.4 + 0.4 = \square \times .4$
$2 \times \square = 1.0$
$0.5 \times \square = 1.5$
$\square \times 0.7 = 7$
$\square \times 1.3 = 1.3$

Pupils should solve equations like those shown above until they understand the pattern. They should discover this generalization: *The product of a whole number and a one-place decimal is a one-place decimal.*

Multiplying Ones and Hundredths

Initial work with multiplication of a whole number and a decimal begins with tenths and is extended to hundredths. Use as many of the procedures described for multiplying ones and tenths as the class needs to discover how to find the product of ones and hundredths.

Pupils should discover that the product of ones and hundredths is hundredths. Similarly, the product of ones and thousandths is thousandths. Thousandths requires three decimal places.

The class can approximate to find the position of the decimal point in the product or apply the rule that the product of ones and tenths is tenths, ones and hundredths is hundredths, and so on.

MASTERY LEVEL

Pupils achieve mastery level in multiplying a whole number and a decimal when they no longer rely on place value to determine the position of the decimal point in the product. Pupils discover that the product contains as many decimal places as the decimal factor. Thus, the product $7 \times .345$ will contain three decimal places because the decimal factor .345 contains three decimal places. It is important that the *class* discover this rule for finding the position of the point in the product. The teacher should not give the rule and then have the class demonstrate its application in a mechanical way. When pupils use this shortcut to locate the point in the product, they should check the answer either by approximation to see if it is sensible or by use of place value. Advanced pupils should be encouraged to use both methods.

The Product of Two Decimals

A typical real-life problem might be encountered at the meat counter of a supermarket, where a computerized scale states the price of 1.35 pounds of meat at $1.89 per pound. The solution may be written:

1 pound $\rightarrow$ $1.89
1.35 pounds $\rightarrow$ $1.35 \times 1.89 = 2.5515$
      The cost of 1.35 pounds is $2.55.

The $2.55 is obtained by standard rounding procedures, although some stores round up and charge $2.56. (Note that 2.56 is between 1×1 and 2×2.)

SYMBOLIC LEVEL

Multiplication of two decimals begins at the symbolic level because the activities outlined for the product of whole numbers do not apply. It is difficult to demonstrate how to take .2 of a group of .3 except perhaps by using the number line. We feel that if pupils have an understanding of the product of a whole number and a decimal, it is more efficient to introduce multiplication of two decimals at the symbolic level.

Pupils should use previous experience with whole numbers and common fractions to find the product of two decimals. For ex-

ample, to find the product of .2 and .3, the students would rename each decimal as a common fraction and multiply:

(a) $0.2 \times 0.3 = \dfrac{2}{10} \times \dfrac{3}{10} = \dfrac{6}{\square} = .06$

(b) $0.2 \times 0.3 = 2$ tenths $\times 3$ tenths $=$
$(2 \times 3) \times ($tenths $\times$ tenths$) = 6 \times (\dfrac{1}{10} \times$
$\dfrac{1}{10)} = 6 \times \dfrac{1}{\square} = \dfrac{6}{\square} = .06$

Example (b) can help pupils discover that tenths $\times$ tenths $=$ hundredths, a statement that is analogous to tens $\times$ tens $=$ hundreds.

(c) $0.3 \times 0.4 = \dfrac{3}{\square} \times \dfrac{4}{\square} = \dfrac{12}{\triangle} = .12$

(d) $0.3 \times 0.4 = 3$ tenths $\times 4$ tenths $=$
$(3 \times 4) \times ($tenths $\times$ tenths$) = 12$ hundredths $= .12$

(e) $1.2 \times .23 = \dfrac{12}{10} \times \dfrac{\square}{100} = \dfrac{276}{\triangle} = .276$

(f) $1.2 \times .23 = 12$ tenths $\times 23$ hundredths $= (12 \times 23) \times ($tenths $\times$ hundredths$) = 276$ thousands $= \square$.

This example leads students to draw the conclusion that tenths $\times$ hundredths $=$ thousandths, a useful generalization. Point out that $1.2 \times .23$ must be more than 1×0.2 or 0.2. The answer .276 is sensible.

By working examples like this, pupils discover that the number of decimal places in the product is equal to the sum of the number of places in the two factors. After the pupils make this discovery, they no longer rely on place value for locating the decimal point in the product.

The Multiplication Algorithm

Have the students multiply two decimals containing two or more digits. Use the multiplication algorithm as shown in (a) and (b) on page 272 and determine the decimal point by estimation.

(a)   4.5   (b)   35
      × 1.5   × .23
       225   105
        45   70
      6.75   8.05

To multiply two decimals, the students should proceed as follows:

1. Multiply as with whole numbers.

2. Find the sum of the number of decimal places in the two factors.

3. Counting from the right, mark off as many places in the product as are found in step 2.

4. Estimate to determine if the answer is sensible that is, between 1×4 and 2×5.

The pupils now operate at the mastery level, because they are applying a rule that does not require the use of place value. The pupils now understand the mathematical basis of the shortcuts; hence use of the rule does not constitute rote learning.

Often pupils do not understand why the product of two decimals, such as $0.2 \times 0.4 = .08$, is less than either factor. The solution with fractional numbers will show clearly that the product is smaller than either factor.

$$\frac{2}{10} \times \frac{4}{10} = \frac{8}{100} \text{ or } .08.$$

Another approach is to use the part of a whole concept of a fraction such as ⅔ of 8. Pupils should recognize that the product of a proper fraction and any number must be less than that number, even when that number is a fraction.

Division by a Fraction

Dividing a Whole Number by a Unit Fraction

Start with a problem: Susan wants to make a pair of signs of equal size out of a piece of cardboard. Refer to (A). How many signs does she make? How many halves are in a whole?

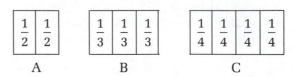

A   B   C

Refer to (B): How many thirds in 1?
Refer to (C) How many fourths in 1?
Use the multiplication–division relation to complete the following:
  If $2 \times ½ = 1$ then $1 \div ½ = \square$
  If $3 \times ⅓ = 1$ then $1 \div ⅓ = \square$
  If $1 \div ¼ = 4$ then $4 \div ¼ = \square$
The above activities indicate that there are 2 halves in 1, 3 thirds in 1, and four fourths in 1. Use this pattern to complete the following:
  (a) The number of fifths in 1 is $\square$
  (b) The number of fifths in 3 = $\square$
  (c) The number of tenths in 1 = $\square$
  (d) The number of tenths in 4 = $\square$
  (e) $1 \div ⅙ = \square$ (f) $1 \div 1/20 = \square$
  (g) $2 \div ½ = \square$

Dividing a Number by a Fraction

VISUAL LEVEL

(a) Start with a problem: How many pieces of ribbon ¾ of a yard long can be cut from a piece that is 3 yards in length? Have the class analyze the problem to recognize that the solution requires the division: $3 \div ¾$. It may help to restate the problem with whole numbers to help the class recognize that the problem solution requires finding how many ¾s are in 3, a measurement division. The class should also recognize that this is their first encounter with division by a fraction.

Draw a line 3 feet long on the chalkboard and mark a point on the line that is ¾ of a foot from the left end. Let pupils use string to discover that there are four ¾s in 3.

Pupils discover the number of ¾s in 3 by measuring.   *(Photo by Leland Perry)*

Have pupils use a ruler to count how many ¾s of an inch in 3 inches.

Each pupil should draw a number line, as illustrated in Fig. 13.6.

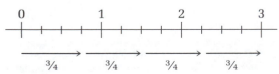

Figure 13.6

SYMBOLIC LEVEL

Review the following four ways of representing division to illustrate that multiplying the dividend and divisor or the numerator and denominator by the same number does not change the quotient.

$$\frac{6}{2} = 3 \qquad\qquad 6 \div 2 = 3$$

$$6/2 = 3 \qquad\qquad 2\overline{)6}$$

$$\frac{6 \times 2}{2 \times 2} = 3 \qquad (6 \times 2) \div (2 \times 2) = 3$$

$$(6 \times 2)/(2 \times 2) = 3 \qquad 2 \times 2\overline{)6 \times 2}^{\,3}$$

Use exercises similar to the following to establish a nonverbal procedure for multiplying two fractions to obtain a product of 1.

$$\frac{2}{3} \times \frac{3}{2} = \square \qquad \frac{3}{4} \times \square = 1$$

$$\square \times \frac{3}{5} = 1 \qquad 4 \times \square = 1$$

Use guided discovery to help the class to recognize that:

Division by 1 is the easiest division: N ÷ 1 = N for all N.

Multiplying the divisor in 3 ÷ ¾ by ⁴⁄₃ will give a divisor of 1.

Ask what must be done to compensate for multiplying the divisor of 3 ÷ ¾ by ⁴⁄₃. Use the following sequence:

$$3 \div \frac{3}{4} = \frac{3}{4}\overline{)3}$$

$$= \frac{3}{4} \times \frac{4}{3}\overline{)3 \times \frac{4}{3}}$$

$$= 1\overline{)4}$$

$$3 \div \frac{3}{4} = 3 \times \frac{4}{3} = 4$$

Check the division by multiplying the quotient by the divisor: 4 × ¾ = 3.

Check to see if the answer is sensible. The quotient (4) must be greater than the dividend (3) because the divisor (¾) is less than the dividend.

Use example (a) as a pattern to complete the remaining examples:

(a) $3 \div \dfrac{3}{4} = \left(3 \times \dfrac{4}{3}\right) \div \left(\dfrac{3}{4} \times \dfrac{4}{3}\right)$

$$= 4 \div 1 = 4$$

(b) $6 \div \dfrac{2}{3}$ (c) $\dfrac{1}{2} \div 3$ (d) $5 \div \dfrac{3}{5}$

Use class discussion to help the class recognize that multiplying the dividend and divisor to obtain a divisor of 1 accomplishes the following:

(a) It changes division by a fraction into division by 1.

(b) It changes division by a fraction into multiplication.[3]

Use illustrative patterns in examples (a) and (b) to complete the examples (c) through (f).

(a) $2 \div \dfrac{2}{3} = \left(2 \times \dfrac{3}{2}\right) \div \left(\dfrac{2}{3} \times \dfrac{3}{2}\right)$

$$= 3 \div 1 = 3$$

(b) $\dfrac{1}{3} \div \dfrac{3}{5} = \left(\dfrac{1}{3} \times \dfrac{5}{3}\right) \div \left(\dfrac{3}{5} \times \dfrac{5}{3}\right)$

$$= \dfrac{5}{9} \div 1 = \dfrac{5}{9}$$

(c) $3 \div \dfrac{1}{2}$ (d) $\dfrac{1}{4} \div 5$

(e) $\dfrac{2}{3} \div \dfrac{3}{4}$ (f) $\dfrac{2}{5} \div \dfrac{3}{5}$

MASTERY LEVEL

The mastery level is not reached until the pupil can directly transform the division example into the corresponding multiplication example. Use the pattern in (a) and in (b) to complete examples (c–g.)

(a) $3 \div \dfrac{3}{4} = 3 \times \dfrac{4}{3} = 4$ (e) $\dfrac{4}{7} \div \dfrac{4}{5}$

(b) $\dfrac{2}{3} \div \dfrac{3}{5} = \dfrac{2}{3} \times \dfrac{5}{3}$ (f) $\dfrac{3}{4} \div \dfrac{1}{5}$

(c) $8 \div \dfrac{1}{2}$ (g) $\dfrac{2}{5} \div 5$

(d) $7 \div \dfrac{2}{3}$ (h) $\dfrac{a}{b} \div \dfrac{c}{d}$

3. Grossnickle, Foster, and Leland M. Perry, "Division with Common Fraction and Decimal Divisors," *School Science and Mathematics,* 85 (November 1985): 556–566.

(i) Instead of dividing by ⅔ multiply by?

(j) Instead of dividing by ¾ multiply by?

(k) Instead of dividing by 4 multiply by?

(l) Instead of dividing by ⁵⁄ᵈ multiply by?

The Reciprocal and the Division Algorithm

If $A \times B = 1$, then by definition A is the reciprocal of B and B is the reciprocal of A. Every number except zero has a reciprocal. The product of a number and its reciprocal is equal to 1. Initial work with division of fractions requires the reciprocal concept but the patterns illustrated in the previous sections are more important than the name.

The word *invert* is often used in connection with the concept of reciprocal. Inverting ⅗ gives the reciprocal ⁵⁄₃: $⅗ \times ⁵⁄₃ = 1$. The reciprocal of 3 is ⅓. It must be recognized that $3 = ³⁄₁$: $3 \times ⅓ = 1$.

In the past, the expression *invert and multiply* was often taught by rote and pupils sometimes inverted the wrong fraction. If the word *invert* is used, it should be delayed until the reciprocal concept is understood.

(a) If $3 \times ⅓ = 1$, then 3 is the reciprocal of ⅓ and ⅓ is the ____ of 3.

(b) If $⅔ \times ³⁄₂ = 1$, then ⅔ is the reciprocal of ____ and ³⁄₂ is the reciprocal of ____.

(c) Instead of dividing by ¾, multiply by the ____ of ¾.

(d) Instead of dividing by ⅘, multiply by the ____ of ⅘.

(e) Instead of dividing by ⅓, multiply by the ____ of ⅓.

In addition to the concept of the reciprocal, two principles are required to obtain the division algorithm:

1. Multiplying the dividend and divisor by the same number does not change the quotient.

2. We get a divisor of one by multiplying both the dividend and the divisor by the reciprocal of the divisor.

The algorithm may be stated in words as follows:

To divide a number by a fraction, multiply that number by the reciprocal of the fraction (divisor).

The algorithm may be restated using *invert* instead of *reciprocal*:

To divide a number by a fraction, multiply the number by the inverted divisor. This is often abbreviated as *invert the divisor and multiply.*

Multiply the dividend and divisor of $ᵃ⁄ᵇ \div ᶜ⁄ᵈ$ by $ᵈ⁄ᶜ$ to obtain the symbolic form of the division algorithm $ᵃ⁄ᵇ \div ᶜ⁄ᵈ = ᵃ⁄ᵇ \times ᵈ⁄ᶜ$.

If $A = B$, then $B = A$. Algebraic sentences can be read from right to left as well as from left to right, therefore: $ᵃ⁄ᵇ \times ᵈ⁄ᶜ = ᵃ⁄ᵇ \div ᶜ⁄ᵈ$

The division algorithm also tells us how to change multiplication into division so that the product $4 \times ½$ can be obtained with the division $4 \div 2$.

Determining if the Answer is Sensible

The final step in computation and problem solution should be to see if the answer is sensible.

The ability to estimate with reasonable accuracy is one of the best ways to check when the activity involves whole numbers. Such estimates may not detect small errors but will guard against costly large ones. Estimates that place the correct answer between two limits are particularly helpful.

The following basic principles involving fractions help in determining if the answer is sensible:

1. If a number is multiplied by a proper fraction, the product is always smaller than that number. This principle leads to the following:

$$⁹⁄₁₀ \times 100 < 100 \qquad .9 \times 8 < 8$$

2. The product of two proper fractions is always less than either fraction.

$\frac{2}{3} \times \frac{3}{4}$ is less than $\frac{2}{3}$ *and* is less than $\frac{3}{4}$

$.06 \times .23$ is less than .06 *and* is less than .23

3. Division by a proper fraction always gives a quotient larger than the dividend. This applies when the dividend is a proper fraction.

$8 \div \frac{2}{3} > 8$

$\frac{2}{3} \div \frac{8}{9} > \frac{2}{3}$

$.07 \div .89 > .07$

4. Any number divided by a smaller number is greater than 1. Any number divided by a larger number is less than 1.

$12 \div 17 < 1$

$\frac{2}{3} \div \frac{3}{4} < 1$

$.14/.2 < 1$

$.07 \div .3 < 1$

Complex Fractions

A complex fraction contains a fraction in the numerator, in the denominator, or in both the numerator and denominator. The examples used in the previous section are designed to help pupils understand the division algorithm. However, the expression $3 \div \frac{3}{4} = 3 \times \frac{4}{3} \div \frac{3}{4} \times \frac{4}{3}$ may be better understood by using complex fractions as follows:

$$\frac{3}{\frac{3}{4}} = \frac{3 \times \frac{4}{3}}{\frac{3}{4} \times \frac{4}{3}} = \frac{3 \times \frac{4}{3}}{1} = \frac{4}{1} = 4$$

Similarly, it may be easier to understand the division algorithm, as derived by multiplying dividend and divisor of $\frac{a}{b} \div \frac{c}{d}$ by $\frac{d}{c}$, by representing this multiplication in the form of complex fractions.

$$\frac{a}{b} \div \frac{c}{d} = \frac{\frac{a}{b}}{\frac{c}{d}} \times \frac{\frac{d}{c}}{\frac{d}{c}} = \frac{\frac{a}{b} \times \frac{d}{c}}{1} = \frac{a}{b} \times \frac{d}{c}$$

Mixed Numbers

The expression $1\frac{2}{3}$ has always been known as a mixed number. Some purists object to this terminology because $1\frac{2}{3}$ is a numeral. This level of distinguishing between a numeral and a number is no longer practiced on the elementary level and the term *mixed number* is still used because no better term has been found. The mixed number $1\frac{2}{3}$ is an abbreviation for $1 + \frac{2}{3}$.

Mixed numbers rarely occur in business and industry, where decimals are prevalent, but the New York Stock Exchange still lists stock prices as mixed numbers with the fractions having denominators of 2, 4, or 8.

In recognition of the real world, computation with mixed numbers should be held to a minimum. Except in special situations, a mixed number should be changed to a decimal. Many calculators will change a mixed number such as $1\frac{3}{4}$ to a decimal by entering the following: $1 + \frac{3}{4}$ and press = to get 1.75. Changing $1\frac{2}{3}$ to a decimal follows the same pattern but produces the nonterminating decimal 1.66666667. The number of decimal places varies with the calculator. Calculator logic differs and some calculators may require a different sequence such as $\frac{1}{2} + 1$. Because $1\frac{1}{2} + 1\frac{1}{3} = 1 + \frac{1}{2} + 1 + \frac{1}{3}$, addition of mixed numbers involves no new operations.

Reduce calculator rounding errors to a minimum for a sequence of operations by not rounding until the final answer. This procedure allows the calculator to use its maximum number of decimal places.

All mixed numbers can be converted to improper fractions. Computation with improper fractions is discussed in the next sections.

Use the pattern in (a) to change mixed numbers to improper fractions in examples (b) through (e).

(a) $3\frac{3}{5} = 3 + \frac{3}{5} = \frac{15}{5} + \frac{3}{5} = \frac{18}{5}.$

(b) $2\frac{3}{4}$ (c) $4\frac{1}{2}$ (d) $1\frac{1}{5}$ (e) $5\frac{1}{3}$

Improper Fractions

An *improper fraction* has a numerator equal to or greater than its denominator. Adding, subtracting, multiplying, and dividing improper fractions involve no new concepts or operations. In most cases, operations with any fraction having a denominator larger than 16 and many with denominators less than that should be done as decimals on a calculator or computer.

In the elementary school, tradition requires that improper fractions be changed to a mixed number as the final answer to a problem. Improper fractions in science are rarely changed to mixed numbers. The fraction ¹⁰⁄₉ is often more useful than the mixed number 1⅑. Pupils should not lose credit for a correct answer expressed as an improper fraction unless instructions have clearly stated that improper fractions must be expressed as mixed numbers.

Division Involving Decimals

It has been traditional to consider four types of examples involving decimals:

(1) $2\overline{)6.2}$ Decimal divided by a whole number.

(2) $4\overline{)6}$ Whole number divided by a whole number, decimal quotient.

(3) $.4\overline{)3}$ Whole number divided by a decimal.

(4) $.2\overline{).14}$ Decimal divided by a decimal.

Multiplying the dividend and divisor by the same number enables the reduction of the four types just listed to the following two types:

Type 1: Division of a decimal by a whole number. Example (4), $.2\overline{).14}$, can be changed

to a type 1 example by multiplying dividend and divisor by 10 to get $2\overline{)1.4}$

Type 2: The division of a whole number by a whole number with a decimal quotient. Example (3), $.4\overline{)3}$, can be changed to a type 2 example by multiplying dividend and divisor by 10 to get $4\overline{)30}$.

Use examples (a), (b), (c), and (d) as models. Indicate for each example (e)–(j) whether it is type 1 (T1), type 2 (T2), or can be changed to type 1 (C-T1) or type 2 (C-T2):

(a) $5\overline{)1.2}$ T1   (f) $.4\overline{)1.7}$
(b) $5\overline{)19}$ T2   (g) $6\overline{)8.6}$
(c) $.5\overline{)1.05}$ C-T1   (h) $.12\overline{).2}$
(d) $.8\overline{)2}$ C-T2   (i) $1.2\overline{).1}$
(e) $5\overline{)3}$ (j) $.23\overline{).123}$

Dividing a Decimal by a Whole Number

To teach how to divide a decimal by a whole number, start with a problem: Joe wishes to divide 6.2 kilograms of candy equally into two bags. What is the weight of the candy in each bag? The problem solution requires the division $2\overline{)6.2}$

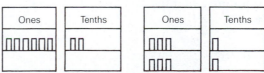

6.2 → divided into 2 parts = 3.1 in each part

Work with the pocket chart leads to the solution $2\overline{)6.2}$ or 6.2 ÷ 2 = 3.1. Each bag contains 3.1 kilograms of candy.
Check: 2 × 3.1 = 6.2.

SYMBOLIC LEVEL

Use the check with the multiplication–division relation:

$$2 \times 3.1 = 6.2 \rightarrow 6.2 \div 2 = 3.1$$

Use the distributive property:

$$6.2 \div 2 = (6 + .2) \div 2$$
$$= (6 \div 2) + (.2 \div 2) = 3 + .1 = 3.1$$

Estimate: Recognize that the answer is more than 3.

Guess and test: $3 \times 2 = 6$; $3.1 \times 2 = 6.2$

Write in the form of the standard algorithm:

$$\begin{array}{r} 3.1 \\ 2\overline{)6.2} \\ \underline{6} \\ 2 \\ \underline{2} \end{array}$$

Dividing a Whole Number by a Whole Number with a Decimal Quotient

EXPLORATORY LEVEL

To teach how to divide a whole number by a whole number with a decimal quotient, start with a problem: Convert ⅖ into a decimal fraction. The solution requires completing the division $5\overline{)2}$.

Help the pupil think: 2 ones cannot be divided by 5 ones, so we change 2 ones into 20 tenths: 20 tenths divided by 5 equals 4 tenths.

The pocket chart below indicates that 20 tenths can be separated into 5 groups, each containing 4 tenths: $2 \div 5 = .4$ Check: $5 \times .4 = 2$

SYMBOLIC LEVEL

Apply the multiplication–division relation to the check:

1. $5 \times .4 = 2 \rightarrow 2 \div 5 = .4$

2. Estimate: Early estimation of this type is difficult, but it should be clear that the quotient is less than 1. Selective use of guess and test can begin to establish a basis for such estimates.

3. Guess and test: $.1 \times 5 = .5$; $.2 \times 5 = 1$; $.3 \times 5 = 1.5$; $.4 \times 5 = 2$

Guessing and testing often implies lack of availability of a calculator. A calculator would enable the direct solution. Selective use of guess and test should test only $.1 \times 5$ and $.5 \times 5$. This pair will enable most pupils to guess the answer of .4 with fewer trials.

4. Write the standard algorithm:

$$\begin{array}{r} .4 \\ 5\overline{)2.0} \\ \underline{2\,0} \end{array}$$

Always check. Guess and test provides the check in this example.

MASTERY LEVEL

Pupils achieve the mastery level for division with decimals when:

1. They can divide a decimal by a whole number and divide a whole number by a whole number to obtain a decimal quotient.

2. They can change other examples to one of the two types just described by multiplying dividend and divisor by a power of 10.

It is often necessary to annex zeros to the

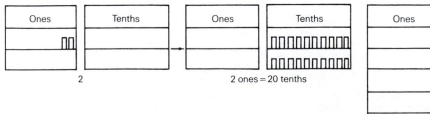

2   2 ones = 20 tenths

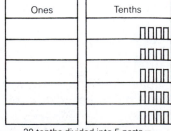

20 tenths divided into 5 parts =
4 tenths in each part

dividend to complete the division. The location of the decimal point is fixed by finding each quotient digit as tens, ones, or tenths and the like and placing the digit in the quotient to indicate its place value. Annexing zeros does not affect the position of the decimal point with this procedure.

Refer to example A.

1. Think 28 tenths divided by 8 ones is 3 tenths. Write 3 in the tenths place in the quotient. Multiply and subtract to obtain a remainder of 4 tenths.

Example A

$$\begin{array}{r} .3 \\ 8\overline{)2.8} \\ 2\ 4 \\ \hline 4 \end{array}$$

2. Consider example B. The 4 tenths remaining cannot be divided by 8 ones. Change the 4 tenths to 40 hundredths, divide by 8 ones to obtain the quotient 5 hundredths. Write 5 in the hundredths place in the quotient. Multiply and subtract as illustrated in example B.

Example B

$$\begin{array}{r} .35 \\ 8\overline{)2.80} \\ 2\ 4 \\ \hline 40 \\ 40 \end{array}$$

The procedure just outlined ensures that

when a decimal is divided by a whole number, the decimal point in the quotient is placed above the decimal point in the dividend.

For many division examples that the pupil will encounter, it may be more efficient to place the decimal point by estimation. It should be clear that $28 \div 8$ is between 3 and 4. When the quotient of 35 is obtained without regard to place value it should be clear that the correct answer is 3.5. If the check is performed with 35 to get the product $8 \times 35 = 280$, inspection shows that rewriting 35 as 3.5 will give the required check, $8 \times 3.5 = 28$. This procedure illustrates the value of a check in division involving decimals. The check not only verifies the correct use of facts in the computation but also verifies the position of the decimal point. An error in computation may be minor or major, but an error in the position of the decimal point is never minor.

Exercise 13.1

1. Divide as indicated. If a division is not type 1 or type 2 multiply by the appropriate power of 10 to change it to one of these two types.
   (a) $4\overline{)1.8}$ (b) $6\overline{)27}$ (c) $.12\overline{).27}$ (d) $.8\overline{).36}$
   (e) $5\overline{)14}$ (f) $.5\overline{).22}$ (g) $6\overline{)21}$ (h) $.08\overline{).6}$

2. Place the decimal point in each of the following by estimating the quotient and then multiply the quotient by the divisor to check your result.

   (a) $4\overline{)3.6}^{\,9}$ (b) $5\overline{)17}^{\,34}$ (c) $.6\overline{).33}^{\,55}$ (d) $12\overline{)105}^{\,875}$

   (e) $8\overline{)164}^{\,205}$ (f) $.08\overline{).1}^{\,125}$ (g) $16\overline{).04}^{\,25}$ (h) $1.2\overline{)450}^{\,375}$

Standard Percent Situations

Three types of problems involving multiplication and division of fractions are related to the basic multiplication situation: "n groups of $a = b$."

a. Find a fractional part of a number such as ½ of 10 (a and n are given and b is to be determined).

b. Find what part one number is of another (a and b are given and n is to be determined).

c. Find a number when a fractional part of it is known, such as ¼ of what number is 10 (n and b are given and a is to be determined).

Because percents are another way of naming fractional (rational) numbers, the three types of percent problems correspond to the three types just listed for multiplication and division of fractions. The three types of percent problems are derived from the basic percent statement $r\%$ of $b = p$ where r is the rate, b the base, and p the percentage. The three types are:

a. Find the percent of a number, such as 5% of 40 (the rate and base are given and the percentage is to be determined).

b. Find what percent one number is of another, such as 3 is what percent of 4 (the base and percentage are given and the rate is to be determined).

c. Find a number when a percent of it is given, such as 2% of what number is 4 (the rate and percentage are given and the base is to be determined).

Table 13.1 identifies the rate, base, and percentage and gives the percent statement in its standard form.

The percentage is obtained by multiplying the base by the rate, or $r \times b = p$. This relation is called the *percent formula* and is usually written as $p = br$ where p is the percentage (a number), b the base, and r the rate (percentage divided by the base). When using the formula, the rate is expressed as a common or decimal fraction.

When the base and rate are known, the formula indicates that the rate is to be multiplied by the base. For problem (a) in the Table 13.1, $p = br = 40 \times .05 = 2$.

When the base and percentage are known, the rate is a missing factor that can be determined by dividing the percentage by the base. For problem (b) in Table 13.1, $b = 4$ and $p = 3$, so $r \times 4 = 3$ or $r = 3 \div 4 = .75 = 75\%$.

When the percentage and rate are known, the base is a missing factor and can be found by dividing the percentage by the rate. For (c) in Table 13.1, $r \times b = p$ becomes $.02 \times b = 4$, so that $b = 4 \div .02 = 200$.

Point out that when using the formula, and any two items are known, the third is found by direct multiplication or by finding a missing factor with the multiplication–division relation.

Teaching Percent Problems

Finding a Percent of a Number

Paying sales tax can be a pupil's first experience with percent. A typical problem might ask the student to find the sales tax and total price of an $8.00 item when the tax rate is 5%.

5% of 8 = .05 × 8 = .40
Tax is $.40 or 40¢.
The total cost is $8.00 + $.40 = $8.40.

Table 13.1 Three Types of Percent Problems

Type	Rate	Base	Percentage	Standard Sentence
(a)	5%	40	p	5% of 40 = p
(b)	r	4	3	$r\%$ of 4 = 3
(c)	2%	b	4	2% of b = 4

The total cost can also be found by taking 105% of $8.00. The total is 100% of the cost plus 5% of the cost or 105% of the cost: 105% of 8 = 1.05 × 8 = 8.40, or $8.40. This approach can be used with a calculator.

Ask pupils to bring in sales slips with the tax listed separately. Verify the results using both paper and pencil and a calculator.

Discount is another common percent situation that involves multiplication of decimals. A typical problem might ask the student to determine the amount saved if a $60 item is purchased at a 20% discount.

20% of 60 = .20 × 60 = 12.
The amount saved is $12.

The problem may also ask for the new price, which is $60 − $12, or $48. Because the new price is 100% of $60 − 20% of $60, it is 80% of 60 or .80 × 60 = 48, or $48.

Interest rates and many other everyday situations involve percent. Pupils should be encouraged to bring in newspaper clippings that use the language of percent.

Exercise 13.2

1. Find the cost of .35 pounds of meat if the cost per pound is $2.45.
2. Find the money saved if a $25 camera is purchased at a discount of 10%.
3. In problem 2, find the actual amount paid in two different ways.
4. If the sales tax is 6%, find the tax on a $7000 car.
5. In problem 4, find the total cost of the car in two ways.

Finding What Percent One Number Is of Another

Previous problems involving division with whole numbers and with common fractions can now be solved by using decimals. The use of decimals often makes the problems more realistic. However, certain aspects of percent cannot be treated effectively until the pupil understands division involving decimals. Use problems whose answers are readily apparent to introduce how to find what percent one number is of another. Do oral work. Have each pupil identify the number to be compared and the number with which it is compared. Then have them write a number sentence for the situation. The following problems illustrate the procedure:

1. 5 is what percent of 100?
   $5 = n\%$ of 100
   5 is compared with 100, or $5/100 = 5\%$
2. 3 is what percent of 10?
   $3 = n\%$ of 10
   3 is compared with 10, or $3/10 = 30/100 = 30\%$
3. What percent of 10 is 7?
   $7 = n\%$ of 10
   7 is compared with 10, or $7/10 = 70/100 = 70\%$

Solving such easy problems enables the pupils to discover the pattern for writing the number sentence in problems of this type. Then they are ready for problems in which the ratio is not so readily determined as a percent.

For example, the class knows how to express ⅝ as the decimal .625. To find what percent 5 is of 8, rename .625 as 62.5%. To find what percent one number is of another, divide one number by another (or write as a common fraction) and express the quotient as a percent. Because division is not commutative, it is vital to know which number to use as the divisor (denominator). This process compares two numbers. One of

them, the base, represents 100%. The number compared with the base is the percentage. There is no single rule that will always identify the base. In the standard form, $r\%$ of $b = p$, the base follows "of."

The terms "percent" and "percentage" often confuse pupils. The percent is a *rate*. The percentage is a *number* obtained by multiplying the base by the rate.

Exercise 13.3

1. What percent of 12 is 3?

2. What percent of 3 is 12?

3. What percent of 7 is 4? Give the answer in the closest whole percent.

4. Give the answer to problem 3 in the nearest tenth of a percent by rounding the division to 3 decimal places and expressing as a percent.

5. Jim has 7 out of 10 answers correct on a test. What percent of his answers are correct?

6. Express what percent 2 is of 3 to the nearest hundredth of a percent.

7. The calculator says that $7 \div 41 = .1707317$. What percent of 41 is 7? Give the answer in:
   a. The closest whole percent.
   b. The closest tenth of a percent.
   c. The closest hundredth of a percent.

8. A man pays a tax of $1 on an article that costs $20. What is the rate of the sales tax in percent?

Estimation and Percent

Because percent is a common occurrence in everyday affairs, the ability to estimate percent is valuable. Pupils should know how to find 1%, 10%, and 50% of a number, almost instantaneously by dividing by 100, 10, or 2: 1% of 167 = 1.67; 1% of 4.8 is .048; 10% of 35 = 3.5; 10% of 48.3 is 4.83; 50% of 467 = 233.5. The ability to find these percents mentally in conjunction with the "guess-and-test" approach will enable a pupil to estimate all three types of problems.

For example, to estimate 17% of 381, a pupil would think: 10% of 381 is 38.1 so 20% is 2 × 38.1 or approximately 76. The answer is clearly closer to 76 than to 38, so any guess between 60 and 70 is reasonable. A more accurate estimate can be found by noting that 1% is about 4, so 17% is 3% less than 20%, or 76 − 12 = 64. The correct answer is 64.77.

When estimating what percent 23 is of 61, one sees clearly that it is less than 50% (½ × 61 = 30.5). 40% is 50% less 10% or 30 − 6 (rounded), or 24. Therefore, an estimate of 38% or 39% is indicated. The correct answer is 37.7% (rounded). Note that 40% is also 4 × 10%, or in this case, 4 × 6.1, or 24.4.

To estimate 13% of what number is 119, find 10% of 100 = 10, 10% of 1000 = 100, 13% of 1000 = 100 + 30 or 130 (10% + 3 × 1%). Therefore, 1000 is too large. Similarly, 13% of 900 = 90 + 27, or 117, so the correct answer is just over 900. Any estimate between 910 and 920 is excellent. The correct answer is 915.4 (rounded). This is a guess-and-test procedure.

The Proportion Method

The percent formula, as described in the previous section, has been the traditional method for solving problems in percent. In the 1960s the proportion method became popular, and is still widely used. A proportion has two equal quotients.[4]

Solving Proportions

The following approach to solving proportions depends upon the following three principles.

(a) The identity property for multiplication.

(b) If denominators are equal in a proportion, numerators are equal.

(c) The multiplication–division relation: If $2 \times N = 8$ then $N = 8 \div 2$.

We must accept that equal denominators imply equal numerators on an inductive basis. Use a brief lesson to guide the pupils to discover this concept.

Proceed as follows for phase I:

4. Traditionally, a proportion in geometry has been defined as having two or more equal ratios. A ratio is often interpreted as a quotient for numbers representing similar things, whereas a rate is a quotient of numbers representing different types of things. We make no such distinction for this topic, but the use of rate in problem-solving discussions does imply a quotient of numbers representing unlike quantities.

1. Use the identity property:
$$\frac{n}{3} = \frac{4}{5} \longrightarrow \frac{n}{3} \times \frac{5}{5} = \frac{4}{5} \times \frac{3}{3}$$

2. Multiply fractions:
$$\frac{5 \times n}{15} \qquad \frac{4 \times 3}{15}$$

3. Equal denominators → $\quad 5 \times n = 12$

4. Mult.–division relation → $n = 12 \div 5$
$$= 2.4$$

Provide enough examples to establish the pattern so that the correct performance of step 1 always leads to equal denominators. Then the equations in step 2 can be omitted without loss of understanding.

Phase II:

1. $\dfrac{n}{7} = \dfrac{8}{9} \rightarrow \dfrac{n}{7} \times \dfrac{9}{9} = \dfrac{8}{9} \times \dfrac{7}{7}$

2. $\qquad\quad 9 \times n = 8 \times 7$

3. $\qquad\quad n = 56 \div 9 = 6\tfrac{2}{9} =$
$\qquad$ 6.22 approximately

The following leads to a generalization on the right of the numerical example on the left:

$$\frac{2}{3} = \frac{4}{6} \qquad\qquad \frac{a}{b} = \frac{c}{d}$$

$$\frac{2}{3} \times \frac{6}{6} = \frac{4}{6} \times \frac{3}{3} \qquad \frac{a}{b} \times \frac{d}{d} = \frac{c}{d} \times \frac{b}{b}$$

$$\frac{2 \times 6}{18} = \frac{4 \times 3}{18} \qquad \frac{a \times d}{b \times d} = \frac{c \times b}{b \times d}$$

Equal denominators imply equal numerators, Therefore:

$$2 \times 6 = 3 \times 4 \qquad a \times d = b \times c$$

The equation $a \times d = b \times c$ is often described as *cross multiplication* as indicated by:

$$\frac{a}{b} \times \frac{c}{d}$$

The *cross-multiply method* has often been taught by rote, an unacceptable practice when the central principle in our approach to mathematics is *meaning*. However, now that we have established a sound foundation for it, we will use it in the remainder of the chapter as it is the most efficient method. Pupils should use the Phase II method until they can understand that the cross-multiply method is a natural outgrowth of Phase II.

Using Proportions for Percent Problems

If $R \times B = P$, then $R = P \div B$. If R is expressed as a common fraction:

$$\frac{R}{100} = \frac{P}{B}$$

To find the percentage P if $R = 7\%$ and $B = 150$, proceed as follows:

$$\frac{7}{100} = \frac{P}{150}$$
$$100 \times P = 7 \times 150$$
$$P = 1050 \div 100 = 10.5$$

It is essential that in the proportion method, a rate of 7% requires that R be en-

tered as 7. In the formula we must use $R = .07$.

Find the rate if the base is 80 and the percentage is 16.

$$\frac{R}{100} = \frac{16}{80} \rightarrow 80 \times R = 16 \times 100$$
$$R = 1600 \div 80 = 20$$
$$\text{rate} = 20\%$$

Find the base if the rate is 12% and the percentage is 72.

$$\frac{12}{100} = \frac{72}{B} \rightarrow 12 \times B = 72 \times 100$$
$$B = \frac{72 \times 100}{12}$$
$$B = 600$$

The statement: "If $A = B$ then $A \times N = B \times N$ is often described verbally *as equals multiplied by equals give equals* and is a basic concept in algebra. If this is available, the proof of *cross multiply* can be given as follows:

$$\frac{a}{b} = \frac{c}{d} \rightarrow \frac{a}{b} \times b \times d = \frac{c}{d} \times b \times d$$
$$\left(\frac{a}{b} \times \frac{b}{1}\right) \times d = \left(\frac{c}{d} \times \frac{d}{1}\right) \times b$$
$$a \times d = c \times b$$

Exercise 13.4

1. Use the identity property to find the missing quantity in each of the following percent situations:
   (a) $B = 10$; $R = 5\%$; $P = ?$ (d) $B = 120$; $R = 7\%$; $P = ?$
   (b) $P = 20$; $R = 20\%$; $B = ?$ (e) $P = 11$; $B = 12.5$; $R = ?$
   (c) $P = 40$; $B = 160$; $R = ?$ (f) $P = 300$; $R = 12\%$; $B = ?$

2. Use the cross-multiply method to perform the examples in exercise 1.

   Solve the following problems by proportion:

3. Find the cost of 10 pounds of seed if the cost of 3 pounds is $12.

4. Sue can travel 10 miles in an hour and one-half on her bicycle.
   a. At this rate, how long will it take her to travel 15 miles?
   b. At this rate, how far will she travel in seven and one-half hours?

5. Jill can save $20 dollars in five weeks. At this rate, how long will it take to save $160?

6. Solve example 5 as a two-step problem.

Calculator Activities

When pupils begin to multiply and divide fractions on a symbolic level, the calculator can be valuable for strengthening the relation between fractions and decimals. It is not practical to check every computation with a calculator, but the teacher should be alert for situations when a calculator check will provide an additional understanding of the concept involved.

It has always been difficult to teach, with understanding, the "invert and multiply" method for division of fractions. The calculator can help verify valid procedures.

Enter 1 into the calculator and subtract 0.2. Enter the repeat mode and continue to subtract .2 until an answer of 0 is obtained. Be certain that the pupils count the number of subtractions necessary to get zero. An alternate approach is to enter 0.2 and add in the repeat mode until the total is 1. With either method, the pupils can be guided to recognize that $5 \times .2 = 1$ or $1 \div .2 = 5$. Now proceed as follows:

1. Have pupils rename .2 as $\frac{2}{10}$ and reduce to $\frac{1}{5}$.

2. Rewrite the last equation as $1 \div 1/5 = 5$.

3. Compare the last equation with $1 \times 5 = 5$ to see that this verifies the invert-and-multiply procedure.

This approach can be used with 1 and .25, 2 and .5, and others but the number of subtractions should probably not exceed five or six. This is not a proof, but it does rationalize the process. Routine division with fractions should be checked occasionally by converting to decimals. Terminating decimals should be used in the beginning but nonterminating decimals should not be avoided after the method is established. Nonterminating decimals naturally lead to a discussion of rounding. There is no single rule that tells how many places to round decimals. This decision depends on the situation and requires experience. When computing with measurements, the basic rule is that the answer should never contain more decimal places than the least accurate of the measurements.

A minimum amount of time should be spent on computation with mixed numbers. They have probably always consumed more pupil learning time than merited in terms of usage in everyday situations. Computation with mixed numbers should be done by converting to improper fractions or to decimals. There are many variations in the way calculators accept entries. Experiment to discover the sequence necessary to obtain correct results. The following procedure will usually change $3\frac{4}{7}$ to a decimal: Divide 4 by 7, press +, press 3 and then press =. To multiply $3\frac{4}{7}$ by $1\frac{1}{3}$, it may be necessary to record the decimal value of the first number and key it in after a second number has been entered into the calculator. If the calculator has a memory, the following procedure can eliminate any writing. Proceed as follows:

1. Obtain $3\frac{4}{7} = 3.571428$ as before and place it in memory.

2. Obtain $1\frac{1}{3} = 1.3333333$ as before.

3. With 1.3333333 on display, press "$\times$" and recall 3.571428.

4. Press = to get the product.

By placing this number in memory, another fraction or mixed number can be entered and added, multiplied, and so on. In this way there is no limit to the number of fractions and/or mixed numbers that can be computed efficiently without a paper-and-pencil record.

If the calculator has an accumulative memory, often labeled M+, the procedure is easier. Convert each fraction or mixed number into a decimal and enter it into memory. The recall will give the sum of the decimals that have been entered.

The immediate mode of a computer is similar to a calculator in many ways but has one advantage that few calculators have as demonstrated by the following:

Enter PRINT (1 + ⅓) * (3 + 4/7). Press return to get: 4.76190.

The number of decimal places displayed will vary with the computer. Different sequences may produce a difference in the fifth or sixth place due to rounding of errors.

The advantage of the computer is that the complete entry remains visible so that any errors or questions about the procedure can be answered. Use of nonterminating decimals causes no difficulty other than some discrepancy in the last decimal place. This can happen with whole numbers and terminating decimals.

Use the repeating property of the calculator for the following:

(1) Find a pair of consecutive three-digit multiples of 11 such that the larger multiple is divisible by the sum of the digits in the smaller multiple.

The numbers 121 and 132 meet the condition because 1 + 2 + 1 = 4 and 132 is divisible by 4.

(2) Find the smallest number that has a remainder of 7 when divisible by 13 that is a multiple of 12. Enter 7 and press +. Now enter 13 and press =. Successive pressing of the = key will now give numbers that have a remainder of 7 when divided by 13: 20, 33, 46, 59, 72, 85, 98. . .

The multiples of 12 are: 12, 24, 36, 48, 60, 72. . ., so 72 is the first number in the previous sequence that is a multiple of 12.

(3) Find the smallest two-digit prime number that has a remainder of 5 when divisible by 11. The sequence is 5, 16, 27, . . .

The first prime number in this sequence is 71.

(4) Find the first three prime numbers greater than 300. Remember to check by dividing each number by 2, 3, 5, 7, 11, 13, and 17. Stop after 17, which is the largest prime less than the square root of 300.

The numbers are 307, 311, and 313.

Computer Activities

Program P13.1 provides practice in the basic algorithm for multiplying fractions. No dividing out of common factors is performed before multiplying numerator and denominator but a three-line computer program reduces the fraction of the final product to lowest terms. It is easier to program the computer to divide out the common fator after multiplication than before.

```
P 13.1
 10 HOME : VTAB 8
 20 A = 2 + INT(5 * RND(1))
 30 B = 5 + INT(7 * RND(1))
 40 C = 1 + INT(4 * RND(1))
 50 D = 4 + INT(6 * RND(1))
 60 PRINT
 70 PRINT A;"/";B;" X ";C;
    "/";D;"= ";A;" X ";
    C;"/";
 80 INPUT "";Z$
 90 PRINT A;"/";B;" X ";C;
    "/";D;"= ";A;" X ";C;
    "/";B;" X ";D
100 PRINT TAB (11) "=";
110 INPUT "";Z$
120 PRINT TAB(11) " = ";
    A * C;"/"; B * D
130 FOR J = B*D TO 1
    STEP - 1
```

```
140 X = A * C /J : Y =
    B * D / J
150 IF J = 1 THEN END
160 IF INT (X) = X AND
    INT(Y) = Y THEN 180
170 NEXT
180 PRINT TAB(11)" = ";
    X;"/";Y
```

Program P13.2 provides practice in placing the decimal point when given the product without it.

P13.2
```
 10 HOME : VTAB 6
 20 A = 40 + INT(20 *
    RND(1))
 30 B = 10 * INT(40 *
    RND(1))
 40 C = 1 + INT(2 * RND(1))
 50 D = 1 + INT(3 * RND(1))
 60 A1 = A/10 ^ C:B1 = B /
    10 ^ D
 70 PRINT "PLACE DECIMAL
    POINT IN FOLLOWING:"
 80 PRINT
 90 PRINT A1;" X ";B1;
    TAB(13);" -> ";A * B
100 INPUT
              ";Z$
110 PRINT A1;" X ";B1;
    TAB(13);" = ";
    A1 * B1
120 PRINT: PRINT
130 PRINT A1 * B;" / ";B1;
    TAB(13);" -> ";A
140 INPUT
              ";Z$
150 PRINT A1 * B;" / ";B1;
    TAB(13)" = ";A1 * 10
    ^ D
```

Problem Solving

(a) Phil bought a book at a 12% discount and saved $1.80. What is the list price of the book?

(b) What will be saved if a $30 coat is purchased at a 20% discount?

(c) At a 12% discount, what amount is saved from a list price of $N dollars?

(d) Write a FOR-NEXT loop that will solve problem (a).

Answers: (a) 12% of N = 1.80 → N = 1.80 ÷ .12 = 15 (b) 20% of 30 = .2 × 30 = 6. $6 will be saved. (c) 12% of N or .12 × N (d) Program follows and shows that a list price of $15 will save $1.80 with a 12% discount.

```
10 FOR N = 1 TO 20
20 PRINT N, .12*N
30 NEXT
RUN
1          .12
2          .24
------------------------
10         1.20
------------------------
15         1.80
------------------------
```

(e) What is the list price of a coat if its discount price is $240 with a discount of 20%?

(f) If the list price is $400 and the discount is 10%, what is the amount of the discount? the selling price?

(g) For an item sold at a 20% discount: The selling price is what percent of the list price?

(h) Find the list price for a selling price of $400 with a discount of 20%. Use an equation and verify the answer with a FOR-NEXT loop.

Answers: (e) 80% of N = $240 → N = 240 ÷ .8 = 300, list price is $300. (f) 10% of 400 = 40, discount is $40, selling price is $360; (g) A discount of 20% → discount price is 80% of list price; (h) .8 × N = 400 → N = 400 ÷ .80 = 500. List price is $500.

```
10 FOR N = 400 TO 600
20 PRINT N, .8 X N
30 NEXT
```

The output of this loop verifies that for a discount price of $400 with a discount of 20%, the list price will be $500.

```
- - - - - - - - - - - - - - - - - - - - - - - - - - -
- -
500        400
```

Sandy planned a trip to the mall on bargain day when the discounts were 20, 30, and 40 percent. She planned to buy several items with list prices in the $200-to-$400 range and printed the following table for reference with her computer:

```
200        160        140        120
220        176        154        132
- - - - - - - - - - - - - - - - - - - - - - - - - - -
400        320        280        240
```

The left-hand column represents the list price and the next three items in any row represent the discount prices at 20, 30, and 40 percent discounts.

Complete the following program that will tell the computer to make this table. The answer is given on page 289.

```
10 FOR N = 200 TO 400 STEP 20
```

Patterns

The following magic squares all follow the same pattern. Any three numbers can be entered in the top three rows and the pattern dictates the center element. When that number is entered, the remainder of the square can be completed by completing the diagonals and the remaining two squares. Experiment to find the pattern. Start with patterns involving whole numbers and then move to fractions. Use your calculator if necessary.

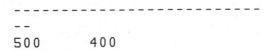

```
A. 2  3  4    B. 1  3  0    C. 4  5  3
   □  3  □       □ ⅓ □        □  4  □
   □  □  □       □  □  □       □  □  □
```

The squares E and F are derived from square D. Tell how it is done. See page 289.

```
D. 1  2  3    E. .5  1  1.5   F. −1  0   1
   4  2  □        2  1   0        2  0  −2
   1  2  3       .5  1  1.5      −1  0   1
```

Read Carefully

(a) Is it legal for a man to marry his widow's sister in the United States?

(b) A fly averages 50 mph when flying straight, turning left or right, or making a U turn. Two cars head toward each other, one at 50 mph and the other at 30 mph. The fly leaves one car and flies to the other, makes a U turn, and goes back to the first car and so on, maintaining its average speed. When the two cars meet, having traveled an hour since the fly began the round trips, how far will the fly have traveled?

(c) Alphonse found coins in a box. He did not take coins and did not leave coins. How many coins were in the box?

(d) If three people meet and all shake hands with each other, how many handshakes are there? Remember that it takes two people to make one handshake.

Answers: (a) There is no law against it but a man with a widow is dead.

(b) The fly, having flown for one hour, traveled 50 miles. The car speeds are unnecessary.

(c) There were two coins in the box. He took one coin so he did not take coins. He left one coin so he did not leave coins.

(d) There are three handshakes. It may be easiest to visualize as three people standing at the three vertices of a triangle so that each side of the triangle represents a handshake.

Write an Equation

(a) A boy has three fewer marbles than half of his brother's. The total number of marbles for both boys is 72. How many marbles does each boy have?

(b) In ten years a girl will be twice as old as she is now. How old is she now?

(c) Solve b by guess and test.

(d) The cost of a bottle and its cork is $1.10. The bottle costs one dollar more than the cork. What is the cost of each? Try to solve this before writing the equation.

Answers: (a) N + N ÷ 2 − 3 = 72, N = 50. Brother: 50 marbles. Boy: 22. (b) Age now: A, Age in 10 years: A + 10. A + 10 = 2 * A; A = 10 (c) 10 FOR A = 1 TO 20: PRINT A, A + 10 : NEXT A Output shows that for A = 10, A + 10 is twice A or 20 (d) Cork = N; Bottle = 110 − N; (110 − N) − N = 100; N = 5; 110 − N = 105.

The following computation can be performed on most computers in the immediate mode by entering PRINT 2E + 3 *2 E + 2 and pressing return. You should be able to do these without the calculator or computer if you understand the notation. There is a long way and a short way. Try to find the short way and check the results with a calculator or computer. The calculator may not be able to do the work the short way but it can do it the long way.

(a) $(2E + 3) \div (2E + 3)$
(b) $(4E + 4) \times (2E + 3)$
(c) $(2E + 2) + (3E + 2)$
(d) $(3E + 3) \times (2E + 2)$
(e) $(3E - 2) \times (2E + 2)$
(f) $(2E + 3)^2$
(g) $(6E + 5) \div (2E + 3)$
(h) $(8E + 5) \times (7E + 4)$
(i) $(8E + 12) \div (2E + 12)$

PROGRAM FOR ANSWER TO SANDY'S PROBLEM

```
10 FOR N = 200 TO 400 STEP
   20
20 PRINT N;" ";.8 * N;"
   ";.7 * N :" ";.6 * N
30 NEXT N
```

The program illustrates how to make a FOR-NEXT loop start with a desired number and use an increment larger than 1.

Some computers allow three commas for four columns of output, while others use two commas for three columns. The quotes used in line 20 allow a more flexible output.

MAGIC SQUARES PATTERNS

The pattern for the magic squares A, B, and C was developed algebraically. The center square is ⅓ the sum of the elements in the first row. The only hazard in its use is that it may require negative numbers and some rather difficult fractions, but a calculator can help.

Square E is derived from square D by multiplying each element in D by 5 and then dividing by 10. Square F is derived from square D by subtracting 2 from each element in D.

Summary

Elementary school pupils have difficulty with multiplication and division of fractions and decimals. Further, their achievement is typically low on tests. The major reason for this is the overall lack of understanding of fractions and decimals in multiplication and division problems.

To learn to multiply and divide fractions and decimals, pupils should be given a variety of word problems to solve. In the early stage of learning, pupils need to explore solutions to problems with manipulatives and visuals to develop an understanding of the thinking strategies involved.

Exploration at the symbolic level should help pupils discover patterns and relationships. Solving multiplication and division problems expressed with both common fractions and decimals should reinforce the meanings of these numbers. Practice estimation prior to calculation.

The language of percent is common in everyday affairs as well as in business and industry. The percent sign is equivalent to one-hundredth, the basis for changing to and from percent. The percent sign is used mainly for descriptive purposes and rarely in computation. There are three basic percent situations. Percent problems can be solved by use of the formula or by use of proportions. Both methods are in common use.

Extensive use should be made of calculators and computer programs.

Exercise 13.5

Part I

1. If the product of a and b is 1, then a is the _____ of b and b is the _____ of a.

2. What number does not have a reciprocal?

3. Complete the following statement of the division algorithm: Rather than divide by a number, _____.

4. In everyday language, rational numbers are called _____.

5. What is the cost of 2½ pounds of nuts at $4 per pound?

6. Which analysis is correct for problem 5: Given 2½, find 1, or given 1, find 2½?

7. A football halfback gained 108 yards in 24 carries. What is his average yardage per carry?

8. Which analysis is correct for problem 7: Given 1, find 24, or given 24, find 1?

9. Joe drinks ⅓ of a quart of milk per day. If his family drinks 10 quarts of milk per week, how many quarts does the rest of the family drink in a week? in a day?

10. Gus runs the marathon at a rate of 5½ miles per hour. How long will it take him to finish the race if the total distance is 26⁷⁄₁₂ miles?

Part II

Give the pattern you would use to teach these problems to a class of average achievers at the grade 6 level:

1. The length of a bookshelf is 2.75 feet. What is the length of three of these shelves?

2. A gardener planted 60 rose bushes. If 90% of them grew, how many did not grow?

3. How many pieces of ribbon 1.5 yards in length can be cut from a roll of ribbon containing 24 yards?

4. A team won 13 of the 20 games it played. What percent of the games played did that team win?

5. A team won 12 games and lost 13 games. What percent of the games played did that team win?

6. A tank contains 48 gallons of fuel oil when it is 30% filled. How many gallons will the tank hold when completely filled?

7. A manufacturer advertises that the cutting edge of a razor blade is 17 millionths of an inch thick. Write the decimal for this number.

8. What is the largest possible number of digits in the repetend of the decimal representation of the fraction $\frac{1}{n}$? Check your answer by finding the repetend for $\frac{1}{7}$, $\frac{1}{13}$, and $\frac{1}{17}$.

9. If two numbers (not zero) are equal, their reciprocals are equal. Show this to be true by multiplying both sides of the equation $\frac{1}{n} = \frac{1}{m}$ by mn.

10. Show how the statement in problem 9 applies to $\frac{3}{4} = \frac{12}{n}$.

11. A teacher introduced division by a decimal divisor using a caret to shift the decimal point, as illustrated in the example: $.3_\wedge)\overline{.1_\wedge 8}$ Evaluate this technique.

12. Solve by formula: 30% of what number is 48?

13. Solve problem 12 by the proportion method.

14. What is the cost of a book selling for $9 if it is sold at 20% above cost? A student gave the following solution:

    20% of $9 = $1.80. The cost is $9 − $1.80 or $7.20.

As a teacher, how would you evaluate this solution?

15. The total prize money in a golf tournament is $600,000. The first prize is $108,000; the second is $64,800; the third is $40,000. Each prize is what percent of the total?

Selected Readings

Ashlock, Robert B., et. al. *Guiding Each Child's Learning of Mathematics*. Columbus, OH: Charles E. Merrill, 1983. Chapters 13 and 14.

Bitter, Gary G., et. al. *Mathematics Methods for the Elementary and Middle School: A Comprehensive Approach*. Needham Heights, MA: Allyn & Bacon, 1989. Chapters 10 and 11.

Grossnickle, Foster, and Leland M. Perry, "Division with Common Fraction and Decimal Divisors, " *School Science and Mathematics*, 85 (November 1985): 556–566.

Heddens, James W., and William R. Speer. *Today's Mathematics*, 6th ed. Chicago: Science Research Associates, 1988. Units 10 and 11.

Kennedy, Leonard M., and Steve Tipps. *Guiding Children's Learning of Mathematics*, 5th ed. Belmont, CA: Wadsworth, 1988. Chapters 11 and 12.

Marks, John L., et. al. *Teaching Elementary School Mathematics for Understanding*, 5th ed. New York: McGraw-Hill, 1985. Chapters 8 and 9.

Post, Thomas R. *Teaching Mathematics in Grades K–8*. Needham Heights, MA: Allyn & Bacon, 1988. Chapter 7.

Reys, Robert E., et. al. *Helping Children Learn Mathematics*, 2nd ed. Englewood Cliffs, NJ: Prentice-Hall, 1989. Chapters 11 and 12.

Riedesel, C. Alan. *Teaching Elementary School Mathematics*, 4th ed. Englewood Cliffs, NJ: Prentice-Hall, 1985. Chapters 10, 11, and 12.

14

Systems of Numeration and of Number

ACHIEVEMENT GOALS

After studying this chapter you should be able to:

1. Describe how number concepts were communicated in ancient civilizations.

2. Rename Egyptian and Roman numerals in Hindu–Arabic notation and rename Hindu–Arabic numerals in Egyptian and Roman numerals.

3. Identify the characteristics of the Hindu–Arabic decimal system of notation.

4. Name five elements of an effective system of numeration.

5. List and discuss the special properties of zero and 1.

6. Describe the properties of addition and multiplication and give the identities for these operations.

7. Discuss the role of prime and composite numbers in the elementary mathematics program.

8. Distinguish between whole numbers and integers and between whole numbers and rationals. Arrange the following sets of numbers in order of inclusiveness: whole numbers, integers, real numbers, counting numbers, and rational numbers.

VOCABULARY

These terms are defined or illustrated in the Glossary.

Abacus	Identity element
Addend	Integer
Array	Inverse operation
Associative	Negative number
property	Number line
Base (system of	Number period
numeration)	Open sentence
Binary operation	Ordinal number
Cardinal number	Overloaded place
Commutative	Place value
property	Rational numbers
Digit	Real numbers
Distributive	Signed number
property	Total value (digit)

History shows that mathematics has been a central part of the everyday lives of mankind for thousands of years. In the beginning, mathematics was developed to cope with quantity and with space. The methods of dealing with quantity or number developed into the science of arithmetic, whereas the methods of dealing with space developed into the field of geometry. This chapter is concerned with the development and structure of arithmetic. Chapter 16 treats the many aspects of geometry.

The Earliest Concepts of Number

The idea of number, saying numbers, and recording numbers took thousands of years to develop. Number has several characteristics. First, it is abstract and exists only in the mind of man. No one has ever seen the number 3 but we are all familiar with three things.

E. T. Bell describes some great thinkers in mathematics and quotes Bertrand Russell's observation that "it must have taken many ages to discover that a brace of pheasants and a couple of days were both instances of the number two."[1] Bell does not mention an unknown who should rank with the pioneer thinkers in this field. This unknown discovered that the wings of a bird have something in common with a man and his wife. The genius who discovered "twoness" between two wings and two people and expressed it symbolically made a great contribution to civilization. This discovery helped us express magnitude with abstract names such as *one* and *two* without using concrete names such as *head* and *wing*.[2]

1. E. T. Bell, *Men and Mathematics* (New York: Simon & Schuster, 1937), p. 14.

2. Foster E. Grossnickle and Leland M. Perry, "Man's Romance with Number," *School Science and Mathematics*, 87 (January 1987): 7–11.

Matching

Early civilizations used systems of matching to keep track of the number of items, such as the number of sheep in a flock. As each animal left the pen, a pebble was placed in a container. When the flock returned, a pebble was removed as each animal re-entered the pen. If no pebbles remained after the last animal entered the pen, no sheep was missing. The set of pebbles matched the set of sheep.

This type of one-to-one matching is still useful today. When setting a table, you don't count the napkins you need, but merely place a napkin at each place setting. Counting is related to the matching process but requires names for numbers.

Early Number Concepts

Number was first used to communicate how many things were involved, such as how many animals, how many warriors, and the like. Fingers, pebbles, marks in the sand, and similar devices made symbolic communication possible before there were names for number, which enabled such information to be transmitted verbally. Historians of mathematics agree that humans chose a base of ten for their system of communicating "how many" because of the ease of matching fingers with things. Soon it became expedient to name quantities represented by common groupings of things. In one early culture the phrase "taking the thumb" indicated the quantity five. Historical records show other common names for small groupings.

Young children learn to assign number names to small quantities and often show numbers with fingers. When asked "How old are you?," a young child will show his or her age with fingers.

Counting—A Major Invention

After number names were assigned to small numbers of things, man discovered that these collections could be arranged in an increase-by-one fashion. Number, as it evolved over the years, took on the characteristics of being *orderly*, of following a *pattern*, and of using *symbols* to represent number values.

Saying Numbers

In our system of base-ten numeration (the way we say numbers), there are names for sets from zero to nine, then the name of the base, which is ten (the point of regrouping into one collection and renaming), and names for multiples of the ten—twenty, thirty, forty, and so forth.

Writing Numerals

For a system of notation (the way we record numbers), there must be *symbols* (digits), a *base* (ten), and *place value*. Place value makes it possible to write any quantity with only ten different digits. Place value was the creation of the great minds of Hindu priests in central India over twelve hundred years ago. To be self-contained—to function without a supplementary aid, such as an abacus—there must be a symbol to hold a vacant place in a numeral. The Hindus gave us the symbol zero for that purpose.

As children learn to count meaningfully in the Hindu–Arabic system, they discover the *pattern* of the repetition of the number names. When they learn to write numbers with digits, they discover the *pattern* of the repetition of the digits, the idea of place value, and the use of zero as a place holder. These things now seem very simple, but as Bell points out, "our way of writing numbers . . . with its 'place system' of value and the introduction of a symbol for zero [must have] . . . cost incredible labor to invent."[3]

3. E. T. Bell, p. 14.

Uses of Number in Measurement

During the Stone Age people were involved in making, inventing, and developing ways to communicate in words, perhaps in written symbols, a limited number of quantitative ideas. The motivation to do this was probably a need to answer the questions "How many?" and Which one?"

Numbers soon took on an additional task—to measure, or describe "how much." For example, to talk and write about how many days had passed, a prehistoric person could merely use counting numbers. But to describe how far it was to the next village, the person had to use counting numbers in conjunction with a measurement unit, such as so many steps, so many pole lengths, or how many days it took to walk the distance. Ten Sleeps, an Indian settlement in Wyoming, took its name from the process of applying number to measurement.

Symbolization of Numbers

Earlier civilizations developed number systems to suit their needs. The set of counting, or natural, numbers was the first set to be developed. The symbols (numerals) used to represent these numbers differed according to each culture. To some extent, the complexity of a civilization corresponds to the number of sets beyond the counting numbers that were used.

The Egyptian System of Notation

The culture that built the pyramids also produced a system of numeration and notation. It is likely that the Egyptian number system arose out of need. By about 3000 B.C. prosperous cities had grown up along the Nile River. Markets, businesses, and government activities demanded a system of records, and record keeping required numbers.

The ancient Egyptian system of numeration used a new symbol to represent each

Table 14.1 Egyptian Number Symbols and Their Values

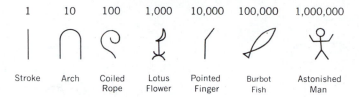

1	10	100	1,000	10,000	100,000	1,000,000
Stroke	Arch	Coiled Rope	Lotus Flower	Pointed Finger	Burbot Fish	Astonished Man

power of 10. Table 14.1 shows the different symbols used by the Egyptians and their corresponding values in our number system.

In the Egyptian system, ten strokes had the same value as one arch. Each new symbol, as we move from left to right in the table, represents a number ten times larger than the preceding symbol.

The number represented by a numeral is the sum of the numbers represented by its various symbols. For example, consider the numeral for 14,375:

Using Egyptian symbols, the number represented is the sum of 10,000, 4000, 300, 70, and 5, or 14,375.

The symbols in this numeral are arranged in order of their value. The symbol of greatest value is on the left, and the symbol of least value is on the right. The symbols could have been in the reverse order or placed randomly. Therefore, the position or place of a symbol in a numeral did not affect the value of that symbol. The Egyptian system of numeration used neither order nor place value.

The Egyptian numeral for 14,375 contains twenty symbols. In contrast, our numeral for this amount contains only five symbols.

The Egyptian system is adequate to describe "how many," but it is not suited for computation. This is also true of the Roman system.

The Roman System of Notation

One ancient number system that has lasted until modern times is the Roman system of notation, commonly called *Roman numerals*. The ancient Romans used the abacus to perform computations and Roman numerals to record the answers. Because it has no zero and is not a place-value system, the Roman system is very inefficient for computations with paper and pencil.

The Roman system uses a new symbol for each succeeding greater group. The symbols used in Roman notation are:

I	V	X	L	C	D	M
1	5	10	50	100	500	1000

A bar placed above a numeral multiplies the value of the number by 1000. Thus $\overline{C}$ represents 100,000, rather than 100.

The plan of counting by five, as in tallying votes, suggests how the symbols I, V, and X came to be used in Roman notation. Four vertical strokes and one cross stroke suggest V, to represent five. The representation for the numbers 5 through 10 would be as follows:

Tally	ⵊ	ⵊ I	ⵊ II	ⵊ III	ⵊ IIII	ⵊ ⵊ
Numeral	V	VI	VII	VIII	VIIII	X

The Roman system operates according to four principles:

Exercise 14.1
1. What number is represented by each of these Egyptian numerals?

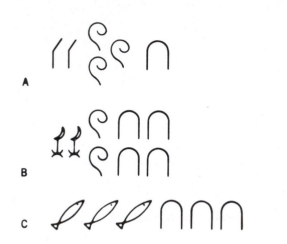

2. Use Egyptian numerals to represent the following numbers:
   (a) 32
   (b) 320
   (c) 203
   (d) 1560
   (e) 1,001,001
   (f) this year

Repetition: A symbol is repeated to indicate the number value.

Subtraction (not a part of early Roman usage): For the numbers 4, 40, 400 and 9, 90, 900, subtraction is done by writing a symbol representing a smaller value to the *left* of a symbol of greater value.

Multiplication: A bar drawn over any Roman numeral indicates that the value is to be multiplied by 1000.

Addition: All the values of the symbols written are added to get the total value of the number.

The Roman system used a "cycle of numerals" in a "times 5, times 2" sequence:

$$I \times 5 = V \quad X \times 5 = L \quad C \times 5 = D$$
$$V \times 2 = X \quad L \times 2 = C \quad D \times 2 = M$$

This cycle may have stemmed from thinking of fingers and arms, but it has no use today except perhaps as an aid in learning and remembering Roman numerals.

The value of a number represented in Roman numerals is the sum of the numbers represented by each symbol, except when subtraction is involved. Thus the number represented by MMCCCXXVI is 2326, which is the sum of the numbers represented by each symbol:

MM   CCC   XX   V   I
2000 + 300 + 20 + 5 + 1 = 2326

The Hindu–Arabic System of Notation

During the Middle Ages the Roman system was replaced by the Hindu–Arabic system in most major civilizations. Because it is a place-value system with zero, efficient pa-

Exercise 14.2

1. Find the number represented by these Roman numerals:

   (a) CCXLV   (f) $\overline{\text{C}}$ CXLIX
   (b) CDXL   (g) $\overline{\text{MM}}$
   (c) MMDCXLV   (h) DCCIV
   (d) $\overline{\text{M}}$ MDC   (i) $\overline{\text{DC}}$
   (e) DLXXXIV   (j) $\overline{\text{DC}}$

2. Represent the following numbers in Roman numerals:

   (a) 105   (d) 1001
   (b) 2250   (e) 1,000,000
   (c) 1440   (f) 200,000

per-and-pencil computation in the Hindu–Arabic system is possible.

The Hindu–Arabic system was invented by Hindu priests in central India and was spread to the West by the Arabs. Its distinctive feature is *place value*. The Hindus invented place value sometime between the sixth and seventh centuries A.D. Later, after the system reached the West, the Hindus discovered the digit *zero*, which could be used as a place holder for an empty groove on their clay counting boards, as shown in Figure 14.1. The system was complete with the distinctive features of place value and zero.

We can illustrate the principle of place value with the aid of the counting board. Counting was accomplished by a one-to-one matching of pebbles with the items being counted. Before the invention of place value, when the "counter" reached ten, or the base of the system, the things being used to represent ones were exchanged for *one* object of *another* type, usually bigger in size or at least visually different. In modern times, exchanging ten pennies for one dime is the same general idea.

The Hindus did not exchange a pebble or marker for a pebble or marker of a different size. With the aid of a counting board, when the first groove on the right had ten pebbles—usually all that would fit—the Hindus would exchange the ten pebbles for *one* of the *same* kind and place that one pebble in the groove to the left of the first place. This groove then became the *tens place*. Any single pebble in that position represented ten pebbles in the *ones place*. The position of a pebble on the counting board determined its total numerical value.

Of the systems discussed in this chapter, only the Hindu–Arabic decimal, place-value system is convenient for paper-and-pencil computation. For just this reason it

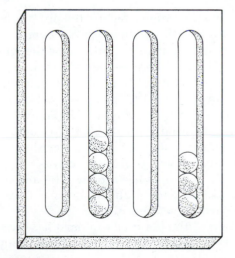

Figure 14.1
A Hindu Counting Board—
An Abacus-like Device

replaced the Roman system in Europe during the Middle Ages.

Complete Place Value

The English language abounds with words that have different meanings in different contexts. For example, the word *frog* represents an amphibian, part of a horse's hoof, a temporary obstruction in the throat, and a closing on a coat. To give more than one meaning to a numeral would seem to confound matters, but this is done in our Hindu–Arabic system. We give a value to the *place* occupied by the digit as well as to the value of the digit itself. For example, 3 in 234 is in the *tens place*, indicating that the place contains 3 *tens* or 30 ones.

Rods on an abacus instead of zero are used to hold an empty place and thus make place value possible. The Hindu–Arabic system has place value because zero is used to hold a vacant place in a numeral. This system is superior to all ancient systems of numeration.

Zero

Many historians regard the introduction of zero into the number system as an invention with as much importance as the wheel. The origins of both are equally obscure. According to Swiss-American mathematician Florian Cajori, the Egyptian astronomer-mathematician-geographer Ptolemy (A.D. 100–170) used the Greek letter omicron (o) to represent blanks in the sexagesimal system about 130 A.D. But this o was not used exactly as zero is used today. The first modern use of zero probably occurred during the seventh century A.D.[4]

Each of the ten digits in our place system holds a place and indicates the frequency or

4. Vera Sanford, "Hindu Arabic Numerals," *Arithmetic Teacher,* (2 December 1955):115.

number of items in that place. Zero is often referred to as a placeholder because it is the symbolic equivalent of an empty column in the abacus. It is this property of zero that makes it possible to distinguish between the numerals 31, 301, and 3001 and makes possible efficient computation with paper and pencil.

Because the Roman and Egyptian systems do not contain a symbol for zero, efficient paper-and-pencil computation is not possible. Computation in these two systems was done on an abacus.

Characteristics of a Place-Value System

There are eight main characteristics of the decimal system of numeration for whole numbers. These are:

1. The base of the system is ten, as there are exactly 10 digits in the system.

2. The digits used are 1, 2, 3, 4, 5, 6, 7, 8, 9, 0.

3. Each digit in a numeral performs two functions: It holds a place and it shows the frequency of that place.

4. Each digit in a two-or-more-place numeral that names a whole number has three values:
   a. *cardinal value,* sometimes called the *face value*
   b. *positional value*
   c. *total value*

The positional value is the value of the place the digit holds in a numeral. This value is a power of the base. The power is the same as the number of places the digit is to the left of the ones place. The total value is the product of the cardinal and the positional values.

We can illustrate the different values of a digit by considering the numeral 732. The *cardinal value:*

of 7 is 7; of 3 is 3; of 2 is 2.

The *positional value:*

of 7 is 100; of 3 is 10; of 2 is 1.

The *total value:*

of 7 is 700; of 3 is 30; of 2 is 2.

The cardinal and total values of a digit are the same for each digit in the ones place. These two values are also the same for the digit 0 in all places, because the product of 0 and a number is 0.

5. The number is the sum of the total values of the digits in the different places.

6. Moving a digit to the left in a whole number multiplies its place value and total value by a power of 10. If 3 is moved two places to the left, the value of the 3 has been multiplied by 10^2. We read the numeral 10^2 as "ten to the second power," or "ten squared."

7. Moving a digit to the right divides its place value by a power of 10. Since dividing by 10 is the same as multiplying by $\frac{1}{10}$, or 10^{-1}, moving a digit to the right in a numeral multiplies the value of that digit by a power of $\frac{1}{10}$. The power is the same as the number of places the digit is moved.

8. Every two-or-more-place numeral can be named in different ways. The *standard numeral* for three hundred forty-nine is 349. This number may be written as:
   a. 349 = 3 hundreds, 4 tens, 9 ones = 34 tens, 9 ones = 349 ones
   b. 349 = 300 + 40 + 9
   c. $349 = 3 \times 10^2 + 4 \times 10^1 + 9 \times 10^0$.

   Example (a) illustrates place value. Example (b) shows how to rename 349 to illustrate total values. The 3 in 349 represents 3 hundreds, or 3×100, the 4 represents 4 tens, or 4×10, while the 9 represents 9 ones, or 9×1. The total value of 3 is 300, of 4 is 40, and of 9 is 9. Example (c) illustrates the base-ten aspect of our system by using *exponential* notation.

Elements of a Numeration System

By examining the ancient Egyptian and Roman systems of numeration, we can see that they are deficient in many respects. If we compare these systems with the Hindu–Arabic, we can easily identify the essential elements of an effective system of numeration. Such a system must have the property of completeness so that it can function without the use of supplementary aids. The elements of a complete system include:

1. A base

2. Symbols or numerals

3. A fixed value for a place in a numeral

4. Zero

5. A decimal point

Man invented all five of these elements in order to deal effectively with numbers.

Ten is the base of the decimal system, and so ten symbols are needed. The base of most ancient numeration systems was a multiple of five—5, 10, or 20. The Babylonian numeration system used a base of sixty. We measure time on this scale today.

A symbol used in a numeration system must have a *name*, as well as a *design*, or *form*. The names of the digits, which vary in different languages, are used in enumeration. Table 14.2 gives the number names of the first ten counting numbers in three different languages.

Although different societies in the West have different names for the digits, the symbols used to represent numbers are the same, except for 7 and 1. Many Europeans write the numeral one as *1* and so must write the numeral seven as *7* to avoid confusion.

The third and fourth essential elements in a system of numeration are place value and zero, which we have already described. The fifth element is a point, such as the decimal point, used to locate the ones place. The use of a decimal point extends place value to the right of the ones place in the decimal

Table 14.2 Number Names in Different Languages

English	one	two	three	four	five	six	seven	eight	nine	ten
German	ein	zwei	drei	vier	fünf	sechs	sieben	acht	neun	zehn
Spanish	uno	dos	tres	cuatro	cinco	seis	siete	ocho	nueve	diez

system. Any digit, except 0, written to the right of that point has a value less than one but greater than zero.

Periods in Numerals

It is difficult to read the numeral 371495 as it is written here. To make it easier to read large numbers, we use *periods* in the numerals. Beginning on the right, three consecutive places constitute a period. A comma, or a single space, is used to separate periods in numerals containing five or more digits. The space is used in the metric system. A four-place numeral can be separated into two periods by a comma, or a space, provided that the numeral does not represent a date or a time interval.

The first period designates ones. This period and each succeeding full period to the left contain three places, designated as ones, tens, and hundreds. Every period must contain three places except the first period on the left, as is seen in the third period of the numeral 8,371,495.

Table 14.3 lists the first four periods in grouping numerals. Each period to the left has a value 1000 times the value of the period to the right. There are 1000 thousands in a million and 1000 millions in a billion. It is possible, therefore, to represent a million as 1000 thousands. Similarly, 1000 millions represents a billion.

The value of a billion is not the same in all countries. In our country a billion is equal to 1000 millions, while in England a billion is equal to a million millions. A billion of this value is 1000 times as large as our billion.

There are other period names that can be used to designate a period to the left of the group for billions. For a numeral to represent a value greater than a numeral in the group or period for billions, that numeral must have at least thirteen places. Any numeral representing trillions has at least 13 places.

Overloading a Place

Efficient computation is possible in the Hindu–Arabic decimal, place-value system not only because each place can be calculated as easily as the ones place, but also because it is possible to *overload* a place as needed. A place is overloaded when the number at that place is greater than 9. Consequently, to subtract 23 from 71, the 71 could be renamed 6 tens 11 ones, so that subtraction can be done at both the ones place and the tens place.

Table 14.3 Use of Periods in Grouping Numerals

Billions	Millions	Thousands	Ones
Hundreds-Tens-Ones	Hundreds-Tens-Ones	Hundreds-Tens-Ones	Hundreds-Tens-Ones

Exercise 14.3

1. Write the standard numeral for the following:
   (a) 7000 + 300 + 50 + 6
   (b) $(5 \times 10^3) + (1 \times 10^2) + (6 \times 10) + 5$
   (c) 7 hundreds 35 ones
   (d) 20 tens 9 ones
   (e) 3 thousands 26 ones

2. Write place-value names as shown in 1(a):
   (a) 3782   (b) 4025

3. Rename in terms of powers of ten:
   (a) 4730
   (b) 29,100

4. Rename 732 in three different ways so that every digit is used once in each numeral:
   $732 = 7$ hundreds $+ \square$ tens $+ 2\square$
   $\square$ tens $+ 2$ ones
   $\square$ ones

5. Use the pattern in problem 4 to rename the following:
   (a) 378   (b) 2235

6. Give the value of the following:
   (a) 3×10^3 (c) 10^0
   (b) 5×10^2 (d) $(2 \times 10^2) + (3 \times 10^0)$

Properties of Number and Number Operations

Sets

Set concepts and notation were introduced into the elementary mathematics curriculum in the 1960s as New Math became popular. Unfortunately, too much emphasis was placed on many of the technical aspects of sets, especially the abstract notation of sets, subsets, union, intersection, Cartesian product, and the like. Both teachers and parents questioned the value of this emphasis, given that the mathematics curriculum was already overcrowded and children were unable to learn what many considered more important and more basic subject matter.

Set concepts are basic to mathematics. On advanced levels, set theory is very complex. Set ideas in elementary mathematics are useful in relating abstract number concepts to the world of objects. Collections of things occur naturally in our lives—for example, "sets of books," "a set of dishes," "a herd of cattle." This text uses *set* in the everyday sense.

Number and Numeral

A number is an abstract idea. It cannot be seen, touched, or erased. The number two is an idea common to all pairs of things.

A *numeral* is a written symbol that represents a number. It can be seen, touched, and erased. The numeral 2 is one of many symbols that can be used to represent the intangible number two.

The New Math programs of the 1960s placed great emphasis on having children learn the fine distinction between "number" and "numeral." In many cases, the language was overdetailed and confusing. The simplest solution is for a teacher to make this distinction when it comes up naturally in conversation and helps to clarify an idea. Otherwise, just keep in mind that we think with numbers and record with numerals.

Possibly the most useful concept associated with the number–numeral distinction is that each number has many names (numerals) and that renaming numbers is one of the most common mathematical activities. Renaming 23 as 20 + 3 or (2 × 10) + 3 sometimes makes it easier to understand arithmetic operations.

Equalities and Inequalities

The word *equal* means "names the same number." Forming an equality usually involves discovering another name for the same number. The equality 1 + 1 = 2 indicates that *1 + 1* and *2* are different symbols or names for the same number.

The statement 2 ≠ 3 indicates that the numerals name different numbers but gives no information as to which is larger. The inequalities 2 < 3 and 3 > 2 indicate that 2 is less than 3 and that 3 is greater than 2. These inequalities are equivalent to one another, since each can be read from right to left as well as from left to right, a characteristic of mathematical sentences. The tip of the arrow always points to the smaller number.

Properties of Number Operations

In the past, mathematics was taught largely by rote rules, such as "invert and multiply," with little or no effort to make the rules meaningful. In the 1950s and 1960s, there was concerted effort to use sound mathematical number properties in place of such rules.

Understanding certain properties of number reduces the task of learning the basic facts in addition and subtraction. Similarly, discovering certain properties or relationships between multiplication and division

helps the pupil to work with these operations. In the following sections we discuss some of the most important properties of number, beginning with zero.

SPECIAL PROPERTIES OF ZERO

Zero has very special number properties:

1. 0 + 1 = 1 + 0 = 1. Zero is the *additive identity*; the sum of zero and any number is that number.

2. $0 \times N = N \times 0$. The product of zero and any number is zero. A consequence of this is that for $N \neq 0$, $0 \div N = 0 \times \frac{1}{N} = 0$.

3. $^{+}N + {}^{-}N = 0$. The sum of any number and its opposite is zero. This is the most fundamental fact for dealing with signed numbers. The word *opposite* is an everyday term for the technical term *additive inverse*.

4. Division by zero is impossible and is often described as undefined. If a nonzero number N divided by 0 equals K, as in $N \div 0 = K$, then it must follow that $N = 0 \times K$, which contradicts the statement $0 \times K = 0$.

SPECIAL PROPERTIES OF ONE

The number one has some very special properties:

1. Where N is a counting number, $N + 1$ is the next counting number.

2. $N \times 1 = N$. Any number multiplied by one equals that number. The equation $N \times 1 = N$ expresses the *identity property* for multiplication. Renaming 1 as $\frac{2}{2}$ is often useful in examples such as: $\frac{3}{4} \times 1 = \frac{3}{4} \times \frac{2}{2} = \frac{6}{8}$.

3. If N is a nonzero number, $N \div N = 1$. Any nonzero number divided by itself equals one.

4. Any fractional number in the form of $\frac{a}{b}$, where a and $b \neq 0$, multiplied by its *reciprocal* equals one. The reciprocal of $\frac{a}{b}$ is $\frac{b}{a}$ or $\frac{a}{b} \times \frac{b}{a} = 1$.

THE IDENTITY PROPERTY

The identity property can be introduced by tables of the following type:

(a) 1 + 0 = 1   (b) 1 × 1 = 1
    2 + 0 = 2   2 × 1 = 2
    3 + 0 = 3   3 × 1 = 3
    4 + 0 = □   4 × 1 = □
    5 + □ = 5   5 × □ = 5

The pattern in (a) shows that 0 is the identity element for addition; the sum of any number and 0 is that number.

The pattern in (b) shows that 1 is the identity element for multiplication; the product of any number and 1 is that number.

Tables (a) and (b) illustrate that the number 0 in addition behaves just as 1 behaves in multiplication.

Elementary pupils should become familiar with the identity concept through the renaming process. They should learn to rename 2 as 2 + 0 or 0 + 2 and, when multiplication has been introduced, 2 × 1 and 1 × 2. Renaming 5 as 5 + 0 can be useful in helping pupils to learn that 4 + 1 = 5 and 3 + 2 = 5. Renaming ½ as ½ × 1 is useful in helping pupils recognize that one-half and two-fourths name the same number.

THE INVERSE PROPERTY

The inverse property is probably the most complex number operation we will discuss.

It can be illustrated by the following patterns:

(a)   0 + 0 = 0   (b) 1 × 1 = 1

$^{-}$1 + 1 = 0 $\dfrac{2}{1} \times \dfrac{1}{2} = 1$

$^{-}$2 + 2 = 0 $\dfrac{3}{1} \times \dfrac{1}{3} = 1$

$^{-}$3 + 3 = 0 $\dfrac{4}{1} \times \dfrac{1}{4} = 1$

$^{-}$4 + 4 = 0

The pattern in (a) shows pairs of *inverse numbers* for addition. A pair of inverse numbers in addition has a sum of 0 (the identity element for addition). The pattern in (b) shows pairs of inverse numbers in multiplication. A pair of inverse numbers in multiplication has a product of 1 (the identity element for multiplication).

Our number system is said to have the *inverse property for addition* because for every number X in the system there is a number $^{-}$X, such that $^{-}$X + X = X + $^{-}$X = 0.

Our number system is said to have the *inverse property for multiplication* because for every number X there is a number $\dfrac{1}{X}$ such that: $\dfrac{X}{1} \times \dfrac{1}{X} = \dfrac{1}{X} \times \dfrac{X}{1} = \dfrac{X}{X} = 1$, where X cannot equal *zero.*

Exercise 14.4

1. A common property of 0 and 1 discussed in this chapter is the _____ property.

2. Show how the number one behaves in multiplication just as the number zero behaves in addition.

3. Rename 5 in four different ways, using the identity for addition and multiplication.

4. Use the equality $1 = \dfrac{2}{2}$ to show that $\dfrac{3}{4} = \dfrac{6}{8}$.

5. Illustrate that zero is not the identity element for subtraction.

6. Complete each of the sentences below by writing the correct numeral in the frame or frames.

(a) $\square + 3 = 3$.

(b) $4 \times \square = 4$.

(c) $\dfrac{2}{3} \times \dfrac{\square}{\square} = \dfrac{8}{12}$.

(d) $\dfrac{4}{5} \times \dfrac{2}{\square} = \dfrac{8}{\triangle}$.

(e) $0 + 3 = \square$.

(f) $5 + (3 - 3) = 8 - \square$.

(g) $5 - \square = 5$.

(h) $5 \div \triangle = 5$.

(i) $\dfrac{3}{3} \times \dfrac{2}{3} = 1 \times \dfrac{\triangle}{\square}$.

(j) $\dfrac{5}{6} + 0 = \square$.

(k) $\dfrac{2}{5} \times \square = \dfrac{2}{5}$.

(l) $3 \times \square = \square \times 3$.

THE COMMUTATIVE PROPERTY

Our number system is commutative for addition because the sum of any two numbers is the same regardless of the order in which they are added. This property can be stated more concisely in algebraic terms: For every x and y in our system of numbers:

$$x + y = y + x.$$

By comparing the two given statements, we see why properties of number systems are frequently stated with algebraic symbolism rather than in purely verbal form. Modern programs use more algebraic language than do traditional programs, although the difference between the newer and older programs is not as apparent at the elementary level as at the secondary level.

All the number systems of elementary mathematics are commutative for addition and multiplication but not for subtraction and division.

The commutative property of number systems is simple enough to be understood by pupils in the lower elementary grades and important enough to be referred to at all levels of mathematics. Pupils in the elementary grades should recognize the commutative property as a nonverbal pattern. The teacher may refer to it by name, but pupils should not be required to do so.

THE ASSOCIATIVE PROPERTY

The associative property of our number system for addition and multiplication can be stated as follows: For all x, y, and z in our number system:

$$(x + y) + z = x + (y + z)$$
$$x(yz) = (xy)z$$

The associative property is important because of the *binary* nature of addition and multiplication.[5] These two operations are binary because each operation can be performed on only two numbers at a time.

When more than two numbers are to be added, the binary nature of addition requires that the operation first be performed on two numbers. The associative property of addition states that when three numbers are to be added, the result of adding the sum of the first and second numbers to the third number is the same as adding the first number to the sum of the second and third numbers. A similar statement can be made for multiplication.

Exercise 14.5

1. Rename $3 + 4$ using the commutative property.

2. Rename $3 + (4 - 1)$ using only the commutative property.

3. Rename $3 + (4 + 1)$ in two different ways by using only the commutative property.

4. How can understanding the commutative property reduce the memory load for addition and multiplication facts?

The associative property makes it easy to handle addition combinations with sums greater than 10. Using the associative property, we can rename the second addend to create an addend that, when added to the first number of the addition example, has a sum of 10. Then it is easy to find the sum of the combination.

1. Example: $7 + 5 = \square$

2. Question: $7 + \square = 10$; Answer 3

3. So rename the 5 as $3 + 2$

4. Now the example is: $7 + (3 + 2) = \square$

5. Apply the associative property: $7 + (3 + 2) = (7 + 3) + 2 = 10 + 2 = 12$.

5. Subtraction and division are also binary operations, but do not have the associative or commutative property, as illustrated by the following counterexamples:

$6 - 5 \neq 5 - 6$

$(6 - 3) - 2 \neq 6 - (3 - 2)$

$6 \div 2 \neq 2 \div 6$

$(8 \div 4) \div 2 \neq 8 \div (4 \div 2)$

ACTIVITIES

The following is a list of some useful activities involving the associative and commutative properties.

1. Ask students to rename $2 + 3$. A response of 5 is natural and correct at any grade level, but with teacher guidance the response of $3 + 2$ should be common as early as grade 1. Answers of $(1 + 1) + 3$ and $2 + (2 + 1)$ should also be obtained by first-grade pupils.

Pupils should be able to rename $76 + 234$ as $234 + 76$ long before they can determine the sum of 310. Exercises of this nature help pupils learn the basic pattern of the commutative property long before a name is attached to it. When a pattern is understood, it is much easier to give it a name.

2. Ask the class to rename $4 + (6 + 1)$. Again, $4 + 7$ and 11 are correct, but examples of this type should be given often enough so that $(4 + 6) + 1$ will also be given. In a renaming activity any correct answer should be accepted, but pupils should be encouraged to give others until the name or numeral desired by the teacher is obtained. If the desired answer is not given in a reasonable time, the teacher should give the answer and then immediately give several similar examples to see if the class understands the idea involved. Renaming sessions should be frequent and brief and should usually have a specific goal.

3. Both of the stated activities can be repeated with examples such as 3×4 and $4 \times (5 \times 3)$ when the multiplication concept has been introduced.

4. The following exercise involves pupil recognition of an equation as true or false. The correct answers are given in parentheses.

$5 - 3 = 3 - 5$	(False)
$3 \times 5 = 5 \times 3$	(True)
$3(4 + 5) = 3 \times 4 + 5$	(False)
$32 \times 25 = 8 \times (4 \times 25)$	(True)
$4 \times (7 \times 25) = (4 \times 25) \times 7$	(True)
$89 + 43 = (89 + 11) + 32$	(True)

A teacher should use similar examples and discuss why they are *true* or *false* in terms of the properties of the number systems under discussion.

Exercise 14.6

1. Which of the following words is frequently used to describe the application of the associative property?
   (a) Change   (b) Regroup   (c) Rearrange

2. Rename by applying the associative property: $2 + (8 + 7)$.

3. Give one property for each of the following statements: (A) Commutative; (B) Associative; (C) Commutative and associative:
   (a) $2 + 3 = 3 + 2$
   (b) $4 + (5 + 7) = 4 + (7 + 5)$
   (c) $4 + (5 + 7) = (4 + 5) + 7$
   (d) $4 + (5 + 7) = (7 + 5) + 4$
   (e) $4 + (5 + 7) = (4 + 7) + 5$

4. Complete the sentences below by writing the correct answer in each of the frames. Indicate the property illustrated in each sentence:
   (a) $2 + (3 + 5) = 2 + (\square + 3)$ Property _____

   (b) $3 + (4 + \triangle) = (4 + 0) + 3$ Property _____

   (c) $(2 + 5) + \square = 2 + (5 + 3)$ Property _____

   (d) $(2 + 7) + 8 = (2 + 8) + \square$ Property _____

The *commutative* property is probably learned most readily on a nonverbal level by most children. The *associative* property is more subtle and not learned as easily. Two words that are useful in dealing with these two properties are *rearrange* and *regroup*. Rearranging can apply to only the commutative property (changing the order of the addends or factors) or both the commutative and associative properties (changing both the order and the grouping of the addends or factors). For example, if 2 + 3 is rearranged as 3 + 2, only the commutative property is involved. If 7 + 4 + 6 is rearranged as 4 + 6 + 7, both the associative and the commutative properties are involved. Although this distinction can and should be made later in the elementary grades, possibly the most useful feature during the early stages of learning the associative and commutative properties is the combined effect that: *Addends (or factors) can be rearranged and regrouped in any manner without changing the sum (or product).*

Pupils should learn quickly that rearranging and regrouping *does* affect the answer in subtraction and division examples, as seen in the following examples:

5 − 4 is not equal to 4 − 5
6 ÷ 2 is not equal to 2 ÷ 6
(6 − 4) − 2 is not equal to 6 − (4 − 2)
(6 ÷ 4) ÷ 2 is not equal to 6 ÷ (4 ÷ 2)

The four operations are binary. As the following example illustrates, this fact is useful in dealing with the order of operations:

(1) 3 + 4 × 2
(2) 3 + 4 ÷ 2

When no parentheses are used, many students solve (1) as 3 + 4 = 7, 7 × 2 = 14. This answer is incorrect because of the universal convention that in an expression involving both addition (or subtraction) and multiplication (or division), multiplication (or division) is done before addition (or subtraction).

Expressions with more than two operations rarely occur in the elementary textbooks. When they do, parentheses should be used to remove any ambiguity.

When dealing with expressions that involve more than two numbers, pupils should recognize that the choice of the numbers used to start the series of operations can affect the results.

THE DISTRIBUTIVE PROPERTY

The associative and commutative properties are defined in terms of a set of numbers and *one* binary operation. Our number system is commutative with respect to addition and not for subtraction. The distributive property is defined in terms of a set of numbers and *two* operations. The distributive property is the only property discussed in this chapter that is defined in terms of two operations.

The distributive property—of multiplication over addition for our number system—can be defined as follows: For all x, y, and z in our number system, $x(y + z) = xy + xz$.

The distributive property indicates that 3(4 + 5) can be renamed as (3 × 4) + (3 × 5). There are many other names for the number represented by 3(4 + 5), including 3 × 9. The distributive property indicates that if multiplication is to be performed before addition in 3(4 + 5), the *multiplication must be distributed over both addends.*

Pupils should be reminded periodically that in (3 × 4) + (3 × 5) the multiplication is to be performed before the addition.

Multiplication is also distributive over subtraction, but this fact is not usually stated in the definition of the distributive property. It can be stated: for all x, y, and z in our number system, $x(y − z) = (xy) − (xz)$. For example:

$$3 \times (9 − 2) = (3 \times 9) − (3 \times 2)$$
$$= 27 − 6 = 21$$

Worked another way:

$$3 \times (9 − 2) = 3 \times 7 = 21$$

A very good visual way to show the distributive property of multiplication over addition is with an *array*. For example, the number fact 2 × 3 = ? can be visualized in an array as:

• • •
• • •

Likewise, the number array 5 × 8 can be shown visually as:

```
• • • • • • • •
• • • • • • • •
• • • • • • • •
• • • • • • • •
• • • • • • • •
```

Then 8 can be renamed as 4 + 4 and the array for 5 (4 + 4) can be shown as:

```
• • • • x x x x
• • • • x x x x
• • • • x x x x
• • • • x x x x
• • • • x x x x
```

This technique enables one to take a difficult number combination and break it into two easier number facts; in this case (5 × 4) + (5 × 4) = 20 + 20 = 40.

ACTIVITIES

The following are some typical activities that can help pupils obtain a better understanding of the distributive property.

1. Ask pupils to rename 4(5 + 10). Continue the activity until (4 × 5) + (4 × 10) is obtained. If it is necessary to give the answer, use several other examples to be certain that the basic pattern is understood. Talk about multiplying each addend or distributing the multiplication over both addends.

2. The activity in item 1 can be performed before pupils know the name of the distributive property. After pupils have learned this property by name, the following activity, and others like it, can be introduced. Ask pupils to rename the following using the distributive property. Correct answers are given in parentheses.

4(10 + 7)	(4 × 10) + (4 × 7)
4 × 23	(4 × 20) + (4 × 3)
5 × 8	(5 × 5) + (5 × 3)

Other answers are possible.

3. When pupils learn that multiplication is also distributive with respect to subtraction, they can rename 7(30 − 2) as 7 × 30 − 7 × 2. This can be done beneficially both before and after pupils have learned the meaning of the word *distributive*.

4. Pupils should learn that the expression 7(3 + 7) can be solved most easily as 7 × 10, while for most people 7(20 − 1) can be solved most readily if renamed (7 × 20) − (7 × 1). A list similar to the following can be given and pupils asked whether to add (subtract) or multiply first. Keep in mind that this is a subjective question and different pupils may give different answers, as a result of their attitudes and skills. Pupil disagreements that provoke discussions should be encouraged.

10(8 + 9)

Adding first is easier (comparing two choices), but multiplying first is not much more difficult.

17(4 + 6)

Adding first is shorter.

11(40 − 1)

Multiplying first is probably easier for most pupils.

5. If $a = b$, the renaming concept allows a to be renamed as b or b to be renamed as a. Therefore, since 3(4 + 5) = (3 × 4) + (3 × 5), the left-hand member of the equation can be renamed as (3 × 4) + (3 × 5) or the right-hand member renamed as 3(4 + 5). Pupils will tend not to do the latter renaming without guidance. The following situations illustrate the advantage of this renaming:

(7 × 12) + (7 × 8)
Rename as 7(12 + 8) or 7 × 20

$(\frac{1}{4} \times 49) + (\frac{1}{4} \times 51)$

Rename as $\frac{1}{4}(49 + 51)$ or $\frac{1}{4} \times 100$

The value of this activity cannot be over-emphasized.

CLOSURE

The final property to be discussed is closure. The whole numbers are closed with respect to addition because the sum of two whole numbers is always a whole number. The whole numbers are not closed with re-spect to subtraction because the difference $6 - 8$ is not a whole number.

The whole numbers are closed with re-spect to multiplication but not with respect to division since $2 \div 3$ is not a whole num-ber. One counterexample is sufficient to prove that a set of numbers is not closed for a given operation.

The closure property has very few direct applications, but understanding this con-cept helps one gain a knowledge of the de-velopment of number systems.

Exercise 14.7

1. What is the most important and apparent difference between the dis-tributive property and the associative and commutative properties?

2. Why is it not appropriate to say that the operation of addition is dis-tributive?

3. Rename each of the following using the distributive property:
   (a) $3(4 + 5)$
   (b) $(4 \times 5) + (4 \times 15)$
   (c) $(2 \times \frac{1}{7}) + (3 \times \frac{1}{7})$
   (d) $2x + 3x$

4. Use the distributive property of multiplication over subtraction to re-name $(18 \times \frac{1}{7}) - (4 \times \frac{1}{7})$.

5. To illustrate the distributive property of multiplication over addition for the example $3(4 + 5)$, we multiply each of the terms in parenthe-ses by 3 and then add the results. Use the expression $3 + 4 \times 5$ to show that addition is not distributive over multiplication.

6. Using the expressions $(8 - 4) \div 2$ and $2 \div (8 - 4)$, show that the right-hand distributive property of division over subtraction applies, but not the left-hand, because division is not commutative.

7. Complete the open sentences below by writing the correct numerals in the frames:
   (a) $(2 \times 3) + (2 \times 4) = 2(3 + \square)$.
   (b) $3(4 + 5) = 3 \times 4 + \triangle \times 5$.
   (c) $(8 \times \frac{1}{7}) - (5 \times \frac{1}{7}) = \square \times \frac{1}{7}$.

8. Just as the frame $\square$ holds a place for a numeral, the circle $\bigcirc$ is fre-quently used to hold a place for an operation. For example, the state-ment $2 \bigcirc 3 = 6$ becomes a true statement when the symbol for mul-

tiplication is placed in the circle. Write a symbol for multiplication, division, addition, or subtraction in each of the following circles so that the sentence will be true:

(a) $2(3 + 4) = 2 \bigcirc (3 + 4)$.
(b) $4(3 \bigcirc 5) = (4 \times 3) + (4 \times 5)$.
(c) $5(3 + 6) = (5 \bigcirc 3) + (5 \bigcirc 6)$.
(d) $7(8 - 5) = (7 \times 8) \bigcirc (7 \times 5)$.

9. The parentheses in $(2 \times 3) + (2 \times 5)$ are sometimes omitted because of the almost universal convention that multiplication and division are performed before addition and subtraction in expressions of this type. Place parentheses in each of the following expressions so that a person not familiar with the order of operations will not make an error:

(a) $3 \times 5 + 2$ (f) $5 \times 7 - 5 \times 2$
(b) $4 + 3 \times 4$ (g) $7 - 4 \div 2$
(c) $9 - 2 \times 3$ (h) $6 \div 2 + 6 \div 3$
(d) $8 \div 4 + 2$ (i) $6 \times 2 - 6 \div 3$
(e) $2 \times 3 + 2 \times 4$ (j) $12 \times 3 - 8 + 5$

Kinds of Numbers in the Real Number System

The Natural Numbers

The natural numbers, also called the *counting numbers*, were the first to be discovered by any civilization. The natural numbers are 1, 2, 3, 4, 5, . . . Figure 14.2 presents a graph of the natural numbers.

The properties of natural numbers are such that addition and multiplication can always be performed with the set of natural numbers and yield a natural number answer. However, that subtraction and division cannot always be performed. The difference $2 - 6$ and the quotient $2 \div 6$ do not exist in the set of natural numbers. In traditional programs pupils were frequently told that it was impossible to subtract 6 from 2. In a modern program pupils are told that 6

cannot be subtracted from 2 in the set of natural numbers (the subtraction is always possible in the set of integers).

The natural numbers are more than adequate to meet the needs of a primitive civilization. These numbers even serve the everyday needs of somewhat advanced civilizations. The Roman system of numeration is a set of numerals representing the natural numbers. Since 0 is not involved, this system met the needs of Roman merchants (with the help of an abacus or similar device).

When a civilization begins to advance technically the natural numbers quickly become inadequate. At this point a resourceful civilization extends the number system. The next logical developments are *whole numbers* and *integers*.

The Whole Numbers

The *whole numbers* include the natural numbers plus zero. Zero was first introduced by the Hindus as a place holder in a numeral. Its name comes from the Arabic

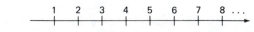

Figure 14.2
Counting Numbers

word *sifr,* which means "vacant." Later zero was considered a whole number.

The Integers

The *integers* are numbers as:

$$\ldots\ ^-3,\ ^-2,\ ^-1,\ 0,\ ^+1,\ ^+2,\ ^+3,\ \ldots$$

Figure 14.3 presents a graph of the integers.

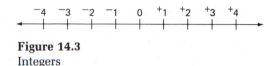

Figure 14.3
Integers

Every integer has an inverse element for addition. Pairs of inverse numbers are shown on the graph in Figure 14.4.

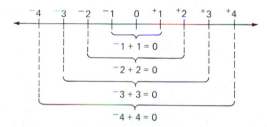

Figure 14.4

The mathematical consequence of the existence of inverses for addition is that the integers are now closed with respect to subtraction. The difference $2 - 6$ can be translated into the sum $2 + {}^-6$ or $^-4$. The difference $2 - {}^-6$ can be translated into the sum $2 + 6$, or 8.

The integers are not much more useful for everyday purposes than are the natural numbers. Negative numbers have relatively few everyday applications. They are useful in business for representing profit and loss, and in reading temperature and changes in altitude.

From a mathematical standpoint, the major deficiency of the integers is that division

cannot always be performed, since $2 \div 6$ is not an integer. This fact provides the basis for the next logical progression: to the rational numbers.

The Rational Numbers

The set of rational numbers includes $^-\frac{3}{4}$, $^-\frac{1}{2}$, 0, $\frac{2}{3}$, 1, $^{17}\!/_3$, 203. Figure 14.5 presents a graph of the set of rational numbers.

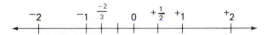

It is not possible to label all the points on the graph to make clear which numbers do and which do not belong to the graph.

Figure 14.5

It is not possible to define natural numbers or integers suitably for elementary pupils. A *rational number* can be defined as the quotient of two integers with the divisor not equal to 0. In everyday language, rational numbers are known as *fractions.*

Listing some typical rational numbers, as was done above, is somewhat misleading in terms of suggesting the range of the set. For example, the number $^{17}\!/_3$ does not make it clear that $^{234}\!/_{418}$ is also a rational number.

Also, the graph of the rational numbers is deceptive. It appears to be a complete line because rational numbers are so "close" together (dense) that the physical points representing these numbers merge to make an apparently continuous line. The graph of the rational numbers is actually full of "holes." One "hole" is at the point $\sqrt{2}$. The proof that $\sqrt{2}$ is not rational is now included in many secondary textbooks, as well as in those designed for elementary school teachers.

Every rational number except 0 has an inverse for multiplication. Thus the rational numbers are closed with respect to division, except for division by 0. The graph in Figure 14.6 indicates some pairs of inverses for multiplication.

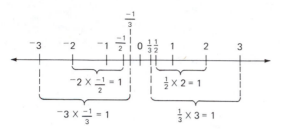

Figure 14.6

The rational numbers are adequate to meet almost all the everyday needs of individuals and businesses in modern society, but these numbers do not suffice for many scientific and technical needs. Since $\sqrt{2}$ is not a rational number, it is not possible to find a rational number to describe the length of the hypotenuse of a right triangle whose other two sides are equal to 1, as shown in Figure 14.7. This fact leads to the next extension, *the real numbers*.

Figure 14.7

The Real Numbers

The *real numbers* include all the rational numbers (and therefore all the integers and natural numbers). A real number that is not rational, such as $\sqrt{2}$, is an *irrational number*. The real numbers consist of the *rational numbers* and the *irrational numbers*. Typical real numbers are $^-3$, $^-\sqrt{2}$, $^-\frac{1}{2}$, 0, 1, $\sqrt{2}$, 7, $^{18}/_7$.

The real numbers are closed with respect to addition, subtraction, multiplication, and division (except for division by 0). The op-

eration of square root is possible for all *positive* reals. The operation of square root of a negative real does not yield a real number. Thus, some operations are still not possible in the reals.

The real numbers are adequate to meet most modern technical and industrial needs. For some scientific purposes, however, real numbers are insufficient.

The Complex Numbers

Complex numbers are of the form $a + bi$ where $i = \sqrt{^-1}$ and a and b are real numbers. The graph of the complex numbers covers the entire plane. The complex numbers include the real numbers (and therefore the rationals, integers, and naturals). Typical complex numbers are -13, $\sqrt{^-1}$, $2 + \sqrt{^-1}$, 0, $\sqrt{7}$, $^-5$, $+ \sqrt{^-13}$.

It is possible to find the square root of any complex number, but inequalities do not always make sense in this system. For example, it is not possible to decide consistently whether $3 - 2i$ is greater or less than $2 + 3i$.

The set of complex numbers is the most complete number system that has thus far been devised. Complex numbers have practical uses in describing the properties of electricity, as well as many important theoretical applications.

Summary

Our number system evolved over many centuries and is now a major component of our cultural heritage. Understanding how to use addition, subtraction, multiplication, and division in problem solving is a basic requirement for every educated person in today's technological society. The ready availability of calculators and computers makes it more important than ever to understand concepts associated with these operations. It is less important today to be able to compute with pencil-and-paper because individuals in business, industry, and science cannot afford the time required for most paper-and-pencil computation. Careless and inaccurate computation are just as undesirable as ever.

Various civilizations invented different systems of numeration, but the Hindu–Arabic system is now universal because the use of zero as a place holder enables this system to be used for efficient paper-and-pencil computation. The Roman system of numeration is still in use for specialized display and outlines but not for computation. Before the Hindu–Arabic system replaced previous systems, computation was performed on an abacus or its equivalent. Current computing devices usually perform computation in the binary system of numeration but display results in our base-ten system.

In the 1960s it was popular for a time to be very precise in the distinction between number and numeral, until it was realized that this practice was often more confusing than helpful. Current practice avoids referring to this distinction unless it clarifies the concept under discussion. The renaming process uses this distinction in a useful way without specifically referring to number or numeral. The key idea is that each number has many numerals and that it is important to realize which numeral to use for a specific purpose. The number one-half can be represented by many numerals, among them .5, ½, and ²⁄₄. The numerals .5 and ½ are considered more appropriate than ²⁄₄ for a final answer, but the latter is required if the number is to be added to ¾.

The growth of our number system occurred to meet the requirements of industry and science as our knowledge and technology developed. An ordinary citizen usually has no need for complex numbers but would be loath to give up many of the benefits that the use of these numbers has given to society.

Exercise 14.8

1. Identify the property used to rename each of the following numbers.
    (a) $3 + 6 = 6 + 3$
    (b) $4 = 4 + 0$
    (c) $5 \times 3 = 3 \times 5$
    (d) $3 = 3 \times 1$
    (e) $23 = 3 + 20$
    (f) $4 \times \dfrac{1}{4} = 1$
    (g) $3(30 + 2) = (3 \times 30) + (3 \times 2)$
    (h) $50 = 10 \times 5$
    (i) $99 + 18 = (99 + 1) + 17$
    (j) $28 \times 25 = 7(4 \times 25)$
    (k) $^{+}3 + {}^{-}3 = 0$

2. Indicate which of the following statements are true for all replacements of the variable.
    (a) $\square + 3 = (\square + 2) + 1$
    (b) $3(1 + \square) = 3 + 3 \times \square$
    (c) $3 \times \square = \square + 2$
    (d) $8 \times \square = 2 \times (4 \times \square)$
    (e) $4 \div 2 = \square$

(f) $\Box \div 3 = 3 \div \Box$
(g) $4 + \Box = 2 - \Box$
(h) $4 \times \Box = \Box \times 4$

3. List the property illustrated in each part of Problem 2 that is true for all replacements of the variable.

4. Complete each of the following statements by writing the correct numeral in each frame.

(a) $2 \div 3 = 2 \times \Box$

(b) $3 \div \dfrac{3}{4} = 3 \times \Box$

(c) $4 \times \dfrac{1}{2} = 4 \div \Box$

(d) $3 + {}^{-}2 = 3 - \Box$

(e) $5 - 2 = 5 + \Box$

(f) $2 + \Box = 0$

Selected Readings

Bennett, Albert B., Jr., and Leonard T. Nelson. *Mathematics: An Informal Approach*, 2nd ed. Needham Heights, MA: Allyn & Bacon, 1985.

Bettinger, Marion L. and Mervin L. Kudy. *Essential Mathematics*. Reading, MA: Addison-Wesley, 1984.

Eves, Howard. *An Introduction to the History of Mathematics*, 4th ed. New York: Holt, Rinehart and Winston, 1976. Pp. 7–43.

Heintz, Ruth. *Mathematics for Elementary Teachers: A Content Approach*. Reading, MA: Addison-Wesley, 1980.

Laycock, Mary, and Gene Watson. *The Fabric of Mathematics: A Resource Book for Teachers*. Hayward, CA: Activity Resources Company, 1975.

Miller, Charles D., and Vern E. Heeren. *Mathematical Ideas*, 3rd ed. Glenview, IL: Scott, Foresman, 1978. Chapter 3.

Willerding, Margaret F. *Elementary Mathematics: Its Structure and Concepts*, 2nd ed. New York: Wiley, 1970. Chapters 3 and 4.

Measurement: Metric and U.S. Customary Systems

ACHIEVEMENT GOALS

After studying this chapter, you should be able to:

1. Enumerate the features of the Metric Conversion Act of 1975 and the Omnibus Trade Bill of 1988.

2. Enumerate the essential features of the U.S. Customary system of measurement, formerly known as the English system.

3. Enumerate the essential features of the metric system, including SI units.

4. List major objectives for teaching measurement in the primary and upper grades.

5. Describe various approaches to teaching measurement in the elementary school.

6. Draw up plans to provide measurement activities, particularly for (a) length, (b) mass (weight), (c) capacity, and (d) temperature.

VOCABULARY

These terms are defined or illustrated in the Glossary.

Accuracy in
  measurement
Centi-
Degree Celsius
Density
Gram
Kilo-
Liter

Mass
Meter
Milli-
Nonstandard units
Precision
SI metric units
Standard units

The language of mathematics expresses itself in three different ways: by *counting, estimating,* and *measuring.* We count 12 pupils in a group; this is an exact number. A newspaper reporter estimates the attendance at a sports event to be 75,000. If the stadium seats 75,000 and the stadium is full, the estimate is good. If the stadium holds 80,000 and it is not full, the estimate may be correct to the nearest thousand. Some boys measure a distance of 60 feet between two bases for a softball diamond. The accuracy of this measure depends upon the measuring instrument used and how careful the boys are in using the instrument. There is always an error in measurement.

In this chapter we deal with measurement. Two systems of measurement are known as the *International Metric System* and the *U.S. Customary System.* Although it has been legal in the United States to use metric measures since 1866, the general public has resisted changing from the U.S. Customary System because people have become so accustomed to using it over the years. The Omnibus Trade and Competitiveness Act of 1988 directs government agencies to convert to the metric system by 1992, so it is just a matter of time until the United States will convert to the metric system. However, the U.S. Customary units of measure will continue to be used for a long time. Elementary pupils must consequently learn both systems.

The Metric Conversion Act of 1975

On December 23, 1975, the Metric Conversion Act of 1975 (PL 94–1680) became law. It declared that the policy of the United States shall be to "coordinate and plan . . . the voluntary conversion to the metric system." The act established a seventeen-member U.S. metric board to set overall policy for converting to metric. It charged the Secretary of Commerce with the responsibility of interpreting or modifying metric stan-

dards. It was the intention of the government to be converted to metric by 1985. This did not happen for several reasons.

First, although the seventeen-member metric board was given a $3-million annual budget and had more than 100 employees, it ran into many obstacles because of the "voluntary" aspect of the Metric Conversion Act. A few years later the board's funds were cut off and the responsibilities of guiding the nation toward metrication was turned over to the Office of Metric programs within the Commerce Department.

Second, there was a general revolt against metrication by the United States public. When Shell Oil spent more than $2 million converting thousands of gasoline stations to metric, the company found that the general public would not buy its products in liters, so the company was forced to change back to selling gasoline by the gallon.

Third, small manufacturers found it very expensive to change equipment and dies to produce new metric sizes that probably won't be accepted by the U.S. consumer.

Fourth, teachers, who were themselves uncertain about metric measurements, were happy to keep on teaching the U.S. Customary System of measurement, knowing they would have the support of most parents.

The Omnibus Trade Bill of 1988

On August 23, 1988, the Omnibus Trade and Competitiveness Act of 1988 became law. As a part of the Omnibus Trade Act, the Metric Conversion Act of 1975 was revised. The new law stipulated that the federal government would assist industry and small business as they voluntarily convert to the metric system of measurement. It also designated the metric system of measurement as the preferred system of weights and measures for United States trade and commerce. The act directed each federal agency to be using the metric system of measurement in its procurements, grants, and other business-related activities insofar as possible by the end of the fiscal year 1992.

During the last decade the United States has been gradually converting to the metric system. Almost all American cars are now built to metric specifications. Most other companies have followed suit. Following the Department of Commerce order, all wine and liquor sold in the United States is packaged in metric units. The Defense Department has set a policy of using metric for all new development. Almost all goods sold in the food markets are marked in both U.S. Customary and metric units. Many state highway signs show both miles and kilometers. In most states public school children must be instructed in metric measure.

There is still much to be done before the United States public accepts and willingly uses the metric system. The key to change is for pupils in the elementary school to learn the metric system. Teachers must know and understand the metric system and be able to teach metrics to children in a meaningful, interesting, and effective way, and be able to relate metric units to the U.S. Customary system.

Origins of Measurement Systems

In early times measurement was indefinite and crude. Just as the decimal system of numeration grew out of the use of the fingers of the hand, measures of various kinds were derived from natural events, parts of the body, and units that were easy to manage and understand. The movements of the stars and planets provided an easy way to *reckon time*. A day was the time that elapsed from sunrise to sunrise, a month the time between a certain phase of the moon and its recurrence, and a year the time it took the sun to pass through successive changes from one position in the heavens back to the same position.

The length of objects was first measured by using parts of the human body. A *cubit* was equal to the length of the arm from the middle finger to the bend of the elbow. A *foot* was the length of a real foot—in eighth-century Rome, Charlemagne's foot. In the eleventh century, King Henry I of England established the *yard* as the distance from his nose to the end of his outstretched hand.

The human stride was a convenient way of measuring distances. People measured short distances by the number of steps taken to cover them. Longer distances were described by the number of days it took to make a journey.

Capacity was measured with bowls and cups, and mass was determined by balancing with grains of wheat or barley. For thousands of years, barter was the means of exchange, and so definite units of value were not needed. The use of these nonstandard units made trading difficult.

Development of Standard Units

Measurement is the process by which a *unit of measure* is compared with the thing being measured. A *standard unit* of measure is needed to make measurements consistent that are done by different individuals. Standard units of measure were established by law by governments throughout the world. In the United States, the U.S. Bureau of Standards is the official agency that regulates and maintains standard units of measure.

Before trade and industry were widespread there was little concern that methods and units of measure were nonstandard. However, when people formed groups to conduct business, industry, and construction, and began to trade, there came a need for *standard units* with a common meaning. The English System of Weights and Measures, adopted by the United States during the eighteenth century, had evolved in Britain and was used throughout the world.

Origins of the Metric System

A scientific report made in 1790 to the French National Assembly proposed a decimal system of money, weights, and measures. In 1791 the Academy of Sciences designated the standard of length as one ten-millionth of the distance from the Equator to the North Pole, running through Paris. This distance was to be determined by first measuring the meridian arc from near Dunkirk on the English Channel to Barcelona on the Mediterranean, in Spain. From this measured distance, the length of one ten-millionth of a quarter meridian could be calculated.

In addition to the standard *meter*, the French Academy created a standard unit of *mass* equal to a cubic decimeter (1000 cubic centimeters) of distilled water lowered to the temperature of 4°C. The new standard was called a *kilogram*, and a platinum-iridium cylindrical bar was constructed with a height and a diameter of 3.9 centimeters. The standard for capacity later became the cubic decimeter, which was named *liter*. The metric system was designed specifically to make measurement easier by creating a system, rather than a collection, of units of measure.

Essential Features of the Metric System

The metric system is superior to all other previous systems of weights and measures for several reasons. First, the system has a base of ten. That is, each basic unit is subdivided into powers of ten. The ratio between consecutive units of the metric system is the same as the decimal ratio of consecutive places in our number system. Computation with metric units is much easier because decimals are used rather than "denominate" numbers and common fractions.

Second, the basic units of length, mass, and capacity are consistently related to each other. Once the meter was standardized, it was subdivided into ten parts (each called a decimeter), 100 parts (centimeters), and 1000 parts (millimeters). The basic unit of mass is the kilogram, which is the mass of a decimeter cube (10 centimeters on each edge) filled with distilled water at a temperature of 4°C. Capacity is the amount of substance it takes to fill a decimeter cube, and its basic unit is the *liter*.

Third, the names of the consecutive units are consistent for all of the units of metric measure. The same prefixes are used for subdivisions of every unit and for the multiples of ten of every unit. (For purposes of discussing prefixes, the gram will be used as the basic name of mass, even though the basic standard is the kilogram.) The prefix for any subdivision of a metric unit that is divided into 1000 parts is *milli*—as in millimeter, milliliter, and milligram. Each basic metric unit multiplied times 1000 has the prefix *kilo*, as in kilometer, kiloliter, and kilogram. See Table 15.1 for the prefixes commonly taught in the elementary school.

Fourth, the standards of the metric system are uniform throughout the world, a uniformity that is made possible by the International Bureau of Weights and Measures under the aegis of the General Conference on Weights and Measures, with delegates from forty-three nations. All countries that use the metric system are able to trade manufactured articles with consistent measurements.

International System of Metric Units (SI)

Metric measurement refers to the *International System of Units* (SI), known as the modernized metric system, as approved by the General Conference on Weights and Measures held in Paris in 1960. This system includes seven basic SI units—meter, kilo-

Table 15.1 SI Prefixes Commonly Taught in Elementary Schools

Factor	Prefix	Symbol	Pronunciation
$1\ 000\ 000 = 10^6$	mega	M	meg-a-
$1\ 000 = 10^3$	kilo	k	kill-o-
$100 = 10^2$	hecto	h	hec-toe-
$10 = 10^1$	deka	da	deck-a-
$1 = 10^0$	(basic unit)		
$0.1 = 10^{-1}$	deci	d	dess-ie-
$0.01 = 10^{-2}$	centi	c	sen-ta-
$0.001 = 10^{-3}$	milli	m	mill-ie-
$0.000\ 001 = 10^{-6}$	micro	μ	mi-cro

Note: Prefixes 10^1 to 10^6 are derived from Greek words; prefixes 10^{-1} to 10^{-6} are derived from Latin words.

gram, second, ampere, kelvin, mole, and candela—two supplementary SI units—radian, steradian—and almost sixty derived SI units with special names.

Metric Rules

There are precise rules for using SI metric symbols. Metric words for units of measure start with lower-case letters, except when the unit is taken from the name of a person, such as Celsius. The prefixes are pronounced with the accent on the first syllable, as in ki-lo-gram. The units for length and capacity are meter and liter.

Word names for SI basic units all begin with lower-case letters, and the letter symbol for each is a lower-case letter, except for two units—K (kelvin) and A (ampere), as shown in Table 15.2, page 320.

When used as words, the prefixes to metric SI units are all lower-case letters. The letter designations are capitalized for prefixes denoting a million or more, and those less than a million are lower-case letters.

Prefixes can be used only in combination with names of units; it is correct to say 13 kilograms, but not 13 kilos.

The letter designations for metric units are not followed by a period except at the end of a sentence. The symbols for units are never pluralized; for example, 250 meters = 250 m, not 250 ms.

Large numbers should be divided into groups of three digits counting to the left or right of the decimal position, and these periods should be separated by a space, and not with a comma. A group of four digits may or may not be grouped. The numeral for "forty-six thousand two hundred thirty-five" is written as 46 235, rather than 46,235. For numbers less than one, a zero is written before the decimal point, such as 0.637, not .637. An exception is the case in which amounts of money are written on legal documents and checks. In these situations, each number period should be separated by a comma to avoid a space that can be filled with a digit.

Common fraction notation is not used in

Table 15.2 International System of Units (SI)

SI BASE UNITS

Physical Quantity	Unit	Symbol
length	meter	m
mass	kilogram	kg
time	second	s
electric current	ampere	A
thermodynamic temperature	kelvin	K
amount of substance	mole	mol
luminous intensity	candela	cd

Source: *Metric Units of Measure and Study Guide—SI* (Boulder, CO: U.S. Metric Association, 1976), pp. 10–11.

metric measurements. A measure of 25 centimeters, for example, should be in terms of meters, as 0.25 m, not as ¼ meter.

A space is left between the numeral and the metric letter symbol, as in 23 cm, not 23cm. In names or symbols for units with prefixes, no space is left between the letter for the prefix and the letter for the metric unit; for example, 46 milliliters is written as 46 mL, not 46 m L. The symbol for degree Celsius is °C with no space between ° and C. Temperature should be written as 22 °C not 22°C.

Metric measurements can be expressed in different degrees of precision. The smaller the measuring unit used, the more precise the measurement. The greatest possible error in a measure is ± 0.5 of the smallest unit used on the measuring instrument.

Approaches to Teaching Measurement in the Elementary School

There are three possible approaches to teaching measurement in the elementary school. First, teach the customary system as currently used in society, and then discuss the metric system as a secondary system. Second, teach the metric system as the primary system, and then cover the customary system. Third, teach only the metric system. State and local policies determine how a local district decides which approach is to be used. We recommend that elementary pupils be instructed in the measurement process using nonstandard, customary, and metric units. Reference should be made to customary measures in terms of how these units are used in daily life. Students in the upper grades should learn the metric system as the primary system of measurement, along with a study of how metric units and measurements relate to the most common customary units.

In the elementary school, there should be little emphasis on conversion from customary to metric units. Conversion from U.S. Customary to metric units is now practical with a calculator. To be able to convert within any system or from one system to another, a pupil must know two things: whether to divide or multiply and the conversion factor. Common sense should dictate that one needs more smaller units to measure a given quantity than larger units, meaning that multiplication is required. For example, most pupils know that 4 ft. = 4 × 12, or 48 inches. They can use this example as a guide telling them whether to multiply or divide in converting in other situations.

Calculators minimize computation, and so make conversion a practical and useful activity, provided that pupils are not required to memorize conversion factors. Also, this activity, when supplemented by conversion in the metric system, helps pupils recognize why the metric system is desirable. If calculators are not available, conversion should be done mostly by estimation, except where conversion factors are small whole numbers.

Measurement in the Primary Grades

Children learn about measurement by making measurements. Their first contact with measurement is in everyday life, with regard to time, length, capacity, weight (mass), and so on. Beginning at an early age, the customary system of measurement becomes part of their language—they drink a cupful of orange juice, weigh 46 pounds, walk a half-mile to school, and have recess at a quarter past ten. These and many other measurement terms are incidental but necessary aspects of a child's life.

The first contact most pupils have with the metric system is in school activities—often, in the development of concepts and skills in metric measurements. Any customary units of measurement that are included in the instructional program should be related to metric units and to everyday usage. Show pupils that the units present in daily life can be labeled with metric units.

The following is a list of the most common objectives in measurement for pupils in the primary grades (K–3). Children should be able to:

1. Use nonstandard units of measure to estimate and verify length, mass, capacity, and time.

2. Identify typical parts of the body, objects, and containers that measure approximately a meter, a centimeter, a gram, a kilogram, a liter, and so on.

3. Know and understand the relationships between units of measure, such as 100 cm = 1 m; 1000 g = 1 kg; and 1000 L = 1 kL.

4. Measure objects using standard units to a specified degree of accuracy, such as measuring a pencil to the nearest centimeter and to the nearest inch.

5. Tell time on the hour and half hour and know the days of the week and months of the year. The child should know how to read a digital clock.

6. Use words to describe variations of hot or cold and be able to read and record temperature readings in degrees Celsius.

Measurement in the Upper Grades

Pupils in the grades 4 to 6 should have had a variety of measurement experiences. They still need exploratory activities of actually measuring length and distance, capacity and volume, mass, and time. They should be expected to estimate measures and then measure to a certain degree of accuracy. Pupils at this level are introduced to structural aspects of metric measures at the symbolic level and can be expected to perform computations with metric measurements. They should be expected to investigate the history and science of both the metric and customary systems of measurement.

We recommend that metric measures be treated as the primary system of measurement in the upper grades. Because pupils will still come in contact with various aspects of the customary system, these units should be presented and pupils given the opportunity to build charts of relationships. They should not be expected to convert from metric to customary units except to build a relationships chart with the use of a calculator. Encourage pupils to find uses of metric measures in everyday life and in newspapers and magazines.

The following is a list of the most common objectives for teaching measurement to pupils in grades 4 to 6. Pupils should be able to do the following:

1. Given specific things to measure (length, capacity, mass), (a) select the appropriate unit of measure, (b) estimate the measurement, (c) measure to a specified degree of accuracy, and (d) calculate the difference between the estimate and the measure.

2. Given the basic units of meter, liter, and gram, understand the structure and relationships between the various prefixes for each unit and change a particular measure from one designation to another, such as from centimeters to meters, meters to kilometers, milliliters to liters, grams to kilograms, and grams to milligrams.

3. Understand and use metric symbols in writing metric measures.

4. Become proficient in calculating with metric units in problem-solving situations.

5. Be able to relate metric measures to customary measures by building and using an equivalents chart.

6. Become aware of the uses of metric measures in business and industry and in everyday life, and in other school subjects.[1]

---

1. See James E. Inskeep, Jr., "Teaching Measurement to Elementary School Children," in *Measurement in School Mathematics*, 1976 Yearbook (Reston, VA: National Council of Teachers of Mathematics, 1976), Chapter 4, pp. 60–86.

Measurement Activities Through the Grades

Measuring Length with Nonstandard Units

In the primary grades, pupils begin to measure, using nonstandard units, by a process of comparing and counting. Measuring units should be introduced through everyday usage that can be demonstrated with concrete materials. Let pupils choose their unit of measure—such as a paper clip, the width of a hand, or a drinking straw. Once the unit has been selected, various things can be measured by counting how many times the unit is contained in the thing being measured.

One of the basic problems in measurement a child faces is to discover that the length of an object does not change regardless of its position in space. Piaget called this property *conservation of length*. The unit of measure selected also must be constant.

Pupils also must learn to use the measuring unit. The unit must be placed at the end of the object to be measured and moved end to end until it reaches the other end of the object. Each move must be counted.

In addition, pupils must learn that the object measured may not contain the unit of measure an exact number of times. Young children will call this phenomenon "coming out uneven." The child will need to be directed first to count the whole number of times, and if the object measures a little bit but not a whole unit more, then just to report the measure the whole number of times plus "a little bit more."

Finally, pupils who measure the same object with different units of measure obviously will obtain different answers. The length of a table may be 29 straw lengths, or 35 hands wide, or 5 steps. This situation will lead pupils to conclude that to get the same number of units, the unit of measure being used needs to be the same length.

Laboratory Activities

To teach measurement with nonstandard units, provide laboratory activities and have the pupils measure different lengths with different units. Set up a table with several lengths of doweling (unmarked) measuring from 1 centimeter to 1 meter. Pick one piece of about average length and paint it a color, perhaps red. This rod is the *comparison unit*. On the left-hand side of the table, put a sign reading SHORTER THAN RED ROD and on the right-hand side a sign LONGER THAN RED ROD. The task for each child is to take each piece of doweling, compare it with the red rod, and place it on the appropriate side of the table. Children can work together in pairs, with one child estimating those that are shorter and the other estimating those that are longer. Then they can measure to find out if their guesses were correct.

A variation of this laboratory activity is to fill the table with various objects of different length, such as chalk, pencils, erasers, string, sticks, paper strips, and so on. The reference unit could be something picked by the child, such as the "width of a hand," or "distance between tips of two outstretched adjacent fingers."

Measuring Length with Standard Units

Beginning at the third-grade level, children learn to measure with *standard units* "to the nearest unit." Upper-grade pupils need to learn to select appropriate units to measure different lengths; they need to learn to make estimates before measuring; and they need to develop a sense of length. They should measure and label various things in the classroom, such as tabletops, books, and desks.

Beginning experiences with measuring long distances around the school should include measuring distances from one place to another and putting up signs. For example, put up a sign to indicate a point 55 METERS TO CAFETERIA, or about 60 yards. To emphasize metric measures distances along a length of the playground could be marked off in lengths of 10 meters from 0 to 1000 meters or 1 kilometer, if the school yard is large enough. Pupils should be aware that metric measures are used in the Olympic games. The distances to the walls on a baseball field should be marked in meters. You might mark off other distances for games and races in meters, or measure the "ball throw" in meters, and so on.

Upper-grade pupils should collect model objects that have certain measurements.

A dime measures 1 millimeter thick.

The diameter of a nickel is 2 centimeters.

A large paper clip is 1 centimeter wide.

A meter is the height of the teacher's chair.

To measure length, the classroom should be equipped with: (a) 30-cm rulers (about a foot long), (b) meter sticks, and (c) trundle wheels for measuring longer distances. Rulers should also be marked in millimeters for measuring very small objects.

Have pupils fill out a special chart, "My measurements in metrics." Have them record their height in centimeters, mass (weight) in kilograms, head size in millimeters, length of foot in centimeters, and the like. (see Exercise 15.1, page 325.)

TEACHING THE MEANING OF PREFIXES

The prefixes used most often to measure length and distances are, for very short lengths, the millimeter and centimeter, and for long distances, the meter and kilometer. Upper-grade children should frequently be asked to show the relationship among these prefixes.

RELATION OF METRIC UNITS TO CUSTOMARY UNITS

For some time to come, pupils will continue to have contact with distances in customary units. Road signs, mileage on road maps, dimensions printed on models, and the like will continue to be printed in these units.

Students and adults who have learned to measure with customary units often need to have on hand a reference of equivalents to metric units. With a calculator and an equivalent table, it is easy to convert individual measures from customary to metric units. We do not recommend mathematical conversion from one system to another without a calculator. Prepare a visual chart showing patterns and relationships that can be used when customary units are given and metric units are desired, or vice versa. However, in many cases precise conversions are not necessary. When this happens, pupils should be able to approximate equivalents for comparison purposes. For example, they should know that a quart is a little less than a liter, a yard is a little less than a meter, and a pound is a little less than one-half of a kilogram. The chart format shown in Table 15.3 can be used to show the ap-

proximate relationship between miles and kilometers.

Suppose that a map of a country is marked in miles. For a class project, have students convert distances from one city to another. The chart shows that for every 5 miles there are approximately 8 kilometers. To determine the number of kilometers for 85 miles, the pupil would divide by 5 (85 ÷ 5 = 17) and multiply by 8 (17 × 8 = 136). Therefore, 85 mi. ≈ 136 km. (The symbol ≈ means that the two measures are approximately equal.) Another method is to find two numbers under miles that have a sum of 85—for example, 50 and 35. Write the corresponding kilometers for each—80 and 56—and then find the sum of 136 km. With the aid of a calculator, miles can be converted to kilometers by multiplying the number of miles by 1.6093 and rounding off to the nearest tenth.

Children in the upper grades enjoy taking different things that are marked in customary units and translating them into metric units. They can do this by using standard conversion tables (see inside back cover) and calculators to prepare charts of equivalent measures.

Table 15.3 Approximate Relationships Between Miles and Kilometers

Miles	Kilometers
5	8
10	16
15	24
20	32
25	40
30	48
35	56
40	64
45	72
50	80

Measuring Mass

The unit for mass in the metric system is the *kilogram*. This unit is the only basic unit in SI that has a prefix. Prefixes are applied to the *gram*, which is a very light measure, about equal to the mass of a small paper clip. To find the mass of a very light object, the gram is appropriate. A four-ounce candy bar has a mass of 113.4 grams. A one-pound box of candy has a mass of 453.6 grams. One thousand grams equal one kilogram. The one-pound box of candy would have a mass of 0.45 kilograms.

Most people do not like to use the word *mass* to describe an object. The term *weight* is so well established in our vocabulary that for practical purposes it is useless to try to

Customary to Metric	Metric to Customary
1 inch = 2.54 centimeters	1 centimeter = 0.3937 inch
1 foot = 30.48 centimeters	1 meter = 3.2808 feet
1 yard = 0.9144 meter	1 meter = 1.0936 yards
1 mile = 1609.33 meters	1 kilometer = 0.6214 mile
1 mile = 1.609 kilometers	

Exercise 15.1

1. Estimate metric measurements, then use a metric tape and find actual dimensions:

	Estimate	Measured
a. My height	___ cm	___ cm
b. My head size	___ mm	___ mm
c. The length of one of my shoes	___ cm	___ cm
d. My waist size	___ cm	___ cm
e. The length of my arm	___ cm	___ cm
f. My arm span	___ m	___ m
g. My chest size	___ mm	___ mm

2. First estimate the length of each of the following line segments to the nearest millimeter. Then use a ruler graduated in millimeters to measure each to the nearest centimeter:

	Estimate	Measured
a. _____	___ mm	___ cm
b. _____	___ mm	___ cm
c. _____	___ mm	___ cm
d. _____	___ mm	___ cm
e. _____	___ mm	___ cm

3. Obtain a road map for your state. Select four major cities. Ask students to find the distance in miles between each pair of major cities and use a calculator to convert these distances to kilometers.

change it to mass. What did the baby weigh? How much does that roast weigh? Will you weigh this package to find out the amount of postage required? Mass and weight are equal at the equator, at sea level, or in a vacuum. A person's weight varies very little from one place on earth to another. The two measures are approximately the same on earth. But on the moon, a person's mass would remain the same but his weight would be much less than on earth.

A child's first experiences with weight involve finding his or her own weight. Beyond that, young children do not often refer to weight. Provide experiences with balance scales to determine which objects weigh more or less than the comparison unit. Set up a table with a type of "pan balance." Have on the table several different objects. Pick one as the *reference unit* and have students compare each of the other things to this unit in order to sort the objects into groups of "heavier than," "lighter than," or "same as" the reference unit. As in other lab activities, the children should be encouraged to estimate before they make their comparisons and keep some written record of their work to share later with other members of the class.

Measuring Mass Activities in Grades 4 to 6

Pupils should engage in some of the same activities suggested for primary-grade pupils. In addition, activities such as the following should be provided.

1. Encourage pupils to find things that weigh 1 gram, 5 grams, 10 grams, 20 grams, 28 grams (about an ounce), 100 grams, 500 grams, and 1 kilogram.

2. Have pupils weigh and label common objects in the classroom, such as books, chalk, erasers, notebooks, and blocks.

3. Have pupils weigh cubes of the same size but made from different materials. Do they weigh the same? Is this why a kilogram is defined as the mass of a cubic decimeter of distilled water at sea level at the temperature of 4 °C?

Converting to Metric

Pupils will find that many of the articles in stores are now double-labeled, that is, with both customary and metric units. For objects that are labeled only in customary units, pupils can use the table of equivalents with a calculator, prepare their own equivalents charts for conversion purposes.

Measuring Capacity

One cubic decimeter of distilled water at the temperature of 4 °C at sea level would weigh one *kilogram* and would be equal to one *liter* of liquid. Under these conditions, one cubic centimeter weighs one *gram*. Because different types of liquid have different *densities* (the mass of a substance per unit volume), a cubic decimeter of milk will not weigh exactly one kilogram, although it will be one *liter* of milk.

The unit *liter* was most probably named after Claude Émile Jean-Baptiste Litre (1716–1778). In 1736, Litre was alleged to have gone to Sandwich, where he met Josiah Barrel, who wanted to design a vessel in which to measure his cranberry crop. Together they created a "cranberry barrel."

Customary to Metric	Metric to Customary
1 ounce* = 28.35 grams	1 gram = 0.0353 ounce
1 pound = 0.4536 kilogram	1 kilogram = 2.2046 pounds
1 ton = 0.9072 metric ton	1 metric ton = 1.102 tons (2000 lb)

*This is the *avoirdupois* ounce, which is equal to 28.35 grams. The *troy* ounce, which is equal to 31.103 48 grams, is 10 percent larger than the avoirdupois ounce. Gold is sold on the international market by the troy ounce. A *fluid* ounce equals 29.6 mL.

Exercise 15.2

1. Have pupils first estimate the weight (mass) of each of the following personal things. Then have them use a metric scale graduated in grams to measure each.

	Estimate	*Measured*
a. My weight	_____ kg	_____ kg
b. Both my shoes	_____ g	_____ g
c. My textbook	_____ g	_____ g
d. My pencil or pen	_____ g	_____ g
e. My wallet or purse	_____ g	_____ g
f. A nickel	_____ g	_____ g

2. Ask pupils to visit their local grocery store and find five articles that are marked in both ounces and grams. Have them make a record:

		ounces	*grams*
Article	_____	_____	_____
	_____	_____	_____
	_____	_____	_____
	_____	_____	_____
	_____	_____	_____

Later Litre made a fortune with the graduated cylinders he designed and sold throughout Europe during the 1770s.

Pupils learn about liters and milliliters by pouring activities. Provide a variety of different containers, both small and large, such as juice cans, bottles, distilled-water jugs, milk cartons, plastic containers, and coffee cans, to use for measuring capacity. The child's first experience with capacity should be with nonstandard units.

Set up a table with containers of different shapes and sizes. Select a small juice can as the measuring unit. Fill a large container with some material, such as sand. (Water is good, but makes a mess.) Have children work in pairs to answer the question "How many cans does it take to fill each container?" For activities like this, label each container with some symbol and prepare a sheet for children to use in recording their answers.

Have pupils find containers that hold about a liter. Collect plastic containers and have the pupils mark them in milliliters and liters.

Figure 15.1 illustrates cardboard models of a 125 mL container that pupils can make from patterns. The 125 mL container measures 5 cm on each edge. A 1000 mL (1 liter) container can be made from the pattern that measures 10 cm on each edge. Children will find that it takes eight 125 mL containers to fill the 1000 mL container.[2]

Graduated beakers up to one liter should be available for upper-grade pupils to use in measuring various materials. Instead of water, lima beans, sand, corn, rice, and the like can be used for different measuring activities.

2. The original symbol for liter was the script "l" or ℓ. This was changed by the General Conference on Weights and Measures to a capital "L" to avoid confusion with other symbols.

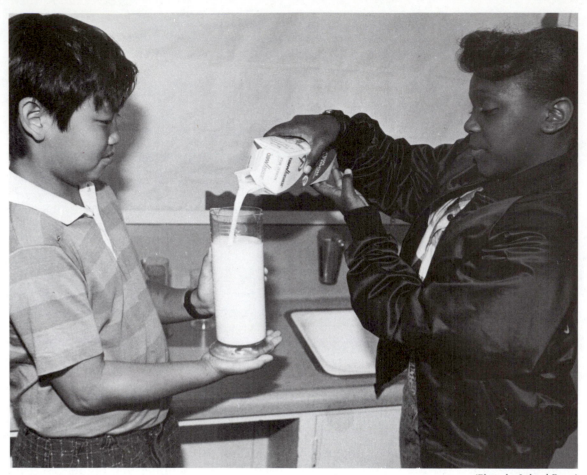

Pupils discover the number of mL in a quart.

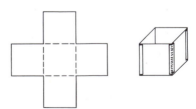

Figure 15.1
Models of a 125-mL container (5 cm per edge) and a 1000-mL container (10 cm per edge). The volume of a 125-mL container is 125 cm³, and the volume of a 1000-mL container is 1000 cm³.

Have the pupils pick different containers—various sizes of bottles and cans—and fill each with some type of material that will pour. Then have each pupil transfer the material from one container to a graduated beaker and record the measure in milliliters. Have them record the measures in the following way:

A coffee cup of rice = _____ mL
A glass of corn   = _____ mL
A can of beans   = _____ mL
A quart of milk   = _____ mL

CONVERTING TO METRIC MEASURES

Pupils may notice that some containers in the grocery store are marked in customary units with the metric equivalent given. For example, a quart of milk may be marked 0.9463 liter. At gas stations, a sign may read 1 GALLON = 3.785 LITERS. Have pupils look for different items that are "double-labeled" and make a list, writing the measure in both customary and metric units for each item.

Have capable pupils use a calculator and the table of equivalents at the bottom of the page to make a chart of liquid measure equivalents similar to that in Table 15.4.

Measuring Temperature

For many years, the unit for measuring temperature in the United States was degree Fahrenheit. On this scale, water freezes at

Table 15.4 A Chart of Equivalents of Gallons to Liters

Gal to L	10	20	30
	37.8	75.7	113.6
1	3.785		
2	7.6		83.3
3	11.4		124.9
4	15.1		
5	18.9	56.8	
6	22.7		
7	26.5		
8	30.3		
9	34.1	71.9	

(Gallons, vertical label at left)

32 °F and boils at 212 °F. One degree of Celsius = 5/9 Fahrenheit. That is, every 5 degrees Celsius represent 9 degrees Fahrenheit.

The 100-unit scale thermometer invented by Anders Celsius set the melting point of snow as 100 °C and the point of boiling water as 0 °C. After Celsius died, the points were reversed.

For practical reasons, elementary school children should not be expected to convert from one scale to another by the formula: C = 5/9 (F − 32) and F = (9/5 × C) + 32. Using a calculator, one would convert from Fahrenheit to Celsius by the sequence: °F − 32 × 5 ÷ 9 = °C. To

Customary to Metric	Metric to Customary
1 ounce = 0.0296 liter	1 liter = 33.815 ounces
1 pint (16 oz) = 0.4732 liter	1 liter = 2.1134 pints
1 quart (32 oz) = 0.9463 liter	1 liter = 1.0567 quarts
1 gallon = 3.785 liters	1 liter = 0.2642 gallons

Note: 1 barrel (of petroleum) = 159 L
1 metric ton (tonne) of petroleum = 7.32 barrels, or 1.164 m^3

Exercise 15.3

1. With a calculator complete the equivalents chart shown in Table 15.4.
2. Given: One fluid ounce = 29.574 mL in volume. Make a chart of equivalents to fit the pattern below, rounding off to the nearest tenths place. Use a calculator.

(a) 8 fl oz = _____ mL
(b) 16 fl oz = _____ mL
(c) 32 fl oz = _____ mL
(d) 12 fl oz = _____ mL
(e) 18 fl oz = _____ mL

Ounces to mL		10	20	30
		295.7		
1	29.57			
2				946.24
3				
4				
5				
6		473.2		
7				
8	236.6			
9				

3. The public may dislike purchasing gasoline by the liter because distances are still measured in miles and people will want to know how many miles per gallon they are getting. Complete the table below to convert miles per gallon to kilometers per liter.

(a) 10 mi/gal = _____ km/L
(b) 15 mi/gal = _____ km/L
(c) 20 mi/gal = _____ km/L
(d) 22 mi/gal = _____ km/L
(e) 32 mi/gal = _____ km/L

Mi/gal to km/L		10	20	30
		4.25	8.5	12.75
.1	0.425			
2				
3				
4				
5	2.12	6.38	10.62	14.88
6				
7				
8				
8				
9				

convert from Celsius to Fahrenheit, the formula is:
°C × 1.8 + 32 = °F.

Teaching Temperature

Many weather reports give temperatures in degrees Fahrenheit and then in degrees Celsius. Very soon, most temperatures will be given in degrees Celsius, without the conversion to degrees Fahrenheit. In the el-

ementary school, pupils should become accustomed to what different temperatures *feel* like.

100 °C Water boils. Boil some water and measure the temperature with a cooking thermometer.

37 °C Body temperature. Use a clinical thermometer and take the temperature of at least six children.

22 °C   Comfortable room temperature. Have an outdoor-indoor thermometer and have pupils keep a record of hourly temperatures.

0 °C   Water freezes. Bring in a bucket of ice and measure the temperature.

You can set up a weather station center to keep records of temperatures in degrees Celsius, rainfall in millimeters, and wind velocity in km/h (kilometers per hour).

Exercise 15.4

Here is a simple technique for developing a table of equivalents for Fahrenheit to Celsius:

1. On a sheet of lined paper, start near the bottom and record 32 °F = 0 °C.

2. For each increase or decrease of 9 °F, there will be a corresponding 5 °C increase or decrease. Fill in a table such as the one below:

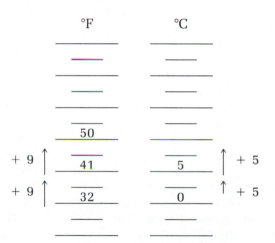

3. For each increase or decrease of 4.5 °F, there will be a corresponding 2.5 °C increase or decrease. Fill in these values on your table.

4. For every 2 °F, there is approximately 1 °C.

5. A rule for quick estimation for changing from C to F is double C and add 30; to change from F to C subtract 30 from F and divide by two. This gives satisfactory approximations for most normal temperatures. Try this rule on the values in the table in exercise 2 above and observe the differences.

Calculator Activities

The metric system came into existence to utilize the ease of multiplying and dividing by powers of 10.

The calculator can be used as a tool for discovering a wide variety of number patterns. Discovering the shortcut for multiplying and dividing by powers of 10 may be the most useful. To guide pupils in the discovery of this procedure, start with each pupil having a calculator. Place a column of numbers on the chalkboard, some decimals and some whole numbers. Allow room for at least two additional columns. Ask the class to multiply each number by 10 and then by 100. Record the results in a manner similar to the following:

$$32.4, \ 10 \times 32.4 = 324, \ 100 \times 32.4 = 3240$$

$$.038, \ 10 \times .038 = .38, \ 100 \times .038 = 3.8$$

$$42, \ 10 \times 42 = 420, \quad 100 \times 42 = 4200$$

As the work continues, encourage discussion and guide the class to discover the pattern that is developing. When a pupil makes a guess, ask for confirmation or rejection and the reason for doing so. This should lead to the discovery that multiplying by 10 moves the decimal point one place to the right and multiplying by 100 moves the decimal point two places to the right. Some pupils may be able to multiply whole numbers by powers of 10. Help them discover that annexing two zeros to 42 is the equivalent of moving the decimal point two places to the right. Ask where the decimal point is in 42 and then ask where it is in 4200 to help the pupils recognize that annexing zeros is the equivalent of moving the decimal point.

This activity provides an opportunity to recognize the necessity for accurate statements in mathematics. Ask the pupils what happens to the number when two zeros are annexed. If a pupil says the number is multiplied by 100, ask if .4200 is 100 times 0.42. Annexing two zeros to a whole number does multiply it by 100, but annexing two zeros to a decimal such as 0.42 does not.

Note that many people say that we add two zeros rather than annex two zeros. Adding zero to a number does not change the number.

After the class discovers the rule for multiplying by a power of 10, a similar activity

can lead to the discovery that dividing by a power of 10 moves the decimal point to the left, one place for each power of 10.

Some purists object to "moving the decimal point" as a rote rule. An automatic procedure or shortcut is not a rote process if it is obtained on the basis of meaningful experience. Any algorithm is a rote process when it is learned by following rules without understanding. An algorithm should be automatic but the automatic response should result from activities based on sound mathematical principles.

The calculator should be used to convert units that are not related by powers of 10, such as feet to inches or inches to feet, but such problems should stem from practical situations rather than theoretical ones that are not within the experience of the pupils.

The rationale for changing from smaller to larger and larger to smaller is discussed in the next section, on computer activities.

Use information on commercial packages and the calculator to check the relation between customary and metric units. The print on a half-gallon carton of milk indicates that it contains 1.89 liters. Use this information to find how many liters in a gallon, how many liters in a quart, and how many quarts in a liter.

Stress that these are standard rate problems to strengthen the concept of rate and of unit conversion by recording results as follows:

1 gallon → 1.89/.5 = 3.78 liters
1 liter → .5/1.89 = .26 gallons
3.78 liters = 4 quarts
1 liter → 4/3.78 or 1.06 quarts
1.06 quarts = 1 liter
1 quart → 1/1.06 = .94 liters

Use highway signs that show both miles and kilometers and be alert for other displays in books, magazines, and signs that link the two systems.

As a change of pace, try this with the class as a calculator activity. Ask each pupil to enter a two-digit number in the calculator and proceed as follows: annex four zeros, press the addition key, enter the same two-digit number, followed by two zeros multiply by 100, press the addition key again, enter the two-digit number and press the equal key. Now divide that sum by 91 and go from pupil to pupil and divide the number in each calculator by 111 to get the original entry in the calculator window.

Challenge the pupils to discover how it works. Demonstrate on the chalkboard that the process is equivalent to multiplying by 10101, which has factors of 111 and 91. After the pupil divides by 91, the teacher division by 111 will yield the original two-digit number for the quotient. This occurs because dividing successively by 91 and 111 is the equivalent of dividing by 10101 to undo the original multiplication by 10101 and return to the original number. Note that it will work with any size number that does not overload the calculator.

Computer Activities

The computational advantage of the metric system is lost if the pupil cannot multiply and divide by powers of 10 efficiently. The calculator section of this chapter suggests activities to help pupils discover how to multiply and divide efficiently by powers of 10. Program P15.1 provides practice for sharpening these skills mentally.

```
PROGRAM P15.1
  10 GOSUB 200
  20 PRINT A;" X ";10^B;" = ";
  30 INPUT "";Z$
  40 PRINT A;" X ";10 ^ B;"
     = ";A * 10 ^ B
  50 INPUT Z$
  60 GOSUB 200
  70 PRINT D;"/";10 ^ C;" = ";
  80 INPUT "";Z$
  90 PRINT D; "/";10 ^ C;" =
```

```
     "; D / 10 ^ C
 100 INPUT Z$
 110 GOTO 10
 200 HOME : VTAB 10
 210 A = INT(1000 + 1000 *
     RND(1))/100
 220 B = 1 + INT(3 *
     RND(1))
 230 C = 1 = INT(4 *RND(1))
 240 D = INT(10000 + 30000
     * RND(1))
 250 RETURN
```

Adding a repeat routine at the end of the program will not work because the RETURN instruction in line 250 will prevent the computer from executing it. Therefore it has to be placed in lines 100 and 110. This is the option that makes the program repeat indefinitely and requires a CTRL-C or BREAK to exit the program. To use a FOR-NEXT repeat option, replace line 110 with 110 NEXT J, and insert line 5: 5 FOR J = 1 TO 5.

Two things are necessary to convert from one unit to another in a given system:

1. The conversion factor or rate.

2. Whether to multiply or divide.

Using pure rote memory as a basis for deciding whether to multiply or divide is difficult. Far too often this has been taught so as to be learned by rote. Common sense should provide the rationale. Ask pupils which requires the greatest number of units for measuring the length of a table, feet or inches. If you know the number of feet, it should be clear that the number representing feet must be *multiplied* by 12 to obtain the number of inches. The number of inches required to describe a given distance must be greater than the number of feet. The following should help pupils recognize the conversion process as a multiplication or division situation.

1 ft $\rightarrow$ 12 in	6 ft $\rightarrow$ 6 $\times$ 12 $\rightarrow$ 72 in
2 in $\rightarrow$ 1 ft	72 in $\rightarrow$ 72/12 $\rightarrow$ 6 ft

Reference to a familiar situation such as feet and inches should enable one to choose the correct operation.

Program P15.2 implements the ideas in the previous discussion. It asks for the names of the larger unit, the smaller unit, and the conversion factor (rate). When this information is entered, the pupil must tell the computer whether the conversion is from smaller to larger or the reverse. The computer will then perform the conversion.

```
PROGRAM P15.2
  10 HOME :VTAB 5
  20 PRINT "THIS PROGRAM
     CONVERTS ANY UNIT TO
     ANY OTHER UNIT WHEN YOU
     KNOW THE CONVERSION
     FACTOR(RATE) AND WHICH
     UNIT IS LARGER."
  30 PRINT
  40 INPUT "ENTER NAME OF
     LARGER UNIT   "; A$
  50 INPUT "ENTER NAME OF
     SMALLER UNIT ";B$
  60 INPUT "ENTER THE CON-
     VERSION FACTOR ";R
  70 PRINT
  80 PRINT "ENTER 1 FOR
     SMALLER TO LARGER "
  90 PRINT "ENTER 2 FOR
     LARGER TO SMALLER "
 100 PRINT
 110 INPUT "ENTER CHOICE
     HERE -> ";X
 120 ON X GOTO 130, 180
 130 PRINT
 140 PRINT "ENTER NUMBER OF "
     ; B$;" -> ";
 150 INPUT "";N
 160 PRINT N;" ";B$;" = "
     ;INT(100 * N/R + .5)
     /100;" ";A$
 170 END
 180 PRINT
 190 PRINT "ENTER NUMBER OF "
     ;A$;" -> ";
```

```
 200 INPUT "";M
 210 PRINT M;" ";A$;" = ";
     M*R ;" ";B$
```

Problem Solving

(a) Write a program that will make a table that will enable you to immediately convert any number of inches, 1 to 20, to centimeters.

(b) Change one line of the program for part (a) so that it will convert centimeters to inches.

(c) Change the program in part (a) so that it will convert square feet to square inches.

(d) Change the program in part (a) so that it will convert miles to kilometers.

(e) What name is used for this type of table?

Answers: (a)
```
 10 FOR N = 1 TO 20
 20 PRINT N;" IN=
    ";2.54*N;" CM"
 30 NEXT N
```
(b) `20 PRINT N;" CM = "; INT(100* N/2.54 + .5)/100;"IN"`

(c) `20 PRINT N;" SQ FT = "; 144 * N; " SQ IN`

(d) `PRINT N;" MI = "; 1.6 * N;" KM"` (The conversion factor of 1.6 is correct to the nearest 10th, accurate enough for most needs.)

(e) In everyday language, it is a conversion table. In mathematical language, it is a function table listing a set of ordered pairs.

Look for Patterns

(a) How many terms in the sequence: $1 + 2 + 3 + \ldots + 20$?

(b) How many terms in the sequence: $0 + 1 + 2 + \ldots + 20$?

(c) How many terms in the sequence: $5 + 6 + 7 + \ldots + 31 + 32$?

(d) How many terms in the sequence: $1 + 2 + 3 + \ldots + N$?

(e) How many terms in the sequence: 0 + 1 + 2 + . . . + N?

(f) How many terms in the sequence: 5 + 6 + 7 + . . . + N?

(g) How many terms in the sequence: a + a+1 + a+2 + a+3 + , , , + N?

(h) 1 + 2 + 3 + 4 + . . . + 40 = □ × (1 + 40)

(i) 11 + 12 + 13 + . . . + 58 + 59 + 60 = □ × (11 + 60)

(j) 23 + 24 + 25 + . . . + 56 + 57 + 58 = □ × (23 + 58)

(k) 1 + 2 + 3 + . . . + 13 + 14 + 15
= 7 × (1 + 15) + □
= □ × (1 + 15)

(l) 13 + 14 + 15 + 16 + 17 + 18 + 19
= 3 × (13 + 19) + □
= □ × 32

(m) 1 + 2 + 3 + . . . + N = □ × (1 + △)

(n) 11 + 12 + 13 + . . . + N = □ × (11 + △)

(o) Write a FOR-NEXT loop that will find all sums from part h to part l.

Answers: **(a)** 20; **(b)** 21; **(c)** 32 − 5 + 1 = 28 or 32 for sequence from 1 to 32 − 4 in sequence from 1 to 4 = 32−4 = 28; **(d)** N; **(e)** N + 1; **(f)** N − 5 + 1 or N − 4; **(g)** N − a + 1; **(h)** 20 × 41 = 820; **(i)** 25 × 71 = 1775; **(j)** 18 × 81 = 1458; **(k)** 8, the middle term. The sequence has 15 terms. 7 × 16 + 8 = 15/2 × 24; **(l)** 3 × 32 + 16 = 7/2 × 32; **(m)** N (N + 1)/2 **(n)** (N − 10) (11 + N)/2

```
(o) 10 INPUT "ENTER 1ST
       TERM  ";A
    20 INPUT "ENTER LAST
       TERM ";B
    30 FOR N = A TO B
    40 T = T + N
    50 NEXT N
    60 PRINT "SUM FROM ";A;
       " TO ";B; " = ";T
```

The above program will find the sum of

any sequence of whole numbers beginning with A and ending with B and will find the sum of the sequences labeled from part (h) to part (l).

Formulas

The previous work with patterns leads to the following formulas:

1. The sum of the first N natural numbers is N × (N + 1)/2

2. The sum of a set of counting numbers from A to B is (B − A + 1)(A + B)/2

Apply these formulas as a check on your previous work.

Inverse Operations

The following problems can be solved by starting with the end result and working backward, often a useful procedure.

(a) A boy subtracted 7 instead of adding 7 to get 0. What is the correct answer?

(b) If you multiply by 10 instead of dividing by 10 and add 5 instead of subtracting 5 to get an answer of 605, what is the original number? the correct answer?

(c) If you subtract 10 instead of adding 10 and divide by 2 instead of multiplying by 2 to get 14, what is the original number? the correct answer?

(d) If you add 3 instead of subtracting 3 and multiply by 2 instead of dividing by 2 and subtract 4 instead of adding 4 to get 34, what is the original number? the correct answer?

(e) If you multiply by 2 instead of subtracting 2 and divide by 3 instead of adding 3 to get 8, what is the original number? the correct number?

Answers: (a) original number: 0 + 7 = 7, correct answer: 7 + 7 = 14.
(b) Original number: (605 − 5) ÷ 10 = 60, correct answer: 60/10 − 5 = 1

(c) Original number $14 \times 2 + 10 = 38$; $(38 + 10) \div 2 = 24$

(d) Original number: $(34 + 4) \div 2 - 3 = 16$, correct number $(16 - 3) \div 2 - 4 = 2.5$

(e) Original number $= 3 \times 8 \div 2 = 12$; correct number $= 12 - 2 + 3 = 13$

Summary

The Metric Conversion Act of 1975 was meant to convert the United States to the metric system by 1985, a goal that obviously was not met. Some of the reasons for this failure are:

1. Many aspects of the program were voluntary.

2. The general public refused to accept the replacement of familiar units with new ones. Shell Oil spent over two million dollars to convert its pumps but changed back to gallons when the public refused to buy liters.

3. Many small businesses found the changeover was not cost-effective.

4. The change of administration and bureaucratic red tape also contributed to lack of success.

The Omnibus Trade Bill of 1988 was designed to make the United States more competitive in world trade and specifies that the metric system shall be the preferred system of weights and measures for United States trade and commerce. The act requires each federal agency to make every effort to effect this conversion by 1992. However, continued use of the traditional system is permitted for noncommercial purposes.

International industrial corporations have been exclusively metric for many years to avoid the necessity of different sets of tools and machine parts.

With all government agencies and most businesses converted to metrics, the system will filter into schools and everyday affairs but, as past experience indicates, there is little probability of complete conversion in the near future.

The best way to teach measurement to pupils in the elementary school is to emphasize measurement activities designed to develop both concepts and skills, such as the following:

1. Have pupils actually measure various things using nonstandard units. Discuss variations. Laboratory activities are essential to learning to measure.

2. Introduce only the most commonly used customary and metric units. Have pupils learn to select the appropriate units and measure the same things with both systems. Discuss historical points of interest about how measurement units were discovered and used by our ancestors.

3. Have pupils estimate a measure before measuring an object. Pupils who can make a close guess at a measurement demonstrate their understanding of the process.

4. Discuss the approximate nature of measurement results. Develop the idea of accuracy of a measurement to one-half of the smallest unit represented on the measurement instrument.

5. Have pupils discover the advantages of the metric system over the customary system by having them change from smaller to larger units, or the reverse. They will see that all that is required in the metric system is to move the decimal point, whereas the customary system requires division or multiplication.

6. Have pupils discover that in daily life, only a limited number of units in a metric table are used, such as centimeters, meters, and kilometers for linear measure. The other units are included to show that the ratio between any two consecutive places is ten.

7. Have students develop a "feel" for approximate equivalents of both customary and metric measures. For the next several years, pupils will be using both systems. They need to understand the approximate relationships between corresponding units of measurement.

8. Enrichment may include converting from one system to the other with a table of equivalents and a minicalculator. Otherwise, this activity should not be used for drill purposes.

Exercise 15.5

1. Examine the scope and sequence chart of a recently published series of elementary mathematics textbooks and determine the sequence and grade placement of metric topics.

2. Make a list of the measuring devices and aids needed in typical primary and upper-grade classrooms.

3. Prepare a learning-center project for one or more aspects of metric measures: (a) Design worksheets for pupils to use; (b) Have available required materials; and (c) Provide for discussion and evaluation.

4. Outline the advantages and disadvantages of the United States' conversion to the metric system by 1992.

5. List the advantages and disadvantages of teaching only metric measures in the elementary schools.

Selected Readings

Donovan, Frank. *Prepare Now for a Metric Future.* New York: Weybright and Talley, 1970.

Goldbecker, Sheralyn S. *Metric Education.* Washington, D.C.: National Education Association, 1976.

Higgins, Jon L. (ed.). *A Metric Handbook for Teachers.* Reston, VA: National Council of Teachers of Mathematics (no date).

Kurtz, Ray V. *Metrics for Elementary and Middle Schools.* Washington D.C.: National Education Association, 1978.

Leffin, Walter W. *Going Metric, Grades K-8.* Reston, VA: National Council of Teachers of Mathematics, 1975.

Metric Units of Measure and Style Guide—SI. Boulder, CO: U.S. Metric Association, Inc., 1976.

Nelson, Doyal (ed.). *Measurement in School Mathematics,* 1976 Yearbook. Reston, VA: National Council of Teachers of Mathematics, 1976.

Trafton, Paul R., and Albert P. Shulte. *New Directions for Elementary School Mathematics,* 1989 Yearbook. Reston, VA: National Council of Teachers of Mathematics, 1989. Chapter 12.

Youngpeter, John M., and Dennis P. Davan. *Meter—Suggested Activities to Motivate the Teaching of the Metric System,* Spice Series. Stevensville, MI: Educational Service, 1975.

Agencies to Contact for Up-to-Date Metric Information

United States Metric Board
1600 Wilson Boulevard
Arlington, VA 22209

U.S. Metric Association
10245 Andasol Avenue
Northridge, CA 91325

American National Metric Council
1625 Massachusetts Avenue NW
Washington, DC 20036

Geometry

ACHIEVEMENT GOALS

After studying this chapter, you should be able to:

1. Justify the inclusion of geometry in the elementary curriculum.

2. Summarize the objectives for teaching geometry to primary and upper-grade pupils in the elementary school.

3. Describe and illustrate the meaning of various concepts and terms of geometry (see Vocabulary).

4. Identify and illustrate one-dimensional figures, two-dimensional figures, and three-dimensional figures.

5. Describe common properties of geometric figures.

6. Outline activities for teaching concepts and skills for dealing with one-dimensional figures, such as lines, segments, rays, and angles.

7. Design activities to teach concepts and skills for working with two-dimensional figures, such as circles, and various polygons, such as triangles, squares, rectangles, trapezoids, and parallelograms.

8. Design activities to teach concepts and skills for dealing with three-dimensional figures such as prisms, pyramids, cylinders, cones, and spheres.

VOCABULARY

These terms are defined or illustrated in the Glossary.

Acute angle	Polygon
Adjacent angles	Polyhedron
Angle	Protractor
Area	Quadrilateral
Circumference	Ray
Cylinder	Region
Equilateral triangle	Rhombus
Isosceles triangle	Scalene triangle
Obtuse angle	Similar figures
Parallel lines	Solid
Parallelogram	Symmetry
Perimeter	Tetrahedron
Perpendicular	Trapezoid
Pi (π)	Volume

The study of geometry at the elementary school level is quite different from high school and college geometry, which emphasizes definitions and formal proofs. At the elementary school level, pupils are informally taught concepts and general notions about geometric figures, without formal definitions and proofs. Both the nonmetric and metric aspects of geometry are included at the elementary school level. Nonmetric geometry deals with the concepts and representations of sets of points in space, whereas metric geometry uses numbers to measure and describe the various properties of geometric figures.

Objectives for Geometry

Children encounter many geometric shapes in their everyday environment. The elementary school pupil begins to learn geometry by developing concepts at the exploratory level with manipulative materials, such as logic blocks, geoboards, and models of geometric shapes. Students first learn to recognize different figures and their names. Then they learn to work with drawings of geometric shapes as they use the number line and rectangular and circular regions in working with number operations and with fractions. Also, pupils learn to draw geometric figures to represent geometric concepts and to assist them in problem solving.

The major objectives of teaching geometry in the primary grades are to enable pupils to:

1. Identify various geometric figures from physical models, including the square, rectangle, circle, triangle, cube, cylinder, pyramid, cone, and sphere.

2. Recognize certain properties of shapes from physical models and drawings, with some attention to type of regions, edges, angles, sides, and so on.

3. Sort, compare, measure, and draw various geometric plane figures.

Pupils in the upper grades study geometry at the concrete, visual, and symbolic levels. They are able to examine models of geometric figures and identify properties and relationships. They form generalizations about the relationships of geometric figures to one another. Upper-grade pupils use the instruments of geometry—compass, straight edge, protractor—to measure and draw simple geometric figures. These learners become proficient in finding perimeters and areas of simple plane figures and the volumes of rectangular solids.

The major objectives of teaching geometry to upper-grade children include further study and understanding of primary grade objectives, plus enabling the students to:

1. Classify and rearrange geometric shapes by pattern and in terms of symmetry and simple geometric transformations.

2. Describe properties of geometric figures in precise language with appropriate models.

3. Demonstrate an understanding of concepts, such as perpendicular, parallel, congruency, symmetry, and simple transformations.

4. Reproduce models of plane and solid geometric figures, describe their properties, and measure and calculate perimeter, area, and volume of common shapes.

Beginning Geometric Concepts and Terms

Geometry deals with abstract notions of *points* in space that make up various geometric figures, such as *lines*, *segments*, *planes*, and *solids*. Drawings and models of geometric figures enable pupils to discover properties and relationships.

Pupils discover properties of polygons.

(Photo by Leland Perry)

Points

The term *point* is undefined in geometry. It is usually described as a "nondimensional position in space." That is, it locates a position in space without taking up space. On paper, a point is represented by a "dot," which represents the idea of a point, although in fact the point cannot be seen or touched. A point is usually named with a capital letter.

One-Dimensional Figures

One-dimensional figures in geometry are called *curves*. A curve can be thought of as the *path* of a moving point, which has only length, and not width. A curve may or may not be straight. It may or may not lie in the same plane. It may or may not cross itself, and may or may not end where it started.

All the drawings in Exercises 16.1 are curves because curves in mathematics include straight lines. However, elementary school pupils should not use the term "curve" in this sense. To elementary school pupils, the word "curve" generally means something that "changes directions continuously," as in examples (a), (c), and (f) of Exercises 16.1. Therefore, you should name the geometric figures that are straight with their specific names; (b) line segment, (e) broken segment, (g) line, and (h) ray.

A curve that does not cross itself is called a *simple curve*. The curve in example (c) is *not* simple.

A curve that ends where it starts is called a *closed curve*. Examples (f) and (i) are *simple, closed curves*.

Elementary school children can learn about points, curves, and line segments by working with and talking about the pictorial aspects of geometric figures, not from abstract definitions and symbolic notations. Laboratory activities adapted from the exercises found in each section of this chapter should help children to understand the basic geometric ideas involved.

MEASURING LINE SEGMENTS

The line segment AB in Figure 16.1 is marked off in units equal in length to CD. We can thus take the length of $\overline{CD}$ as the

Exercise 16.1
Which of the following drawings are geometric curves?

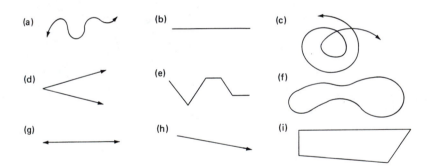

Line Segments

A *line segment* can be defined as the shortest path between two points. Only one line segment can be drawn to connect any two points in space. A point on a line segment (except an end point) is said to be *between* the end points. The end points are usually named with capital letters, such as in A _____ B, and the entire line segment is named by two capital letters with a bar above them, such as $\overline{AB}$.

unit of measure. Since $\overline{CD}$ measures $\overline{AB}$ four times, the length of $\overline{AB}$ is 4 $\overline{CD}$.

The *centimeter* is a commonly used unit for measuring short lengths in the metric system of measurement. The length of $\overline{EF}$, shown in Figure 16.1, is approximately 2 centimeters. The line segment is partitioned into two line segments of equal measure. Two line segments that are of equal measure are known as *congruent* line segments. The measure of $\overline{EF}$ is 2. The *length* of a line segment is the number of units in the segment named with the unit used in measuring. Thus, the length of $\overline{EF}$ is 2 cm.

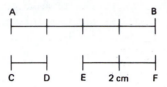

Figure 16.1
The measure of line segments

Lines

A *line* in geometry is a straight, one-dimensional figure that extends indefinitely in both directions. The idea of a "nonending" straight line is represented by writing an *arrow* on each end of the line to signify that the figure continues without end. Any two points on a line can be identified and labeled with capital letters that are then used to name the line. The drawing in Figure 16.2 illustrates the line PQ. In symbolic notation, the line would be named by the two letters that name the identified points on the line, with a drawing of a line above; in this case, $\overleftrightarrow{PQ}$.

Figure 16.2
Line PQ

RELATIONS BETWEEN LINES

Two lines in the same plane must intersect or be parallel. Two lines intersect at no more than *one* point. Two lines that intersect are either *oblique* or *perpendicular*. Perpendicular lines intersect at right angles (90°), and oblique lines intersect at an angle other than a right angle.

Rays and Angles

A *ray* has a starting point and extends indefinitely in one straight direction. In symbolic notation, a ray is named by the starting point with a capital letter and any other point located on the ray. Figure 16.3 illustrates ray GH. Point G is the starting point, and point H is a point on the ray that is used to name it. The symbol for ray GH consists of the two capital letters identifying the points and a drawing of a ray above the letters, or $\overrightarrow{GH}$.

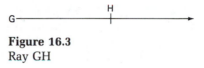

Figure 16.3
Ray GH

An *angle* is formed by two rays with the same starting point. Angles can be measured in degrees, using a *protractor*, and classified accordingly. An *acute* angle measures more than zero degrees and less than 90°. A *right* angle measures 90°. An *obtuse* angle measures more than 90° and less than 180°.

Angles are named with three capital letters. The first letter is a point located on one of the sides of the angle (ray), the second letter names the common starting point of the rays (called the *vertex*), and the third letter is a point located on the other side of the angle. Sometimes an angle is named by the letter of its vertex. Figure 16.4 illustrates angle DEF, or angle E. It is named by the symbols $\angle$ DEF, $\angle$ FED, or $\angle$ E.

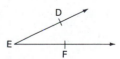

Figure 16.4
Angle DEF

Measuring Angles

The standard unit of angular measure is the *degree*, symbolized as 1° and read "one degree." If we rotate a ray 360° about a point in a plane, the entire plane will be covered. The unit for angular measure came to us from the Babylonians, who probably based the angular measure for a complete surface on the number of days in a year.

A PROTRACTOR

The instrument used to measure an angle is the *protractor*, which is shown in Figure 16.5. The rounded edge of a protractor contains two scales, an outer and an inner scale, both graduated to 180 degrees. The two scales make it easy to measure an angle in any position. In the protractor of Figure 16.5, the zero point on the outer scale is on the left and of the inner scale on the right. The center is always placed on the vertex of

the angle to be measured and the zero point is placed on one side of the angle. The point on the scale that is cut by the other side of the angle indicates the number of degrees in the angle. The protractor in Figure 16.5 is set to show the measure of angle BOC, which is 45. We write this fact as ∠BOC = 45°. Indicate the measures of ∠COD and ∠COG.

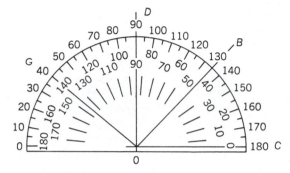

Figure 16.5
A protractor

Exercise 16.2
Given the following angles:

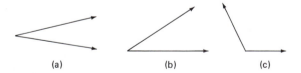

(a)   (b)   (c)

1. Estimate the measure of each: (a) _____ (b) _____ (c) _____
2. With a protractor measure each of the angles: (a) _____ (b) _____ (c) _____
3. With only a straight edge and a pencil, estimate and draw angles equal to the following measures:
   (a) 35°   (b) 55°   (c) 100°
4. With a protractor measure each of the angles approximated and drawn in exercise 3: (a) _____ (b) _____ (c) _____

Classroom Activities

Classroom activities should include laboratory sessions in which various geometric figures are drawn, labeled, and described. It is worthwhile to have pupils assist in creating bulletin-board displays for the ideas of points, line segments, lines, rays, curves, angles, and the like. Then have pupils help to develop a list of everyday representations of each concept, such as:

Points: Illustrated by a small dot, the end of a pin, the corner of a sheet of paper, a position on a map, etc. None is a real point but each represents an idea that approximates a point.

Line segments: Illustrated by a drawing, edge of a sheet of paper, intersection of a wall with the ceiling, etc.

Rays: Illustrated by a drawing, a ray of light from the sun or a flashlight, a radio beam from a transmitter, etc.

Angles: Illustrated by a drawing, two rays of light from the sun in different directions, corner and adjacent sides of a table, etc.

Curved line segments: Illustrated by a drawing, boundaries on a map, a river on a map, veins of leaves, etc.

Two-Dimensional Figures in a Plane

A *plane* can be described as a flat surface, as suggested by a tabletop or the floor of a room—which are actually parts of a plane. A plane region has length and width but no thickness. A *region* is a part of a plane. The most common two-dimensional figures studied in the elementary school are *polygons* and *circles* with their interior regions. Without the interior regions, polygons and circles are one-dimensional figures.

Polygons

A *polygon* is a simple, closed one-dimensional figure in a plane formed by three or more line segments with no two adjacent line segments on the same line.

Pupils in the primary grades can identify triangles, squares, and rectangles, but the study of special properties of polygons should be delayed until the upper grades. Pupils must rely entirely on shape for their earliest identification of geometric figures, based on general perceptions of characteristic features. For example, in the early stages, pupils should be able to distinguish between triangles and squares on the basis of the number of sides: triangles have three sides and squares have four. The special features of the square are that the sides must be *congruent* (equal in measure) and the angles *right angles* (measure 90°). Children learn to name geometric figures that are squares long before they are able to understand these two properties.

Current textbooks provide numerous opportunities to identify geometric figures. Sometimes it helps to supplement the textbook work with the following laboratory activities. These laboratory activities require readiness, which the teacher can achieve by first showing and discussing models of the various figures, before pupils draw them.

1. Give each child a piece of blank, unlined paper, a sharp pencil, and a straight edge.

2. Have each child place three different dots on the paper, not in a straight line.

3. Then have each child use the straight edge to connect the three points with line segments.

4. Let each child show and tell about her or his drawing. Make note of the fact that each drawing is a triangle.

5. Have precut cardboard models of different-sized square regions, and give each child a different one.

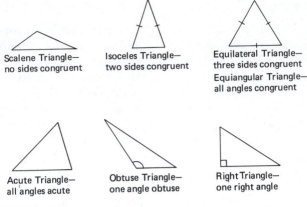

Figure 16.6
Types of triangles

6. Have each child trace around the edges of his or her own square region on a blank, unlined piece of paper.

7. Let each child show and tell about his or her drawing. Remind students of the fact that each drawing is a square, and talk about various features of squares.

Triangles

Elementary textbooks generally refer to six different kinds of triangles. Figure 16.6 depicts these different kinds of triangles, and lists their names and special features.

Elementary school pupils are usually able to identify only a few of these types of triangles. In general, students can be expected to distinguish between right triangles and nonright triangles. Nonright triangles are either *acute* or *obtuse*.

Quadrilaterals

Quadrilaterals are polygons that have four sides, four angles, and four vertexes. Textbooks refer to several different kinds of quadrilaterals. The different kinds, and their names and special features, are shown in Figure 16.7.

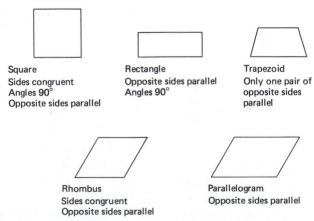

Figure 16.7
Some properties of five quadrilaterals

A good activity for teaching the various appropriate names for different quadrilaterals is to furnish patterns and from them have each student cut out of cardboard the following quadrilaterals:

1. Two different-sized trapezoids

2. Two different-sized parallelograms (not rhombuses or squares)

3. Two different-sized rectangles (not squares)

4. Two different-sized rhombuses (not squares)

5. Two different-sized squares

In addition, the teacher should prepare a "classification board" using Figure 16.7 as a pattern.

Have each pupil pick a quadrilateral region at random and place it on the classification board with its appropriate name. Then ask pupils to give the distinguishing characteristics of each figure. If pupils can answer questions such as the following, they will understand the concept of the measures of the sides and angles of these polygons:

1. How many sides are there in a quadrilateral?

2. How many sides are there in (a) a square? (b) a rectangle? (c) a trapezoid? (d) a parallelogram? (e) a rhombus?

3. Are opposite sides congruent in (a) a square? (b) a rectangle? (c) a trapezoid? (d) a parallelogram? (e) a rhombus?

4. What kind of angle is formed by the adjacent sides of (a) a square, (b) a rectangle?

5. Is a square a rectangle?

6. Is a rectangle a square?

7. How can a parallelogram differ from a rectangle?

8. Is a rectangle a parallelogram?

9. Is a parallelogram a rectangle?

Activities with Tangrams

Tangrams are valuable in helping children visualize spatial relationships with polygons. Tangram pieces are made up of seven regions cut from a square region of heavy cardboard, as shown in Figure 16.8. The teacher should provide young children with the pieces but encourage upper-grade pupils to make their own tangrams.

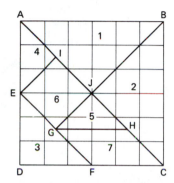

Figure 16.8
Pattern for tangram pieces

If you are teaching young children, you should draw the boundary of a polygon to be created on the front of a brown envelope containing the needed pieces. In the beginning phases, kindergarten children need to have an outline of each piece.

Upper-grade pupils should make their own tangram pieces by following the pattern shown in Figure 16.8. Square ABCD can be any size. We recommend a square with sides of 10 cm for primary pupils. The pieces should be numbered from 1 to 7 for identification purposes, as shown in Figure 16.8. The cut-out pieces should be stored in an envelope. Have pupils do Exercise 16.3.

Activities on a Geoboard

The geoboard is an excellent instructional aid to help children understand different characteristics of polygons. Geoboards can

Exercise 16.3

Make a set of tangrams and number the pieces as shown in Figure 16.8.

1. Make a *triangle* with the following set of pieces:
   (a) 1, 2 (b) 4, 5, 7 (c) 1, 4, 5, 7 (d) 3, 4, 5, 6, 7 (e) all seven pieces

2. Make a *square* with the following set of pieces:
   (a) 4, 5 (b) 3, 4, 5 (c) 1, 3, 4, 5 (d) 3, 4, 5, 6, 7 (e) all seven pieces

3. Make a *parallelogram* or a *rectangle* with the following set of pieces:
   (a) 1, 2 (b) 4, 5, 6 (c) 1, 4, 5, 7 (d) 4, 5, 6, 7 (e) 1, 2, 4, 5, 6 (f) 1, 2, 3, 4, 5 (g) 1, 3, 4, 5, 6, 7 (h) all seven pieces

4. Make a *trapezoid* with the following set of pieces:
   (a) 5, 6, 7 (b) 4, 5, 6, 7 (c) 1, 2, 4, 5, 6 (d) 1, 2, 3, 4, 5, 6 (e) all seven pieces

be purchased commercially or made from a piece of plywood and nails. A 25-nail board is recommended. Here are some beginning activities with the geoboard. Have pupils make:

1. A three-sided figure with one right angle and describe the figure.

2. A three-sided figure with two sides of equal length. Describe the figure.

3. A four-sided figure with four equal sides. Describe the figure.

4. A four-sided figure that has all right angles. Describe.

5. A four-sided figure with no right angles. Describe.

6. A four-sided figure that has only two parallel sides. Describe.

7. The smallest square you can using only one rubber band. This is one square unit.

8. A quadrilateral (four-sided figure) that contains eight square units. Describe.

9. A rectangle that has four square units (not a square).

10. A square that has sixteen square units. Describe. How many units are there around the square (perimeter)?

11. A rectangle that has six square units. Describe. What is its perimeter?

12. A square with an area of one. What is its perimeter?

13. A square with a perimeter of twelve units. What is its area?

14. A square with a perimeter that measures the same as its area. Describe the figure.

Symmetry

A geometric figure can have either point or line *symmetry*. A geometric shape has point symmetry if every line segment through the point of symmetry connecting two points on the shape is bisected by the point of symmetry.[1] A circle has point symmetry with respect to its center. Line symmetry exists if a line can be located such that all line segments perpendicular to the given line connecting two points on the shape are bisected by the given line. A circle has line symmetry with respect to any diameter. Figure 16.9 presents examples of geometric figures that have line symmetry. The geoboard and geobands can be used to illustrate symmetry.

An interesting project for children is to have them collect pictures from old maga-

---

1. A point *bisects* a line segment if it separated the segment into two congruent parts.

zines. Then have them cut each picture along a line of symmetry and paste it onto a piece of construction paper. The task is for the child to draw the "other half" of the picture.

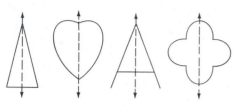

Figure 16.9
Figures with line symmetry

Similar Geometric Figures

Two geometric figures are *similar* if they have the same shape. All circles are similar. Two triangles are similar if their corresponding angles are congruent or if their corresponding sides are in the same proportion. Figure 16.10 presents examples of similar geometric shapes.

Figure 16.10
Similar geometric shapes

Circles

A *circle* is a one-dimensional plane figure that is a simple, closed curve. It is not a polygon because it is not made up of line segments. It has an *interior* region and an *exterior* region. The distance from the center of the interior region to the circle is called the *radius*. A circle is a set of points equidistant from a point in the center. The circle and its interior region form a two-dimensional figure.

A circle can be drawn by tracing a circular surface, such as a coin or the base of a

bottle. A circle of any given radius can be drawn by using a compass, as shown in Figure 16.11.

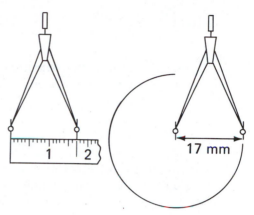

Figure 16.11
Drawing a circle with a compass

Perimeters and Areas

Finding Perimeters

The *perimeter* of a polygon (measure of the "rim") is the sum of the measures of the sides of the figure.[2]

A textbook problem may ask the student to find a perimeter, either giving the dimensions of the figure or requiring the student to measure the sides. The length of a side can be found by direct measurement with a ruler or by using a compass and a ruler.

Figure 16.12 shows how to find the perimeter of a polygon by using a compass. Lay off in succession the measures of the sides *a*, *b*, and *c* of the triangle as illustrated. The sum of these measures is the perimeter of the triangle. Open the compass to the length of these line segments and find the distance between the points of the compass with a ruler.

2. A *measure* is a number, and a *length* contains a label such as inches or centimeters. We add numbers and not inches. This distinction is not usually made in current elementary programs.

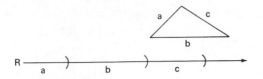

Figure 16.12

Students begin dealing with perimeters of polygons at the exploratory level and continue at the symbolic level.

VISUAL LEVEL

Pupils at the visual level perform activities such as the following in dealing with perimeters:

1. Find the perimeter in centimeters of each of the polygons in Figure 16.13.

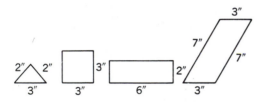

Figure 16.13

2. Draw figures having the same shape as those in problem 1. Then measure the sides with a ruler and find the perimeter.

3. Find the perimeter of triangle DEF in Figure 16.14, by using the method illustrated in Figure 16.12.

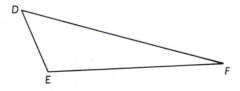

Figure 16.14

SYMBOLIC LEVEL

At the symbolic level, pupils in the upper grades find perimeters of polygons by developing and using formulas.

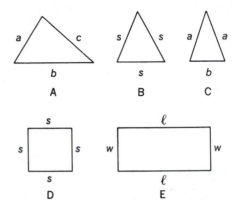

Figure 16.15

4. Find the perimeters of the polygons in Figure 16.15. From demonstrations of the type given at the exploratory level, have the class explain the sequence of steps in finding a perimeter, such as the triangle in Figure 16.14. Have the class tell how a letter can be used to represent each side of a triangle. Then have the students develop a rule and a formula for finding the perimeter of a triangle.

a. The perimeter of any triangle is equal to the sum of the measures of the three sides. The formula is:

$$p = a + b + c$$

b. The perimeter of an equilateral triangle is equal to three times the measure of one side. The formula is:

$$p = 3s$$

The formula for the perimeter of an equilateral triangle is an application of the distributive property and the identity property for multiplication:

$p = s + s + s$
$\quad = (1 \times s) + (1 \times s) + (1 \times s)$
$\quad = (1 + 1 + 1)s$
$p = 3s$

c. The formula for the perimeter of an isosceles triangle is:

$p = 2a + b$

d. The perimeter of a square is equal to four times the measure of one side. The formula is:

$p = s + s + s + s$, or $p = 4s$

The formula for the perimeter of a square follows the pattern given in (b):

$p = s + s + s + s$
$\quad = (1 \times s) + (1 \times s) + (1 \times s)$
$\quad \qquad\qquad\qquad + (1 \times s)$
$\quad = (1 + 1 + 1 + 1)s$
$p = 4s$

e. The perimeter of a rectangle is equal to the sum of the measures of the four sides. The formula is:

$p = \ell + w + \ell + w$
$p = 2l + 2w$
$p = 2(l + w)$

The students demonstrate that all three formulas for the perimeter of a rectangle are equivalent by replacing *l* and *w* with numerals and then doing the indicated operations. They also identify the formula *p = 2(l + w)* as an application of the distributive property of multiplication over addition.

Unit of Measure for Area

Finding the area of a plane surface is the same as measuring its region. For example, the rectangle ABCD in Figure 16.16 encloses a region. The rectangle itself has no area, as it consists of line segments. When we say "Find the area of a rectangle," we mean

"Find the area of the region enclosed by a rectangle."

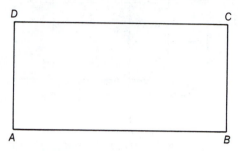

Figure 16.16

The unit of measure for a region is another region that is used to cover the enclosed space. The standard unit of measure for a plane surface is a unit square (having a side of one). One standard unit of area is a square centimeter (cm^2), as shown in B, Figure 16.17.

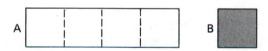

Figure 16.17

Rectangle A of Figure 16.17 is divided into four squares, each of which is congruent to square B. The area of square B is 1 cm^2, and so the area of rectangle A is 4 cm^2.

Finding the Area of a Rectangle

CONCRETE AND VISUAL LEVELS

In the rectangular region shown in Figure 16.18, each square region is equal to 1 cm^2, the unit of measure. The teacher should direct pupils to use the square regions to cover the rectangular surface—for example, as one "tiles" the floor. Allow them to discover that each row has the same number of

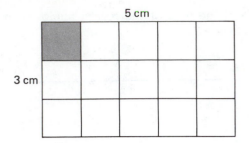

Figure 16.18

square units. The total number of square units is the number in each row times the number of rows.

Students begin work on finding the area of a rectangular region at the exploratory level. The class should participate in the following kinds of activities:

1. Divide several rectangular surfaces drawn on the chalkboard into square regions and have the pupils find the area of each by finding the number of squares in one row times the number of rows. Each area is represented by the number of squares plus the symbol for the unit of measure (square units).

2. Show the class a picture in which a rectangular surface is divided into square units. Ask the class to find the area, expressed in square units, of the entire region.

3. Have each pupil draw a rectangle having measures expressed as whole numbers, such as 2 cm by 4 cm, and divide the figure into 1-cm squares. Then have each student find the number of squares by multiplying the number in a row by the number of rows.

4. On the chalkboard, draw several rectangular regions labeled in whole-number dimensions. Have the class find the area, expressed in square units, of each figure.

SYMBOLIC LEVEL

Pupils at the symbolic level can derive a rule and a formula for finding the area of a rec-

tangular region. The rule for the area of a rectangular region is: *The number of square units in the area of a rectangular surface is the product of the number of units in length and width.* Both dimensions must be expressed in the same linear unit. The area must be expressed in square units. The formula for the area of a rectangle is $A = \ell \times w$.

The *square* is a special kind of rectangle whose sides are of equal measure. The letter s is generally used to represent the side of a square; hence, the formula for the area of a square becomes $A = s \times s$, or $A = s^2$. The measure of the area of a 4-cm square is 4×4, or 16, and the area is 16 cm^2.

The class should apply the rule or formula for finding the area of a square and other rectangular regions that are given in the textbook.

MASTERY LEVEL

The pupils have achieved mastery when they can apply the formula for finding the area of a rectangle with skill and understanding. The amount of time spent on a topic helps to determine how fast elementary students achieve mastery.

Finding the Area of Other Plane Figures

The elementary school curriculum may or may not include finding the area of plane figures such as triangles, parallelograms, trapezoids, or circles. If a teacher introduces this topic for any or all of these figures, the same pattern should be followed as for finding the area of a rectangle. The introductory work is at the exploratory level. Have pupils cut parallelograms or triangles from paper and arrange or transform them so as to form rectangles. Then have them compare the area of the triangle or the parallelogram with the area of the rectangle. Have them use a picture or make a drawing of a figure and transform it so that they can find the area of the enclosed region.

At the symbolic level, the class can derive a rule or formula for finding the area of a figure. The formulas for finding the area of four figures using a minicalculator are:

Area of a triangle = base × height ÷ 2 or $A = b \times h \div 2 = \frac{1}{2} \times b \times h$

Area of a parallelogram = base × height or $A = b \times h$

Area of a trapezoid = the sum of the measures of the parallel bases (b_1 and b_2) divided by 2 and multiplied by the height or $A = b_1 + b_2 \div 2 \times h$.

Area of a circle = pi times radius squared, or $3.14 \times r \times r$ or $A = \pi r^2$.

Height

The height of a triangle is a perpendicular segment from a vertex of the triangle to the line containing the opposite side. In Figure 16.19, the height of triangle ABC is BD. Name the height of each of the other triangles in the figure. If there is more than one height, name all of them. Height is sometimes called altitude.

The height in a parallelogram is a perpendicular segment from a point on one side to the line containing the opposite side. More than one height is drawn in each of the parallelograms shown in Figure 16.20.

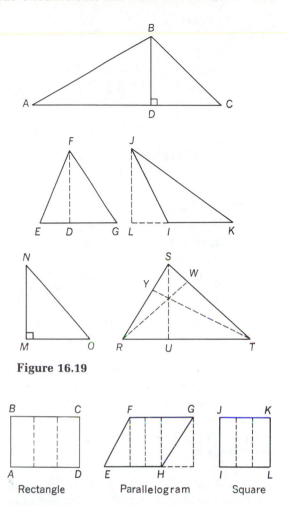

Figure 16.19

Figure 16.20

Rectangle   Parallelogram   Square

The Circumference and Diameter of a Circle

Each student or small group of students should use a cylindrical can or a wheel to find the ratio of the circumference of a circle to the diameter. The class should compare the ratios of different-size cans or wheels. The value of each ratio should be a little more than 3. Then the teacher should have a class demonstration with a 7-inch wooden disk to show how to find the ratio of the circumference to the diameter. A student should mark a point on the circumfer-

ence and then roll the disk along a yardstick until the marked point touches the stick. The scaled value of this point should be approximately 22 inches. This distance divided by the diameter would give a quotient of $^{22}/_7$, or $3\frac{1}{7}$, which may be expressed approximately as 3.14.

The diagram in Figure 16.21 shows an effective instructional aid for demonstrating the method of finding the ratio of the circumference to the diameter. In the diagram, XY is a board about 24 inches long and MN is part of a yardstick or a cloth tape fastened to the side of the board. At the base of XY

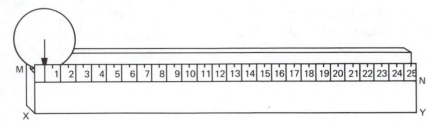

Figure 16.21
Coordinate axes

there is a groove about ⅜ inch wide in which circular disks of plywood about ¼ inch thick can be rolled. If the teacher has disks of 3″, 4″, and 7″ in diameter, a student can give a demonstration to show the circumference of each circular disk. Then the class can find the ratio of the circumference to the diameter for each disk. The experiment should show that the circumference is about 3.1 times the diameter.

The teacher should have the students compare the results of their experiments with the ratio 3⅐. Most of the results should be approximately 3.1. The ratio of the circumference to the diameter is π and its value is approximately 3⅐, or 3.14. The exact value of π cannot be determined, but in beginning work with this symbol, π is usually given the value of 3⅐, or 3.14. The more precise value, 3.1416, is used when greater accuracy is demanded than that used at the junior high school level.

The pupils should discover that the circumference of any circle is equal to π times its diameter, or π times twice the radius.

The formula for the circumference of a circle is

$$C = \pi d \text{ or } C = 2\pi 2r$$

The teacher should have the students make a graph, similar to the graph shown in Figure 16.22, to display on the bulletin board. If the radius is 3½ inches, the diameter will be 7 inches, and the circumference will be 22 inches. Metric units should also be used. The superior students should discover that the circumference of a circle is a function of its diameter.

The Area of a Circular Region

The formula for the area of a circular region can be derived or verified by transforming a circle so as to approximate a parallelogram and showing that the formula, $A = \pi r^2$, gives the area of the circular region.

The teacher should have a circular disk, cut from heavy cardboard, about 6 inches in diameter and cut into at least 8 equal sec-

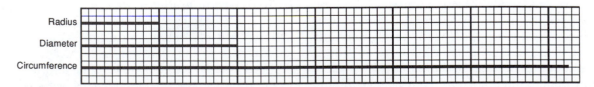

Radius

Diameter

Circumference

Figure 16.22

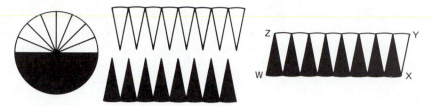

Figure 16.23

tors, preferably 12 or 16 equal sectors. The sectors should be arranged as shown. The resulting figure will approximate a parallelogram as represented by *WXYZ* in Figure 16.23. The greater the number of equal sectors into which the disk is cut, the closer will the figure formed by these sectors approximate a parallelogram. The altitude of the parallelogram is equal to the radius of the circle. The base of the parallelogram is approximately half of the circumference, or $\frac{2\pi r}{2}$, or πr. Substituting r for h and πr for b in the formula, $A = bh$, the formula for the area of a circular region is shown to be:

$$A = \pi r \times r, \text{ or } A = \pi r^2$$

This method is not satisfactory as a strict mathematical proof but is appropriate for this grade level.

The circle inscribed in the square in Figure 16.24 provides a method for verifying the approximate value of π as 3.14.

By inspection there are approximately 78½ square units in one quadrant of the circular region. Four times 78.5 equals 314 square units, the area of the circular region. In the corresponding quadrant, the square region has a side of 10, which is also the radius of the circle. The area of the square region equals 100 square units. If we multiply 100 (which is r^2) times 3.14 (the approximate value of π), the result is 314 square units.

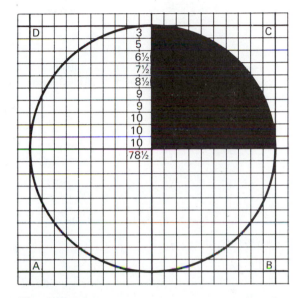

Figure 16.24

Locating Points on a Grid

Elementary school pupils can be taught to make various kinds of graphs—bar, circle, and line. Both bar and broken-line graphs involve a form of coordinate graphing. As pupils become capable of constructing these graphs, it is essential that they gain an understanding of coordinate graphing.

One type of graphing involves locating points on a plane grid. The plane grid is formed out of a horizontal and a vertical line that intersect to form right angles. The point of intersection is zero. To the right of the point of intersection, several other points are marked off at equal distances from one another and numbered from left to right 1, 2. . . . On the vertical line above zero points are marked off at equal distances from one another and numbered 1, 2, . . . In geometry, the two number lines are called the *coordinate axes,* as shown in Figure 16.25.

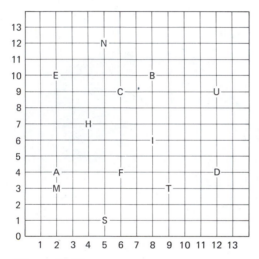

Figure 16.25

To locate a point with the *coordinates* of (2,4) means to move to the right along the horizontal axis 2 units and up parallel to the vertical axis 4 spaces. Point A in Figure 16.25 has the coordinates of (2,4). Many interesting activities can be devised for upper-grade children by using the techniques of coordinate geometry.

Three-Dimensional Figures

A three-dimensional geometric figure is a *solid.* Some solids are bounded by faces (flat surfaces) that are polygonal regions, such as cubes, prisms, and pyramids. Other solids are bounded by "curved surfaces," such as cylinders, cones, and spheres. Pupils at the elementary level should hear few formal

statements of the properties of each of these solids. However, pupils should be expected to identify each of the kinds of solids listed before.

Activities

1. Discuss with the class the number of line segments needed to enclose a region and help them discover that at least three line segments are needed. Ask them for the smallest number of sides needed to form a polygon and help them recognize that this is the same as the preceding question.

2. Discuss with the class the number of plane surfaces necessary to enclose a portion of space. Have some physical models of solids or some pictures of them on hand for reference and help the class discover that at least four surfaces are needed, or that the fewest possible faces that a solid may have is four. Have pupils give answers before they refer to the physical models so that they have the opportunity to visualize geometric situations mentally.

3. A triangular piece of paper (with all angles less than 90°) can be used to make a solid of four sides (a tetrahedron). Start with triangle *ABC,* as is illustrated in Figure 16.26. Determine the three midpoints of the three sides, *X, Y,* and *Z.* Fold firmly along the line segments $\overline{XY}$, $\overline{XZ}$, and $\overline{YZ}$. With careful and proper folding, the three vertexes of the triangle—*A, B,* and *C*—will then meet to form the fourth vertex of a tet-

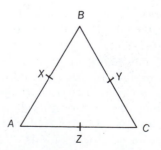

Figure 16.26

Exercise 16.4

Use Figure 16.25 and decode the following message:

    (2,3) (2,4) (9,3) (4,7) (8,6) (5,1) (6,4) (12,9) (5,12)

LETTERS: _____ _____ _____ _____ _____ _____ _____ _____ _____

rahedron whose other vertexes are *X, Y,* and *Z.*

If you use triangles of different shapes (all acute triangles), tetrahedrons of different shapes will result. If you use a right triangle, two of the faces will fold over to equal the third and form a rectangle. If an obtuse triangle is used, a tetrahedron cannot be formed. If an equilateral triangle is used, a regular tetrahedron will result (with all edges equal and all faces with the same size and shape).

4. Have the class make other solids by folding on the basis of patterns drawn on paper (see Figure 16.27 for patterns for familiar figures).

5. Use soda straws, toothpicks, pipe cleaners, or similar materials to construct models of polyhedrons.

6. Have the class count the faces, vertexes, and edges of a tetrahedron and other polyhedrons and make a table (see Table 16.1).

Table 16.1

	Faces	Edges	Vertexes
Tetrahedron	4	6	4
Cube	6	12	8
Pyramid with square bases	5	8	5

When the table has been completed for all the polyhedrons that are available, ask pupils if they can discover a pattern or relationship among the number of faces, vertexes, and edges. This relationship was first formulated more than two hundred years

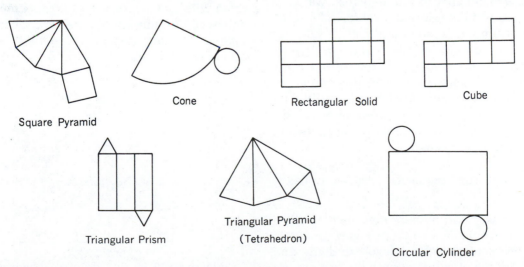

Square Pyramid

Cone

Rectangular Solid

Cube

Triangular Prism

Triangular Pyramid
(Tetrahedron)

Circular Cylinder

Figure 16.27

ago by the Swiss mathematician Leonhard Euler as $F + V = E + 2$, where F represents the number of faces, V the number of vertexes, and E the number of edges.

Surface Area of a Solid

Each geometric solid has a *surface* measured in square units. The surface area of a solid is the sum of the areas of its faces. For example, a cube with 2-cm edges has an area of 4 cm^2 for each face. A cube has 6 faces. The surface area of this cube is 6 × 4 cm^2 = 24 cm^2. Although there is a formula for finding the surface of each of the regular space figures called solids, pupils at the elementary school level should not be expected to find the surface of solids other than for a cube and a rectangular prism. We recommend that pupils find the surface of these solids by calculating the area of each face of the square or prism and taking the sum of the area of the faces.

Volume of a Solid

When we find the *volume* of a solid, we measure its interior. A solid is a figure that has dimensions of length, width, and height. Just as we used a square region to measure the area of plane figures, we use a cubic unit to measure the volume of a solid. For example, a standard metric unit for finding volume is the cubic centimeter (cm^3). For any given solid, the volume is the number of cubic centimeters it contains.

Finding the volume of a solid will be restricted to a rectangular prism because most curriculums do not deal with other solids in the elementary school.

FINDING THE VOLUME OF A RECTANGULAR PRISM

Each face and base of a rectangular prism is a rectangle, as shown in Figure 16.28. At the elementary school level, students find the volume of solids at both the exploratory

and symbolic levels. The classroom should be equipped with approximately 125 1-cm cubes and several small rectangular boxes having unlike dimensions. The inside dimensions of each box should be a whole number of centimeters. The class should participate in activities such as the following to gain the background needed to formulate a rule for finding the volume of a rectangular solid.

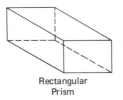

Rectangular Prism

Figure 16.28

EXPLORATORY LEVEL

1. Have the class select a box and find the number of 1-cm cubes needed to fill it. The dimensions of the box in centimeters may be 2 × 5 × 3. A member of the class puts one layer of cubes in the box, as shown in Figure 16.29. The teacher has the class note that there are 10 cubes in one layer (5 cubes in each row and 2 rows = 10 cubes). Since there will be 3 layers, it will take 3 times 10 cubes, or 30 cubes, to fill the box. The volume is 30 cm^3. Repeat this activity with other boxes of different sizes.

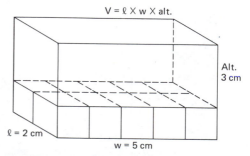

$V = \ell \times w \times \text{alt.}$

Alt. 3 cm

$\ell = 2$ cm

$w = 5$ cm

Figure 16.29

2. Draw figures of rectangular prisms on the chalkboard or show pictures of them. Have the class find the number of cubic units in a layer of a prism and then multiply by the number of layers. Be sure the pupils discover that the number of cubic units in a layer is equal to the product of the number of linear units in length and width. Also, the number of layers is the same as the number of linear units in the height.

3. Have the class derive a rule for finding the volume of a rectangular prism. The rule can be stated as: The number of cubic units in the measure of a rectangular prism is equal to the product of the dimensions (expressed in the same units of linear measure), and the volume is that number with the cubic unit used.

4. Have the class derive a formula for the rule: $V = \ell \times w \times h$ where ℓ = length, w = width, and h = height.

5. Have the pupils substitute numbers in the formula and calculate the product. Point out that the calculation of $\ell \times w \times h$ will result in a number, whereas the volume is that number along with the symbol for the cubic unit used. For example, if $\ell = 6$ cm, $w = 4$ cm, and $h = 3$ cm, the number of cubes is $6 \times 4 \times 3$, or 72, and the volume of the prism is 72 cm^3.

Problem Solving

(a) Arrange three coins so that every coin touches every other coin.

(b) Arrange four coins so that they all touch each other.

(c) Place six coins in a straight line. Move three of them in any manner necessary to obtain two rows of four coins each.

(d) Make four equilateral triangles with six matches.

(e) Place nine sheep in four pens with an odd number in each pen.

Answers: (a) Place two coins to touch each other and place the third coin on top. (b) Place the three coins tangent to each other and place the fourth coin on top. (c) Place an end coin on top of its neighbor and take two coins from the other end to make a T. (d) Make an equilateral tetrahedron with the six matches to obtain a six-sided tetrahedron with four equilateral triangular faces. (e) Place three of the pens in a fourth pen and place three sheep in each of the interior pens. There are then three sheep in each of the interior pens and nine in the exterior pen.

Read Carefully

(a) If 14 stamps cost 3 cents and a quarter, what is the cost of 100 stamps?

(b) When is the quotient larger than the dividend?

Answers: (a) $2.00 (b) When the divisor is less than one.

Polygons and Handshakes

(a) Define a diagonal of a polygon; a side of a polygon.

(b) Why does a triangle have no diagonals?

(c) For any vertex in a rectangle, how many nonadjacent vertices are there?

(d) How many diagonals can be drawn from any one vertex in a rectangle?

(e) A rectangle has four vertices and a diagonal is drawn from each. Why does a rectangle have only two diagonals?

(f) How many adjacent vertices does each vertex in a polygon have?

(g) Describe the relation between the number of sides in a polygon and the number of diagonals that can be drawn from any vertex.

(h) If a polygon has N vertices, how many diagonals can be drawn from each vertex?

(i) How many diagonals does a five-sided polygon, a pentagon, have?

(j) How many diagonals does a polygon of N sides have?

Answers: (a) A diagonal of a polygon is a line segment connecting two nonadjacent vertices. A side connects two adjacent vertices. (b) The triangle has no nonadjacent vertices. Every vertex is adjacent to each of the others. (c) Each vertex in a rectangle has two adjacent vertices, so each vertex has only one nonadjacent vertex. (d) Because each vertex in a rectangle has one nonadjacent vertex, only one diagonal can be drawn from each vertex. (e) Diagonals connect two vertices. When diagonals are counted in terms of vertices, each diagonal is counted twice. (f) Each vertex has two adjacent vertices. (g) The number of diagonals that can be drawn from a given vertex is three fewer than the number of sides of the polygon. No diagonal can be drawn from the vertex to itself or to either of its two adjacent vertices. (h) The number of diagonals that can be drawn from a vertex is $N - 3$. (i) The number of diagonals that can be drawn from each vertex in a pentagon is $5 - 3$ or 2. Draw a pentagon and check. With two diagonals from each vertex, multiplied by 5, we have counted each diagonal twice, so there are five diagonals. (j) An N-sided polygon will have $N(N - 3)/2$ diagonals.

Handshakes

(a) Relate the number of handshakes between three people and four people to polygons.

(b) How many handshakes will there be for a group of three people? for a group of four people?

Answers: (a) If we visualize three people, each standing at the vertex of a triangle, there will be one handshake for each of the three sides of the triangle. If we visualize four people, each standing at the vertex of a rectangle, there will be one handshake for each side as well as one for each diagonal.

(b) Three—one for each side of the triangle. Six, one for each of four sides and one for each diagonal.

The number of handshakes for a group of N people, each shaking hands once with everyone else in the group, is N, the number of sides in a polygon of N sides, plus $N \times (N - 3)/2$, the number of diagonals in an N-sided polygon. Algebraically $N + N \times (N - 3)/2 = N(N - 1)/2$. The fact that these two expressions are identical can be verified by the following FOR-NEXT loop:

```
10 FOR N = 1 TO 20: PRINT
   N + N * (N - 3) / 2,N *
   (N - 1) / 2: NEXT N
```

We have just solved the handshake problem by relating to the problem of finding the number of diagonals in a polygon, a classic example of translating a new problem into an old one.

The expression $N \times (N-1)/2$ is the formula for the sum of the $N-1$ natural number as well as the formula for the $N-1$ triangular number.

The formula will also solve the problem of how many wires must be used to connect N telephones and similar connectivity problems, illustrating one of the most interesting aspects of mathematics, where new problems are sometimes found to be old problems in disguise. This approach to the handshake problem is an excellent example of translating an apparently new problem into a familiar one.

Computer Activities

Program P 16.1 illustrates how a READ-DATA program can provide practice in becoming familiar with facts that must be learned. This program asks for the area of a circle and displays the formula after the pupil presses the return key. The formula may be typed in before the return key is pressed.

```
PROGRAM P 16.1
  10 HOME : VTAB 5
  20 FOR J = 1 TO 5
  30 PRINT "IDENTIFY THE
     FORMULA REQUIRED:"
  40 PRINT
  50 READ A$,B$
  60 PRINT A$;"-> ";
  70 INPUT "";Z$
  80 PRINT A$;"-> ";B$
  90 INPUT Z$: HOME : VTAB 5
 100 NEXT
 110 DATA AREA OF CIRCLE,
     A = PI X R^2 PI=3.14..
 120 DATA AREA OF A RECTAN-
     GLE, A = L X W
 130 DATA AREA OF A TRIAN-
     GLE, A = (1/2) X B X H
 140 DATA VOLUME OF A CUBE,
     V = S^3
 150 DATA AREA OF A TRAPE-
     ZOID,A = (H/2) X (A +
     B)
```

Program P 16.2 uses the STOP instruction in line 50 to tell the computer to exit the program without removing it from memory, allowing computation in the immediate mode. When the computation is complete, the instruction GOTO 100 tells the computer to process line 100, placing it back in the program. The pupil can now enter the area and see if the computation is performed and rounded correctly.

```
PROGRAM P 16.2
  10 HOME : VTAB 4
  20 R = INT (20 + 70 *
     RND(1)) / 10
  30 PRINT "FIND THE AREA
     OF A CIRCLE WITH A RA-
     DIUS ";R;" TO THE NEAR-
     EST 10TH OF A SQUARE
     FOOT.
  40 PRINT "THE BREAK MES-
     SAGE PLACES THE COM-
     PUTER IN ITS IMMEDIATE
     MODE. PERFORM THE COM-
     PUTATION AND THEN ENTER
     GOTO 100.
  50 STOP
 100 INPUT "ENTER AREA ->"
     ";A$
 110 PRINT "AREA -> "; INT
     (10 * 3.14 * R * R +
     .5) / 10
 120 PRINT "THE ANSWER
     SHOULD NOT CONTAIN
     MORE THAN ONE DECIMAL
     PLACE BECAUSE ";R;" IS
     A ONE PLACE DECIMAL."
 180 REM    P16.2
```

Summary

A study of geometry gives pupils the opportunity to explore their environment. It is an interesting subject that pupils in the elementary school study eagerly. You can foster this enthusiasm by relating geometry to everyday experiences and by providing activities designed to develop each child's interest. Teaching geometry at the elementary level should take an informal, activity-oriented approach. Pupils need not be bombarded with formal definitions of many geometric terms. The language of geometry is important, but it should be developed gradually and with reference to geometric models made from concrete materials and shown with drawings. It is essential that pupils studying geometry be allowed the time to discover basic concepts from exploratory activities.

Primary-grade children should learn to identify various geometric figures from physical models. They should be able to sort, compare, measure, describe, and draw various geometric figures. Upper-grade pupils study more advanced concepts of geometry, such as perpendicularity, parallelism, congruency, and symmetry. At this level pupils also learn to measure and calculate perimeters and areas of common polygons and circles. They study various solids, such as cones, cylinders, spheres, prisms, pyramids, and rectangular solids, including the cube. They learn to find the surface area and volume of a rectangular solid.

Pupils should be given the opportunity to use the computer program LOGO to draw lines, angles, polygons, and a variety of other geometric figures (see Appendix B).

Exercise 16.5

1. What is a geometric figure?

2. What is the simplest geometric figure?

3. Identify the ten line segments in the figure below:

4. How many "curved" lines can be drawn from point A to point B?

5. How many line segments can be drawn from point A to point B?

6. Name each of the geometric figures below:

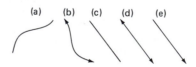

7. Differentiate between a figure and its region; between the area of a figure and its volume.

8. Illustrate the difference between drawing and constructing an equilateral triangle.

9. Use a carpenter's rule to illustrate different kinds of triangles; different kinds of quadrilaterals.

10. Draw a circle having a radius of 6 centimeters. With that radius, mark off in succession six arcs on the circle. Connect these points to form a hexagon. What is the perimeter of the hexagon?

11. The measure of an acute angle is between what two numbers? The measure of an obtuse angle is between what two numbers?

12. Under what conditions will a height of a triangle fall without the triangle? Coincide with a side of the triangle?

13. The perimeter of an isosceles triangle is 21 centimeters. If the length of the base is 5 centimeters, what is the length of each congruent side?

Selected Readings

Aichele, Douglas B., and Melfried Olson. *Geometric Selections for Middle School Teachers (5–9)*. Washington, D.C.: National Education Association, 1981.

Brydegaard, Marguerite, and James E. Inskeep, Jr. (eds.). *Readings in Geometry from the Arithmetic Teacher*. Reston, VA: National Council of Teachers of Mathematics, 1970.

Glenn, J. A. (ed.). *Children Learning Geometry*. New York: Harper, 1979.

Hill, James M. (ed.). *Geometry for Grades K–6, Readings from the* Arithmetic Teacher. Reston, VA: National Council of Teachers of Mathematics, 1987.

Kespohl, Ruth Carwell. *Geometry Problems My Students Have Written*. Reston, VA: National Council of Teachers of Mathematics, 1979.

Lesh, Richard (ed.). *Recent Research Concerning the Development of Spatial and Geometric Concepts*. Columbus, OH: ERIC Science, Mathematics and Environmental Education Clearinghouse, May 1978.

O'Daffer, Phares. "Geometry: What Shape for a Comprehensive, Balanced Curriculum?" In *Selected Issues in Mathematics Education*, 1981 Yearbook of the National Society for the Study of Education. Berkeley, CA: McCutchan, 1981. Chapter 7.

Watt, Daniel. *Learning with LOGO*. New York: McGraw-Hill, 1985.

Young, John E., and Grace A. Bush. *Geometry for Elementary Teachers*. San Francisco: Holden-Day, 1971.

Statistics and Probability

ACHIEVEMENT GOALS

After studying this chapter you should be able to:

1. List the objectives of statistics and probability for upper-grade pupils.

2. Assess readiness and provide motivation for the appropriate topics in statistics and probability.

3. Plan and provide suitable experiences for pupils in statistics and probability.

4. Recognize the role of and make effective use of the calculator and computer for promoting understanding and reducing computation drudgery.

5. Recognize the importance of making pupils aware of the difference between experimental and theoretical probability.

VOCABULARY

These terms are defined or illustrated in the Glossary.

And (as used in probability)
Average
Equally likely events
Dependent events
Impossible events
Independent events
Inferential statistics
Mean
Mode
Or (as used in probability)
Probability formula
Random events
Range

The topics of statistics and probability are now included in most mathematics programs in the elementary school. Important activities for elementary pupils include the collection of data, organization and interpretation of data in the form of tables and graphs, and making predictions.

The fourth National Assessment of Educational Progress in Mathematics found that third- and seventh-grade pupils could make direct readings from tables and graphs. However, they had difficulty in determining relationships among the data shown.

Only 50 percent of the seventh-grade pupils tested could calculate an average from given data and only 40 percent could determine a mean and a median for numbers less than 20. Meaningful existence in a modern society requires an understanding of elementary statistics and probability. Pupils should be provided with activities that will lead to an understanding of these topics.[1]

Statistics and probability became a part of the elementary curriculum when New Math was introduced in the 1960s. They have remained in the elementary school mathematics curriculum since that time, with most elementary mathematics series including some study of these topics in their materials. During primary grades, pupils are introduced to statistics and probability.[2]

Objectives

Pupils in elementary school should study statistics and probability to accomplish these goals:

1. Vicky L. Kouba, et. al., "Results of the Fourth NAEP Assessment of Mathematics, Measurement, Geometry, Data Interpretation, Attitudes and Other Topics," *Arithmetic Teacher*, 35 (May 1988):15.

2. *Curriculum and Evaluation Standards for School Mathematics* (Reston, VA: National Council of Teachers of Mathematics, October 1989), pp. 54–56.

1. To be able to collect, organize, and describe data.

2. To learn to construct and interpret tables.

3. To be able to make inferences, convincing arguments, and evaluate arguments based on data analysis.

4. To make simulations involving probability.

5. To use experimental probability to make reasonable predictions.

The objectives for early grades are similar to those for the upper grades but are implemented at a more elementary level.

Readiness and Motivation

Young pupils usually enjoy activities involving the collection, organization, and interpretation of data. Many enjoy making and interpreting graphs. Coin tossing, using spinners, throwing number blocks, and making computer simulations usually arouse interest. These activities should be simple and interesting and within the attention span of the group.

Upper-grade pupils study statistics and probability on a higher level but still require some manipulatives or computer simulations to validate many of the procedures. Motivation can often be obtained with the following activities:

1. Collect data from familiar everyday situations.

2. Devise original ways to represent data with tables and graphs.

3. Use class discussion for guided discovery to learn how to develop methods that use data to make predictions.

4. Use everyday situations and computer simulations to determine experimental probabilities for different situations.

5. Search for examples in newspapers and magazines of statistics and probability.

Teaching Graphing

Graphing involves collecting, organizing, and interpreting data. At any grade level, information about hobbies, pets, food, height, recreational activities, and similar projects may be collected and interpreted graphically. A good activity for early elementary pupils is the collection of information about favorite pets. After a preliminary survey, choose three of the most popular and make a table and and graphs similar to those in the following exhibits.

Table 17.1

Puppy	12
Kitty	8
Hamster	4

Figure 17.1

Puppy	xxxxx xxxxx xx
Kitty	xxxxx xxx
Hamster	xxxx

Figure 17.2

	x		
	x		
	x		
	x		
Each	x	x	
x	x	x	
represents	x	x	
one			
vote.	x	x	
	x	x	x
	x	x	x
	x	x	x
	x	x	x
	Puppy	Kitty	Hamster

Table 17.1 and the graphs in Figures 17.1 and 17.2 offer an excellent opportunity for discussing advantages of each different representation of the same information. Finding a value listed in a table is more accurate and usually quicker than reading from a graph. On the other hand, a glance at either graph allows instant recognition that puppies and hamsters are, respectively, the most popular and least popular. Determining the exact vote in either graph requires counting by fives, a worthwhile activity for early elementary pupils. Later graphs may have a scale and require ability to interpolate. Interpreting the graph and table can provide practice in the use of difference, more than and less than.

Each member of an elementary class can fill out a questionnaire about sports preference, food preference, the best-liked television show and the like. Many problems arise when collecting, recording, and organizing the results with a variety of viable decisions available. It is wise to start with small well-structured projects and gradually provide the opportunity for pupils to make and implement decisions. As this type of work proceeds, one graph marker may represent five, ten, or more items before a scale is used to indicate the value.

At the upper-grade level, students should be encouraged to select topics for investigation and, with minimum supervision, decide on how to collect, record, and interpret the data. However, the teacher must be aware of pupil progress so that help can be given when pupils need it.

It would be interesting to find how much time each pupil requires to get to and from a school without bus service. Another related study is to find the distance each pupil travels to and from the school. Comparing the two results may be another interesting study.

Teaching Descriptive Statistics

Descriptive statistics is usually taught in the fifth and sixth grade. The term *statistics* is often used to refer to a set of numbers: the number of runs scored by a team, the average temperatures for a given location, and the like. However, as a branch of mathematics, statistics provides a set of measures that helps to describe and interpret numerical data.

We are overwhelmed by sets of numbers in our everyday lives. Pupils should be encouraged to collect data on a wide variety of topics, including:

1. Batting averages for teams and individuals
2. Cost of living index
3. Federal, state, and local budgets
4. Number of passes attempted and completed per football game
5. Earned runs per baseball game
6. Number of basketball foul shots attempted and made

The most common statistical measures that help us describe sets of numbers are the:

mean or average

median

mode

range

The Mean

In everyday language, the mean is called the average and is the most familiar of the statistical measures. To find the mean of a set of N numbers, find the sum of these numbers and divide that sum by N.

The mean (average) for the set of numbers {10, 12, 15, 8, 20, 6, 13} equals: (10 + 12 +

15 + 8 + 20 + 6 + 13)/7 = 84/7 = 12.

Involve pupils in discussions of many topics, including average salary, average rainfall, average temperature, average output for bushels of corn and wheat, and the like. In these situations, the mean or average is often used as the *single number* that characterizes a set of numbers. The mean is one of several measures of the *central tendency* of a set of numbers. Generally, a set cannot be completely and accurately characterized by a single number. If the average rainfall for an area you plan to visit is 1 inch per month, you cannot predict when you will need an umbrella. However, if you plan to stay for a month, you should take one. If the average snowfall for a given month is half an inch, that area is not likely to provide good skiing.

A = {1,2,3,4,5,6,7,8,9}   B = {3,5,7,9,11}
C = {4,4,4,4}

Use sets A, B, and C to answer the following questions:

1. Find the average or mean of set A.
2. The addition of what number to set A will make its average or mean equal to 6?
3. Compute the average or mean of set B.
4. The addition of what number to set B will make its average or mean equal to 8?
5. Find the average or mean for set C.

The Median

The median is the middle number in a set that has an odd number of members and is the average of the two middle numbers for a set that has an even number of members.

Set A = {3, 5, 6, 12, 19}
Set B = {5, 11, 14, 18, 20, 22}

The median of set A (the middle number) is 6.

The median of set B (average of the 2 middle numbers) is 16.

The mean or average of set A is 45/5 or 9.

The mean or average of set B is 90/6 or 15.

In some instances, people prefer to use the median rather than the mean as the single number for characterizing a set. When a set contains a few members much larger than the others, the median is usually a better representation of central tendency than the mean.

Making a large increase in a single number in a set can have a substantial effect on the mean. Changing the set 3, 4, 5 to the set 3, 4, 98 will change the mean from 4 to 35 but will not change the median.

C = {3,4,5,6}   D = (4, 6, 8, 10, 12}
E = {7, 7, 7, 7, 7, 7, 7, 7, 7}

Use sets C, D, and E to answer the following questions:

1. Find the mean and median for set C.

2. What number must be added to set C so that it will have its average or mean that is equal to 6? What will the median be after the addition of that number to set C?

3. Find the mean and median for set D.

4. What will the new median for Set D be if a number larger than 10 is added to set D?

5. What will the new median for set D be if a number smaller than 6 is added to set D?

6. Find the mean and median for set E.

7. How will adding the number 1000 change the mean and median for set E?

8. How will the mean and median be changed if several numbers are removed from set E?

The Mode

The *mode* is the number in a set that occurs most frequently. It is one of the least used of the elementary statistical measures. (The term is used in a non-numerical sense in the garment industry to assess such items as the style or color that is used most frequently in a given season.)

The Range

The *range* is the difference between the highest and lowest numbers in the set. The range gives an indication of the variation in the set. The range of {3, 4, 5} is 2. The range of {2, 4, 98} is 96. The range is useful for determining the scale for a graph.

The number of items in a set is not always included in the set of elementary statistical measures. The more items in a set, the less effect annexing or deleting a single number is likely to have on the measures discussed in this chapter.

No one number can accurately characterize a set of numbers. The more information available about a set, the more accurately one can understand the composition of that set. Mathematical statistics includes many more statistical measures than we can deal with at this level. One of the most important of these is standard deviation; that is discussed in detail in any standard text on statistics.

Exercise 17.1

Sets of numbers obtained from practical situations rarely have the unusual composition as the ones used in the following examples. These sets allow the reader to obtain a better understanding of the statistical measures we are discussing.

Find the *mean, median,* and *range* for the sets in exercises 1–8

1. {3, 7, 10, 24, 29}

2. (3, 7, 10, 20, 26, 30}

3. The rainfall for town A for seven days in the middle of summer was 0, 0, 0, 0, 0, 0, and 7 inches respectively.

4. For seven consecutive days, Jim earned 35, 20, 45, 30, 44, 50, and 0 dollars respectively.

5. The average snowfall for each of six fall and winter months is 3, 10, 11, 10, 7, and 8 inches.

6. A set has 10 numbers, 9 of which equal 100 and the tenth is equal to 1000.

7. A set has 1000 numbers, 999 of which equal 100. The thousandth number is equal to 1100.

8. What set of numbers added to set A will not change the range?

9. Describe a set with a range of zero.

10. Describe the mean, median, and mode of a set with a range of zero.

11. Choose a set of five scores for basketball, football, baseball, or a similar sport. Find the average score and median score of the losing teams, the average score and the median score of the winning teams, the average and the median of the differences between winning and losing scores.

Statistical Inference

Many industries test the quality of their total production by testing sets of samples selected at random. This process, called quality control or statistical inference, is based on probability and statistics. Much effort has been expended to determine the size of the smallest sample necessary to obtain an accurate assessment of the entire production.

Any one of the many polls that precede our elections is an example of statistical inference. Each of these polls collects samples of a small segment of the voting population, scientifically determined, and uses this information to predict the outcome of the election. A poll predicting the presidential election of 1936 failed badly because it contacted only people with telephones and automobiles, definitely not a random sample of an entire population in a depression. Getting small samples that accurately mirror the composition of an entire population of people is a complex process. The sample must take into consideration such things as economic situation, gender, ethnic background, and so on. Current polls will often indicate the percent of maximum error such as 3 percent or 5 percent.

The mathematics of predicting elections by examining samples has much in common with the quality-control procedures used in industry but is more complex because it is easier to sample a homogeneous set, such as the items from a production line, than a complex set of people.

Program P17.5 allows examination of random samples for the set {1, 2, 3, 4, . . ., 99, 100}. By experimenting with different-size samples, some indication may be obtained about the sample size and the number of samples necessary to give a reasonable representation of the entire set. Run the program and enter 10 at the input prompt. The program will display 10 random numbers selected from the set 1–100. If this sample is a *true* representative of the entire set, it will have five odd numbers and five even numbers because the parent set is half even and half odd. Similarly, there should be three multiples of 3, two multiples of 5, and one multiple of 10. Experiment to discover the approximate number and size necessary to give a reasonable picture of the parent set, but remember that one sample is not enough. Run the program a half-dozen times with an entry of 10 to see the wide variation in a single random sample. Refer to activity 9 on page 376 for an example of a simplified approach to the sampling process. Although Program P17.5 provides an opportunity to get a glimpse of sampling procedures, inferential statistics is too complex to examine in more detail at this level.

Functions

The set of numbers {60,65,70,80,90} is just that, a set of numbers. However, if each number in the set represents the temperature at 8, 9, 10, 11, and 12 o'clock, we have a set of ordered pairs, a *function*.

We work with functions in three ways: formulas, tables, and graphs. Each has its advantages and disadvantages.

A formula is the most compact way to represent a function, but it may take complex computations to find ordered pairs.

A table is a convenient way to list selected ordered pairs of a function, but it is impossible to list all the ordered pairs of the inch–centimeter function described by the formula: in. = 2.54 cm.

Graphs give an excellent overall view of a function, but obtaining accurate information from them is often difficult.

As noted in Chapter 2, every school should have a graph program available that can take the data pupils enter into the computer and print professional-looking bar graphs and circle graphs as well as graphs of mathematical functions. A given set of data can be represented in three or more styles so that the pupils can begin to recognize the

Figure 17.3

Time	Temperature
8	***** ****
9	***** *****
10	***** ***** **
11	***** ***** ***
12	***** ***** ***** *

Each * represents 5 degrees

advantages and shortcomings of each. The ability to see graphs of data pupils have collected will generate enthusiasm for such projects.

A graphics program, often called a *paint program*, can be valuable for constructing dictinctive graphs as well as many mathematics figures and diagrams. The graphs in exercises 4 and 5 below were constructed with a paint program.

Determining the Scale

Determining the scale is an important part of creating a graph to represent a set of ordered pairs.

To determine the scale for the first elements of the set (0, 11), (5, 7), (10, 13), (15, 27), and (20, 53), find the range to be 20 − 0 = 20 so that a scale with four intervals of five with endpoints labled 0, 5, 10, 15, and 20 is the most natural. For some purposes, a scale of two intervals of ten with endpoints 0, 10, and 20 may be reasonable. The latter scale is acceptable when accuracy in determining specific values is not important.

To determine the scale for the set of second elements, note that the range is 53 − 7 = 45. Divide 45 by 10 and round to 5 to indicate a scale with five intervals of ten with endpoints of 0, 10, 20, 30, 40, and 50.

A scale interval of 5 requires endpoints of 0, 5, 10, 15, 20, 25, 30, 35, 40, 45, and 50.

The range is the key statistical measure for determing the scale of a graph. However, the required accuracy and the space available for the graph must also be considered.

Exercise 17.2

1. Find temperature at 8 o'clock and 12 o'clock for graph in Figure 17.3

2. Draw a graph similar to that in Figure 17.3 to represent temperatures 35, 40, 40, 45, and 50 at 8, 9, 10, 11, and 12 o'clock respectively.

3. A company's production for the years 1975, 1980, 1985, and 1990 was 1,000,000, 1,500,000, 2,000,000, and 2,000,000 units respectively. Draw a graph to represent this information.

4. Use the line graph in Figure 17.4.
   a. What were sales for 1980?
   b. In what year were sales the lowest?
   c. In what year were sales the highest?

Figure 17.4

5. Use the bar graph in Figure 17.5
   a. Give the output of the Diamond mine.
   b. Give the output of the Loadstone mine.

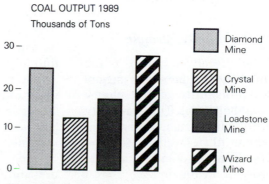

Figure 17.5

Teaching Probability

An individual may look at the sky and predict that it probably will rain. Even though the prediction is based on experience, it is just a guess. The weather bureau, however, predicts the probability of rain on a much more scientific basis by using such factors as humidity, atmospheric pressure, dewpoint, and wind patterns. When the weather bureau states that there is a 30 percent probability of rain, it means that rain has occurred on three out of ten days in the past when the measurable conditions were about the same as on the day of the prediction.

Probability and statistics are often very closely related. Statistics helps us analyze the past and present while probability may, in a limited way, help us predict the future.

Theoretical Probability: The Formula

The probability of an event is the ratio of the number of equally likely ways that it can succeed (S) to the total number of equally likely ways that it can happen (H).

The total number of ways an event can happen (H) is equal to the sum of the number of ways that it can succeed (S) and the number of ways that it can fail (F). Therefore: $H = S + F$.

Because of the relation $H = S + F$, the probability formula appears in the literature in both of the following ways:

(1) $P = S/H$ (2) $P = S/(S + F)$

Applying the Probability Formula

Half of the whole numbers from 1 to 100 are even. If one of these numbers is chosen at random, the probability of the choice being even is one-half (1/2). There are fifty ways in which the choice can succeed and fifty ways in which it can fail, $S = 50$, $F = 50$, and $H = 100$. The use of either formula gives a probability of 50/100 or 1/2.

A coin toss is frequently used to decide which team receives or kicks off in football and for similar choices in other sports. For the choice of either heads or tails with a coin, $S = 1$, $F = 1$, and $H = 2$. Therefore the probability of either a head or a tail is 1/2.

A pair of dice is used for many board games, including backgammon and Monopoly. A single die is used for others, such as Trivial Pursuit. A die (the singular of *dice*) is a cube with six faces numbered from 1 to 6. For the probability of obtaining a 6, $S = 1$, $F = 5$, and $H = 6$. Therefore the probability of throwing a 6 with a single toss is one-sixth (1/6). It follows that the probability for tossing a 1 or 2 or 3 or 4 or 5 is also 1/6.

Many board games use a spinner in which an arrow is attached to a circle containing congruent sectors, often 6. When spun, the arrow will stop on one of the numbered sectors. The probability of its stopping in any sector is 1/A where A is the number of congruent sectors in which the circle has been divided, $S = 1$, $F = A - 1$, and $H = A$.

A box contains five objects, numbered from 1 to 5, with identical size and feel. If an object is drawn at random so that the number cannot be identified until it is removed, the probability of drawing object number 5 is one-fifth (1/5). $S = 1$; $F = 4$; $H = 5$; $P = 1/5$

Experimental Probability

There are many situations in which the information required for the formula cannot be calculated because there is no count to find S and F other than by experiment. One example is the statement that the probability of rain is 10 percent. This statement can be made with reasonable accuracy only on the basis of experience and careful record-keeping.

Two additional examples of experimental probability are:

1. It is often said in baseball that a player is a 300 hitter, indicating that the probability that he will get a hit is at least 300/1000 or .3. This is an example of the many things in baseball that are based on experimental probability. The designation as a 300 hitter is based on the past performance of obtaining an average of three or more hits for every ten times at bat. Managers will change a pitcher from a left-hander to a right-hander to face a given batter, based on experience—often called playing the percentages, which is pure experimental probability.

2. A die with five numbered faces is in the form of an irregular polyhedron. It is tossed 10,000 times with the following results:

1 − 1490; 2 − 2510; 3 − 3000;
4 − 996; 5 − 2004;

For the probability of obtaining a 1, S = 1490, F = 8410, N = 10,000. Therefore P = 1490/10,000 or .149 or 14.9%

Find the remaining probabilities to the nearest thousandth.

Equally Likely Choices

The importance of the condition that the events must be equally likely cannot be overemphasized. One can argue that the probability of becoming a millionaire is 1/2 because there are only two possibilities: You will or will not become a millionaire. Therefore S = 1, F = 1, and P = 1/2. The obvious fallacy is that the two events are not *equally* likely. This illustration should make it clear that the probability formula is meaningless unless it is applied to events that are equally likely.

A random choice is one that has no other factor than chance involved in its selection. A random selection requires that every item in the selection set must have an equal chance of being chosen. Random selection is as important to probability as the concept of equally likely possibilities. Industry rarely tests every item that it manufactures to identify defective products. Instead, companies rely on random choice of samples. Experience has shown that by testing an appropriate number of *random* samples, the number of defective items in the entire production can be predicted quite accurately.

If one wants to find the probability of choosing a pupil who can swim from an entire student body, it is not a random choice to ask only members of the swimming team. A sample poll at a political rally for a given party would be of little value in predicting the election.

Counting and Probability

Counting various possible situations for computing probabilities is an important mathematical activity. The counting process varies from simple to complex. Many beginners will not count correctly in the situation where a coin is tossed twice. A superficial count indicates three situations: two heads, two tails, and a head and a tail. The correct count is four: two heads, two tails, a head and tail, and finally a tail and a head, as indicated by the following tree diagram.

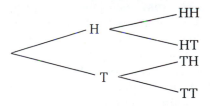

Because there are four possibilities (as seen in the diagram), there are two ways in which the requirement that the coins are not both heads or both tails succeeds, HT and TH(S = 2), and two ways in which it can fail, HH and TT(F = 2). Therefore P = 2/ (2 + 2) = 1/2,

Experimental Versus Theoretical Probability

Theoretical probability uses the formula and *experimental probability* uses past experience to predict the number of successes that will occur for a sequence of random events.

Neither type of probability can predict the outcome of a single random event. The predictions of the two types may differ substantially for a small number of trials but they usually give reliable approximations for the number of successes obtained with a large number of random events. As the number of trials increases, the difference between theoretical and experimental probability approaches zero.

Theoretical probability is unreliable when the counting of possible successes is incorrect. For example, as indicated previously, an individual may count three possibilities for the toss of two coins: (1) 2 heads; (2) 2 tails; (3) a head and a tail. For this count, the formula gives a probability of 1/3 for obtaining unlike results. With a sufficient number of trials, the experimental approach will indicate that the probability is 1/2 rather than 1/3 so that a reassessment of the theoretical approach is in order.

Experimental probability can be tedious. The task of tossing a coin 1000 times and recording each toss is time-consuming. Computer simulations that replace the activity of tossing a coin are available and give an excellent approximation of physical experimental results. The computer activities at the end of this chapter offer programs that simulate coin-tossing as well as other activities.

Situations Involving **and** *and* **or**

In the following discussion we will use the abbreviations:

$P(A)$ = the probability of an event A

$P(B)$ = the probability of an event B

$P(A$ or $B)$ represents the probability of "A or B"

$P(A$ and $B)$ represents the probability of "A and B"

Two of the most fundamental problems in elementary probability are:

Given: $P(A)$ and $P(B)$

1. Find $P(A$ or $B)$
2. Find $P(A$ and $B)$

A request for $P(A$ or $B)$ implies that if A occurs then B cannot occur and if B occurs, then A cannot. In this situation, A and B are often described as mutually exclusive events.

A request for $P(A$ and $B)$ implies that if A occurs, B may or may not occur and if B occurs, then A may or may not occur. In this situation, A and B are often described as independent events.

1. Find the probability of obtaining a head or a tail on the single toss of a coin: $P(A) = 1/2$ and $P(B) = 1/2 \rightarrow P(A$ or $B) = 1/2 + 1/2 = 1$.

A probability of 1 indicates that an event is *certain*. A single coin toss must give either a head or tail. The two events are mutually exclusive.

2. Find the probability of obtaining a head on each of two successive coin tosses: $P(A) = 1/2$ $P(B) = 1/2 \rightarrow P(A$ and $B)$ $1/2 \times 1/2 = 1/4$.

Obtaining a head on the first toss has no effect on the result of the second toss. The events are independent.

A problem may involve both *and* and *or* without specifically mentioning either of them, as in finding the probability that the result of two successive tosses will be the same. This requires that both tosses be heads *or* that both tosses be tails. The probability that both tosses will be heads is the same as finding the probability of a head *and* a head, which is $1/2 \times 1/2$ or $1/4$. The same argument indicates that the probability of a tail *and* a tail is 1/4. Therefore the probability of a head *and* a head *or* a tail *and* a tail is 1/4 + 1/4 or 1/2. This conclusion can be verified by referring to the tree diagram on page 373.

Complementary Probabilities

We know that the probability of obtaining a 6 on the single toss of a die is 1/6. Therefore the probability of not obtaining a 6 is 1 − 1/6 = 5/6. This can be verified by asking the probability of obtaining 1 *or* 2 *or* 3 *or* 4 *or* 5, which is equal to 1/6 + 1/6 + 1/6 + 1/6 + 1/6 = 5/6.

A and B are complementary events:

1. If A occurs, then B cannot occur. If B occurs, then A cannot occur.

2. The probability of A not occurring is 1 − P(A) = P(B).

3. The probability of B not occurring is 1 − P(B) = P(A).

The birthday problem is famous because it defies intuition. It asks for the probability that two people will have the same birthday if they are in a room with N people. Another variation asks how many people must be in a room for the probability of two people having the same birthday to be more than 1/2. Complementary probability combined with the *and* concept leads to a solution that is simple in theory but difficult in computation.

The plan is to find the probability that no two people in the group have the same birthday. The complementary probability then indicates the probability that at least two people have the same birthday.

We start with a group containing individuals which we will call A, B, C, D, E, and so on. B will have a different birthday than A for 364 out of 365 days in the year. If P(B) is the probability that B has a different birthday than A, then P(B) = 364/365. If P(C) is the probability that C has a different

birthday than A or B, then P(C) = 363/365. Therefore P(B *and* C) = P(B) × P(C), the probability that A, B, and C have different birthdays. Therefore:

P(B and C) = 364/365 × 363/365
P(B and C and D) = 364/365 × 363/365 × 362/365

From this pattern it follows that the probability that N people will have different birthdays is the product of N − 1 fractions, each with a denominator of 365 and with numerators starting with 364 and decreasing by 1. When this computation is completed, we have the probability of N different people all having different birthdays. The resulting fraction must be subtracted from 1 to find the probability that at least two people in the group will have the same birthday.

Paper-and-pencil computation is out of the question, but Program P17.5 performs this computation in seconds. It lists pairs of complementary probabilities (refer to page 379 for details). The surprising fact is that if twenty-three people are in a room the probability that at least two have the same birthday is about 1/2.

Fallacies

The most common fallacy with regard to probability is the belief that if five heads are obtained in five tosses, the probability of a tail on the next toss is greater than 1/2. Coins have no memory. The probability of obtaining a head on any toss, whether it is the first or the millionth, is 1/2.

The probability of obtaining a head *and* a head *and* a head *and* a head *and* a head is 1/2 × 1/2 × 1/2 × 1/2 × 1/2 = 1/32. In more convenient language, the probability of obtaining five heads in five consecutive tosses of the coin is 1/32. The probability of obtaining N heads from N successive tosses is $(1/2)^N$. Program 17.1 on page 377 is a computer simulation of tossing a coin and allows one to see the simulated result of tossing a coin 100 times in a few seconds.

The second fallacy is that the probability of 1/2 for heads in a coin toss means that every time the coin is tossed ten times, there will always be five heads and, therefore, five tails. Understanding the difference between theoretical and experimental probability should make it clear that this is a false concept. Program P17.2 is also a coin-tossing simulation but displays the result of each toss and shows the consecutive occurrence of heads and tails. Run P17.2 often enough to see that a sequence of five or more consecutive heads or tails is not unusual.

Activities

1. Have every member of the class open a book at random and give the page number on the right-hand page. Record whether the number is even or odd until it is discovered that all the numbers are odd.

2. The lack of randomness in exercise 1 can be eliminated by being certain that the pupils use both right- and left-hand pages at random. These first two exercises offer the opportunity for stressing the importance of random selection.

3. Obtain a spinner like the one frequently used with board games. Spin it dozens of times or so a day and record the result. As the number of spins increases, each number should occur approximately the same number of times. A mechanical defect in the spinner might affect its randomness.

4. Place marbles or markers of two different colors in a container so that one or more can be withdrawn without knowing the color. Place twice as many of one color as of the other and mix thoroughly. Then have each pupil withdraw a marble without looking and record the results. If the marbles are well mixed, the results should approach a 2-to-1 ratio. Experiment with different ratios having probabilities of 1/4 and 1/5.

5. Lack of randomness may be demonstrated by deliberately placing all the marbles of each color together.

6. Reverse the process and don't tell the pupils the ratio. This provides an introduction to sampling by seeing how many marbles must be drawn before the pupils can guess the approximate ratio.

7. Place a set of ten thumbtacks in a container and empty the container. Repeat and record results over a period of time to determine the experimental probability of the position that a thumbtack will land with point up or on its side. Pupils must handle the thumbtacks with care.

8. Toss four pennies at a time several times a day over a period of time and record how many times each of the following is obtained: four heads and no tails, three heads and a tail, two heads and two tails, one head and three tails, and no heads and four tails. Compare your results with the following theoretical ratios of probability: 1 : 4 : 6 : 4 : 1 for four heads, three heads, two heads, one head, and no heads respectively.

9. Use Program P17.5 on page 379. Run the program three times and insert 10 at the input prompt on each run. Complete a table similar to the one on page 377, which was obtained in this manner.

Because 10 is 1/10 of 100, if the above results mirror the population of 100, multiplying each average by 10 should give the corresponding number of that item in the parent set. Therefore, from the above table we infer that the set {1-100} contains 53 even numbers, 30 primes, 33 multiples of 3, and 17 multiples of 5. When these results are compared with the actual 50 even numbers, 25 primes, 33 multiples of 3, and 20 multiples of 5, the estimate is not exact but is a reasonable approximation.

	Run #1	Run #2	Run #3	Mean
Even numbers	4	7	5	5.3
Primes	2	4	3	3
Multiples of 3	2	5	3	3.3
Multiples of 5	1	1	3	1.7

When you have completed your three runs and filled out the table, compare your results with the correct values, just illustrated, to help you understand a simplified approach to the sampling procedure.

Computer Activities

Program P17.1 requires an entry of the number of tosses desired. It then displays the total number of heads and tails without displaying the results of individual tosses.

```
PROGRAM P17.1
 10 HOME: VTAB 8
 20 CLEAR
 30 INPUT "INDICATE THE
    NUMBER OF TOSSES";R
 35 PRINT
 36 PRINT "WAIT!!!"
 37 PRINT
 40 N = RND(1)
 50 IF N <.5 THEN 90
 60 K = K + 1
 70 IF K + W > R - 1 THEN 120
 80 GOTO 40
 90 W = W + 1
100 IF K + W > R - 1 THEN 120
110 GOTO 40
120 PRINT
130 PRINT "HEADS-> ";K;"
    TAILS-> ";W
```

Program P17.2 is also a coin-tossing simulation but displays the result of each toss so that sequences of consecutive tosses can be observed.

Obtain Program P17.2 from P17.1 by making the following changes:

Delete lines 35, 36, and 37 by typing the line numbers and pressing RETURN without any keyboard entry.

Retype line 30 as: FOR J = 1 + R1 TO 10 + R1
Retype line 70 as: PRINT "H";
Retype line 100 as: PRINT "T";
Retype line 110 as: NEXT
Insert line 115 as: R1 = R1 + 10
Enter line 140 as: INPUT Z$
Enter line 150 as: GOTO 30

This program is a continuous or infinite loop. It will stop after every 10 tails occur (or after 10 cycles of the FOR-NEXT loop) to display totals. If there are ten heads with the ten tails, there will be twenty lines of output between pauses. If there are five heads with the ten tails, there will be fifteen lines of output between pauses. A CTRL-C or equivalent instruction is required to exit the program.

One measure of the difference between experimental and theoretical probability is the difference between the expected and actual number of successes. When fifty heads are expected from 100 tosses and forty occur, the difference is ten, which is 10 percent of the 100 tosses. In a million tosses the difference might be 100, ten times the difference of ten with 100 tosses but one-

one-hundredth of 1 percent of 1,000,000 tosses.

Program P17.3 is a birthday-distribution simulation. When 20 is entered at the input prompt, twenty numbers from 1 to 365 are displayed. Each number is interpreted as a birthday. The number 200 indicates that a person in the group has a birthday on the 200th day of the year. The program is designed to show how often one might expect to find two or more people in a group with the same birthday. With a sufficient number of trials, Program P17.3 will confirm that, given a group of twenty-three people, the probability that two people will have the same birthday is about 1/2.

```
PROGRAM P17.3
  10 HOME: VTAB 8
  20 INPUT "ENTER NUMBER OF
     PEOPLE ";N
  30 DIM T(N)
  40 FOR J = 1 TO N
  50 T(J) = 1 + INT(365
     *RND(1))
  60 NEXT J
  70 PRINT
  80 R = 0
  90 FOR L = 1 to N - 1
 100 IF T(L) < = T(L + 1)
     THEN 150
 110 Z = T(L)
 120 T(L) = T(L + 1)
 130 T(L + 1) = Z
 140 R = 1
 150 NEXT L
 160 IF R = 1 THEN 80
 170 FOR L = 1 TO N
 180 IF T(L) <> 0 THEN PRINT
     T(L);" ";
 190 NEXT L
```

The length of Program P17.3 is necessary in order to display the numbers in sequence to make it easier to tell when two people have the same birthday.

Program P17.4 performs the computation for the birthday probability described on page 375. Few, if any, programs in the text demonstrate the computational power of the computer better this this one. In seconds the program finds the product of more than twenty fractions. Each has a denominator of 365, with all numerators greater than 300.

The program starts with the division 364/354 and then multiplies the quotient by 363. This product is then divided by 365. The pattern of divide, multiply, divide is repeated until the computation is completed. Encourage pupils to perform the multiplication for three of these fractions to learn a useful method of dealing with such products.

If 23 is the INPUT in line 20 for the number of people, the program will display 22 pairs of complementary probabilities with the last pair being .494 and .596. The .494 indicates the probability that all birthdays in the group of 23 will be different. Therefore the complementary probability of .506 indicates that the probability that at least two people will have the same birthday is about 1/2. Note that .494 + .506 = 1.

If 50 is entered at the input prompt, the program indicates that the probability of at least two people having the same birthday is .971, almost certain.

```
PROGRAM P17.4
  10 T = 1
  20 HOME: VTAB 8
  30 PRINT "ENTER THE NUMBER
OF PEOPLE IN THE GROUP";N
  40 PRINT
  50 PRINT
  60 INPUT Z$ : HOME
  70 FOR J = 1 TO N-1
  80 B = 365 - J
  90 B1 = B/365
 100 T = T*B1
 110 PRINT J + 1; TAB(8) :
```

```
       T ; TAB(20) ; 1 - T
 120 NEXT J
```

Program P17.5 offers a very elementary approach to statistical inference. It allows the pupil to choose a random sample from the set 1-100. The sample may then be examined to see how its composition compares with the entire set. If 10 is entered at the input prompt, a set of ten random numbers from 1 to 100 is displayed. If this set mirrors the entire population, it will contain five even and five odd numbers, two or three prime numbers, three multiples of 3, two multiples of 5, and so on. This analysis is excellent reenforcement for recognizing primes, multiples, and the like. The program includes the list of all twenty-five prime numbers less than 100 as a reference to help pupils check the sample for primes. This feature may be eliminated by omitting lines 80 to 160.

```
PROGRAM P17.5
  10 HOME : VTAB 3
  20 INPUT "ENTER N TO OBTAIN
     A RANDOM SAMPLE OF N
     ITEMS FROM {1-100}";N
  30 PRINT
  40 FOR J = 1 TO N
  50 PRINT INT(1 + 100 *
     RND(1));" ";
  60 NEXT N
  70 PRINT : PRINT
  80 PRINT "A LIST OF THE 25
     PRIMES LESS THAN 100
     FOLLOWS FOR CONVENIENT
     REFERENCE:"
  90 PRINT
 100 PRINT "2 3 ";
 110 FOR B = 5 TO 100 STEP 2
 120 FOR C = 3 TO SQR(B)
     STEP 2
 130 IF B/C = INT (B/C)
     THEN 160
 140 NEXT C
```

```
 150 PRINT B;" ";
 160 NEXT B
```

Summary

Statistics and probability are more evident in everyday living than ever before. We are flooded with information, much of it numerical. Simple statistical measures, such as mean (average) and median, help to keep things in perspective, but it is important to realize their limitations. It is possible to drown in a pond with an average depth of 1 inch. This old saying should remind us of the limitation of using a single measure to describe a set of numbers.

It is often easier to find a major newspaper with one or more graphs than without any. Graphs help us digest some aspects of a large amount of information at a glance, but their limitations must also be recognized. A table or formula can provide much more specific information when it is needed, but many functions have no formula and the table is useless if it does not cover the area of interest.

Probability is most meaningful to elementary pupils when learned by experience. It has predictive value with major limitations. If these limitations are not understood, conclusions obtained from data can be pure fiction. The computer makes it easier and provides a broader range of activities for understanding probability.

The chapter covers an introduction to graphing and the basic statistical measures of mean, median, mode, and range. The probability section introduces the probability formula and emphasizes the distinction between theoretical and experimental probability. Each is of little or no help for predicting the outcome of a single event but can be very useful in predicting the result of many events.

Exercise 17.3

1. Find the mean, median, and range of {2, 3, 5, 7, 8}.

2. Find the mean, median, and range of {6, 12, 18, 24}.

3. Explain why the median is usually considered a better single characterization of {1, 2, 3, 4, 5, 6, 7, 1000} than the mean.

4. List three ways of describing a function and an advantage and disadvantage for each.

5. If a coin is tossed twice, what is the probability of both tosses giving the same result?

6. What is the probability for five consecutive tosses of a coin that the result of all five tosses will be the same? not the same?

7. What is the probability that for three tosses of the coin that the results will not all be the same?

The following questions assume that a container contains three white markers, four yellow markers, and seven red markers.

8. If one marker is drawn at random, what is the probability of drawing a white marker? a yellow marker? a red marker?

9. If one marker is drawn at random, what is the probability of drawing a white or yellow marker? What is the probability of not drawing a red marker?

10. What is the probability of drawing a white and a red marker if the first marker is replaced before the second is drawn?

Selected Readings

Bennett, Albert B., Jr. and Leonard T. Nelson. *Mathematics—An Informal Approach.* Needham Heights, MA: Allyn & Bacon, 1985. Chapter 10.

Bitter, Gary G., et. al. *Mathematics Methods for the Elementary and Middle School.* Needham Heights, MA: Allyn & Bacon, 1989. Chapter 12.

Choate, L. D., and J. K. Okey. "Graphically Speaking: Primary-level Graphing Experiences," in *Teaching Statistics and Probability,* 1981 Yearbook. Reston, VA: National Council of Teachers of Mathematics, 1981. Pp. 1–7.

Collins, B. "Using Your Children's First Names for a Graphing Project," *Journal of the British Columbia Primary Teachers Association, 22* (February 1981): 52–56.

Heddens, James W., and William R. Speer. *Today's Mathematics,* 6th ed. Chicago: Science Research Associates, 1988. Unit 16.

Kennedy, Leonard M., and Steve Tipps. *Guiding Children's Learning of Mathematics,* 5th ed. Belmont, CA: Wadsworth, 1988. Chapter 14.

Pereira-Mendoza, L., and J. Swift. "Why Teach Statistics and Probability: A Rationale," in *Teaching Statistics and Probability,* 1981 Yearbook. Reston, VA: National Council of Teachers of Mathematics, 1981. Pp. 33–40.

Reys, Robert E., et. al. *Helping Children Learn Mathematics,* 2nd ed. Englewood Cliffs, NJ: Prentice-Hall, 1989. Chapter 14.

Riedesel, C. Alan. *Teaching Elementary School Mathematics,* 4th ed. Englewood Cliffs, NJ: Prentice-Hall, 1985. Chapter 12.

Shulte, Albert P., and James R. Smart (eds.). *Teaching Statistics and Probability,* 1981 Yearbook. Reston, Va: National Council of Teachers of Mathematics, 1981.

Sobel, Max A., and Evan M. Maletsky. *Teaching Mathematics,* 2nd ed. Englewood Cliffs, NJ: Prentice-Hall, 1988. Chapter 8.

Souviney, Randall. *Learning to Teach Mathematics.* Columbus, OH: Merrill, 1989. Chapter 14.

Wiebe, James H. *Teaching Elementary Mathematics in a Technological Age.* Scottsdale, AZ: Gorsuch Scarisbriek, 1989. Chapter 18.

Teaching Minorities and Limited-English-Proficient Pupils

ACHIEVEMENT GOALS

After studying this chapter, you should be able to:

1. Summarize data regarding the number and percent of pupils in the schools who speak languages other than English.

2. Discuss the achievement in mathematics of minorities and limited-English-proficient pupils.

3. Describe bilingual approaches, including advantages and disadvantages, to teaching limited-English-speaking pupils mathematics.

4. Describe English as a Second Language (ESL) approaches to teaching mathematics, including a description of their advantages and disadvantages.

5. Outline special instructional approaches that are successful in teaching limited-English-proficient pupils.

6. List suggested ways of working with parents of minority and limited-English-proficient pupils.

VOCABULARY

These terms are defined or illustrated in the context of their use.

Bilingual
  education
  program
Chapter 1
  programs
English as a
  Second
  Language (ESL)
  approach
Hispanic

Immersion
  approach
Limited-English-
  proficient
Maintenance
  approach
Minority
Transitional
  program

The elementary school of the 1990s will continue to be faced with the very difficult task of trying to offset the forces of poverty, racial isolation, and limited English proficiency that plague many elementary school pupils of America. The number of limited-English-speaking pupils from the age of 5 to 14 will increase from 2.4 million in 1980 to over 3.4 million in the year 2000.[1]

It is estimated that in 1988 one of every four students enrolled in the schools of the United States came from a family living in poverty. More than 15 percent of America's elementary school pupils cannot speak English. "After the year 2000, one out of every three Americans will be non-white. Teachers daily encounter learning problems related to students' race, class, and gender."[2]

Providing for individualized differences (as discussed in Chapter 4), if appropriately implemented, will lead to success in mathematics for most elementary school pupils. However, there is a growing number of poor, minority and/or limited-English-proficient pupils who must be provided special instruction to develop proficiency in mathematics. Over the past fifteen years a large immigration to the United States has resulted in record numbers of limited-English-speaking pupils in the public schools. As Joan First points out, the extraordinary cultural diversity and backgrounds of these new arrivals present difficult challenges that must be met if this country is to benefit from their vital resources. It is important to teach mathematics to minority and limited-English-proficient pupils so that their primary language and culture is respected.[3]

Major forces associated with the underachievement of minorities are created by the status of the family, which is affected by income, occupational level, educational level, home climate, and parental attitudes. These factors must be addressed by society at large and cannot generally be changed by the schools except over a long period in very indirect ways.

In this chapter we define *minorities* to include blacks, Hispanics, Native Americans, Eskimos, whites living in poverty, and other ethnic groups whose achievement is unsatisfactory due to limited English proficiency.

Languages Spoken by 5- To 17-Year-Olds

According to the 1989 edition of the *World Almanac* there are 47,494,000 children and youth from the age of 5 to 17 years in the United States. Of this number, about 14 percent (4,568,000) speak a language other than English; of these about 65 percent speak Spanish (2,952,000 individuals).[4]

In 1978 there were more than 3 million Hispanics enrolled in United States schools.[5] This represented about 7 percent of the school population in 1978. (In 1987 it was 9 percent.) Thirty percent of students in New York City speak Spanish. More than 50 percent of the school population in San Diego, Los Angeles, and Miami speak Spanish. Texas has more than one million students in the schools who speak Spanish. Bernard McFadden concludes that "a significant and growing proportion of American children are entering school with a knowl-

1. F. H. Nelson, "Issues in State Funding for Bilingual Education," *The Urban Review, 16* (4), 1984, pp. 195–205.

2. Carl A. Grant, "Race, Class, Gender," *The Elementary School Journal*, 88 (May 1988): 561–569.

3. Joan M. First, "Immigrant Students in U.S. Public Schools: Challenges with Solutions," *Phi Delta Kappan*, 70 (November 1988): 205–206.

4. *The World Almanac* (New York: Pharos Books, 1989), p. 222.

5. Hispanics are Spanish-speaking people from such groups as Mexican-American, Puerto Rican, Cuban, and others from the Caribbean Basin and Central and South America.

edge of English that is insufficient to comprehend what is taught in an English-language-only-classroom."[6] If pupils cannot understand English they will have difficulty learning mathematics, especially problem-solving aspects that rely so heavily on language and meaning skills.

Minorities in the United States

In 1987, of the almost 245 million people in the United States, about 30 million were enrolled in the public elementary schools. Of this number, about 71 percent were white, 16 percent were black, 9 percent were Hispanic, 2.5 percent were Asian or Pacific Islanders, and 0.9 percent were Native Americans.[7]

The density of minority population varies from state to state:

35 percent or more—California, New Mexico, Texas, Louisiana, Mississippi, South Carolina

25 to 34 percent— Arizona, Alabama, Georgia, Florida, North Carolina, Virginia, Delaware, Maryland, Washington D.C., New Jersey, New York, Illinois, Hawaii

10 to 24 percent— Alaska, Washington, Montana, Colorado, Nebraska, Kansas, Oklahoma, Tennessee, Michigan

All the other states have less than 10 percent minorities.[8]

Achievement of Minorities in Mathematics

According to John Dorsey, a majority of the pupils classified as minority in American schools are blacks and Hispanics. Data from the 1986 National Assessment of Educational Progress in Mathematics showed that black and Hispanic students improved in their performance over the 1978 assessment, but the difference in achievement between these minority groups and their white peers still remained substantial. Asian-American students, on the other hand, performed equal to or better than their white peers. Dorsey reports that the low achievement of black and Hispanic pupils in the 9-, 13-, and 17-year-old groups is a major concern for the schools.[9]

When children from minority groups enter school, their achievement is about the same as normal class achievement. By the end of the sixth grade, however, the median mathematics score for these minority children is about half a grade level below that of their white peers. By the end of the eighth grade, on the average, there is at least one whole grade-level difference.

A study involving 28,000 elementary school students in the Montgomery County Public Schools in Maryland found that by the end of the sixth grade 50 percent of the black and Hispanic students lacked the

6. Bernard J. McFadden, "Bilingual Education and the Law," *Journal of Law and Education*, 12 (January 1983): 1–27.

7. *Digest of Educational Statistics* (Washington, DC: U.S. Office of Education, Office of Educational Research and Improvement, 1987).

8. Leonard Olguin, "The Prize of American Life and Education: Minority Gains and Losses," *Action in Teacher Education*, 10 (Summer 1988): 2.

9. John A. Dorsey, *The Mathematics Report Card—Are We Measuring Up? Trends and Achievement Based on the 1986 National Assessment* (Princeton, NJ: Educational Testing Service, June 1988), pp. 21–24.

skills needed for advanced mathematics courses.[10]

The Legal Basis for Bilingual Programs

The *Lau v. Nichols* Supreme Court decision handed down in 1974 was based on a case in which limited-English-proficient Chinese-American students in San Francisco received no special instruction to meet their linguistic needs. The Court ruled that these students were denied equal educational opportunities because they were taught in a language they could not understand. When limited-English-proficient students are enrolled in a classroom where English is the only language of instruction, the schools must make special provisions for them. Since that decision, every state has implemented plans to teach English to limited-English-proficient students. Several approaches have been utilized, including bilingual education approaches and English as a second language approaches.

Bilingual Education Approaches

A "full" bilingual education is a program of instruction in which pupils develop competence in their primary language, while at the same time they learn a second language. The teacher knows and uses both languages. In most bilingual programs in the United States, the two languages are Spanish and English. The class is made up of some pupils whose primary language is Spanish and some pupils whose primary language is English. The goal is for the Spanish-speaking pupils to learn English and the English-speaking students to learn Spanish. Not

10. Robert Rothman, "Blacks, Hispanics Lag in Math by 3rd Grade," *Education Week*, August 3, 1988, p. 7.

more than 60 percent of the pupils should be from either language group. Instructional materials are in both languages.

This type of program received the federal government's endorsement with the passage of the Bilingual Education Act of 1968. This act required special programs in districts with large numbers of limited-English-proficient pupils. Title VII of the Elementary and Secondary Act of 1968 provided funding for bilingual programs.

Maintenance Bilingual Program

The hope of early proponents of bilingual education was for the students to learn school subjects in both their primary language and in a second language throughout their school years. The goal of the bilingual program is to teach English to those who have limited achievement in that language. English is then used to teach other school subjects and at the same time help to maintain proficiency in the primary language. The goal is not to teach the English-speaking pupils a second language. Both limited-English and fluent-English-speaking pupils are enrolled in the same class to avoid isolating the limited-English-speaking pupils from the fluent-English-speaking students. Besides, the English-speaking students provide useful models for the limited-English-proficient children.

Transitional Bilingual Program

In the transitional bilingual program, limited-English-proficient pupils receive initial instruction in their primary language at the same time they are learning English. When they become sufficiently proficient in English, no attempt is made to maintain their native language. As in other types of bilingual programs, at least 40 percent of the pupils enrolled in the class should be English-speaking. Public support for providing instruction in a pupil's primary language has declined in recent years. In the 1988 Gallup *Phi Kappa Deltan* Poll, 42 percent of the respondents favored bilingual education, 49 percent opposed it, and 9 percent were unsure.[11]

However, Dr. Lauro Cavazos, U.S. Secretary of Education (appointed in 1988), strongly supports bilingual education. He believes that children should be taught English as soon as possible while maintaining their own culture and primary language. He suggests that teachers need to:

1. Be linguistically and culturally sensitive to children's needs.

2. Have high expectations.

3. Take home backgrounds into account.

4. Integrate specialized services.

5. Provide parent education[12].

English as a Second Language (ESL)

In the English as a Second Language (ESL) approach, the children's primary language is not taught. The teacher or aide uses the children's first language to assist them in understanding English. It is not necessary for the teacher to know the primary language(s) of the students, but it is necessary for the teacher to understand the culture and ethnic beliefs of these pupils. It is also necessary for the teacher to understand and implement an effective ESL program with appropriate instructional materials. Special staff development programs should be provided at the school and district levels for ESL teachers and aides.

English as the Key to Learning Mathematics

Pupils must develop English competence to ensure success in mathematics. Minorities who are competent in English tend to perform at or near grade level, regardless of what language is spoken in the home. Robert Rothman asserts "It would appear that whether or not one comes from a home where a second language is frequently spoken is not an important issue in itself, but whether or not one is competent in English."[13]

Improving Mathematics Instruction for Bilinguals

Bilingual programs tend to emphasize the development of language skills—listening, speaking, reading, and writing. These skills are important in learning mathematics. Mary Jo Lass offers several suggestions for improving mathematics instruction for bilinguals based on research. Some of her chief suggestions are:

1. First develop bilingual students' first-language competence, then develop their English-language proficiency. This approach is especially important to improve later mathematical ability in English.

2. Teach mathematics to bilingual children bilingually. The role of language is vital in problem solving. Mathematics vocabulary should be taught directly and systematically.

3. Consider pairing English-dominant students with limited-English-proficient students for English mathematics instruction as one grouping method. Social-interaction patterns can affect mathematics achievement.

11. Alex M. Gallup and Stanley M. Elam, "The 20th Annual Gallup Poll of the Pupils' Attitude Toward the Schools," *Phi Delta Kappan*, 70 (September 1988): 39.

12. "Bilingual Education," *The Education Digest, 54* (January 1989): 68–69.

13. Robert Rothman, "English Fluency Attainment Linked in the New NAEP Study," *Education Week*, November 9, 1988, p. 1.

4. Teach problem solving directly. Use culturally relevant situations and illustrations.

5. Use individualized instruction and a diagnostic-prescriptive approach.

6. Provide extensive staff development, including opportunities for bilingual mathematics teachers to develop their own materials.

7. Develop a planned, parent-participation model.[14]

Develop First-Language Competence

When possible, limited-English-proficient pupils should learn mathematics concepts in their own language in order to improve later mathematics reasoning. It is desirable for the teacher or aide to know the primary language of the pupils and explain in simple terms the concepts involved. Extensive use should be made of manipulatives and visuals during the learning process. The emphasis should be placed on understanding.

Systematically Teach English

When pupils learn mathematics concepts in their own language they should discover the English words used to describe the concepts. During the initial stages of learning, emphasis should be placed on listening to the English words and then on saying them. Make a list of key mathematics terms and develop vocabulary systematically.

Have Available a Primary Language Helper

During instruction in mathematics, if the teacher does not know the primary language of the pupils, someone should be available—adult, parent, aide, tutor, or peer—who can explain the concept or skill to the pupils in their native language. If pupils understand words in their own language, they will learn the corresponding English words more readily.

Use the "Total Physical Response"

Limited-English-proficient pupils go through three preliminary stages in language acquisition:

1. Comprehension state. Listening, pointing, nodding.

2. Early speech state. One word or yes/no responses.

3. Speech emergence stage. Use of short phrases without fluency.

In learning mathematics pupils should use structured concrete materials and visual aids. The teacher should talk to the children about what they are doing and seeing. Capitalize on *actions* with concrete instructional materials. Show, do, and tell in the pupils' primary language and in English. Keep the language simple and directly related to the concept or skill being taught. Listening ability serves as the basis for speaking ability; therefore the emphasis should be placed first on comprehension rather than on production of language.[15]

Accommodate Individual Differences in the Self-Contained Classroom

Chapter 4 deals with individual differences in a self-contained classroom. It expresses the view that pupils should be kept together for the introduction of each unit in mathematics. Then various kinds of adjustments in time, space, people, curriculum, instructional materials, and teaching meth-

14. Mary Jo Lass, "Suggestions from Research for Improving Mathematics Instruction for Bilinguals," *School Science and Mathematics*, 88 (October 1988): 480–487.

15. Carmen T. Elenbaas, "Putting Language Acquisition Theory to Practice in the Classroom," *Resources in Education*, July 1983. ED226587.

ods are introduced. In grouping of minority and limited-English-proficient pupils, care should be taken to avoid assigning them to groups based upon such factors as ethnicity, sex, or physical or mental handicaps.[16]

Utilize Cooperative Learning Approaches

Limited-English pupils should be grouped with fluent-English-speaking pupils in pairs or groups of four as they are learning mathematics. Children learn from each other and the limited-English children will learn a great amount of English by working with fluent-English pupils. Research has shown that both groups profit academically from such grouping practices.

Implement a Mastery-Learning Plan

Group-paced mastery learning can be effectively used to help minority and limited-English-proficient pupils achieve a higher level of mastery. According to research by Herbert Walberg, the factors that tend to lead to higher achievement are:

1. Attentive behavior during class dicussions.

2. Active participation during follow-up activities.

3. Attention to individual tasks.

4. Positive motivation—wanting to learn.

5. Success[17].

Provide a Diagnostic-Prescriptive Approach

Individualized, self-paced learning based upon effective diagnosis should be used for those pupils who are still having difficulty after the teacher has implemented other approaches. Prescriptive activities should follow discovery experiences, directed teaching, and mastery-learning approaches. Individualized activities should be tracked by a structured hierarchy of concepts and skills in mathematics.

Utilize a "Talking Computer" Laboratory

Language is the foundation of literacy, and literacy is the mark of an educated person. In America today every citizen needs to be fluent in reading and writing English. Language proficiency also facilitates learning mathematics. The use of the "talking computer" may well be one of the school's most powerful resources for helping limited-English-proficient pupils learn English and mathematics.

Research has shown that it is highly feasible, practical, and educationally sound to use state-of-the-art "talking computers" and well-designed software to teach limited-English-proficient pupils. Upgrading current computer systems and purchasing new computers with voice synthesizers, combined with the use of specially designed software, greatly increases the value of the computer as a teaching tool. Pupils should be scheduled to work in the computer laboratory at least two fifty-minute periods per week. Schools that have used computer laboratories for computer-assisted instruction have witnessed a dramatic improvement in achievement in mathematics.[18]

16. See Louis Fischer and Gail Paulus Sorenson, "Legal Bases of Individualization," in *Individual Differences and the Common Curriculum,* Eighty-second Yearbook of the National Society for the Study of Education (Chicago: University of Chicago Press, 1983), pp. 75–100.

17. Herbert J. Walberg, "Synthesis of Research on Time and Learning," *Educational Leadership,* 45 (March 1988): 76–85.

18. Pat Ordovensky, "In School, Computers Get Good Feedback," in *USA Today,* January 17, 1989, p. 4D.

Involve Parents in the Instructional Program

There should be a close relationship between the school and parents. Schools can develop a well-planned parent-education program in which parents are involved in the following ways:

1. Become informed about school activities and specific instructional objectives.

2. Utilize materials sent home by the teacher to help their child learn.

3. Provide a home environment where everyday activities are used to develop children's behavior and attitudes toward high achievement in school.

4. Provide a home climate conducive to studying and completing assigned homework.

5. Monitor the television habits of their children and put a limit on the amount of time set aside for watching TV.

6. Volunteer to help in the classroom.

7. Attend parent-teacher conferences and parent-education meetings.[19]

Programs of the past for limited-English-proficient students have made a positive impact on their achievement. Research reported by James Crawford shows that Spanish-speakers in the United States are learning English more rapidly today than in previous generations. After fifteen years in the United States, 75 percent of Hispanic immigrants are speaking English on a daily basis.[20]

Government-Funded Compensatory Education

Poverty, racial isolation, and limited English ability are serious deterrents to becoming an educated person. A good education usually fosters economic security and social success. Children who grow up in poverty and are racially segregated often have low self-concepts and have difficulty learning.

The U.S. Supreme Court's decision *Brown v. Board of Education of Topeka* led to court-ordered integration of minorities in the public schools. The Court said that education was "perhaps the most important function of state and local governments. . . . In these days, it is doubtful that any child may reasonably be expected to succeed in life if he is denied the opportunity of an education . . . which must be made available to all on equal terms."[21]

In an effort to provide educational opportunities on an equal basis for all pupils, Congress initiated the Head Start and Title I programs.

Head Start

The Head Start program was initiated under the Economic Opportunity Act of 1964. Its main purpose was to provide educational experiences for poor, disadvantaged preschool children as an early intervention strategy to prepare them for school. Parent and community involvement was required. Later the federal government introduced Project Follow Through to help Head Start participants continue to learn in the primary grades.

The Elementary and Secondary Act

The *Elementary and Secondary Act of 1965* included the provision called Title I to provide funding for disadvantaged and under-

19. See Adriana de Kanter, et. al., "Parent Involvement Strategies: A New Emphasis on Traditional Parent Roles," *Resources in Education*, December 1986. ED233919.

20. James Crawford, "Study Charts Hispanics' Acquisition of English," *Education Week*, May 18, 1988, p. 4.

21. *Brown v. Board of Education of Topeka*, 347 U.S. 483 (1954).

achieving children. These programs, now called Chapter 1 and still in effect, are administered by state governments under federal guidelines. Money is allocated to school districts by the state based on the number of families receiving aid to dependent children. At the school level, pupils qualify for Chapter 1 services if they fall below a certain percentile on a nationally normed standardized test.

Early Programs for Poor and Underachieving Pupils

Instructional programs under Chapter 1 are of two types: (1) Pull-out programs and (2) in-class models. Most of the early programs were of the first type. A pull-out program generally is coordinated by a reading/ mathematics specialist assisted by several instructional aides. Identified pupils at each grade level are pulled out of the self-contained classroom for a period of thirty to fifty minutes each day. Pupils work in a specially equipped learning laboratory under the general direction of the specialist but usually with the instructional aid. The approach most frequently used is the "diagnostic-prescriptive individualized learning plan." In this plan pupils are tested in basic skills and placed on a continuum. Learning activities are directly related to helping the pupils learn what they missed on the test.

Nancy Madden and Robert Slavin reviewed research on effective pull-out programs and found three types: (1) diagnostic-prescriptive programs, (2) tutoring programs, and (3) computer-assisted instruction.[22]

Some researchers and school professionals questioned the practice of removing pupils from their classroom for instruction because they felt that while students were out of the room they were missing important activities. Also, it was felt that the pull-out program emphasized the idea that the identified pupils were "slow," thus contributing to a low self-image. Further, many felt that too much of the directed instruction was provided by untrained aides. There was therefore a movement to provide Chapter 1 services to identified pupils within the self-contained classroom.

In the in-class models the Chapter 1 specialist and/or the instructional aide worked in the classroom alongside the regular classroom teacher. The diagnostic-prescriptive, self-paced approach was still used as the instructional vehicle. Researchers have been unable to establish the superiority of either approach. What is important is the way the program is organized and implemented.

In-School Features of Effective Chapter 1 Programs

Robert Slavin made a comprehensive study of Chapter 1 programs that were identified as "exemplary" by the U.S. Department of Education. He found the following five features of effective Chapter 1 programs.[23]

Comprehensive Approach

The comprehensive approach is one in which the regular classroom is reorganized to enable the teacher to accommodate the wide range of student needs. The various techniques discussed in Chapter 4 to accommodate individual differences within the self-contained classroom have the great-

---

22. Nancy A. Madden and Robert E. Slavin, "Effective Pull-out Programs for Students at Risk," *Resources in Education*, April 1988. ED288921.

23. Robert E. Slavin, "Making Chapter 1 Make a Difference," *Phi Delta Kappan, 69* (October 1987): 110–119.

est potential for helping Chapter 1 pupils improve their achievement.

Continuous Progress Models

In the continuous progress model the pupils proceed at their own pace through a sequence of well-defined objectives. They are taught in small groups composed of pupils with like needs. Grouping is flexible and learners are regrouped as needed according to their achievement and needs.

Cooperative Learning Groups

As discussed in Chapter 4, cooperative learning groups of three to five are formed from mixed-ability students into teams that work together to accomplish specific tasks. Cooperative learning groups can work effectively as part of the mastery learning approach (also discussed in Chapter 4).

Tutoring Programs

The use of tutors is an effective way to increase the achievement of Chapter 1 pupils. Parent tutoring in home-based situations has been found to be effective for educationally disadvantaged children.[24] Tutoring programs use specially trained tutors to work individually with indentified pupils on specific mathematics concepts and skills. Tutors may be cross-age tutors, peer tutors, or adult tutors.

Computer-Assisted Instruction

One of the best approaches for completely individualizing the learning of mathematics for Chapter 1 pupils is to provide computer-assisted instruction.

Parent Support of Compensatory Education

For compensatory education to work, parents should be actively involved. Modes of participation should be developed whereby parents are directly involved in the education of their own children. Parents need to serve actively on school-site councils, participate in parent-education activities, and serve as tutors of their children. According to research by Dorothy Rich, the parent-as-tutor approach has high promise.[25]

Electronic Learning Aids

The Cassette Recorder

The cassette recorder can be valuable in a number of ways, particularly for recording the speech of a limited-English-proficient pupil. If the pronounciation of the pupil and a proper rendition of a sentence are recorded on the same tape, the pupil can get a repeated comparison of the difference between the two versions. If this is repeated over a period of time, progress can be accurately assessed. It is helpful for pupils to hear their voices and compare them with accepted models.

A recorded sentence for pupils to enter into a computer, as suggested in the following paragraph, can also be a valuable instructional aid. The computer can display the correct sentence for comparison with the pupil entry of the spoken sentence.

Computer Activities

Most computers in the schools have had talking capability for several years. With appropriate software they can reproduce speech typed into the keyboard. Additional

24. Milbrey W. McLaughlin and Parrick M. Shields, "Involving Parents in the Schools: Lessons for Policy", in Designs for Compensatory Education, *Resources in Education*, December 1986. ED293920.

25. Dorothy Rich, "The Parent Gap in Compensatory Education and How to Bridge It," *Resources in Education*, September 1988. ED293921.

speakers may be necessary, but even then the speech tends to sound more like a robot than a person. There has been constant improvement in this field. Computers with speech capability should be in a computer laboratory to be used by limited-English-proficiency pupils. Programs can be designed to allow pupils to read words or sentences on the computer screen and listen to them spoken by the computer. In a companion activity, the pupil types in words or sentences and hears the computer speak as this input is displayed on the screen. Some software packages also allow speech entry with the use of a phonetic alphabet, which can produce more natural-sounding speech when programmed by an expert.

Now becoming available is software that will enable the computer to translate the spoken word into digital data that can be stored in the computer for reproduction whenever desired. This enables pupils to speak to the computer and then see their spoken words translated into written form and displayed on the computer screen.

Computers without voice capability can be useful in a variety of ways. Program P18.1 demonstrates this versatility. The data pairs in lines 400-440 are deliberately diverse for illustrative purposes. Lines 10-100 with the DATA in lines 400-440 make a complete one-way program. Lines 200-300 give the reverse program. The initial program asks the pupil to enter the second member of a DATA pair in response to the display of the first. The second part of the program reverses this procedure.

By retyping the DATA in line 400-440 into equivalent pairs, dozens of programs illustrating specific concepts can be obtained. This is an ideal program for learning English vocabulary from Spanish or any other language. Enter each word and its equivalent as a DATA pair and the program will display the first word in the pair and ask for the second and reverse the procedure in the second part of the program.

Enter a set of sentences on a cassette program and time it so that the computer displays the sentence as it is spoken. If this sentence and its translation are placed as a DATA pair in P18.1, a correlation between spoken and written word similar to that described with the talking computer may be obtained. An alternate approach is for the teacher or aide to read the sentence as it is displayed on the computer.

The program is relatively easy to enter into a computer but, as with any program, strict accuracy is required. It is fairly long but the lines are not complicated.

```
PROGRAM P18.1
  10 FOR J = 1 TO 5
  20 HOME : VTAB 10
  30 PRINT "TRANSLATE"
  40 PRINT
  50 READ A$, B$
  60 PRINT A$;"-> ";
  70 INPUT " ";Z$
  80 PRINT A$; "-> ";B$
  90 INPUT Z$
 100 NEXT
 200 RESTORE
 210 FOR J = 1 TO 5
 220 HOME : VTAB 10
 230 PRINT "TRANSLATE"
 240 PRINT
 250 READ A$,B$
 260 PRINT B$;"-> ";
 270 INPUT " ";Z$
 280 PRINT B$; "-> ";A$
 290 INPUT Z$
 300 NEXT
 400 DATA 3,THREE
 410 DATA CINCO, 5 OR FIVE
 420 DATA 1 + 2 = 3,ONE PLUS
     TWO EQUALS THREE
 430 DATA CASA ROJA,RED HOUSE
 440 DATA 6/2=3,SIX DIVIDED
     BY TWO EQUALS THREE
```

Summary

During the past fifteen years there has been a heavy influx of immigrants to the United States, many of whose children come to school with limited English proficiency. A large majority of these children come from Hispanic families. This places a major responsibility upon the schools to provide special instructional adjustments so these children can learn English. Further, the black population is growing in America. Test scores of minorities are below class norms in mathematics. Special instructional adjustments must be made to accommodate these low-achieving pupils.

The *Lau v. Nichols* Supreme Court decision of 1974 led to the implementation of bilingual and English as a second language programs to assist limited-English-proficient pupils to learn English. In terms of learning mathematics, pupils should learn early concepts with manipulatives with someone present who can explain the ideas in the pupils' native language. English words should be added gradually and systematically. Cooperative learning groups where fluent-English pupils are paired with limited-English-proficient pupils have been found very helpful. A diagnostic-prescriptive approach should be implemented. The "talking computer" has been found to be a very effective instructional aid. Parents must be involved in a variety of ways in the instructional program.

Compensatory education is sponsored by the federal government to provide over-and-above instructional services to low-achieving pupils from high-poverty areas. Head Start and Chapter 1 programs are funded by the federal government. Chapter 1 programs are of two types: (1) pull-out and (2) in-class models. Both models require the assistance of specialist teachers and trained instructional aides. Features of effective Chapter 1 programs include: (1) a comprehensive approach, (2) a continuous progress model, (3) cooperative learning groups, (4) tutorial programs, (5) computer-assisted instruction, and (6) parent education and parent participation.

Selected Readings

Contreras, A. Reynaldo (ed.). *Bilingual Education*. Bloomington, IN: Phi Delta Kappa, April 1988.

Cocking, Rodney R., and Jose P. Mestre (eds.). *Linguistic and Cultural Influences on Learning Mathematics*. Hillsdale, NJ: Lawrence Erlbaum Associates, 1988.

Cox, T., and G. Jones. *Disadvantaged 11 Year Olds*. New York: Pergamon, 1983.

First, Joan M., et. al. *New Voices: Immigrant Students in U.S. Public Schools*. Boston: National Coalition of Advocates for Students, 1988.

Krause, Marina C. *Multicultural Mathematics Materials*. Reston, VA: National Council of Teachers of Mathematics, 1983.

Mathews, W. (ed.). "Minorities and Mathematics", special issue of the *Journal for Research in Mathematics Education*, 15 (March 1984).

Miller, Thomas, and Thomas Espenshade. *The Fourth Wave*. Washington, DC: Urban Institute Press, 1985.

Schofield, Janet Ward. *Black and White in School—Trust, Tension, or Tolerance?*. New York: Praeger, 1982.

Trafton, Paul R., and Albert P. Shulte. *New Directions for Elementary School Mathematics*, 1989 Yearbook. Reston, VA: National Council of Teachers of Mathematics, 1989. Chapter 19.

Troike, G. R. *Research Evidence for the Effectiveness of Bilingual Education.* Washington, DC: National Clearinghouse for Bilingual Education, 1978.

Widlake, Paul. *Reducing Educational Disadvantage.* Philadelphia: Open University Press, 1986.

Programming in Basic

When we use the word computer in this text, we are referring to a microcomputer, the most recent addition to the computer family that is entering schools, homes, and small businesses in ever-increasing numbers.

A computer receives information and instructions from different sources (input), processes it, and sends the result (output) to a video screen (monitor), a printer, or some other output device. We assume that your computer has the following components:

1. A central processing unit, commonly abbreviated as CPU, and its associated electronic circuit. The CPU is the heart of the computer and controls all input, output, and processing for the computer.

2. A keyboard containing all the keys found on a typewriter as well as certain additional keys necessary for operating the computer. The keyboard is an important device for entering information and instructions into the computer.

3. A cathode ray tube or video screen, usually referred to as a monitor or CRT. We use CRT as the abbreviation for the cathode ray tube, video screen, or monitor.

4. A disk drive that can store information from computer memory to a magnetic disk or send information stored on disk to the computer. Using a computer without a disk drive severely limits what you can do with the computer.

Computer Languages

Computer language use in the elementary school is almost entirely confined to BASIC and LOGO. BASIC is used in secondary schools but is being supplemented or replaced by Pascal, the language required for the advanced placement program that enables pupils to obtain college credit in computer science in many universities. Pascal is also used in commercial programming. A language called C rivals Pascal as a popular current language. Old standbys, such as Fortran and COBAL, are still used in science and business, respectively, as well as many others. Each language has its advantages and disadvantages.

Learn By Doing

Dozens of varieties of computers are on the market. Although they have many features in common, each has its own procedures. It is imperative that you read the manual for your computer and have it available for reference.

Computing is a "Learn By Doing" activity. You must enter instructions and programs into the computer as you read.

Computers can be frustrating. Although they are often referred to as giant brains, they are not very smart unless someone tells them what to do. They have a very limited vocabulary and refuse to recognize instructions that do not use this vocabulary.

Be prepared to make mistakes. Learning to recognize and correct errors is an essential part of the computing process.

Prompt and Cursor

Refer to your manual to determine how to activate BASIC on your computer. When BASIC is activated a **prompt** will appear, usually in the upper left hand corner of your CRT. "OK" and "]" are prompts that some computers use to indicate that the computer is waiting for instructions in BASIC.

The variations among computer brands and types are immense. Learn to activate BASIC on *your* computer and recognize the symbol on the CRT that tells you that BASIC is waiting for input. Be prepared to make minor adjustments in the instructions given here; the instructions your computer will accept may be slightly—or greatly—different. Refer to your computer manual when instructions given here do not produce the expected results.

Most computers display a **cursor** immediately to the right of or below the prompt. Often a blinking square or vertical line, the cursor indicates where the next character typed on the keyboard will appear on the CRT.

A prompt indicates the status of your computer. The cursor indicates the position of the next entry from the keyboard. Some computers display only the cursor.

Carriage Return

In reference to a typewriter, the term *carriage return* refers to the typewriter carriage

that, having reached the right margin, is moved down a space and returned to the left margin so that the next character typed will appear at the beginning of the following line.

On a computer, the "carriage return" moves the cursor to the beginning of the next line but also tells the computer to process or store the information typed since the last carriage return. Use the manual, if necessary, to identify the key on your computer that initiates a carriage return. It often has the label RETURN or ENTER.

COMPUTERS DO NOT PROCESS INFORMATION TYPED ON THE KEYBOARD UNTIL A CARRIAGE RETURN IS ACTIVATED.

WE USE <CR> TO TELL YOU TO INITIATE A CARRIAGE RETURN BY PRESSING THE APPROPRIATE KEY ON YOUR COMPUTER.

Let's Begin

Activate BASIC and type AAA.

The letters AAA appear on the CRT followed by the cursor.

Activate the carriage return (<CR>). On many computers the message SYNTAX ERROR will appear on the CRT immediately below AAA.

Remember, the computer only understands instructions that use its limited vocabulary. When a <CR> tells the computer to process an instruction that it does not understand, the **SYNTAX ERROR** message is displayed on the CRT.

In addition to variations among computers, there are different versions of BASIC. When your computer does not behave as described in the text, the most probable cause is:

1. You may have made an error.

2. The computer may require a different instruction or procedure. If this is the case, you must refer to your manual.

Backspace

Type AAA without a carriage return and find the key on your computer that will move the cursor to the left. It often has a left pointing arrow or is marked DELETE. Refer to your manual if these are not available.

Use the backspace key to move the cursor back to its initial position and then type ABC to replace AAA. As you move the cursor back, the letters AAA may or may not be erased but they will be replaced when you type ABC.

When you learn to move the cursor to any position on the CRT, you can use the backspace key to replace the letter, word, or group of words preceding the cursor by moving the cursor to the left and retyping.

Print/print

Type PRINT 3 + 4 <Cr> to obtain following display on your CRT.

```
PRINT 3 + 4
7
```

PRINT tells the computer to display information on the CRT, as shown above, and allows the computer to act as a calculator.

Now use lower case to type print 3 + 4 <CR>. If you get a SYNTAX ERROR message, your computer will not accept BASIC instructions in lower case. You must then use the upper case mode when you enter programs in BASIC.

Now type: ? 3 + 4 <CR>

The above instruction may produce a display of 7. Most versions of BASIC use the question mark as an abbreviation for PRINT. This is an important time saver for inexperienced typists.

Experiment with additional examples and other items that may occur to you. You cannot damage the computer by pressing the wrong key but doing so may destroy information in the computer. Never experiment with an important program in memory if the program has not been saved to disk.

Immediate and Programming Modes

Type PRINT 3 * 4 <CR> to obtain following display:

```
PRINT 3*4
12
```

The symbol * is the universal computer symbol for multiplication. The everyday symbol x cannot be used for multiplication because the computer cannot tell when x is a letter and when it is a symbol for multiplication. Now type 10 PRINT 8 - 3 <CR>. Nothing will appear to happen.

Type RUN <Cr> to obtain the following display:

```
10 PRINT 8 - 3 <CR>
RUN
5
```

You have just entered and run your first BASIC program.

A computer program uses the computer's limited vocabulary to provide a set of instructions that makes it perform a desired task. The 10 preceding PRINT is called a line number. Every instruction in early versions of BASIC must have a line number.

Refer to your manual to learn how to save this program to disk and how to recall it from disk to computer memory. Save this one-line program to disk. Type NEW to clear the computer memory; then, recall the program from the disk and run it to learn this important procedure.

Punctuation: The Colon

The **colon** makes it possible to use more than one instruction with a single line number. We demonstrate this in the immediate mode because the result is displayed as soon as a carriage return is initiated.

Example A1, in the immediate mode, shows how we can use colons so that one <CR> will process four separate instructions.

EXAMPLE A1

```
PRINT 3 + 4: PRINT 3 * 4:PRINT
6 - 3:PRINT 6/3 <CR>

   7
  12
   3
   2
```

Example A2 illustrates the use of four instructions with one line number in the programming mode. These two examples illustrate standard computer symbols for addition, subtraction, multiplication and division.

EXAMPLE A2

```
10 PRINT 3+4:PRINT 3*4:PRINT
6-3:PRINT 6/3 <CR>
RUN
   7
  12
   3
   2
```

Displaying Words

Example A3 illustrates that when quotation marks follow a PRINT instruction, the computer displays exactly what is typed between the quotes, including the spaces.

EXAMPLE A3

```
PRINT "HELLO":PRINT"1  +2  =
3":PRINT 1+2=3" <CR>
HELLO
1  +2  =  3
1+2=3
```

Example A4 illustrates how the first instruction (before the colon) tells the computer to multiply 2 by 3 while the second (after the colon) tells the computer to display the symbols typed between quotes, "2*3".

EXAMPLE A4

```
PRINT 2*3:PRINT "2*3" <CR>
6
2*3
```

Punctuation: The Semicolon

Example A5 illustrates how the semicolon tells the computer to display the output of two successive instructions on the same line. Some computers place a space between the two outputs and some do not.

Example A5

```
PRINT 2*15;3 + 4 <CR>
307 or 30 7 The spacing varies with
```
the computer.

Example A5 requires only one PRINT instruction because of the semicolon. Example A4 requires two PRINT instructions because the colon interprets the two instructions as though they are on separate lines, even though the second instruction does not require a line number.

Line 20 of the program in Example A6 shows how to insert a space between two outputs when the computer does not. Line 30 illustrates an important combined use of the semicolon and quotation marks. Remember, the computer displays exactly what is entered between quotes that follow a print instruction.

Example A6

```
10  PRINT 2*15;3+4 <CR>
20  PRINT 2*15;" ";3+4 <CR>
30  PRINT "2X15=";2*15
RUN <Cr>
307 OR 30 7 Spacing varies with
computers.
30 7 OR 30   7
2 X 15 = 30
```

The immediate mode is often neglected but can provide much useful information. It is more versatile than most calculators found in the elementary schools and can display the entire expression in detail: EXAMPLE A7

```
PRINT "3*4+88/11 - 3^2 =
";3*4;" + ";88/11 ;"-
";3^2;"=";  3*4+88/11;  - 3^2
<CR>  3*4+88/11 - 3^2 = 12 +
8 - 9 = 11
```

The expression 3^2 is computer notation for the square of 3. Example A7 illustrates the order of operation in a manner that is impossible for a calculator. The ability to see the entire expression enables one to verify that an error in entry has not been made.

Variables can be entered into computer memory in the immediate mode but the resulting computations cannot be saved to disk. The following is excellent practice for typing entries of the type that are frequently required in programs. Colons save space by allowing a single line entry.

```
A=3:B=4:PRINT A;"X";B;"=";
A*B <CR>
3 X 4 = 12
```

This type of entry is often difficult for beginning programmers. The advantage of using the immediate mode is that the computer indicates a syntax error instantly rather than after the entire program has been entered and run.

Many recent versions of BASIC will accept PRINT A" × ""B" = ""A*B, without the semicolons, as well as PRINT A;" × "";B;" = "";A*B. If your computer accepts the former without a SYNTAX ERROR, entering text programs will be easier and have fewer errors once you learn the pattern. You may make a few more errors in learning the pattern but much time will be saved in the long run.

Generally, do not eliminate end semicolons that place two outputs on the same line or the semicolon in INPUT "";N. You can practice with example A7.

Exercise

1. For each of the following examples, try to anticipate the output and then use your computer to check your answer:

A. `10 PRINT 0 + 4:PRINT 0 * 4`

　　OUTPUT for 1A: _____

B. `10 PRINT 0 + 4`
　　`20 PRINT 0 * 4`

　　OUTPUT for 1B: _____

C. `10 PRNT 3 * 3`

　　OUTPUT for 1C: _____

D. `10 PRINT 3 + 4 * 5`

　　OUTPUT for 1D: _____

E. `10 PRINT 4 * 4`
　　`20 PRINT 6/2`

　　OUTPUT _____

F. `10 PRINT 4 * 4; " ";`
　　`20 PRINT 6/2`

　　OUTPUT _____

G. `10 PRINT 24/4;`
　　`20 PRINT 2 * 3`

　　OUTPUT _____

H. `10 PRINT 24/4:;PRINT 2 * 3`

ANSWERS

A & B: 4　　A and B show two different
　　　　0　　ways of writing the same program.

C. `SYNTAX ERROR`　　`PRINT` is Misspelled

D. 23　　Multiplication is performed before addition.

E. 16
   3

F. 16 3   Semicolon in line 10 tells computer to place output for line 20 on same line as output for line 10.
             Run program without quotation marks in line 10.

G & H. 66   There is no space between the output of the two instructions without quotation marks

Modification of Text Programs for IBM and Compatibles

The simplest way to illustrate the difference between APPLESOFT BASIC, as used in this text, and GWBASIC, the most common form of BASIC in IBM and compatible computers, is to translate a simple program from one language to the other The REM in line 15 is a **rem**ark that helps you understand the program. These remarks have no effect on the running of the program and can be seen only when the program is listed by entering the instruction LIST. We use lower case for remarks to set them aside from the program instructions.

Illustrative Program Named Square in APPLESOFT

```
10 HOME:VTAB 8
15 REM Home clears the
screen and returns the cur-
sor to the upper left hand
corner. VTAB 8 (vertical tab
8) places initial output on
the 1st line of the 8th row.
20 A = 1 + INT(20 * RND(1))
30 PRINT "THE SQUARE of";A;
" = ";
40 INPUT "";N$
50 PRINT "THE SQUARE of";A;
" = ";A*A
```

Translation of APPLESOFT Program Square to GWBASIC

```
10 CLS:RANDOMIZE TIMER:
LOCATE 8,1
15 REM CLS is equivalent
to APPLESOFT HOME. RANDOMIZE
TIMER is essential to give
different random number on
each run. LOCATE 8,1 places
initial output in 1st column
of 8th row.
20 A = 1 + INT(20 * RND)
30 PRINT "THE SQUARE OF";A;
"=";
40 INPUT "",N
50 PRINT "THE SQUARE OF";A;
"=";A*A
```

To place the initial output for APPLESOFT in the tenth column of the fifth row, line 10 becomes: 10 HOME:VTAB 5:HTAB 10

For GWBASIC use: 10 CLS:RANDOMIZE TIMER:LOCATE 5, 10

RANDOMIZE TIMER is essential whenever random variables are used in the program.

The colon allows more than one instruction on a single line, implemented with a single carriage return. Without the colon, we would need three lines as follows:

```
APPLESOFT          GWBASIC
10 HOME     10 CLS
11 VTAB 5  11 RANDOMIZE TIMER
12 HTAB 10 12 LOCATE 5, 10
```

RANDOMIZE TIMER can be omitted FOR GWBASIC if there are no random variables in the program.

APPLESOFT uses RND(1) for a random number between 0 and 1

GWBASIC uses RND, a simpler notation that does not require double parentheses as required for line 20 in the APPLESOFT program.

Line 20 in each program generates random numbers in range 1–20.

Lines 30 and 50 are identical in the two programs.

N$ is called a string variable and will accept numeric and nonnumeric characters. N is called a real variable and will accept only numeric characters. N$ in APPLESOFT line 40 allows the program to proceed without a keyboard entry, with a carriage return. This is desirable to encourage mental arithmetic. Refer to your manual for other characteristics of string variables.

Line 40 in APPLESOFT uses a pair of empty quotes, a semicolon and a string variable, N$. If N replaces N$, the APPLESOFT program will not continue without a keyboard entry. The empty quotes and semicolon eliminate the question mark so that only the flashing cursor indicates that the computer is waiting for a keyboard entry. GWBASIC requires the empty quotes and a comma to accomplish the same result. The GWBASIC program will continue without a carriage return with no keyboard entry with N or N$.

Advantages of BASIC

1. BASIC is the most accessible language because it is included as part of the software that comes with practically every computer found in elementary schools. BASIC is activated on many computers as soon as they are turned on; others require a brief set of instructions.

2. Simple programs, as those illustrated in this text, produce the widest variety of output for the least amount of typing. A good example, which requires about 70 keystrokes, is the following 4-line factor program that is discussed more fully in Chapter 6.

```
10 INPUT N
20 FOR J = 1 TO SQR(N)
30 IF N/J = INT(N/J) THEN
```

```
PRINT J, N/J
40 NEXT J
```

This program displays all the factors of any whole number entered at the input prompt. Entering 111111 will display 16 pairs of factors. The program will indicate that a number is prime by displaying exactly one pair of factors, the number and 1. The same program in Pascal requires twice as many lines because of its formal nature. Basic is less formal and more flexible but the formality of Pascal provides a structure that is valuable when writing large programs. There are many more examples of the versatility of the FOR-NEXT loop in the problem-solving sections of the end of the chapters that follow Chapter 5.

3. BASIC is still one of the most popular programming languages for educational and home use. A beginner can find more BASIC programs to copy and modify in books, journals, and magazines than for any other computer language. Moderate sized programs for educational, recreational or home use are available to be copied or modified. Public Domain programs are available from user groups. Some companies collect these programs and sell them, with many programs on a disk, for a small fee. A computer magazine dedicated to a given computer will have advertisements for these programs for that computer.

4. Any elementary pupil who learns to use the FOR-NEXT loop to solve the variety of problems illustrated in this text has acquired many of the skills required for more advanced computer use. A 3- to 6-line FOR-NEXT loop can solve an amazing variety of problems.

Disadvantages of BASIC

1. BASIC is called an interpretive language because it must change each instruction to machine language, using only zeros and ones, every time the program is run. For this

reason, BASIC is relatively slow. Currently popular languages, such as Pascal and C, are compiled. A compiled language is translated only once. After the language is compiled, no additional translation is necessary and the program is executed more rapidly.

2. BASIC is inefficient for programs containing hundreds of lines. The use of GOTO in such programs becomes difficult to control and can lead to many complications. Pascal and C rarely use GOTO but build their programs as independent modules. This procedure is illustrated in the LOGO program called ROTATE on page 406. The use of these modules is called structured programming.

3. Basic is not as powerful as more recent languages. It has a much more limited set of instructions. Pascal and C are more powerful because they have a wider range of instructions.

However, more recent versions of BASIC have most of the capabilities of Pascal and C. They can be compiled, have a wider set of instructions and can program with modules without line numbers.

Programming in LOGO

Logo was created at MIT by Seymour Papert in 1943 with a computer directing a mechanical turtle that recorded a path on the floor as it followed computer instructions. The current computer versions uses a cursor, called a turtle, that follows instructions to move on the screen (CRT). The LOGO cursor (turtle) differs from the cursor for BASIC in two ways:

(1) The turtle has position and direction. It is triangular in shape and acts as an arrow that clearly indicates the direction it will move. The command FD 20 moves the turtle 20 units in the direction that it is pointing. FD is the standard abbreviation for FORWARD. RT, LT and BK are standard abbreviations for right, left and back, respectively.

(2) The turtle's initial position is in the center of the screen pointing up so that the command FD 20 will move the turtle 20 units up or, "north." It is desirable to use east in place of 90, south in place 180 and west in place of 270 to help pupils interpret geography maps.

Drawing Geometric Figures

Insert the LOGO disk into the drive and turn on the computer. When loading is complete, a WELCOME TO LOGO message may appear with the prompt, usually a question mark, followed by a blinking cursor. Each of the various versions of LOGO has its own characteristics. A manual for your version is essential because variation exists among procedural commands, such as editing or saving to disk. However, little variation exists in the following geometric activities, the hallmark of LOGO.

Type: FD 40 <CR>

The graphics screen will appear with the display shown in Figure B-1.

Type RT 90 <CR>

Look carefully to see that the turtle has turned 90 degrees to the right so that the FD instruction will now tell it to move in a horizontal direction or east, from left to right. Watch for mistakes in typing as you go; some versions of LOGO use the ESCAPE key as the backspace key while others use the left arrow key.

Type FD 40 RT 90 <CR>

You have combined two steps into a single command to get the output shown in Figure B-2 with the turtle moved to the right

Figure B-1
FD 40

Figure B-2
B1 + RT90

Figure B-4
B3 + HOME HIDETURTLE

and pointed down. LOGO allows you to put many such instructions on the same line but there is a limit that varies from computer to computer. Experiment. If an instruction is too long, break it into two or more lines. The advantage of two or more instructions on a single line is that only one carriage return is required and screen space is used more efficiently.

Type `FD 40 RT 90` <CR> to get the output shown in Figure B-3.

Type `HOME HIDETURTLE` <CR> to get the display in Figure B-4. The `HOME` command returns the turtle to its initial position and direction. The `HIDETURTLE` command does just that, hides the turtle. You will also get the display in Figure B-4 if you type `FD 40` <CR> except the turtle will be visible and pointing west instead of north. It is usually desirable to have the turtle showing when the program is executed so that the result of each command can be seen. It is desirable to hide the turtle for the final display for aesthetic purposes and for printing. It is very important to be aware of the direction the turtle is pointing when giving instructions.

Type `DRAW` <CR> and the screen will be erased and the turtle returned to its initial position. The command `HOME` will perform the same action on some versions of LOGO and `CLEARSCREEN` may clear the screen without returning the turtle to its original position.

Type `FD 40 RT 90 FD 40 RT 90 Fd 40 RT 90 FD 40 RT 90 HIDE-TURTLE` <CR> to the same display shown in Figure B-4. This illustrates the use of many instructions with a single carriage return.

Type `RT 45 FD 50 RT 130 FD 70 HOME HIDETURTLE` <CR> to get the output shown in Figure B-5. The command `RT 45` turns the turtle 45 degrees to the right. The `RT 130` rotates the turtle 130 degrees to the right from its position established after the `FD 50` command. It may be helpful to use five separate steps with five carriage returns, with the turtle visible, to see the effect of each command.

Figure B-3
B2 + FD40 RT90

Figure B-5
RT45 FD50 RT130 FD70 HOME HIDETURTLE

The Repeat Loop

Type REPEAT 4[FD 40 RT 90] HIDETURTLE <Cr>. This uses a minimum of typing to get the same square displayed in Figure B-4. The REPEAT N instruction tells the computer to perform a loop of N cycles where the instructions between the brackets, [ ], are executed on each cycle of the loop. More recent computers have the brackets on the keyboard to the right of the P key and do not require the shift key. Earlier computers have the brackets in different locations. Parentheses or braces will not work.

The previous activities have been executed in the "immediate mode," a term that is not usually used in LOGO because there is little difference between the immediate mode and the programming mode. Many programming instructions for BASIC, such as FOR-NEXT, are not available in its immediate mode. However, information cannot be saved to disk in the immediate mode in either language.

Entering Programs in LOGO

LOGO has three screens, the text screen, the graphics screen and the edit screen. Programming, editing, and computer output take place on the same screen in BASIC except for graphics. The graphics screen in LOGO will have four lines of text at the bottom unless an appropriate command, varying with the computer, tells the computer to display the entire screen. Programming in LOGO takes place on the edit screen.

Type TO SQUARE <CR> and the edit screen appears, placing the computer in the programming mode. The following program, called SQUARE, will display the same square shown in Figure B-4. Every LOGO program must start with TO XXX where XXX is the name of the program. This name can then be used as a module in other pro-

grams, as illustrated in the program ROTATE on page 406.

```
TO SQUARE
REPEAT 4[FD 40 RT 90] HIDE-
TURTLE <CR>
END <CR>
CTRL-C <CR>
```

The CTRL-C command tells the computer to place in its memory the program called SQUARE. The computer will not place a program in memory without the END command telling the computer that the module is complete. If the computer finds the program conforms to its limited vocabulary, the CTRL-C command changes the screen back to the text screen which, after a slight delay, displays the message: SQUARE DEFINED. If the program is unacceptable, an error message is displayed. Type EDIT SQUARE <CR> to return the computer to the edit screen.

After the computer displays SQUARE DEFINED on the text screen, type SQUARE <CR> at the cursor. The computer then returns to the graphics screen and executes the program. The program named SQUARE will remain in computer memory until the computer is turned off or until the command GOODBYE or its equivalent is entered. Storing the program on disk will allow you to recall the program as needed. See the computer manual for instructions on how to save to and recall programs from disk.

When a program is in memory with the name RECTANGLE, typing RECTANGLE <CR> at the cursor on the text screen tells the computer to execute the program named RECTANGLE.

LOGO does not use line numbers. It changes normal program progressing by using the name of a module that is in computer memory. In the program ROTATE, the use of the single word SQUARE eliminates the retyping of the entire program SQUARE.

We will no longer indicate a carriage return at the end of each line as this standard practice should be understood by now. ENTER is often used instead of TYPE as a reminder of the combination of activities: First the information is typed, then it is entered by pressing the key on your computer that is equivalent to the carriage return.

Programming with Modules

With SQUARE in memory, enter the program ROTATE as follows:

```
TO ROTATE
REPEAT 10[SQUARE RT 36]
END
CTRL-C
```

The text screen will now appear and display: ROTATE DEFINED.

Enter ROTATE at the cursor on the text screen and the computer will move to the graphic screen and display the figure shown in Figure B-6.

The output starts with the original square and rotates it 36 degrees in each cycle of the REPEAT loop. With careful examination, you can identify the separate squares.

When the program SQUARE is used in another program, as in ROTATE, we will

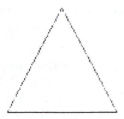

Figure B-7
TO TRI

refer to it as a module. The program ROTATE calls for the module SQUARE 10 separate times, once in each cycle of the REPEAT loop.

Obtain Program TRI as follows:

```
TO TRI
RT 90 FD 50 LT 120 FD 50
LT 120 FD 50
END
```

Enter CTRL-C and get the text screen with the message: TRI DEFINED.

Enter TRI at the prompt and get the display in Figure B-7.

Program TRI can now be used as module in Program ROTATE2, whose output is shown in Figure B-8.

```
TO ROTATE 2
REPEAT 12[TRI]
END
```

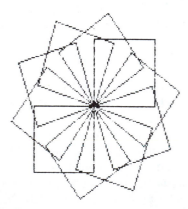

Figure B-6
TO ROTATE

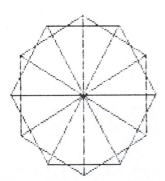

Figure B-8
TO ROTATE 2 REPEAT 12[TRI]

It is natural to wonder why the triangle in ROTATE 2 is rotated as there is no visible ROTATE instruction. The reason is that the turtle is pointed in a different direction after each cycle of the loop. Run TRI with the turtle visible, with ten separate steps, to see the position of the turtle at the end of each step.

The advantage of LOGO for young learners is that an instruction, such as FD 20, is implemented immediately with a carriage return and the display on the CRT clearly follows the instruction. This provides a geometric interaction between the pupil and the computer that is not available in BASIC. The display of geometric figures in BASIC requires a much higher level of programming.

Recursion

Recursion is the process of using the original program as a module within that program. The program named RECURSION illustrates this procedure. Be warned that RECURSION is an infinite loop and requires CTRL-G or an equivalent command to exit the program. **Do not** use RESET or CTRL-RESET. **These commands may crash the system and erase every program in memory.** Either of the latter commands usually is equivalent to turning off the computer and then reloading LOGO. It may be wise to experiment with commands for your computer when there are no important programs in memory. One of the most basic computer procedures is to save important programs to disk before experimenting.

```
TO RECURSION
TRI
RT 20
RECURSION
END
```

The RECURSION module in the next-to-last line of Program RECURSION sends the computer back to the beginning of the pro-

gram and forms an infinite or continuous loop that must be stopped with an appropriate command. Except for demonstration purposes, infinite loops should be avoided.

If-Then

LOGO has a command similar to IF-THEN in BASIC. However, it does not require the THEN, although most versions will accept it. Using the IF conditional, we can stop RECURSION from being an infinite loop as shown in Program RECURSION2. The turtle points in a different direction in each cycle of the RECURSION loop. When the heading becomes zero (north), the instruction following IF tells the computer to stop the program.

```
TO RECURSION2
TRI
RT 20
IF HEADING=0 STOP
RECURSION
END
```

Note that we must use STOP instead of END as the latter has a special function for indicating the end of a module in LOGO. The display for Program RECURSION2 is shown in Figure B-9.

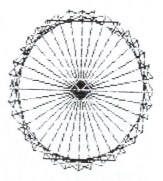

Figure B-9
RECURSION2

Variables

Variables are usually associated with geometry but can be useful in graphic programs. LOGO requires that a colon be placed before each variable to allow the computer to distinguish it from ordinary words and letters. Because LOGO was invented for children, it normally uses descriptive words rather than single letters for variables to make the program easier to understand. This procedure is often used in BASIC for the same reason. Using a word rather than a single letter may help understanding, but it is an added burden for the inexperienced typist.

LOGO requires that the program variables be listed after the name of the program as shown in Program POLY. The variable :N represents the number of sides of the regular polygon and the variable :SIDE represents the length of each of the congruent sides.

```
TO POLY :N :SIDE
REPEAT :N [FD :SIDE RT 360 /
:N]
END
```

To tell the program to display a regular pentagon with a side of length 40, enter POLY 5 40 at the cursor on the text screen after POLY DEFINED is displayed there.

It is quite remarkable than a single-line program, other than the necessary beginning and end, can do so much. Figure B-10 shows the output for various value of :N and :SIDE.

The formula uses the fundamental theorem from geometry that the sum of the exterior angles of a convex polygon is always 360 degrees. Figure B-10 illustrates that after Program POLY generates a polygon with the first direction being north (up), the angle it makes with the side it has just drawn is the exterior angle of the polygon. Program POLY tells the computer to turn right 360 / :N, precisely the exterior angle of an :N-sided regular polygon.

The theorem on exterior angles leads to the proof that the sum of the interior angles of a convex polygon is $180 \times N - 360$. If the exterior angle of a triangle is 360/N, the corresponding interior angle is $180 - 360/N$. Therefore the sum of the N interior angles is $N \times (180 - 360/N)$. Simple algebraic manipulation shows this sum to be $180 \times N - 360$.

Mathematicians have often approximated a circle by thinking of it a regular polygon with a large number of sides, each with a very small length. Program POLY can demonstrate this. Enter POLY 360 1 and obtain an approximation for a circle as shown in

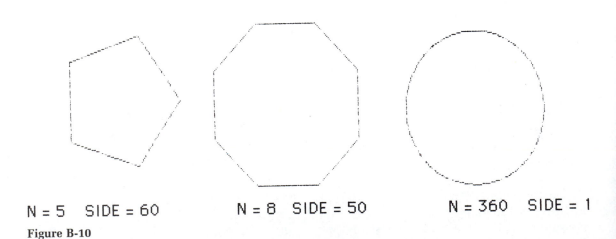

N = 5   SIDE = 60   N = 8   SIDE = 50   N = 360   SIDE = 1

Figure B-10

Figure B-10. The accuracy of the approximation varies with the computer and the printer.

Estimating Angles

Logo can provide an understanding of angles in an efficient manner. A simple configuration for this activity is shown in Figure B.11, obtained with the commands: HOME FD 50 RT 90 FD 70 BK 70 HOME. The purpose of the first HOME command is to be sure that the turtle is heading north in its standard position. The purpose of the last two commands is to return the turtle to its home position. The task of the pupil is to enter a command of the form RT A FD B HOME where A is the estimate of the angle and B is the estimate of the distance. The second HOME command places the turtle in its standard position ready for the second estimate if it is needed. The second attempt should be an improvement over the first. There is no limit to the number of attempts, but it should rarely take more than three tries to come very close to the mark. The Program ANGLE can provide practice with a variety of angles and distances.

```
TO ANGLE :A  :B
HOME FD :A  RT 90  FD :B  Bk
:B  HOME
END
```

Entering ANGLE 50 70 at the prompt will give the same display shown in Figure B-11. However, each time the program is

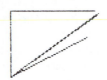

Figure B-12
Estimate Angle

run, a different figure can be obtained by using a different pair of numbers following ANGLE, such as ANGLE 30 100. Therefore, the program offers an unlimited number of examples. In estimating angles, it is useful to first decide if the angle is more or less than 45 degrees. When the pupil is unfamiliar with the scale, it may help a beginner to enter RT 45 FD 100 HOME to obtain a line of length 100 at a 45 degree angle as a basis for making an estimate.

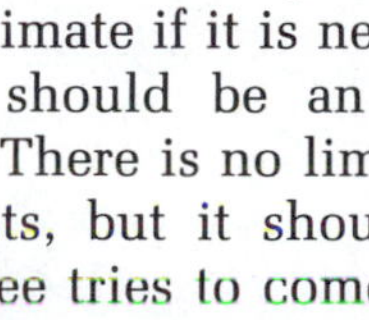

Figure B-12 shows a first guess of RT 65 FD 70, which is then followed by an almost perfect second guess of BK 70 HOME RT 55 FD 85.

Figure B-13 shows an alternate approach after the first guess in Figure B-12. Rather than returning to the home position and guessing again, the second guess starts where the first guess ends and proceeds with a second guess of LT 50 FD 20 to come very close to the mark.

When the topic of scale drawing has been introduced, it can be very useful to have the pupil make a scale drawing and use a protractor to measure the angle and use the scale to determine the distance. LOGO can then be used to check the accuracy of the drawing.

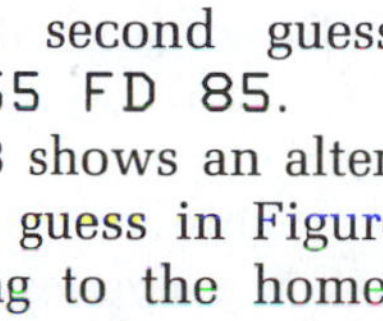

Figure B-11
Estimate Angle

Figure B-13
Estimate Angle

Fast learners may use the arctangent function, available on many calculators and almost all computers, to find the angle. The Theorem of Pythagoras can determine the distance.

read maps with understanding. Setheading 90 tells the turtle to point in an easterly direction no matter which way it was heading when the command is initiated. Use of this command can help pupils interpret maps.

Advantages of LOGO

1. LOGO is unrivaled for its interactive approach to geometry, which is so intuitive that most early elementary pupils can use it immediately and grow with it to generate some remarkable programs. LOGO programs and associated activities are appearing with greater frequency in professional journals but do not occur often in the general computer magazines.

2. LOGO is more powerful than BASIC. It does not require line numbers because it uses modules for structured programming. Its ability to use recursion, as in the program RECURSION on page 407, allows the construction of more complex programs with less typing.

3. LOGO is valuable for helping pupils to understand angles, polygons and a variety of geometric figures. Its use of 0–360 to describe directions and changes in directions provides a background that helps pupils to

Disadvantages of LOGO

1. LOGO must be purchased on a separate disk, creating storage problems. It requires much more memory than BASIC and takes longer to activate.

2. While practically everybody agrees on LOGO's value for geometry, there is less agreement on its value for other purposes. It takes a higher level of programming to construct the equivalent of a three-line FOR-NEXT loop in BASIC.

3. Variables are more difficult to use in LOGO. Each variable must be preceded with a colon, as :A, a procedure that causes early difficulty when pupils forget to insert the colon.

There are many versions of LOGO and new ones are being introduced with specialized objectives. The advice for choosing a version of LOGO is the same as for choosing any software: See it in action before deciding.

Answers to Selected Exercises

CHAPTER 6

5. 21 − 3 = 7; 1 item costs $7.00; 7 × 7 = 49; 7 items cost $49.00. **6.** (a) $11.50 + $5.00 = $16.50; 20 − 16.50 = $3.50 change. (b) 20 − (11.5 + 5.00) = $3.50. On a calculator, enter 20, press −, enter 11.5, press −, enter 5, press =; 10. $167,772.15

CHAPTER 8

7. (a) 100 − 55 = n; 45¢ (b) 25 + 42 = n; 67 papers (c) 54 − 15 = n; 39 (d) 56 − (21 + 18) = n; 17 cm **8.** Dec.: "9 from 12, 3; 0 from 9, 9; 3 from 9, 6; 1 from 4, 3" EA: "9 from 12, 3; 1 from 10, 9; 4 from 10, 6; 2 from 5, 3"

CHAPTER 9

Exercise 9.1

1. (a) 6 + 9; 8 + 7 (b) 5 + 5 + 5; 3 + 3 + 3 + 3 + 3 (c) 3 × 5 = 15; 5 × 3 = 15; (d) 15 ÷ 3 = 5; 15 ÷ 5 = 3 **2.** (a) M, 4 × 8 = n (b) D-M, 35 ÷ 5 = n (c) M, 2 × 8 = n (d) D-M, 12 ÷ 4 = n (e) D-P, 10 ÷ 5 = n (f) D-P, 25 ÷ 5 = n

Exercise 9.2

1. 4 × 5 = n; 20 players **2.** 3 × 8 = n; 24 feet. **3.** 18 ÷ 6 = n; 3 hrs. **4.** 35 ÷ 5 = n; 7 packages **5.** 5 × 8 = n; 40 trees **6.** 400 ÷ 25 = n; 16 stamps. **7.** commutative and associative; both addition and multiplication used in distributive **8.** 3 × (30 + 2) **9.** **11.** (a) measurement (b) measurement (c) measurement (d) partition (e) partition **13.** 10, 100; 10 = (9 + 1)

CHAPTER 10

Exercise 10.1

1. (a) $70 per ton (b) $140 per ton (c) $105,000 **2.** Not enough information. The miles per gallon for the car is not needed. The 3 hours is unnecessary. **3.** M/950 =

13/285. The solution, which is not asked for, is 43 miles, rounded. **4.** 12 posts. There are 11 spaces of 3 feet between posts, but there must be 12 posts. **5.** 11 seconds **6.** M/t miles per minute. **7.** An estimate of 100 × 50, the middle number is very good. **8.** 50 × 101 = 5050.

Exercise 10.2

1. 360 stars **2.** 35 gallons **3.** $10.10 change **4.** 56° average temperature **5.** 7 pieces **6.** 15 **7.** (30 + 4) × (50 + 7) = (30 + 4) × 50 + (30 + 4) × 7 = 30 × 50 + 4 × 50 + 30 × 7 + 4 × 7 = 1500 + 200 + 210 + 28 = 1938 **8.** lower limit 1500; upper limit 2400 **9.** It eliminates estimation; usually takes longer; requires more space; useful for slow learners. **10.** Similar to multiple method but need not require all multiples to be written. For a quotient of 12, at most the first 3 multiples would be required. **11.** (a) 12 × 15 = 180; 15 × 12 = 180; 180 ÷ 15 = 12; 180 ÷ 12 = 15 (b) 57 × 16 = 912; 16 × 57 = 912; 912 ÷ 16 = 57; 912 ÷ 57 = 16 **12.** Slow learners: use the multiple method; use the pyramid or subtractive method; write 1 × divisor, 5 × divisor and 10 × divisor as guides in estimation. Fast learners: Stress mental estimation with as little paper and pencil work as possible. **13.** (a) For a given multiplicand, the larger the multiplier the larger the product. (b) For a given multiplier, the larger the multiplicand, the larger the product. **14.** (a) For a given dividend, the larger the divisor the smaller the quotient. (b) For a given divisor, the larger the dividend the larger the quotient. **15.** (a) 6 × 68 or 9 × 45 (b) 8 × 47 (c) 8 × 89 **16.** (a) given 4, find 1 (b) how many 4s are in 32 (c) given 1, find 8 (d) given 1, find 4 (e) how many 8s are in 32 (f) given 8, find 1

CHAPTER 11

Exercise 11.1

4. a. ¾, 0.75, 75% b. ⅜, .375, 37½% c. ⅝, .625, 62½% **5** (a) $12/5 lb = ? / 3 lb; 12 × 3/ 5 = 36/5 = 7 1/5 =

$7.20 (b) 5 men, 4 women, 9 students 5 men/ 9 students = ? men/ 1800 students = 5 × 1800/9 = 1000 men (c) 5 miles/ 3 sec = ? miles/ 3600 sec = 5 × 3600/ 3 = 6,000 mph.

CHAPTER 12

Exercise 12.1

1. (a) 2 (b) 3 (c) 5 (d) 4 (e) 12 (f) 3   **2.** (a) 8 = 2, 4, 8; 24 = 2, 3, 4, 6, 8, 12, 24; gcf = 8 (b) 9 = 3, 9; 12 = 2, 3, 4, 6, 12; gcf = 3 (c) 12 = 2, 3, 4, 6, 12; 15 = 3, 5, 15; gcf = 3 (d) 8 = 2, 4, 8; 18 = 2, 3, 6, 9, 18; gcf = 2. (e) 12 = 2, 4, 6, 12; 20 = 2, 4, 5, 10, 20; gcf = 4; 16 = 2, 4, 8, 16; 22 = 2, 11; gcf = 2   **3.** (a) 18 = 2 × 3 × 3; 24 = 2 × 2 × 2 × 3; gcf = 2 × 3 = 6 (b) 21 = 3 × 7; 28 = 2 × 2 × 7; gcf = 7 (c) 24 = 2 × 2 × 2 × 3; 36 = 2 × 2 × 3 × 3; gcf = 12 (d) 28 = 2 × 2 × 7; 52 = 2 × 2 × 13; gcf = 4 (e) 30 = 2 × 3 × 5; 50 = 2 × 5 × 5; gcf = 2 × 5 = 10 (f) 35 = 5 × 7; 42 = 2 × 3 × 7; gcf = 7   **4.** 3. (a) ¾ (b) ¾ (c) ⅔ (d) ⁷⁄₁₃ (e) ⅗ (f) ⅚

Exercise 12.2

1. (a) 12, 24, 36, 48, 60
　　30, 60
　　LCM = 60
　(b)　8, 16, 24, 32, 40, 48, 56
　　14, 28, 42, 56
　　LCM = 56
2. (a) 10 = 2 × 5
　　12 = 2 × 2 × 3
　　LCD = 2 × 2 × 3 × 5 = 60
　(b)　8 = 2 × 2 × 2
　　12 = 2 × 2 × 3
　　LCD = 2 × 2 × 3 × 2 = 24
　(c)　9 = 3 × 3
　　15 = 3 × 5
　　LCD = 3 × 5 × 3 = 45
3. (a) 126 is divisible by 6 (b) 348 is divisible by both 4 and 6 (c) 740 is divisible by 4 (d) 462 is divisible by 6 (e) 144 is divisible by both 4 and 6 (f) 772 is divisible by 4 (g) 276 is divisible by both 4 and 6   **4.** (c) 2808 (e) 40680   **5.** (a) 231 = 3 × 7 × 11 (b) 137 is prime (c) 167 is prime (d)1001 = 7 × 11 × 13 (e) 1573 = 11 × 11 × 13   **6.** (a) 117 (b) 666 (c) 180 (d) 333 (e) 1818 (f) 1008

Exercise 12.3

2. (a) 2/3 + 3/5 = 10/15 + 9/15 = 19/15 = 1 4/15
　(b) 0.67
　　0.60
　　‾‾‾‾
　　1.27
3. (a) $10/24 = \dfrac{2 \times 5}{2 \times 2 \times 2 \times 3} = 5/12$
　(b) $12/30 = \dfrac{2 \times 2 \times 3}{2 \times 3 \times 5} = 2/5$

(c) $18/40 = \dfrac{2 \times 3 \times 3}{2 \times 2 \times 2 \times 5} = 9/20$

4. 5/8 = 25/40 = 62.5/100 = 0.625
7/12 = 35/60 = 58.$\overline{3}$ /100 = 0.583
4/15 = 12/45 = 26.$\overline{6}$ ./100 = 0.266

5. (a) 3/8 + 2/8 = 5/8
　　0.375
　　+ 0.250
　　‾‾‾‾‾
　　0.625
　(b) 2/3 + 5/6 = 4/6 + 5/6 = 9/6 = 1 1/2
　　0.67
　　+ 0.83
　　‾‾‾‾
　　1.50

6. (a) 3/4 − 3/8 = 6/8 − 3/8 = 3/8; 3/8 = 0.375
　　0.750
　　− 0.375
　　‾‾‾‾‾
　　0.375
　(b) 5/6 − 2/3 = 5/6 − 4/6 = 1/6; 1/6 = 0.16
　　0.83
　　− 0.66
　　‾‾‾‾
　　0.17
　(c) 3 3/4 − 1 3/8 = 3 6/8 − 1 3/8 = 2 3/8; 2 3/8 = 2.375.
　　3.750
　　− 1.375
　　‾‾‾‾‾
　　2.375

7. (a) 12　24　36　48　60
　　15　30　45　60　　　　LCM = 60
　(b) 12 = 2 × 2 × 3
　　15 = 3 × 5　　LCM = 2 × 2 × 3 × 5 = 60
　(c) 3)12　15
　　　4　　5　　LCM = 3 × 4 × 5 = 60

8. (a) 12　24　36
　　18　36　　　　LCM = 36
　　12 = 2 × 2 × 3
　　18 = 2 × 3 × 3　　LCM = 2 × 2 × 3 × 3
　　= 36
　　2)12　18
　　3) 6　　9
　　　2　　3　　LCM = 2 × 3 × 2 × 3 = 36
　(b) 20　40　60　80　100　120　140
　　35　70　105　140　　　　LCM = 140
　　20 = 2 × 2 × 5
　　35 = 5 × 7　　LCM = 2 × 2 × 5 × 7
　　= 140
　　5)20　35
　　　4　　7　　LCM = 5 × 4 × 7 = 140
　(c) 10　20　30　40　50　60　70　80　90
　　15　30　45　60　75　90
　　18　36　54　72　90
　　LCM = 90
　　10 = 2 × 5
　　15 = 3 × 5
　　18 = 2 × 3 × 3　　LCM = 2 × 5 × 3 × 3
　　= 90

CHAPTER 13

Exercise 13.2

1. \$.86 or 86¢ **2.** \$2.50 **3.** \$25 − \$2.50 = \$22.50; 90% of 25 = 22.50; \$22.50 paid **4.** \$420 **5.** \$7000 + \$420 = \$7420; 106% of 7000 = 7420 or \$7420 paid

Exercise 13.3

1. 25% **2.** 400% **3.** 57% **4.** 57.1% **5.** 70% **6.** 66.67% **7.** (a) 17% (b) 17.1% (c) 17.07% **8.** 5%

Exercise 13.4

1. (a) 0.5 (b) 100 (c) 25% (d) 8.4 (e) 88% (f) 2500 **3.** \$40 **4.** (a) $2\frac{1}{4}$ hours (b) 50 miles **5.** 40 weeks

Exercise 13.5

Part I: 1. reciprocal (multiplicative inverse); reciprocal **2.** zero **3.** multiply by its reciprocal **4.** fractions **5.** n = $2\frac{1}{2}$ × 4 = 10; total is \$10 **6.** given 1, find $2\frac{1}{2}$ **7.** 4.5 yards per carry. **8.** given 24, find 1. **9.** $7\frac{2}{3}$ qt. 1.1 qt. **10.** $4\frac{5}{6}$ hours or 5 hours and 50 minutes
Part II: 1. 8.25 ft. **2.** 6 roses **3.** 16 pieces **4.** 65% **5.** 48% **6.** 160 gallons (30% of n = 48) **7.** .000017 **8.** n − 1 **10.** $\frac{n}{12} = \frac{4}{3} = \frac{16}{12}$; n = 16 **12.** .3 × n = 48; n = 48 ÷ .3; n = 160 **13.** $\frac{30}{100} = \frac{48}{n}$; 30n = 4800; n = 160 **14.** Solution is incorrect as 9 is used for base instead of cost. Correct answer comes from 120% of n = 9; cost is \$7.50 **15.** 18%; 10.8%; 6.8%.

CHAPTER 14

Exercise 14.1

1. (a) 20,310 (b) 2,240 (c)300,030 (d) 468 (e) 2,022,040
2. (a) (b) (c) (d) (e)

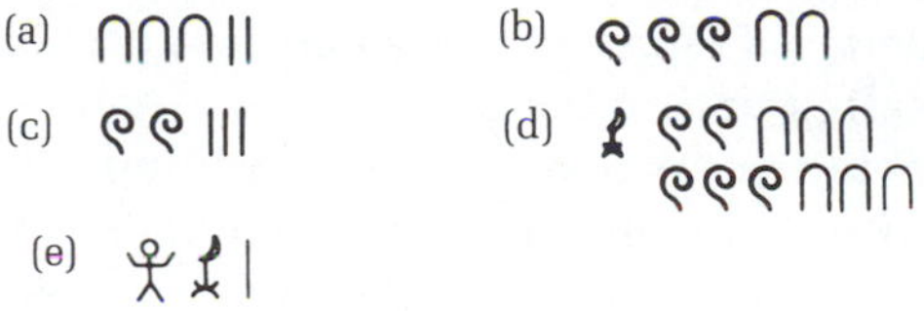

Exercise 14.2

1. (a) 245 (b) 440 (c) 2645 (d) 1,001,600 (e) 584 (f) 100,149 (g) 2,000,000 (h) 704 (i) 600,000 (j) 500,100 **2.** (a) CV (b) MMCCL (c) MCDXL (d) MI (e) $\overline{\text{M}}$ (f) $\overline{\text{CC}}$

Exercise 14.3

1. (a) 7356 (b) 5165 (c) 735 (d) 209 (e) 3026 **2.** (a) 3 thousands + 7 hundreds + 8 tens + 2 ones (b) 4 thousands + 2 tens + 5 ones **3.** (a) $(4 \times 10^3) + (7 \times 10^2) + (3 \times 10^1)$ (b) $(2 \times 10^4) + (9 \times 10^3) + (1 \times 10^2)$ **4.** 732 = 7 hundreds + 3 tens + 2 ones; 73 tens + 2 ones; 732 ones. **5.** (a) 378 = 3 hundreds + 7 tens + 8 ones; 37 tens + 8 ones; 378 ones (b) 2235 = 2 thousands + 2 hundreds + 3 tens + 5 ones; 22 hundreds + 3 tens + 5 ones; 223 tens + 5 ones; 2235 ones **6.** (a) 3000 (b) 500 (c) 1 (d) 203

Exercise 14.4

1. Identity **2.** n + 0 = 0 + n = n; n × 1 = 1 × n = n for all n **3.** 5 + 0; 0 + 5; 1 × 5; 5 × 1; many other answers **4.** $\frac{3}{4} \times \frac{2}{2} = \frac{6}{8}$ **5.** 1 − 0 ≠ 0 − 1 **6.** (a) 0 (b) 1 (c) $\frac{4}{4}$ (d) 2, 10 (e) 3 (f) 3 (g) 0 (h) 1 (i) $\frac{2}{3}$ (j) $\frac{5}{6}$ (k) 1 (l) n

Exercise 14.5

1. 4 + 3 **2.** (4 − 1) + 3 **3.** (4 + 1) + 3; 3 + (1 + 4); (1 + 4) + 3 **4.** Reduce the number almost by half.

Exercise 14.6

1. b **2.** (2 + 8) + 7 **3.** (a) A (b) A (c) B (d) A (e) C **4.** (a) 5, A (b) 0, A (c) 3, B (d) 7, C

Exercise 14.7

1 and **2.** Two operations are needed to apply the distributive property **3.** (a) (3 × 4) + (3 × 5) (b) 4 (5 + 15) (c) $\frac{1}{7}$ (2 + 3) (d) X (2 + 3) **4.** $\frac{1}{7}$ (18 − 4) = $\frac{1}{7}$ × 14 = 2 **5.** 3 + (4 × 5) ≠ (3 + 4) × (3 + 5) **6.** (8 − 4) ÷ 2 = (8 ÷ 2) − (4 ÷ 2); 2 ÷ (8 − 4) ≠ (8 ÷ 2) − (4 ÷ 2) **7.** (a) 4 (b) 3 (c) 3 **8.** (a) × (b) + (c) × (d) − **9.** (a) (3 × 5) + 2 (b) 4 + (3 × 4) (c) 9 − (2 × 3) (d) (8 ÷ 4) + 2 (e) (2 × 3) + (2 × 4) (f) (5 × 7) − (5 × 2) (g) 7 − (4 ÷ 2) (h) (6 ÷ 2) + (6 ÷ 3) (i) (6 × 2) − (6 ÷ 3) (j) (12 × 3) − 8 + 5

Exercise 14.8

1. (a) commutative (b) identity (c) commutative (d) identity (e) commutative (f) inverse (g) distributive (h) commutative (i) associative (j) associative (k) inverse **2.** (a), (b), (d), (h) **3.** (a) associative (b) distributive (d) associative (h) commutative **4.** (a) $\frac{1}{3}$ (b) $\frac{4}{3}$ (c) 2 (d) 2 (e) $^-2$ (f) $^-2$

CHAPTER 17

Exercise 17.1

1. Mean = 14.6; Median = 10; Range = 26 **2.** Mean = 16; Median = 15; Range = 27 **3.** Mean = 1; Median = 0; Range = 7 **4.** Mean = 32; Median = 35; Range = 50 **5.** Mean = 8.17 Median = 9; Range = 8 **6.** Mean = 190; Median = 100; Range = 1000 **7.** Mean = 101; Median = 100; Range = 1000

Exercise 17.3

1. Mean = 5; Median = 5; Range = 6 **2.** Mean = 15; Median = 15; Range = 18 **3.** Use the median when there are one or more extremely low or high scores in the distribution. **5.** 1/2 **6.** 1/16; 15/16 **7.** 3/4 **8.** 3/14; 2/7; 1/2 **9.** 1/2; 1/2 **10.** 3/28

Glossary

The following is a compendium of vocabulary terms highlighted at the beginning of each chapter. When a precise definition is too technical or complex, we use a description rather than a definition.

Abacus An ancient device for calculating that consists of movable beads on parallel rods. Each rod holds a place in a numeral. An empty rod represents a place holder in the same manner that zero does in a numeral.

Academic acceleration The process that allows pupils to complete a subject or program in less than the usual allotted time.

Accuracy in measurement Measure M is more accurate than measurement N if the relative error of M is less than that of N. See Precision.

Acute Angle An angle that has a measure between 0 and 90 degrees.

Addend A number that is added. The addends in 4 + 5 = 9 are 4 and 5.

Adding by endings The process of adding a two-digit number and a one-digit number as 17 + 6, 27 + 6, 37 + 6 in one mental operation to recognize that the first digit of the sum is in the next decade and the last digit of the sum is the ending 3. If you add 7 + 6 and then 1 + 1, you are not adding by endings.

Additive inverse Often referred to as the opposite; the sum of any number and its additive inverse is zero.

Adjacent angles Two angles that have a common vertex and common side (ray).

Algorithm A procedure or series of steps that enables efficient computation of an operation, such as addition.

And (probability) The probability of an event A **and** the probability of an event B is the product of the two probabilities.

And (logic) The statement A **and** B is true if and only if both A and B are true.

Angle A geometric figure formed by two rays starting from the same point.

Approximation A process, often using short cuts, designed to obtain an answer that is not exact but usable for many practical purposes.

Area The measure of the interior region of a closed plane figure.

Arithmetic expression A set of symbols that represent numbers. Examples of arithmetics expressions are: 5, 3 + 7, 2 × 6 and 18/3.

Array An arrangement of elements in rows and columns with the same number of elements in each row and column.

Assessment The process of accumulating comprehensive information for evaluating a pupil's performance.

Associative picture A picture that is related to a topic such as a car for a problem dealing with mileage.

Associative property for addition The process of regrouping three addends without changing the sum. Best stated algebraically: $a + (b + c) = (a + b) + c$.

Associative property for multiplication The process of regrouping three factors without changing the product: $a \times (b \times c) = (a \times b) \times c$.

Average See Mean.

Back to Basics The name frequently given to the elementary mathematics program of the 1970s.

Base (percentage formula) In the expression A% of B, B is the base.

Base (place system) The number of digits in a place system. The base, in a place system, indicates the number of items in any place required to make one unit in the place immediately to the left.

Basic A widely used computer language.

Basic fact Any true equation containing the sum or product of a pair of single digit numbers.

Binary operation. An operation performed on two numbers to obtain a third. Addition, subtraction, multiplication and division are binary operations that are performed on exactly two numbers at a time.

Bridging the decade Addition of a one-digit number to a two-digit number, giving a sum in the next decade. The sum 18 + 5 = 23 bridges the decade. *See Adding by endings.*

Calculator logic The process that determines which keys must be pressed to perform a given operation.

Cardinal number A number that indicates how many items are in a set.

Carriage return(<CR>) With computers, the key or procedure that moves the cursor to the beginning of the next line, and causes information to be processed or stored; may be initiated by pressing a single key that is often labeled as RETURN or ENTER.

Centi A metric prefix meaning hundredths, as in centimeters.

Circle The set of all points in a plane equidistant from a fixed point called the center.

Circumference The length or distance around a circle.

Closure An operation is closed with respect to a set of numbers if that operation always produces a member of the set.

Cognitive The process of knowing based on perception, introspection, and or memory.

Colon A standard punctuation symbol that allows placement of more than one instruction on a line in a computer program.

Column impasse When the difference in a subtraction for a particular column is less than zero.

Common fraction See Fraction

Common multiple A common multiple of A and B is divisible by both A and B. It may or may not be the least or lowest common multiple.

Commutative property of addition The order of adding two numbers does not affect the sum: a + b = b + a.

Commutative property of multiplication The order of multiplying two numbers does not affect the product: $a \times b = b \times a$

Comparative subtraction A subtraction that determines how much more or less one number is than another.

Complex fraction It has one of the following: a fraction in the numerator, a fraction in the denominator, or a fraction in both the numerator and denominator.

Composite number A whole number that is divisible by a number other than itself and 1.

Computer memory That part of the computer that enables it to store information.

Computer program A series of instructions that tells the computer how to perform a specific task.

Conceptual Associated with understanding basic ideas; relating to a mental image of an action or thing.

Congruent Geometric figures that have the same size and shape.

Continuum A set of sequential skills that proceed from simple to difficult in an uninterrupted progression.

Correlation A measure of the relation between two sets of measurements. The closer the relation the higher the correlation.

Counting numbers The set of whole numbers greater than zero; also known as natural numbers or positive integers: 1, 2,3,4 . . . .

CPU An abbreviation for the central processing unit of a computer.

Criterion-reference test A test designed to

determine the degree of mastery for specific objectives.

CRT An abbreviation for cathode ray tube, the technical name for a computer screen.

Cursor The symbol on the screen that indicates the position for the display of the next entry from the keyboard or computer memory. It is often a blinking square, vertical or horizontal line segment.

Customary System of Measurement Units such as feet and inches obtained from the English system of measurement. By habit, it is often referred to as the English system.

Cylinder On the elementary level, a shape similar to the standard tin can.

Decade A set of 10 consecutive whole numbers beginning with a multiple of 10. The decade of the 20s: 20–29.

Decimal A fractional numeral in which the denominator is not written but is indicated by the position of the decimal point.

Decimal fraction Same as decimal.

Decomposition A method of subtraction that requires regrouping of the minuend in order to complete the operation.

Deductive Reasoning A logical process using an "if-then" pattern.

Degree Celsius The metric unit for measuring temperature, based on the temperature change of water from freezing at 0 ° C. to boiling at 100 ° C.

Degree Fahrenheit The English unit for measuring temperature, now referred to as customary. Water freezes at 32 ° F. and boils at 212 ° F.

Denominator In the fractional numeral a/b, the denominator is b.

Density The weight of an object divided by its volume.

Diagnosis A process that enables teachers to locate the causes of pupil difficulty in the learning process.

Difference The answer obtained by subtracting two numbers.

Digit The symbols contained in the base of a place system. In base 10 the digits are 0,1,2,3,4,5,6,7,8,9.

Direct measurement A measurement obtained by applying the measuring instrument directly to the object being measured.

Directed numbers See Integers, Signed numbers.

Disk A thin, magnetic, coated, circular plate that enables the computer to store information from the computer and that allows the computer to retrieve the information.

Disk drive The mechanism that holds the disk and enables it to perform the process of storing and retrieval of information.

Distributive property Best stated algebraically: a(b + c) = ab + ac. It indicates that to multiply before adding, one must multiply each term.

Dividend The dividend is divided by the divisor to get the quotient. In the division, a ÷ b = c, a is the dividend.

Divisible In the set of whole numbers, a is divisible by b if there is a whole number c such that a = c × b. The divisor b and the quotient c are factors of the dividend. The dividend is a multiple of divisor and quotient.

Divisor In the division a ÷ b = c, b is the divisor, but b cannot be 0.

Equal additions method A method of subtraction that adds a number, usually a power of 10, to each number in the subtraction.

Equally likely events (probability) A set of events such that each event is as likely to occur as any of the other events in that set.

Equation A statement indicating that two expressions name the same number, 1 + 2 = 3 is a true statement. 2 = 3 is false.

Equal fractions Synonymous with equivalent fractions.

Equilateral triangle A triangle with congruent sides.

Error pattern Computational errors that follow the same pattern.

Expanded notation In expanded notation, 234 = 2 hundreds + 3 tens + 4 ones or 200 + 30 + 4.

Exploratory activity Use of concrete objects and visuals to promote early learning before introducing the verbal level.

Exponent In the expression n^x, the whole number x is the exponent. When x is a whole number, it tells how many times n is used as a factor.

Expository method The teacher tells the pupils what is to be learned. It is the opposite procedure of discovery.

Expressive vocabulary The vocabulary used in speaking and writing.

Face value (digit) The cardinal value of a digit in a numeral. In 27, 2 has a face value of 2 and a total value of 20.

Fact Finder A manipulative device used to model basic facts.

Factor When two or more whole numbers are multiplied, each is a factor of the product.

Formative evaluation Evaluation used by a teacher to direct and develop learning.

Formula An algebraic expression, such as A = BH, that shows how different quantities are related.

FOR-NEXT LOOP An important pair of computer instructions that tells the computer to repeat a specific number of times. *See* Loop.

Fraction A rational number or the numeral that represents it. To say that we add or multiply fractions, indicates that *fraction* is used as a number. To talk about a numerator indicates that *fraction* is used as a numeral. We add or multiply numbers. Fractional numerals have numerators and denominators.

Frame An elementary form of a variable designed to help pupils recognize its role as a place holder as in □ + 3 = 5.

Function A set of ordered pairs with no two first elements alike. We use tables, graphs and formulas to work with functions.

Functional picture A picture that contains information required for solving a problem.

Geoboard A board with an array of pegs or nails used to create geometric figures with rubber bands.

Geometric figure a set of one or more points in space.

Gram A metric unit of weight equal to the weight of one cubic centimeter of distilled water at 4 ° Celsius.

Greatest common factor The largest factor (divisor) of two or more numbers.

Guess and test A strategy for problem solving. The name describes the process. This procedure has become more viable with access to a computer using a FOR-NEXT loop.

Guided discovery A learning procedure guided by the teacher using a variety of materials, activities, questions, and class discussion that enables pupils to learn without being told.

Hardware The computer and any physical device attached to it, such as a printer.

Heterogeneous class A class containing pupils with a wide range of abilities and background.

Heuristic A problem solving procedure using intuition, experience, and general strategies. Unlike an algorithm, it does not guarantee success.

Higher-decade addition See adding by endings.

Higher-decade multiplication Multiplication to obtain products in decades higher than the 30s, usually with factors 6,7,8, or 9.

Horizontal enrichment Learning activities involving subject matter, not usually found in textbooks, for enrichment.

Identity element for addition The identity element for addition is zero because: 0 + n = n + 0 = n for all n.

Identity element for multiplication The

identity element for multiplication is 1 because: $1 \times n = n \times 1$ for all n.

Immediate mode The computer mode that allows the computer to be used as a calculator. Information placed in computer memory in the immediate mode cannot be saved on disk.

Improper fraction A fraction equal to or greater than 1.

Independent events When the occurrence of any event in a set has no effect on the occurrence of any other member of that set.

Indirect measurement Measurement in which the measuring instrument is not applied directly to the object being measured.

Inductive reasoning A logical procedure that draws a conclusion based on observation.

Inequality A number sentence that indicates that two numerals or expressions are names for different numbers.

Inferential statistics Statistical procedures that predict the outcome of an event, such as the poll for an election.

Integer The set of integers includes the set of positive whole numbers, negative whole numbers, and zero.

Interpretive vocabulary The vocabulary used in listening and reading.

Inverse operation An operation which "undoes" a given operation. Addition-subtraction and multiplication-division are pairs of inverse operations.

Isosceles triangle A triangle with two congruent sides.

Key word approach A word that may help a pupil identify the operation necessary to solve a problem. Failure to recognize limitations of keywords will lead to incorrect solutions.

Kilo A metric prefix meaning 1000 times the base unit.

Kilobyte The most common unit used to describe the amount of computer memory. An approximation, a kilobyte is actually equal to 2^{10} or 1024 bytes rather than 1000 bytes.

Learning laboratory or center A place where pupils can handle materials, practice skills, and become involved in the process of learning mathematics.

Least (lowest) common denominator The smallest denominator divisible by each number in a set of denominators. It is the lowest common multiple of the denominators.

Least (lowest) common multiple The smallest number divisible by each number of a set of numbers.

Like fractions Fractions that have the same denominator.

Line segment A set of points forming a path that is the shortest distance between the two end points.

Liter A basic metric unit of capacity, equal to 1000 cm^3. 1 liter $\approx$ 1.1 quart.

LOGO A computer language that is often used in early elementary grades because of it ease in programming to display geometric figures.

Lowest terms A fraction is in its lowest terms if its numerator and denominator have no common factor greater than 1.

Loop A computer procedure that repeats a set of instructions a specified number of times. An infinite loop runs indefinitely until special steps are taken to end it.

Mainframe computers A class of large computers used by government and industry.

Mass Absolute quantity of matter as opposed to weight, which varies with gravitational force.

Mastery level of understanding A pupil performs at the mastery level when the response is automatic with understanding.

Mathematical problem A problem that cannot be solved by a habitual response.

Mathematical sentence An equation or inequality.

Mathematical structure A system, often with one or more operations, characterized by a set of properties and definitions.

Mean The sum of the numbers in a set divided by the number of elements (numbers) in the set.

Median The middle value in a set, either the middle number or the average of the two middle numbers.

Measurement The process of finding the number of standard units in the object or quantity.

Measurement division The process of using division to find how many sets of a specific size are in a given set.

Meter The standard metric unit of length, equal to 39.37 inches to nearest hundredth of an inch.

Microcomputer The class of smallest computers found in schools, homes, and small businesses.

Milli The metric prefix meaning one-thousandth of the standard units.

Minicomputers A class of intermediate sized computers.

Minuend The number from which another number is subtracted.

Mixed number A numeral in the form of the sum of a whole number and a fraction, as $3\frac{2}{5}$, an abbreviation for $3 + \frac{2}{5}$.

Mode A statistical measure indicating the item that occurs most frequently in a set.

Motivation A set of circumstances that makes pupils want to learn.

Multiple A multiple of 6 is the product of any integer and 6.

Multiplicand The number that is being multiplied, a factor.

Multiplication-division pattern. In verbal form: if factor × factor = product, then the product divided by factor = factor. For the pair of numbers 3 and 4: $3 \times 4 = 12 <-> 12/3 = 4 <-> 12/4 = 3 <-> 4 \times 3 = 12$.

Multiplicative identity The multiplicative identity is 1: $1 \times n = n \times 1 = n$ for all n.

Multiplicative inverse *See* Reciprocal.

Multiplier The number that multiplies the multiplicand.

Natural number *See* Counting number.

Negative number A number less than zero.

New math A term often used for the mathematics curriculum of the 1960s because it involved many changes from the traditional curriculum of the 1950s.

Nonstandard unit An arbitrary unit selected to introduce the concept of measurement.

Nonterminating decimal The term is self descriptive. A digit or series of digits repeats endlessly, the decimal representation for 1/3, 0.3333333 . . . ; 1/11 = .090909 . . .

Norm-referenced test A standardized test that has statistical information available, such as percentiles and grade equivalents, which may be used to interpret the score of an individual.

Number family A set of addition facts with the same sum.

Number line A line with each of its points corresponding to a number.

Number pattern An arrangement of numbers that illustrates a mathematical concept.

Number period The system of grouping digits in a numeral to facilitate reading it.

Number property A fundamental characteristic of a number or number operation.

Number system A set of numbers with one or more operations.

Numeral A symbol that represents a number.

Numeration system A systematic set of symbols used to represent numbers such as our base 10 or the Roman system.

Numerator In the fraction a/b, a is the numerator.

Obtuse angle An angle with a measure between 90 and 180 degrees.

Open sentence A sentence that contains one or more variables.

Or (probability) The probability of an event A or an event B is the sum of the probabilities. P(A or B) = P(A) + P(B).

Ordered pair The ordered pair (2,3) is different than the ordered pair (3,2).

Ordinal number A number that indicates a specific member of a set, such as the third.

Overloaded place A place is overloaded when the number of items in that place cannot be expressed with a single digit.

Parallel Two lines in a plane are parallel if they do not intersect.

Parallelogram A four-sided figure (quadrilateral) with opposite sides parallel.

Partial dividend The remainder used to determine each quotient digit after the first, when the quotient contains more than one digit.

Partitive division Divison that finds the number in each part that results from breaking the original set into equal parts.

Pattern blocks A set of wooden blocks in various geometric shapes, such as rectangles, which are useful for counting, sorting, measurement and problem solving.

Percent Another word for hundredths: 11 percent = 11% = 11 hundredths = 0.11.

Percentage The result of finding the percent of a number by multiplying the base by the rate. Do not confuse it with the rate.

Percentage formula $P = B \times R$ where P is the percentage, B is the base and R is the rate (often referred to as the percent).

Perimeter The sum of the measures of the sides of a polygon.

Peripherals Hardware that can be attached to a computer, such as a printer.

Personal attributes The visible characteristics of a person.

Perpendicular Perpendicular lines intersect at right angles.

Pi (π) The ratio obtained by dividing the circumference of any circle by its diameter. It is an irrational number represented by a nonterminating decimal, often approximated as 3.14, 3.1416 or $3\frac{1}{7}$.

Place value The property of our numeration system that assigns a value to a digit depending on its position in a numeral.

Polygon A closed plane figure formed by line segments. A closed broken line in a plane.

Polyhedron A closed three-dimensional figure having four or more faces with each face consisting of a polygon and its interior.

Positional value The same as place value. The positional value of 7 in 176 is 10.

Positive number A number greater than zero.

Power of 10 A number in the form 10^n. When referring to numeration, n must be a whole number.

Precision Measurement A is more precise than a measurement B if the absolute error in A is less than that of B. When the measurement 100 has an error of 1, it has an absolute error of 1 and a relative error of 1%. When a measurement of 1000 has an error of 1, it has an absolute error of 1 and a relative error of 0.1%. Both measurements have the same precision but the latter has greater accuracy.

Preoperational A period in the cognitive development of a child identified by Piaget as occurring from ages two to seven.

Prime factorization Expressing a number as the product of its prime factors.

Prime number A whole number greater than 1 with exactly two distinct factors, itself and 1.

PRINT (computer) The PRINT instruction tells the computer to display information on the computer screen (CRT).

Probability The quotient of the number of ways in which an event can succeed divided by the total number of ways that the event can succeed or fail.

Probability formula $P = s/(s + f)$ where s is the number of ways in which an event can succeed and f is the number of ways it can fail. The formula is also written as $P = s/h$ where h is the total number of ways that an event can happen: h = s + f.

Product The result of multiplying two or more numbers (factors).

Programming mode Computer mode that allows information in computer memory to be transferred to disk.

Prompt A symbol on the computer screen that indicates the computer mode.

Proper fraction A fraction with a value between 0 and 1.

Proportion In its simplest form, a proportion consists of the statement that two rates or ratios are equal.

Protractor An instrument for measuring angles.

Quadrilateral A four-sided polygon.

Quality control A process used by industry to determine the quality of an entire production by testing small random samples.

Quantitative thinking The ability to understand and interpret numbers when expressed in verbal or written form.

Quotation marks Standard punctuation symbols important in computer programming. The computer displays exactly what is included between the quotation marks in PRINT statements, including the spaces.

Quotient The answer obtained by dividing one number by another.

Ragged decimals Addition or subtraction of decimals containing a different number of places.

Random event A random event has no other factor than chance in its occurrence or selection. Each item in the set has an equal chance of being selected.

Range The difference between the largest and smallest numbers in a set.

Rate (percent) The product of the rate and base is the percentage. The rate is usually expressed with the percent sign but may be expressed as a decimal. Because 3% is read as 3 percent, the rate is often confused with the percentage.

Rate A quotient, sometimes used interchangeably with ratio, but usually indicates division with numbers representing unlike quantities (partition division).

Ratio A quotient, sometimes used interchangeably with rate, but usually indicates division with numbers representing like quantities (measurement division).

Rational counting Counting with an understanding of the pattern.

Rational number The quotient of two integers with the divisor not zero.

Ray Any part of a line beginning at a point on the line and extending indefinitely in one direction.

Real numbers The set of numbers consisting of the rational and irrational numbers. They can be placed in one to one correspondence with points on a line.

Reciprocal The multiplicative inverse. The product of any number, other than 0, and its reciprocal is 1. If $n \neq 0$, then the reciprocal of N is 1/N. The reciprocal of a/b is b/a.

Region In two dimensions: a part of a plane. In three dimensions: a portion of space.

Regrouping Using the fact that any item in a place, in our base 10 system, is equal to 10 items in the place immediately to its right. One ten equals 10 ones. One thousand equal 10 hundreds.

Reinforcement The process of providing additional activity to enable the pupil to use a procedure efficiently.

Relative error See Precision.

Reliability The reliability of a test reflects the consistency of results when the test is repeated.

Remainder The difference between the dividend and the largest multiple of the divisor that is contained in the dividend.

Renaming The process of replacing one numeral with another without changing the number.

Repeating decimal Any rational number with a denominator that has a factor other than 2 or 5, such as 1/3 or 2/11, has an equivalent decimal that is nonterminating and *repeating*. An irrational number is represented by a nonterminating, *nonrepeating* decimal.

Repetend The sequence of digits in a nonterminating decimal that repeats. The repetend in .090909 . . . is "09". A bar is sometimes used to indicate the repetend as in 1/11 = .09̄.

Rhombus an equilateral quadrilateral. A square is a special case of a rhombus in the same way that a trapezoid is a special case of a quadrilateral.

Right angle An angle with a measure of 90 degrees. An angle formed by two perpendicular lines.

Rote counting Counting by pure memory without understanding.

Scalene triangle A triangle with no two sides congruent.

Scope and sequence Reference to the amount of material to be covered (scope) at a given grade level and the order in which the material is to be taught (sequence).

Segment *See* Line segment.

Sequence A set of numbers, as 2, 3, 4, . . . , usually having a recognizable pattern for elementary grades.

Seriation The process of placing numbers in order of magnitude.

Signed numbers See integers.

SI metrics A modernized metric system known as the international system of units.

Similar figures Figures with the same shape. Similar polygons have corresponding angles equal and corresponding sides proportional.

Software A computer program or set of programs.

Solid A three-dimensional figure and its interior.

Standard units Officially designated units of measure with standards established and kept by a government.

Standardized test A test that is administered to a large heterogeneous group to establish norms.

Strand Refers to the content of mathematics being taught such as computation, estimation, problem solving and geometry.

Strategy A procedure that provides a pupil with guides for problem analysis and the choice of the correct operation.

Subtrahend The number which is subtracted from the minuend.

Summative evaluation Evaluation made at the end of a unit or course to determine a pupil's overall achievement.

Surface A table top is a typical model for a plane surface. The surface of a sphere is a typical model for a curved surface.

Symbolic level of learning Pupils operate at the symbolic level of learning when they can use numerals and symbols with understanding.

Symmetry A mirror-like relation between parts of a figure with respect to a point, a line, or a plane. Line segments, joining corresponding points of the two parts, are bisected by the point, line, or plane. The circle is symmetrical with respect to its center, which bisects every diameter. The circle is also symmetrical to each of its diameters. A sphere is symmetrical to any plane through its center.

System of numeration See Numeration system.

Terms of a fraction The numerator and denominator.

Tetrahedron A polyhedron with four faces, a triangular pyramid.

Tolerance The allowable error in a measurement.

Total value (digit) The product of the cardinal value of the digit and its place value. The 7 in 176 has a total value of 70.

Trapezoid A quadrilateral with one pair of parallel sides.

Twin primes Two consecutive odd prime numbers, such as 3 and 5.

Unit fraction A fraction with a numerator of 1.

Unlike fractions Fractions that have different denominators.

Unlike but related fractions *See* Related fractions.

Validity The validity of a test indicates its ability to measure what it is intended to measure. Validity indicates the extent to which the test results agree with true achievement.

Variable A variable holds a place for a numeral. In the equation $x + 3 = 7$, x is the variable. A frame is a particular type of variable used in elementary programs to provide visual reinforcement of the concept.

Vertical enrichment Enrichment that provides more advanced content than is typical for a given class.

Volume The measure of the interior of a closed three-dimensional figure, usually expressed in cubic units.

Whole numbers The common name for cardinal numbers: 0,1,2,3 . . . .

Index

A

ability tracking, 57
abstraction levels, 5, 7–9
academic acceleration, 66–67
achievement differences, 55
activities, situations for
 angles, 345
 associative property, 305–306
 calculator, *see* calculators
 circles, 130, 349
 commutative property, 306–307
 computer, *see* computers
 counting, 78–79, 92,
 distributive property, 307–309
 drill, *see* drill activities
 measurement, 322–331
 metric system, 322–331, 331–333, 333–336
 points, 345
 probability, 376–379
 rays, 343
 two-dimensional figures, 347–348
 three-dimensional figures, 356–359
acute angle, 343
addend(s), 152, 169
addition
 alternative approaches to, 151–152
 associative property, 304–305
 basic facts in, 117, 118, 119–122
 calculators in, 152–153
 checks for, 151
 column, 131, 147–148
 commutative property, 304
 computer in, 259
 of decimals, 243–245
 by endings, 193–194
 estimates for, 154–155
 of fractions, 243–245, 253, 256–257
 higher-decade, 145–148, 193–194
 inverses for, 303
 of mixed numbers, 257–259

of multidigit numbers, 139–145
and multiplication, relationship, 161
problem solving and, 126, 131–134
recommended grade placement in, 117–118
regrouping in, 11–14
reinforcement in, 127–131
and subtraction, relationship, 127, 161
use of, in teaching, 90
addition crows, 128–129
algorism(s)
 for division, 187–215, 275
 for multiplication, 187–215, 271–272
algorithm((s), *see* algorism(s)
analytical diagnosis, 49
and (probability), 374–375
angle(s)
 activities involving, 345
 acute, 343
 definition of, 343
 measurement of, 344
 right, 343
area
 of a circular region, finding, 354–355
 of plane figures, finding, 352–353
 of a rectangle, finding, 351–352
 of a solid, finding surface, 358
 unit of measurement for, 351
arithmetic average, 43
arithmetic, mental, *see* mental arithmetic
Arithmetic Teacher, The, 34
associative property, *see* properties
attitude, pupil, toward mathematics
 evaluation of, 47–48
attitudinal objectives, 5
attribute blocks, 23

B

Back-to-Basics movement, 4, 15
bar graph, 355
Barrel, Josiah, 326
base(s), numeration system
 ten, 23–24, 138–139, 294, 318
base 10 blocks, 11, 23–24, 198
base 10 type materials, 142, 229
BASIC, programming in, 395–402
basic facts
 in addition, 117, 118, 119–122
 in division, 166–169, 171–173
 drill activities and, 128–131
 less than ten, 118–119
 in multiplication, 161–166, 171–173
 in subtraction, 118, 122–125
Begle, Edward C., 3, 65
bilingual education
 approaches to, 385–386
 comprehensive, 390–391
 computer-assisted, 391–392
 cooperative learning in, 388
 electronic learning aids in, 391–392
 government-funded compensatory, 389
 in-school features of, 390–391
 legal basis of, 385
 maintenance programs in, 385
 mathematics improvement in, 386–389
 parental involvement in, 389
 for poor and underachieving pupils, 390
 transitional programs, 385–386
 see also minority pupils
Bilingual Education Act (1968), 385
binary (operation), 305
Bloom, Benjamin B., 59–60, 73
bridging the decade, 146
broken-line graph, 355
Brooks, Douglas M., 56